Air Transport Economics

Air Transport Economics: From Theory to Applications uniquely merges the institutional and technical aspects of the aviation industry with their theoretical economic underpinnings. Its integrative approach offers a fresh point of view that will find favor with many students of aviation.

This fourth edition has undergone extensive updates throughout. It features new material addressing the impact of COVID-19 on the air transport industry, and the efforts made by both the industry and governments to facilitate recovery. A new chapter examines the impact of air transport on climate change and how government policies to address this issue could reshape the industry. Additionally, alongside expanded coverage of revenue management and pricing decisions, this fourth edition incorporates case studies that give real-world examples to reflect current industry practices. Moreover, there is a discussion of the latest computer applications that enhance the effectiveness of the new techniques.

This book offers a self-contained theory and applications-oriented text for individuals aspiring to enter the aviation industry as a practicing professional in the management area. It will be of the greatest relevance to undergraduate and graduate students aiming to acquire a comprehensive grasp of the economics of the aviation industry. The review questions at the end of each chapter have been expanded considerably, and an online assignment has been introduced for each chapter. This book will also appeal to many professionals who seek an accessible and practical explanation of the underlying economic forces that shape the industry.

Bijan Vasigh is Professor of Economics and Finance in the College of Business at Embry-Riddle Aeronautical University, Daytona Beach, Florida. He received a Ph.D. in Economics from the State University of New York and has published many articles concerning the aviation industry.

Brian Pearce is Honorary Professor at University College London Bartlett School's Air Transportation Systems Laboratory and also a Visiting Professor at the Centre for Air Transport Management at Cranfield University. He previously served as the Chief Economist of the International Air Transport Association (IATA).

Air Transport Economics

From Theory to Applications

Fourth Edition

Bijan Vasigh and Brian Pearce

LONDON AND NEW YORK

Designed cover image: © Getty Images

Fourth edition published 2024
by Routledge
4 Park Square, Milton Park, Abingdon, Oxon, OX14 4RN

and by Routledge
605 Third Avenue, New York, NY 10158

Routledge is an imprint of the Taylor & Francis Group, an informa business

First edition published by Routledge 2008
Third edition published by Routledge 2018

British Library Cataloguing-in-Publication Data
A catalogue record for this book is available from the British Library

ISBN: 9781032482552 (hbk)
ISBN: 9781032482538 (pbk)
ISBN: 9781003388135 (ebk)

DOI: 10.4324/9781003388135

Typeset in Times New Roman
by codeMantra

Contents

Figures

Tables

Preface to the Fourth Edition

The fourth edition of this text has been extensively updated to reflect developments in air transport markets and the industry since the publication of the third edition in 2018, notably including the impact of COVID-19. All tables and figures have been updated with the latest available data, and new examples illustrating key concepts and issues have been included.

However, the underlying economics of air transport remain unchanged. Despite the recent pandemic and rising concerns over the impact on climate change, preferences for air transport remain largely unchanged and a strong rebound in demand occurred once border restrictions were lifted. Perhaps one major lesson from COVID-19 is the inevitability of periodic unpredictable shocks. The chapter on forecasting has been updated to incorporate a section on radical uncertainty and how forecasts can still be useful for decision making. Industry developments continue to be driven by the particular economics of production, with consolidation on many markets driven by the prevalence of density economies, the development of ancillary services by the large proportion of fixed costs, and pricing by the low marginal costs of providing airline services and openness to competition on most city-pair markets.

The impact of government policy on the industry covering various issues has been covered extensively in various chapters, including ownership, market regulation, safety, and security. However, a new chapter has been added on a policy issue that could pose an existential challenge for the industry, climate change. In this chapter, we examine the greenhouse gases produced by flight due to the combustion of jet kerosene, the climate science explaining and quantifying the surface temperature impact of CO_2 emissions and condensation trails. Climate change itself exerts impacts on the industry, through sea level rise and more volatile weather conditions. However, the major impact may be felt in the industry through government policy measures, aimed at reducing the use of fossil fuels. We consider the effectiveness of various government policy instruments, including carbon taxation, emission trading schemes, and baseline and offset schemes, such as ICAO's CORSIA scheme. The aim of such policies is to encourage, or force, a change to new low- or no-carbon fuels. We explore options such as drop-in sustainable aviation fuels (SAF), liquid hydrogen, and electrification.

Overall, the theme of this book remains the same. As pointed out in earlier editions of the text, our preferred approach is to apply economic principles to the industry, since here is the area where we see the need to have a basic text that brings together many of the unique aspects of the aviation industry. Again, it is our hope that the text will appeal to interested readers within aviation, as well as to students who hope to enter the industry.

Foreword

Air transport plays a vital role in the development of the global economy with its strong impact on economic growth through connecting people and business activities across continents. However, rapid technological changes, environmental concerns, and worldwide crises affect the air transport sector significantly in terms of traffic, capacity, and performance. Companies in the industry must understand the economic principles underlying successful strategy, restructuring, and recovery.

In this book, the author Dr. Vasigh and the co-author Brian Pearce present a comprehensive and insightful analysis of the economic principles and market dynamics that govern the air transport industry. They bring a unique perspective to the subject, showcasing real-world examples and case studies to explain key concepts with their extensive industry experiences and expertise.

The authors cover fundamental issues such as entry into the aviation industry, demand and supply, competitive market structure, and forecasting in the aviation industry, both theoretically and practically. In this book, they practically touch on issues such as how to determine the optimal ticket price by embodying the effects of fuel prices and deregulations with examples, by considering the supply and demand curves according to certain constraints. In addition, this book includes the current effects of new technologies, and global and social events on air transport.

Turkish Airlines is certainly aware of the complexity and nuances of the aviation industry. We have witnessed the evolution of the airline business from humble beginnings to becoming a major global industry connecting people and cultures around the world. Our strategies, strong character, and future plans have accepted the fundamental principles in this book as its basis.

Dr. Vasigh and Brian Pearce offer valuable insights and perspectives on economic factors and the aviation industry's adaptation to a rapidly changing environment. With its theoretical and practical content, this book is an important resource for students, researchers, policy makers, and industry professionals. The authors' expertise and coherence, as well as examples of recent trends, make this book an essential resource for those seeking to understand the complex economic principles in the industry.

Prof. Ahmet Bolat
Turkish Airlines
Chairman of the Board of Directors and the Executive Committee

Acknowledgments

The development and writing of any textbook is a long and trying experience — a sentiment that will resonate with all aspiring authors! Our effort has been no exception. And, as with any other text, we have received a great deal of assistance and encouragement from a number of individuals whose efforts we would like to acknowledge. We would like to express our heartfelt thanks to the following people who have supported and encouraged us throughout the writing of this book.

We owe a special debt to the graduate assistants who helped with the preparation of this manuscript: Nicolás Pombo, Liam Mackay, G. Wiscombe, Aakanksha Mannam, Ageel Alageel, Sharath Sashikumar Bindu, Pascal Lawrence, Myra Ann Wee, Christian Vogel, James Cirino, Chris Weeden, and Duane Miner. These students spent countless hours collecting data, editing graphs, and updating tables and figures.

We also express our appreciation to our publishers for their patience and help in transforming the raw manuscript into an actual textbook. The authors gratefully acknowledge the support of Andrew Harrison (Senior Editor, Economics) and Helena Parkinson (Editorial Assistant, Economics) at Routledge who encouraged and helped us to deliver a top-quality product. Further appreciation goes to many other people who have helped make this book a reality, including Ahmet Bolat, Levent Konukcu, Rasih Kahraman, Tae Oum, Irwin Price, Zane Rowe, Barry Humphreys, and Darryl Jenkins. We appreciate your support and input.

Last but not least, we would like to thank our readers, whose encouragement and inspiration drive us to continue writing. Your support holds immense value to us, and we trust that this book will meet your expectations.

About the Authors

Bijan Vasigh is Professor of Economics and Finance in the College of Business at Embry-Riddle Aeronautical University, Daytona Beach, Florida. He received a Ph.D. in Economics from the State University of New York and has published many articles concerning the aviation industry. The articles were published in numerous academic journals, including the *Journal of Economics and Finance*, *Journal of Transportation Management*, *National Aeronautics and Space Administration (NASA) Scientific and Technical Aerospace Reports*, *Transportation Quarterly*, *Airport Business*, *Journal of Business and Economics*, and *Journal of Travel Research.* He has been quoted in major newspapers and magazines around the world. In 2006, his paper, "A Total Factor Productivity Based for Tactical Cluster Assessment: Empirical Investigation in the Airline Industry," was awarded the Dr. Frank E. Sorenson Award for outstanding achievement of excellence in aviation research scholarship. Bijan is the author of *Aircraft Finance: Strategies for Managing Capital Costs in a Turbulent Industry* and *The Foundations of Airline Finance: Methodology and Practice.*

Brian Pearce is an economist specializing in the economics of air transport, environmental policy, financial markets, and macroeconomic forecasting. He was Chief Economist at IATA, until taking early retirement in July 2021, where he sat on the senior leadership team and was President of its pension foundation. He was acting SVP of IATA's Member & External Relations division from 2019 to early 2020. He is currently a Visiting Professor at the Department of Air Transport, Cranfield University, oversight committee member of Skytra, and a fellow of the Royal Aeronautical Society. Previously, he has been a member of the expert panel of the UK Airports Commission, an expert adviser to ICAO on market-based instruments, a member of AirNZ's sustainability panel, head of Global Economics at SBC Warburg Dillon Read, and Chief Economist at Ernst & Young's ITEM Club, among other appointments.

About the Authors

1 Evolution of the Air Transport Industry

The airline industry is not only highly cyclical and seasonal but also is significantly impacted by exogenous shocks, such as the spread of communicable diseases, terrorism, and economic shocks. In recent times, the airline industry has faced financial turmoil, leading to many airlines entering Chapter 11 bankruptcy protection. The global financial crisis of 2008 resulted in more than $5 billion losses for the airline industry. The decade before 2020 was the most profitable in the airline history, characterized by consolidation and lower fuel prices that facilitated the industry to enjoy the longest period of profitability. However, the COVID-19 pandemic disrupted international travel as nations closed their borders and imposed strict travel restrictions. The industry incurred a loss of nearly $140 billion in 2020, and the cumulative losses over the 2020–2022 period could surpass $200 billion totally. According to the International Air Transport Association (IATA), the global airline industry reported a loss of $51.8 billion in 2021. In 2022, the industry managed to reduce its losses by 78% to $12 billion, reflecting a slow recovery from the pandemic.

In response to the industry's poor financial performance, airlines have consolidated in many parts of the world. A series of mega-mergers has led to the dominance of the four largest US airlines, namely, American, Delta, United, and Southwest, controlling about 80% of the total domestic passenger traffic. This wave of merger activity within the airline sector began with the merger between USAir and America West in 2005, followed by Delta–Northwest in 2008, United Airlines–Continental in 2010, Southwest–AirTran in 2011, and US Airways–American Airlines in 2013. The concentration of airline markets often leads to several consequences, including higher ticket prices, higher level of profitability, and in some cases lower service levels.

The typically poor financial performance of airlines, both in absolute terms and compared to other economic sectors, contrasts sharply with the exceptional growth in demand for air transport observed in recent decades. Despite some exceptions among individual airlines, the airline sector generates one of the lowest returns on capital for investors. However, the demand for its cargo and passenger services is so strong, that it is one of the fastest growing economic sectors. Although COVID-19-related border restrictions brought international air travel almost to a halt, the lifting of these restraints has resulted in higher demand. This robust rebound seems to include business travel, despite the concerns about substitution by technologies such as Zoom and other video conferencing tools. Air cargo, in contrast, barely experienced any decline during the pandemic and rapidly reached record levels of activity. This sector played a major role in connecting global supply chains and transporting goods of essential items such as pharmaceuticals. One measure of the perceived value of air transport, to economies as well as individual users, is evident from the $230 billion financial aid provided to airlines by governments to prevent widespread failures during the pandemic.

DOI: 10.4324/9781003388135-1

A key evolutionary factor lies in the gradual shift of passenger domination, moving from North America and Europe to the ever-growing Asia-Pacific market. The annual number of passengers flown within the United States increased from 665 million in 1990 to 927 million in 2019.[1] However, the situation changed in 2020, with US airlines carrying 369 million passengers, a sharp drop from 927 million in 2019 and 889 million in 2018. This decline in passenger traffic in 2020 represented the lowest figures for US airlines since the mid-1980s.[2] Global passenger traffic exhibited a modest recovery in 2021, with the number of passengers worldwide reaching 2.3 billion—a 49% reduction from pre-pandemic (2019) levels. Due to improving economic conditions of populous nations such as China and India, it is anticipated that they will lead the dominant air transport markets in the future. This anticipation is well supported by the surge in air passengers in China, increasing from 72.7 million in 2001 to 417 million in 2020. This astonishing expansion translates to an average annual growth rate of 10.64%.

In 2021, approximately 440.6 million passengers traveled by air in China, reflecting a 36% decline compared to the figures from 2019 (660 million), primarily attributed to the impact of the pandemic.

The purpose of this chapter is to outline the evolution of the air transport industry, including airlines and airports. The following topics will be covered:

- The Airline Industry
- Financial Condition of the Airline Industry
- Consolidation and Bankruptcies
- Factors Affecting World Air Traffic Growth
- Economic Impacts of the Air Transport Industry
    - Direct Impact
    - Indirect Impact
    - Induced Impact
    - Total Impact
- Outlook for the Air Transport Industry
- Summary
- Discussion Questions

The Airline Industry

Due to its relatively minimal profit margins, the financial health of the aviation industry is highly dependent on the global economic conditions and the level of competition. Throughout history, the airline industry has typically generated an average return on invested capital (ROIC) significantly lower than the weighted average cost of capital (WACC). Furthermore, the industry's demand is highly seasonal, cyclical, and impacted by external shocks, such as natural disaster and acts of terrorism.

In the initial months following the onset of COVID-19 pandemic in early 2020, the aviation industry experienced an outbreak of bankruptcies. Since 2020, about 68 airlines have either entered or exited bankruptcy, or been forced into liquidation.[3] By January 2023, Norwegian airline filed for bankruptcy after failing to raise the funds needed to sustain its operations.

Profits tend to soar during times of economic boom, while times of economic distress can lead carriers to reduce their capacity and can possibly face bankruptcy. Although there were some exceptions such as Southwest Airlines and Ryanair, the airline sector has been regarded as a challenging sector for investors due to its inherent volatility and low returns. Nevertheless, recent trends indicate that the industry might at last be seen moving toward a sustainable, long-term equilibrium, where overall airline profits—may be normal, though not spectacular,—aligned with other industries. The year 2015 marked a significant turning point for the industry, facilitated by the oil price decline and industry consolidation, leading to improved financial rewards for equity owners. Furthermore, over the past decade, a series of bankruptcies and mergers has reduced the number of mega-carriers from ten to four. In 2015, four US carriers, namely, American Airlines, Southwest Airlines, Delta Air Lines, and United Airlines, controlled about 80% of the market share. Prior to the onset of the COVID-19 pandemic, from 2015 to 2019, the ROIC surpassed WACC, indicating that the airline industry was generating a substantial value for its investors during this period.

On July 5, 2022, the Scandinavian airline (SAS) filed for Chapter 11 bankruptcy protection.[4]

Since the enactment of the US Airline Deregulation Act of 1978, the airline industry has been characterized by significant volatility. This volatility has resulted in bankruptcies, substantial layoffs, salary cuts for employees, loss of shareholder wealth, and major market uncertainty. Periods of strong revenue generation are often followed by periods of economic drought. The most recent economic downturns were brought about by the COVID-19 pandemic in 2019.

IATA anticipates that the total passenger count will reach 4.0 billion by 2024. This number is predicted to double within the next 20 years. Historically, households with higher incomes travel more frequently compared to those of lower incomes. Furthermore, the emerging economies, such as Asia Pacific and Latin America, will likely see the strongest growth in passenger traffic. Projections indicate that the United States will experience a rise in passenger numbers from 798 million in 2016 to 1.45 billion by 2035.

Prior to deregulation, the airline industry exhibited a relatively stable pattern with minimal losses during economic downturns and enjoying healthy profits during periods of growth. However, it was evident that this stability was mainly due to government regulation that effectively eliminated any competition between airlines and certainly prevented new competitors from entering the market. This situation definitely proved to be the biggest disadvantage for the passenger who had to pay ticket prices designed to cover average airline costs, with no competitive discounts permitted. While this process of deregulation might have appeared to cause huge financial setbacks for numerous airlines, it also exposed those airlines that could not measure up to their first bout of meaningful competition.

On the other hand, deregulation created the opportunity for some carriers, such as Southwest Airlines and Ryanair, to post some of the greatest profits in the history of the industry. Figure 1.1 displays this trend of volatility.

The significant international impact of airline deregulation in the United States can be attributed to the historical dominance of the North American airline industry in the global aviation landscape. As depicted in Table 1.1, the North American market, while still currently securing its position of being the largest in terms of aircraft movement (37.99%), has experienced a decline in its market share concerning passengers and cargo.

In 2019, the Asia-Pacific region recorded a total of 3.38 billion air passengers, representing 37% of the global volume of 9.16 billion passengers. This growth in passenger count was attributed to the explosive economic expansion in those regions, particularly China and India. However, in 2020, the region witnessed only 1.57 billion passengers owing to pandemic-induced restrictions across the globe, an unprecedented 53% crash in traffic.[5] Both Boeing and Airbus

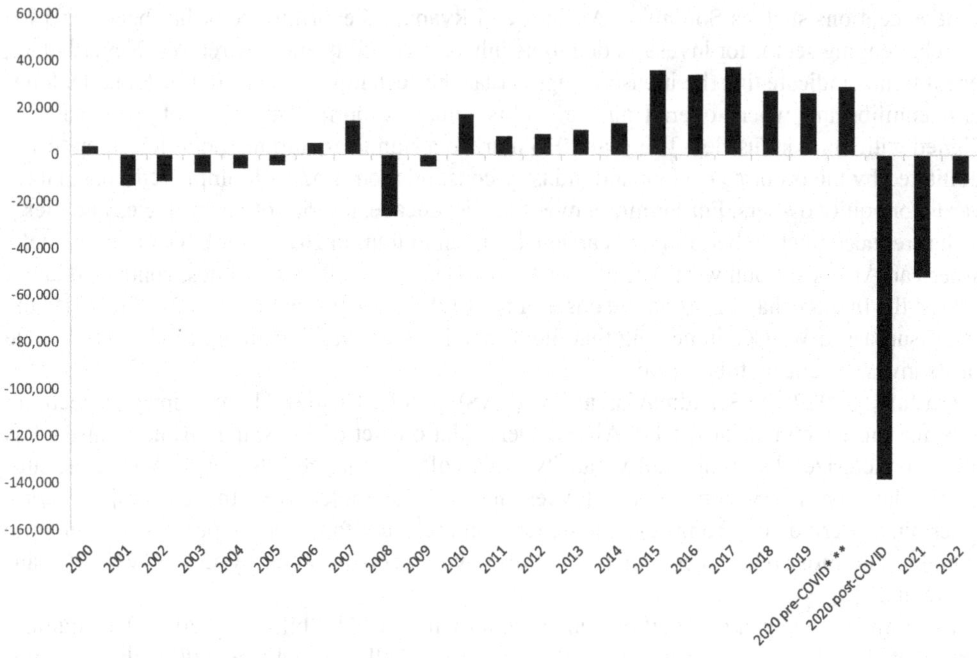

Figure 1.1 World Airline Operating Profits (in Billions).

Source: Compiled by the authors

Table 1.1 World Airlines Passenger and Cargo Traffic, 2021

	Movements	*% Change*	*Passengers*	*% Change*	*Cargo*	*% Change*
Africa	1,542,603	(53.00)	77,029,748	(0.67)	1,895,377	−$24.74
Asia-Pacific	17,065,900	(37.00)	1,568,094,878	(53.46)	41,210,568	−$0.12
Europe	13,275,794	(48.83)	760,011,138	(68.00)	18,914,841	−$0.12
Latin American	4,668,127	(46.00)	276,742,239	(59.00)	4,588,393	−$0.19
Middle East	1,614,966	(48.00)	135,653,825	(66.00)	6,712,560	−$0.23
North America	23,619,770	(32.00)	783,256,482	(61.00)	35,160,317	−$0.02
Total	**61,787,160**	**(40.0)**	**3,600,788,310**	**(62.61)**	**108,482,056**	**−$0.14**

Source: ICAO–ACI Airport Data.

Cargo is quoted in metric tons.

market forecasts point out that the Asia-Pacific region is expected to surpass North America in the next 20 years, with over half of the world's air traffic growth driven by travel to, from, or within the Asia-Pacific region.

In terms of international passengers, both the Asia-Pacific and European markets have far surpassed North America as depicted in Table 1.2. The supremacy of North America in the domain of international air transportation is mainly attributed to its robust economy and extensive geographical area. On the other hand, Europe emerged as the second biggest market in 2020 due to the presence of numerous small countries and significant government support for surface transportation, mainly railroads. As a result, most of the domestic aviation markets in Europe remain relatively small, causing European airlines to heavily rely on international travel

Table 1.2 International Passengers and Cargo Traffic, 2021

	Passengers	*% Change*	*Freight*
Africa	44,045,995	(16.5)	1,835,006
Asia-Pacific	178,030,972	(68.3)	37,114,600
Europe	451,999,206	(37.5)	18,093,529
Latin American	69,685,288	(56.3)	4,432,345
Middle East	83,412,500	(77.3)	6,653,036
North America	82,668,361	(45.0)	33,926,760
Total	**909,842,322**	**75%**	**102,055,276**

Source: Airports Council International, 2020. https://data.icao.int/newDataPlus/Dataplus/App_ACIAirportTraffic.

for sustenance. The growth of economies in Eastern Europe will also undoubtedly increase the region's share of international travel. Growth is also gaining momentum in the Middle East, transforming it into a major global transport hub.

Another trend in air transportation is the rapid growth and expansion of the regional and international cargo industries, as outlined in Tables 1.1 and 1.2. Asia-Pacific asserts its dominance, particularly in the domain of international cargo, with a current market share of 37.9% of the global cargo market. Much of this growth is a result of China's burgeoning economy, coupled with considerable growth in exports originating from this region.

Air cargo has played a key role as a catalyst and beneficiary in the rapid globalization of manufacturing supply chains, especially during the 1990s and 2000s. This acceleration was intensified by China's joining the World Trade Organization (WTO), which facilitated rapid transport links to enable just-in-time manufacturing and assembly. However, the rapid growth during this period slowed following the rise in protectionist measures that followed the post-Global Financial Crisis. Now air cargo growth is adversely affected by the fracturing and reorientation of trade relations resulting from military conflict in Europe and wider geopolitical concerns. This undermines the earlier consensus regarding the benefits of globalization.

Another way of perceiving the global distribution of air transportation is by examining the quantity of in-service aircraft. Table 1.3 classifies aircraft into two categories based on their age: new and middle, or old. While the North American market comprises the highest number of commercial aircraft, it also contains a relatively high percentage of older aircraft (47%). Both North America and the Asia-Pacific region attract the aircraft manufacturers, as many of the older aircraft are expected to be replaced, generating new demand in the coming years. Europe, on the other hand, exhibits a smaller share of old aircraft (27%). This is arguably a result of the stringent noise regulations implemented by the European Community that banned many older-generation aircraft. Finally, some correlation can be discerned between the number of new aircraft and the region's economic growth.

A final method for analyzing the composition of the air transport industry involves examining traffic data based on airports. Tables 1.4 and 1.5 present a list of the top 15 airports ranked by total passengers, total international passengers, and total cargo volume. The prominent rankings mirror the distribution of passengers according to their regions, as *evidenced* by the two leading airports in terms of passenger numbers. Given North America constitutes the second-largest passenger market, it is not surprising that Atlanta holds the top spot for the highest passenger count. Similarly, the Middle East is experiencing robust growth, while Europe is a prominent hub for international passengers. Thus, it should come as no surprise that Dubai and London claim the top two airports for international passengers traffic. Additionally, many of the airports listed in Table 1.4 are located in countries with relatively smaller or nonexistent domestic air

Table 1.3 Number of Aircraft in Service

Region	*As of August 2022*		
	Number of Fleet in Service	*Average Fleet Age*	*Median Fleet Age*
Asia-Pacific	9,152	11.8	9.2
Africa	1,471	21.7	20.6
Europe	7,472	14.3	12.3
Latin America	2,369	17.9	12.7
Middle East	1,532	12.7	9.1
North America	10,261	18.7	17.7

Source: https://centreforaviation.com/data.

Table 1.4 Airport Passenger Traffic, 2021

Total Passenger Traffic				*Aircraft Movements*			
Rank	*Airport*	*Total*	*% Change*	*Rank*	*Airport*	*Total*	*% Change*
1	Atlanta (ATL)	75,704,760	76.4	1	Atlanta (ATL)	707,661	29.10
2	Dalla/Fort Worth (DFW)	62,465,756	58.7	2	Chicago (ORD)	684,201	27.10
3	Denver (DEN)	58,828,552	74.4	3	Dalla/Fort Worth (DFW)	651,895	26.70
4	Chicago (ORD)	54,020,399	75.1	4	Denver (DEN)	580,866	32.90
5	Los Angeles (LAX)	49,007,284	66.8	5	Charlotte NC (CLT)	519,895	33.60
6	Charlotte, NC (CLT)	43,302,230	59.2	6	Los Angeles (LAX)	506,769	33.60
7	Orlando (MCO)	40,351,068	86.7	7	Las Vegas (LAS)	486,540	50.40
8	Guangzhou (CAN)	40,259,401	(8.0)	8	Phoenix (PHX)	408,285	31.06
9	Chengdu (CTU)	40,117,496	(1.5)	9	Miami (MIA)	387,973	16.30
10	Las Vegas (LAS)	39,754,366	78.6	10	Houston, TX	378,562	11.10
11	Phoenix (PHX)	38,846,713	77.2	11	Seattle, WA	374,510	26.50
12	Miami (MIA)	37,302,456	99.9	12	Guangzhou (CAN)	362,470	(2.90)
13	New Delhi (DEL)	37,139,957	30.3	13	Long Beach, US (LGB)	350,022	21.80
14	Istanbul (IST)	36,988,067	58.5	14	Shanghai, CN (PVG)	349,524	(0.80)
15	Shenzhen (SZX)	36,358,185	(4.1)	15	Grand Fork ND. US (SLC)	249,524	41.60

travel markets. Similar to the airline market, the airport sector in the Asia-Pacific region is undergoing remarkable expansion. For example, Beijing Capital International Airport ranks as the second busiest in the world in terms of total passenger traffic, closely followed by Tokyo International Airport in Japan, which secures the fourth place.

Much of the airport development in the Asia-Pacific region remains concentrated in China and India, with notable projects already underway in Vietnam, the Philippines, and Indonesia. The distribution of airports by region in terms of cargo volume is not clear-cut, but facilities in North America, Asia-Pacific, and Europe are well represented in the top 15. Notably, Hong Kong is the busiest cargo airport in the world. In the Asia-Pacific region, the large amount of

Table 1.5 Cargo Traffic at Major International Airports, 2021

Rank	*Airport*	*Cargo (Metric Tons)*	*% Change*
1	Hong Kong (HKG)	5,025,495	12.2
2	Memphis (MEM)	4,480,465	(2.9)
3	Shanghai (PVG)	3,982,616	8.0
4	Anchorage (ANC)	3,555,160	12.6
5	Incheaon (ICN)	3,329,292	18.0
6	Louisville (SDF)	3,052,269	4.6
7	Taipei (TPE)	2,812,065	20.0
8	Los Angeles (LAX)	2,691,830	20.7
9	Tokyo (NRT)	2,644,074	31.1
10	Doha (DOH)	2,620,095	20.50
11	Chicago (ORD)	2,536,576	26.7
12	Miami (MIA)	2,520,859	17.9
13	Dubai (DXB)	2,319,185	20.0
14	Frankfurt (FRA)	2,274,969	18.8
15	Paris (CDG)	2,062,433	18.1

export trade has spurred cargo growth, especially in Hong Kong and Shanghai, which occupy the first and third positions, respectively.

Financial Condition of the Airline Industry

The U.S. Airline Deregulation Act of 1978 dramatically transformed the financial landscape of the global airline industry. Following the United States' lead, other countries also began the process of deregulating their own aviation markets. Prior to 1978, commercial aviation was relatively stable mainly based on the government's enforcement of non-competitive behavior and pricing control. In the post-deregulation era, the industry adopted a more cyclical nature of a competitive industry, where periods of robust financial profitability could be followed by periods of severe economic distress. Akin to other competitive industries, the financial health of the airline industry is strongly related to economic growth. Therefore, it is not surprising that the airlines suffer in the face of economic slowdowns.

More fundamentally, the structure of costs within most airlines poses challenges in achieving a sufficient price to generate a normal return on capital. Numerous costs are fixed, influenced by the process of setting flight schedules for half-year seasons. The marginal cost of flying an additional passenger can be minimal as a result, including just a small quantity of fuel and perhaps catering to some seat classes. In the face of strong actual or potential competition, fares and cargo rates get driven down toward these low marginal costs. This level can sometimes go below average costs due to large fixed costs, ultimately yielding operational losses.

Of course, airlines make efforts to ensure routes and flights are profitable. However, the characteristics of air transport services present additional challenges in this endeavor. One characteristic is that aircraft seats or cargo hold space is 'perishable.' In essence, once a flight takes off, any unsold seat on that flight is worthless. Unlike other industries, unsold seats cannot be retained in inventory for future sale. As a result, there is considerable pressure to fill seats and cargo holds at any price, even if it generates cash rather than profit. A further characteristic that drives pricing downward is that most airline seats and schedules are similar, homogenous, lacking in differentiation. Most air passengers willingly switch between airlines on a route if the fare is lower. Airlines have tried to address this lack of significant product differentiation with frequent flier programs and, more recently, the introduction of ancillary services. However, for most airlines, it remains the case that these fundamental cost and product characteristics make it difficult to maintain unit revenues significantly higher than unit costs.

In the early 1980s, shortly after deregulation of the US airline industry, the sector suffered a minor crisis as a result of the economy slowdown and rising competition. More specifically, the US domestic industry experienced overcapacity, as the many new airlines that were formed out of deregulation either went bankrupt or merged with other carriers. Consequently, the industry endured a span of four years of global net losses, largely based on the situation in the United States. A similar situation unfolded in the early 1990s, driven by an economic downturn coupled with additional pressures arising from political uncertainty resulting from the first Gulf War and increased fuel costs.

Although the early stages of each decade following deregulation have posed challenges for the airlines, the industry has managed to recover and achieve record short-term profits in the late 1980s and again in the late 1990s. This comeback was driven not only by the overall improvement in the global economy, but also by the impetus of financial distress and heightened competition, which prompted airlines to adopt innovative approaches and maintain stricter cost controls. During these periods, strategies such as revenue management and passenger loyalty programs were developed to boost profitability. Additionally, technological innovations allowed the airlines to improve their profit margins. Given that fuel constitutes a substantial cost, the industry's overall focus lies in improving efficiency. For example, better engine design has reduced the number of engines needed to fly an aircraft. All of these technologies have enabled airlines to reduce their costs and/or increase revenue. A more recent technological innovation has been e-ticketing, which has enabled airlines to reduce their ticket distribution costs.

The post-deregulation pattern of profitability continued into the new century, with the global industry experiencing its worst downturn to date. While the terrorist attacks of 2001 and the 2007/2008 financial crisis were secondary contributors, the root causes were low yields and exceptionally high costs. Specifically, the industry grappled with escalating prices for fuel and airport security, coupled with the impact of domestic overcapacity that drove up operating costs. In fact, airlines were facing trouble before the September 11 disaster, with many carriers operating at a loss and lacking significant initiatives to reduce expenses or increase productivity. This resulted in an industry-wide net loss from 2001 to 2005, followed by an economic resurgence in 2006 and 2007. These profits were short lived. However, the year 2008 was arguably one of the worst in the history of commercial aviation. Subsequent to this, the industry suffered losses due to the COVID-19 pandemic, surpassing $200 billion in the period from 2020 to 2022, as shown in Table 1.6.

However, the road to recovery has been slow for the airline industry due to various reasons, such as political instability in various parts of the world, rising fuel prices, and persistent competition between network and low-cost carriers. This situation has been most evident in the North American market. The industry bore witness to high-profile bankruptcies of US Airways, United, Delta, Northwest, and then American. These bankruptcies highlighted the increasing impacts of fierce competition from lower-cost airlines and the ungainly cost structures of the more traditional carriers. This scenario led to a trend of consolidation in the industry over recent years.

In the United States, bankruptcy protection enabled several carriers to restructure their costs and force wage concessions from labor groups. Moreover, carriers reduced overcapacity and shifted capacity to international markets that offered new opportunities. Several low-cost carriers (LCCs) have also remained successful and profitable by continuing to expand while keeping costs relatively constant. Innovations such as e-ticketing and fleet rationalization have been instrumental in helping airlines achieve cost reductions, thereby narrowing the cost gap between network airlines and LCCs. Figure 1.2 provides a comparison in terms of Cost per Available Seat Mile (CASM).

Table 1.6 Scheduled Airlines Financial Performance

	2006	*2010*	*2016*	*2017*	*2018*	*2019*	*2020*	*2021*	*2022*
Revenues, $ billion	**465**	**564**	**709**	**755**	**812**	**838**	**373**	**472**	**658**
Passenger	365	445	545	581	605	607	189	227	378
Cargo	53.2	66.1	80.8	95.9	113.3	100.8	128.8	175.0	168.9
Other	46.8	52.9	83.2	78.1	93.7	130.2	55.2	70.0	111.1
Sched. passengers, millions	2,258	2,700	3,817	4,095	4,378	4,543	1,807	2,277	3,432
Freight tonnes, millions	43.4	49.1	57.0	61.5	63.5	61.5	56.1	66.2	69.3
Passenger yield, %	6.6	9.5	(7.0)	(1.3)	(3.0)	(3.7)	(8.8)	2.0	10.0
Cargo yield, %	4.4	14.4	(7.4)	8.2	14.0	(8.2)	40.0	15.0	(8.0)
Expenses, $ billion	**450**	**536**	**649**	**698**	**766**	**795**	**484**	**526**	**676**
Fuel	127	152	135	150	178	186	78	100	132
Crude oil price, Brent, $/b	65.1	79.4	44.6	54.9	71.6	65.0	43.5	69.6	67.0
Jet kerosene price, $/b	81.9	91.4	52.1	66.7	86.1	77.0	46.6	74.5	77.8
Non-fuel	324	384	514	549	588	608	405	426	544
cents per ATK (non-fuel unit cost)	36.6	40.0	38.5	38.9	39.3	39.4	47.1	43.3	44.2
Break-even weight load factor, %	60.7	63.5	62.8	65.0	66.5	66.4	77.4	68.7	65.9
Weight load factor achieved, %	62.7	66.8	68.6	70.3	70.5	70.0	59.7	61.7	64.1
Passenger load factor achieved, %	76.1	78.7	80.5	81.6	82.0	82.6	65.1	67.1	75.1
Operating profit, $ billion	**15.0**	**27.6**	**60.1**	**56.6**	**45.9**	**43.2**	**(110.8)**	**(53.8)**	**(18.0)**
% margin	3.2	4.9	8.5	7.5	5.7	5.2	(29.7)	(11.4)	(2.7)
Net profit, $ billion	**5.0**	**17.3**	**34.2**	**37.6**	**27.3**	**26.4**	**(137.7)**	**(51.8)**	**(11.6)**
% margin	1.1	3.1	4.8	5.0	3.4	3.1	(37.0)	(11.0)	(1.8)

Source: Compiled by the authors from ICAO and IATA airline financial data.

Air transport unit costs have experienced a substantial decline in real terms due to technological and business model innovation. Contrary to the notion that poor profitability is driven by high costs, the root challenge for airline financial performance lies elsewhere. While substantial cost reductions have been achieved, these benefits have been often transferred to consumers through lower air fares and cargo rates. This phenomenon is due to competitive pressure within the industry and the economic structure of costs and products, as previously discussed.

Among network carriers in 2019, before the onset of COVID-19 pandemic, Delta Air Lines generated the most revenue (Table 1.7). During the pandemic in 2020, air cargo thrived, while passenger services were severely curtailed due to border restriction and other control measures; this resulted in FedEx generating the highest revenues.

Consolidation and Bankruptcies

The airline industry serves as a good example of an oligopoly, wherein a few airlines hold the significant portion of the market share. Examples such as Delta Air Lines, Singapore Airlines, and Air France operate their routes with limited direct competitors, especially in long-haul

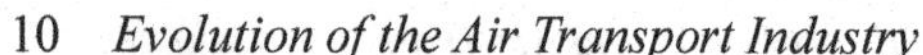

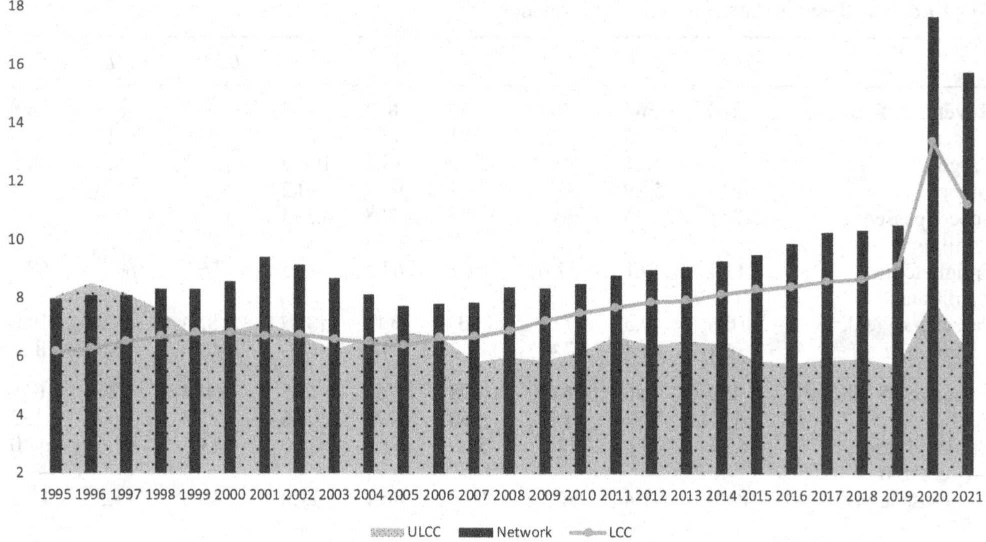

Figure 1.2 Cost Comparison between Ultra-Low-Cost, Low-Cost, and Legacy Carriers (CASM).
Source: Compiled from MIT Airline Data Project

Table 1.7 Top 10 Airlines by Revenue, 2020 and 2021

2020			*2021*		
Rank	*Airline*	*Revenue in Billions*	*Rank*	*Airline*	*Revenue in Billions*
1	Lufthansa	17.86	1	American Airlines	29.90
2	American Airlines	17.34	2	Delta Air Lines	29.90
3	Delta Air Lines	17.10	3	United Airlines	24.60
4	United Airlines	15.36	4	Air France-KLM	16.58
5	China Southern	13.44	5	China Southern	16.40
6	Air France-KLM	12.70	6	Lufthansa Group	15.40
7	Air China	10.72	7	Air China	10.90
8	Emirates Group	9.69	8	China Eastern Airlines	10.80
9	China Eastern Airlines	9.35	9	Southwest Airlines	9.10
10	Southwest Airlines	9.05	10	ANA	8.00

markets. However, the intricate economics of the airline sector, marked by economic recession, rising fuel costs, and stiff competition, have forced many carriers to face financial distress. This has resulted in the liquidation of companies such as Eastern Airlines, Pan American, and Piedmont. Additionally, American Airlines, US Airways, United Airlines, Delta Air Lines, and Northwest Airlines have sought bankruptcy protection to navigate through the financial challenges. The period immediately following deregulation, particularly in the 1980s, was one of the most turbulent periods for commercial aviation in the United States and produced the greatest rate of airline bankruptcies. The number of mergers rapidly increased following deregulation in 1978, and over the next ten years, a total of 51 airline mergers and acquisitions took place. Consequently, these consolidations yielded six legacy carriers from the initial 15 independent carriers that had nearly 80% of the US market share in 1987.

Since 1990, more than 189 airlines have filed for bankruptcy. Most recently filed airlines were Delta and Northwest in 2005. These carriers eventually merged, followed by United and Continental in 2010.

In response to the challenges they faced, airlines adopted the strategies of mergers and consolidations. Over the past few years, several mergers have changed the competitive landscape of the market, particularly Delta–Northwest, United–Continental, Southwest–AirTran, and US Airways–American. The merger between Delta and Northwest in 2008 resulted in the creation of the largest commercial airline in the world, boasting a fleet of 822 aircraft.[6] The merger of American and US Airways increased American's market share at Philadelphia airport to 77%.[7] While in the United States, the top four carriers have around 70% of the market share, in Europe, they just have 45% of the market share.[8]

Most recently, Alaska Air Group closed the $2.6-billion acquisition of Virgin America following approval from the Justice Department.[9] The newly merged carrier will create the fifth largest airline in the United States, uniting the two carriers and serving a combined customer base of 40 million individuals.[10]

A merger and consolidation are the act of joining of two corporations to form a new larger entity, to reduce competition and enjoy broader economies of scale or scope.

Table 1.8 displays the domestic market share for various US carriers. In 2008, Southwest Airlines surpassed Delta Air Lines to emerge as the largest domestic carrier (in terms of passengers flown) in the United States. Southwest Airlines maintained its ranking until 2010 when Delta merged with Northwest. In 2015, American Airlines ranked first with 23% market share, followed closely by Southwest Airlines. Although small when compared to Southwest, JetBlue, and Spirit, both enjoyed a gradual rise in the market share as well. Clearly, LCCs are capturing more of the domestic market share, while legacy network carriers are losing theirs. This is mainly due to the LCCs' ongoing expansion and the advantages stemming from their lower-cost structures.

While the frequency of mergers reduced during the 1990s, critics still assert that most mergers were part of well-planned strategies to lessen competition in various markets. As a result, starting in 1985, the Department of Transportation (DOT) assumed the approval authority for all airline mergers. This decision mandated that the DOT must now balance the consumer benefits against the potential negative effects stemming from increased market concentration. On the other hand, the extraordinary financial problems of legacy carriers suggest that reductions in capacity, whether through mergers or alliances, may be inevitable. Some economists contend that reducing competition through consolidation and coordination can actually benefit passengers by allowing airlines to build more efficient networks with greater economies of scale, scope, and density. Figure 1.3 provides a framework of the major airline mergers that have transpired in the United States since the advent of deregulation. As of October 2016, a mere four airlines control 85% of the US air travel market. As such, some consumers feel that the merger between Virgin America and Alaska Air Group (ALK) have made the market less competitive.[11]

The Herfindahl-Hirschman index (HHI) serves as a measure of US market consolidation within the airline industry. This trend of consolidation has been a common strategy in recent years, as airlines endeavor to establish a competitive advantage through market power and efficiency. As highlighted in Table 1.8, the trend toward consolidation has grown more pronounced since 2011.[12] The combined market dominance of four airlines, namely, American Airlines,

Table 1.8 US Airline Industry Domestic Market Share, 2004–2021

Airlines	*2004*	*2005*	*2008*	*2010*	*2011*	*2016*	*2017*	*2018*	*2019*	*2020*	*2021*
American	18.51%	18.00%	16.34%	15.91%	15.43%	20.31%	15.66%	15.32%	15.49%	16.83%	18.30%
Continental	7.90%	7.88%	8.50%	8.33%	8.54%						
Delta	15.48%	15.39%	11.65%	18.80%	18.32%	20.74%	16.26%	16.24%	16.76%	14.37%	17.10%
Northwest	8.84%	8.64%	7.25%								
United	14.68%	13.11%	12.42%	11.53%	10.50%	12.86%	10.83%	11.03%	10.76%	8.92%	14.30%
US Airways	6.36%	6.27%	9.32%	9.00%	8.95%						
America West	4.58%	4.59%									
Southwest	12.10%	13.34%	16.60%	16.83%	17.50%	25.91%	20.68%	20.40%	19.47%	19.78%	17.10%
jetBlue	2.95%	3.70%	4.97%	5.05%	5.32%	5.44%	4.35%	4.35%	4.14%	3.30%	5.40%
AirTran	1.89%	2.40%	3.82%	3.93%	3.95%						
Frontier	1.29%	1.34%	1.79%	1.76%	1.92%	2.45%	2.14%	0.00%	2.68%	3.24%	3.20%
Virgin America	0.0%	0.0%	0.72%	1.31%	1.60%	1.37%					
Alaska	3.17%	3.16%	3.50%	3.86%	4.09%	3.94%	3.23%	4.04%	4.13%	3.37%	5.70%
Hawaiian	1.07%	1.11%	1.38%	1.53%	1.52%	1.70%	1.34%	1.32%	1.25%	0.89%	1.80%
Spirit	0.99%	0.83%	1.04%	1.12%	1.32%	3.34%	2.95%	3.37%	3.77%	4.99%	4.70%
Allegiant	0.18%	0.25%	0.69%	1.03%	1.04%	1.94%	1.65%	1.76%	1.85%	2.58%	2.25%
HHI	1,172.6	1,141.0	1,103.2	1,238.8	1,215.5	1,750.0	1,389.6	1,412.7	1,316.6	1,311.7	1,340.7

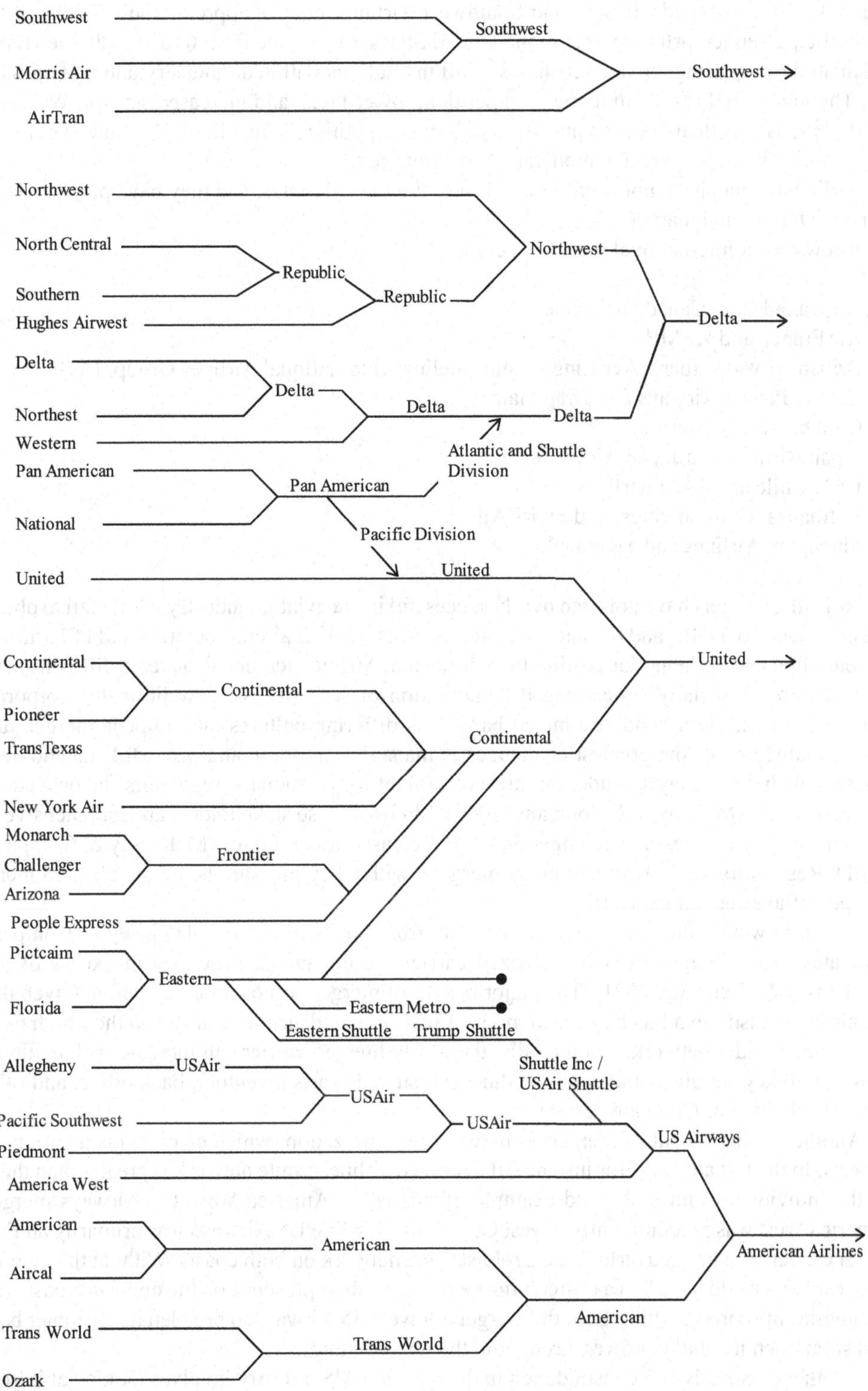

Figure 1.3 Evolution of US Airline Industry.

Delta Air Lines, United Airlines, and Southwest Airlines, control approximately 74.3% of the domestic passenger airline market in the United States. On a scale from 0 to 10,000, the HHI is calculated by squaring the market shares of all institutions within an industry and adding them up. The lower HHI results in higher competition, lower fares, and increased service. When the HHI value is less than 100, the market is highly competitive. When the HHI value is between 1,000 and 1,800, the market is moderately concentrated.

Airline mergers have not been limited just to the United States, and they have played a large part in international market.

A few recent international mergers include:

- Air Canada and Canadian Airlines
- Air France and KLM[13]
- British Airways, Iberia Aer Lingus, and Vueling (International Airlines Group, IAG)
- Cathay Pacific Airways and Dragonair
- Cimber Air and Sterling
- Japan Airlines and Japan Air System
- LAN Chile and TAM Airlines[14]
- Lufthansa, Germanwings, and Swiss Air
- Singapore Airlines and Tigerair[15]

Historically, mergers have not been overly successful in the aviation industry. Many fail to obtain the envisioned benefits, and the one-time merger costs, such as aircraft painting and IT harmonization, often end up being far costlier than projected. Airline mergers also create difficulty with labor groups, especially concerning the integration of seniority lists. Additionally, corporate culture can be a highly underestimated barrier, as differing cultures may impede merger success. Finally, one of the greatest challenges is managing multiple and powerful stakeholders. These stakeholders may include, but are not limited to, politicians, regulators, labor leaders, and consumers (McKinsey & Company, 2001). Many of these stakeholders are apprehensive of mergers as they fear lessened competition and increased travel prices (McKinsey & Company, 2001). Regulators have prevented many mergers, with a key measure being the planned mergers' potential effect on the HHI.

Again, however, there are potential benefits from airline mergers. McKinsey & Company estimates that a merger of two mid-sized carriers could unlock synergies in excess of 7% (McKinsey & Company, 2001). The major benefit of mergers is cost rationalization. Given that the airline industry exhibits large economies of scale, merged airlines can spread their high fixed costs over a wider network. Additionally, the newly merged carrier can increase its bargaining power with key suppliers and combine functions such as parts inventory, back office, and sales force (McKinsey & Company, 2001).

Another major benefit of mergers is network harmonization, which can include a variety of aspects. In the last analysis, for instance, the merged airline's route network is greater than those of the individual airlines. A good example of this is the America West–US Airways merger. America West was predominantly a West Coast carrier, while US Airways was primarily an East Coast carrier. The merged airline had a robust route network on both coasts. Without the merger, both carriers would have had a difficult time expanding their presence on the opposite coast. The economies of scope resulting from the merger allowed US Airways to broaden its customer base and strengthen its market power throughout the United States.

Another perspective on consolidation in the domestic US industry involves looking at it from the airport level. Following deregulation, the major carriers adopted a hub-and-spoke system, channeling passengers through a few key airports. Consequently, some carriers gained dominant positions at specific hub airports across the United States. Table 1.9 depicts the concentration by enplanement and operating carrier at the ten largest airports in the United States.

The general trend in airport consolidation from 2004 through 2023 shows the increasing dominance of the largest carrier. In Dallas, Delta's withdrawal left American Airlines as the only major airline still in operation (with a 67.64% market share in 2023). Simultaneously, this change rendered Dallas one of the most consolidated domestic airports between 2005 and 2023.

The reduction in consolidation at US airports is largely attributable to two factors:

1 Increased competition, particularly from LCCs.
2 Major carriers pushing more flying to regional affiliates.

LCC$_s$, Southwest, Frontier, and Spirit have positioned themselves in the dominant hubs of Denver and Atlanta, effectively capturing market share at those airports. With the emergence of regional jets, major carriers have been redirecting capacity toward regional carriers in an attempt to reduce costs. As an indication of this trend, in May 2007, Bombardier Aerospace introduced the next-generation versions of its CRJ700, CRJ900, and CRJ1000 regional jets. These new CRJ NextGen aircraft featured significant operating cost improvements and an increased use

Table 1.9a Major US Airports Concentration (with Enplanements by Operating Carrier)

		2004	*2005*	*2006*	*2007*	*2008*	*2009*
Atlanta	Largest carrier %	68.4	66.8	60.0	56.8	56.7	56.1
(ATL)	Largest carrier	DL	DL	DL	DL	DL	DL
	Herfindahl index	4,916	4,794	4,063	3,771	3,764	3,707
Chicago	Largest carrier %	40.7	36.5	36.4	36.2	36.4	34.2
(ORD)	Largest carrier	UA	UA	UA	UA	UA	UA
	Herfindahl index	2,716	2,421	2,352	2,339	2,320	2,091
Dallas	Largest carrier %	65.8	73.8	73.8	74.1	74.6	74.6
(DFW)	Largest carrier	AA	AA	AA	AA	AA	AA
	Herfindahl index	4,521	5,607	5,612	5,665	5,730	5,708
Denver	Largest carrier %	48.8	44.5	44.0	41.6	38.0	32.8
(DEN)	Largest carrier	UA	UA	UA	UA	UA	UA
	Herfindahl Index	2,729	2,432	2,468	2,340	2,140	1,838
Detroit	Largest carrier %	67.4	64.6	63.7	62.4	58.4	52.2
(DTW)	Largest carrier	NW	NW	NW	NW	NW	NW
	Herfindahl Index	4,684	4,338	4,220	4,086	3,640	3,028
Houston	Largest carrier %	66.7	64.6	63.7	65.1	65.6	65.1
(IAH)	Largest carrier	CO	CO	CO	CO	CO	CO
	Herfindahl Index	4,855	4,711	4,715	4,653	4,695	4,712
Las Vegas	Largest carrier %	33.9	33.7	36.5	37.1	38.8	41.5
(LAS)	Largest carrier	WN	WN	WN	WN	WN	WN
	Herfindahl Index	1,705	1,701	1,835	1,753	1,982	2,097
Los Angeles	Largest carrier %	21.9	20.5	21.1	19.7	19.5	19.6
(LAX)	Largest carrier	UA	UA	UA	AA	AA	AA
	Herfindahl Index	1,268	1,290	1,303	1,214	1,191	1,180
Minneapolis	Largest carrier %	69.4	67.1	67.4	67.2	62.0	54.3
(MSP)	Largest carrier	NW	NW	NW	NW	NW	NW
	Herfindahl Index	4,930	4,625	4,663	4,632	3,997	3,170
Phoenix	Largest carrier %	38.1	37.5	35.8	30.4	39.3	39.7
(PHX)	Largest carrier	HP	HP	HP	WN	US	US
	Herfindahl Index	2,387	2,411	2,360	1,893	2,555	2,604

Source: Compiled by the authors using Form 41 data.

Table 1.9b Major US Airports Concentration (with Enplanements by Operating Carrier)

		2017	*2018*	*2019*	*2020*	*2021*
Atlanta (ATL)	Largest carrier %	72.75	72.71	72.82	67.59	69.29
	Largest carrier	DL	DL	DL	DL	DL
	Herfindahl Index	4,708.0	4,713.8	4,697.8	5,432.0	5,199.4
Chicago (ORD)	Largest carrier %	32.08	31.80	31.35	26.61	27.99
	Largest carrier	UA	UA	UA	UA	UA
	Herfindahl Index	8,971.0	8,988.9	9,017.3	9,292.0	9,216.6
Dallas (DFW)	Largest carrier %	68.60	68.29	68.06	64.66	66.03
	Largest carrier	AA	AA	AA	AA	AA
	Herfindahl Index	5,294.5	5,336.9	5,368.3	5,819.5	5,640.5
Denver (DEN)	Largest carrier %	30.34	30.52	31.50	31.03	30.30
	Largest carrier	UA	UA	UA	UA	UA
	Herfindahl Index	9,079.6	9,068.6	9,007.8	9,037.2	9,082.0
Detroit (DTW)	Largest carrier %	47.10	46.96	49.51	45.12	49.45
	Largest carrier	DL	DL	DL	DL	DL
	Herfindahl Index	7,781.8	7,795.0	7,549.0	7,964.4	7,554.9
Houston (IAH)	Largest carrier %	52.92	53.22	50.89	44.87	46.70
	Largest carrier	UA	UA	UA	UA	UA
	Herfindahl Index	7,199.8	7,167.9	7,410.5	7,986.9	7,819.3
Las Vegas (LAS)	Largest carrier %	41.25	40.27	37.31	36.86	36.77
	Largest carrier	WN	WN	WN	WN	WN
	Herfindahl Index	8,298.6	8,378.5	8,608.1	8,641.5	8,648.1
Los Angeles (LAX)	Largest carrier %	18.77	19.32	20.32	21.75	21.56
	Largest carrier	AA	AA	AA	AA	AA
	Herfindahl Index	9,647.7	9,626.8	9,587.1	9,527.0	9,535.2
Minneapolis (MSP)	Largest carrier %	52.50	52.92	53.55	48.28	51.01
	Largest carrier	DL	DL	DL	DL	DL
	Herfindahl Index	7,244.0	7,199.8	7,132.7	7,669.3	7,398.2
Phoenix (PHX)	Largest carrier %	37.36	36.99	37.46	35.54	35.37
	Largest carrier	WN	WN	WN	WN	WN
	Herfindahl Index	8,604.4	8,631.9	8,596.9	8,737.0	8,749.1

Source: https://www.transtats.bts.gov/airports.asp?20=E.
Source: Compiled by the authors using Form 41 data.

of composite materials. On June 25, 2019, Bombardier reached an agreement with Mitsubishi Heavy Industries (MHI) to sell the CRJ program, with the deal anticipated to close in early 2020 subject to regulatory approval. Bombardier concluded sale of the CRJ Series Regional Jet program to MHI in 2020.

Because the Form 41 data used in Table 1.9 breaks down data by operating carriers, regional carriers are handled separately. For example, ExpressJet's operations at Houston are treated separately, even though the flights are marketed by United Airlines. This could potentially distort the level of consolidation at airports with a significant regional carrier presence.

As shown in Table 1.9, the HHI indicates a decline in consolidation within the US domestic airline industry when consolidation is analyzed on an airport basis. However, it is important to remember that the degree of consolidation at major US airports far surpasses that of industry-wide consolidation. The airport with the lowest level of consolidation on the list is Los Angeles (1,935), while Atlanta Airport stands out as the most consolidated with a value of 5,454. Therefore, in at least a few markets, airline mergers have led to diminished competition and increased consolidation at major US airports.

Airlines have aimed to address poor profitability through consolidation with domestic market mergers and increasingly closer business partnerships (code shares, alliance, joint ventures) on international markets, where cross-border mergers are generally prohibited. However, subsequent chapters will illustrate why this approach has often not been successful. Scale economies in fleet are quickly attained—where bigger is not always more beautiful—although very significant economies from more dense traffic flows, allowing larger aircraft and higher load factors, can be achieved through smart network mergers. Lower unit costs due to scale or density will not improve profitability if these are fully passed through to consumers at lower fares. Therefore, the impact of consolidation in reducing competitive pressures has been significant. Equally important for recent profitability has been the introduction of ancillary services, as new business models treat the aircraft or seat as a 'platform' for selling multiple goods and services to consumers.

Factors Affecting World Air Traffic Growth

The factors influencing air traffic growth are numerous and complex, and operate on global, national, and regional levels. This diversity helps explain why air travel can experience significant growth in one country or city while remaining stagnant in another. Growth factors include:

- Gross Domestic Product
- Lower travel costs
- Political factors
- Random events
- Trade liberalization and open skies

> Gross Domestic Product (GDP) is the total dollar value of all goods and services produced over a specific time in a given economy.

Indicators such as Gross Domestic Product (GDP) and Gross National Product (GNP) measure the level of economic prosperity. GDP represents the total market value of all final goods and services produced in a country in a given year. Increased prosperity drives increased demand for air travel in two separate but concurrent ways. First, increased economic activity helps generate employment and trade, leading to an increase in business travel, the most important segment for airlines. Business travel is the primary reason why world financial centers, such as London and New York, have experienced robust air traffic growth. Additionally, increased economic activity also spurs air cargo growth.

The second outcome of economic prosperity is a decrease in unemployment along with a concurrent increase in household income. People possess more discretionary income and are more often able to afford leisure travel trips. An illustrative example of this can be observed in China, where a growing middle class has driven a significant expansion of air travel within the country.

A reduction in the real cost of air travel will also result in increased air traffic. Remarkable advancements in fuel efficiency, originating from engine technologies, brought about this change. This change was first witnessed in the 1970s when deregulation resulted in a substantial decline in ticket prices. Air travel became affordable to a greater number of people, and they took full advantage of the opportunity. Fares were particularly low after new business models and competition were introduced by the LCCs, and airports experienced tremendous growth in their passenger statistics once a low-cost airline initiated service. This phenomenon has been coined the "Southwest Effect." Ryanair is accomplishing similar feats in Europe where weekend getaways are now affordable to almost everyone. Norwegian is trying to join forces with Ryanair and easyJet to challenge the long-haul routes of full-service airlines.[16]

Travel cost for the consumer encompasses not only the fare but also the duration of journey times. While this might be primarily an inconvenience for the leisure passenger, it holds a material financial impact for business travelers or their employers. Technological and business model advancements have facilitated the direct connection of an increasing number of cities, thereby reducing journey times and, therefore, overall expenses for consumers. Reducing travel times through direct city-pair connections has boosted air travel demand in recent decades.

Another factor influencing world air traffic is population. Robust population growth in developing countries, such as India and China, has played a pivotal role in driving the expansion of air travel growth. However, this only occurs when population growth is accompanied by income growth.

The substantial growth of air travel in these densely populated Asian markets illustrates how the inclination to travel for individuals rises dramatically once incomes exceed certain thresholds. These thresholds act as multipliers on the influence of large populations on the demand for air travel. In contrast, as income levels rise to those typical of a developed country, the inclination to fly stabilizes. Individuals appear to reach a limit to the number of times they wish to fly annually, despite their higher living standards.

Trade liberalization is another significant factor influencing air transportation. The liberalization of air travel and implementation of Open Sky Agreements enhance both traffic and economy. On the contrary, restrictive bilateral air services agreements between countries reduce air travel, tourism, and business. An Open Skies agreement establishes an open market between two or more signatory nations. The establishment of the Single European Aviation Market led to an average annual growth rate in traffic between 1995 and 2004 that was almost double the rate observed between 1990 and 1994.[17] When such artificial barriers are lifted, the marketplace dictates demand for goods and services, often resulting in increased air travel. The reason is that government regulation in the aviation industry usually involves ticket prices and market access. In this context, preferred airlines (usually a national airline) are granted monopoly access with some sort of a fare structure to cover average costs. This effectively eliminates competition and restricts the growth of air traffic. The United States itself serves as a good example of economic liberalization. Following deregulation, airfares plummeted, and air traffic growth increased significantly. Moreover, the freedom for airlines to fly to any destination made flying more convenient for passengers by providing more non-stop flights with greater frequency. Likewise, recent air transport liberalization in Europe and India has led to a tremendous growth in air traffic within these countries.

Politics and political stability also play a role in air travel. Not surprisingly, traffic growth is slow in countries that follow protectionist policies. In these cases, the government restricts air travel as a matter of political policy. Political instability can also greatly influence air travel, as people do not want to travel to regions where they feel unsafe. This is arguably the reason for the poor air traffic growth in parts of Africa where governments are in constant turmoil. Finally, political instability reduces and/or restricts business activities within the country.

Terrorist attacks can also impact air travel. Following the tragic events of September 11, traffic reduced drastically as passengers no longer felt safe traveling within the United States. Additionally, many were hesitant to travel to international destinations in fear of a similar attack taking place.

Ransom shocks, such as terrorism, have significant impacts on air transport demand. An economic study from Cornell University demonstrated that following the terrorist attacks on September 11, 2001, a 9% reduction in the nation's busiest airports was evidenced, totaling a nearly $1 billion loss for the airline industry.

Finally, the amount of leisure time can affect demand. Typically, individuals who possess greater discretionary free time have a greater desire for leisure and/or vacation flights. Tourism promotion can also help spur an increased demand for air travel to a particular destination. For example, Walt Disney World has turned Orlando into the number one destination airport in the United States.

Economic Impacts of the Air Transport Industry

Direct economic impacts are the outcomes of what might be termed first-tier economic activities carried out by an industry in the local area. The global air transport industry supports nearly 63 million jobs worldwide and contributes $2.7 trillion to global GDP.

The global air transport industry is a complex network, encompassing commercial airlines, aircraft manufacturers, air navigation providers, commercial and civilian airports, and other service providers. By 2038, aviation industry is projected to contribute directly $1.7 trillion to the world GDP. Nearly 88 million jobs were supported worldwide in aviation and related tourism before the impact of COVID-19 on the industry. Of this, 11.3 million individuals were directly employed in the aviation industry.[18]

Typically, commercial air travel closely tracks the movement of the domestic economy. After deregulation, the large US commercial air carriers averaged an annual revenue growth rate of 4.8%, compared to the US GDP average growth rate of 2.6%. In 2021, roughly 23,880 commercial aircraft served the market, and this number is expected to reach to 47,080 over the next 20 years.[19]

The Federal Aviation Administration (FAA) estimates long-term growth in enplanements for large US carriers to average 2.7% domestically and 4.2% internationally by 2030. For regional and commuter airlines, an average growth of 2.9% is anticipated.

We mentioned earlier that international aviation continues to grow and this is largely due to the soaring economies in the Asia-Pacific region.[20] The total economic effect on the community depends on whether the influence is direct, indirect, or induced.

Direct Impact

In 2011, aviation and related tourism employed 56 million people worldwide. It is projected that by 2026, the industry will contribute $1 trillion to the global GDP. The direct impact represents economic activities that would not have occurred in the absence of air transportation. Both airlines and airports contribute directly to the economy. For instance, they pay for fuel, landing fees, and salaries of local residents. The direct economic impacts are the consequences of what might be termed first-tier economic activities carried out by an industry within the local area. Numerous activities at airports, for instance, directly involve the local economy.

Expenditures made by airlines, fixed-based operators, and tenants are also classified as direct impacts, but only those expenditures leading to local business activity hold relevance for regional assessments. Therefore, it is important to distinguish between the local value-added component of expenditures and the regional import component. Consider the fuel expenses of an airline. This involves local storage, distribution systems, and transportation of fuel into the region. In most parts of the country, only the former component is relevant for any local economic impact analysis. Additionally, large aircraft manufacturers offer substantial economic benefits by establishing their production facilities in a particular community or state (Smith, 2012). For example, the Boeing 787 Dreamliner project in Washington State was slated to create approximately 11,470 jobs, contributing to an economic output of $2.268 billion. If the aviation industry were treated as a country, it would hold the 19th position in the world's GDP rankings, generating around $540 billion worth of product and services annually.[21]

Indirect Impact

Indirect impacts arise from off-site economic activities that share a causal relationship with the aviation industry. Examples include travel agencies, hotels, rental car companies, restaurants, and retail establishments. Some companies have strong ties to airlines, and, like airport businesses, employ labor, purchase locally produced goods and services, and invest in capital projects. Indirect impacts differ from direct impacts in that they originate entirely from off-site sources. Furthermore, a significant portion of the economic activity is generated by tourists who travel to a location by air. The resultant demand for local hotel accommodation generates jobs and may require the construction of more hotels, thereby creating more economic impact. This precisely explains why most major airports are surrounded by a variety of hotels.

Induced Impact

Finally, the induced economic impact represents the multiplier effect of direct and indirect impacts. This refers to secondary spending that increases sales within a city or region. Imagine a new airline employee who purchases a house in the local community. The income of builder of the house is then used to purchase other goods and services, and the income of the suppliers of these goods and services is spent locally. This framework of expenditures forms the basis behind the multiplier effect, where one transaction leads to multiple economic transactions (Jenkins and Vasigh, 2013).

Regions that are more economically self-sufficient generally tend to have higher multipliers than those relying more on regional imports, since more of the spending and re-spending is within the region. Therefore, the larger the region, the higher the multiplier. Some examples of the induced impact of aviation encompass:

- Job creation
- Increased economic activity
- Tourism
- Knowledge exchange[22]
- Community development

Total Impact

Total economic impact is defined as the sum of direct, indirect, and induced impacts. It measures the importance of an industry based on the employment it generates and the goods and services it consumes. Total economic impact is usually expressed in terms of economic output, earnings, or employment (sometimes full-time equivalents). The basic formula is

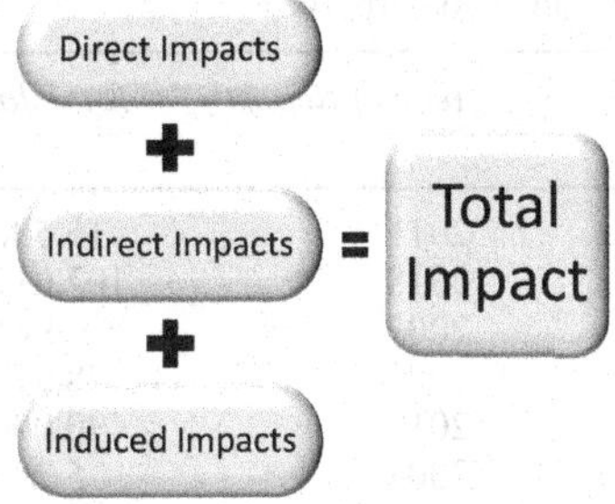

Table 1.10 provides a comparison of the total economic impact in terms of employment for 11 airports located in the United States.

The airport reports were conducted independently and at different times, yet the methodology used for each is similar. Although the 11 airports vary in size, they all deliver strong economic benefits to their communities. When normalized in terms of commercial departures, Memphis generates one job per departure. In other words, an additional daily flight would generate approximately 365 new jobs for the region. Wichita's extremely high ratio of three is likely attributable to the large local manufacturing and maintenance facilities for Cessna and Bombardier. Likewise, the presence of Federal Express in Memphis explains the high economic impact to departure ratio. Finally, much of Seattle's economy revolves around tourism and the presence of aircraft manufacturing giant, Boeing.

The economic "impact" described above employs the widely used 'input-output' methodology to track the flow of spending, output, and employment within economic sectors. It highlights the footprint of air transport on an economy or region. However, this should not be taken as a measure of what the economy would lose in its absence. It has been observed that when adding the indirect and induced economic impacts from various sectors in an economy, the sum can surpass 100% of the size of the economy. This phenomenon of double counting emerges because this methodology examines spending on air transport, primarily from the demand-side. Tourism is perceived solely as overseas residents spending being the equivalent of domestic consumer spending. Yet, rather than creating new jobs, this approach could lead to shifting of workers from other sectors or put upward pressure on wages and inflation. Consequently, the overall impact on jobs and GDP might be relatively smaller than cumulative result of adding direct, indirect, and induced impacts together would suggest.

Another approach to measuring the economic value of air transport, which avoids this double-counting issue, involves examining the micro-economic and supply-side effects of the industry. Air transport reduces journey times and costs between cities, both at home and overseas, for goods and people alike. Additionally, it influences less visible economic drivers such as competition and the exchange of ideas and innovation. These factors constitute the fundamental source of economic value derived from air transport for both consumers and the wider economy. There exist 'agglomeration' economic benefits from rapid air transport connections allowing increased density in labor markets in cities, as well as business clusters, which boosts productivity and economic capacity. Furthermore, 'gains from trade' economic benefits arise as air cargo allows the trade of goods to reap economies of scale and wider competition to improve productivity as well.

In addition to the broader economic benefits from air transport, there are also associated costs. Air travel can transmit or accelerate the transmission of diseases, as evident during the COVID-19 pandemic. Air transport is also an intensive user of fossil fuels, therefore contributing

Table 1.10 The Economic Impact of Selected Airports

Airport	*Year of Report*	*Total Jobs*	*Total Jobs per Commercial Departure*
Anchorage International	2011	15,500	0.115
Beijing Capital Intl	2018	102,012	0.342
Central Wisconsin Airport	2007	981	0.075
Cincinnati/Northern Kentucky	2000	78,573	0.651
Dubai International	2019	490,000	1.313
Greenville-Spartanburg	2003	5,787	0.246
Haneda International Airport	2019	264,079	1.152
Hartsfield-Jackson Atlanta Int Airport	2019	511,000	0.010
Memphis	2004	165,901	1.010
Minneapolis-St. Paul	2004	153,376	0.630
Portland International	2007	38,571	0.429
San Francisco International Airport	2018	330,215	0.720
Seattle-Tacoma	2003	160,174	0.964
Southwest Florida International	2010	41,588	0.979
T.F. Green Rhode Island	2006	21,857	0.781
Wichita	2002	41,634	3.184

Source: Compiled by the authors using numerous sources.

to climate change, a significant public policy challenge in contemporary times. The substantial benefits from air transport led to widespread government support for airlines during the recent pandemic. However, these broader costs will also influence the approach of governments to regulate the development of the air transport industry, both presently and in the future.

Outlook for the Air Transport Industry

Presently, the global airline industry consists of over 1,500 commercial airlines, offering service to over 4,000 airports with commercial flights and operating a fleet of more than 24,000 aircraft.[23] As the demand for the air transport industry is highly correlated with overall economic growth, it is not surprising that the global perspective on the air transportation mirrors the global economic outlook. Following a robust rebound in 2003, the airline industry faced substantial challenges in 2007–2008 due to its persistent financial problems.[24] Therefore, the industry is expected to grow significantly in developing economies, such as the Asia-Pacific region, while growth in other regions is expected to be steadier. GDP and economic growth serve as strong indicators for short-term measures. However, direct correlations between GDP and air transport growth are never absolute due to the structural barriers in the industry. A prime example of this can be seen in the impact of deregulation in the United States, a major structural change that led to rapid growth within the industry compared to the overall economy.

Airport capacity and, in the United States, antiquated air traffic control are also potential structural barriers. Some major international airports in the United States and Europe grapple with severe capacity issues. When reaching capacity thresholds, airport delays increase exponentially. These delays, especially if they are ongoing, discourage demand and constrain growth.[25] Similar capacity issues could plague airports in the Asia-Pacific region, especially in India, China, and Japan. This capacity barrier is a prime reason why Airbus embarked on the creation of its new super-jumbo A380 aircraft.

The two primary sources for long-term air transport outlook are Boeing and Airbus. Both aircraft manufacturers generally present similar growth estimates. According to Boeing's forecast,

Table 1.11 Regional Economic Growth Forecast, 2019–2041

Region	*GDP (%)*	*RPK (%)*	*Fleet 2041*
North America	2.0	2.6	10,810
Latin America	2.5	4.4	2,880
Europe	1.4	3.0	9,360
CIS	2.5	3.7	1,400
Middle East	2.7	4.0	3,400
Asia	4.0	6.0	18,280
Africa	3.1	5.2	1,570
World	2.6	3.8	47,800

Source: Compiled by the authors using Boeing Current Market Outlook, 2019–2041.

world revenue passenger kilometers (RPK) will grow at 5% per annum over the next 20 years (see Table 1.11).

Both Airbus and Boeing also forecast worldwide demand for new aircraft over the next 20 years. However, these forecasts vary slightly according to each company's strategic plan and product offerings. Boeing estimates that airlines will receive delivery of 19,575 aircraft by 2031. Deliveries over the 20 years until 2041 are projected to reach 41,170 airplanes.[26] Airbus, on the other hand, predicts a demand for 39.490 new passenger and freighter aircraft during the next 20 years (including 2,440 new-build or converted freighters). Among these, 31,620 are typically single-aisle and 7,870 are typically wide-body.[27]

The demand for freighters is anticipated to reach 4,100 aircraft by 2041, with nearly half of these newly built. Boeing, on the other hand, estimates that the remaining 30% of demand will be for small and medium wide-body aircraft. Airbus also forecasts the need for 1,331 very large aircraft. Additionally, the two companies differ on where the demand will be. Boeing still believes that North America will remain the largest market for new aircraft (mostly narrow-body), while Airbus anticipates a shift to the Asian-Pacific region. Additionally, Airbus foresees greater LCC growth in this region to spur narrow-body sales.

Another sector worth mentioning is air cargo. Both Boeing and Airbus forecast that global air cargo will grow by about 6% per year over the next 20 years. This growth is much higher than passenger growth forecasts and holds especially relevance in international markets where the air cargo industry has not developed to the extent as passenger traffic. As a result, demand for cargo aircraft (new or second-hand) is expected to be strong, especially for wide-body aircraft. China is poised to lead this sector in growth, both domestically and internationally. The US domestic air cargo market, on the other hand, appears to be mature, with Airbus forecasting a modest 2.8% annual growth rate and Boeing projecting 4.8% growth.

These projections made by aircraft manufacturers of future substantial demand for their products from prospective air passengers and shippers are reasonable from the perspective of the populous but underdeveloped air transport markets of Asia and Africa. This projected future largely mirrors a continuation of the past, though with a shift from past demand growth which came largely from Europe and the Americas. However, certain factors may cause the future to differ from the past in important, if unpredictable, ways. The long and substantial fall in the real cost of air transport could potentially reverse course as the costs associated with climate change are factored in through taxation, emissions trading costs, or the higher cost of sustainable fuels. Protectionist policies and the fracturing of trade and global supply chains might reverse some of the gains through globalization, impacting both long-haul air travel and cargo.

Considering the outlook for both the airline industry and air transport demand is interesting. In previous decades, market liberalization, privatization, and globalization facilitated the entry of new players, fostered competition, and led to the development of new business models such as hub and spoke, LCCs, and global interconnectors. These changes shifted the industry's focus toward Asia, resulting in a very different landscape compared to the past. In contrast, the future dynamics presents a contrasting picture. Growing protectionism or focus on national interests implies limited potential for further market liberalization and reduced support for international consolidation through joint ventures. Alongside this, the impact of the policy response to climate change suggests that air transport may become significantly more expensive in the coming decades, in contrast to the significantly cheaper as seen in the past. Nonetheless, this does not necessarily imply diminished profitability for airlines, as this depends on how the industry addresses some of the fundamental cost and product-related issues, which are explored in subsequent chapters.

Summary

Air transport economics is an important subject that guides policy makers in promoting sustainable and efficient air travel and air cargo services. This covers the analysis of the economic factors influencing the aviation industry, including the supply and demand for air travel, pricing strategies, market structure, and regulation. The COVID-19 pandemic had a devastating impact on the international aviation industry. In the United States, passenger traffic in April 2020 plummeted 96% compared to April 2019, and throughout 2021, it remained significantly below the 2019 levels. The purpose of this chapter is to describe the evolution of the air transport industry, assess the economic impact of aviation, and provide forecasts for future growth. Many internal as well as external factors affect the profitability of the airline industry. The fortune of global air passenger traffic will undoubtedly be subject to numerous exogenous shocks from pandemics to terrorism. This chapter introduced the present state of the air transport industry, with a representative data set covering traffic volume, finances, mergers, bankruptcies, and concentration levels. Over the past decade in the United States, mega-mergers among airlines have reduced the nation's major carriers from nine to just four (American, United, Delta, and Southwest). These four largest airlines hold a roughly 80% market share in the United States.

As the preceding discussion and statistics amply demonstrate, airlines and airports comprise a large and growing segment of the domestic and international economies. Although aviation is similar to other large industries, it has some peculiar characteristics that can best be understood in the context of standard economic analysis.

This text aims to apply economic analysis to the air transport industry and to explain and illuminate those characteristics. To that end, the first four chapters of this book introduce readers to basic economic theory, including demand, supply, costs, and production analysis. These ideas are presented in the context of the aviation and with applicable examples from the industry.

Discussion Questions

1 What are the factors influencing world air traffic growth?
2 Identify some of the characteristics of the US airline industry before deregulation.
   a How did this era affect airlines and passengers?
   b Was deregulation successful?
   c What are direct and indirect economic impacts related to air transportation and how do they differ? Provide an example of each.

3 Which regions serve the largest number of passengers, movements, and cargo?
4 Is regional aviation activity reflected in the average age of aircraft by region?
5 What are some trends with respect to consolidation in the industry? How does this consolidation manifest at airports? How is this demonstrated through the HHI?
6 Mergers have been an important part of the airline industry. Have they been successful? Why have so many been unsuccessful?
7 Which regions are forecasted to have the highest growth in aviation over the next 20 years?
8 How were airline ticket prices set during the period of regulation? From an economic point of view, what would be the predicted outcome of setting prices in this way?
9 Explain how the airline industry is affected or unaffected by the rate of economic growth.
10 What is the difference between indirect and induced economic effects?
11 Explain how you might set up an economic impact study for a proposed airport construction project.
12 Explain why low-cost carriers have cost advantages over legacy carriers.
13 Why are international airlines so much less competitive than domestic airlines?
14 List some of the inherent advantages of air travel compared to other modes of transportation.
15 List some of the economic factors that make the airline industry different from other industries and some that make it the same as far as economic analysis is concerned.
16 Discuss the prospects for the airline industry in the next few years.
17 Explain what is meant by induced economic effects and give an example.

Notes

1 United States Department of Transportation. Bureau of Transportation Statistics, April 30, 2020.
2 United States Department of Transportation. Bureau of Transportation Statistics, Release Number: BTS 18-21, March 11, 2021.
3 The Airlines Still Facing Risk of Bankruptcy as Travel Returns, Bloomberg, February 24, 2022.
4 SAS, the Scandinavian airline, files for bankruptcy protection after pilots strike. *The New York Times*, July 5, 2022.
5 Airports Council International (ACI). Asia-Pacific set to lose status as world's largest aviation market, September 19, 2022.
6 Delta Air Lines, Annual Report, 2016.
7 *The Economist*, April 22, 2017.
8 *The Economist*, April 22, 2017.
9 Alaska Airlines' parent finishes buying Virgin America, but the airlines will operate separately for now. *Los Angeles Times*. January 12, 2017.
10 Meet America's 5th largest airline: The newly merged Alaska Air and Virgin America. *Business Insider*. December 16, 2016.
11 Lawsuit aims to prevent Alaska Airlines-Virgin America deal, Las Vegas Sun, September 16, 2016.
12 For more information on HHI see Chapter 9.
13 The Air France-KLM group was created in 2004.
14 LAN signed an agreement with Brazilian airline TAM Airlines to merge on August 13, 2010, forming the LATAM Airlines Group.
15 CAPA, May 19, 2016.
16 *The Telegraph*. February 2, 2017.
17 The Economic Impact of Air Service Liberalization, Inter*VISTAS* Consulting, 2014.
18 Air Transport Action Group (ATAG), Facts and Figure, 2023.
19 Boeing, Current Market Outlook, 2022–2041.
20 IATA: Confident Businesses, Travelers Drive Airline Demand. May 2, 2017.
21 Air Transport Action Group (ATAG), 2012.
22 Air travel enables people to travel for business, academic, and cultural exchange purposes, facilitating the sharing of knowledge and ideas across borders.
23 Air Transport Action Group (ATAG), Aviation Benefits Beyond Border. July 2020.
24 Zacks Equity Research, January 10, 2012.
25 See Chapter 5 for an analytical discussion of this issue.
26 Boeing Commercial market Outlook, 2022–2041.
27 Airbus, Global Market Forecast, 20221–2041.

References

Jenkins, D. and Vasigh, B. (2013). *The Economic Impact of Unmanned Aircraft Systems Integration in the United States*. Association for Unmanned Vehicle Systems International (AUVSI). http://www.portseattle.org/downloads/business/POS2003EIS_Final.pdf.

McKinsey & Company. (2001). Making Mergers Work. *Airline Business*. Retrieved on August 31, 2006 from Air Transport Intelligence.

Smith, C.D.M. (2012). The Economic Impact of Commercial Airports in 2010. Airports Council International–North America. Retrieved February 8, 2017.

2 Principles of Economics with Applications in Air Transport

This chapter introduces the readers to the economic theories that can help us understand air transport markets. Essentially, the idea is that people respond to incentives in a generally predictable manner. The notion that people tend to logically respond to costs and benefits may not seem profound, but it is surprising how much insight can be gained by carefully tracing the logical impact of incentives. We can also better understand why some markets work and others do not, and how the cost structure can drive the nature of competition in those markets. Although many people think of economics as being wildly controversial, this is not the case at all. While there certainly are some controversies, most of the ideas presented in this chapter involve principles of applied economics that have been settled for many years. Applied economics is the use of economic theory to make better decisions and solve real aviation problems. Many of the consensus points explained here may initially surprise you, but will hopefully make sense in the end.

The subject of economics is generally divided into two major categories: microeconomics and macroeconomics. Macroeconomics focuses on the overall economy, addressing issues such as economic growth, inflation, and overall unemployment, and it is covered in more detail in the last chapter of this book. This chapter focuses more on microeconomics, tracing the logic of incentives on decision-making by individual consumers and business firms—what drives the output of competing producers, how they interact on markets and sell different goods and services, and how these goods and services are allocated to different consumers. Throughout this chapter, we will examine the key economic concepts of scarcity, choice, and opportunity cost.

This basic economic framework can then be applied to issues in aviation, including the role of government in aviation, deregulation, operating costs, foreign operations, and certification. We then present economics as a discipline for informing and critiquing economic policy. The main topics covered in the chapter are as follows:

- Basic Economics
- Scope of Economics
    - Microeconomics
    - Macroeconomics
- The Role of Economic Systems
    - Markets
    - Government and Aviation

DOI: 10.4324/9781003388135-2

- Economic Failures
  - Market Failures
  - Government Failures
- Summary
- Discussion Questions

Basic Economics

Economics may be defined as the science of decision-making and allocating scare resources among competing demands. Many decisions carried out in the aviation industry are prime examples of economic decisions where scarce or limited resources have to be allocated. An example of this was the decision to construct a $1.28 billion fifth runway at Atlanta's Hartsfield-Jackson airport (ATL) to increase operational capacity. Broadly speaking, every resource is scarce, and the allocation of resources under a variety of incentives and decision-making parameters forms the core of economic analysis. An important feature of economic analysis is the assumption that people understand and can act in their own best interest. That is, people respond predictably to a given set of choices in order to maximize their benefits or minimize their losses. Though this is an assumption, it holds true in many, though not all, circumstances. For instance, individuals will engage in a search process to find the lowest ticket price for a given itinerary and set of requirements like flexibility, refundability, and service level. However, there is a limit to the amount of time they will spend in such market research since the time spent searching for the best price has a cost, as it is time that could be spent in doing something else.

Scope of Economics

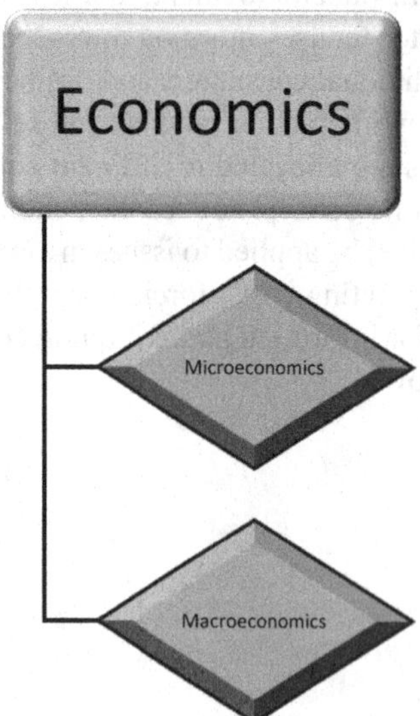

If we read different books on economics, we might come across various definitions for the subject, but they all share two common factors. First, there is the notion of scarcity, and second, the concept of plentiful and competing wants. Therefore, we can define economics as the art or science of using limited productive resources, such as land, capital, labor, and technology, to produce various goods and services that satisfy plentiful and competing human wants. At its core, economics involves choices and tradeoffs; choices matter because resources are limited while human wants can be unlimited. The economic method of thinking centers on analyzing the decisions of individuals and corporations, and how they interact in markets in light of incentives and choices. Economics has many subdivisions and specialties, but the broadest distinction has been between "macro" and "micro" economics. These respective fields are covered in the subsequent sections.

Microeconomics deals with the behavior of individual households and business firms in making decisions regarding prices and the level of production.

Microeconomics

Microeconomics deals with the behavior of individual households and businesses (decision-making units) and with the production, exchange, allocation, or consumption of goods and services. It depends heavily on the concepts of supply and demand; that is, the way in which the market determines the price of goods and services and the level of production. Airlines provide particularly good examples for the decision-making aspect of microeconomics since they respond swiftly to changing market conditions by altering supply and/or prices with sophisticated pricing techniques. Capacity (quantity) management is a prime instance of microeconomic decisions. During the Gulf War, airlines experienced a significant decline in traffic so they reduced their capacity (supply) by 10% over a period of about one year. In India, the low-cost carrier (LCC) JetLite Airways, which ceased operations in 2012, a subsidiary of Jet Airways, slashed fares on all sectors by up to 40% to increase quantity demanded.[1] Airline revenue management is another good example of a microeconomic decision-making. Airbus and Boeing are two tough rivals in the aircraft industry; they compete with each other to capture a bigger market share by introducing more efficient aircraft. Boeing's 737 family of aircraft and Airbus's A320 family of aircraft are the two dominant platforms in the narrow-body aircraft market. The competition between Boeing and Airbus is expected to continue, with both companies working to develop new and more advanced aircraft to meet the needs of airlines and passengers.

Opportunity Cost

This implicit cost of resources is known as opportunity cost and is yet another fundamental concept in economics. Opportunity cost is defined as the alternative cost of using a resource; that is, the benefits that would accrue if the resource were being utilized in its next best allocation. In other words, the next best use of the resource is the economic cost of using it in the current allocation. For instance, in the earlier example, the opportunity cost of the time spent searching for the best ticket price is the next best use of that time, perhaps running a company, generating greater sales, or spending time with family. For an airline, the opportunity costs of acquiring a new aircraft could involve an alternative use for that money, such as acquiring another type of aircraft, opening a new route, or restructuring. When an airline purchases or leases an aircraft, the airline economists evaluate the opportunity cost involved. Acquiring one aircraft comes at the expense of acquiring another. Management usually opts to purchase or lease the aircraft that will provide them the highest value for the available resources.

The opportunity costs of a resource determine the eventual allocation of those resources. Continuing with the example above, as long as the opportunity costs of time do not exceed the potential cost savings that can be achieved, the individual will continue the search. Once the opportunity cost of time surpasses the potential cost savings, the individual will cease the search and opt for the best available price.

Continuing the example, travel aggregators like Expedia.com and Travelocity have massively reduced the search costs associated with booking airline tickets. By aggregating the various ticket prices into a convenient form, the time spent searching for the best fare is reduced, along with the opportunity costs of travel arrangements. Effectively, travel has been made affordable due to information provided by a knowledgeable middleman.

International Trade

Opportunity cost is also a critical driver of cross-border or international trade. The microeconomics of international trade matters for aviation because the pattern of the flow of goods across borders influences air cargo markets. During the COVID-19 pandemic, this aspect of the air transport business was not restricted by border controls and became a vital source of demand and cash flow for many airlines. Historically, air cargo has been relatively small compared to the passenger business for most airlines, but it has often exhibited rapid growth and, with different seasonality, offers a useful diversification of revenue sources.

In the past, the pattern of international trade in goods was determined by the industries in which a county has a comparative advantage. Comparative advantage is shaped by the opportunity costs of production, discussed earlier. This is quite a subtle concept. It could be the case that one country can manufacture all goods more efficiently than another country. However, it turns out that both countries can gain from trade with each other if they each produce and trade the good(s) they excel at making. Taiwan might excel at producing textiles compared to India, but it pays for Taiwan to specialize in semi-conductors and import textiles from India. Semiconductors are just the sort of high-value, low-volume products that constitute a key market for the rapid, though relatively costly, service offered by air cargo businesses.

In the past, comparative advantage was determined by factors such as weather and resources. However, today there is a substantial amount of international trade occurring within the same industries, driven by specialization and different capabilities that result in a variety of brands offering the same type of product. Cross-border trade frequently involves components, rather than finished goods, reflecting the fragmentation and globalization of manufacturing supply chains in recent decades. Different countries specialize and gain economies of scale in producing or assembling different parts of products, for example, laptop computers or smartphones. Both of these goods and their components constitute significant sources of demand for air cargo services. The COVID-19 pandemic has had a significant negative impact on international trade, causing disruptions in global supply chains and trade flows. The pandemic has disrupted supply chains around the world, leading to delays in the production and delivery of cars, as well as an increase in prices due to the scarcity of certain components.

Pricing Decisions

Another fundamental concept of economic thinking is pricing. Prices constitute the central allocation mechanism of economics and serve as the decision-making parameters by which individuals organize their actions. For example, consider the price of oil. Millions of people use the price of oil to make decisions that impact both business and personal consumer interests. Large corporate firms, such as airlines, use it as a benchmark to make important decisions regarding their pricing strategies. Exploration and development activities depend upon the present price of oil, as do numerous transportation-related decisions. Naturally, consumers adjust their behavior based directly on the price of gasoline and oil. In many instances, individuals are unaware of the influence that prices have on their decision-making processes, as prices can be implicit as well as explicit. In the case of the oil, prices are explicitly given in the marketplace; however, there are also implicit prices that must be considered within the economic way of thinking. For example, the price of flying from Orlando to Houston is $293 on Southwest Airlines, while the cost of driving there is $147.17.[2] On the surface, driving might appear far cheaper. However, the true price of driving does not consider the cost of 14 hours and 53 minutes of the passenger's time. Assuming a median income of $67,521 (U.S. Census Bureau, 2016), which translates into roughly $32.46 per hour, the true cost of driving is $480.41 + $147.17 = $627.78. This makes driving 209% more expensive than flying. Therefore, when factoring in the implicit price of driving, flying becomes the more efficient alternative.

Revenue management will be explored in more depth in a subsequent chapter, but the basic concept is that airlines price seats differently based on several variables, including service level, time before flight, and day of the week. The idea is to charge each consumer the maximum he/she is willing to pay based on his/her personal characteristics. A business traveler with limited flexibility and last-minute travel needs would be willing to pay significantly more than a casual vacationer who is much more price sensitive. Airlines separate the aircraft into cabins (economy, business, and first in the typical three-class system) that are further segmented into classes, each with its own price point and often slightly different ticket characteristics like flexibility and refundability. Pricing the cabins according to class allows the airline to maximize its revenue based on traveler preferences, as it can set a higher price for those who are willing to pay it. Essentially, they use high-priced tickets to subsidize revenue from those who are more price sensitive. The entire process of revenue management is built on microeconomic decision-making—travelers with certain characteristics are likely to support a higher price than others, and tailoring pricing to those characteristics benefits both the airline and the consumers.

Decisions regarding aircraft acquisition, fleet selection, and route planning all fall within the realm of microeconomic activities. Will this new aircraft achieve a justifiably high load factor if deployed on this route? Considering route characteristics, will adding this new aircraft to the fleet yield an optimal mix? Does the market size on this route suffice to support the entry of a new airline? All these decisions are rooted in the behavior of individual consumers and the effect that changing certain variables will exert on individual preferences.

Output Decisions

Output decisions for an airline involve various aspects such as capacity, seat pitch, aircraft size, aircraft type, and schedule selection. Establishing schedules for a six-month season is a particularly important decision, affecting the economics of airlines. This decision fixes in part many costs, making them difficult to adjust if demand were to suddenly decline due to demand or cost shocks. This is particularly applicable on congested or capacity-constrained routes, where regulations regarding take-off and landing slots often apply, though less so on uncongested markets. Capacity decisions fall within the scope of microeconomic decisions. In recent years, airlines have shifted capacity away from domestic US markets to more profitable international markets. In April 2008, Emirates Airline commenced New York service with a double-deck aircraft, only to replace it with the smaller Boeing 777 two months later.[3] In response to soaring fuel costs, Frontier reduced one-third of its daily departures from Milwaukee from 67 to 45. In addition, the carrier suspended non-stop service to six cities.[4] In May 2011, Ryanair announced a capacity cut by grounding 80 aircraft in the winter schedules between November 2011 and April 2012 due to the high cost of fuel and continuing weak economic conditions.[5] Ryanair clearly pursued a strategy centered on a low-cost structure, which allowed them to offer low fares. Global airline capacity in 2021 ended at 5.7 billion seats compared to the 8.7 billion reported in 2019, representing a 35% decrease from pre-Covid levels, and of course, demand is considerably lower for these 5.7 billion seats.

Markets

Decisions by companies regarding pricing and supply levels for a particular good, as well as the extent to which consumers desire to purchase it, are made within a market specific to that good or service. While the market for Boeing's latest narrow-body aircraft might span the globe, the airline markets are quite different. Most air passengers, whether for a holiday or to visit friends or relatives, aim to travel between their originating city and their destination city. If they are traveling from New York to London, a flight from Seattle to Montreal or even New York to Frankfurt will be a poor substitute. The "market" for airlines in this case is air travel between New York and London.

Microeconomic analysis can be instrumental in understanding competitive dynamics among airlines within a specific market. The pricing or output decisions made by airlines operating between Seattle and Montreal would not exert any influence on the choices made by airlines in the New York-London market. However, other airlines flying direct or via a connecting hub airport will influence the setting of pricing and supply levels.

Markets for air cargo transportation differ somewhat from those for air passenger travel. Passengers, excepting the budget-conscious students, typically care about the routing with a preference for direct connections. Conversely, the cargo boxes being transported by air do not hold such preferences. Therefore, the number of routes is higher and thus the size of the market for transporting air cargo between two cities is usually much broader. Air cargo markets also tend to be unidirectional. Air passengers usually will fly back to their point of origin, but cargo containers do not, posing challenges for airlines needing to fully utilize return cargo flights. Some types of air travel also produce markets wider than a typical city-pair, such as holiday travel to sunny destinations where passengers may not have a strong preference for the destination as long as there is a beach and warm weather.

Macroeconomics

Macroeconomics studies the decision-making processes for the entire economy, focusing on the performance of economies and changes in areas such as inflation, unemployment, interest rate, balance of trades, and economic growth. In contrast to microeconomics, macroeconomics serves as a field that becomes relevant during the decision-making processes of airlines and aircraft manufacturers as a structural variable. This implies that macroeconomics presents circumstances and parameters that may be uncontrollable, but are key drivers of their business operations.

In contrast, macroeconomics studies decision-making processes for the entire economy in terms of inflation, employment, and economic growth.

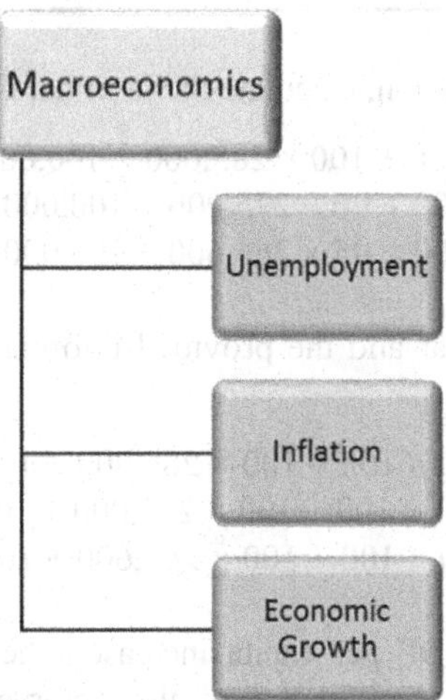

Gross Domestic Product (GDP) represents the total dollar value of all goods and services produced in a specific economy during a given period. For instance, movements in GDP and economic activity have implications for travel. The microeconomic decisions made by individuals are impacted by the overall economy, which, in turn, affects household incomes and consumer confidence. As a result, airline and airport managers must take into account these circumstances while making decisions.

In a slow economic climate, for instance, introducing discounted fares or sales promotions might be more effective strategies for generating demand than introducing a new luxury class. Airport and airline managers also have to deal with seasonality—travel is typically slow during the winter months, but picks up during the holiday season, and prices may have to be altered to account for the effects. Cargo flows exhibit different seasonality, with demand usually rising toward the end of the year due to the new product launches of consumer electronics, such as smart phones. Similarly, the impact of taxes and passenger fees on airline tickets is a major issue that airlines have to contend with. Figure 2.1 provides a comparison between the GDP per capita and the number of passengers carried annually per population for various countries and regions around the world. It is clear that the higher the GDP per capita, the higher the number of passengers carried. Moreover, as GDP increases, the number of passengers is expected to increase along the trendline.

Example

Suppose that a country produces three goods: aircraft (AC), agricultural product (AP), and housing (HS). The following hypothetical table provides information about the prices and output for these three goods for the years 2021, 2022, and 2023.

Year	*Price of AC*	*Quantity of AC*	*Price of AP*	*Quantity of AP*	***Price of HS***	***Unit of Housing***
2021	$37,000,000	100	$100	285,000	$100,000	300
2022	$37,500,000	100	$90	275,000	$150,000	250
2023	$39,000,000	100	$95	266,600	$106,000	700

a Using the provided information, calculate the nominal GDP for 2016, 2017, and 2018.

$$GDP_{2021} = \$35{,}000{,}000 \times 100 + 100 \times 285{,}000 + 100{,}000 \times 300 = \$3{,}558{,}500{,}000$$
$$GDP_{2022} = \$37{,}500{,}000 \times 100 + 90 \times 275{,}000 + 100{,}000 \times 250 = \$3{,}427{,}375{,}000$$
$$GDP_{2023} = \$39{,}000{,}000 \times 100 + 95 \times 266{,}600 + 106{,}000 \times 700 = \$3{,}806{,}393{,}000$$

b Using 2016 as the base year and the provided information, calculate the real GDP for 2016, 2017, and 2018.

$$\text{Real GDP}_{2021} = \$35{,}000{,}000 \times 100 + 100 \times 285{,}000 + 100{,}000 \times 300 = \$3{,}558{,}500{,}000$$
$$\text{Real GDP}_{2022} = \$35{,}000{,}000 \times 100 + 100 \times 275{,}000 + 100{,}000 \times 250 = \$3{,}202{,}500{,}000$$
$$\text{Real GDP}_{2023} = \$35{,}000{,}000 \times 100 + 100 \times 266{,}600 + 100{,}000 \times 700 = \$3{,}421{,}660{,}000$$

As depicted in Figure 2.1, as GDP per capita increases, the passengers carried per population also increases. The overall significance of the observed trend is an impressive 61% ($R^2 = 0.6134$). In the future, countries like China and Russia are expected to follow a similar pattern. The higher end of the spectrum consists of countries such as Singapore, the United States, and New Zealand, all of which carry more passengers per population due to their location and significantly higher GDP per capita. For aircraft manufacturers, macroeconomic variables become crucial

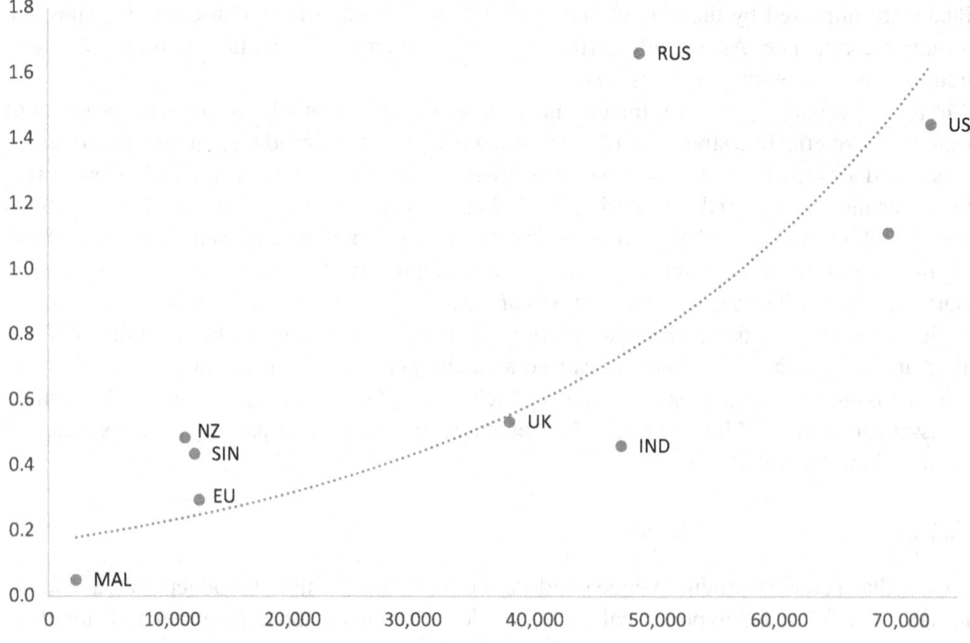

Figure 2.1 GDP per Capita versus Passengers/Population, 2022.

Source: World Bank, World Development Indicators Databank

in terms of predicting the demand for aircraft over the long term, as the financial health of airlines is highly dependent on economic cyclicality. According to the most recent forecast by Boeing, in the two decades leading up to 2035, the world will need 39,620 new planes. China alone will require at least 6,000 aircraft, worth some $1 trillion.[6] Therefore, forecasting when the demand for aircraft is likely to fall off and/or pick up again will determine the timing of expected cash flows on aircraft, and consequently, the breakeven year and quantity that will determine project success or failure.

Three of the major measures of macroeconomics are inflation, unemployment, and the business cycle.

Inflation

Inflation matters for airlines mainly due to its impact on interest rates. Many airlines finance their activities mainly through issuing debt, and changes in interest rates can critically affect cash flows. Price inflation can be defined as the general rise in prices of goods and services in an economy over time. It is not concerned with relative price changes, such as oil prices rising sharply compared to manufactured goods, or air ticket prices falling compared to a basket of goods and services. In 1980, for example, an airline ticket cost on average $250. By 2023, the average price of the same ticket had risen to $900 without adjusting by inflation. The inflation rate can be measured by the consumer price index (CPI), which estimates the annual percentage change in the cost to the average consumer of acquiring a basket of goods and services representative of average consumer purchases, possibly fixed at specified intervals.[7] The Bureau of Labor Statistics (BLS) publishes CPI monthly. A CPI of 108, for example, indicates that representative basket of prices are 8% higher than they were in the base period.

> **Inflation** is an increase in the general price level of goods and services in an economy. **Hyperinflation** is used to describe situations where the prices of all goods and services rise uncontrollably over a short period of time.

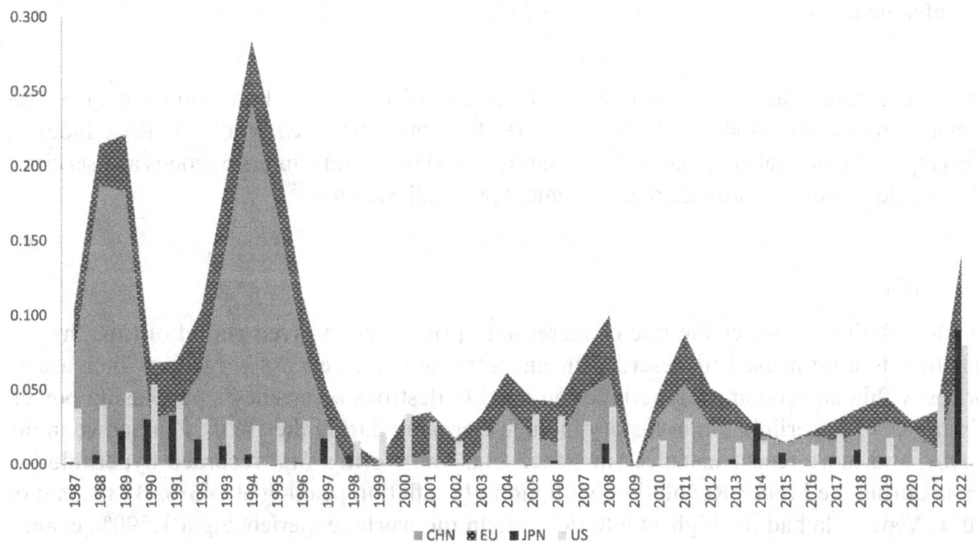

Figure 2.2 Annual Percent Change in CPI, 1987–2022.

Source: World Bank, World Development Indicators Databank

Figure 2.2 depicts historical inflation rates, highlighting the surge in inflation during the 1970s in the United States, Europe, and Japan. In 1971, the industrialized world abandoned the last official link between paper currencies and gold. The goal was to let the market decide the exchange rates, similar to how it decides the price and quantity of nearly everything else. By doing so, this policy effectively liberated governments to create as much paper money, resulting inflation, as they deemed fit. The dominant economic theory of the time saw inflation as a potential stimulant of economic growth. However, the results of this experiment in the 1970s were highly disappointing, leading to a shift in attitudes toward inflation. This shift was reflected in the changes in monetary policy, resulting in significantly lower inflation rates in the industrialized world from the 1980s through the early 2020s. The shocks to the global economy from COVID-19 and the impact of the war in Ukraine have generated a resurgence of inflation in many economies. According to the US Bureau of Labor Statistics, the CPI, which measures the change in prices of a basket of goods and services, increased by 7.0% over the 12 months ending in January 2022.

Although many factors can influence the rate of inflation, one is the supply of paper currency and other liquid assets, such as cash deposited in checking accounts—the money supply. Inflation is sometimes thought to be caused by governments "printing too much money." However, financial innovation has rather destroyed the ability of central banks to measure, let alone control, the "supply" of money. Most central banks assess inflation pressures by the degree of spare capacity in labor and output markets, the "natural" rate of unemployment and the "output gap."

Assume that the CPI of January 2020 was 115 and the index for January 2023 is listed as 140. To make the calculations, we take the more recent CPI, subtract the oldest CPI, and then divide by the oldest CPI.

$$\text{Inflation rate} = \frac{CPI_{2023} - CPI_{2020}}{CPI_{2020}} \times 100$$

$$\text{Inflation rate} = \frac{140 - 115}{115} \times 100 = 0.21 \text{ or } 21\%$$

Thus, the inflation rate from January 2020 to January 2023 was 21%. Furthermore, the US BLS regularly reports the Producer Price Indexes (PPIs). Formerly called Wholesale Price Indexes, PPIs represent the change in the selling prices received by manufacturers of goods and services. These indexes are primarily used to implement price adjustments.

Hyperinflation

While inflation measures the rate of increase in prices over a given period of time, hyperinflation is a term used to describe an uncontrollable and excessive general increase in prices within an economy. Hyperinflation quickly destroys a currency's purchasing power. Examples of hyperinflation in history include Germany during the 1920s, Zimbabwe in the 2000s, and more recent instances in Venezuela. The world's first recorded hyperinflation came during the French Revolution, with monthly inflation peaking at 143%. By the end of 2021, Venezuela had the highest inflation rate in the world, experiencing a 1,590% change compared to the previous year. In Zimbabwe, prices doubled every day during its hyperinflation period.

Unemployment

The unemployment rate is defined as the percentage of the total labor force who are currently without a job but actively seeking employment and willing to work. Unemployment is relevant in the context of air transport, partly, because it serves as a good indicator of the consumer confidence in an economy. Therefore, this confidence indicates their willingness to increase spending on air transport beyond what their incomes would justify. Using the BLS's classifications, individuals are considered unemployed if they do not have a job, have actively searched for work in the past four weeks, and are currently available for employment. Individuals who are not working and are waiting to be recalled to a job from which they had been temporarily laid off are also classified as unemployed. The unemployment rate is expressed as a percentage of the labor force. The labor force includes the number of persons in the economy who are either employed or seeking a job, at least 16 years old, not serving in the military, and not institutionalized.

The Bureau of Labor Statistics supplies the following definitions:

Employed persons are all persons who, during the reference week (the week including the twelfth day of the month):

- Did any work as paid employees, worked in their own business or profession or on their own farm, or worked 15 hours or more as unpaid workers in an enterprise operated by a member of their family, or
- People who were not working but who had jobs from which they were temporarily absent because of vacation, illness, bad weather, childcare problems, maternity or paternity leave, labor-management dispute job training, or other family or personal reasons, whether or not they were paid for the time off or were seeking other jobs.

In other words, the labor force includes all people who are eligible to work in the everyday US economy.

$$\text{Unemployment rate} = \frac{\text{Number of unemployed persons}}{\text{Total labor force}}$$

Consider a country that has a population of 1,000,000, with 40,000 unemployed. Fifteen percent of the total population is less than 16 years old, and 5% of the total population is retired and not working. Hence, the unemployment rate is calculated as follows:

Population less than sixteen = 0.15 × 1,000,000 = 150,000
Number of people retired = 0.05 × 1,000,000 = 50,000
Number of people in the labor force = 1,000,000 − (150,000 + 50,000) = 800,000
Unemployment rate = 40,000 ÷ 800,000 = **5%**

Figure 2.3 illustrates historical trends in unemployment rates, with some estimated projections for the years beyond 2015. The ups and downs of the unemployment rate reflect the state of the economy, and they roughly mirror the ups and downs of real GDP.

It might appear that achieving 0% unemployment would be ideal, but this is not the case. Economic growth inherently leads to the elimination of some jobs as technology advances, resulting in temporary unemployment for some individuals. Technological advancements often increase output per worker in a given industry, which can lead to need for fewer workers in that industry. As a result, some individuals lose jobs. Two centuries ago, for example, most people

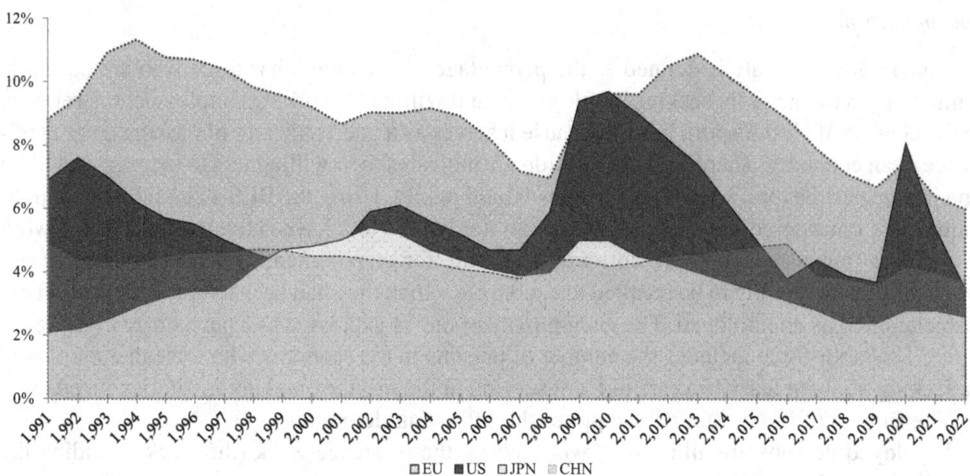

Figure 2.3 Historical Unemployment Rates, 1991–2022.

Source: World Bank Database

were employed in agriculture. As technology improved, vast numbers of farm jobs were eliminated, and now, very few people in the United States work in agriculture. Technological progress enables us to produce more food with fewer people working on the field. Those freed up resources and labor hours are now redirected to produce airplanes, cars, computers, and many other products. Indeed, the essence of an advancing economy is the requirement for increased output per worker achieve higher real wages, thus creating more consumption per worker and an elevated standard of living.

Unemployment can be further classified as *structural unemployment*, *cyclical unemployment*, and *frictional unemployment.*

The *structural* rate of unemployment is an inherent rate that exists in an economy, independent of unemployment resulting from business cycles. This type of unemployment arises due to a mismatch between skills and qualification that companies need and what the available

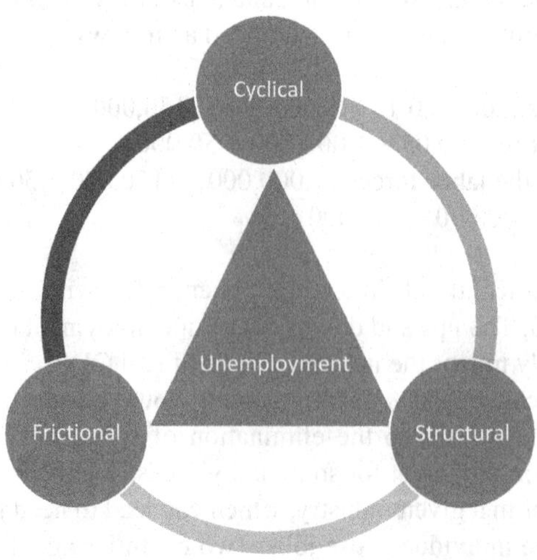

workforce can offer. Structural unemployment is more serious than cyclical, frictional, or seasonal unemployment.

Cyclical unemployment occurs as a result of business cycles. When the business cycle is at its peak (maximum economic output), cyclical employment is low. Conversely, higher rates exist when consumer expenditure is low, leading to inadequate demand for employers to hire all individuals seeking jobs. Similarly, when the business cycle is low and economic output decreases, cyclical unemployment increases.

Frictional unemployment is also referred to as transitional unemployment. This form of unemployment is consistently present in the economy as a result of persons transitioning between jobs and new workers entering the labor force. Frictional unemployment occurs as a result of the time it takes for the labor market to match the available jobs with individuals in the labor force.

Economic Growth (Business Cycles)

From an economic point of view, a business cycle is defined as the movement of economic activities, such as unemployment, inflation, and economic growth. This constitutes perhaps the most critical macroeconomic influence on air transport, because both demand and airline profits are highly leveraged to the business cycle. The demand for air cargo, in particular, as well as airline profits, exhibits considerably higher sensitivity to the overall economy, falling sharply during a recession and rising substantially during a boom. A business cycle has four distinct phases:[8]

1 *Expansion or recovery*: During this phase of the business cycle, real GDP begins to increase, unemployment falls, and consumer and business spending rises. Historically, the annual growth in air travel has been about twice the annual growth in GDP, with increased growth during periods of economic expansion.
2 *Peak*: The peak occurs at the highest point between economic expansion and the start of economic contraction.
3 *Contraction or recession*: This is a phase when real GDP begins to decline, and unemployment starts to increase. Contractions start at the peak of a business cycle and end at the trough. They are marked by a significant decline in economic activity spread across the economy, lasting more than a few years.
4 *Trough*: The trough signals the end of a period of declining business activity and the transition to expansion. This is the beginning of economic recovery.

Figure 2.4 illustrates each of the four phases, showing passenger enplanements from January 1996 to January 2022.

From 1996 to 2001, the airline industry underwent an expansion marked by a rising number of enplanements. Notably, there was a peak in August 2001; however, the terrorist attack the following month had a dramatic impact on the number of passengers. This resulted in a slight recession and a trough, but the industry bounced back fairly well and once again experienced an expansion until the onset of the 2008 economic crisis. With the crisis spreading globally, a trough was observed in the latter part of 2009, after which the economy embarked on a slow recovery. The airline industry is currently experiencing an expansion and might soon reach its peak before falling into the recession phase of the cycle. The impact of COVID-19 has surpassed the 2003 SARS outbreak, which had resulted in reduction of annual Revenue Passenger Miles (RPMs) by 8%. In 2021, due to the coronavirus pandemic, the global airline industry boarded just over 2.2 billion scheduled passengers. This represents a 50% loss in global air passenger traffic compared to 2019.

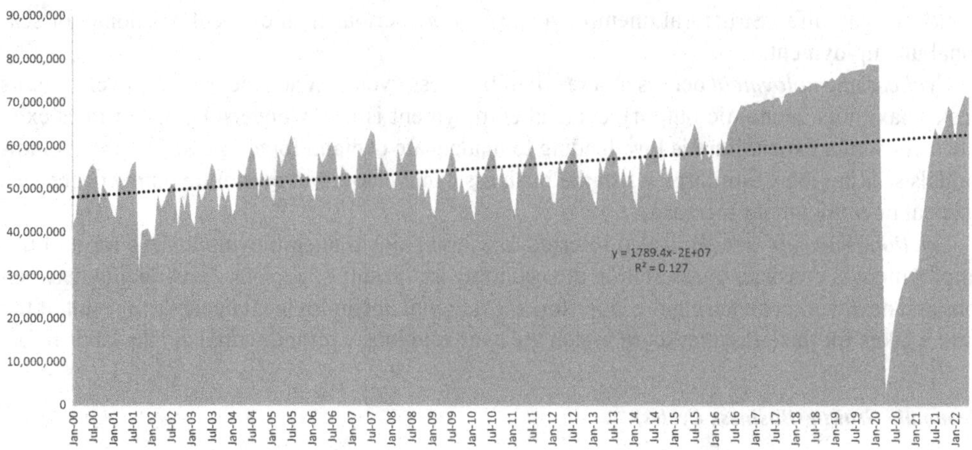

Figure 2.4 Monthly Passenger Enplanements, 1996–2022.

Source: BTS National Transportation Statistics

The Role of Economic Systems

Any economic system serves as a framework within which individuals and corporates make decisions and choices about goods and services. These systems contain explicit or implicit rules for production, exchange, and the assignment, also known as who gets what, according to economists. The effectiveness of an economic system will depend on its ability to utilize the comparative advantages of an economy and its people, and the division of labor. Comparative advantage requires focusing on what an entity does best, rather than what it merely does better than others or other economies. Corporations specialize either by exploiting economies of scale or by their distinctive capabilities. In air transport, typically different corporations specialize in running airports, manufacturing aircraft, or flying passengers. Regarding the division of labor, competitive markets should, in theory, automatically determine the allocation of job based on the needs of corporations and the abilities of individuals.

Broadly speaking, modern economic systems can be characterized by the extent of the market and the prevalence of government in decision-making and resource allocation.

At one end of the spectrum lies hypothetical laissez-faire capitalism, in which the economy is primarily driven by the market with limited government involvement, and the market dictates resource allocation. A key feature of this system is pluralism and discipline. Numerous business trial and errors occur in a pluralist, market-based system, and where bad decisions are inevitably made because of radical uncertainty, those activities are quickly ended. Additionally, decentralization of activities and decision-making is another key feature of these market-based systems, allowing information on changing consumer demands and competitive pressures to be transmitted and responded to with changing output, prices, and innovation.

On the other end of the spectrum lies a pure command economy, where resources are allocated with reference to a central authority or a government, without any reference to a market. A key feature of these economies is that decision-making is centralized, which leads to the absence of the key information which trial and error and decentralization provide.

In the middle of the continuum is a mixed economy. The mixed economy is a combination of private enterprise with a larger government sector (usually involved with income transfer). In a mixed economy, there coexists freedom of ownership, pricing policy, and profit earning.

Historically, no economies have ever achieved either of these extreme ends. The beginnings of the post-industrial revolution in nineteenth-century America were close to pure capitalism, although there was still some government involvement in the economy. The Soviet Union's communist economy for the much part of the twentieth century was very close to a complete command economy, although some market forces existed in the form of black markets. Over time, however, every modern economy has come to some form of mixed system, with varying degrees of reliance on government involvement.

Markets

Markets and market-based decisions play a prevalent and often dominant role in various aspects of air transport, and in particular, the airline business. Output and pricing decisions made by airlines mostly take place in markets subject to competition from other airlines, and with minimal interference from governments. This is the case in the US domestic market, across the Atlantic and in most of Europe for example. Outcomes for consumers and corporations are market-based, decentralized, and anonymous. On either side of the market, if consumers or producers are not satisfied, they will exit the market.

Even within these liberalized markets, certain decisions and economic outcomes are not market-based. For example, allocation of landing and take-off slots at congested airports in Europe is determined by a political process and a 'slots coordinator'. The same holds true for establishing airport charges, although economic regulators often try, imperfectly, to mimic market conditions. In situation where markets are not fully liberalized and bilateral air service agreements are in place between the governments at either end, access, capacity, and pricing are often explicitly determined by the Government or Civil Aviation Authority. Here outcomes and decision-making are political, centralized, and personalized in contrast to market-based economic systems. If anyone is dissatisfied in this process, the mechanism of complaint is "voice."

Government and Aviation

Within every economy, industries subject to varying degrees of government supervision exist. Industries like the financial sector have historically faced less regulation than manufacturing, pharmaceuticals, or aviation. Therefore, while the US government might be less involved in economic activities than that of the French government, the US aviation industry could be more regulated than the country as a whole, albeit less regulated than the French aviation industry.

Further, even within the aviation industry, there exists a range of regulations. For instance, airline deregulation in the 1970s brought airlines firmly within the sphere of the free market. However, aircraft manufacturing and certification have simultaneously grown more highly regulated over time due to liability concerns. Further still, different parts of the aviation industry might be regulated differently. In Europe, for instance, more airports are being privatized. This is less common in the United States. Therefore, US airports are arguably subject to greater regulation than their European counterparts. On the other hand, in Europe, operational restrictions due to environmental and noise concerns might be less stringent compared to those in the United States.

Overall, the current push is toward reducing government involvement in aviation. For instance, the various Open Skies agreements between the European Union (EU) and the United States enable any US airline to fly from any point in the United States to any point in Europe. This EU–US Open Skies agreement was first signed in April 2007 and became effective in March 2008. A second phase of the agreement, aimed at reducing further barriers in the transatlantic aviation market, was signed in June 2010.[9] This phase aims to reduce the involvement of governments in the decisions of individual carriers to offer transcontinental service, and foster increased competition among airlines from different countries. However, the agreement is by no means comprehensive. It does not allow European carriers to operate flights within two points in the United States, but it does allow American carriers to operate intra-European flights. Initiatives have been undertaken to create a completely Open Skies agreement between the two entities, which would represent a significant withdrawal of government influence from air transportation.

An economic incentive is best described as a force or circumstance that encourages an individual to engage in a particular activity. For instance, a tax credit on home ownership will incentivize a certain kind of economic activity, specifically home ownership. Similarly, the emergence of LCCs as a competitive threat incentivized the legacy carriers like American Airlines to become more competitive and adopt practices like revenue management. In contrast, a disincentive discourages an individual from engaging in a particular activity. Raising the tax on jet fuel would necessitate higher ticket prices for the consumer as a result of cost pass through and would give consumers a disincentive for air travel.

Incentives can be both economic and noneconomic in nature. The threat of litigation has incentivized the Federal Aviation Administrator (FAA) to institute ever more stringent tests for aircraft certification, which has, in turn, disincentivized many general aviation manufacturers from major or frequent innovation. The economic way of thought centers on analyzing incentives and predicting human behavior when dealing with clearly defined incentives.

Incentives serve as a powerful tool for analyzing public policy. Phrasing these policies using the language of incentives can shed a lot of light on potential benefits or consequences. While airline regulation allowed carriers to make a normal profit and maintain stable operations, it also incentivized inefficient operations. No matter how low the load factor is on approved routes, inefficiency generates a relatively predictable amount of costs and revenues. While airline deregulation may have caused airlines' operational structures to become unpredictable, their revenue to fall and their costs to rise it, in turn, incentivized competition and highly efficient operational practices like revenue management and route profitability analysis. As a result, airline consumers reap the benefits of such operations in terms of new routes, new airline options, and vastly reduced ticket prices. We will return to airline regulation and deregulation with an example later in this chapter.

The air transport industry plays a substantial role in the national economy, and government plays an important role in aviation safety, security, and the operations of critical infrastructure. For example, the European Aviation Safety Agency (EASA) was created by the European Union in 2002 with the objective of enhancing safety for the European citizen in Europe and worldwide.[10] Throughout the world, aviation has always been deeply intertwined with government. In the United States, the FAA serves as the regulator of all the nation's civil aviation activities, including management of air traffic in US airspace. FAA Office of Aviation Safety (AVS) is responsible for the aircraft certification; continued airworthiness of aircraft; and certification of pilots, mechanics, and others in safety-related positions.

Since the beginning of commercial aviation in the 1920s and 1930s, governments on both sides of the Atlantic supported and subsidized the fledgling industry. They accomplished this by improving the continued airworthiness of civil aircraft through lucrative mail contracts, and later through military contracts. The tragic crashes of Lion Air Flight 610 and the subsequent crash of Ethiopian Airlines Flight 302 in March 2019 led to the worldwide grounding of the 737 Max fleet. Over a span of five months, 346 lives were lost in the crashes, first in Indonesia in late 2018 and then a few months later in Ethiopia. The causes of the two accidents were linked mainly to the 737's maneuvering characteristics augmentation system (MCAS), which was introduced to the 737 Max to manage changes in behavior created by the plane having much larger engines than 737NG. At the outset, Boeing CEO Muilenburg puts at least some of the blame for the crashes at the feet of the pilots of the two ill-fated 737 MAX aircraft. On the other hand, Boeing blames Muilenburg for skimping safety to expedite the 737's market roll out, and Muilenburg was fired shortly after.

The economics of early commercial aviation were extremely unattractive. Planes could not fly at night or during extreme weather, and speeds rarely exceeded 90 miles an hour at best. As such, commercial aviation in the early 1920s was hardly viable without government assistance. Both France and Germany laid the foundations for their industries with flag carriers Air France and the Deutsche Luft Reederei, which would later become Lufthansa.[11] The American and British governments were more cautious about direct government support; instead, they took the route of indirect subsidies through mail contracts. This pattern is observed to this very day, with the styles of support afforded to Boeing and Airbus by the respective governments in the United States and Europe. Both are subsidized, albeit through different mechanisms. Airbus is arguably subsidized more directly, while others argue that Boeing receives an indirect cross-subsidization through its defense contracts.

Aircraft and engine manufacturing, on the other hand, have received government subsidies through direct contracts with the military since the First World War. Numerous developments in aircraft design were conducted by Boeing, Lockheed Martin, McDonnell Douglas, Fokker, De Havilland, and Northrop Grumman. The Contract Air Mail Act of 1925 and the subsequent Air Commerce Act of 1926 put commercial aviation squarely into the hands of the private sector. However, they offered it massive government support and reserved the power of regulatory oversight in the determination and disposition of those contracts. It was under this umbrella that commercial aviation would truly flourished—monoplane design for higher cruise speeds, which would enable airmail to become an attractive competition for traditional mail routes. Lockheed's famous Orion and Vega, and Boeing's Monomail were all developed to maximize the profits by efficiently transporting government mail. Since the airmail subsidies were based on weight, the greater the capacity of the airplanes and the greater their useful load, the higher the potential earnings for an airline. This had two effects. First, it shifted significant volume of mail traffic from railroads to airplanes. Second, it spurred manufacturers/airlines to focus on building and operating airplanes capable of carrying substantial weight at high speed, leading to design innovations that poised aircraft to take over high-speed passenger transportation in the future.

Another significant milestone in aviation legislation took place with the 1930 Watres Act, championed by Congressman Walter Brown. Effectively, the Watres Act changed the nature of the subsidies for airmail from weight to mileage. This shifted the focus of aircraft manufacturers toward building large planes with an extended range. The Act also shifted the subsidy from freight to passengers. When airlines were paid by the mile regardless of the weight of the mail it transported, it turned out advantageous to fly aircraft with long-range capabilities. This, in turn, would incentivize intercontinental travel. Further, since the demand for mail was fairly static, and longer ranges usually necessitated larger aircraft, airlines had the incentive to use the extra space to transport passengers. The government's intention was for successful airlines to gradually shift revenues from mail to passengers, and that the subsidies for the industry could slowly be phased out. Further, the Watres Act granted the government broad discretionary power to award airmail contracts as it deemed fit, removing some of the competitive bidding associated with the mail contracts. This aligned with Congressman Watres' vision, which sought to bring order to the seemingly chaotic development of aviation in the United States. This consolidated the competition in the airline industry into a few major players, establishing the stage for airlines that would eventually become known as the legacy carriers. This shift led to the creation of the Civil Aeronautics Board (CAB). Therefore, the inception of aviation and the direction that the industry took were incentivized and controlled by governments.

An increased number of passengers and aircraft in the skies necessitated the development of extensive infrastructure and a solid air traffic management system. The Federal Airways Act of 1946 implemented key navigational elements, such as the Instrument Landing System (ILS), Very-High-Frequency Omnidirectional Range (the VORs), the designation of specific airways, and the increasing use of radar (Fried and Myron, 1997). Direct pilot-to-controller communication followed in 1955, shortly before a tragic midair collision at the Grand Canyon in 1956. A United Airlines DC-7 and a TWA Super Constellation collided while both were operating under visual flight rules in uncontrolled airspace. This led to the adoption of positively controlled airspace above 24,000 feet and the abandonment of visual flight rules by commercial airliners.[12]

In 1959, airports were modernized under the direction of the Federal Aviation Authority (created from the Civil Aviation Authority in 1958). Further regulation was enacted in 1960 following a midair collision over Brooklyn that mirrored the Grand Canyon accident of 1956. At this point, aviation infrastructure, navigational aids, airports, and aviation safety became tightly regulated, and airlines remained under the regulatory umbrella until 1975.

Prior to 1975, the United States was primarily served by four major airlines: United, American, Eastern, and TWA. On the international front, Pan Am held the position of the largest international carrier. The CAB regulated the routes and fares of these airlines, and any new market entrant had to apply for permission, which could be contested by the existing carriers. Furthermore, an airline wishing to expand service into a new route had to fill out a petition with the CAB. Again, existing carriers had the right to dispute these petitions, many of which made it all the way to court.

Every aspect of airline operations was regulated, including aircraft acquisitions, the types and disposition of freight carried, the choice to offer refundable tickets, the decision to add a stopover to a direct route, flight attendant uniforms, and so forth. While none of the carriers went bankrupt under government control, they lack the flexibility to conduct business on their own terms without extensive approval processes.

Arguably, it was airline deregulation that introduced the practice of revenue management, which was a byproduct of competition engendered by the emergence of LCCs. Revenue management, as discussed earlier, minimizes consumer surplus by charging each consumer what he/she is willing to pay, as opposed to applying a blanket single fare across consumer characteristics. Furthermore, the decrease in ticket prices and the increase in route choices point to a distinct benefit for consumers. On the other side, airlines, especially legacy carriers, had to operate in an environment of much more heated competition, with narrower margins and the potential for price wars, all while maintaining much the same cost and managerial structure that they had utilized during the days of regulation.

This pattern is by no means restricted to the United States—every country has a comparable aviation regulation framework reflective of its economic and political development. Throughout the world and in any political or economic framework, aviation remains a tightly regulated industry with heavy government involvement. For example, there has been a push for privatization of airports, especially in Europe, which is triggering a similar call in America. Simultaneously, however, the costs of certifying non-experimental aircraft have steadily increased over the past few decades, although there has been an attempt to address this trend in the United States through the introduction of a new Light Sport Aircraft category that bypasses most of the heavy certification and pilot licensure burden imposed on other aircraft.

With this degree of government involvement, no discussion of aviation economics would be complete without an analysis of the economics of government, its incentives, and its impact on commercial aviation. Governments are a function of the political system and philosophy that each country has come to adopt. In the United States, this encompasses the development of the FAA, airline regulation and deregulation, and the historically unrestricted nature of general aviation. All are intimately linked to the political climate and prevalent philosophy at the time. In order to better understand the nature of government involvement in aviation, it is necessary to discuss the broader picture—market-driven political and economic systems in comparison to command economies.

Economic Failures

Not all of the impacts of air transport are reflected in market costs. While a factory might have to pay cleanup costs following the pollution of a river, the emissions from burning aviation fuel that contribute to greenhouse gases in the atmosphere and climate change are mostly not priced or charged to the airline or traveler. Until recently, there have been no markets for greenhouse gases. The same is true for the impacts or costs imposed on residents around airports due to the noise made by aircraft landing and taking off. Neither are there payments made to air transport for any beneficial spillovers into local and national economies from gains from trade and other wider economic benefits. In this sense, the market fails and intervention is required to prevent sub-optimal outcomes for households and the economy.

Broadly speaking, there might be two kinds of economic failures: market failures and government failures.

Market Failure

Market failure occurs when the market forces (supply and demand) do not lead to efficient distribution of productive resources. It can occur due to a variety of reasons, such as monopoly, negative externalities, and public goods. Market failure happens when the market does not allocate resources to their most efficient use. Put another way, equity failure occurs when the market does not allocate resources to their most perceived equitable distribution. In this case, the market would allocate more or less than "a perceived optimum." In economic terms, market failures indicate that the market is somehow not operating as it should. The two main categories of market failures are externalities and a lack of competition.

Externalities are hidden costs and benefits associated with the production of a good or service that are not fully experienced by the individual producing or consuming it but exist as a byproduct of such production or consumption. A negative externality is an undesirable consequence of production that is not experienced directly by the producer, and climate change is the ultimate negative externality. According to a Brookings report:

> The economic cost of climate change is high: an annual $12 billion increase in electricity bills due to added air conditioning; $66 billion to $106 billion worth of coastal property damage due to rising seas; and billions in lost wages for farmers and construction workers forced to take the day off or risk suffering from heat stroke or worse.

Flying a tube of aluminum or composites full of people and cargo at 30,000 feet is energy intensive and burns fossils fuels, which emit greenhouse gases such as carbon dioxide. This external cost of air transport from the climate change it contributes to is starting to prompt governments to attempt to establish missing markets in greenhouse gases. This is achieved through the implementation of market-based policy measures such as carbon taxes, or the requirement to buy allowances or offsets in cap-and-trade schemes. This will be dealt with in more detail in a later chapter.

A classical aviation example of externalities would be the congestion costs imposed by increased general aviation activity. In the United States, the number of active general aviation aircraft increased from 131,743 to 204,980 from 1970 to 2021. General aviation traffic does not pay user fees for its share of consumption of airport and air traffic control resources. These expenses are subsidized by the federal government, or in the case of large airports, by landing charges and other fees imposed on commercial airlines. However, a high volume of general aviation traffic may lead to increased congestion at large airports, tie up air traffic control resources, and impose costs on all aircraft. If there were user fees for general aviation and the pilot experienced the full cost of his/her consumption of resources, the volume of such activity would drop off. Since the general aviation pilots only experience a part of the true costs of flying, they tend to *overproduce*, in this case by flying a lot more than they would under the full costs of flying.

Similarly, positive externalities exist when a remote city or rural area is connected to the rest of the country by air travel. Apart from the revenues generated by ticket sales to and from the area, the hidden benefits of air travel include job creation from the airline and airports in the area, increased possibilities for commerce and enterprise due to increased connectivity, the possibility of emergency relief and aid in times of natural disaster, and so forth. These externalities are not experienced by the airlines aiming to provide service to the region—all they experience are low revenues and high costs associated with operating in a limited market. Therefore, they *underproduce*, by choosing not to operate that route since it will have poor profitability. This is where the role of the Essential Air Service Program comes into play; it subsidizes unprofitable routes due to the presence of substantial positive externalities. These subsidies pass on some of the benefits of the positive externalities to airlines, allowing them to operate in such limited markets.

The second kind of market failure is a lack of competition, leading toward monopoly. A few industries involve such high level of fixed cost investment, high entry barriers, and great economies of scale that natural monopolies or duopolies are the only sustainable firm structure. Large aircraft manufacturing serve as a prime example of such an industry. Developing the Airbus A380 cost approximately $14 billion. The Boeing 777 cost approximately $5.5 billion to develop, and it was based on an existing product platform. This example highlights the high barriers of entry into the industry and the economies of scale that are derived from mass production. These factors make vigorous competition extremely challenging. Further, the uncertainty of the revenue stream from such development is always extremely high. In other words, even though the manufacturer might collaborate with its customers in designing and building the aircraft, the volatile nature of the airline industry, the unstable competitive structure due to bankruptcies, and the changes in economic circumstances make the end revenues of a product extremely uncertain while raising the cost of investment. Therefore, the manufacturing industry is dominated by a few major players, and to sustain the competition, even if it devolves into a duopoly, a stable source of income is required that may effectively cross-subsidize the business of manufacturing large jets. In the case of Boeing and Airbus, this takes the shape of government defense and civilian contracts, as well as direct government subsidies. Many pundits argue that the commercial airports possess significant monopoly power, and to prevent monopolistic profit, airport charges such as landing fees must be regulated. Globally, many airports face little or no competition, and without regulation, they may impose monopolistic prices.

Government Failure

Government failure occurs when a government intervention in the economy results in allocation of resources being inferior to that achieved by the free market. The economic collapse of the former Soviet Union on December 26, 1991 indicated the failure of command economies as a means of allocating resources among competing uses. The absence of a system providing financial incentives or price signals to direct economic activity led economic inefficiencies.

Most large airports are dominated by a single major carrier, with monopoly or near-monopoly pricing power. Therefore, the premium associated with a hub airport is usually higher than the premium associated with smaller airports in terms of passenger yield. Arguably, small community airports have benefited the most from deregulation in terms of passenger yield. Further, the total number of scheduled departures in small, medium, and large hubs has also historically increased, although recent trends have shown a decrease, as Figure 2.5 demonstrates.

However, studies like Brenner (1988) and Anderson, Gong, and Lakshmanan (2005) have found decreasing competition in the airline market due to bankruptcies and consolidations, as well as deteriorating competition in major hub airports as a result of the dominance of major hub airlines. While this trend was indeed the case through the first 20 years of deregulation, the hub dominance of airlines like Delta at Atlanta has slowly diminished over time. Delta's market share at Atlanta (percentage of scheduled revenue passengers enplaned through Delta as a percentage of total scheduled revenue passengers) rose from 49.96% to 83.70% from 1977 to 1993, and subsequently declined to 69.29% in 2021 (Table 2.1). This is primarily due to the emergence of viable competitors like Southwest and other LLCs, which are now responsible for over 13% of the market share at Atlanta. Therefore, it could be argued that in

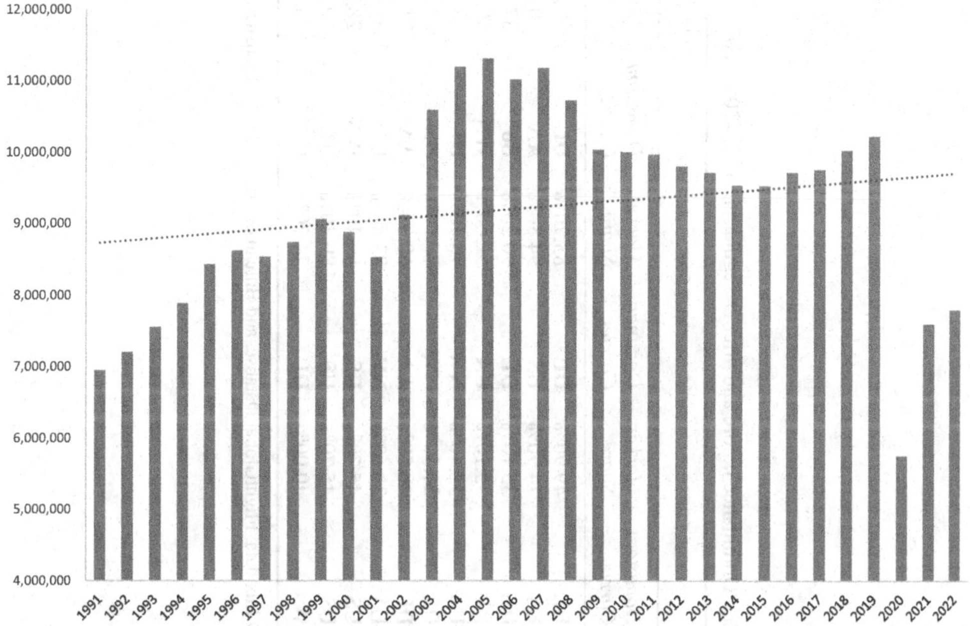

Figure 2.5 Scheduled Departures within the United States, 1991–2022.

Source: Compiled by the authors using Form 41

Table 2.1 Hub Dominance before and after Deregulation: 1977, 2017–2021

	1977		*1993*		*2016*		*2018*		*2020*		*2022*		
Airports	*Dominant Carrier*	*Market Share*	*Dominant Carrier*	*Market Share*	*Dominant Carrier*	*Market Share*	*Airports*	*Dominant Carrier*	*Market Share*	*Dominant Carrier*	*Market Share*	*Dominant Carrier*	
ATL	**DL**	49.90%	**DL**	83.70%	**DL**	72.57%	**DL**	72.71%	**DL**	67.59%	**DL**	69.29%	
CLT	**EA**	74.90%	**US**	94.80%	**AA**	60.22%	**AA**	60.17%	**AA**	58.12%	**AA**	60.46%	
CVG	**DL**	35.10%	**DL**	90.20%	**B6**	37.54%	**B6**	36.95%	**B6**	38.47%	**B6**	38.22%	
DEN	**DL**	35.10%	**UA**	52.60%	**WN**	30.58%	**UA**	30.52%	**WN**	31.03%	**WN**	32.47%	
DTW	**UA**	32.40%	**NW**	78.10%	**DL**	47.36%	**DL**	46.96%	**DL**	45.12%	**DL**	49.45%	
MEM	**DL**	21.30%	**NW**	76.60%	**DL**	26.27%	**DL**	25.37%	**DL**	19.64%	**DL**	20.46%	
MIA	**DL**	40.50%	**AA**	60.00%	**AA**	71.92%	**AA**	69.09%	**AA**	66.64%	**AA**	59.07%	
MSP	**EA**	30.60%	**NW**	83.80%	**DL**	51.05%	**DL**	52.92%	**DL**	48.28%	**DL**	51.01%	
PIT	**US**	45.70%	**US**	89.40%	**WN**	28.83%	**WN**	27.49%	**WN**	26.99%	**WN**	28.10%	
SLC	**US**	45.70%	**US**	89.40%	**DL**	49.57%	**DL**	51.20%	**DL**	52.89%	**DL**	54.42%	
STL	**WA**	40.00%	**DL**	74.70%	**WN**	56.21%	**WN**	61.86%	**WN**	63.36%	**WN**	58.73%	

Source: O&D Lux data, FlightGlobal Databse, and Bureau of Transportation Statistics.

the long term, airlines return to a more or less competitive state in a deregulated environment due to the threat of new entrants, reduced entry barriers, and the accountability fostered by market forces.

It is notable that airline bankruptcies since deregulation have increased dramatically. No airline was allowed to go bankrupt under the CAB's fares and competitive strategies. As of April 2012, there had been about 47 airline bankruptcies in the United States, 17 of which resulted in ceased operations. According to a US General Accounting Office Study in 1996, quality of service indicators have emerged with mixed results at various airports across the nation. Was deregulation a government success or failure? The answer seems to depend on one's perspective. Air travelers today possess more choices for carriers, a greater number of routes, and lower fares, all of which point to greater competition in the airline industry. On the other hand, airline profitability has declined considerably, as has the compensation of employees. However, taken in its entirety, airline deregulation can be considered a government success, or rather, a success of the free market over the organizational power of the government in aviation.

A more unqualified government success in terms of effective regulation lies in the field of aviation safety. Since the creation of the FAA in 1958, accident rates dropped almost 92.5%, from approximately one every 12.5 million aircraft miles to one in every 166.67 million aircraft miles flown. Figure 2.6 illustrates the striking decline in air traffic accidents between 1960 and 2021. This achievement can be attributed to extensive regulation in terms of pilot certification, training, aircraft airworthiness, operational directives, the institution of controlled airspaces, navigational aids, sophisticated weather and flight planning tools, and the standardization of scheduled air carrier operations. Moreover, these factors have contributed considerably to the development of aviation by establishing an excellent track record for safety and accountability.

It could also be contended that a significant portion of this decline in commercial aviation accidents and fatalities can be attributed to factors other than government regulation, such as the

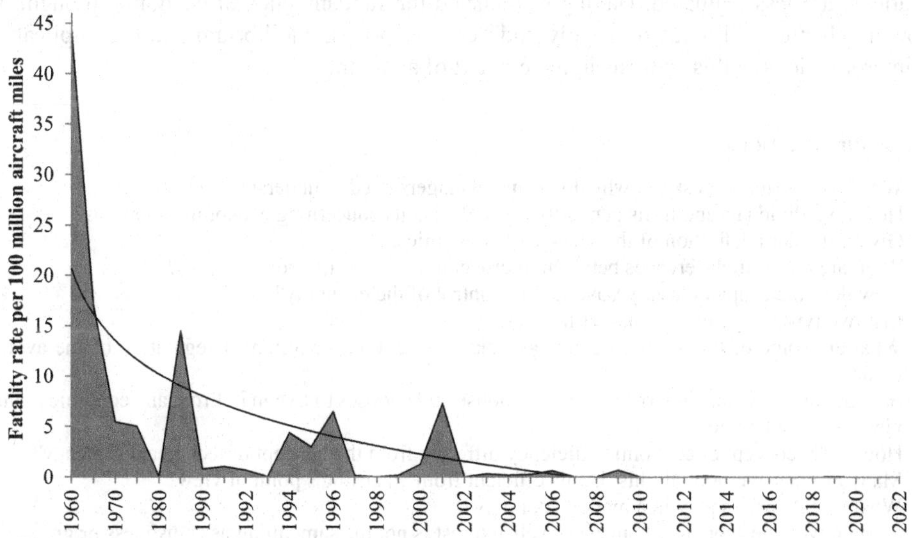

Figure 2.6 Fatality Rates per Million Aircraft Miles Flown, 1960–2020.

Source: BTS National Transportation statistics, Table 2.9: U.S. Carrier Safety Data

introduction of jet engines, improvements in avionics instituted by the private sector, improvements in pilot training, and the rising number of simulators as a flight-training tool. These are factors that could have arguably emerged even without government regulation. However, regardless of the relative percentages of aviation safety attributable to the market or the government, the dramatic decline in aviation accidents and fatalities since the 1960s, coupled with robust regulatory pressures on airlines and aircraft manufacturers to emphasize safety, presents a remarkable example of the government and the market working in tandem to achieve an optimal result.

Summary

This chapter introduced the reader to the economic way of thinking in the context of aviation. Economics is presented as a science of choice amidst the scarcity of resources. Economics is divided into two major categories: microeconomics and macroeconomics. Macroeconomics focuses on the overall economy, addressing issues such as economic growth, inflation, and overall unemployment, and is covered in more detail in the last chapter of this book. Microeconomics deals with the behavior of individual households and businesses (decision-making units) and with the production, exchange and allocation, or consumption, of goods and services. We also explored the concepts of incentives and opportunity costs, which are fundamental to economic decision-making.

Furthermore, we discussed the role and history of government regulation in an economy, economic failure, within the context of aviation. The 2007–2009 financial crisis began years earlier due to lax government financial regulation, cheap credit that fueled a housing bubble. Following the collapse of air travel caused by COVID-19 in early 2020, US carriers received federal funds from a dedicated program, amounting to approximately $54 billion. Air France-KLM was set to receive up to $12 billion in state aid to cope with the impact of COVID-19. Overall, government influence is non-uniform, varying across industries with some being more highly regulated than others. Even within an industry like aviation, some aspects, such as airline operations, are less regulated. Having established the fundamentals of economic thought, the following chapter will focus on supply and demand, prices, equilibrium and the implications and interpretations of this analysis in the context of aviation.

Discussion Questions

1 What is opportunity cost and why do airline managers need to understand it?
2 How do individuals and firms generally make decisions concerning economic situations?
3 Give a standard definition of the science of economics.
4 What are the main differences between microeconomics and macroeconomics?
5 How does the chapter classify government control of the economy?
6 List two types of perceived market failures.
7 What are some of the main problems associated with total government regulation of the aviation industry?
8 Suppose an individual inherits a $500,000 house and chooses to live in it. From an economic point of view, is this a free good?
9 How is the concept of economic efficiency different from the concept of technical efficiency?
10 Many airlines overbook flights. Is this efficient from an airline's point of view?
11 What role do prices play in a market economy?
12 Explain why the economic concept of self-interest is not the same thing as selfishness or greed.
13 Suppose a freeway has one lane that is devoted only to people with important business (as defined by the people themselves). Do you think that lane would be any less crowded than the other lanes?

14 Do you think that the problem of scarcity will ever be solved? Why or why not?
15 How is unemployment defined in the United States?
16 Why is some amount of unemployment essential to the functioning of a market economy?
17 What is cyclical unemployment?
18 Define inflation. Is it possible for all prices to increase at the same rate?
19 Suppose a credit company would like to lend money at a 3% rate of interest, but there is an inflation rate of 10%. What rate would they charge and why?
20 Define the economic concept of externality. How might an externality be addressed in the marketplace?
21 As an airport manager, provide examples of opportunity costs from your professional prospective.
22 When you are deciding how much money to spend on air travel, what factors affect your decision? Does your decision depend on how much money you have? Does your action depend on whether you are on a business trip or a personal trip?
23 Suppose there are only three goods that households consume: clothes, food, and weapon. Given the information below, find the CPI in the base year and the current year using a 100-point scale.

	Weapon		***Food***		***Clothes***	
Year	***Price***	***Quantity***	***Price***	***Quantity***	***Price***	***Quantity***
Base Year	$10,000	1	$10	2,000	$5	1,500
Current Year	$5,000	2	$12	6,000	$10	1,500

24 Calculate the labor force participation and the unemployment rate in the following cases:

a Population 20 million; labor force 11 million and 10 million employed.
b Population 20 million; employed 9 million and 1 million unemployed.
c Population 8 million; labor force 3 million and 300,000 unemployed.

25 Find the unemployment rate for the following employees with each level of education.

	Total Population	*In Labor Force*	*Employed*
High School	35,450,000	23,042,500	21,199,100
Bachelor's Degree	45,233,000	29,401,450	27,343,349
Post Graduate	41,150,000	26,747,500	25,945,075

Notes

1 Oasis Hong Kong Airline was launched in 2006 and is a now-defunct long-haul low-cost airline.
2 Retrieved from Trvelmath.com on September 4, 2022, for travel on February 15, 2017, assuming fuel burn of 24 miles per gallon and a gas price of $3.82 per gallon.
3 *The National Business*, September 1, 2009.
4 Airlines cut flights as jet-fuel costs climb. *Denver Post*, October 24, 2011.
5 *The Financial Times*, Ryanair to cut capacity for first time, May 23, 2011.
6 *Asian Review*, August 26, 2016.
7 The CPI measures the cost of goods and services to a typical consumer, based on the costs of the same goods and services at a base period.
8 Duration of periods and contractions can be found from a variety of sources including the National Bureau of Economic Research.
9 Open Skies Treaty, United States Department of State Bureau of Arms Control. March 23, 2012.
10 Commission of the European Communities. Amending Regulation (EC), No. 216/2008.
11 Deutsche Lufthansa timetable at timetableimages.com.
12 Civil Aeronautics Board. Accident Investigation Report. File No. 1-009, April 17, 1957.

References

Anderson, W.P., Gong, G., and Lakshmanan, T.R. (2005). Competition in a Deregulated Market for Air Travel: The US Domestic Experience and Lessons for Global Markets. *Research in Transportation Economics*, 13, 3–25.

Brenner, M. (1988). Airline Deregulation: A Case Study in Public Policy Failure. *Transportation Law Journal*, 16, 179.

Bureau of Transportation Statistics (BTS). (2016). *Number of US Aircraft, Vehicles, Vessels, and Other Conveyances*, pp. Tables 1–11. Retrieved on January 27, 2016 from https://www.rita.dot.gov/bts/sites/rita.dot.gov.bts/files/publications/national_transportation_statistics/html/table_01_11.html

Fried, W. and Myron, K. (1997). *Avionics Navigation Systems* (2nd ed.). New York: John Wiley & Sons.

3 Supply, Demand, and Elasticity

Analysis in the Airline Industry

In economics, elasticity measures how reactive the market is to a change in one variable (price, income, price of other goods and services) for a given product. Price elasticity of demand is employed by airlines to launch their optimal pricing strategy and maximize revenue. The elasticity of demand for air travel is an important consideration for airlines when setting prices and devising marketing strategies. In this chapter, we apply the tools of supply and demand analysis to aviation markets, airlines, airports, and aircraft manufacturers. On the demand side, our focus lies in analyzing passenger responses to changes in ticket prices, along with other relevant factors, such as changes in income. The management perspective then incorporates demand information through tools such as price and income elasticity, with further information about supply helping to maximize profits. As usual, careful economic analysis reveals some surprising truths. We present examples of the efficiency of market allocation of resources and contrast this with a regulated allocation. We employ general aviation user fees and airport landing slot allocation as a way to illustrate the importance of a thorough understanding of the factors influencing supply and demand for an aviation manager. The perishability of inventory (i.e., once an empty seat has flown, it is worthless) leaves the airline manager in a disadvantage compared to the manufacturing sector. Thus, determining market equilibrium necessitates an analysis of fuel costs, ticket price, and other characteristics of supply and demand. The price of oil, for example, has a dramatic impact on ticket prices, and substantial changes in oil prices have led to volatile swings in traffic.

This chapter explores the following specific topics:

- Basic Elements of Demand
  - Law of Demand
  - Demand Schedule
  - Demand Curve
- Derived Demand
- Direct Demand
- Demand Function
  - Implicit Demand Functions
  - Explicit Demand Functions
  - Other Demand Functions
  - Inverse Demand Function
  - Determinants of Demand for Air Transportation

DOI: 10.4324/9781003388135-3

Basic Elements of Demand

Demand in economic terms can be defined as the ability and willingness to buy specific quantities of a good or a service at alternative prices in a given time period under *ceteris paribus*[1] conditions. Airlines determine airfares in response to both passenger demand and market competition. Understanding demand theory and the demand function is one of the more important aspects for any business, as the characteristics of demand will dictate the patterns and characteristics of sales. For the airlines, the principal objective in setting airfares is to maximize the revenue for every flight. For example, if an airline were to drop ticket prices, would the resulting increase in passenger demand cause an increase or decrease in passenger revenue? When would the increased sales generated by low ticket prices start to impact passenger yield? Numerous macroeconomic variables and external industry factors affect air transport demand significantly. The airline industry has been one of the hardest hit sectors during the COVID-19 pandemic; by April 2020, more than 140 airlines slashed capacity down to 10% of pre-pandemic levels or less. The pandemic has also accelerated aircraft retirements, marking the end of the jumbo jet era, such as Airbus A340-600s, Airbus A380s, and Boeing 747-400s. However, as COVID-19 restrictions are lifted, travel demand has bounced back. Economic recovery leads to increased corporate profits, enabling more spending on air travel, while stronger household incomes encourage more leisure travel. Demand analysis will shed light on these and other critical business decisions.

Law of Demand

Air transport managers must attempt to understand the true nature of passenger demand and improve competitive positions to maintain profitability and growth. The law of demand states that, *ceteris paribus*, as price increases, the quantity demanded decreases. In other words, quantity demanded has a negative relationship with price. Additionally, prices are crucial in determining supply and demand for a given product or service. The law of demand states that if all other factors remain equal, the lower the price of a product, the greater the quantity people will buy.

The law of demand states that, all else equal, consumers will buy less at a given time period when price of a product increases and buy more as price decreases.

To comprehend the law of demand's practicality, let's consider a transcontinental flight from New York to Los Angeles. For this round-trip flight, what would be the maximum price a passenger would be willing to pay? $500? $1,000? $5,000? The fact is that, at some point, the passenger would consider the price to be too expensive and would not take the trip. This decision to not fly is the law of demand in practice; that is, at some price, the quantity demanded for the individual will decrease. The amount by which the quantity demanded decreases with ticket prices will vary by consumer characteristics and preferences. This responsiveness of quantity demanded to price is termed demand elasticity, a concept we will explore at length later in the chapter. Regardless of the degree of the response to demand, the law of demand states that an increase in price leads to a decrease in quantity demanded.

When this decision is presented to all possible travelers, different responses can be expected due to different incomes, urgency, and purposes for travel. These different responses help create a demand schedule, which is simply a table showing the quantities of a product that customers are willing and able to buy at varying prices in a given time period, *ceteris paribus*. Specifically, such a table highlights the number of customers who would purchase a product or service at a given price. It is important to remember that demand is cumulative. In other words, a consumer who is willing to pay $1,000 for the flight would certainly also be willing to pay $500 for the same flight.

Demand Schedule

A demand schedule illustrates the quantity that will be demanded at every price level. This concept can be easily related to our daily lives. Let's consider the hypothetical demand schedule in Table 3.1 for a flight from New York to Los Angeles. Cheaper ticket prices attract more passengers. According to the schedule, if an airline charges $5,000 round trip, it cannot sell more than 15 seats. However, if the same tickets are priced at $4,000, customers will buy 95 tickets. Further decrease to ticket price of $200 leads to even more seats being sold at this price. This is, in essence, what constitutes a demand curve. The demand schedule outlined in Table 3.1 highlights the law of demand, as the quantity demanded (number of passengers) for the $200 airfare is significantly higher than the quantity demanded for the expensive $5,000 airfare.

Table 3.1 Hypothetical Demand Schedule for JFK–LAX

Ticket Prices	*Quantity Demanded*
New York-Los Angeles	Number of Passengers
$200	735
$500	690
$1,000	615
$1,500	540
$2,000	465
$2,500	390
$3,000	315
$3,500	240
$4,000	165
$4,500	90
$5,000	15

Demand Curve

The law of demand can be further understood with the help of certain concepts, such as a demand schedule, a demand curve, and a demand function. A demand curve can be constructed from the aforementioned demand schedules and is a graphical description of the demand schedule, illustrating the quantities of a good that customers are willing and able to buy at varying prices in a given period of time. Demand curves are always graphed with the price per unit on the vertical axis and the quantity demanded on the horizontal axis. The law of demand is then shown by this schedule as downward sloping curve.[2] It should be noted that the demand curve does not portray actual purchases, but rather indicates what consumers would be willing and able to purchase. Figure 3.1 provides the demand curve for the New York to Los Angeles trip. In this example, the curve is a linear negative sloping line.

The demand curve in this example is linear and downward sloping. Also, both vertical and horizontal intercepts have an economic interpretation. The vertical intercept is called a "choke price," which is defined as the price at which demand shrinks to zero. In other words, this price is above what every consumer in the market would be willing to pay for the trip between JFK and LAX. The horizontal intercept is the demand limit. This could represent the entire size of the market as, as discussed below, the demand for air transportation is a derived demand. In other words, it's based on individuals' willingness to travel, which is itself contingent on their reasons for travel. Even if the trip between JFK and LAX were to be offered free of charge, the quantity demanded would increase due to a corresponding increase in vacationers and other leisure travelers. But it would eventually reach a limit, as the underlying factors affecting the desire for travel have not changed. In economics, consumer demand can also be subdivided into direct demand and derived demand.

Direct Demand

Direct demand is the demand for products or services used directly for consumption. The demand for goods does not depend on the demand for any other service or commodity. For example, the direct demand for an internet comes from its ability to provide communication and information services. Consumers subscribe to internet directly for these features, without the need for any other product or service to facilitate its use.

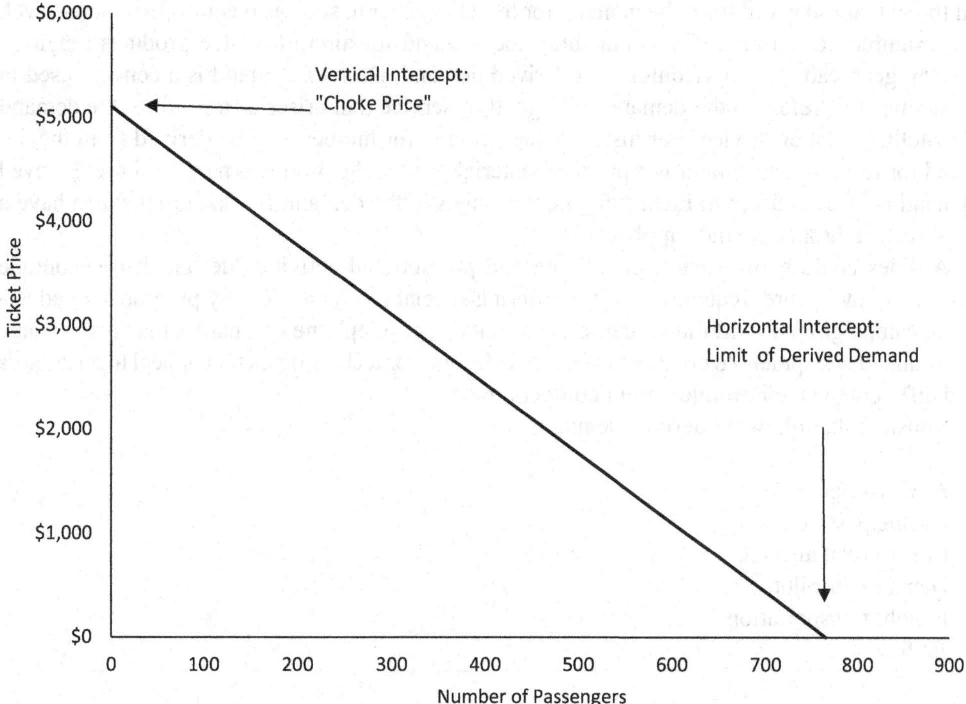

Figure 3.1 Abstract Demand Curve for JFK–LAX Flight.

Direct demand refers to demand for goods and services meant for final consumption. For example, if you use general aviation aircraft for recreational purposes, then your demand for aircraft is a direct demand. For commercial airlines, each aircraft has a unique cost/revenue factor that makes it suitable for certain airlines. The pricing implication of this is that a decrease in the price of that aircraft will lead to an increased demand for the aircraft. This primarily translates into market growth for airlines that were previously unable to afford the aircraft due to fixed cost constraints but are now able to purchase. Itineraries that were previously deemed uneconomical might suddenly become profitable, and the size of the market could grow. Therefore, a managerial implication is that for the manufacturer, demand and market size can be directly influenced by decisions about aircraft type, and competition is not necessarily a zero-sum game. Introducing a significant degree of technological differentiation into the equation, both Boeing and Airbus can create and capture entirely different market segments. Although both companies compete for the same customers, high levels of product differentiation and a direct demand for aircraft make them both able to segment the market and benefit from the increasing numbers of customers.

Derived Demand

In contrast to direct demand, there exists the concept of demand for a good or service stemming from the demand for a different, or related, good or service. As income increases, people start traveling more, leading to increased demand for aircraft, jet fuel, pilots, and labor accordingly. When the demand for a particular product depends on the demand for another product or service, it is called a derived demand. In the case of airlines, derived demand refers to the demand for air travel that is derived from the demand for travel in general, such as business or leisure travel. For example, for an aircraft manufacturer, the demand for aircraft-related products (engines, landing gear, cables, and avionics) is a derived demand. Derived demand is a concept used in economics that refers to the demand for a good or service that arises as a result of the demand for another good or service. For instance, the demand for lumber may be derived from the demand for furniture, as lumber is a primary material used in the production of furniture. Derived demand is a key concept to identifying how changes in the demand for one product can have a ripple effect throughout the supply chain.

Airlines could apply various marketing and promotional activities designed to encourage people to travel more frequently, such as offering special discounts, loyalty programs, or advertising campaigns. Aircraft manufactures, automakers, or telephone companies may also engage in product development to create new features, designs, or technologies that appeal to customers and differentiate their products from competitors.

Consider the following derived demands:

- Advertising
- Airline passengers
- Commercial aircraft
- Demand for pilots
- Freight transportation
- Jet fuel

Derived demand is the demand for a particular product or service that depends on the demand for another product or service. Airlines provide a good example of derived demand. The demand for air travel is derived from the demand for transportation between two or more locations. When you plan to travel for work or pleasure, demand for air transport is just such an intermediate service. It is derived indirectly from the demand for the final service.

Each of these derives from the demand for another demand or service. This is a key aspect in air transportation demand analysis. In other words, the demand for air transportation arises from factors other than the transportation itself. Individuals do not directly demand travel. Rather, their demand originates from their desire to travel. Derived demand can be characterized by the demand for other goods and services or by the product being demanded to produce other goods.

A managerial implication of this analysis is that an *absolute* decline in prices might not necessarily cause an increase in travel if all the competing airlines on a particular route simultaneously decrease their prices as well. In a derived-demand market, only *relative* price decreases matter, as a drop in prices cannot necessarily increase the overall quantity demanded. If every airline were to cut its prices for the JFK–LAX route by $100 tomorrow, travel might increase slightly due to the leisure segment. Overall, however, few more people would necessarily want to go to LAX from JFK merely because it is cheaper to do so. However, if Virgin America alone were to cut its fares by $100, while American Airlines, Delta, and US Airways kept their prices unchanged, Virgin America could steal away customers and increase the demand for its product.

Demand Function

The demand function represents the functional relationship (a mathematical equation) between the quantity demanded for a commodity and its determinants (independent variables).

The demand function can be constructed using information from the demand schedule or the demand curve. Numerous factors, not only price, influence demand. For example, income, on-time performance, flight frequencies, and aircraft interior are some other factors that impact airline demand. A demand function is simply the functional relationship between the quantity demanded and the other influencing factors. Moreover, demand functions may be implicit or explicit.

Implicit Demand Functions

Implicit demand functions simply state a general relationship between the quantities demanded and the factors affecting demand. Implicit functions do not provide the actual mathematical relationships, but rather, a more generalized statement of the factors influencing demand. An econometric model of airline demand shall yield as many equations as there are fare products, and for simplicity purposes, we shall model demand as

$$Q_D = f\left(P, Y, P_{\text{OG}}, \text{PREF}, \text{EXP}, \text{POP}\right)$$

- **Ticket Price (P)**
  Economic analysis has recognized the role of several fundamental factors in determining demand for a product or service. Price is one of the most fundamental determinants of demand since it is often the first factor that consumers think about when they are planning to purchase. In general, increasing price is likely to result in a decrease in quantity demanded, and lower prices will increase the quantity demanded. Prices can change for various reasons (technology, competition, and consumer preference).
- **Income (Y)**
  Income is an important determinant of demand. Generally, the demand for goods and services is positively related to the level of income and economic activity. Income influences both the willingness and ability to purchase. Consumers with higher incomes are able to purchase more goods and services; therefore, an increase in disposable income will lead to an increase in demand for air travel. Additionally, increased consumer income is usually correlated with increased business activity, indicating a higher demand for business travel. Due to this direct relationship between demand and income, the coefficient for consumer income is positive. Goods for which demand increases as consumer income rises are called normal goods. Contrarily, goods for which demand increases as consumer income declines are called inferior goods, and the income coefficient for consumer income is always a negative number.

In economics, a good is normal if an increase in income raises its consumption; it is said to be inferior if an increase in income lowers its consumption. Inferior goods are the opposite of normal goods.

Inferior goods are the types of products people typically purchase when their income is low.

Airline industry is another common inferior good. When passengers have less disposable income, they're more likely to use low-cost airlines. When their income rises, they may travel by full-service airlines.

Used aircraft, budget hotels, driving (vs flying), and flying out of secondary airports might be other examples of inferior goods. When income is low, it makes sense to fly low-cost or no-frill airlines. However, as income increases, passengers may opt for full-service options. Hence, demand for LCCs (low-cost carriers) declines as income increases. As another concrete example, if average income rises by 10% and demand for Budget Inn Hotels falls 5%, then Budget Inn Hotels can be classified as an inferior good.

- **Price of other related goods and services (P_{OG})**
The demand for a product or a service is also affected by the prices of other goods and services, namely substitutes. For air travel, this includes other modes of transportation. In the United States, driving is a reasonable substitute for several short flights, while in Europe, high-speed rail can greatly impact, resulting in lower demand for the same route by air. However, in situations where there is a lack of other modes of transportation (i.e., air service to remote islands), demand for air travel can be expected to increase. Therefore, the expected coefficient for the availability of substitutes could be either positive or negative.
The final pricing variable that impacts the quantity demanded is the price of a complementary product or service. A complementary product or service is a product or service that is usually used jointly with the primary good. Examples in the airline industry are hotels and rental cars. Since many leisure and business travelers have to stay in hotels while on their trip, the price of the hotel will impact the demand for air travel. This is a case of derived demand. For instance, if the average price of a night's stay in Cancun were to increase, fewer people would want to vacation there, and the flight demand would decrease. Based on this typical example, one would expect the coefficient for the price of a complement to be negative.[3]

- **Consumer's preferences and tastes (PREF)**
Consumer preference also plays a role in demand. Airline passengers often compare and evaluate alternative modes of transportation before making any decisions, including their preference between legacy and low-cost carriers. For example, some people might find that Disney World in Japan is much more accessible and affordable than Disney World in Orlando. Additionally, many disabled and old passengers might prefer surface transit rather than the subway. Passengers may have different preferences for price based on their budget and willingness to pay. For example, some passengers may prefer low-cost airlines that offer lower prices but with fewer cabin amenities, while others may prefer full-service airlines that charge higher prices while offering more amenities.

- **Expectation (EXP)**
Future price estimates also affect demand for many commodities. For example, airlines commonly purchase foreign currencies if they expect the prices of the foreign money to rise in the near future. When consumers have an expectation of higher prices in the future, it can greatly impact their purchasing decisions and the demand for products or services. The airline industry is heavily affected by expectation demand, as passengers' expectations of cabin amenities, comfort, service, and convenience can greatly impact their willingness to purchase airline tickets.

- **Population (POP)**
Commercial air transportation is also largely determined by population and economic growth, and economic growth relies on a number of factors, including capital, technology, and the labor force. Current population will impact both current level of demand and future consumption through the interaction of price and ability to purchase. A larger population obviously

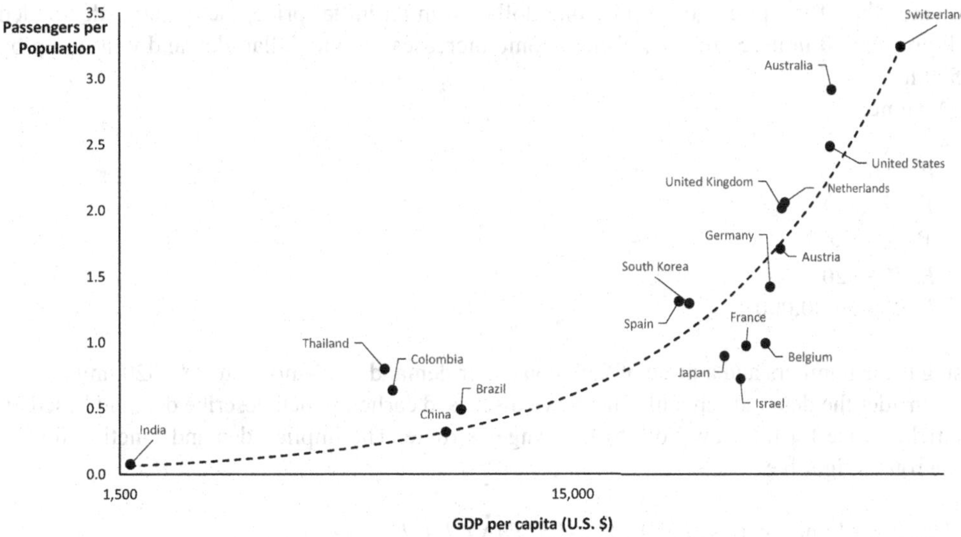

Figure 3.2 Air Transport Passengers Carried per Population and GDP per Capita in USD.

constitutes a larger consumer group, and hence an increase in the demand for different goods and services. An increase in population generally shifts the demand curve to the right, while a decrease in population shifts the demand curve to the left.

As previously discussed in Chapter 2, GDP affects the demand for air travel. Figure 3.2 is another graph demonstrating this relationship; that is, passengers carried per population of various countries plotted against GDP per capita. Again, Switzerland, Australia, and the United States have a high GDP per capita and also carry considerably more passengers relative to their respective populations. On the other hand, countries such as India and China, which have very large populations, carry far fewer passengers per capita, due to less robust economic conditions and lower living standards.

More specifically, domestic air travel rose by 6.3% in 2016, with all markets showing growth. This growth was led by China and India (the first- and second-largest countries in terms of population). Both countries are continuing to add capacity to their networks in order to take advantage of the growing demand for air travel. In fact, China is expected to overtake the United States as the world's largest passenger market by 2029.

Explicit Demand Function

Explicit demand functions provide precise mathematical relationships between the quantity demanded and the variables impacting demand. For the above example, the explicit demand function could be represented as follows:

$$Q_D = -50P + 2.5Y + 10P_{OGS} + 1.50\text{EXP} + 0.005\text{POP}$$

This illustrates the linear demand function as an explicit quantitative relationship among price, income, expectations, price of other goods and services, and quantity. The above equation indicates that if the price goes up by one dollar from an initial price, the quantity demanded will drop by 50 units. Similarly, if the income increases by one dollar, demand will go up by 2.5 units.

Assume:

$P = 60$
$Y = 75{,}000$
$P_{OGS} = 35$
$EXP = -20$
$POP = 2{,}000{,}000$

Using these numbers and a price of \$50, consumer demand will amount to 185,820 units.

Consider the demand schedule and curve discussed earlier, which describe demand based on the ticket price for the New York to Los Angeles route. The implicit demand function for the same route might be:

$$D_{JFK\text{-}LAX} = \text{Function}\ (PX, PZ, Y, ANY\text{-}LA, PANY\text{-}LA, H)$$

where:

- *PX* is the own ticket price,
- *PZ* is the competition's ticket price,
- *Y* is the annual income or state of the economy,
- *ANY-LA* is the availability of other modes of transportation for JFK–LAX,
- *PANY-LA* is the price of other modes of transportation for JFK–LAX,
- *H* is a composition of other factors (i.e., service, customer loyalty, safety, cabin amenities).

The implicit demand function simply states that a relationship exists between a dependent variable and the independent variables; however, it does not state the exact manner in which the variables are related. The numerical relationship that displays the degree of influence that each factor has on the quantity demanded is the explicit demand function. Using the information obtained from the demand schedule and the demand curve, an explicit demand function for JFK–LAX could be:

$$D_{NY\text{-}LA} = 765 - 0.15 \times P$$

Based on this linear function, two statements can be made about the nature of demand for a round-trip JFK–LAX flight. First, when the price of the ticket is \$5,100, demand for this trip drops to zero. In other words, demand for any product or service is always limited by the extent of the market demand (in this case, any price above \$5,100). The other statement concerning the linear demand curve is that the negative price coefficient (or slope) is −0.15, which means that for every dollar increase in the ticket price, the demand drops by 0.15 passengers. This change in demand occurs for all price points, creating a constant negative slope.

Table 3.2 presents data from the BTS O&D Database on ticket prices of the four carriers along the same route. The observed fares were divided into 29 bins of \$150 width. Fares lower than \$100 were omitted from the dataset because of the fact that non-revenue passengers, or airline-subsidized passengers, like crewmembers or family, generally pay artificially low prices. This data is illustrated graphically in Figure 3.3.

Table 3.2 Average Fares for Route JFK–LAX

Average Fare	*Number of Passengers*	*Average Fare*	*Number of Passengers*
$150	95,110	$2,100	210
$300	59,450	$2,250	340
$450	24,250	$2,400	1,130
$600	14,650	$2,550	50
$750	7,550	$2,700	30
$900	4,390	$2,850	20
$1,050	2,020	$3,000	10
$1,200	4,060	$3,150	20
$1,350	4,250	$3,300	10
$1,500	2,470	$3,450	10
$1,650	1,700	$3,600	10
$1,800	1,460	$3,750	10
$1,950	490	$3,900	10

Source: Compiled by the authors using Back Aviation O&D data.

American Airlines, Virgin America, US Airways, Delta Air Lines.

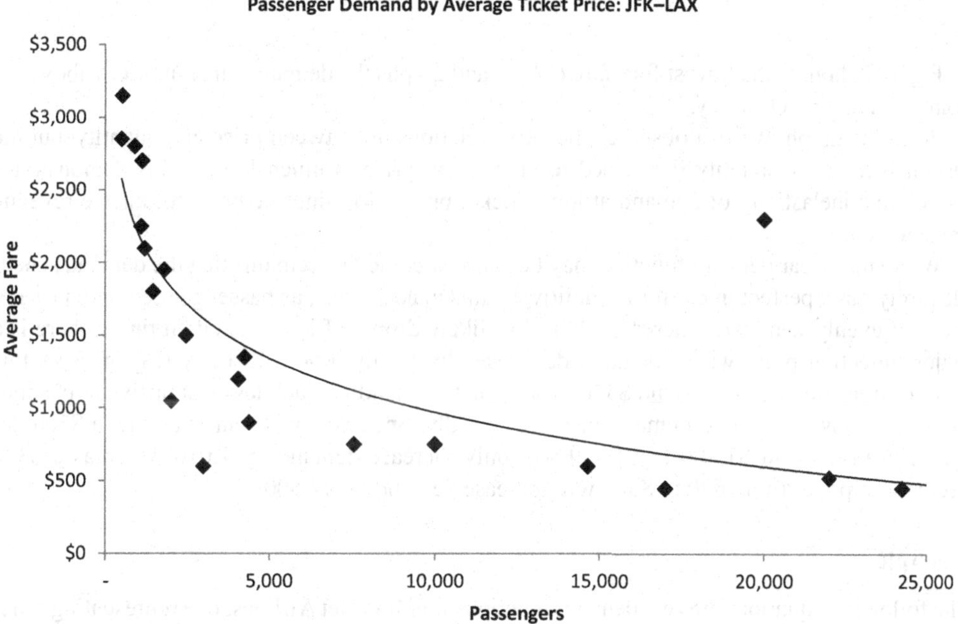

Figure 3.3 Observed Demand Curve for JFK–LAX Route.

Source: Compiled by the authors using Back Aviation O&D data

As can be observed, the empirical demand curve is downward sloping, confirming the law of demand presented above. Moreover, it demonstrates a negative relationship between quantity demanded and price. The curve is concave to the origin, suggesting that at some point, demand increases tremendously as a result of decreasing price. However, above that point, demand is much less responsive to price changes. For JFK–LAX, the abrupt change in demand elasticity occurs somewhere around $350.

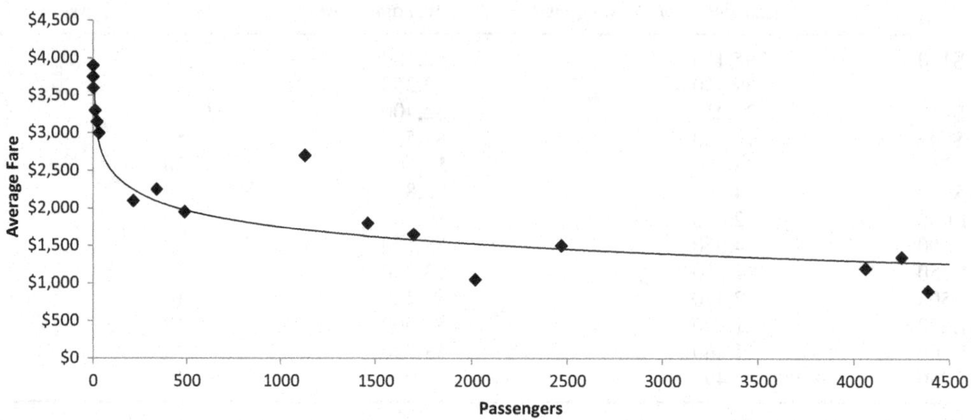

Figure 3.4 Observed Demand Curve for JFK–LAX Route: Omitting Four Lowest Fare Classes.

Source: Compiled by the authors using Back Aviation O&D data

Figure 3.4 omits the lowest four fare classes and graphs the demand curve at prices above the point of changing elasticity.

From the graph, we still observe a negative relationship between price and quantity, but the responsiveness of quantity demanded to changes in price is much lower. This demonstrates the relative inelasticity of demand at lower ticket prices, forming the basis for airline revenue management.

While the linear demand function may be simplistic, the fact remains that the demand schedule rarely has a perfect linear form. Intuitively, this makes sense, as passenger demand does not drop off evenly with price increases, but most likely drops off in steps. Often times, there is a major inflection point where demand decreases drastically. For JFK–LAX (Figure 3.3), this point of inflection occurs around $350. Above that, demand is much less responsive to changes in price. Below that point, demand increases rapidly. Specifically, in our example, a $300 decrease in price from $1,800 to $1,500 will only increase demand by 1,010, whereas a $300 decrease in price from $600 to $300 will increase demand by 44,800.

Example

The following equations are two demand functions for DirectJet Airlines, one representing time-sensitive travelers (a) and the other representing price-sensitive travelers (b). The airline's marginal cost is $60 per passenger.

a $P = 660 - 10Q_{TS}$

b $P = 380 - 5Q_{PS}$

What price should the airlines charge each person if the firm's objective is to maximize profit?

Solution:

To maximize profit, DirectJet needs to set MR = MC.

To find MR for time-sensitive passengers, obtain the first-order derivative of total revenue:

$$TR = P \times Q_{TS}$$

$$TR = (660 - 10Q_{TS}) \times Q_{TS}$$

$$TR = 660Q - 10\,Q_{TS}^{\;2}$$

$$MR = 660 - 20Q_{TS}$$

$$\text{MR} = \text{MC}$$

$$660 - 20Q_{TS} = 60$$

$$Q_{TS} = 30 \text{ seats}$$

$$P_{TS} = 660 - 10\,(30) = \$360$$

We follow the same rule for our price-sensitive passengers:

$$TR = P \times Q_{PS}$$

$$TR = (380 - 5Q_{PS}) \times Q_{PS}$$

$$TR = 380Q_{PS} - 5Q_{PS}^{\;2}$$

$$MR = 380 - 10Q_{PS}$$

$$\text{MR} = \text{MC}$$

$$380 - 10Q_{PS} = 60$$

$$Q_{PS} = 32 \text{ seats}$$

$$P_{PS} = 380 - 5\,(32) = \$180$$

Other Demand Functions

Two other functional forms for demand functions are the semi-log function and the log-linear function:[4]

Semi-log: $\text{Ln}\ Q_D = \beta_0 + \beta_1 P$

Log-linear[5]: $\text{Ln}\ Q_D = \beta_0 + \beta_1 \text{Ln}P$

where:

Q_D = the quantity demanded

P = the ticket price

β_0 = the coefficient for the constant term

β_1 = the price variable

For the airline industry, it is usually assumed that the typical demand function takes the log-linear shape (Figure 3.5).

Unlike a linear demand function where the slope of the function is constant throughout, the slope of a log-linear demand function changes. In Figure 3.5, the initial slope of the function is fairly steep, indicating that a unit drop in the ticket price does not generate a similar increase in

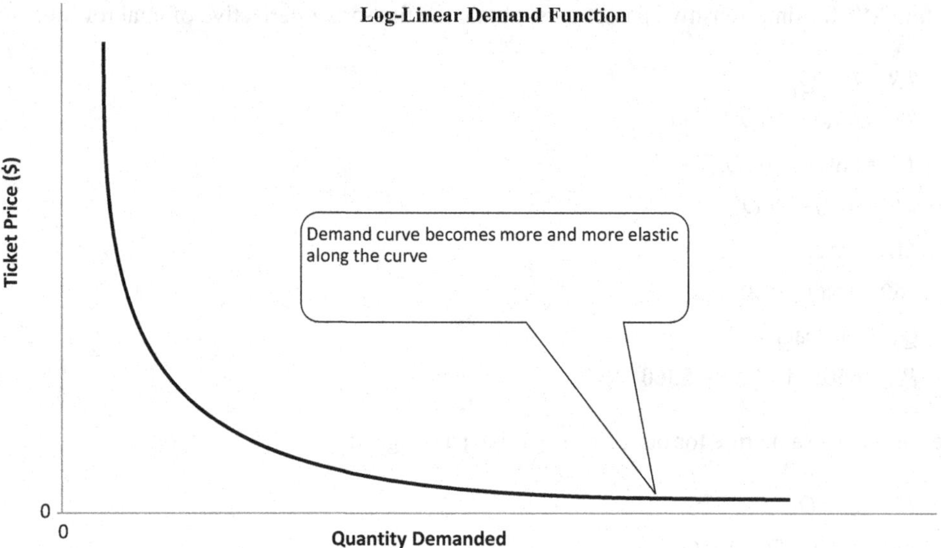

Figure 3.5 Conceptual Log-Linear Demand Curve.

the quantity demanded. This is partly due to the fact that the ticket price is still considered expensive by the majority of potential customers. Eventually, as the price decreases, the quantity demanded becomes greater and greater to the point, reaching the point where a small drop in price generates a significant increase in the quantity demanded. Referring once again to Figure 3.2, the demand curve for the JFK–LAX route can be best approximated by a log-linear function, both before and after the demand inflection point.

The general form of a log-linear demand function can be expanded to explicitly include the competition's price:

$$\text{Ln } Q_D = \beta_0 + \beta_1 \text{Ln}P_X + \beta_2 \text{Ln}P_Z$$

where:

- β_0 is a constant, the intercept
- P_X is the own price.
- P_Z is the competitor's price.
- β_1 and β_2 are the coefficients.

The general log-linear demand function for air transportation can also be expanded to include income (Y):

$$\text{Ln } Q_D = \beta_0 + \beta_1 \text{Ln}P_X + \beta_2 \text{Ln}P_Z + \beta_3 \text{Ln}Y$$

where:

- β_0 is the intercept,
- β_1, β_2, and β_3 are the coefficients.

Inverse Demand Function

In the airline industry, revenue managers are primarily interested in understanding their pricing power and the factors influencing passenger reactions to variations in ticket prices. The inverse demand function is also called the price function, and it treats price as a function of quantity demanded.

$$P(Q) = a + b(Q)$$

where a is the intercept and b is a number always less than zero.

To compute the inverse demand function, simply solve for P in the demand function. For example, if the demand function is

$$Q = 2{,}000 - 0.20 \times P$$

Then the inverse demand function would be

$$P = 10{,}000 - 5 \times Q$$

Suppose the inverse demand function for travel from London Heathrow (LHR) to Beijing (PEK) is given by the above equation. Accordingly, the maximum the airline can charge to sell 100 seats is $5,000 per seat.

For example, if the constant term a is $1,400 and the slope b is −7.5, this implies that for every additional seat demanded, the price of a ticket decreases by $7.50. Thus, if the quantity demanded is 100 seats, the price of a ticket would be:

$$P = \$1{,}400 - (7.5 \times 100) = \$650$$

In this example, if the airline wanted to increase the quantity demanded to 110 seats, it would need to lower the price of a ticket to:

$$P = \$1{,}400 - (7.5 \times 110) = \$575$$

By understanding the inverse demand function, revenue managers can make right decisions about pricing strategies and revenue management to maximize profits and meet customer demand.

Determinants of Demand for Air Transportation

From the demand function examples above, it is perceived that airline travel varies according to a number of factors, or determinants, including

- Aircraft type and location of airport
- Airfare
- Availability of other modes of transportation
- Competitor's ticket prices
- Frequency of service
- In-flight amenities
- Passenger income
- Passenger loyalty
- Random factors (i.e., disease, terrorism, or natural disaster)

- State of the economy
- Safety
- Social and demographic factors

To illustrate the impact that these factors might have on the demand curve, recall the demand schedule for the New York to Los Angeles flight. Table 3.3 provides an updated version.

To emphasize the impact of the ticket price on the demand curve, refer to Figure 3.6. As previously mentioned, a change in the ticket price is always defined as a *ceteris paribus* movement along the demand curve. For example, if the current ticket price for the flight was set at $3,000 and then lowered to $2,000 (all other things remaining constant), the only effect this change would have would be on the quantity demanded. This change is reflected in column two of Table 3.3, where the quantity demanded moves from 315 to 465. Figure 3.6 depicts this movement graphically. As the price decreases, the quantity demanded moves from point A to point B.

By definition, ticket price is the only determinant of demand that causes a movement along the demand curve; changes in the other determinants of the demand cause a shift in the entire demand curve.

> Many airlines including American Airlines, Delta, JetBlue, Southwest Airlines, and Spirit Airlines all have guidelines on how passengers can change their reservations amid warnings about the COVID-19 pandemic.

Continuing the previous example, now suppose a competitor airline rolls out a lower fare structure. This action will cause some consumers to switch, thus increasing demand for the competitor's flights. This increase is illustrated in column three of Table 3.3, where quantity demanded at each price level increases by 210 passengers from column two. The increase in the quantity demanded across all price levels results in a rightward shift in the demand curve

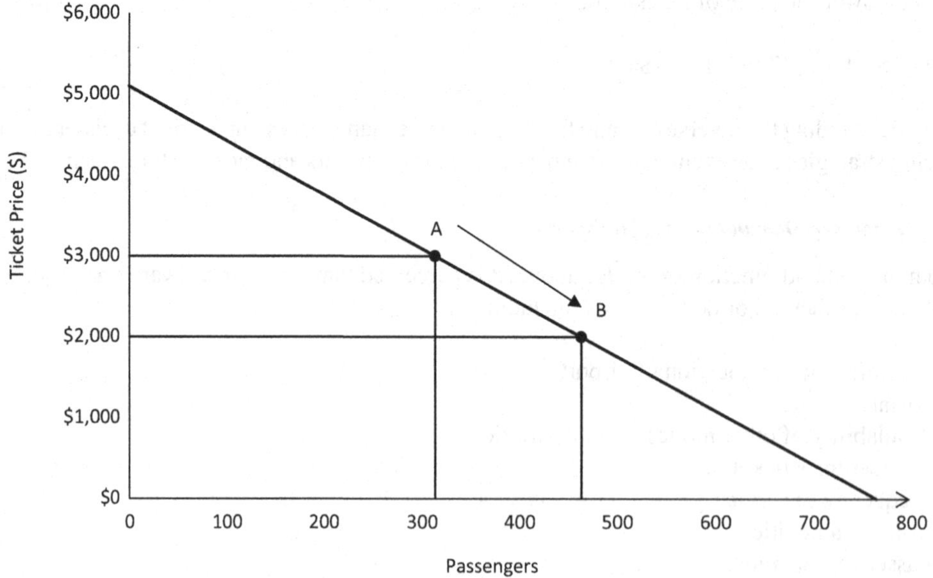

Figure 3.6 Change in Quantity Demanded for JFK–LAX Flight.

Table 3.3 Demand Schedule for JFK–LAX

Ticket Price	*Original Quantity Demanded*	*Quantity Demanded After Competition*
New York–Los Angeles	*(Number of Passengers)*	*(Number of Passengers)*
$0	975	765
$200	945	735
$350	923	713
$500	900	690
$1,000	825	615
$1,500	750	540
$2,000	675	465
$2,500	600	390
$3,000	525	315
$4,000	375	165
$5,000	225	15
$5,100	210	0

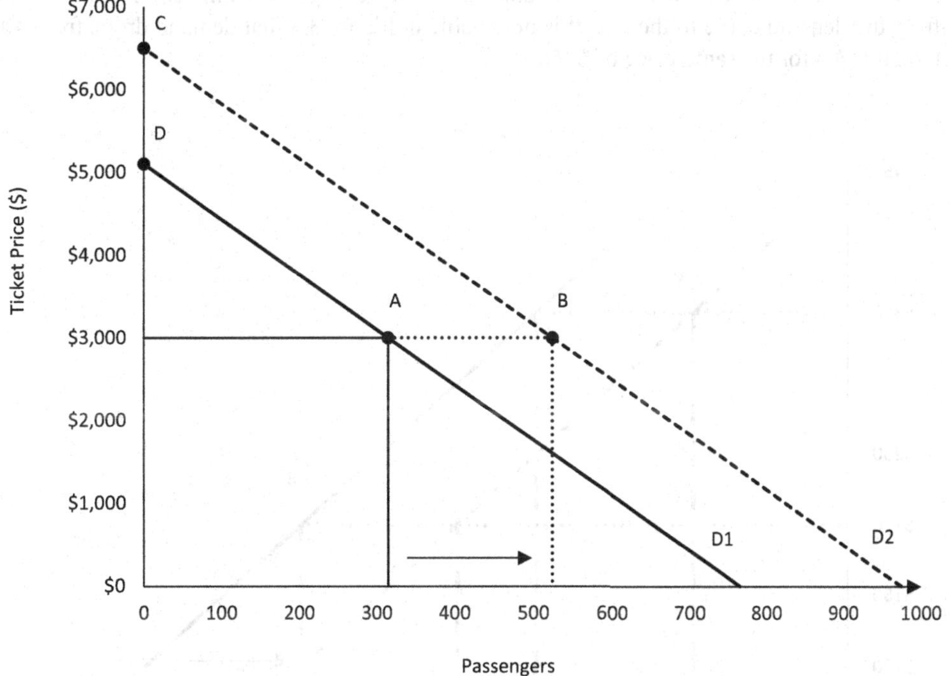

Figure 3.7 Demand Curve (JFK to LAX)—Shift to the Right.

from D_1 to D_2, as depicted in Figure 3.7. For instance, at the price of $3,000, now 525 passengers would be willing to travel from JFK to LAX, instead of 315. This shift is represented by a movement in the demand curve from A to B. Conversely, a negative impact on demand would also lead to a leftward shift in the demand curve. Finally, an increase in demand also causes an increase in the choke price of a market, moving from D to C. In other words, the absolute maximum price beyond which a consumer would not be willing to purchase air travel will increase, since the quantity demanded has increased at every price level.

The demand for a single flight is influenced by multiple factors. However, for many consumers, especially price-sensitive leisure travelers, the price of the flight and the price of competing flights are the most important variables. This became even more apparent with the advent of the internet. Nowadays, price aggregation websites like Expedia and Travelocity make airline ticket price information readily available to potential customers. However, these price variables affect different segments of the population in different ways. For time-sensitive travelers, ticket price versus a competitor's ticket price may not be as important as it is for price-sensitive travelers.

For the competitor's price variable, the coefficient would be expected to be positive, as an increase in the competitor's price would make the competition's product less competitive, and ultimately increase demand for the company's product. Consider airlines A and B, both offering flights on the same route with the same introductory fare of $400. If airline B increases its airfare to $450, it would become less competitive and ultimately increase demand for airline A. Conversely, if airline B drops the price to $350, it would become more competitive and decrease demand for airline A. Regardless of the viewpoint, the price coefficient would be negative, and the cross-price coefficient would be positive.

Apart from price, another determinant that can instantly impact on demand is stochastic or random factors such as disease outbreaks (COVID-19 being the most striking example), natural disasters, or threats of terrorism. Most random factors have a negative impact on demand, thus shifting the demand curve to the left. It is noticeable in Figure 3.8 that demand drops from 400 (A) to 200 (A') for the same price of $350.

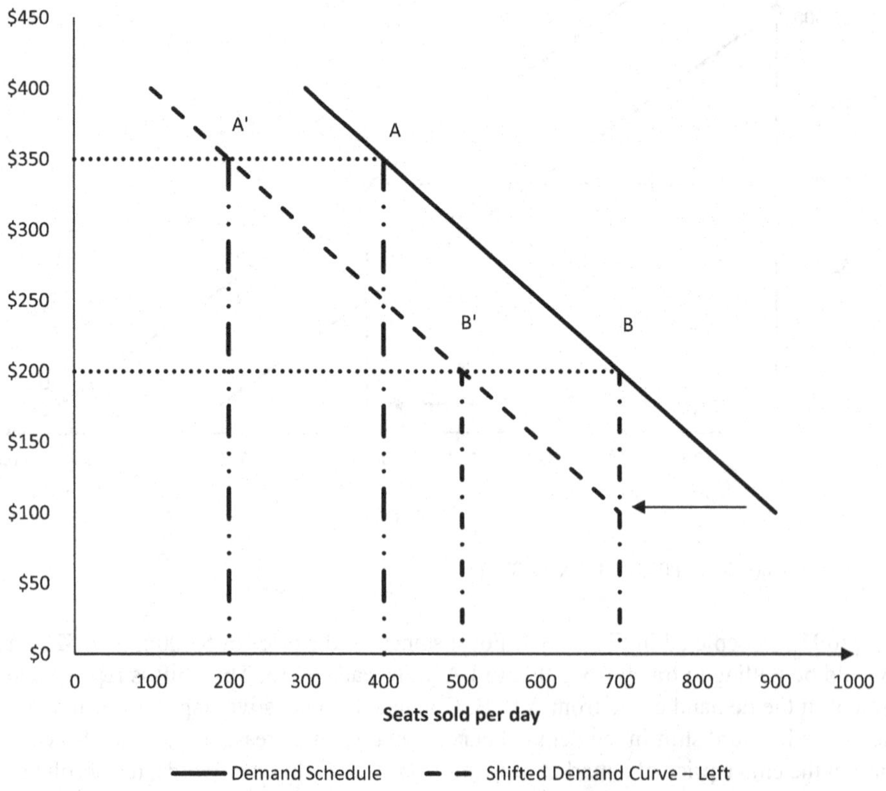

Figure 3.8 Demand Curve – Shift to the Left.

Real-world examples include the financial crisis of 2007–2009 and the Zika virus outbreak in Brazil. Similarly, the 2010 eruption of Iceland's Eyjafjallajökull volcano closed huge swathes of airspace and canceled over 10,000 flights across Europe. More recently, COVID-19, in April 2020, caused international air travel to collapse to just 5% of its pre-pandemic level.

Other variables that might affect the demand for air travel include the quality of service offered, product differentiation, and so forth. These are typically known as "quality" or "hedonic" price determinants and can play an important role in the demand for a good or product. Some of the hedonic indicators for airline demand are:

- **Flight frequency** – This is especially important for business travelers who are generally most time-sensitive. An airline with a large number of flights between two cities has a greater probability of meeting a traveler's demand than does an airline with only a few flights. Moreover, a robust schedule provides the traveler with greater flexibility in case of schedule changes. This is the primary reason why regional jets have become more popular; that is, they enable airlines to provide increased flight frequency while holding the total number of seats offered in the market steady. We would therefore expect a positive coefficient between flight frequency and demand.
- **Connectivity between city-pairs** – The availability of a non-stop flight will generally increase demand more than the availability of a flight with a connection. However, this assumption may not apply to all markets, especially ultra-long-haul markets where passengers may appreciate a stopover. Therefore, generally a non-stop flight variable is expected to have a positive relationship with demand (with some exceptions).
- **Customer loyalty programs** – Frequent flier programs have been one of the most successful marketing tools for airlines. By offering free flights and perks for loyalty, carriers have successfully obtained repeat business, particularly among business travelers.
- **Customer service** – Airlines emphasize service in the form of aircraft seat placement (more room), in-flight entertainment, food and beverages, airport amenities, baggage handling, and friendly customer service. While these are usually intangible variables, they do impact demand. Airlines perceived to have a high level of services usually have a greater demand for their flights. Successful examples include Virgin Atlantic, Emirates, and Singapore Airlines.
- **On-time performance** – The Bureau of Transportation Statistics (BTS) uses on-time performance to rank airlines every quarter. Moreover, this demand variable is often used as a proxy for customer service and is an important determinant in public perception of an airline's quality. Poor on-time performance indicates an unpredictable and inconvenient service as compared to an airline with fewer delays. Airline delays can have significant impacts on passengers, including missed connections, increased stress, and frustration, and lost productivity. Sometimes, a carrier may add extra time to a flight schedule to allow for potential delays or unforeseen circumstances. For example, if a flight from Singapore to Los Angeles is scheduled to take 70 hours, an airline might pad the flight by adding extra hours to the schedule to account for potential delays such as weather, air traffic congestion, or mechanical issues.

Characteristics of Demand for Air Transportation

The demand for air travel also has many unique characteristics that present problems for the industry. These characteristics are:

- Cyclicality
- Directional flow
- Fluctuations

- Perishability
- Seasonality and peaking

The first major characteristic of demand for air transportation is that, unlike the demand for many products, it is constantly fluctuating due to the numerous determinants mentioned earlier. Moreover, no two routes exhibit the same properties of demand.

Cyclicality refers to a long-term trend of peaks and troughs of economic activity. The national and global economies have long been known to experience cyclicality, and since the airline industry is highly correlated, it is not surprising that it also operates through similar cycles. Figure 3.9 depicts the number of passengers carried by US airlines since 1970. While the chart shows overall steady growth, there are four pronounced drops in US airline enplanements: in the early 1980s, early 1990s, post-9/11, and during the COVID-19 pandemic in 2020. The graph reveals a parallel with general economic cycles. It is noticeable that the dip in scheduled revenue passengers around the early 1980s and again in the early 1990s coincides with two recessions. Overall, the slope coefficient of the linear trendline suggests that US enplanements have, on average, increased by 983,939 passengers each quarter.

Another major characteristic of air transport demand is peaking, which is commonly called seasonality. Unlike cyclicality, which is a long-term cycle, peaking is more of a short-term spike in demand. This is illustrated by the quarterly peaks and troughs in Figure 3.9, which represents within-year variations in demand that are nearly independent of economic cycles. The most common form of peaking is seasonality, where demand increases during the summer months and then declines during the winter months. This trend is particularly apparent for leisure destinations where the weather is more favorable, and individuals have more time off. For example, Mediterranean resort destinations are in high demand during the summer months, but lower demand during the winter.

Peaking also affects most domestic routes in the United States. To provide a specific example, let's consider the Chicago to Seattle route. Figure 3.10 displays a 10% sample of the

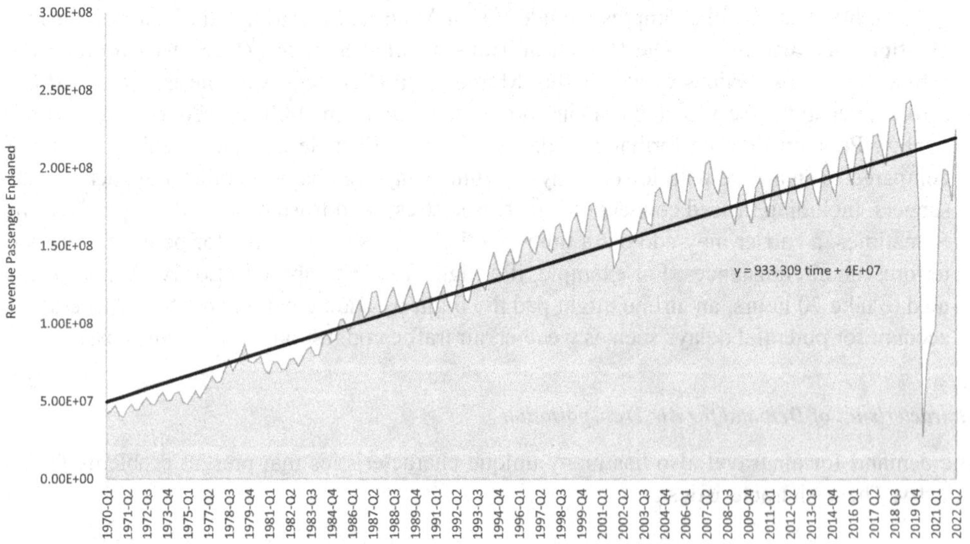

Figure 3.9 US Airline Industry Passenger Enplanements Since 1970.

Source: Compiled by the authors using Back Aviation Form 41 data and US Department of Transportation Statistics

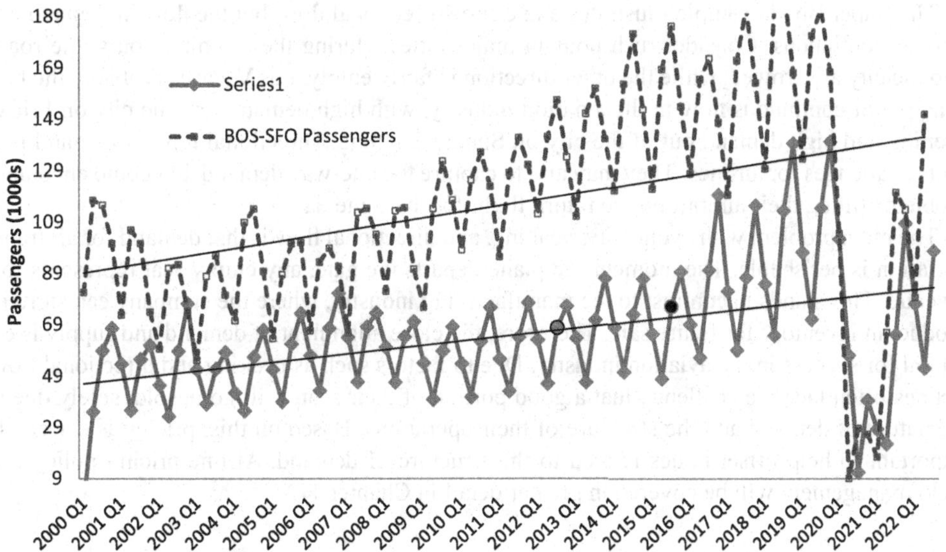

Figure 3.10 Seasonality of Passenger Enplanements, ORD to SEA and BOS to SFO.

Source: Compiled by the authors using Diio O&D data

route's passenger enplanements per quarter since 2001. Clearly, this route experiences tremendous demand during the third quarter of every year, while demand is notably low during the first quarter. This regular pattern can be partly attributed to Seattle's summer cruise ship industry and favorable summer weather. Aside from seasonality, other demand peaks are seen during major holidays like Thanksgiving and Christmas.

Since peaking is fairly predictable, airlines can add capacity by either increasing the frequency of the flights on an existing route or introducing seasonal-only service. However, for an airline to add seasonal capacity, it must either reallocate an aircraft from another route or have excess capacity available, which can be quite expensive. Ideally, the airlines would prefer introducing additional aircraft during the summer months and retire them during the winter. However, short-term leases for aircraft are rare. Therefore, seasonality can present a sizeable financial, operational, and scheduling burden for airlines. They need to meet the seasonal demand while also bearing the assets for the rest of the year. This is one reason why North American carriers have robust aircraft maintenance schedules during the winter months when their schedules are not busy. Some airlines, such as American Airlines and Air Canada, have successfully shifted capacity to Central and South America during the winter season in the northern hemisphere.

Another characteristic of airline demand similar to peaking is directional flow. Directional flow relates to the increased demand of passengers in one direction for a period of time. While cyclicality spans decades and peaking spans years, directional flow is usually assessed on a weekly basis and is fairly short term. An example could be the influx of customers to a city a few days before a major sporting event (i.e., the Super Bowl), followed by a surge in demand for departing flights immediately after the event. The key to note is that directional flow is essentially one way for a short period of time, creating a unique scheduling challenge for airlines. To accommodate the directional flow of passengers, some aircraft might be flown relatively empty in the opposite direction.

The Super Bowl example illustrates a one-time directional flow, but the flow in demand can also be continuous. Consider rush hour in major cities. During the morning hours, the roads into the city are crowed, while the other direction is fairly empty. Las Vegas is probably the best example of continuous flow in the aviation industry, with high demand into the city on Friday evening and high demand out of the city on Sunday evening. Directional flow of demand presents challenges for airlines. They may aim to capture the one-way demand, but could encounter problems filling their aircraft on the return flight for the same day.

The main problem with cyclicality, peaking, and directional flow is that demand for air transportation is perishable. The moment the plane departs the gate, any empty seat represents lost revenue. This stands in contrast to the manufacturing industry, where the company can store its product in inventory for future sale. Therefore, the close alignment of demand and supply is essential for success in the aviation industry. Due to factors such as peaking and directional flow, airlines often face the challenge that a good portion of their seats will go unsold, solely due to the nature of demand and the structure of their operations. Based on this, pricing is extremely important to help offset issues related to the structure of demand. Airline pricing policy and yield management will be covered in greater detail in Chapter 11.

Example

Consider the following demand equation:

$$P = 2{,}000 - 2Q^2$$

a Calculate quantity demanded at a price of \$200.

$$200 = 2{,}000 - 2Q^2$$
$$1{,}800 = 2Q^2$$
$$Q = 30 \text{ units}$$

b At what price demand would be zero.

$$P = 2{,}000 - 2(0)^2$$
$$P = \$2{,}000$$

Market Demand

The market demand is simply the sum of the individual demand. Let us assume an airport served by three airlines. In economics, a market demand curve is a graphical representation that illustrates the quantity of services demanded by all passengers at various price levels. In addition, if more passengers enter the market, then market demand at each price level will rise.

Let's explore the demand illustration for a particular route, say, DAB–JFK, flown by three major carriers: American Airlines (AA), JetBlue Airways (B6), and United Airlines (UA). Figures 3.11–3.13 show the individual demand for the three carriers along this route.

Now let's examine Figure 3.14. This graph combines the three individual linear demand functions to illustrate the market demand across different airlines for this particular route.

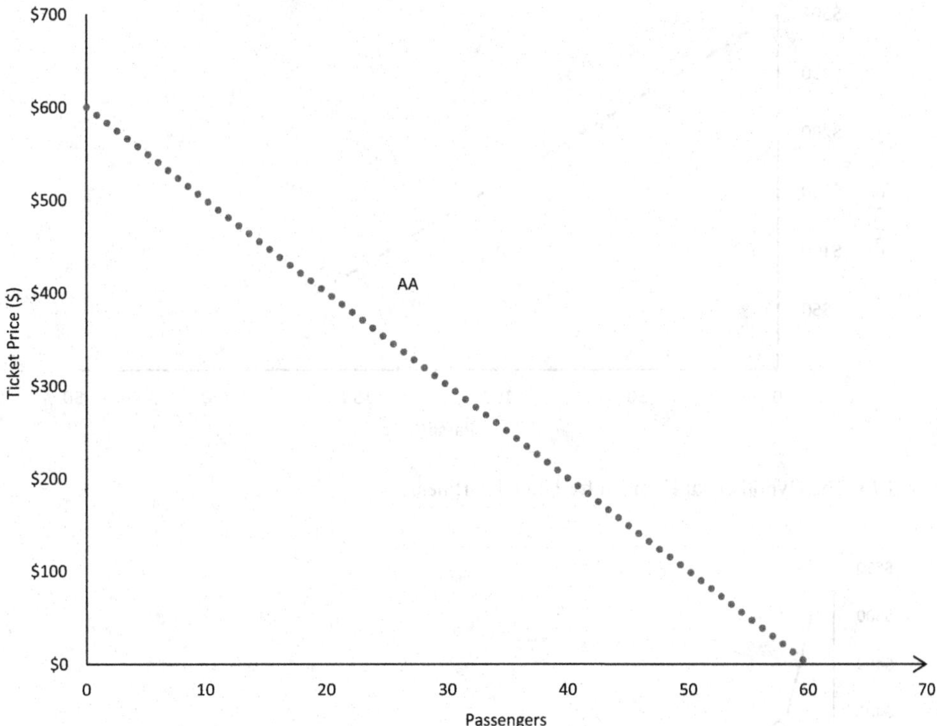

Figure 3.11 Demand for AA.

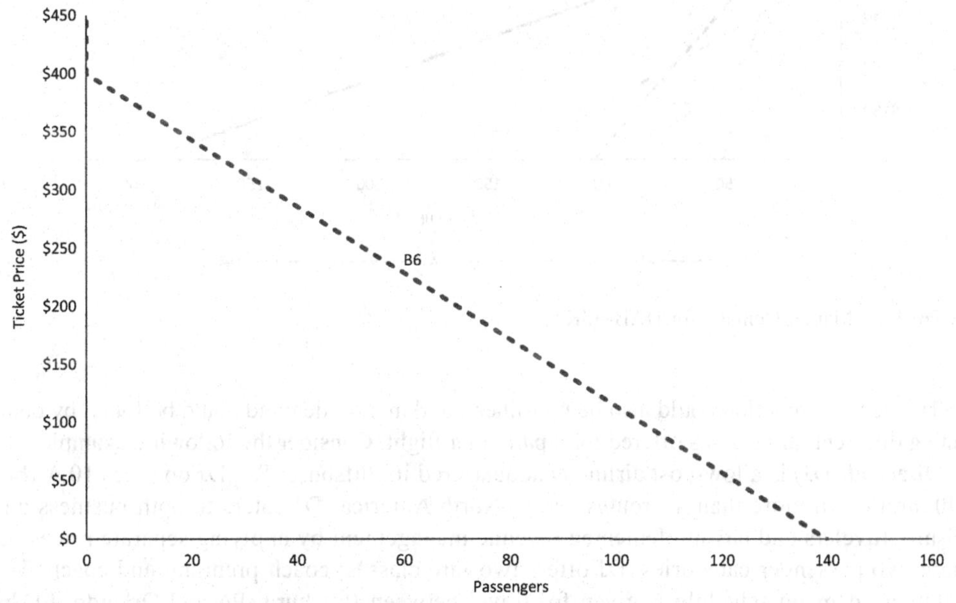

Figure 3.12 The Hypothetical Demand for JetBlue Airways.

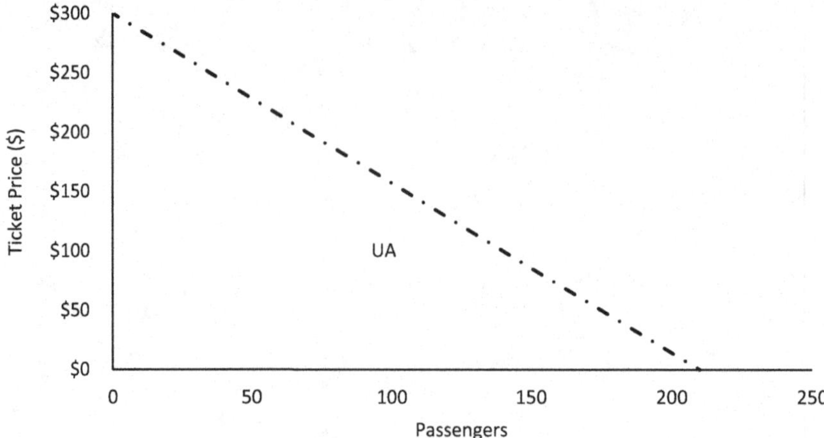

Figure 3.13 The Hypothetical Demand for United Airlines.

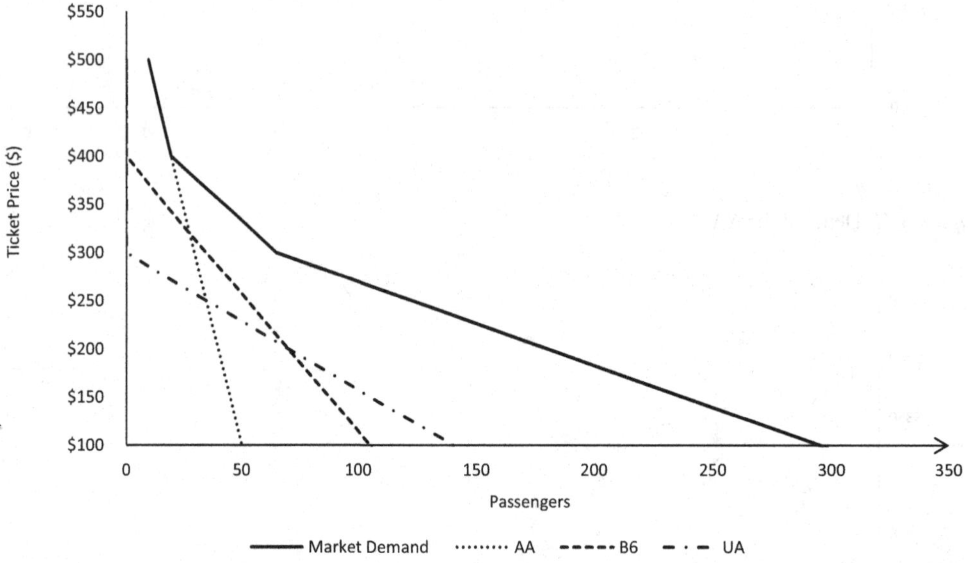

Figure 3.14 Market Demand for DAB–JFK.

The demand function could also be non-linear, and market demand could be found by combining different fare classes offered for a particular flight. Consider the following example.

DirectJet (DJ) is a low-cost airline headquartered in Pittsburg, PA. DJ operates 10 Airbus 340 aircraft on more than 45 routes across North America. DJ caters to both business and leisure travelers and has implemented revenue management by applying separate prices for these two passenger categories. DJ offers two fare classes, coach premium and coach. The following demand schedule is given for travel between Pittsburg, PA and Orlando, FL by DJ's passengers. This flight is served by an A-340 with capacity for 300 travelers. The fixed cost (FC) of operating the flight is $30,000. The total average variable cost per passenger (AVC) is $40.

Price	*Demand*		
	Coach	*Coach Premium*	*Total*
$200	422	157	579
$250	229	104	333
$300	139	75	214
$350	91	56	147
$400	63	44	107
$450	46	35	81
$500	34	29	63
$550	26	24	50
$600	21	21	42
$650	17	18	35
$700	14	16	30
$750	11	14	25
$800	9	12	21

For this airline, estimate a constant elasticity demand function, $D = aP^b$, where demand (D) is a function of price (P), for both fare classes and the total demand. This estimation involves plotting the data on a graph and using the power trendline feature for the three sets of demand. Once plotted, the three curves are depicted as follows:

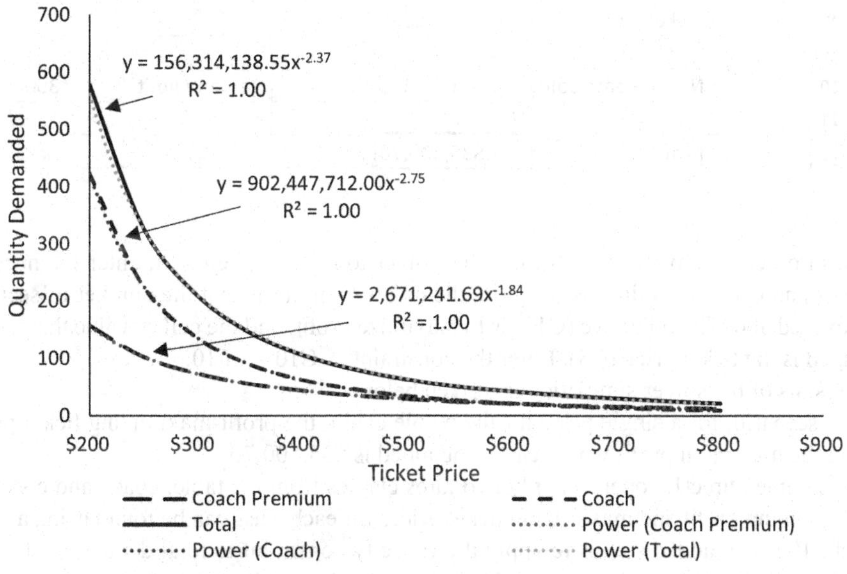

From the trendline equations, the respective demand functions for the two fare classes and the total demand are as shown below:

For Coach, $D = 902{,}447{,}712\ (P)^{-2.75}$

For Coach Premium, $D = 2{,}671{,}241.69\ (P)^{-1.84}$

For Total, $D = 156{,}314{,}138.55\ (P)^{-2.37}$

Note that in this example, the inverse demand function is depicted. To obtain the most viable ticket price, the demand must be found as a function of price, as opposed to the conventional demand curve where price is a function of demand. Now, considering only total demand and a single price for the entire aircraft, the profit-maximizing price for this aircraft can be found, using Excel. In order to do this, the Excel "SOLVER" tool is used. First, set up the demand formula using price (previously obtained), and then establish the profit formula using fixed cost, ticket price, and average variable cost:

Profit = (ticket price – variable cost) × no. of seats sold – fixed cost

The setup for total demand is as shown here. The formula bar in the figure denotes the profit formula given above.

C12 | fx =(C8-C6)*C10-C5

	A	B	C	D	E	F
1		Total Demand				
2		a	156,314,138.55			
3		b	-2.37			
4						
5		Fixed cost	$30,000			
6		VC	$40			
7						
8		Ticket price (P)	$258			
9						
10		No. of seats sold	300		Demand limit	300
11						
12		Profit	$35,500.70			

Now, in order to maximize profit, use the Solver tool shown below to enter the necessary conditions and constraints. In this scenario, the only constraint is that the number of seats sold cannot exceed 300. The objective (C12) is to maximize profit, and the cell or value that needs to be changed is the ticket price (C8). Enter the constraint as C10 <= F10.

The results of the solver simulation are given below.

In this scenario, for a single price for the whole cabin, the profit-maximizing ticket price is $258 and the maximum profit which can be obtained is $35,500.70.

Now, assume DirectJet operates only two fares classes from the table: coach and coach premium. Maximum profit and maximizing ticket prices for each class can be found using a similar approach. The only added step is to apply the capacity constraint to total demand, obtained as sum of the individual number of seats sold in each fare class.

After running Solver, the profit-maximizing ticket price is $342 for coach premium and $245 for coach. Finally, the maximum profit is $37,212.36.

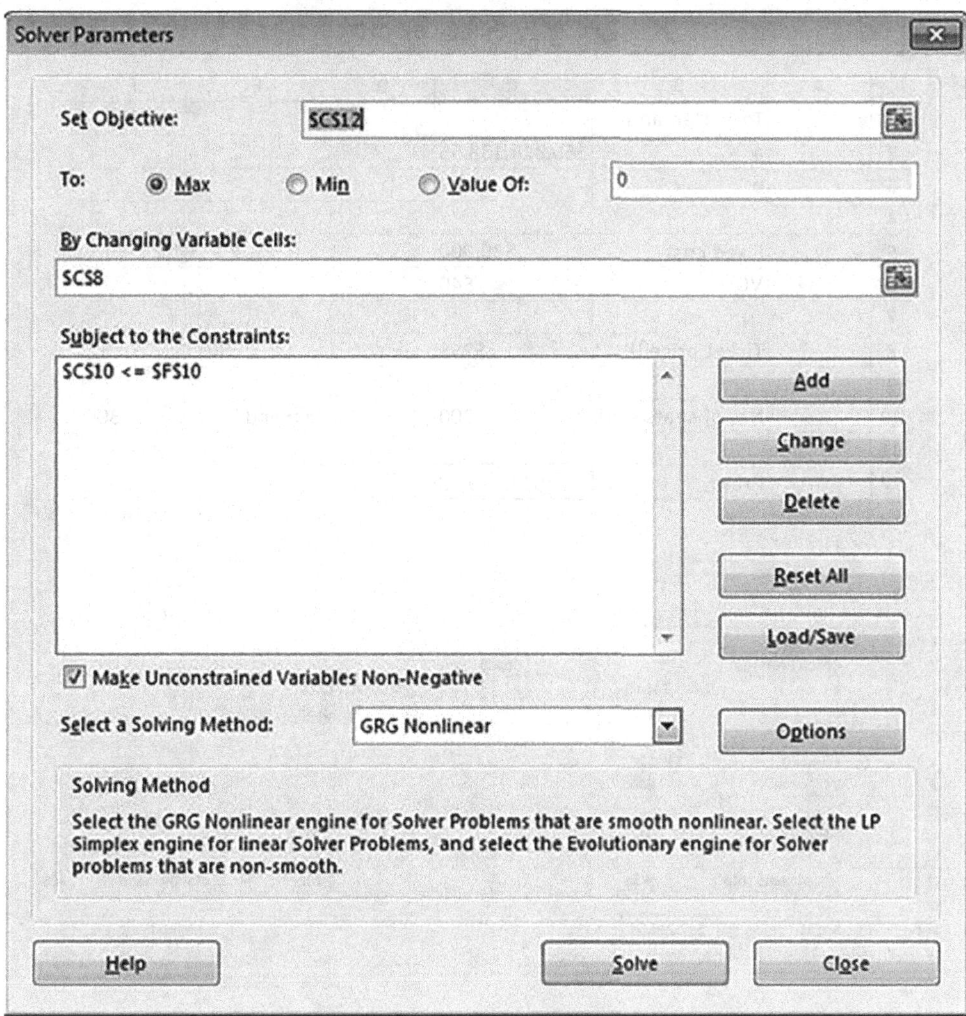

The quantification of demand varies from industry to industry. For airlines, demand and supply are usually expressed in terms of:

- The number of passengers (PAX)
- Available seat miles (ASM)
- Revenue passenger miles (RPMs), which normalizes passenger demand according to the number of miles traveled. For example, if an airline carries 250 paying passengers on a flight that covers 1,000 miles, the airline's revenue passenger miles for that flight would be 250,000 (250 passengers × 1,000 miles).

C12 =(C8-C6)*C10-C5

	A	B	C	D	E	F
1		Total Demand				
2		a	156,314,138.55			
3		b	-2.37			
4						
5		Fixed cost	$30,000			
6		VC	$40			
7						
8		Ticket price (P)	$258			
9						
10		No. of seats sold	300		Demand limit	300
11						
12		Profit	$35,500.70			

C13 =(C9-C7)*C11+(F9-C7)*F11-C6

	A	B	C	D	E	F	G	H	I
1									
2		Coach Premium			Coach				
3		a	2,671,241.69		a	902,447,712.00			
4		b	-1.84		b	-2.75			
5									
6		Fixed cost	$30,000						
7		VC	$40						
8									
9		Ticket price	$342			$245			
10									
11		No. of seats sold	58			242		Total Demand	300
12									
13		Profit	$37,212.36					Demand limit	300
14									

RPM = number of passengers × miles flown

For example, if 250 passengers flew 1,000 miles, it would generate

$RPM = 250 \times 1{,}000 = 250{,}000$ miles

- Revenue passenger kilometers (RPKs), which normalizes passenger demand according to the number of kilometers traveled:

  RPK = number of passengers × number of kilometers flown

- Revenue ton miles (RTMs)

  RTM = tons of cargo × miles flown

- Revenue ton kilometers (RTKs)

  RTK = weight of paid tonnage × total number of kilometers to be transported

Revenue passenger miles (RPMs) are measures of traffic for an airline, obtained by multiplying the number of revenue-paying passengers aboard the aircraft by the distance traveled.

Available seat miles (ASMs) refer to how many seat miles are actually available for purchase on an airline. Hence, ASM captures the total flight passenger capacity of an airline in miles.

The rationale behind normalizing by miles is that raw passenger numbers are only partially informative. A passenger traveling on a 100-mile route from New York, NY to New Haven, CT is not worth the same to an airline as the passenger who travels close to 9,500 miles from New York to Singapore. Therefore, expressing demand in RPMs gives a sense of airline traffic in terms of distance, and is the preferred metric for airline demand analysis. For aircraft manufacturers, demand would be represented as the number of aircraft sold. While demand varies from industry to industry, its characteristics remain similar, and its importance to business is always high. Therefore, it is critical to fully understand the nature of demand.

However, when the other determinants are held constant, the relationship between price and quantity demanded is always negative. If, however, some of the other characteristics are varied, the quantity demanded can change accordingly. For instance, if a drop in the price of airline tickets occurs in conjunction with a global influenza pandemic, the quantity of airline tickets might decrease, even though prices of tickets dropped simultaneously.

Basics of Supply

One of the key reasons why the airline industry has faced financial difficulties and has profit margins well below those of many other industries is that its demand fluctuates constantly, while its supply is relatively fixed. Lack of flexibility in the supply function makes it very difficult to manage capacity effectively. Sometimes passengers may book a flight but fail to show up for their scheduled departure, leaving an empty seat on the plane. Once an aircraft departs, any empty seat becomes worthless, and the revenue that could have been generated from those seats is lost forever. This makes airline seats a perishable asset. The perishability of air transport services, the high fixed costs, and the predetermined capacity in the form of schedules that are published well in advance of the flight, make supply relatively unresponsive since an airline cannot shift its supply on short notice. Given the perishable nature of airline seats, revenue management is a critical function for airlines. Therefore, it is important to have a detailed understanding of the factors that impact airline industry supply. This section introduces these factors, while the following chapter discusses airline production in greater detail.

Factors Affecting Supply of Airline Services

Supply is an economic term that refers to the quantity of a given good or service that suppliers are willing and able to produce at a given price level during a given period. In the airline industry, supply refers to an airline's willingness and ability to provide a specific number of seats at a given price, time period, and market. In the airline industry, supply represents the capacity of an airline to transport passengers, which is a function of offered routes and available aircraft. Supply is usually expressed in available seat miles (ASMs) or available ton miles (ATMs). An ASM is simply one seat carried through the air for one mile, regardless of whether or not it contains a passenger. The presence of a revenue passenger in the seat is the key difference between RPMs (demand) and ASMs (supply), as RPMs only measure seats that have a revenue passenger in them. For example, if an airline has a fleet of 25 aircraft, each with 200 seats, and each plane flies an average of 1,000 miles per day, the airline's daily available seat miles would be:

The law of supply states that at higher prices, producers are willing and able to produce more products. The quantity supplied increases as prices increase and decreases as prices decrease, assuming everything else remains constant. For example, the higher ticket prices give airlines an incentive to provide more flights, assuming their costs are not increasing significantly.

C13 | fx =(C9-C7)*C11+(F9-C7)*F11-C6

	A	B	C	D	E	F	G	H	I
1									
2		Coach Premium			Coach				
3		a	2,671,241.69		a	902,447,712.00			
4		b	-1.84		b	-2.75			
5									
6		Fixed cost	$30,000						
7		VC	$40						
8									
9		Ticket price	$342			$245			
10									
11		No. of seats sold	58			242		Total Demand	300
12									
13		Profit	$37,212.36					Demand limit	300
14									

$$ASM = 25 \times 200 \times 1{,}000 = 5{,}000{,}000$$

Dividing RPMs by ASM gives us a key performance indicator for airlines, the *load factor*. This is defined as the percentage of capacity that has been matched with demand. Similarly, for cargo or freight transportation, the equivalent unit to RPMs is RTM, which may be matched up with ATMs to yield a cargo load factor. For example, if an airline operates a flight with 200 available seats and each passenger on the flight travels a distance of 1,000 miles, the flight's

$$\text{ASM would be } 200 \times 1{,}000 = 200{,}000$$

If the airline generates 150,000 revenue passenger miles on the same flight, the flight's load factor would be:

$$\text{Load factor} = \frac{150{,}000}{200{,}000} = 75\%$$

This means that the airline has filled 75% of its available seats on the flight with paying passengers. Load factors are critical to airline performance, as they determine aircraft utilization, drive the profitability of a given route, and indicate the effective utilization of capacity. In addition to price, factors that affect supply are:

- Price of resource inputs
  - Aircraft costs
  - Fuel prices
  - Labor costs
  - Landing fees
  - Maintenance costs
- Navigation charges
- Technology
- Availability of other modes of transportation
- Government regulation
- Stochastic factors
  - Weather conditions
  - Strikes

The implicit supply function for the airline industry can be written as:

$$Q_s = f(P, P_{RES}, Tech, Comp, Rand, GOV)$$

where:

P is the ticket price
P_{RES} is the price of resources
Tech represents technological improvements
Comp is the behavior of the competition
Rand represents random factors
GOV is the government policy and regulation

The major determinant of supply, similar to demand, is the ticket price of the good or service. This relates to the law of supply, as the quantity of a good supplied in a given time period increases as its price increases, assuming all else is held constant. In the airline industry, this simply means that airlines are willing to supply more seats as ticket prices increase. Based on the law of supply, the supply curve slopes upward, causing any change in price to result in a movement along the curve. This is referred as an increase in the quantity supplied. Table 3.4 provides a hypothetical supply schedule for JFK–LAX.

The next major determinant of supply is the price of resources. For the air transportation industry, production resources encompass, but are not limited to, aircraft, fuel, maintenance, labor, and landing fees. These factors impact supply because they affect the cost of production. If the cost of production increases, then the airline's total costs increase, causing a leftward shift in the supply curve. An increase in the costs of production might force an airline to cut flights that are no longer profitable. This reduction is represented by a leftward shift in the supply curve (fewer seats are offered at the same ticket price). Conversely, if the price of resources decreases, then the supply curve shifts to the right. (More seats are offered at the same ticket price.)

The impact that the price of resources has on supply is significant. For example, during bankruptcy protection, Delta Air Lines was able to significantly reduce its costs by receiving wage

Table 3.4 Supply Schedule for New York to Los Angeles

Ticket Price	*Quantity Supplied*
JFK–LAX	*Number of Passengers*
$200	35
$500	88
$1,000	175
$1,500	263
$2,000	350
$2,500	438
$3,000	525
$3,500	613
$4,000	700
$4,500	788
$5,000	875

concessions and reducing aircraft leasing rates. As a result, Delta dropped many domestic destinations and redeployed resources to new international markets. Similarly, with skyrocketing fuel costs, other airlines eliminated a number of flights that were previously viable, as current revenues could not justify maintaining the routes.

Figure 3.15 exhibits a linear supply curve. As ticket price goes up, so does the number of seats offered. At a price of $3,000 per ticket, an airline would be willing and able to supply 525 seats. The degree of responsiveness of quantity supplied to a change in price is called the price elasticity of supply.

The next major factor determining supply for air transportation is technology. The impact of technology on the supply of air transportation has been vast. Technological advancement has propelled civil aviation to become one of the safest modes of transportation. For example, the introduction of the Boeing 747 in 1970 created a rightward shift in the supply curve as the jumbo jet was able to carry more passengers on a flight than any other aircraft (Boeing, 2007). Similarly, the 787 Dreamliner consumes 20%–25% less fuel, is 30% cheaper to maintain, and costs 15% less to operate (Boeing, 2017). Likewise, Airbus has caused a similar shift in the supply curve. Perhaps one of the best examples of technology's impact on air transportation supply is the introduction of ultra-long-range aircraft—the Boeing 777-200LR and the Airbus A340-500. Prior to these products, routes like Singapore to Los Angeles and New York to Dubai could not be operated. Finally, Extended Twin-Engine Operations (ETOPS) also increased supply over the Atlantic and Pacific Oceans through the use of smaller twin-engine aircraft.

Competitive factors are another important determinant of supply in air transportation. Historically, airlines have aggressively competed for market share, and they regularly adjust supply in response to competition and changing market forces. However, there have been cases where airlines have taken this competition to an extreme. For example, in 1999, American Airlines faced anti-trust lawsuits over its competitive actions against smaller rivals, particularly Vanguard Airlines out of Love Field. The lawsuit alleged that American Airlines had "dumped" capacity on routes where Vanguard Airlines was competing (Flight Global, 2003). Eventually, American was cleared of the charge. Similarly, in 2000, El Salvador-based Group TACA accused Continental Airlines of capacity dumping following a liberalization of the US–El Salvador bilateral air agreement (Knibb, 2000). These examples highlight how the supply curve

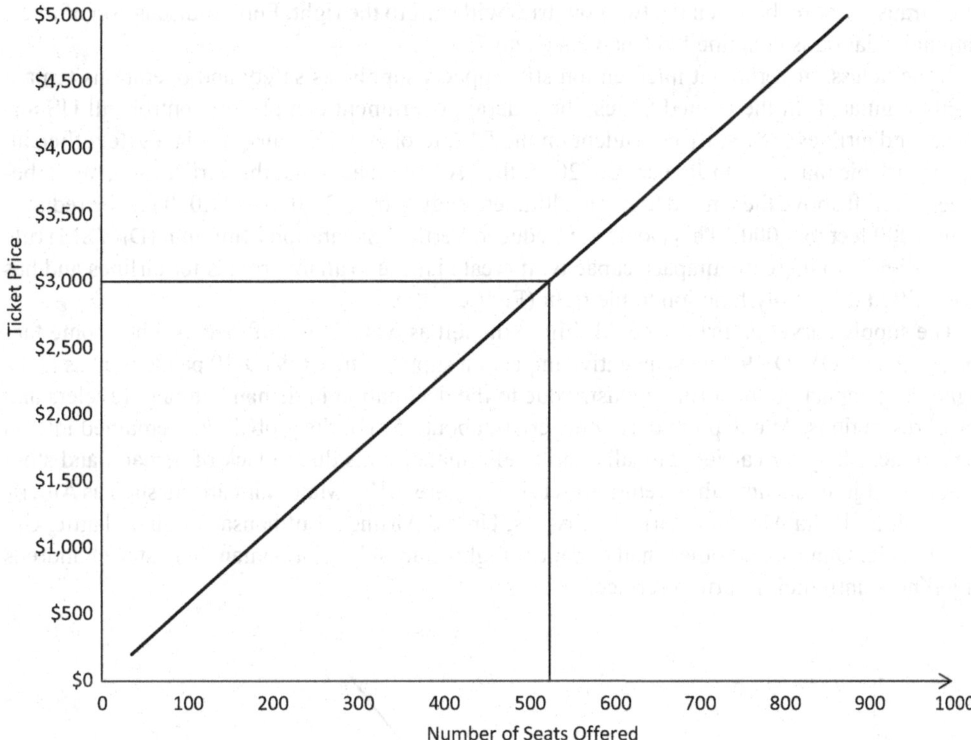

Figure 3.15 Supply Curve of JFK–LAX.

will shift left or right depending on the actions taken by other airlines. Since the 2009 financial downturn in US aviation, airlines have begun to compete less on market share and focus more on profits. Just as in demand, random factors play a large role in supply. The COVID-19 pandemic created a dramatic shift in the demand curve and the supply curve to the left. The pandemic caused a significant leftward shift in the supply curve for airlines, meaning that the quantity of air travel supplied decreased at every given price level. Singapore Airlines was forced to ground a significant portion of its fleet during the pandemic. At the peak of the crisis, more than 90% of SIA's fleet was grounded, with only a few aircraft flying to maintain connections to key destination.

Additionally, for the two carriers involved in the incident, the loss of aircraft reduced their fleet size and ability to transport passengers.[6] Likewise, referring to our previous example, the airspace over Central and Eastern Europe was closed for several days in 2010 following a volcanic eruption in Iceland.

Other factors that have impacted the supply curve are deregulation and liberalization. In general, regulation inhibited market forces, thereby imposing an artificial cap on supply and limiting new entrants. Therefore, when air transport deregulation occurred, this cap was withdrawn and supply subsequently increased. The US–EU Open Skies agreement, which came into effect in 2008, eliminated air service restrictions between the United States and Europe, and allowed airlines to fly for the first time between any EU city and any US city. A more current example is the US–China air transportation agreement. Whenever additional rights are granted, the supply of air transportation between the two countries will shift to the right. Further discussion of international aviation is contained in Chapters 6 and 7.

Nonetheless, government intervention still impacts supply, as safety and operations remain highly regulated. In the United States, the federal government completely controls all US airspace, and airlines are totally dependent on the FAA to operate that airspace in a safe, efficient, and affordable manner. On January 20, 2005, the FAA mandated that the vertical separation between aircraft above the United States at altitudes ranging from 29,000 to 41,000 feet be reduced from 2,000 feet to 1,000.[7] This Domestic Reduced Vertical Separation Minimum (DRVSM) rule was designed to increase airspace capacity. It created more available routes for airlines and has thus shifted the supply function to the right (Figure 3.16).

The supply curve for airlines could shift to the left as well. This shift occurs when some factors, such as COVID-19, have a negative impact on supply. The COVID-19 pandemic has had a significant impact on the airline industry due to the decimation in demand among travelers and travel restrictions. At one point during the crisis, about 75% of the global fleet remained idle on the tarmac. Many air carriers globally had to eliminate flights due to lack of demand and store hundreds of jetliners until their return to service (Figure 3.17). Major air carriers such as American Airlines, Delta Air Lines, British Airways, United Airlines, Lufthansa, Virgin Atlantic, Cathay Pacific, Qantas, and others had to cancel flights due to lack of demand and store hundreds of jetliners until their return to service.

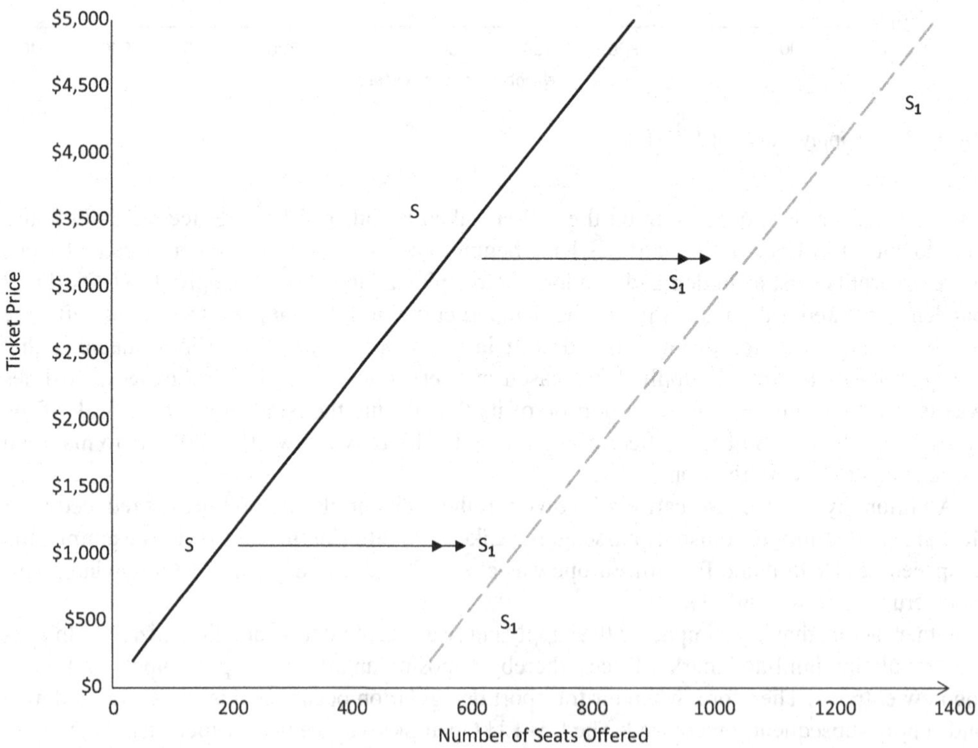

Figure 3.16 Impact of Deregulation on Supply.

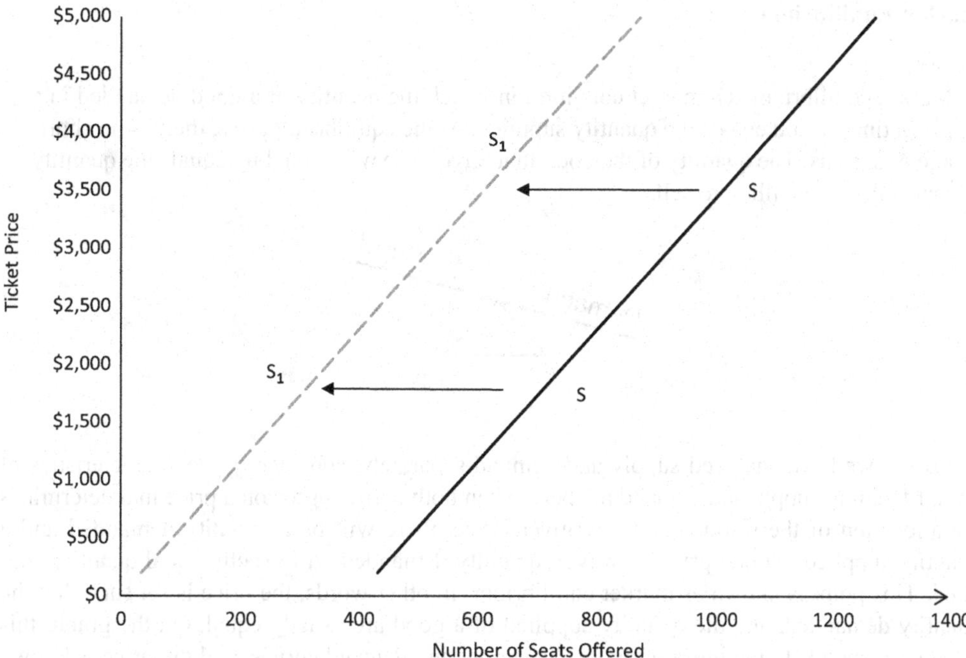

Figure 3.17 Impact of Fuel Shortage on Supply.

Characteristics of Supply for Airline Services

Two major characteristics of supply that significantly influence the air transportation industry are seasonality and rigidity. Both make it challenging for airlines in aligning supply with demand.

The demand for air transportation experiences constant fluctuations, leading airlines to make adjustments in supply to align the passenger demand. To accommodate seasonality, airlines must either pull capacity off existing routes, or have idle capacity available for additional flights. Both options have embedded costs, and airlines typically employ a mix of the two strategies. While the increased costs of a seasonal schedule can be balanced out by increased revenues, carriers have a hard time adjusting supply on a short-term basis due to the second major characteristic of airline supply, rigidity.

An airline's supply tends to be fairly rigid, making it difficult for airlines to reduce and/or increase supply dramatically. This is because an airline creates a schedule of at least six months in advance and accepts bookings up to a year ahead. The carrier must adhere to the schedule or face re-accommodation fees. Fixed costs, such as investment in infrastructure at hub airports, aircraft leases, and labor contracts have to be paid regardless of the schedule. Thus, it is impractical for airlines to reduce capacity on short-term notice. This is a problem particularly for those major US and European carriers that operate in a hub-and-spoke network. It is one reason why non-hub carriers like Southwest Airlines have greater flexibility with supply. Ultimately, this rigidity limits the airlines' ability to match supply and demand effectively.

Market Equilibrium

Market equilibrium is a market condition in which the quantity of a good demanded in a given time period equals the quantity supplied. At the equilibrium price, there is no shortage or surplus. The quantity of the good that buyers are willing to buy equals the quantity that sellers are willing to sell.

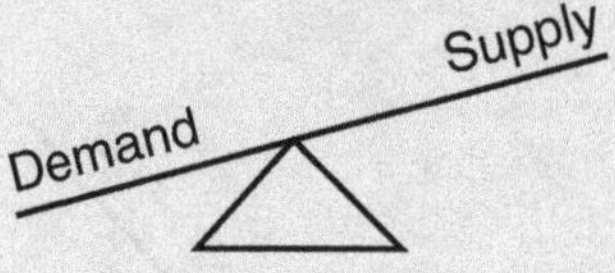

So far, we have analyzed supply and demand separately, considering the characteristics of both. Matching supply and demand happens when both parties agree on a price that determines the allocation of the resource. At any given price, there will be a quantity demanded and a quantity supplied. At one price, however, quantity demanded will exactly equal quantity supplied. This point is known as market equilibrium. In other words, the price is set such that the quantity demanded, and the quantity supplied of a good are exactly equal. On the graph, this point corresponds to the intersection of the supply and demand curves, and the price is known as the market clearing price.

Figure 3.18 illustrates a supply curve and a demand curve on the same set of axes, with price on the y-axis and quantity demanded on the x-axis. We find equilibrium price at *P**, where supply and demand curves intersect. At *P**, buyers want to purchase exactly the same amount that

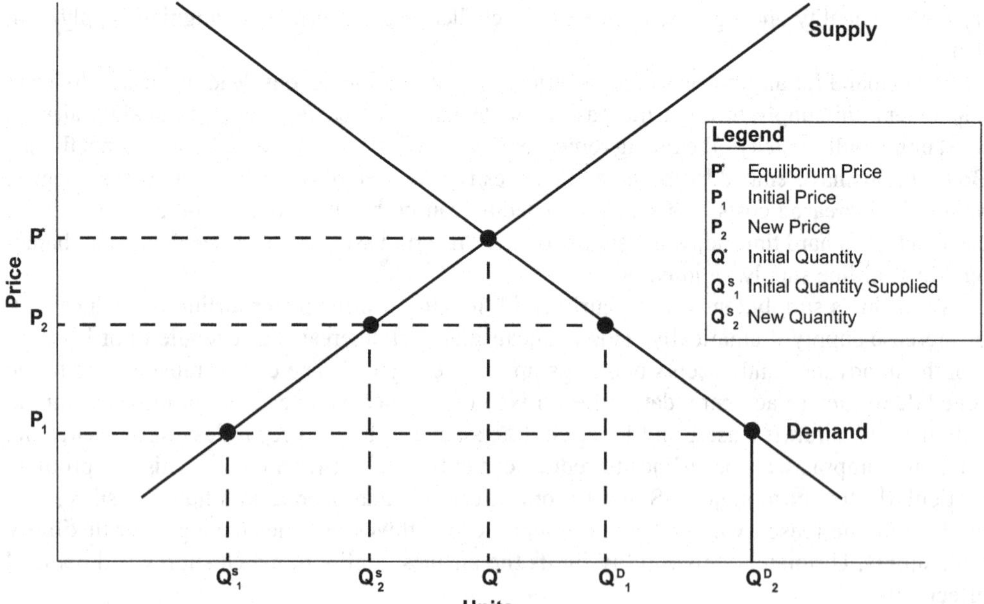

Figure 3.18 Price Movements: Average Fare Is Below Equilibrium.

sellers want to sell. Although we tend to think of businesses as being in control of prices, it is fair to say that consumers also play a role in determining prices. Airlines always want to set higher ticket prices, while passengers always want them at lower prices; P^* is a compromise that forces both sides to take into account the other's needs. Producers must receive a high enough price to cover costs and motivate production, and consumers must pay a price within their budget.

P^* is achieved through a process of trial and error. The firm estimates demand, plans a level of output, and charges a price based on that estimate. Suppose an airline underestimates demand and therefore charges too low a ticket price, P_1, and offers too little output, Q_1^s, as in Figure 3.18. At this low price, the amount demanded by passengers, Q_1^d, is much greater than the output supplied. Airlines, or any other business in this situation, will notice that tickets are sold at unusually high rates; that is, the aircraft will begin to fill up its seats much faster than normal. In fact, if airlines don't respond, there will be a shortage; they will soon sell out seats and start turning away customers. Indeed, airlines do typically respond fairly quickly. They will raise the price and, since the higher price can cover the higher associated per unit costs, they also increase output. Suppose the output is raised to Q_2^s and the average fare to P_2 is increased so that quantity demanded falls to Q_2^d. This is a step in the right direction but there is still excess quantity demanded; the price is still too low, and seats will continue to fill too fast. So, price and output will be raised again and will not settle into equilibrium until P* is reached, at which point Q^s and Q^d are equal, at least approximately, at Q^*. Once the average fare reaches P^*, seat inventories return to a normal pattern and quantity supplied aligns with quantity demanded, achieving balance.

Airlines differ from most businesses due to the fact that their inventories are perishable; empty seats become worthless once the plane takes off. This complication will be addressed in detail in the revenue management section of Chapter 11. For now, let us simply acknowledge that selling air travel is more complex than selling, for instance, smart phones. The producer of a smart phone can maintain inventories for some time, and whatever is unsold today can be sold in the future. Thus, it is possible to more closely match Q^s to Q^d. Since airlines inventories are perishable, it generally isn't feasible to have 100% load factors, or to fill every seat on every flight. So, for airlines, Q^s and Q^d are only approximately equal.

There is a dynamic process for reaching P^*, equilibrium price, if airlines initially overestimate demand. In this case, the average fare is set too high, resulting in very few bookings. If this pattern persists, a surplus of available seats will emerge and aircraft will depart with many more empty seats than normal. Of course, carriers aim to avoid this situation and will therefore bring the price down and reduce capacity until equilibrium is reached at P^*.

Once equilibrium is achieved, then price and quantity will remain at P^* and Q^* as long as both supply and demand remain constant. In practice, supply and demand for air travel tend to shift often, and therefore, almost constant changes in price and quantities are observed.

This concept can also be viewed mathematically. Suppose that the demand and supply functions for DirectJet's flights from New York to Seattle are the following:

$$Q^D = 500 - 5P_X + 2P_Z + 0.01Y$$
$$Q^s = 800 + 3P_X - 2P_{RES}$$

where:

Q^D is the quantity demanded,

P_X is the price of DirectJet's tickets,

P_Z is the price of a competitor airline's tickets,
Y is the consumer income,
P_{RES} is the price of resources, and
Q^s is the quantity supplied.

Assuming that the competitor's ticket price is $300, the annual average income is $50,000, and the cost of resources for the flight is $100, both the demand and supply functions can be rewritten solely in terms of the ticket price:

$$Q^D = 500 - 5P_X + 2(300) + 0.01(50{,}000)$$
$$Q^D = 500 - 5P_X + 600 + 500$$
$$Q^D = 1{,}600 - 5P_X$$
$$Q^S = 800 + 3P_X - 2(100)$$
$$Q^S = 800 + 3P_X - 200$$
$$Q^S = 600 + 3P_X$$

In order to find the market equilibrium price for the flight, the demand and supply functions need to be set equal to each other.

$$Q^D = Q^S$$
$$1{,}600 - 5P_X = 600 + 3P_X$$
$$1{,}000 = 8P_X$$
$$P_X = \$125$$

Based on this calculation, the market equilibrium price for DirectJet's flight between New York and Seattle is $125. At this price point, the quantity demanded equals the quantity supplied. Since the supply and demand curves are equal at the equilibrium price, either the demand or supply function can be used to determine the market equilibrium quantity.

$$Q^D = 1{,}600 - 5P_X \qquad\qquad Q^S = 600 + 3P_X$$
$$Q^D = 1{,}600 - 5(125) \qquad \text{or} \qquad Q^S = 600 + 3(125)$$
$$Q^D = 1{,}600 - 625 \qquad\qquad Q^S = 600 + 375$$
$$Q^D = 975 \qquad\qquad Q^S = 975$$

Now, let us examine Figure 3.19; 975 consumers demand DirectJet's flight between New York and Seattle at a uniform price of $125, while DirectJet supplies 975 seats. At this point, supply and demand are perfectly matched. However, if the price of the flight were to decrease, the quantity demanded would exceed the quantity supplied. This excess demand is depicted by brace "A-B" in Figure 3.19 and is sometimes called spillage. If the price of the flight were to increase from the equilibrium level, the quantity supplied would exceed the quantity demanded. This situation would be represented in the form of empty seats on the aircraft. Since demand is

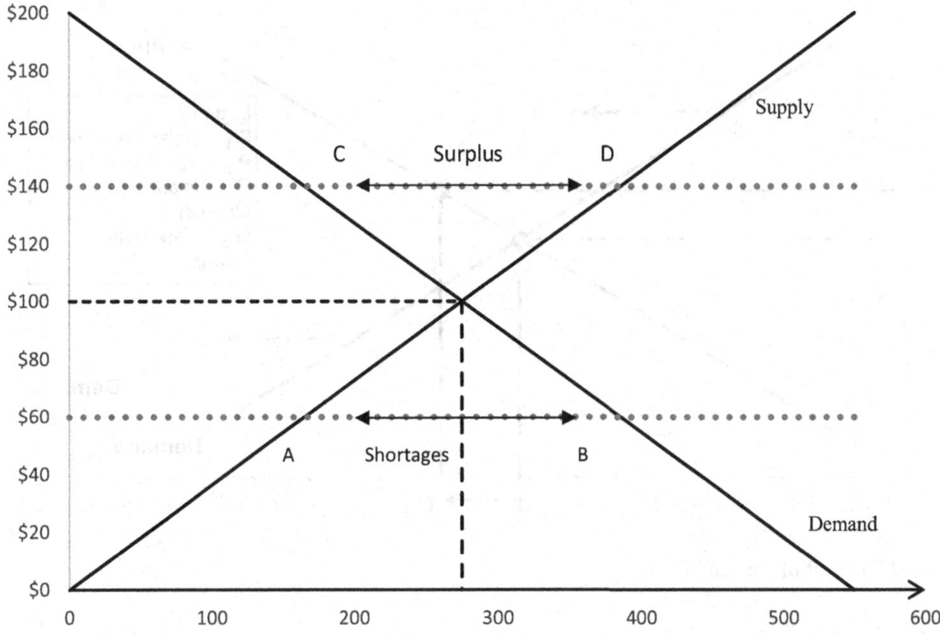

Figure 3.19 Spoilage and Spillage for DirectJet's Flights from New York to Seattle.

perishable, the case of supply exceeding demand is sometimes called spoilage and is depicted by brace "C-D" in Figure 3.19.[8]

The market is an allocating mechanism, as at the equilibrium price of $125, exactly 975 consumers whose willingness to pay is at or above $125 secure airline seats. If a consumer's willingness to pay is below $125, they will decide to opt out of the market and refrain from buying a seat.

Changes in Equilibrium

Analyzing changes in equilibrium is a straightforward process as long as one proceeds by first identifying which curve is shifting and in which direction. For instance, let's consider a scenario where the air travel market is initially in equilibrium and then undergoes changes due to a new event leading passengers to more fully realize how safe commercial flying is compared to other modes of travel. Though the airlines are very pleased with this development, production costs don't change. Therefore, we know that the supply curve doesn't move. It stands to reason that a more realistic assessment of airline safety will result in a greater general willingness to fly—given an acceptable price—than before. This causes an *increase in demand*, as depicted in the curve in Figure 3.20. Interpreting the graph involves examining where the new demand curve, $demand_{new}$, intersects with the supply to observe an increase in both equilibrium price and equilibrium quantity. Supply doesn't change since the supply curve is not shifting, but quantity supplied increases as we move along the existing supply curve.

Next, suppose we are in equilibrium when wages for airline employees increase. This will not shift the demand curve because consumers generally do not *directly* care about the details of airline employee compensation. Since higher wage costs do increase production costs, we will shift the supply curve to the left as presented in Figure 3.21. We observe from the intersection

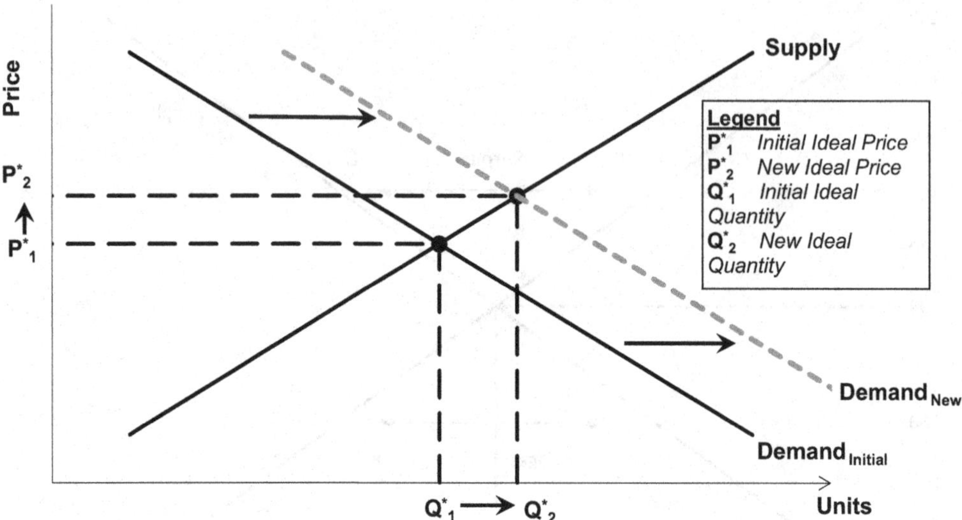

Figure 3.20 Shift of Demand Curve.

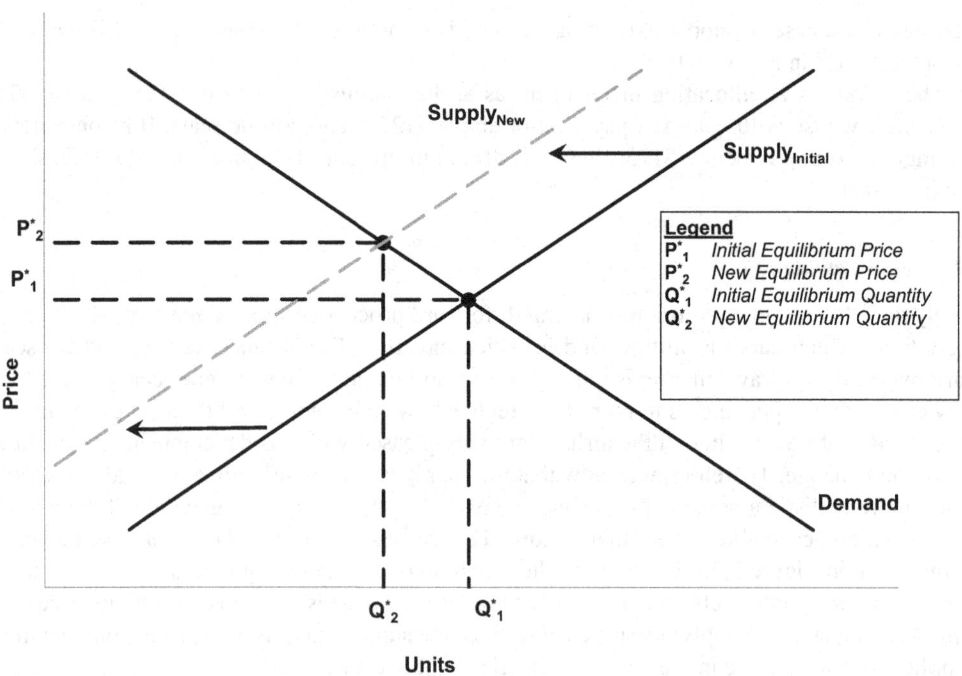

Figure 3.21 Shift of Supply Curve.

of demand and the new supply that equilibrium price rises from P_1^* to P_2^*. Since consumers do of course care about the price of air travel (thus *indirectly* care about how expensive pilots are), *quantity demanded* falls, with equilibrium quantity decreasing from Q_1^* to Q_2^*.

The basic effects of any given shift in supply or demand can be deduced by following these same procedures. As another example, consider the market for oil. The initial supply and demand curves would be at position Supply $_{\text{Initial}}$. If the suppliers decide to collaborate and supply less oil for every price, this causes a backward shift in the supply curve, to Supply$_{\text{New}}$.

Equilibrium Price Maximizes Consumer Well-Being

The equilibrium price generally represents the optimal possible price for consumers given the reality of production costs. While consumers might wish for free air travel, most realize that mandating airlines to provide their service for free would simply result in airlines shutting down. Price must be set high enough to motivate sellers to provide their product at appropriate quality. Sometimes price may seem higher than necessary to motivate needed production, but things are not always as they appear. It is best for consumers to let price move wherever supply and demand may send it.

It is useful to initially illustrate this point outside the realm of the air travel market. Then we can apply a similar reasoning to a more complex aviation scenario. Let us first analyze the widely misunderstood case of pricing crucial consumer goods in the aftermath of a natural disaster. Suppose a severe hurricane knocks out electrical power in an area with drastic consequences for, say, the ice market. Much of the ice supply would have melted, while simultaneously, the demand for ice surges way above normal level. The drastic reduction in supply combined with huge demand will raise equilibrium price far above the norm, as depicted in Figure 3.22. The graph displays an equilibrium price of $20 for a bag of ice that would normally sell for less than $2.

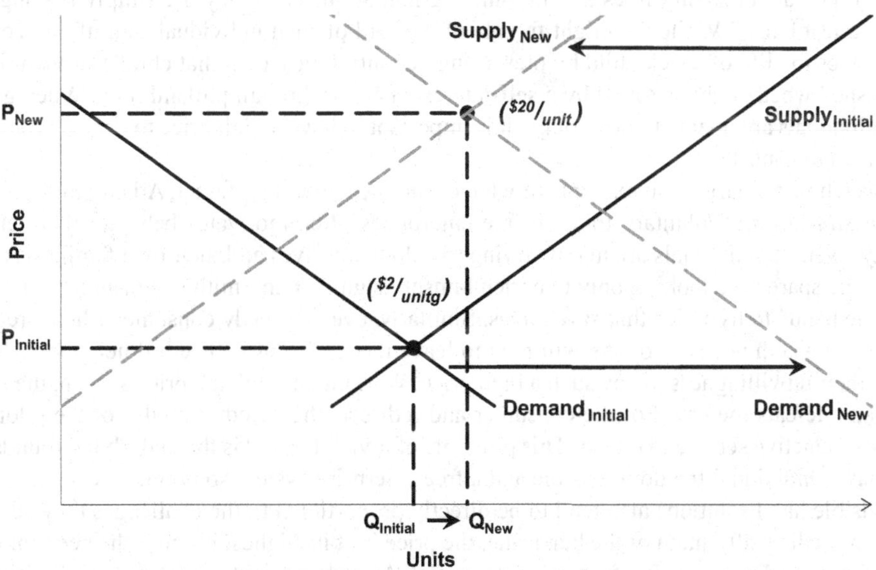

Figure 3.22 Movement of Both Supply and Demand Curves.

The natural, emotional reaction to this is to feel that sellers are engaged in "outrageous price gouging." However, economic logic leads to a very different conclusion. In this case, the high price actually helps consumers to deal with the real problem—the hurricane aftermath—more effectively. The harsh reality is that the hurricane leaves the city with a high demand for ice but only limited ice available. It is impossible to get the product to all who want it, so it is important to guide this crucial resource to those who have the most urgent needs. Everyone desires a cold drink, but there might be some individuals relying on life-saving medicines that could spoil unless they are preserved with ice. The $20 price will convince most of those who are merely thirsty to forgo the ice, while those who face a literal life or death need for ice will not hesitate to pay the exorbitant price. Put another way, the high price rations the good according to need. Of course, to truly minimize human suffering, we need more than just a high price. Charity is also required to buy the ice for those at-risk people who cannot afford it. Again, a high price maximizes the chance of finding ice in time to save lives. In fact, any philanthropist rushing in with ice would do more good to sell it for the $20 than they would by giving it away randomly to those who don't urgently need it. This seemingly unfair price also motivates extreme external measure. For example, young pilots have rented aircraft and flown in ice by helicopter and sea plane, a mode of transport normally unaffordable for most young pilots. But with a bag of ice going for $20, pilots of modest means could afford to rent the aircraft and bring in the life-saving supplies.

It would be ideal if private charities or even government officials could miraculously provide enough ice to solve all problems. But this is inherently not the case. No consumer would be willing to pay $20 for something they could readily receive as a free handout from the Salvation Army or a government relief agency. The high price is conclusive evidence that charities and governments are overwhelmed, demanding an urgent response from anyone capable quickly delivering ice.

It's possible that some individuals bring in the ice are purely motivated by self-interest, unconcerned about saving lives and minimizing human misery. They are simply rushing into "make a fast buck." While we might fret about the soul of such individuals, but if the ice they bring saves the life of a sick child by preserving her antibiotics, then that child's survival is not diminished whether she is saved by a self-interested act or through philanthropy. When generous individuals are unable to do enough, it is important to have a high price to get everyone else motivated to contribute.

This whole scenario is an example of what economics' founding father, Adam Smith, termed the *Invisible Hand.* Voluntary trade in free enterprises often motivates behavior that benefits society, even as individuals are mainly trying to help themselves and their own families. A pilot with some spare time looking only to enrich himself is guided, in Smith's phrasing, "as if by an invisible hand" to fly in ice that saves lives. Similarly, even a greedy consumer who disregards the crucial health needs of others will tend to leave the ice for more needful neighbors simply due to their unwillingness to pay such a high price. Working through the price system, the invisible hand defeats the greed of the consumer and redirects the greedy impulse of the pilot into highly productive service to others. This principle of invisible hand is the underlying foundation that makes individual freedom feasible and a free enterprise system so productive.

Invisible hand solutions also tend to be directly proportional to the challenges they address. In the immediate aftermath of the hurricane, the price is at its highest because the need for careful rationing and new supply efforts is most crucial. As power is restored, demand will decrease while the supply of ice will increase. Both effects will reduce prices so that individuals with lower priority needs will start to buy ice again. If power is completely restored, price will revert to a normal level, perishable medicines will return to refrigerators, and the typical use of ice will be once again for chilling beverages at social gatherings. The high price persists only for as long as its necessity prevails.

Price Controls

It has been argued that the primary objective of price control is to prevent extreme, unchecked inflation and the associated problems, but there might be other negative consequences as well. For example, in the early 1970s, US President Richard Nixon imposed price controls to curb inflation. A controlled price will allocate resources, but not in accordance with supply and demand. Suppose the government mandates reducing the price of ice from \$20 to \$2. The siren call of low prices is appealing to consumers anxious to get a bargain, but the result is tragic. As Figure 3.23 illustrates, the low price will drastically reduce quantity supplied, from Q^* to Q_g^s. Renting helicopters or driving refrigerated trucks from distant locations is no longer as affordable or appealing with an artificially low price of \$2. So, the flow of ice slows to a trickle, while suffering and even death become more likely. At the same time, the quantity demanded surges to Q_g^d because price is depressed. More individuals find it justifiable to spend \$2 to cool a drink, so the limited available ice is mostly purchased for casual use.

Perhaps the greatest irony is that the government price control results in consumers paying more for ice than the market rate of \$20. This follows from the fact that there is more to life than cash; time, in a manner of speaking, is money, too. Figure 3.16 illustrates that the quantity of ice available, Q_g^d, could be sold for *P*', which is obviously well above the \$20 market rate. If *P*' is, say, \$32, then we know consumers would pay that price to buy up all the ice. Normally, consumers compete for scarce products through price, but in this case, errant government

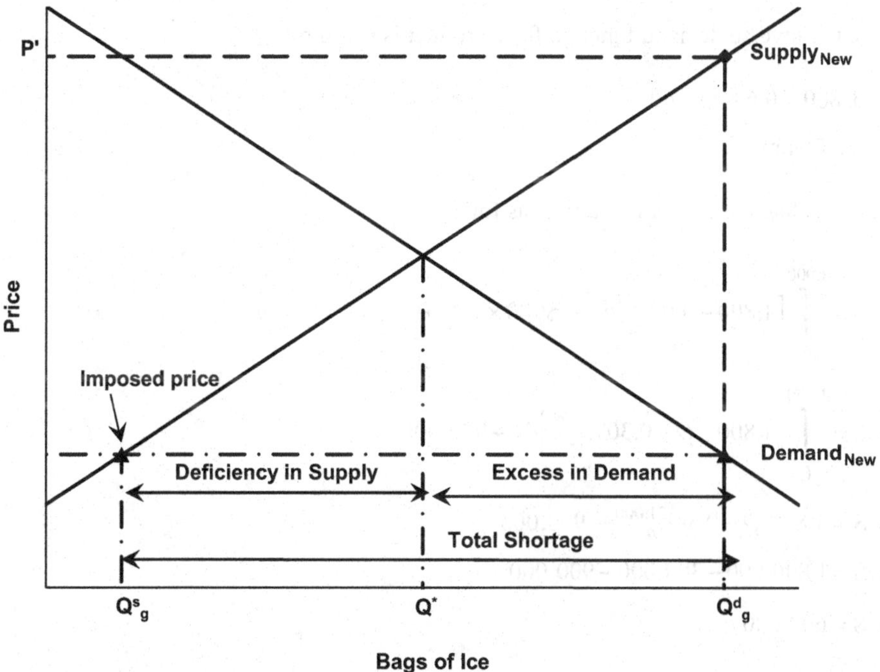

Figure 3.23 Supply Shortage.

regulation precludes that. Instead, consumers compete by getting to limited supplies ahead of the crowd; that is, they arrive early and wait in line. Since the cash price is artificially limited to $2, consumers are willing to use up an additional $30 worth in time. If the average ice consumer values their time at $10 per hour, then the average wait in line will be three hours. Of course, the chaotic uncertainty of the situation will result in some individuals waiting much longer or giving up altogether, while others may luckily stumble into an unexpected delivery and face minimal waiting. But the average price paid will be $30 worth in time in addition to $2 cash. In one way or another, massive demand in the face of minuscule supplies will bid up price. In the absence of regulation, people pay $20 for ice. Under price control, there is much less ice and people pay more, only now the greatest cost is time with a much smaller cash cost. Overall, it is that total cost that counts and renders the price control akin to a sort of "fool's gold."

Consumer and Producer Surplus

Consumer surplus (CS) refers to the benefit accrued by consumers whose willingness to pay exceeds the market equilibrium price. The lower the equilibrium price, the higher the consumer surplus. Referring to Figure 3.24, region C marks the area of consumer surplus—those consumers who "benefit" from the market equilibrium price of $125. *Consumer surplus is defined as the difference between the total amount that consumers are willing and able to pay for a good or service and the total amount that they actually do pay.*

$$\mathrm{CS} = \int_{0}^{Q_e} \left[d(q)\right]\mathrm{dx} - P_e \times Q_e$$

Suppose the inverse demand function for a product is given by:

$P = 1{,}800 - 0.6 \times \mathrm{Q}$, and

$Q = 1{,}000$ units

We can calculate the consumer surplus as follows:

$$\mathrm{CS} = \int_{0}^{1{,}000} \left[1{,}800 - 0.60Q\right]\mathrm{dx} - (\$900 \times 1{,}000)$$

$$\mathrm{CS} = \int_{0}^{1{,}000} \left[1{,}800 \times Q - 0.30 \times Q^2\right]\mathrm{dx} - 900{,}000$$

$$\mathrm{CS} = \left|1{,}800\ Q - 0.3Q^2\right|_{0}^{1{,}000} - 900{,}000$$

$$\mathrm{CS} = 1{,}800{,}000 - 300{,}000 - 900{,}000$$

$$\mathrm{CS} = 600{,}000$$

Similarly, producer surplus is defined as the benefit that gained by producers whose willingness to supply lies below the market equilibrium price. In other words, if airlines were willing to supply the market with seats at prices below the $125 per-seat market equilibrium shown in Figure 3.24, then these airlines would be able to sell their seats at the higher price and therefore reap the benefits. This is depicted as section D in Figure 3.24.

Now, consumer surplus (CS) results only because some consumers in the market have a willingness to pay that lies above the equilibrium price. Supposing an airline could identify these customers and charge them each what they would be willing to pay. They could then derive the benefit of charging higher prices to some consumers, who would be no worse off because they are still paying the price at or below their expressed willingness to pay. Further, with a multi-tiered pricing strategy (known as *price discrimination*), the airline could maximize its producer surplus, since total producer surplus would now equal areas C + D. This forms the basis of revenue management, a topic we will address in detail in Chapter 11.

Airport Landing Fees and Airport Congestion

Following the logic of the preceding discussion, excessive and persistent airport congestion might result from a price that is not in equilibrium; in other words, the landing fee is kept too low by the government. (Most of the world outside the United States is moving toward airport privatization, but major private airports, such as Heathrow, typically have landing fees mandated by the government.) Other factors, of course, may contribute to airport congestion, such as stringent environmental regulations that prevent airport expansion and dated technology that forces aircraft to maintain wider separation. Regardless of other factors, the correct price can eliminate excessive congestion.

The situation is illustrated in Figure 3.25. The supply curve is vertical because, in the short run (and usually the long run as well), airport supply is fixed. Adding runways or ramp capacity takes time and investment, and is not a decision that can be undertaken on short notice. Sometimes expansion may be impossible due to nearby development. Therefore, airport supply is fixed no matter what the price is for its services. Airport demand, on the other hand, is downward sloping, as airlines can choose whether or not to fly into an airport based on the fees to use its resources. Market equilibrium landing fee for airline traffic, P^*, eliminates excessive congestion at the airport, as the price is set such that the number of planes landing at the airport closely aligns with its capacity. However, most airports face government regulations regarding

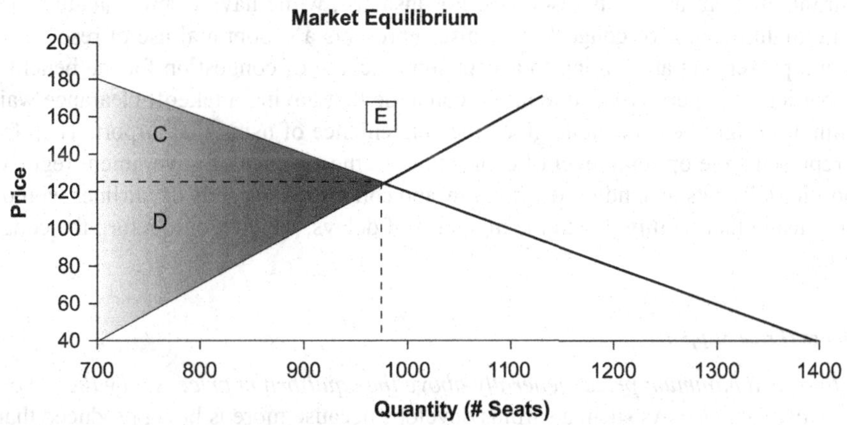

Figure 3.24 Consumer and Producer Surplus at Equilibrium.

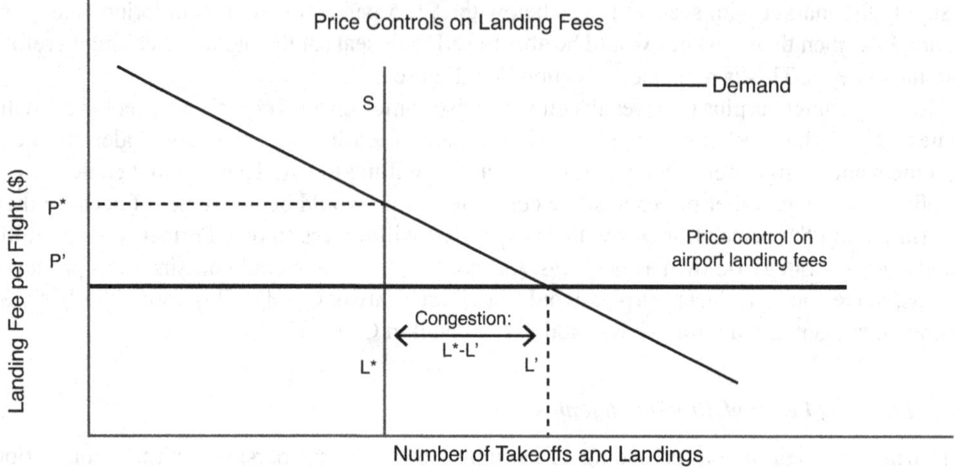

Figure 3.25 Price Controls on Landing Fees in Airports.

the fees that they can charge. In fact, most general aviation traffic at medium or small airports in the United States cannot be charged a landing fee at all, effectively subsidizing the use of airport facilities. However, assume the landing fee for the airport is set at *P'*, below *P**. This implies that *L'* takeoffs and landings will take place at the airport, which is higher than the optimal market quantity *L**. The difference between *L'* and *L** is airport congestion—airport operations in excess of capacity capabilities. Of course, if the government were to set the landing fee at the optimal quantity of *P**, it would naturally eliminate most congestion. However, *P** is usually unobserved and only reached by a process of trial and error by buyer and seller. Furthermore, estimation is near impossible without market data. Mispricing is generally the outcome of price controls, which leads to congestion. Thus, the theoretical optimal landing fee for the airport is *P**, determined by the supply and demand for airport resources.

Of course, it must be noted that *L** does not imply zero congestion, rather merely optimal congestion. It can be optimal for an airport to experience some degree of congestion, if only to represent the efficient use of its resources. For instance, while having fewer landings per day at Atlanta might mean zero congestion, it also represents a suboptimal use of resources. Both airlines and passengers are willing to accept some degree of congestion for the benefit of using that particular airport. An airline might conclude that having a takeoff clearance wait time of ten minutes might be acceptable given the convenience of using that airport. Therefore, *L** merely represents the optimal level of congestion. In the absence of government regulation, if the airport initially sets its landing fees too low and congestion exceeds *L**, airlines would eventually stop using that facility due to the high cost of delays, which would return the congestion level to *L**.

Price Floors (Price Support)

A price floor is a minimum price, generally above the equilibrium price, set by the government on a product or service. As such, a surplus develops because more is being produced than consumers are willing to purchase at that price. When the market price hits the floor, it can fall no lower, in which case market price equals floor price. There is no effect on the price or quantity if the price floor is below the equilibrium. A government may impose a price floor to protect a favored industry. This is particularly common in agricultural price supports. A good example of a price floor in the United States is the minimum wage, or the lowest wage that an employer is allowed to pay a worker.

Suppose the market demand and supply functions are

$$Q_d = 150 - 30P$$

$$Q_s = 30 + 30P$$

yield of the following equilibrium price

$$150 - 30P = 30 + 30P$$

$$60P = 120$$

$$P = \$2$$

To determine the equilibrium quantity, we simply plug this price into either the supply or the demand junction:

$$Q = 30 + 30(2)$$

$$Q = 90 \text{ units.}$$

Now, what would happen if the government imposed a price floor of \$3? Since the price is above the equilibrium price, a surplus would develop. At $P = \$3$,

$$Q_d = 150 - 30(3) = 60 \text{ units}$$

$$Q_s = 30 + 30(3) = 120 \text{ units}$$

Thus, there is a surplus of $120 - 60 = 60$ units.

Price Ceiling

Opposite to a price floor, a price ceiling involves the establishment of a maximum price by the government for a particular good and service. The government may perceive the current price as too high and could potentially harm consumers and the general economy. However, for a price ceiling to be effective, it must be set below the natural equilibrium price. If a price ceiling were imposed above the equilibrium price, it would have no impact on the market. Generally, price ceilings lead to shortages. A possible consequence of a shortage is the generation of a black market where the good is sold illegally above the price ceiling. An example of a price ceiling is the government-mandated price of gasoline during the 1970s. Likewise, President Nixon imposed wage and price controls in 1971. Rent and price controls for utilities are additional examples of price ceilings and are present in many countries around the world. In New York State, rent control has been in effect since 1943, marking the longest continuous implementation in the United States.

Now, suppose that the government imposes a price ceiling of \$1, as shown in Figure 3.26.

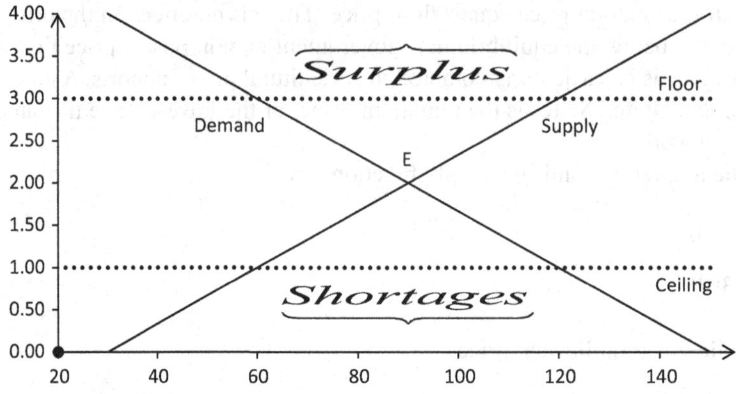

Figure 3.26 Price Controls: Floor and Ceiling.

When P = \$1 quantity supplied and demanded are

$Q_d = 150 - 30(1) = 120$ units

$Q_s = 30 + 30(1) = 600$ units

Thus, there is a shortage of 60 – 120 = −60 units.

Disequilibrium

While markets tend to move toward equilibrium, the process is not always smooth or automatic. Indeed, there can be extended periods of disequilibrium where price does not allocate the quantity demanded or the quantity supplied, even in the absence of government control. Of course, when one adds regulatory pressures to the analysis, the effects of disequilibrium can potentially be extended far longer than they would in a free market.

Disequilibrium can occur as a result of both microeconomic and macroeconomic shocks. The 9/11 terrorist attacks in 2001 and COVID-19 are examples of a macroeconomic shock. Immediately following the 9/11 terrorist attack, all aircraft were grounded in the Continental US, thereby reducing the supply of air transportation to zero within the span of a few hours. There was no equilibrium price because the market lacked any means of supply. Disequilibrium remained until supply was allowed to resume. We are all familiar with the effects of such a disruption. With so many planes grounded on 9/11 until further notice, passengers all over the country were stranded and forced to seek other modes of transportation. Recovery from this disequilibrium was a long process, involving ticket reimbursement, federal aid, and so forth.

The COVID-19 pandemic has had a significant impact on passenger demand for air travel. Airlines have responded to the decline in demand by cutting capacity, reducing flight frequencies, and implementing cost-saving measures. Several airlines ceased almost all their operations, and most supporting companies reduced staffing or shut down their total operations.

On the other hand, weather is a good example of a microeconomic shock, effectively shifting the supply curve to the left. On normal days, traffic can be managed at airports under Visual Flight Rules (VFR). This assists in reducing the burden of maintaining aircraft separation for the controllers, as pilots are essentially tasked with watch out for each other. During normal operations, air traffic regulations and vectoring responsibilities are less stringent in terms of wait times between takeoffs and landings, as well as determining when an aircraft is deemed "clear" of the airspace. Conversely, when an airport encounters bad weather, airport supply is restricted. Bad weather may not always result in a full airport closure. More often than not, Instrument Flight Rules apply and aircraft may still depart from the airport, but under a much more stringent set of rules. Specifically, this means longer separation times between aircraft, close and extensive vectoring by air traffic control, and reduced airspace capacity around the airport. Therefore, the supply curve shifts to the left during periods of bad weather, a phenomenon that could be resolved by an increase in the landing price or a change in technology. When demand outstrips supply, congestion results (Figure 3.27).

When the airport encounters bad weather, the number of aircraft that can be allowed to conduct operations in the airspace falls. This is represented by a shift in the airport supply curve to the left from S to S1. If the weather gets worse, the supply curve would shift all the way to S2, causing the market to go into disequilibrium until the weather clears.

As a broader point, the state of disequilibrium may last a few hours, as in the case of bad weather, or a few days or even years, as in the case of airport landing fees and price control.

Price Sensitivity and Elasticity

Elasticity is an important economic principle that can aid airline and airport managers in their economic decision-making process. The formal definition of elasticity is the percentage change in the dependent variable (quantity demanded) resulting from a 1% change in an independent variable (factor of demand). Informally, elasticity measures the responsiveness of one variable to changes in another. The basic formula for elasticity is:

$$\text{Elasticity} = \frac{\%\Delta Q_D}{\%\Delta P}$$

where:

$\%\Delta Q_D$ = the percentage change in quantity demanded and
$\%\Delta P$ = the percentage change in price.

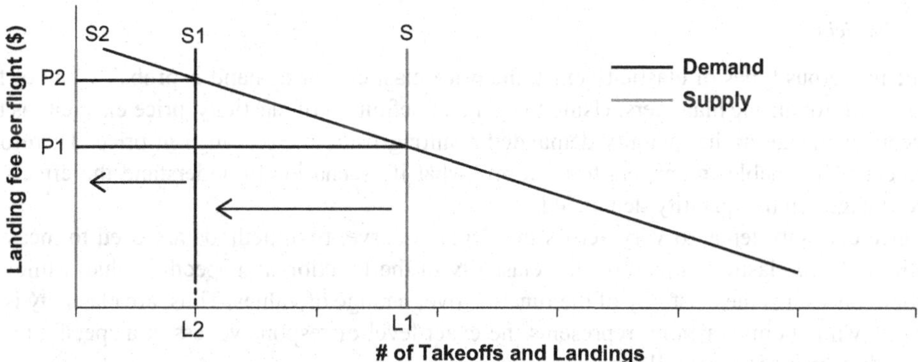

Figure 3.27 Airport under Bad Weather.

For example, suppose that the initial price of a product is \$100, and the initial quantity demanded is 200 units. The new price is \$120, and the new quantity demanded is 160 units. Using the formula above, we can calculate the price elasticity of demand as follows:

$$\%\ \Delta \text{ in quantity demanded} = \frac{(160-200)}{200}\times 100 = -20\%$$

$$\%\ \Delta \text{ in quantity demanded} = \frac{(120-100)}{100}\times 100 = -20\%$$

$$\text{Elasticity} = \frac{-20\%}{20\%} = -1$$

In given example, the price elasticity of demand is −1, which indicates that the demand for this product or service is price elastic. This means that a 1% increase in price would lead to a 1% decrease in quantity demanded.

Elasticity presents the sensitivity of a change in the dependent variable (quantity demanded) resulting from a 1% change in an independent variable (factor of demand).

When measuring elasticity, two types of variables are considered: endogenous and exogenous. Endogenous variables are those directly controlled by the airline, while exogenous variables are beyond the airline's control. In the aviation industry, both price and service are endogenous variables, while factors such as consumer income, competitor's price, and the price of complementary goods are exogenous variables. It is useful to know the effects of these exogenous variables on demand, as this information allows the airline to manage capacity and demand more efficiently. The three major types of elasticities are *price*, *cross price*, and *income*. Let's delve into these concepts in greater detail.

Price Elasticity

While numerous types of elasticity exist, the price elasticity of demand is probably one of the most useful for airline managers. Using the general definition of elasticity, price elasticity is the percentage change in the quantity demanded resulting from a 1% change in price. Therefore, price elasticity enables managers to perform "what-if" scenarios to understand the effects of price changes on the quantity demanded.

Since elasticity tends to vary across the demand curve, two methods are used to measure elasticity. *Point* elasticity measures the elasticity of the function at a specific value, while *arc* elasticity measures the elasticity of the function over a range of values. Thus, arc elasticity is an average, while point elasticity represents the exact level of responsiveness at a specific price. The basic formulae are as follows:

Arc Price Elasticity:

$$E_p = \frac{\dfrac{\Delta Q}{\text{Average } Q}}{\dfrac{\Delta P}{\text{Average } P}}$$

$$E_p = \frac{\Delta Q}{\Delta P} \times \frac{P_2 + P_1}{Q_2 + Q_1}$$

Point Price Elasticity:

$$E_p = \frac{\%\Delta Q}{\%\Delta P}$$

$$E_p = \frac{\Delta Q}{\Delta P} \times \frac{P_A}{Q_A}$$

To illustrate the difference between the two, consider Figure 3.28, which reproduces the demand curve for the JFK–LAX route.

The arc price elasticity of demand in this case is calculated as

$$E_D = \frac{\%\Delta Q_D}{\%\Delta P}$$

$$E_D = \frac{Q_2 - Q_1}{P_2 - P_1} \times \frac{P_2 + P_1}{Q_2 + Q_1}$$

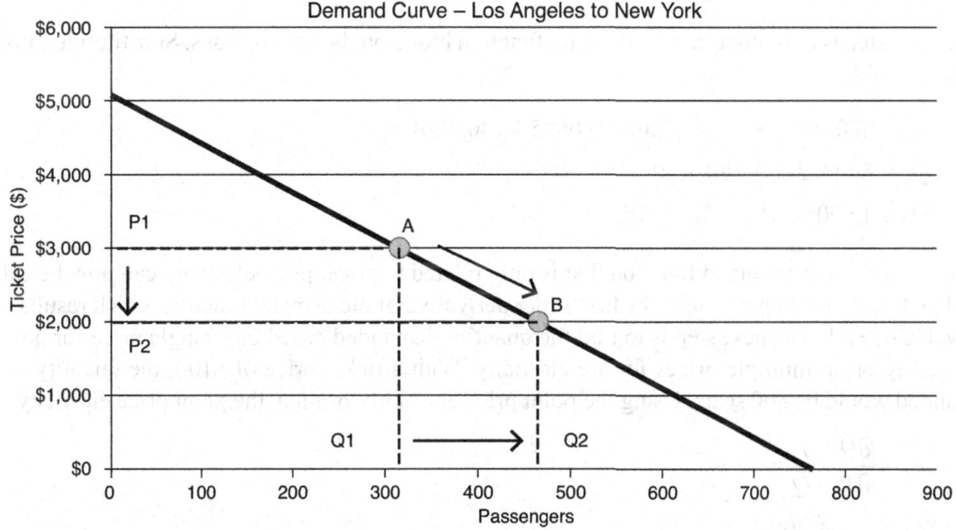

Figure 3.28 Price Elasticity of the JFK–LAX Route.

Assume:

$$Q_2 = 465$$

$$Q_1 = 315$$

$$P_1 = 3{,}000$$

$$P_2 = 2{,}000$$

Therefore, price elasticity is:

$$E_D = \frac{465 - 315}{2{,}000 - 3{,}000} \times \frac{2{,}000 + 3{,}000}{465 + 315}$$

$$E_D = \frac{150}{-1{,}000} \times \frac{5{,}000}{780}$$

$$E_D = -0.96$$

Note the negative sign, which implies that the price of the product is negatively related to the quantity demanded, given by the law of demand. In this case, if the airline decides to raise the ticket price by 1%, it will find that quantity drops by 0.96%. Elasticity can range from zero to infinity. An elasticity equal to zero would indicate no change in demand no matter what the change in price. An infinite elasticity means any price increase will lead to a demand decrease from an infinitely large amount to zero.

In order to calculate price elasticity, we need to calculate the derivative of the demand function.[9] As an illustrative example, let's consider the explicit short-run demand function for a flight, assuming that the competitor's ticket price is $120 and that the average annual income for the market is $40,000.

$$Q_D = 800 - 2P_X + 1.5P_Z + 0.0005Y$$

The first step is to re-compute the demand function based on the assumptions. Substituting those values yields

$$Q_D = 800 - 2P_X + 1.5 \times (120) + 0.0005 \times (40{,}000)$$

$$Q_D = 800 - 2P_X + 180 + 20$$

$$Q_D = 1{,}000 - 2P_X$$

Based on this new demand function that is only related to price, price elasticity can now be calculated. The first step is to take the first-order derivative of the demand function which results in a value of −2.[10] The next step is to find the quantity demanded based on a single price for point elasticity or on multiple prices for arc elasticity. With a ticket price of $100, the quantity demanded would be 800 seats. Using the point price elasticity formula, the point price elasticity is

$$\varepsilon_d = \frac{\partial Q}{\partial P} \times \frac{P}{Q} =$$

$$\varepsilon_d = -2 \times \left(\frac{100}{800}\right)$$

$$\varepsilon_d = -0.25$$

A point price elasticity value of −0.25 means that for every 1% increase in the ticket price, from the $100 level, the quantity demanded would decrease by 0.25%. Next, the arc price elasticity for ticket prices ranging from $100 to $200 can be calculated as follows:

$$E_p = \frac{\Delta Q}{\text{QP}} \times \frac{P_2 + P_1}{Q_2 + Q_1}$$

$$E_p = \frac{-200}{100} \times \frac{200 + 100}{600 + 800}$$

$$E_p = -2 \times \frac{300}{1{,}400}$$

$$E_p = -0.43$$

In this case, if the ticket price goes up by 10%, the volume of traffic will go down by 4.3%. Price elasticity is usually categorized into one of three groups based on its numerical value and its impact on demand:

$|E| > 1$ Elastic

$|E| < 1$ Inelastic

$|E| = 1$ Unitary Elastic

Price elasticity with an absolute value less than one is termed inelastic. Inelastic demand occurs when a 1% increase in price results in decrease in demand by less than a 1% (in the above example, price elasticity would be inelastic since the absolute value of elasticity was calculated as less than one). In these situations, consumers exhibit a strong desire to purchase the good or service. Therefore, price is not a central concern. In price-inelastic situations, firms can increase the price to increase total revenue, as the price effect dominates the quantity effect. However, since point elasticity is not constant across a linear demand curve (we will discuss elastic and inelastic regions of the linear curve later), this practice can only continue up to a certain price where the demand becomes less inelastic (or more elastic). A good example of a price-inelastic product is last-minute air travel. Travelers with immediate plans usually have an important reason for flying and are generally more willing to pay a higher price for convenience.[11]

At the opposite end of the spectrum is elastic demand. This occurs when the coefficient of elasticity has absolute values greater than one. With elastic demand, consumers are more sensitive to changes in price, such that a 1% decrease in price will be offset by percent increase of more than 1% for the quantity demanded. Thus, total revenue increases with price reductions. Again, the benefits of price reductions will be exhausted at some point, as the firm will eventually reach a portion of the demand curve where demand becomes inelastic. Longer-term demand for air travel is more price-elastic than is short-term demand, as many passengers (especially leisure travelers) will choose to take a flight based solely on price.

The final category of elasticity is unitary elastic demand, characterized by an absolute value equal to one. In the case of unitary elastic demand, the quantity and price effects are equal, creating a situation where a 1% increase in price is directly offset by a 1% decrease in the quantity demanded. And, as the preceding discussion indicates, the point at which the company achieves the optimal price level is the point of unitary elasticity. Therefore, the managerial rule of thumb is simple. If demand for the product is inelastic, then the company should raise the price. Likewise, if demand for the product is elastic, then the company should lower prices. Finally, if demand for the product is unitary, then the company should retain the present price. These pricing decisions are displayed graphically in Figure 3.29. For simplicity, the graph focuses only on revenue maximization. The true goal — profit maximization — will be discussed in subsequent chapters.

Since a clear relationship exists between price and total revenue for different states of elasticity, Table 3.5 summarizes the impact that a change in price has on total revenue. As mentioned previously, an increase in price will increase total revenue for goods with inelastic demand, while decreasing total revenue for products that are price elastic. Conversely, the inverse holds true for a decrease in price. For unitary elastic products, a change in price will not affect total revenue as total revenue is maximized at the point where unitary elasticity is achieved.

While elasticity varies along a linear demand curve, certain products and services can be categorized based on their normal price elasticity. As discussed earlier, air travel exhibits tendencies

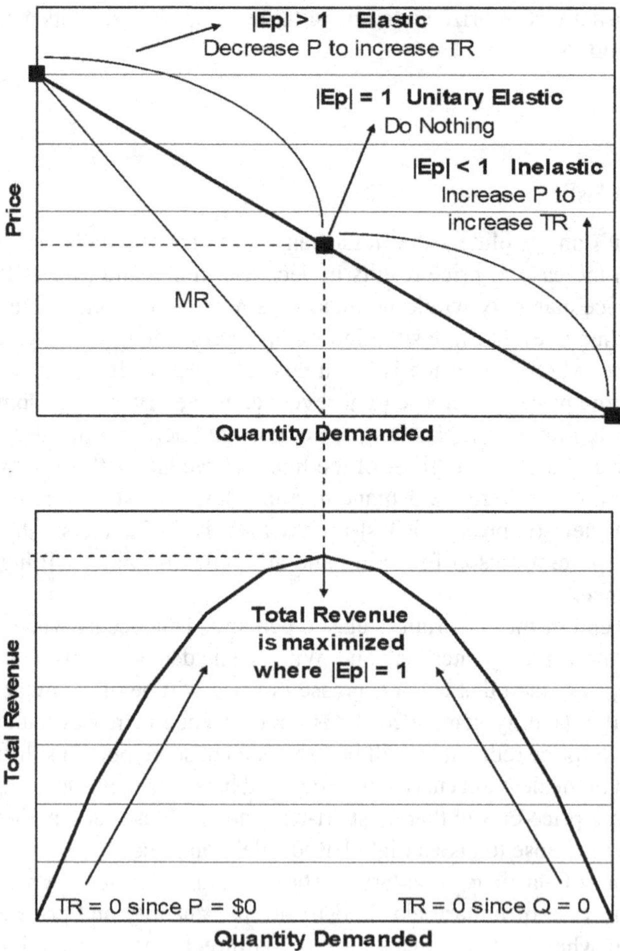

Figure 3.29 Pricing Decision Based on Elasticity.

Table 3.5 Relation between Price Changes, Total Revenue, and Elasticity

	Elastic	*Unitary Elastic*	*Inelastic*
Price increase	↓ in TR	No impact	↑ in TR
Price decrease	↑ in TR	No impact	↓ in TR

Table 3.6 Estimated Price Elasticities of Demand for Various Goods and Services

Goods	*Elasticity of Demand*
Inelastic	
Salt	0.10
Toothpicks	0.10
Airline travel, short run	0.10
Gasoline, short run	0.20
Gasoline, long run	0.70
Coffee	0.25
Tobacco products, short run	0.45
Physician services	0.60
Automobiles, long run	0.20
Approximately Unitary Elastic	
Movies	0.90
Housing, long run	1.20
Private education	1.10
Tires, short run	0.90
Tires, long run	1.20
Elastic	
Restaurant meals	2.30
Foreign travel, long run	4.00
Airline travel, long run	2.40
Automobiles, short run	1.20–1.50
Fresh tomatoes	4.60

Source: Compiled by the authors from Anderson, McLellan, Overton, and Wolfram.

of both inelastic and elastic demand, depending on the time frame. Table 3.6 provides a list of various services and products with their corresponding estimated price elasticity.

An important application of price elasticity for airlines is revenue management. This topic is covered in depth in Chapter 11, but briefly, revenue management involves segmenting the passenger base of an airline into varying price elasticities and pricing each segment differently. For example, last-minute business travelers tend to be relatively insensitive to price as their main priority is reaching to the destination. Thus, their price elasticity will be closer to zero than to one. On the other hand, leisure travelers who book well in advance tend to be more price elastic. Thus, a drop or rise in ticket price will likely cause them to change their travel plans. Although the traveler's characteristics are unobservable, the airline can make a fairly reasonable guess based on observable variables like advance booking, weekend versus weekday booking, number of children, number of people in the party, and so forth. Based on these variables, firms may prefer to price the price-elastic consumer lower than the price-inelastic consumer. In other words, airlines strategize systematic price discrimination in order to maximize revenue and produce surplus. For example, a ticket booked to Chicago, on a Monday, a few days in advance will probably belong to a price-inelastic customer, who may be charged a higher price than someone who books a party of four to Orlando two months in advance. This is the fundamental principle of revenue management.

Cross-Price Elasticity

Another type of elasticity is cross-price elasticity of demand, which measures the responsiveness of demand for one product or a service following a change in the price of another product or service. Cross-price elasticity of demand helps determine if the related firm is either a substitute (competitor) or a complement.

$$\text{Cross elasticity} = \frac{\%\,\Delta \text{ in Quantity Demanded of Good A}}{\%\,\Delta \text{ in Price of Good B}}$$

For example, if the price of train travel goes down, less passenger may choose to fly instead. Conversely, if the price of the related goods (hotels, rental cars, or service) goes down, the demand for air travel is likely to decrease.

Point Cross-Price Elasticity Formula:

$$E_{\mathrm{Dx},y} = \frac{\%\Delta Q_x}{\%\Delta P_y}$$

$$\varepsilon_{\mathrm{xp}} = \frac{\partial Q_X}{\partial P_Y} \times \frac{P_Y}{Q_X}$$

As the following formula indicates, the arc elasticity computes the percentage change between two points in relation to the average of the two prices and the average of the two quantities. This provides the average elasticity between the two points.

Arc Cross-Price Elasticity:

$$E_{\mathrm{xy}} = \frac{\dfrac{\Delta Q}{\text{Average } Q}}{\dfrac{\Delta P_y}{\text{Average } P_y}}$$

$$E_{\mathrm{xy}} = \frac{\Delta Q}{\Delta P_y} \times \frac{P_{y2} + P_{y1}}{Q_2 + Q_1}$$

Using the given formulae and the preceding example, the point cross-price elasticity of demand can be found, assuming that the ticket price of the firm's flight is \$100, the competitor's ticket price is \$120, and the annual income is \$40,000.

$$Q^D = 800 - 2P_X + 1.5P_Y + 0.0005M$$

$$Q^D = 800 - 2(100) + 1.5P_y + 0.0005(40{,}000)$$

$$Q^D = 580 + 1.5P_y$$

$$\varepsilon_{XY} = \frac{\partial Q}{\partial P_Y} \times \frac{P_Y}{Q}$$

$$\varepsilon_{XY} = 1.5 \times \frac{P_Y}{Q}$$

$$\varepsilon_{XY} = 1.5 \times \frac{120}{760}$$

$$\varepsilon_{XY} = 0.24$$

From this example, the cross-price elasticity of 0.24 indicates that the related competitor can be considered a mild substitute to the firm, as the cross-price elasticity of demand is greater than zero. In this situation, a 1% increase in the competitor's ticket price will cause a 0.24% increase in the airlines' ticket sales. In the airline industry, where price competition is fierce, the cross-price elasticity of demand is undoubtedly highly positive. From a revenue management perspective, fare transparency has forced airlines to redouble their efforts to stay competitive. With so much information online, passengers are now able to view almost all the pricing options for their flights, therefore causing many to extremely become price conscious (especially since there is little difference between two products, or seats). As a result, the cross elasticity of demand for the airline industry is generally very high. Furthermore, liberalization and deregulation have created fierce competition. When two airlines compete with each other on the same route, they must consider how the other might react to a competitor price change. Will many passengers switch? Will the other airlines match it? Will they follow a price reduction?

If the cross-price elasticity of demand is found to be less than zero, then the related firm's product is determined to be a complementary good. A complementary good is a good which increases the demand for the firm's good. Examples of complementary goods to the airline industry are hotels and rental cars, as the price of accommodation and transportation directly relates to the demand for air transportation. For instance, if the cross-price elasticity of demand was found to be −0.55, then a 1% increase in the complementary good's price would create a 0.55% decrease in the quantity demanded. As in the case of own price elasticity, cross-price elasticity can be categorized into one of three groups based on its numerical value and its impact of a related firm's price on demand:

$E_{XY} > 0$ Substitute

$E_{XY} < 0$ Complementary

$E_{XY} = 0$ Independent

For example, the cross-price elasticity of demand between Ryan Air and easyJet is expected to be strongly positive. Similarly, when there is a strong complementary relationship between two products (hotels and airlines), the cross-price elasticity will be highly negative. Independent or unrelated products have a zero cross elasticity.

Income Elasticity

A third type of elasticity is income elasticity, which determines the sensitivity that changes in the consumers' annual income to variations in the quantity demanded for a product. Disposable personal income and Gross Domestic Product (GDP) are all good measures for this variable.

Disposable income represents the income available to spend on leisure travel. However, business income is also part of the equation as increased business activity will likely spur an increased need for business travel. Considering the income variable is comprised of two parts for air transportation, GDP is the best proxy variable for income. It takes into consideration both household disposable income and business activity. The formulas for income elasticity are similar to both the price and cross-price elasticity formulas:

Point Income Elasticity:

$$\varepsilon_{xy} = \frac{\%\Delta Q}{\%\Delta Y}$$

$$\varepsilon_{xy} = \frac{\partial Q_X}{\partial P_Y} \times \frac{Y}{Q}$$

Arc Income Elasticity:

$$E_Y = \frac{\frac{\Delta Q}{\text{Average } Q}}{\frac{\Delta Y}{\text{Average } Y}}$$

$$E_Y = \frac{\Delta Q}{\Delta Y} \times \frac{Y_2 + Y_1}{Q_2 + Q_1}$$

Using the same example, assuming that the ticket price is \$100 and the competitor's ticket price is \$120, the arc income elasticity between \$40,000 and \$50,000 is:

$$Q^D = 800 - 2PX + 1.5PY + 0.0005Y$$

$$Q^D = 800 - 2 \times 100 + 1.5 \times 120 + 0.0005Y$$

$$Q^D = 780 + 0.0005Y$$

$$Q_1^D = 780 + 0.0005 \times 40{,}000 = 800$$

$$Q_2^D = 780 + 0.0005 \times 50{,}000 = 805$$

$$E_Y = \frac{\Delta Q}{\Delta Y} \times \frac{Y_2 + Y_1}{Q_2 + Q_1}$$

$$E_Y = \frac{5}{10{,}000} \times \frac{50{,}000 + 40{,}000}{805 + 800}$$

$$E_Y = 0.0005 \times \frac{90{,}000}{1{,}605}$$

$$E_Y = 0.028$$

As with own price elasticity and cross-price elasticity, the good or service can also be classified according to its income elasticity:

$E_Y > 1$ Superior good

$E_Y > 0$ Normal good

$E_Y < 0$ Inferior good

When a product's income elasticity is greater than zero, the good is categorized as a normal good. This implies that the quantity demanded of a normal good increases with any increase in the consumer's income. As anticipated, the majority of goods and services can be classified as normal goods, as in the example mentioned. A sub-category of normal goods are superior goods, whose income elasticity is greater than one. Superior goods have a proportional increase in the quantity demanded that is greater than the increase in consumer income. Superior goods usually encompass high-end luxury products, such as fancy sport cars and business jet travel.

The other goods categorized according to income elasticity are inferior goods. Inferior goods possess income elasticity values lower than zero, indicating that for any increase in income, the quantity demanded decreases. This peculiar situation occurs when products hold a price advantage over competitors but are generally not perceived as quality goods. Therefore, when consumers' income increases, they are more willing to purchase the perceived better product. Examples of inferior goods might include generic products versus brand names or, in some markets, coach travel against first-class seats.

The concept of elasticity is critical to understanding the pricing policies of any industry, especially air transportation. And, as the earlier discussion has shown, elasticity can be used to determine the optimum price level where total revenue is maximized. Ultimately, revenue management is founded in this concept, as elasticity can be used to help manage both pricing and capacity.[12]

Pricing and Elasticity Application

Since the ultimate goal of any pricing policy is to maximize total revenue and total revenue is known to be maximized where price elasticity is unitary elastic, formulas can be derived to determine the optimum price. In order to understand the formula derivation, consider the inverse demand function with the general form of:

$$P = a - b \times Q$$

The basic, general formula for point price elasticity can be slightly modified to reflect an inverse demand function. The derivative of the demand function is simply the inverse of the derivative for the inverse demand function. As the derivative, or slope, of the inverse demand function is (b), the price point elasticity formula can be rewritten as:

$$\varepsilon_p = \frac{\mathrm{dQ}}{\mathrm{dP}} \times \frac{P}{Q}$$

$$\varepsilon_p = \frac{1}{\text{slope}} \times \frac{P}{Q}$$

$$\varepsilon_p = \frac{1}{-b} \times \frac{P}{Q}$$

Additionally, the price variable (*P*) can be replaced by the general form of the inverse demand function. Therefore, the elasticity formula would be:

$$\varepsilon_p = \frac{1}{-b} \times \frac{a - \mathrm{b}Q}{Q}$$

Since the goal is to determine the optimum pricing point where total revenue is maximized, the elasticity formula needs to be set equal to −1, or where unitary elasticity is achieved. Once the equation is set equal to −1, the optimum quantity where total revenue is maximized can be determined:

$$\frac{1}{-b} \times \frac{a - \mathrm{b}Q}{Q} = -1$$

$$\frac{a - \mathrm{b}Q}{Q} = b$$

$$Q = \frac{a}{2b}$$

While this formula provides the optimum quantity demanded where total revenue is maximized, it needs to be placed back into the inverse demand function to obtain the optimum price level. Total revenue is maximized where:

$$P = a - b\left(\frac{a}{2b}\right)$$

$$P = \frac{a}{2}$$

Based on the derivations of the inverse demand function and the price point of elasticity formula, the total revenue maximizing price point can be found. Using the previous example, the revenue maximizing price and quantity would be:

$Q_D = 1{,}000 - 2 \times P_x$

$P = 500 - 0.5 \times Q$

Therefore, the revenue maximizing price is \$250, which creates a demand of 500 seats. At this point, the point price elasticity of demand is −1, or unitary elastic. These formulas are the building block for yield management, which is covered in more detail in Chapter 11.

Summary

In this chapter, we introduced the reader to supply and demand analysis in the context of aviation. Demand is defined as the willingness and ability to pay for a good or service, and the law of demand postulates an inverse relationship between quantity demanded and price. The impacts of the determinants of demand are analyzed in terms of own price, the price of substitutes, the price of complements, and other influences on the demand for a product. Movements along a demand curve are caused by price shifts, and shifts in the curve are caused by other external factors. Peaking and cyclicality are addressed as some of the unique characteristics of airline demand.

Supply is defined as the willingness and ability of a producer to supply a good to the market at a given price. The unique characteristics of airline supply are examined, including product perishability, limited inventories, and constraints in longer-term product provision. Supply movements are analyzed in terms of supply determinants, such as own price, resource prices, technology, and competitive factors. We then elucidate market equilibrium as an interaction between supply and demand, as well as the market clearing price as the price at which the quantity demanded matches the quantity supplied. We emphasize the effects of government price controls in the case of airport congestion pricing, and market disequilibrium is discussed with appropriate examples. Finally, we delve into price elasticity of demand, income elasticity of demand, and the cross elasticity of demand. The formulas and interpretation of elasticities are provided, and revenue management is covered as an application of price elasticity of demand. Supply and demand analysis is the cornerstone of economic thought, and the concepts presented in this chapter will be used as analytical tools throughout the book.

Discussion Questions

1 What is price elasticity of demand? Provide examples of products with elastic demand and products with inelastic demand. Explain your reasoning.
2 Explain the difference between shortage and surplus.
3 Define the law of demand and supply. Explain the difference between demand and quantity demanded.
4 Is price elasticity of demand for the airline industry in short-haul markets more or less than it is in long-haul markets? Why?
5 What are the factors that influence elasticity of demand for pilots?
6 Suppose the income elasticity of demand for a good is −4. Is this a normal good or an inferior good? If it is a normal good, then is it a luxury or a necessity? Why?
7 What are some of the determinants of demand for narrow-body commercial aircraft such as Boeing B-737 and Airbus A-320?
8 With changes in fuel prices, what kind of effects can be witnessed in the market for air travel?
9 Explain direct demand and derived demand. Which of these two types of demand is the airline industry most characterized by?
10 Suppose JetBlue raises the ticket price by 6% and the ASM decreases by 3%. Is the price elasticity of supply elastic, unit elastic, or inelastic? Why?
11 Suppose an airline increases its average ticket price from JFK to CDG from $435 to $515, and consequently, the number of seats sold drops from 800 to 735:
   a What is the price elasticity of demand for this market?
   b Is the demand elastic, unitary elastic, or inelastic in this price range?
   c What is the interpretation of this price elasticity of demand? What does it mean?
   d Suppose the price elasticity of demand calculated in the first bullet above is the exact number representing passengers' responsiveness to a price change for this airline for this market. If there is a 10% decrease in the ticket price, what would the percentage change in the quantity demanded be equal to? If the ticket price were to rise by 15%, what would the percentage change in the quantity demanded be equal to?
   e What happens to the total revenue of the airline when the price rises from $435 to $515? How is this related to the price elasticity of demand for this market?
   f What could cause JFK–CDG to have the elasticity of demand calculated in the first bullet above?
   g Suppose the cross-price elasticity of demand between these two markets is equal to 2. Would these markets be substitutes or complements? Why?
12 Given the following supply and demand functions, calculate consumer surplus.

$P = 600 - Q_d$

$P = 300 + 2Q_S$

13 Assume your demand and cost functions are the following:

$Q = 100 - 0.50P$ and
$TC(Q) = 104 - 14Q + Q^2$

a Find the inverse demand function for your firm's product.
b What price should you charge if you are planning to sell 5 units?
c Calculate your total cost of producing 5 units.

14 The JetGo Company is a major fixed-base operator (FBO) at a regional airport. Management estimates that the demand for the jet fuel is given by the equation:

$Q_{JF} = 10{,}000 - 2{,}000P_{JF} + 0.2Y + 200P_C$

where:

- Q_{JF} is the demand for jet fuel in thousands of gallons per year.
- P_{JF} is the price of jet fuel in dollars per gallon.
- Y is GDP per capita (thousands of dollars).
- P_C is the price of jet fuel in dollars per gallon on the adjacent airport. Initially, the price of jet fuel is set at \$2 per gallon, the income per capita is \$40,000, and the price of competition is \$1.60 per gallon.

a How many gallons of jet fuel will be demanded at the initial prices and income?
b What is the point income elasticity at the initial values?
c What is the point cross elasticity demand? Are these two product substitutes or complements?

15 When the price of airline tickets falls, the supply falls and the demand increases. Using the economic ideas covered in this chapter, critically evaluate this statement.
16 Allegiant Airlines does an excellent job of allocating seats on their point-to-point flights around the United States. What economic concepts do you suppose that they are using as the price of the seats is increased as the departure time for the flight gets closer?
17 The price of oil has been on a downward trend for about six months. How do you think this will affect airline ticket prices and how will this be brought about?
18 Suppose the government mandates that airline ticket prices are too high and that they cannot exceed a certain amount. Using the concepts discussed in this chapter, what would be the short-term results of this policy?
If the policy of the above question were to be continued over a very long time, what would be the results of the policy?
19 Why might an airline that has international routes pay the workers in one country more than the workers in another country for essentially the same job?
20 What is the effect of a price ceiling on the quantity demanded?
21 Consider the market for jet fuel in a remote regional airport. The domestic demand and supply curves are given as (Q_S are gallons in thousands):

$P = 55 - 3Q_D$
$P = 5 + 7\,Q_S.$

a What is the market equilibrium price and quantity?
b If the government imposes a price ceiling of \$28, what will be the shortage of jet fuel at the airport?
c What price floor would yield a surplus of 5,000 gallons of fuel?

22 Consider the following demand curve:

Q	0.00	12.50	25.00	37.50	50.00	62.50
P	\$20.0	\$17.5	\$15.0	\$12.5	\$10.0	\$7.5

and the following supply curve:

Q	62.50	50.00	37.50	25.00	12.50	0.00
P	20	17.5	15	12.5	10	7.5

a What is the equation of demand curve?
b What is the equation of the supply curve?
c Solve for equilibrium price and quantity.

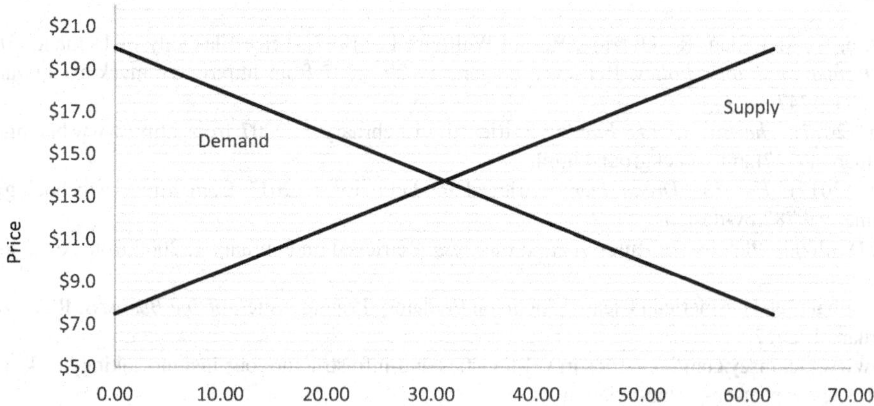

23 Suppose an airline operates a fleet of 50 aircraft with varying seat configurations, ranging from 100 to 300 seats per aircraft. The airline operates an average of ten flights per day, with flight distances ranging from 500 to 1,500 miles.
Calculate the airline's available seat miles (ASM) for the month of January to analyze its capacity and revenue potential.

Notes

1 Ceteris paribus is a Latin term for "all else being equal" or for everything other than the variable of interest being held constant.
2 Stated exceptions to the law of demand usually involve confusion between the perceived quality and/or prestige that a high-priced good confers on the purchaser. Imagine that the exact same quality and/or prestige could be achieved at a lower price. Rational consumers would always select the lower-priced good for the exact same quality and/or prestige since the extra money allows other choices in consumption. Therefore, it is the quality and/or prestige of that good that the consumer is responding to, not the high price.
3 While the coefficient for a competitor's price is positive.
4 The log-linear function is also sometimes referred to as the log-log function.
5 Note that for log-linear demand functions, the elasticities of demand are the coefficient of the variables and are constant. For example, the price elasticity of demand would be simply β_1.
6 American Airlines and United Airlines.
7 FAA November 6, 2009.
8 In the airline industry, the supply is not a smooth upward sloping curve. An aircraft can accommodate only a fixed number of passengers. This would create the situation where the supply curve for a single flight would move up step-wise according to the number of aircraft in the airline's fleet.
9 For those readers who have not taken calculus, the derivative is simply the change in the dependent variable for a one-unit change in the independent variable. In this case, it would be dQ/dP or −2. That is, a one-unit change in P will produce a minus two-unit change in Q.

10 Ibid.
11 That is part of reason why last-minute tickets are expensive and the airlines use revenue management techniques to save seats for last-minute time-sensitive passengers.
12 The principles of elasticity enable managers to see the impact that changes in competitors' prices, advertising campaigns, and economic booms and recessions will have on the airline's operations. From a foundation based on elasticity, a competitive plan and strategy can be created for the airline. Therefore, the concept of elasticity is invaluable to decision-makers in all industries, especially highly volatile industries such as air transportation.

References

Anderson, L., McLellan, R., Overton, P., and Wolfram, L. (1997). Price Elasticity of Demand. *Mackinac Center for Public Policy.* Retrieved on January 29, 2007 from http://www.mackinac.org/article.aspx?ID=1247.

Boeing. (2007). *The Boeing 747 Family*. Retrieved on February 1, 2007 from http://www.boeing.com/commercial/747family/background.html.

Boeing. (2017). *The 787 Dreamliner.* Retrieved on February 1, 2017 from http://www.boeing.com/commercial/787/by-design.

Knibb, D. (2000). Play by the Rules. *Airline Business.* Retrieved on February 1, 2007 from Air Transport Intelligence.

Flight Global (2003). American Cleared Again on Predatory Pricing Issue. *Airline Business.* Retrieved on February 1, 2017.

https://www.mckinsey.com/industries/travel-logistics-and-infrastructure/our-insights/taking-stock-of-the-pandemics-impact-on-global-aviation

4 Cost and Production Analysis

The General Concepts

The value of a business depends on numerous factors, such as revenue and cost structure. Cost is defined as the aggregate monetary value of the inputs used in the production of the goods or services. The airline industry is intensely competitive, and consistent efforts to reduce costs and improve productivity play a pivotal role in the survival of airline. Traditional carriers have struggled against a tradition of high labor costs and high debt under a capital-intensive cost structure. Among the primary expenditures, all airlines have fuel costs as a major expense and are continuously striving to improve fuel efficiency as well as aircraft utilization. In recent years, the surviving legacy carriers have made significant strides in bringing cost structures down toward the range seen in low-cost carriers.

This chapter incorporates a modern approach to the principles and practice of airline cost and production analysis. It introduces prospective airline managers to the technical cost accounting knowledge that can be applied across a whole range of organizations. The scope of cost restructuring surpasses mere reduction of labor costs, and it also involves optimization of all operational and financial strategies. As one important example of this process, airlines may have to restructure their fleets to newer, more fuel-efficient aircraft. This chapter provides a foundation of knowledge that will allow readers to understand the minimization of production costs, through optimal inputs or the reallocation of resources across multiple plants. Furthermore, it also illustrates pertinent costs for specific airline decisions. Lastly, we discuss returns to scale, scope, and density. The specific topics covered in this chapter are the following:

- Cost Classification
  - Historical Costs
  - Current Costs
  - Sunk Costs
  - Opportunity Costs
  - Accounting versus Economic Costs
- Components of Cost
  - Total Costs, Fixed Costs, and Variable Costs
  - Average Costs
  - Marginal Costs
- Cost Functions
  - Linear Cost Functions
  - Cubic Cost Functions
  - Using Cost Functions for Managerial Decisions

DOI: 10.4324/9781003388135-4

- Economies of Scale, Scope, and Density
  - Economies of Scale and Diseconomies of Scale
  - Economies of Scope
  - Economies of Density
- Operating Leverage
- Airline Industry Cost Structure
  - Direct Operating Costs
  - Indirect Operating Costs
  - Non-Operating Costs
- Airline Economies of Scale, Scope, and Density
- Airline Breakeven Analysis
- Airline Operating Leverage
- Summary
- Discussion Questions
- Appendix: Airline Cost Classification and Division

Cost Classification

In 2008, crude oil prices hit an all-time high of $147. However, relief came in 2009 as fuel prices plummeted, and the airline industry started recovering. In the five years before the COVID-19 pandemic, the airlines industry produced its biggest profits ever, owing to lower fuel cost and robust economic growth. The airlines managed to save billions in 2016 thanks to cheaper jet fuel. Specially, American Airlines succeeded in saving more than $5 billion on fuel in 2015, compared to the previous year.[1] Profitability in any industry can be improved by increasing revenues or decreasing costs. One measure of profitability is the difference (contribution margin) between unit revenues and unit costs. To illustrate these concepts concretely, Table 4.1 displays the unit revenue (passenger revenue per available seat mile, RASM), the unit costs (cost per available seat mile, CASM), and the contribution margin for major US airlines in 2021. Alaska Airlines (AS) had the widest spread (RASM-CASM) among US carriers as a result of having the second lowest operating CASM and the fifth highest passenger RASM. JetBlue (B6) enjoyed the second highest contribution margin, despite having one of the lowest passenger RASMs.

Table 4.2 presents the passenger RASM and operating CASM for 2021. From this table, we observe that all the carriers recorded an increase in their RASM-CASM spread from the previous year. Southwest remained the top airline, with a marginal decrease of the passenger RASM but a solid decrease in the operating CASM. However, it is important to note that consistency in profitability is the long-run goal of any airline, and Southwest has consistently achieved this goal.

Table 4.1 Average Cost and Revenue for US Airlines, 2022

	AA	*AS*	*B6*	*DL*	*UA*	*HA*	*WN*
Passenger RASM	14.68	11.78	11.21	15.37	13.79	10.05	13.77
Operating CASM	14.42	10.47	9.92	14.4	14.36	13.36	13.24
RASM – CASM	0.26	1.31	1.29	0.97	−0.57	−3.31	0.53

Data Source: Collected by the authors from SEC fillings form 10-k.

Table 4.2 Average Cost and Revenue for US Airlines, 2022

	AA	*AS*	*B6*	*NK*	*DL*	*UA*	*HA*	*WN*
Passenger RASM	\$0.14	\$0.12	\$0.11	\$0.08	\$0.15	\$0.14	\$0.10	\$0.12
Operating CASM	\$0.14	\$0.10	\$0.11	\$0.08	\$0.14	\$0.14	\$0.12	\$0.11
RASM – CASM	–\$0.005	\$0.013	–\$0.001	–\$0.001	\$0.010	–\$0.006	–\$0.021	\$0.013

Data Source: Collected by the authors from SEC fillings form 10-k.

Example

DirectJet flies a 180-seater Boeing 737-800 aircraft on a long-haul flight of 2,000 mile. There are 135 passengers on board. The total cost of this flight is \$36,000, and the airline generates \$40,500 ticket revenue. We can calculate both CASM and R/RPM as:

$$\text{CASM} = \frac{\text{Cost}}{\text{ASM}} = \frac{\$36{,}000}{180 \times 2{,}000}$$

$$\text{CASM} = \$0.10$$

$$R/\text{RPM} = \frac{\text{Revenue}}{\text{RPM}} = \frac{\$40{,}500}{135 \times 2{,}000}$$

$$R/\text{RPM} = 0.15$$

Recently, US commercial airlines have achieved success at reducing costs and increasing revenues by opening up new routes, dropping unprofitable routes, selecting the most efficient aircraft type, and implementing advanced revenue management practices. Until 2001, airlines lacked a detailed focus on cost reductions; however, downturns in demand have shown that reductions in costs are significant. In an attempt to cut costs, the major airlines have progressively eliminated numerous services and reduced many cabin amenities. Through measures like reduced in-flight amenities, labor outsourcing, automation, and aircraft retirement, legacy carriers have made efforts to lower their cost and optimize their cost structure. Simultaneously, low-cost carriers (LCCs) have also been successful due to their ongoing focus on managing costs. The lesson from the past few years makes it evident that understanding the cost structure and the variables that impact profitability is crucial. The subsequent section of this chapter is devoted to these issues.

In economic terms, cost defined as the opportunity cost is the forgone alternative use of resources in the production, transformation, use, and delivery of services. To illustrate, for a manufacturer, the costs could be the alternative uses of raw materials, labor, buildings, and general overhead supplies. In the airline industry, costs incurred include labor fuel, maintenance, aircraft, catering, and airport landing/usage fees. Typically, fuel, labor, maintenance, and aircraft ownership costs are the four major costs categories for any airline. Furthermore, costs can be separated into different categories and classifications: Historical, Current, Opportunity, Sunk and Accounting, and Economic. Each of these offers a different view of costs suitable for different purposes.

Historical Costs

Costs can be classified and grouped according to time. Historical costs are the costs actually incurred when acquiring an asset, whereas current costs are the costs valuing the asset under prevailing market conditions.[2] For example, when measuring aircraft costs, a decision must be made regarding the usage of historical costs, current costs, or some other measure. Assume DirectJet bought an aircraft in 2023 for $25,000,000, yet today the fair market value of the aircraft may be $23,000,000.

In accordance with Generally Accepted Accounting Principles (GAAP), the book value of a company's assets is based on its historical costs. The book value is determined by deducting a capital consumption allowance (depreciation). Most airlines' depreciable lives for their aircraft hover around 30 years with an estimated residual value of that aircraft of 5% of the historical cost.

Current Costs

Historical costs serve as accounting tools to measure the book value of assets. They provide information on depreciation, depletion, and asset impairment value. However, current costs provide the best representation of the present situation. Moreover, future costs, by their nature, are the expected costs that may be incurred sometime in the future; these will be affected by macroeconomic variables such as the (uncertain) rate of inflation and the rate of interest. Meanwhile, replacement costs are those required to duplicate the productive capabilities using current technology. For example, an older generation 737 aircraft could be replaced by a modern 737 MAX for the cost of the 737 MAX.

Impaired Asset (Impairment Cost)

An impaired asset denoted an asset that has a current market value that falls below the book value listed on the balance sheet. Impaired assets are written down from historical cost to fair market value as a depreciation expense. An asset may become impaired due to various factors, including shifts in economic conditions, technological obsolescence, a decrease in demand for the product or service associated with the asset, or other reasons leading to a decline in the asset's value. A leading aircraft leasing firm, Avolon, recorded a first quarter of 2022 impairment of $304 million to cover the full financial impact of having ten jets still stuck in Russia following European Union sanctions that forced the termination of all Russian leases.[3] When an aircraft is impaired, it must be written down on the balance sheet to reflect its reduced value. In addition, SMBC Aviation Capital has acknowledged that it will not be able to recover 34 owned aircraft stranded in Russia following the country's ongoing invasion of Ukraine and subsequent sanctions, leading the company to recognize a $1.6 billion impairment cost.

> **Impairment Cost** is the drop in the value of an asset on a permanent basis.
> **Sunk costs** are the investments made in the current planes and facilities that can't be recovered. In economics, a sunk cost is an irrelevant cost and must be ignored. For example, the original cost of a runway or a terminal of an airport could be a sunk cost.

Sunk Costs

Finally, and perhaps most importantly, there are the considerations of sunk costs. Sunk costs are the investments that have already been committed, for example, the current aircraft fleet and airport facilities that can't be recovered. These expenses have been incurred in the past and are not recoverable. Since these costs have already occurred and they are unalterable, they should never influence business decisions. Unfortunately, they commonly do. To illustrate this kind of misguided decision-making, suppose an airline has already purchased eight additional lavatory units and is considering installing these units in new aircraft. However, in-depth analysis shows that these lavatory units would increase fuel costs, decrease passenger revenue (by removing seats), and increase maintenance costs. Therefore, the installation of these aircraft lavatories would be costly to the airline, but managers may want to install the lavatories anyway since "we already have them." Let's consider a situation that there is no secondary market for these lavatories. In this example, the pre-purchase of the lavatories has now become a sunk cost and therefore should not affect the final decision of whether or not to install them. Another example of a sunk cost is an empty seat on an airplane. The cost of an airline seat is primarily fixed and sunk with a small portion attributed to variable costs (VC) if one considers the fuel, airport charges, and cabin services.[4] Therefore, sunk costs should not be included in a capital budgeting analysis or any financial decision-making process. Instead, only opportunity costs should be included in the process.

Opportunity Costs

As mentioned earlier, since the pursuit of any economic activity represents a choice between two options, the opportunity cost is the value of the superior alternative. Consequently, the chosen economic activity must provide a better rate of return than the next best alternative. Otherwise, the company would have been better off pursuing the other alternative. For instance, according to Airlines for America (A4A)[5] estimates, the booking of Federal Air Marshals into first-class seats and the displacement of passengers are producing opportunity costs running as high as $180 million annually (Stewart, 2008).

Opportunity cost is defined as the value forgone in order to make one particular investment instead of the next best alternative. If you decided to drive your car along a 2,000-mile route rather than fly, your opportunity costs are lost wages, more maintenance costs, fuel costs, lack of comfort, and higher risk of an accident.

To vividly illustrate opportunity costs, consider the situation an airline faces when deciding between purchasing either a Boeing or Airbus aircraft. Assume that both aircraft have the exact same seating capacity and similar performance characteristics. The Boeing aircraft costs $70 million, while the Airbus aircraft costs $72 million. The fuel costs for each aircraft type have been estimated to be $1,350 per block hour for the Boeing and $1,370 per block hour for the Airbus. Based on these specifications, the airline purchases one Boeing aircraft. In this context, the explicit costs would be the purchase price of $70 million and the hourly fuel consumption rate of $1,350. The opportunity costs in this example would be $2 million in savings on the aircraft purchase price and $20 additional fuel costs per block hour, since the Airbus aircraft was the next best alternative for the airline.

Accounting versus Economic Costs

The final major approach to classifying costs is either accounting or economic costs. Explicit costs are the costs represented by actual out-of-pocket expenditures, while implicit costs are generally non-cash expenditures. For instance, an implicit cost would be the rate of return that an entrepreneur would get in the stock market for capital invested in his own company rather than in the stock market. Implicit costs are the most cost-effective understood in terms of opportunity costs.

Accounting costs generally recognize only explicit costs, while economic costs include both explicit and implicit costs. Therefore, accounting costs do not take into consideration opportunity costs. The two cost approaches also deal with depreciation differently. Accounting costs calculate depreciation based on a predetermined historical usage rate applied against the cost incurred to acquire the asset. Conversely, economic cost is defined as the value of any resource used to produce a good in its best alternative use. Both accounting and economic costs are useful in their respective context, with accounting costs used primarily for financial accounting purposes and economic costs for managerial decision-making process.

Economic cost = accounting cost + opportunity cost[6]

Economic cost = explicit cost + implicit cost[7]

Suppose you have started a small fixed-based operation (FBO) at a regional airport. Your explicit costs are:

Labor	$1,000,000
Materials and supply	$750,000
Finance charge, insurance, and others	$250,000
Total explicit costs (accounting)	$2,000,000

You are not receiving a payment for your services, because the business is new and does not have enough income. Also assume you have rejected a position in which you could have earned $200,000 a year. Hence, in this case: Total Economic Costs = $2,000,000 + $200,000 = $2,200,000 rather than the $2,000,000 of explicit accounting costs.

Components of Cost

Proper application of cost requires a strong understanding of the relationship between the cost and level of production. Cost functions specify the technical relationship between the level of production and the production costs. Production costs can be subdivided as total, fixed, or variable costs.

Fixed Costs, Variable Costs, and Total Cost

While costs categorized by time are important in accounting, the most common and practical method of classifying costs in economics is by their relation to output. In the short run, total costs (TC) consist of two categories: total fixed costs (FC) and total variable costs (VC).

Fixed Cost (FC)

Costs that remain fixed in the short run, irrespective of fluctuations in output levels, are called FCs. In the aviation industry, there are large fixed costs associated with running an airline, an aircraft manufacturer, an airport, or an engine manufacturer. These aviation-related industries require specialized equipment and/or labor that are essentially fixed costs. Such fixed costs may include:

- Aircraft financing
- Aircraft hangar construction
- Aircraft overhaul
- Terminal building

Variable Costs (VC)

Costs that directly vary with changes in production are termed as variable costs. For example, when an aircraft is flown for 10 hours a day, the fuel cost is obviously higher in comparison to non-operational periods, or if a company decides to shut down its plant for a month during summertime, the labor costs will drop to zero. Variable costs may include wages, utilities, and materials used in production. They may also increase at a constant rate, an increasing rate, or a decreasing rate in proportion to the labor and capital used in production.

Total Cost (TC) and its Derivatives

In economics, total cost describes the total economic cost of production. When fixed costs and variable costs are added together, the result is total costs. In simple terms,

$$\text{TC} = \text{FC} + \text{VC}$$

As highlighted earlier, the timeframe is important when categorizing costs based on their relation to output. In the short term, some costs are fixed since they have already been incurred and are not feasible to modify. However, in the long run, all costs are variable, since a company is able to change FCs over time by selling and/or altering the FC asset. An example of this could be long-term aircraft leasing contracts. Airlines are legally and contractually obligated to pay aircraft lease payments to the lessee, the airline would be unable to avoid these payments in the short run no matter how it adjusts output. Therefore, lease payments are fixed in the short run, but variable in the long run, since the contractual obligations are subject to termination. At this point, the airline can cut the aircraft from the fleet in order to adjust capacity. There is usually no set timeframe when FCs will turn into VCs; however, the specific situation will dictate when all costs become variable.

Firms and industries have different ratios of fixed to variable. Notably, the airline industry tends to have high FC, which increases barriers to entry of the industry. The ratio of fixed to variable is called operating leverage, and this topic will be covered later in this chapter. Figure 4.1 displays fixed, variable, and total cost functions.

Average Costs

Comprehending and understanding average cost structure is an important part of pricing and production planning. For measuring unit costs, we should include all fixed costs, variable costs, direct material costs, and direct labor costs involved in production process. Hence, by dividing the TC function by output, we obtain another important category of costs, average total costs. By definition, average TC is the total amount of cost (both fixed and variable) per unit of output. Average fixed cost (AFC) is the FC per unit of output.

$$\text{AFC} = \frac{\text{FC}}{Q}$$

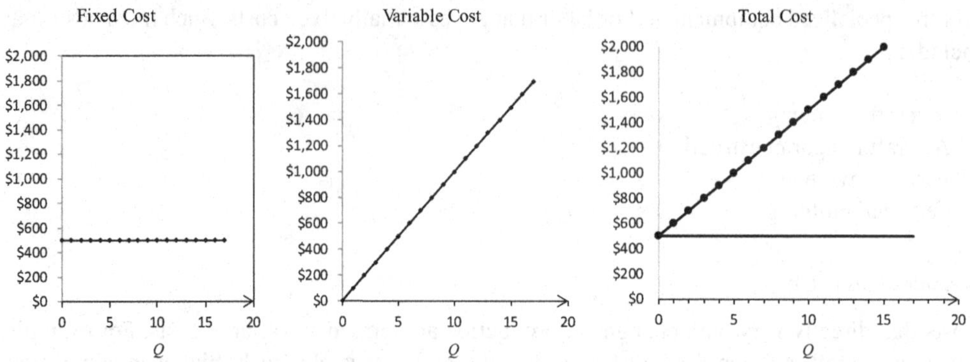

Figure 4.1 Disaggregated Cost Functions.

Because FCs remain constant regardless of output, AFCs will decrease with increases in output, since the FCs are spread out over a greater range of outputs. This provides an incentive for a firm to increase output if it has high levels of FCs. Airlines that fly long-haul markets generally enjoy lower unit or average total cost (CASM). Longer stage lengths allow the FCs of each flight to be distributed over more available seat miles (ASMs). Conversely, an increase in unit cost may be attributed to a shorter stage length.

Average variable cost (AVC) is the VC per unit of output. The AVC function measures the VCs per unit of output. In some cases, AVCs tend to decrease over the first units of production (since so few units are initially produced) and then increase as production increases. Recall that the variable cost is any cost that changes because there is a change in the level of production.

$$AVC = \frac{TVC}{Q}$$

Finally, average total cost (ATC) is the amount calculated by dividing the TC by the units of production. ATC will behave like AVC as it is made up of fixed and variable costs. The following formula describes the relationship between ATCs, AVCs, and AFCs:

$$ATC = \frac{TFC}{Q} + \frac{TVC}{Q}$$

$$ATC = AFC + AVC$$

In the airline industry, the average cost is generally represented by CASM.[8] The output for an airline is passenger miles. CASM is the primary measure unit of cost in the airline industry and is obtained by dividing the operating costs of an airline by ASM.[9]

$$CASM_{Total} = \frac{\text{Total cost}}{ASM}$$

$$CASM_{Operating} = \frac{\text{Operating cost}}{ASM}$$

Another type of cost related to changes in outputs is mixed cost. Mixed costs exhibit characteristics of both FCs and VCs. In other words, the costs are fixed for a certain range of outputs and then increased for a different range of outputs. Although FCs are fixed in the short run for all outputs, mixed costs have smaller bands of FCs and fluctuate to a greater degree. To illustrate, labor can be a mixed cost since it may be difficult to adjust staffing levels to rapidly changing levels of output, but eventually labor costs will have to be adjusted upward or downward to accommodate higher or lower levels of production. Therefore, a mixed cost may appear like a step function with various levels.

Marginal Cost (MC)

Marginal cost (MC) is the cost of producing one more unit of output. In the airline industry, the marginal cost of flying additional passengers is usually just extra fuel-burn and some ground-handling services.

A final and extremely important type of cost relating to output is marginal cost (MC). The term "Marginal" refers to the change in the dependent variable caused by a one unit change in an independent variable. Let's assume that Ryanair offers five daily flights from Liverpool to Dublin, and adding an additional flight increases the cost by £13,000 (or £100 per available seat), and hence the MC of the last flight is £100 per seat. In algebraic terms, the MC is the change in TCs resulting from an increase in one additional unit of output.

$$MC = \frac{dTC}{dQ} = \frac{\Delta TC}{\Delta Q}$$

MCs are determined by simply calculating the change in TCs divided by the change in output. For example, it might cost a company $1,000 to produce 20 units and $1,100 to produce 21 units. In this example, the MC would simply be $100. Additionally, it might cost $1,250 to produce the 22nd unit so that the MC of this unit would be $150, and so forth. It is important to note that MCs generally do not remain constant throughout; therefore, every MC value is unique to that particular change in output.

The airline industry, in broader context, has very high FCs and low MCs. There is a small increase in cost for each additional passenger as, regardless of the number of passengers, airlines have to pay the high FCs associated with aircraft ownership, terminal expenses, and maintenance facilities. Consequently, airline managers find it difficult to cut costs quickly if this becomes necessary.

Cost Functions

A cost function is a mathematical technical relationship between total cost (TC) and units of quantity produced. A cost function is an analytical tool that allows airline managers to predict and estimate cost of operations at different levels of service production, for instance, an airline selling a seat on a particular flight. The production costs depend on the number of passengers, the distance the aircraft is flown, and the volume of cargo that is ferried between destinations. While every company has a unique cost function, there are three more general functional forms: *linear*, *quadratic*, and *cubic cost functions*.

Linear Cost Functions

The linear cost function can be represented by the formula:

$$TC = a + b \times Q$$

$$TC = FC + TVC$$

where a and b are both constants.

In a linear cost function, the constant "a" represents the FC, the constant "b" represents the average variable cost[10] component, and Q represents the total units produced. The fundamental assumption of a linear cost function is the presence of constant returns to scale.[11] This implies that successive units of output can be produced for the same cost (in this case, the constant b) so that the average and MC are equal. Although linear cost functions may not be attainable for all levels of production in the long run, they may be approximated in the short run within a given production range. A linear cost function generally applies best to a mechanized and automated production line where unit costs are approximately the same. For example, if the production capacity of an assembly line is 300 cars per day, a linear cost function can approximate this process up to that point. However, when production surpasses 300 cars a day, a new assembly line would have to be built and the cost function would shift accordingly. Let's consider the following linear cost function:

$$TC = 50 + 5Q$$

We can interpret this function as indicating that when we produce 20 units of this good, the total cost is 50 + 2 × (20) = \$90. Let's assume that the capacity of the production line is 15 units. Table 4.3 breaks down the cost function into the various classifications.

Figure 4.2 displays the FCs for the cost function. Figure 4.3 illustrates the AFC function, and Figure 4.4 demonstrates a vertical summation of the average fixed and AVC functions (ATC). Finally, Figure 4.5 displays the average and MC functions for the linear example, with MC being equal to the AVCs and declining average TCs and FCs for increases in unit output.

To summarize, linear costs occur when the company experiences constant MCs of input charges. Although linear cost functions are not typical of most industries, they may be useful approximations over a given range of outputs.

Table 4.3 Cost Classifications

Units	*TC*	*FC*	*VC*	*AFC*	*AVC*	*ATC*	*MC*
1	55	50	5	50.0	5	55.0	
2	60	50	10	25.0	5	30.0	5
3	65	50	15	16.7	5	21.7	5
4	70	50	20	12.5	5	17.5	5
5	75	50	25	10.0	5	15.0	5
6	80	50	30	8.3	5	13.3	5
7	85	50	35	7.1	5	12.1	5
8	90	50	40	6.3	5	11.3	5
9	95	50	45	5.6	5	10.6	5
10	100	50	50	5.0	5	10.0	5
11	105	50	55	4.5	5	9.5	5
12	110	50	60	4.2	5	9.2	5
13	115	50	65	3.8	5	8.8	5
14	120	50	70	3.6	5	8.6	5
15	125	50	75	3.3	5	8.3	5

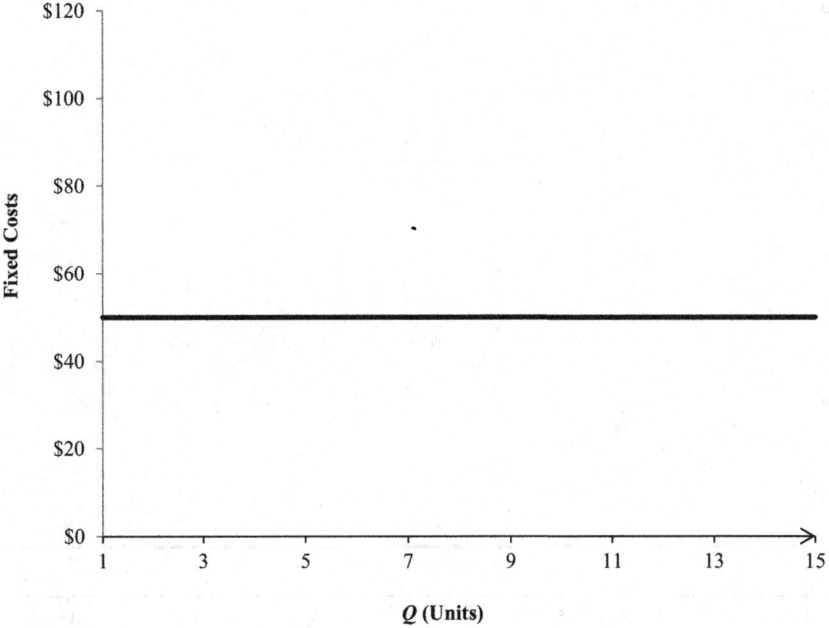

Figure 4.2 Fixed Cost Function.

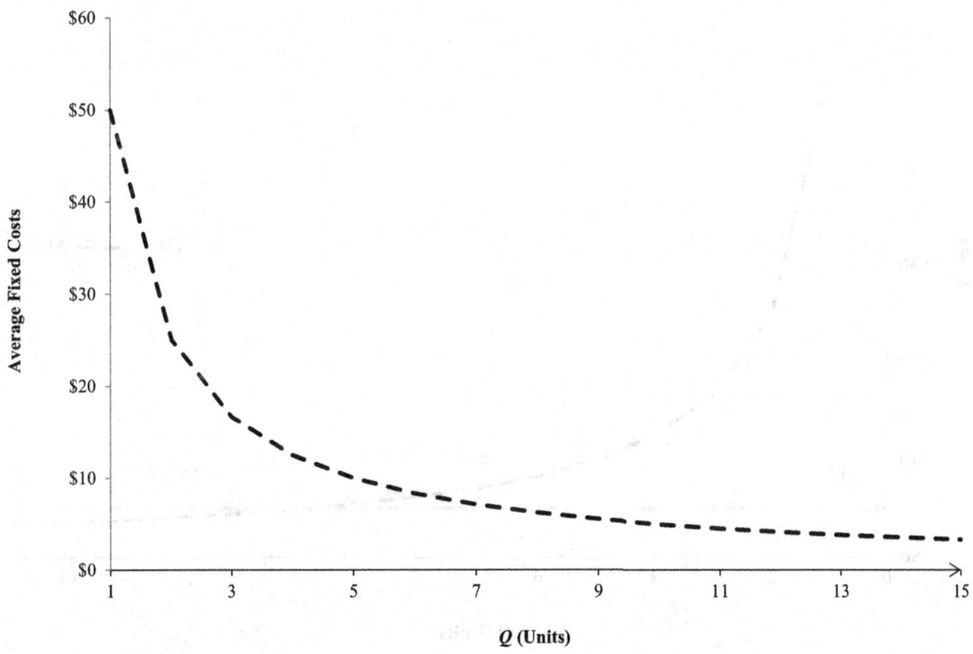

Figure 4.3 Average Fixed Cost Function.

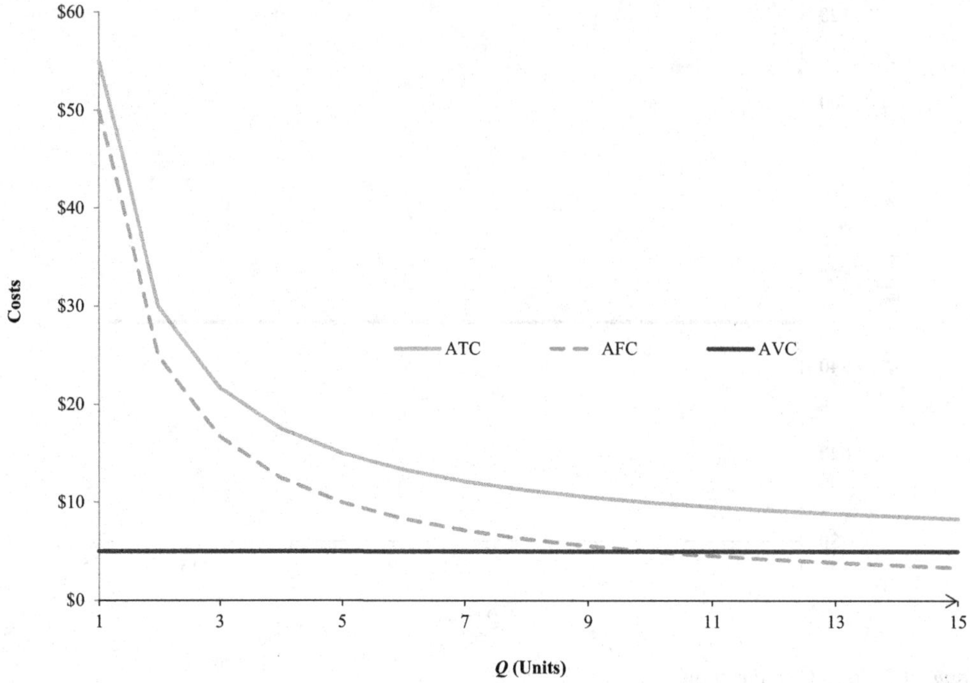

Figure 4.4 Average Variable, Fixed, and Total Cost Functions.

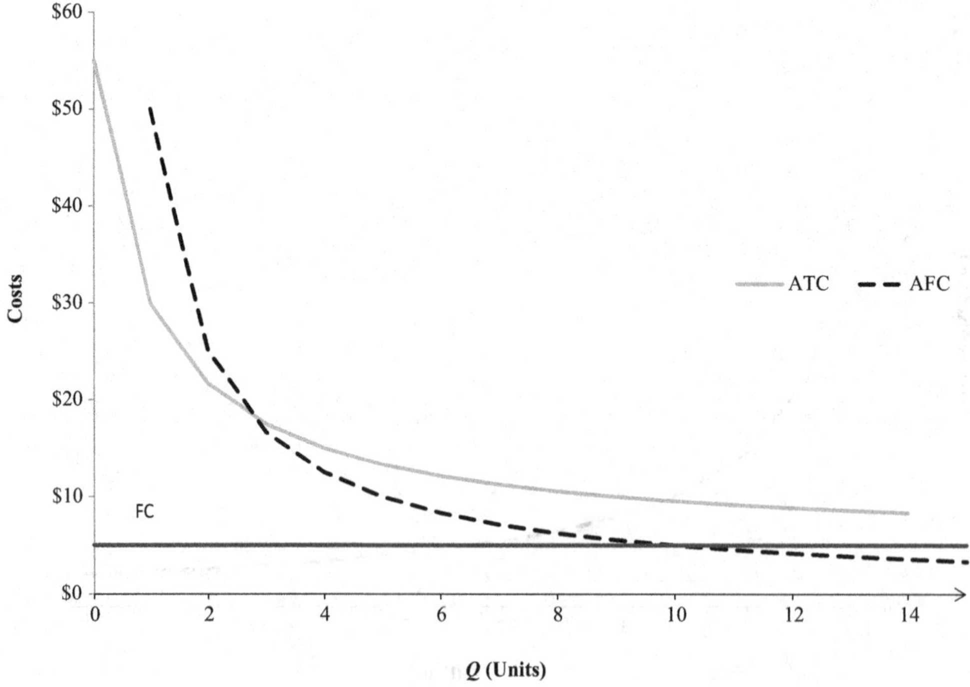

Figure 4.5 Average and Marginal Cost Functions.

Cubic Cost Functions

Another cost functional is the cubic cost function, which often occurs in practice. The general form of a cubic cost function is the following:

$$TC = a + b \times Q + c \times Q^2 + d \times Q^3$$

where

$$FC = a$$

$$a, b, d > 0$$

$$c < 0$$

$$C^2 < 4bd$$

A cubic cost function represents the normal theoretical cost function where the total cost initially rises at a decreasing rate, but then increases at an increasing rate. That is, a cost function first exhibits increasing marginal returns and then diminishing returns to scale as demonstrated by the "U-shaped" average cost function. Consider a company whose TC function is:

$$TC = 100 + 40Q - 8Q^2 + (2/3) \times Q^3$$

From this equation, we can apply the cost definitions covered earlier to review the various categories of cost (Maurice and Thomas, 2005).

FC = constant "*a*" of the general form (in this case, 100)

$$VC = 40Q - 8Q^2 + (2/3) \times Q^3 \text{ (costs that change with output)}$$

$$AFC = \frac{100}{Q}\left(\text{FCs divided by output}\right)$$

For a cubic cost function, both the AVC and MC functions are found to be quadratic. From the equation:

$$TC = 100 + 40Q - 8Q^2 + \frac{2}{3}Q^3$$

The average variable cost function is (VCs divided by output):

$$AVC = 40 - 8Q + \frac{2}{3}Q^2$$

The MC function for the cubic cost function is:

$$MC = \frac{\Delta TC}{\Delta Q} = \frac{TC_n - TC_{n-1}}{Q_n - Q_{n-1}}\left(\text{the change in TCs for a one unit change in output}\right)$$

$$MC = 40 - 16Q + 2Q^2$$

This MC curve is quadratic in nature (U-shaped), indicating that MC drops at the beginning of production, but for every subsequent increase in output, MCs start to increase at a greater rate. This is the basic definition of decreasing returns to scale. Table 4.4 provides the numerical values of the various cost classifications.

In this scenario, the company has FCs of $100, which remain constant regardless of the level of output. Since the FCs remain constant throughout, the AFC declines for every unit increase in output. This cost function also contains a VC function that may include costs such as labor and raw materials. Figure 4.6 illustrates the FC function for this example, while Figure 4.7 demonstrates the typical VC function curve. Figure 4.8 exhibits vertical summation of the cost curves, displaying the TC function and the FC line.

Table 4.4 Cost Classifications

Units	*TC*	*FC*	*VC*	*AFC*	*AVC*	*ATC*	*MC*
1	133	100	32.7	100.0	32.7	132.7	
2	153	100	53.3	50.0	26.7	76.7	20.7
3	166	100	66.0	33.3	22.0	55.3	12.7
4	175	100	74.7	25.0	18.7	43.7	8.7
5	183	100	83.3	20.0	16.7	36.7	8.7
6	196	100	96.0	16.7	16.0	32.7	12.7
7	217	100	116.7	14.3	16.7	31.0	20.7
8	249	100	149.3	12.5	18.7	31.2	32.7
9	298	100	198.0	11.1	22.0	33.1	48.7
10	367	100	266.7	10.0	26.7	36.7	68.7
11	459	100	359.3	9.1	32.7	41.8	92.7
12	580	100	480.0	8.3	40.0	48.3	120.7

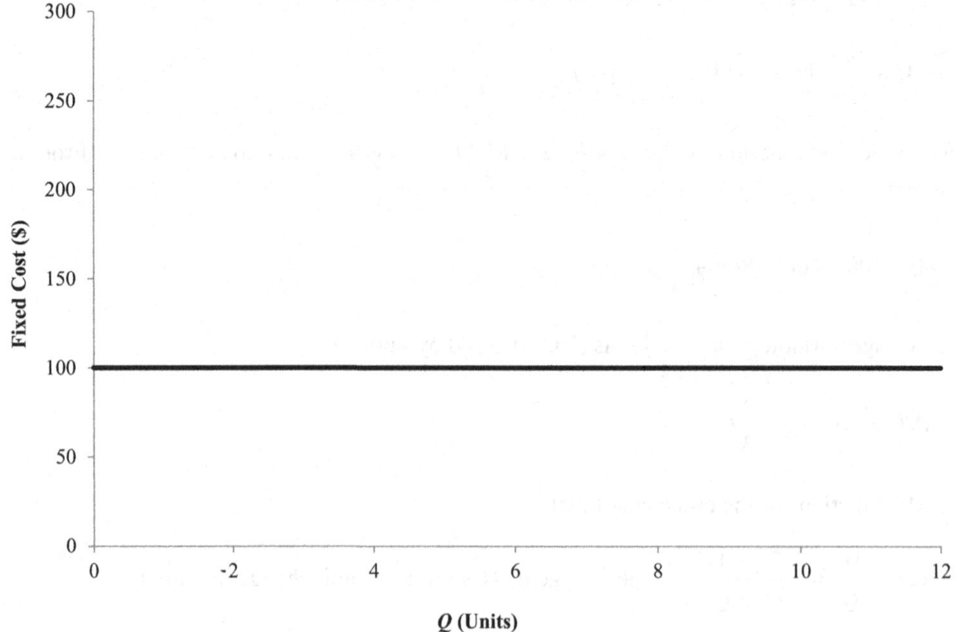

Figure 4.6 Fixed Cost Function.

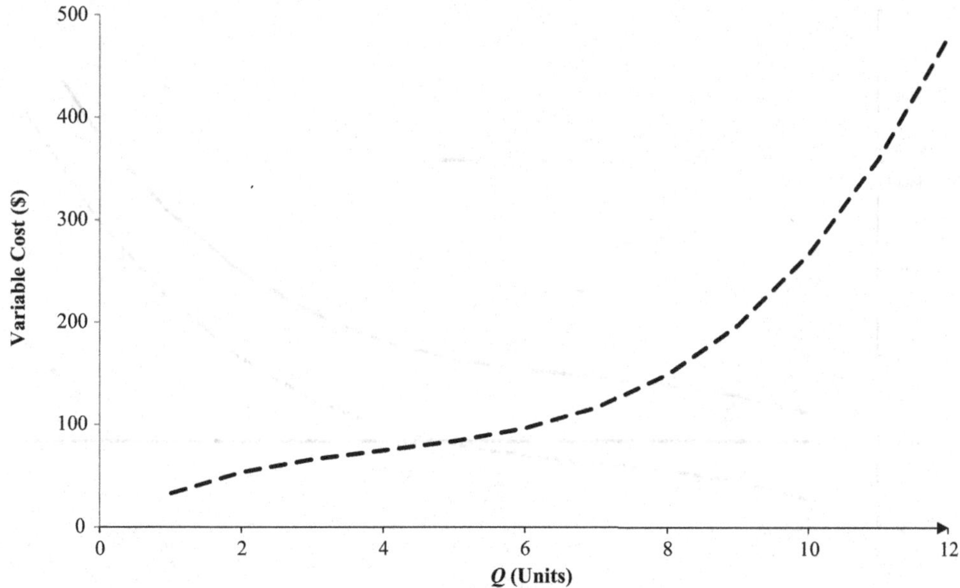

Figure 4.7 Total Variable Cost Function.

Figure 4.8 exemplifies the total, fixed, and variable cost functions for the production facility. Since FCs are the same for all levels of production, the FC line remains horizontal throughout. The VC curve changes slightly for different rates of output, with costs escalating dramatically for higher levels of output. Finally, the TC curve is simply the VC curve shifted upward with the inclusion of the FC line.

Figure 4.9 depicts the MC curve and the average cost curves for all three cost classifications. In Figure 4.9, we observe that the AFC curve will always slope downward at a declining rate and will eventually be asymptotic with the x-axis. The average TC curve is U-shaped which is similar to the AVC as they differ only by the AFC. The MC curve crosses both the AVC and average TC curves at their minimum point and continues above them as output rises. The intuitive reason for this is that, at first, we add unit costs that are less than the average, causing the average costs to fall. Then, as these additional unit costs increase, they eventually are equal to the average (at the minimum of the average). Above this point, we continue adding unit costs that are above the average, hence the rise. A cubic cost function represents the normal theoretical cost function, which exhibits both decreasing marginal and average costs as well as increasing marginal and average costs.

Quadratic Cost Function

Another prevalent form of cost functional structure in the industry is the quadratic function, which has a general form of:

$$TC = a + bQ + cQ^2$$

This can exhibit decreasing returns to scale for the range of production possibilities, as the curve is upward sloping at an increasing rate. The ATC curve then becomes asymptotic at the capacity level of the production range. *If there is diminishing return to the variable factor, the cost function becomes quadratic, which means that the marginal physical product of the variable factor will*

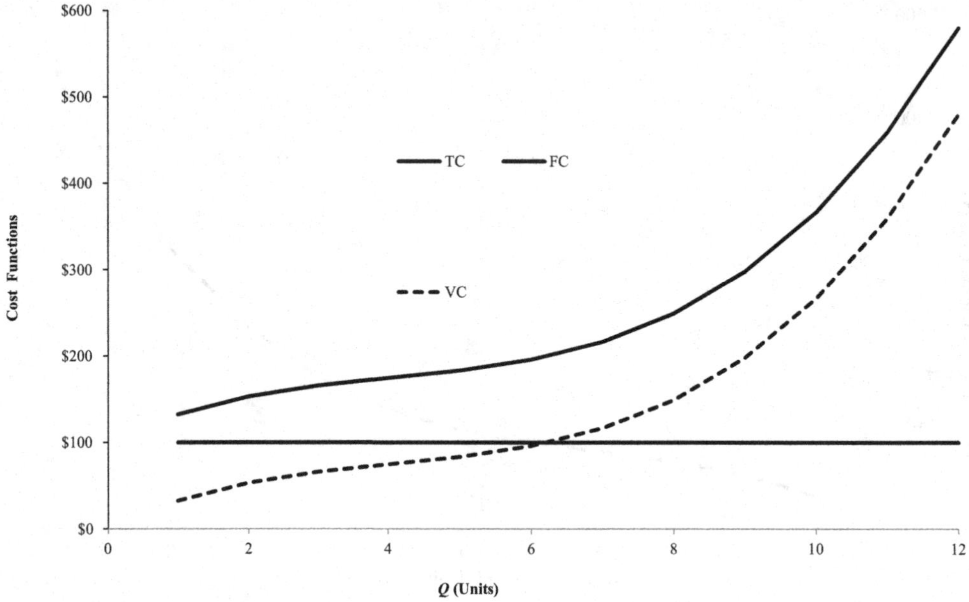

Figure 4.8 Total Cost Function.

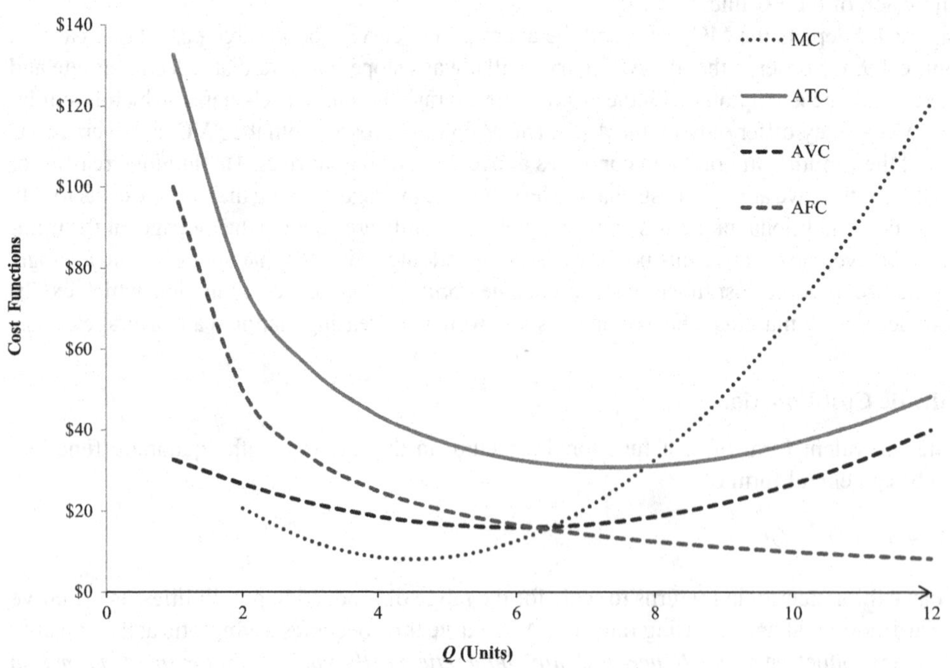

Figure 4.9 Average and Marginal Cost Functions.

diminish. If the cost function is linear, variable cost increases at a constant rate. Quadratic total cost functions have a shape similar to TC curves as depicted in Figure 4.8.

Using Cost Functions for Managerial Decisions

While reviewing the cost categories is instructive, it holds greater significance to understand how they affect managerial decision-making. In this regard, the cost function provides the following information for managerial decision-making:

- When the MC equals to marginal revenue, it guides us in determining where (how much) to produce.
- Comparing average TC to average revenue, it tells us if we should produce in the long run.
- Analyzing AVC, in relation to average revenue, it tells us when we should cease production in the short run.

Given that MC is the cost for extra units of output, it is obvious that, as long as the revenue from the extra unit exceeds its cost, we will want to produce that unit. Conversely, if the cost for that unit exceeds the revenue, then we will not want to produce that unit. Hence, we will continue production up to the point where MC and marginal revenue (MR) are equal but not beyond. So we continue to produce as long as MR ≥ MC.

$$\text{ATC} = \frac{\text{TC}}{Q}$$

$$\text{ATC} = \frac{\text{TFC} + \text{TVC}}{Q}$$

$$\text{TC} = \text{ATC} \times Q$$

Average TC can be multiplied by output to give TCs. As long as total revenues exceed TCs, we will, of course, continue production. In the event that TC falls below total revenue but is still above VCs, then we would still continue production (in the short run) as we are still generating some output to help cover our FCs.[12] It is crucial to remember that FC must be paid in the short run whether we are producing or not. Thus, average VC tells us whether we should continue production in the short run.

To rephrase, AVC can be translated into total VC when multiplied by output. In this case, if our total revenues do not cover our total VCs, we should cease production because we will be losing more money on every unit we produce.

Shutdown	
Short Run	*Long Run*
TC > TR Loss	TR > TC Operate
ATC >P > AVC operate in Short Run	TR < TC Shutdown
ATC >AVC > P Shutdown	

Economies of Scale, Scope, and Density

Having covered the cost curves in some detail, we can now use these concepts to define economies of scale, scope, and density. These factors play a crucial role in managerial decision-making and in shaping not just the cost structure of the company, but also the industry as a whole.

Economies and Diseconomies of Scale

The concept of economies of scale refers to the advantages gained when long-run average costs decrease with an increase in the quantity produced. This phenomenon is common in capital-intensive, high-fixed-cost industries, such as aircraft manufacturing, airlines, railroads, and the steel industry.[13] For example, within the airline industry, network airlines may have an inherent cost advantage over smaller airlines because of economies of scale. Airlines can achieve economies of scale by purchasing or leasing a larger number of aircraft. This strategic move allows them to negotiate better deals with aircraft manufacturers, maintenance providers, and other suppliers, reducing their unit costs. The following list enumerates several sources of economies of scale in the airline industry:

- Higher productivity due to division of labor
- Higher labor productivity due to specialization
- Higher aircraft productivity due to higher aircraft utilization
- Lower average cost due to using uncongested secondary airports
- Lower aircraft price due to quantity purchased
- Lower average cost due to more efficient inventory management

Diseconomies of scale occur when average unit costs increase with an increase in production quantity. The following quotation gives a good illustration of diseconomies of scale. As an airline gets bigger and bigger, it is more difficult to identify a problem and come up with a solution. Some of the causes for diseconomies of scale are:

- Inability to efficiently monitor and coordinate material flows and manage employees' performance at larger facilities
- Slow decision-making ladder
- Increased segregation between workers and management, and communication becoming less effective
- Inflexibility
- Limitations on entrepreneurial skills (hiring qualified employees)

Depending on the firm's cost function, economies of scale usually do not exist for every level of production. Companies encounter stages of quantity where economies of scale are present and levels where diseconomies of scale exist. This is exactly what occurs in cubic cost functions. Referring back to Figure 4.9, the average TC function is U-shaped, indicating economies of scale for production quantities of one through seven, and conversely, indicating diseconomies of scale for production quantities of eight and above.

Economies of Scope

Economies of scope are different from economies of scale in the sense that economies of scale mean producing more of the same product or services, while economies of scope mean more of similar products and services. Consolidation and mergers among airlines lead to better utilization of aircraft, airport gates, and their networks.

Economies of density are achieved through the consolidation of operations. Economies of density exist when the average cost of the airline decreases with the increase in the volume of airline operations. In the airline industry, the economies of scope achieved when adopts the hub-and-spoke network system.

Economies of scope refer to the situation where a company can reduce its unit costs by leveraging efficiencies through sharing of resources for multiple projects or production lines. To put more simply, multiple projects/processes can be more cost-efficient when they are executed together as opposed to individually. As an example, on April 30, 2012, Delta Air Lines announced that it will pay $150 million to acquire a refinery near Philadelphia. This strategic move aimed to cut jet fuel cost by $300 million a year.[14] Delta planned to reduce fuel costs by eliminating speculators and marketing by intermediaries.

The presence of economies of scope benefits a company by allowing it to house activities together and concurrently. Potential synergies achieved through economies of scope could include shared labor, pooled knowledge, and collective capital equipment. For instance, Boeing houses four production lines (747, 767, 777, and 787) at its large Everett production facility (Boeing, 2017). By operating three production lines in the same building, Boeing is able to share resources, such as labor and equipment, across all four lines to maximize resource efficiency. If all four production lines were individually located throughout the country, the company would not be cost-effective in manufacturing aircraft as resources could not be shared among all three production lines. Additionally, Boeing is able to leverage capital knowledge by reducing research and development (R&D) expenses through the utilization of technology developed in other projects. This holds significant value, especially in the development of new aircraft such as the 787-10. Airlines are able to exploit economies of scope by using the same aircraft "platform" to carry passengers on the main deck and cargo in the hold.

Economies of Density

Economies of density refer to the reduction of unit costs achieved by increasing the flow of passengers or cargo in the existing network. This entails heightened capacity utilization or allowing larger, lower unit-cost aircraft, to be used. The airline industry serves as a prime illustration of this concept as it has developed the so-called hub-and-spoke system for air travel. Carriers have found it more cost-effective to consolidate operations at a single airport rather than operate a point-to-point service. Within a hub-and-spoke network, aircraft are more likely to fly at full capacity and can often fly routes more than once a day. For example, consider five airports that could all be connected together either by using one airport as a hub (Figure 4.10) or by flying between each city (Figure 4.11). Opting for a hub-centric approach, all the airports can be connected to each other with a minimum of four flights, while the point-to-point service would require ten flights. The difference in the number of required flights translates into cost savings, as the airline can provide service to all the cities with less resources. This approach also facilitates service to smaller markets. To exemplify, there may be only a few people each day interested in flying from Daytona Beach to New Orleans, not enough to support a nonstop flight. However, passengers heading to New Orleans can fly with many others to the Atlanta hub first, and then fly on to various final destinations. Additionally, the advent of the regional jet has enabled airlines to further strengthen their hub networks by increasing flight frequency as well as connecting markets of smaller capacity that would be unprofitable with larger aircraft. Of course, flying point-to-point services offers its own merits, such as being able to offer nonstop flights for passengers. However, the hub-and-spoke network is still the dominant flying structure in the United States and will probably continue to be so for the foreseeable future.

The mathematical representation of the economies of scope and density of a hub-and-spoke network is also possible. Figure 4.10 displays a typical hub-and-spoke diagram for a network utilizing five airports, while Figure 4.11 depicts a point-to-point route network for the same

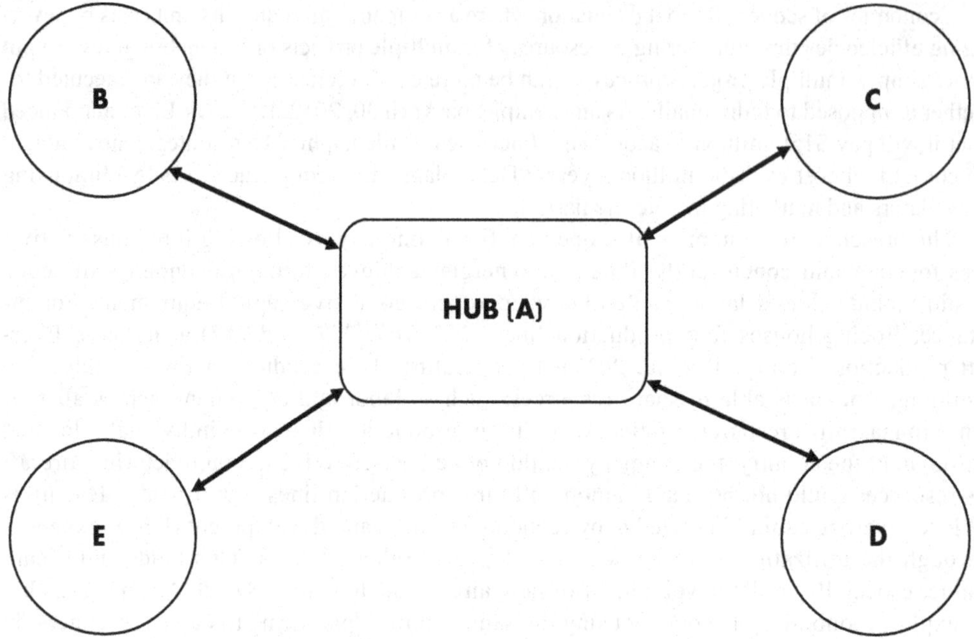

Figure 4.10 Hub-and-Spoke Route Network.

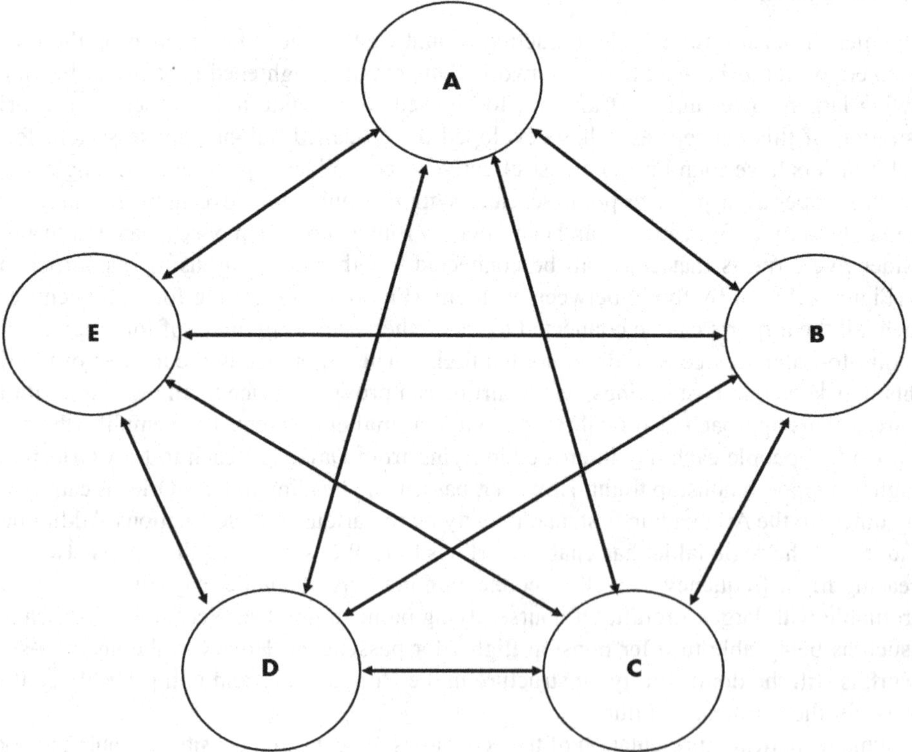

Figure 4.11 Point-to-Point Route Network.

five airports. Clearly, the hub-and-spoke network has significantly fewer flights. The number of flights in a hub-and-spoke network can be calculated by using the formula:

$$\text{Number of flights} = n - 1$$

where n is the number of airports.

Using this formula, the number of flights required to connect five airports in a hub-and-spoke network is 4 (5−1). These four flights are exhibited in Figure 4.10.

The mathematical number of flights required in a point-to-point system can be determined using the formula:

$$\text{Number of flights} = \frac{n \times (n-1)}{2}$$

Using the mentioned formula, the number of flights required in a point-to-point network for five airports is ten. Similarly, a hub-and-spoke network with ten airports requires only nine routes to connect all destinations, while a true point-to-point system would require 45 flights.

$$\text{Number of flights} = \frac{10 \times (10-1)}{2} = 45$$

This reduction in flights is the major reason why the hub-and-spoke network has been adopted by almost all carriers in the United States following deregulation. Among major US carriers, Southwest Airlines is the only operator of a point-to-point route network, yet the majority of Southwest passengers still make connections between flights. A drawback inherent in the aspect of a hub-and-spoke system is the delays at the hub, which can result in delays throughout the network. Similarly, the delays at a spoke can also affect the entire network.

Economies of density are generated because these hub-and-spoke systems, and also joint-business ventures on long-haul markets, allow airlines to concentrate passengers (and cargo) into denser flows on fewer or larger aircraft, raising utilization rates and lowering the cost per passenger carried.

Operating Leverage

> The degree of operating leverage represents the volatility of EBIT relative to a given change in sales, assuming all other variables remain constant. The higher the leverage, the more volatile and unpredictable the EBIT figure, which is relative to a given change in sales.

Operating leverage is a powerful metric that highlights the ratio between operating profit (OP) growth and sales growth. It serves to gauge the proportion of the company's costs that are fixed versus variable. More directly, the degree of operating leverage (DOL) is an elasticity of the company's overall financial health with respect to sales growth. Furthermore, operating leverage can also provide an indication of the company's cost structure, especially with respect to FCs. The general formula for the DOL is:

$$\text{DOL} = \frac{\%\Delta \text{ in EBIT}}{\%\Delta \text{ in Sales}}$$

For example, suppose the EBIT for DirectJet increases by 10% if its combined passenger and cargo sales increases by 5%. The DOL is 0.10/0.05 = 2.0.

The explicit formulae for DOL are as follows:

$$\text{DOL} = \frac{Q(P-V)}{Q(P-V)-\text{FC}}$$

$$\text{DOL} = \frac{S-\text{VC}}{S-\text{VC}-\text{FC}}$$

where

S = Initial Sales in Dollars
P = Sales Price per Unit
Q = Quantity Produced or Sold
V = Variable Cost per Unit
VC = Total Variable Costs
FC = Total Fixed Costs

Example

Assume that Company A sells 5,000 in-flight oxygen masks for $20 per unit. Total sales are $100,000. It costs $10 to manufacture one unit, and fixed costs amount to $30,000.

$$\text{DOL} = \frac{5{,}000(20-10)}{5{,}000(20-10)-30{,}000} = \frac{50{,}000}{20{,}000} = 2.5$$

or

$$\text{DOL} = \frac{100{,}000-50{,}000}{100{,}000-50{,}000-30{,}000} = \frac{50{,}000}{20{,}000} = 2.5$$

The DOL can vary considerably among companies in the same industry. Those with a high DOL are much more reactive to changes in output. This responsiveness stems in part from the company having sizeable FCs, which can either be leveraged effectively during times of increasing sales (because of decreasing average costs) or become a burden to the company when sales decrease. For a concrete numerical example, if the DOL is 2, then this implies that a 1% increase in ticket sales will result in a 2% increase in the airline's OP. In this case, there would be increasing returns to scale. Unfortunately, the reverse is also true during downswings in the economy. Using the same DOL of 2, a 1% decrease in ticket sales would result in a 2% decrease in OP. Therefore, companies with a high DOL experience greater volatility of OP than companies with smaller degrees of operating leverage.

Operating leverage can also take on a negative value, which indicates that the company is experiencing annual FCs greater than annual OPs. This signifies decreasing returns to scale and that the company may have grown too quickly and is not effectively leveraging its FCs. Therefore, to enhance its DOL, the company should reduce its FCs while keeping the same level of output or increase its output with the same FC infrastructure.

Additionally, changes to the company's contribution margin will also dramatically affect the company's DOL. An airline, for instance, may choose between a high level of fixed assets and a

Table 4.5 Effects of Operating Leverage on the Income Statement

	Competition		
	High	*Moderate*	*Low*
	Sales Decrease by 30%	*Sales Remain Unchanged*	*Sales Increase by 30%*
Net sales	$700,000	$1,000,000	$1,300,000
Less: variable costs (70% of sales)	$490,000	$700,000	$910,000
Less: fixed costs	$200,000	$200,000	$200,000
EBIT	$10,000 **EBIT decreases 90%**	$100,000	$190,000 **EBIT increases 90%**
DOL	**−3**		**3**

low level of fixed assets. For example, an airline may substitute self-service check-in machines at different airports for check-in agents. If labor is not replaced with check-in machines, FCs are held lower and VCs higher. Operating with a lower level of operating leverage, the airline shows less growth in profits as sales rise, but faces less risk of loss as sales decline.

To understand the fluctuations in Degree of Operating Leverage (DOL), with a certain percentage increase and decrease in sales, let's consider a company with normal sales of $1,000,000 and variable costs that are 70% of the sales. The ensuing Table 4.5 presents three scenarios under study competition. There exist high competition resulting in drop of sales by 30% and low competition resulting in increase in sales by 30%.

The data highlights that when the sales drop by 30%, the EBIT drops by 90%, resulting in a DOL of −3. Conversely, when the sales increase by 30%, the EBIT increases by 90%, resulting in a DOL of 3. For example, a jet engine manufacturer selling an engine for $10,000,000 per unit has a variable cost per unit of $5,000,000 and fixed operating costs of $300,000,000 per unit per year.

$$\text{DOL} = \frac{S - \text{VC}}{S - \text{VC} - \text{FC}}$$

$$\text{DOL} = \frac{10{,}000{,}000 - 5{,}000{,}000}{10{,}000{,}000 - 5{,}000{,}000 - 3{,}000{,}000}$$

$$\text{DOL} = 2.5$$

This overall understanding of a firm's cost structure is critical in the strategic planning phase of a company. It provides a comparison for the company between sales and OP, and based on the outcome, can help guide strategic direction. It should be noted that operating leverage should not be confused with financial leverage, which deals with how much debt a company is using to finance its activities.

Airline Industry Cost Structure

Given the distinctiveness of each airline's operation is unique, it can be challenging to compare operating costs from airline to airline. Costs are largely dependent on the aircraft size, aircraft type, and the length of a flight. For example, the operating costs of turboprops are much lower than those for regional jets, especially on short-haul routes. The major cost drivers for the world's airlines are fuel, flight equipment, and cost of aircraft and personnel. Airline costs are often divided into three categories to allow comparison between airlines: direct operating costs, indirect operating costs, and overhead costs.

Direct Operating Costs (DOC)

The most common metric used to standardize airline costs is cost per available seat mile (CASM). An available seat mile (ASM) is one aircraft seat flown 1 mile, regardless of whether or not it is carrying a revenue passenger. Costs per ASM, or CASMs, are the costs of flying one aircraft seat for 1 mile. Direct operating costs are those that are directly linked to the airline's operations and are incurred each time the aircraft is flying. The major categories of DOCs are listed below, and they will be discussed in more detail in the following paragraphs.

Example

DirectJet flies a 100-seater turbo-prop aircraft on short-haul flight of 250 mile. There are 80 passengers on board, and hence:

$$\text{ASM} = \text{Seats} \times \text{Miles flown}$$
$$\text{ASM} = 100 \times 250 = 25{,}000$$
$$\text{RPM} = 80 \times 250 = 20{,}000$$

$$\text{LF} = \frac{\text{RPM}}{\text{ASM}} = \frac{20{,}000}{25{,}000} = 80\%$$

- Fuel costs
- Flight deck and cabin crew expenses
- Direct maintenance expenditures
- Other operating costs, including landing fees and capital equipment charges
- En route (Air Traffic Control expenses)
- Aircraft rentals

Fuel Costs

Fuel makes up a significant portion of an airline's total costs, and the fuel efficiency plays a substantial role in airline profitability. When fuel prices remain high, you can expect ticket prices to increase and profitability to decline. The price of fuel is determined by global supply and demand for oil. A sharp rise in the price of fuel is threatening the airline industry's slow recovery from the coronavirus crisis. To reduce fuel costs, airlines must implement effective fuel conservation strategies. The general formula for calculating airline fuel costs is:

$$\text{Fuel costs} = \text{ASM} \times \frac{\text{Fuel price per gallon}}{\dfrac{\text{ASM/block hour}}{\text{Gallons/block hour}}}$$

An airline's fuel cost per ASM is a result of two factors: the price of fuel and fuel efficiency. While the price of fuel is generally beyond the airline's control, airlines can lessen the impact of this cost by using more complex financial or "hedging" strategies, such as purchasing options for the price of oil. By purchasing aviation fuel at the market-bearing rate and offsetting this

Table 4.6 Airline CASM Breakdown, 2021

	AA	*AS*	*B6*	*NK*	*DL*	*UA*	*HA*	*WN*	*BA*	*RYR*
Fuel cost per ASM	3.17	2.44	2.65	2.24	2.90	3.22	1.40	2.51	3.31	1.77
Maintenance cost per ASM	0.92	0.69	1.15	0.39	0.72	0.74	0.34	0.65	1.33	0.00
Salaries and related expenses per ASM	5.51	4.23	4.36	2.61	5.00	5.35	0.48	5.87	5.23	0.01
Other operating costs per ASM	1.86	0.97	2.00	1.30	0.72	2.48	0.06	1.81	1.73	1.98
Total operating costs per ASM	**11.46**	**8.33**	**10.16**	**6.55**	**9.34**	**11.79**	**2.28**	**10.84**	**11.59**	**3.76**
Non-operating costs per ASM	0.69	(0.11)	0.24	1.14	0.77	0.86	0.27	0.97	1.18	1.25
Total costs per ASM	**12.15**	**8.22**	**10.40**	**7.69**	**10.11**	**12.65**	**2.55**	**11.81**	**12.77**	**8.77**

Data Source: Collected by the authors from SEC fillings form 10-k & Financial Reports of Airlines.

with investment gains from oil options, the costs of increases in the price of fuel are lessened. However, these gains are recorded as investment gains in the airline's consolidated financial statements and not as fuel cost benefits.

Airlines can also influence their fuel costs by being more fuel efficient. The simplest way to execute this is to operate new fuel-efficient aircraft in place of older, less fuel-efficient aircraft (as pointed out in the introduction to the chapter). While the capital expenditures required to purchase new aircraft are considerable, they may be outweighed by the fuel costs associated with operating older aircraft. Among the airlines listed in Table 4.6, Alaska has the highest fuel cost per ASM at 3.55 cents. On the other hand, Southwest and Hawaiian operate mostly newer generation aircraft that are more fuel efficient.

Various other fuel efficiency methods center around technological advances, for example, the installation of blended winglets. Aviation Partners Boeing (2017), the joint-venture company that manufacturers blended winglets, estimates that the winglets lower fuel burn by 3.5%–4.0% on flights greater than 1,000 nautical miles for Boeing 737NGs. The winglet technology does not provide substantial savings on short flights as the fuel-burn advantage is offset by the increased weight. Originally introduced for the 737NG aircraft, the success of winglets has led to their installation on a number of different aircraft types.[15] Airbus's A320neo aircraft comes standard with 2.4 m tall winglets called "sharklets" which can cut fuel burn up to 4% by reducing aerodynamic drag. Moreover, when equipped with a New Engine Option, the manufacturer claims the NEO can save up to 20% in fuel burn per seat (Airbus, 2017). According to Boeing, the B737 MAX demonstrates remarkable fuel efficiency, enabling airlines that operate the type to keep their unit costs low. Boeing has estimated that the B737 MAX 8 reduces fuel consumption and CO_2 emissions by 14% compared to the newest B737NG, and it requires 8% less fuel per seat than the A320neo.

While the aforementioned methods usually require substantial capital investments to reduce fuel costs, more subtle fuel management strategies by airlines can also increase fuel efficiency. One common strategy is to use only one engine during normal taxiing procedures, thereby reducing the fuel costs associated with operating an engine during taxi. The more congested the airport is, the greater the amount of taxiing, and the greater amount of savings such a program can provide the airline. Additionally, the airline can selectively shut down an engine(s) during ground delays when the aircraft is sitting idle.

Flight planning also plays a significant role in fuel efficiency, as optimized flight planning can ensure minimum fuel-burn routes and altitudes. This also involves measuring on-board weight more accurately in order to avoid carrying extra fuel. At airports, airlines can strategically impose voluntary ground delays to reduce airborne holding or redesign hubs and schedules to reduce congestion.

Altering the location where fuel is purchased is a further strategy, allowing airlines to take advantage of lower fuel prices in certain regions. Employing this strategy involves a cost-benefit analysis, as the fuel cost savings from lower prices need to be compared with the additional fuel burn generated from the additional weight involved in "tankering" the extra fuel to reach the desired region. Carriers can also pool resources when purchasing fuel in order to achieve bulk discounts. However, it is noteworthy that in some jurisdictions, competition law can prevent such collaboration. This is a strategy that nine African airlines launched in 2012 (AFRAA, 2012).

All these factors have the potential and indeed contribute to airlines being more fuel efficient. Figure 4.12 provides a comparison of fuel efficiency for major US airlines in 2015, in terms of domestic ASMs per gallon. In Figure 4.12, the metric is ASMs per gallons of fuel used; therefore, a higher value is more desirable since airlines want more ASMs to be flown with one gallon of fuel.

The stage length of a flight is important since longer flights burn less fuel per ASM (Figure 4.13). The reason can be attributed to the fact that the takeoff and landing phases of flight consume the most fuel per ASM. Therefore, the longer the flight, there are more fuel-efficient ASMs that help mitigate the impact of less efficient takeoff and landing phase. This correlation between fuel efficiency and average stage length is depicted in Figure 4.14.[16] An anomaly to this correlation was Southwest Airlines and Hawaiian Airlines, both of which exhibited relatively high fuel efficiency despite having the lowest average stage length of all the airlines. Southwest Airlines has managed to overcome its short stage length with operating procedures that conserve fuel; these include using only one engine when taxiing and opting to fly out of less congested airports.

Additionally, from Figure 4.14, it can be noted that JetBlue, Delta, and American, with longer average stage lengths, actually have lower fuel efficiencies. In the case of Delta and American, lower fuel efficiency can be attributed to the high average age of their fleet.

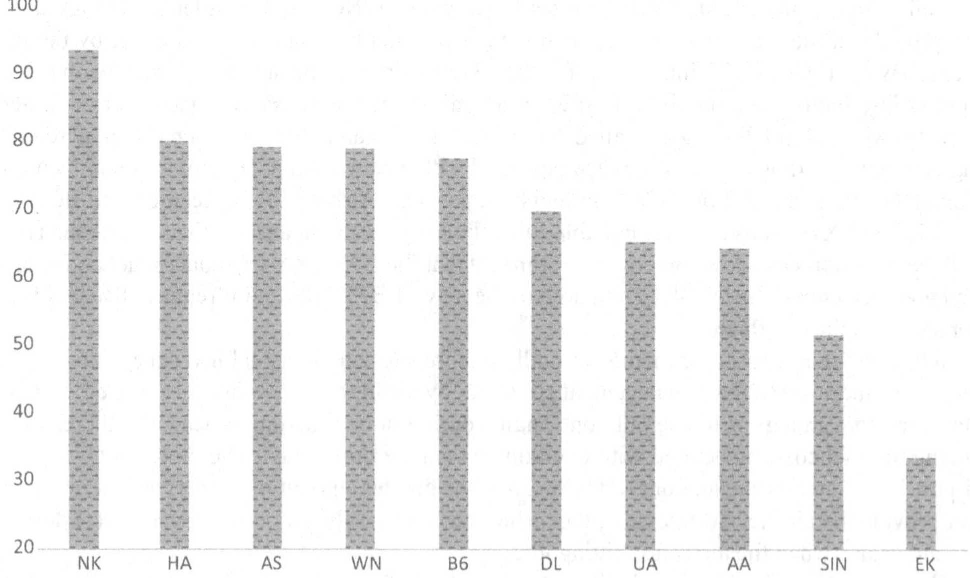

Figure 4.12 US Airlines Fuel Efficiency (ASM per Gallon per Seat), 2022.

Source: Compiled by the authors from OAG Form 41 data

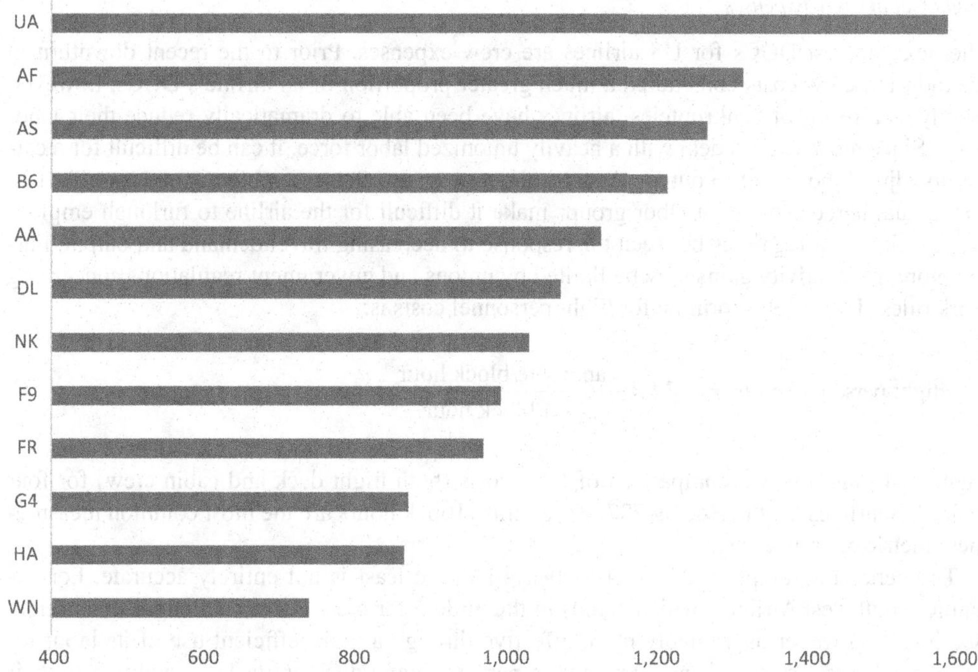

Figure 4.13 US Airlines Average Stage Length, 2022.

Source: Compiled by the authors from US DOT Form 41 data via BTS

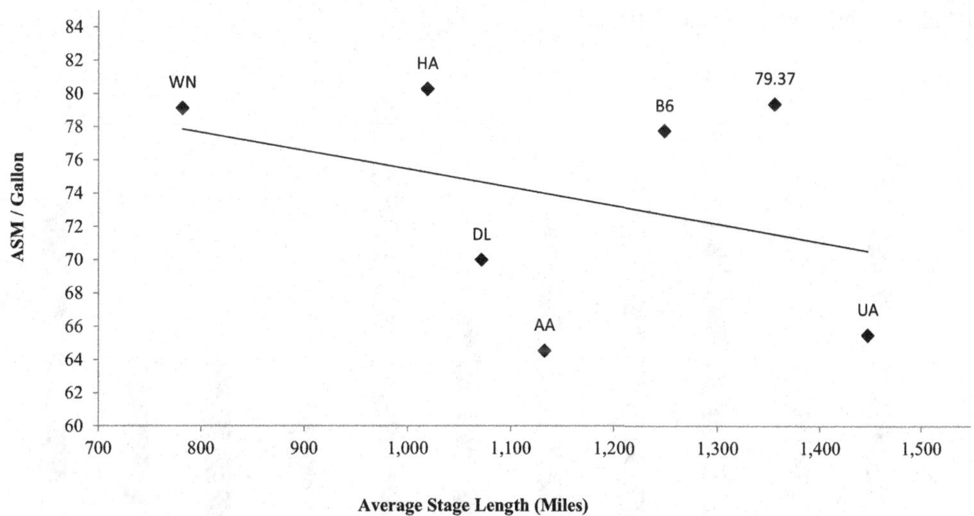

Figure 4.14 Correlation between Fuel Efficiency and Average Stage Length.

Source: Compiled by the authors from DOT Form 41 data via Diio

Flight/Cabin Crew Expenses

The next greatest DOCs for US airlines are crew expenses. Prior to the recent downturn in the industry, crew costs constituted a much greater proportion of an airline's DOCs; however, mainly as a result of bankruptcies, airlines have been able to dramatically reduce their labor costs. Since most airlines deal with a heavily unionized labor force, it can be difficult for a carrier to adjust labor input to output. As a result, crew costs often resemble mixed costs. That is, contractual agreements with labor groups make it difficult for the airline to furlough employees, causing long lag times between the response to decreasing travel demand and output. Furthermore, productivity gains may be limited by unions and government regulations concerning work rules. The general formula for flight personnel costs is:

$$\text{Flight personnel costs} = \text{ASM} \times \frac{\text{Labor rate/block hour}}{\text{ASM/block hour}}$$

Figure 4.15 highlights a comparison of crew costs (both flight deck and cabin crew) for four major US airlines for the Boeing 737-700 aircraft. Block hours are the most common measurement metric of crew costs.

The general assumption that LCCs always pay the least is not entirely accurate. For example, Southwest Airlines, which stands in the middle for crew costs, challenges this notion. Southwest, however, is arguably more effective through a more efficient use of its labor resources. That is, employees are expected to perform many different tasks in addition to their primary duties. These productivity gains help Southwest offset its higher pay rate. Alaska Airlines reaps the benefits from being a relatively young company; therefore, they have a relatively younger workforce with a lower pay rate. In contrast, airlines like United and Delta have been around long enough that many crewmembers are quite senior and command higher wages than junior employees. This factor is enhanced when pension and Medicare issues are included in the crew cost calculations.

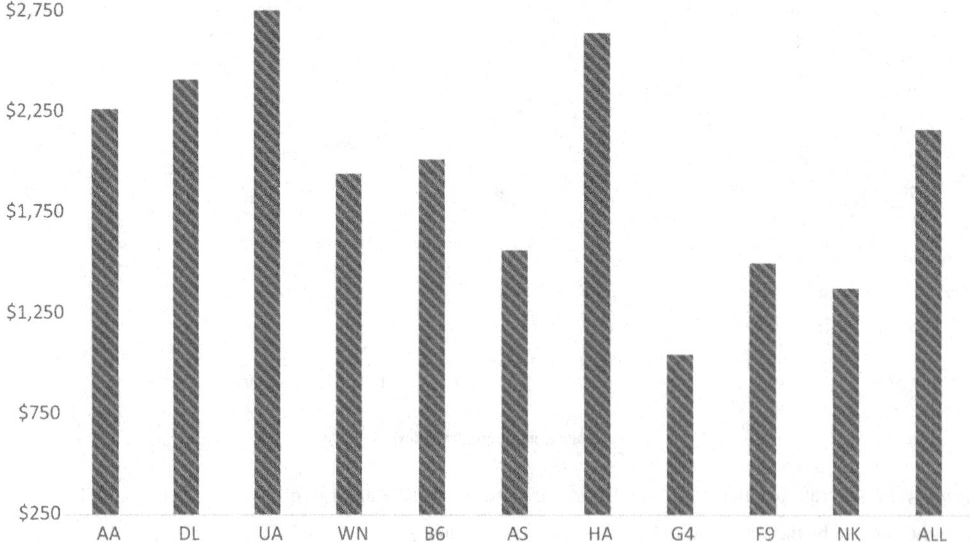

Figure 4.15 Crew Costs per Block Hour, 2022.

Source: Compiled by the authors from Airline Monitor data

Maintenance Costs

> Airline maintenance costs are a significant aspect of the airline industry's operational expenses. These costs encompass all the activities, materials, and personnel required to ensure that aircraft are safe, reliable, and compliant with aviation regulations. Malaysia Airlines placed 25 firm orders and 25 purchase rights for the upgraded version of the Boeing 737 with deliveries commencing in 2019 as it sought to replace some of its aging fleet... the new planes will cut aircraft maintenance costs by 40 percent and fuel costs by 15 percent.[17]

Aircraft undergo regular checks and maintenance as part of daily operations. On top of this, there is a system of heavier A, B, C, and D checks.

- The A check is performed approximately every 400–600 flight hours, or every 200–300 flights, depending on aircraft type.
- The B check is performed approximately every 6–8 months. It is usually completed within 1–3 days at an airport hangar and takes about 160–180 man-hours.
- The C check is performed approximately every 20–24 months, and it is usually requiring about 6,000 man-hours.
- The D check, sometimes known as a heavy maintenance visit (HMV), requires up to 50,000 man-hours.

Preventive maintenance is crucial for keeping aircraft operational. Effective aircraft maintenance management is not just to fix broken aircraft, but also to keep the aircraft flying at the lowest possible cost and at the highest possible quality. Maintenance costs change according to the aircraft type, age, and the size of airline. Modern aircraft have relatively lower fuel burn and lower maintenance costs. Moreover, for smaller airlines, outsourcing maintenance can result in major savings and profitability. Achieving reductions in maintenance costs and fuel burn per seat will result in an overall cost reduction and higher profitability. However, since safety is the number one priority for every airline, maintenance costs are usually not under as much cost-saving scrutiny. The three major components of maintenance costs are:[18]

> Available seat mile (ASM) refers to how many seat miles are available for passengers on a given airline. ASMs are calculated by multiplying the number of seats for a given flight by the number of miles that plane will be flying.
>
> ASM = Number of aircraft seats × Number of miles flown

1 Scheduled maintenance inspections
   a Labor
   b Parts; Airframe/Engine/Avionics
2 Unscheduled maintenance
   a Labor
   b Parts; Airframe/Engine/Avionics
3 Repair of any problems found during scheduled inspections

Nevertheless, airlines must still cost-effectively manage their maintenance operations and staffing levels, while also being safety conscious. In order to accomplish this balance, a major innovation in the maintenance area has been the outsourcing of maintenance activities to third-party vendors, especially for aircraft heavy checks. Maintenance costs can be calculated as:

$$\text{Maintenance costs} = \text{ASM} \times \frac{\text{Maintenance labor and materials/block hour}}{\text{ASM/block hour}}$$

Each airline is unique in the amount of outsourcing that they do. For instance, American Airlines does the majority of its maintenance internally and also does contract maintenance work for other airlines. In contrast, United Airlines does all its wide-body heavy maintenance externally while also having internalized some maintenance operations with the opening of a 757 heavy check line. On the other end of the spectrum, JetBlue externally sources almost all its heavy maintenance and just performs line maintenance internally.

Figure 4.16 displays the maintenance costs for US airlines, including outside labor costs; these costs are standardized per flight hour since flight hours are the primary driver of an aircraft's maintenance cycle. According to the data presented in Figure 4.16, Hawaiian had the highest maintenance costs. At the low end were Southwest, JetBlue, Alaska, and Virgin America. A potential explanation for the great differences in maintenance costs is that the LCC fleets are relatively new. Airlines receive a maintenance honeymoon on new aircraft since their costly heavy checks are delayed for a few years. In contrast, older aircraft have more frequent and costlier heavy checks. Therefore, there is some relation between the airline's average aircraft age and maintenance costs.

Maintenance costs are also influenced by another key factor—maintenance checks. These are more expensive for larger aircraft than for smaller aircraft, thereby benefiting carriers like

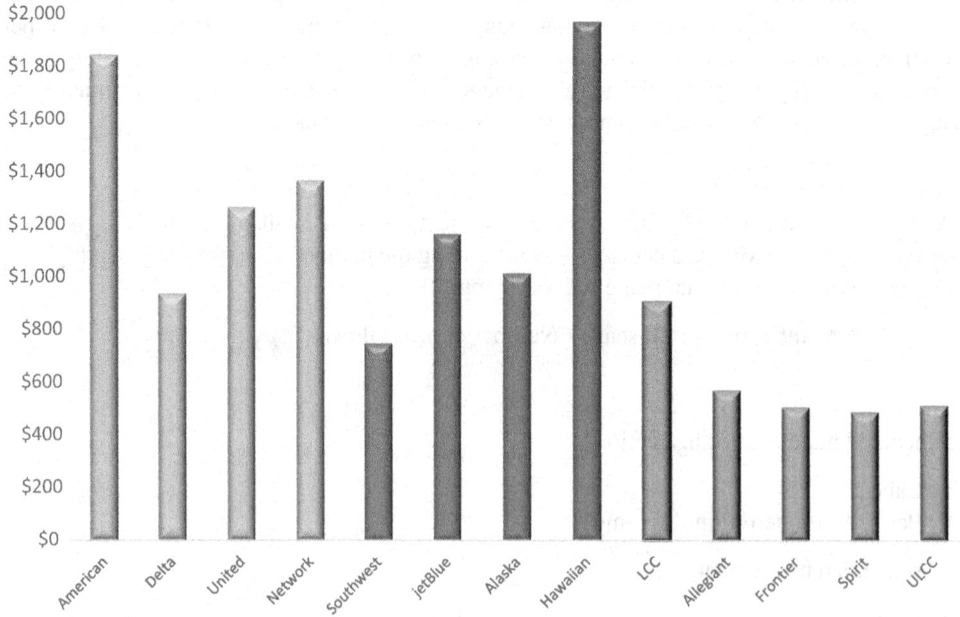

Figure 4.16 US Airline Maintenance Costs per Flight Hour.

Source: Compiled by the authors from US DOT Form 41 data via Diio

Southwest, that only operate narrow-body jets. Finally, the concept of aircraft commonality plays an important role in the maintenance costs for airlines. Airlines with diverse aircraft fleets typically must have spare parts on hand for each aircraft type, thereby requiring a large inventory of parts. One strategy to mitigate this problem is to segment aircraft markets. This is the primary reason why American Airlines decided to operate only certain aircraft types out of certain hubs. For example, MD-80s do not operate out of the Miami hub, 737s do not operate out of Chicago, and the A300s do not fly to either Dallas or Chicago. By employing this rationalized approach, American Airlines need not maintain a spare parts inventory for every aircraft type at every major hub.

Other Operating Costs

Cost per available seat mile (CASM) is a common unit of measurement for the airline industry to calculate and measure the efficiency of various airlines. CASM is calculated as:

CASM = (Total Cost)/ASM

The final category of operating costs includes a variety of aspects, such as airport-related expenditures (i.e., landing fees, gate agents, and baggage handlers) and in-flight catering costs. These areas have seen dramatic reductions, particularly in catering where it is common to make the first cuts. At present, majority of airlines now use third parties to supply their airport and catering services. Table 4.6 presents the CASM breakdown for selected US airlines.

CASMs can be established for a variety of costs, such as operating costs, total operating costs, or simply crew costs. Table 4.6 provides a breakdown of various CASMs for eight major US airlines in 2015, with the TC per ASM representing the direct operating costs (DOC) of fuel, labor, maintenance, and other operating and non-operating costs (typically called overhead costs). Among these, the four DOCs can be considered VCs, while the non-operating costs can be considered FCs. Figure 4.17 displays this information graphically.

For most airlines, salaries and related expenses comprise the major share of total operating costs. In many cases, the other operating costs form close to 50% of the airline's TCs. Acquisitions such as aircraft and investment in airport infrastructure are large capital expenditures; these in turn create an industry with high barriers to entry. However, in recent times, these capital requirements have been lowered with attractive aircraft leasing options, thereby enabling easier entry into the market.

Figure 4.18 provides a time series of per-minute cost of delay for US airlines from 2000 to 2021. Fuel cost appears to be the biggest contributor to per-minute cost of delay, which dropped in 2015 due to the lower oil prices.

Indirect Operating Costs (IOC)

The distinction between direct and indirect operating costs (IOCs) derives from the fact that some costs might change directly with the level of operation, while other costs may not. IOCs are those costs that an airline incurs whether the aircraft flies or not. Numerous instances of indirect costs prevalent in both small and large airlines can be identified. These costs can be grouped as follows:

- Depreciation and maintenance
- Distribution cost (sales and promotion)

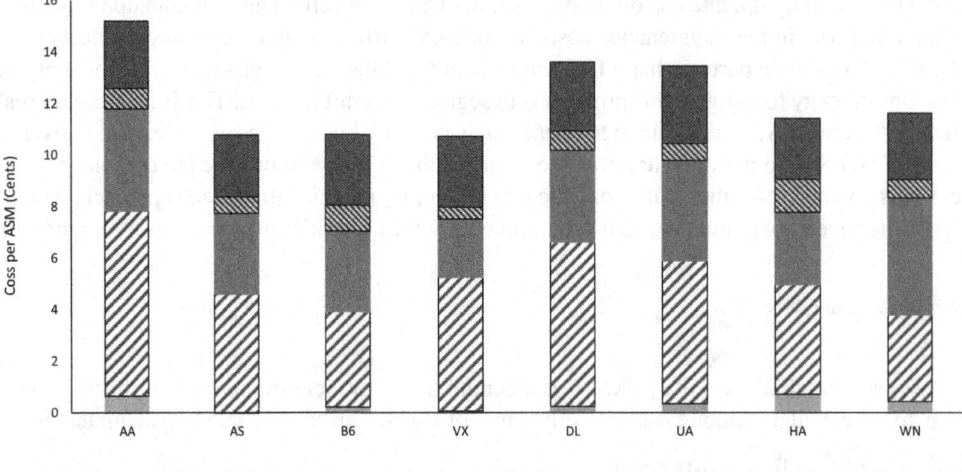

Figure 4.17 US Airlines Cost per Available Seat Mile Breakdown, 2022.

Source: Compiled by the authors from OAG Form 41 data

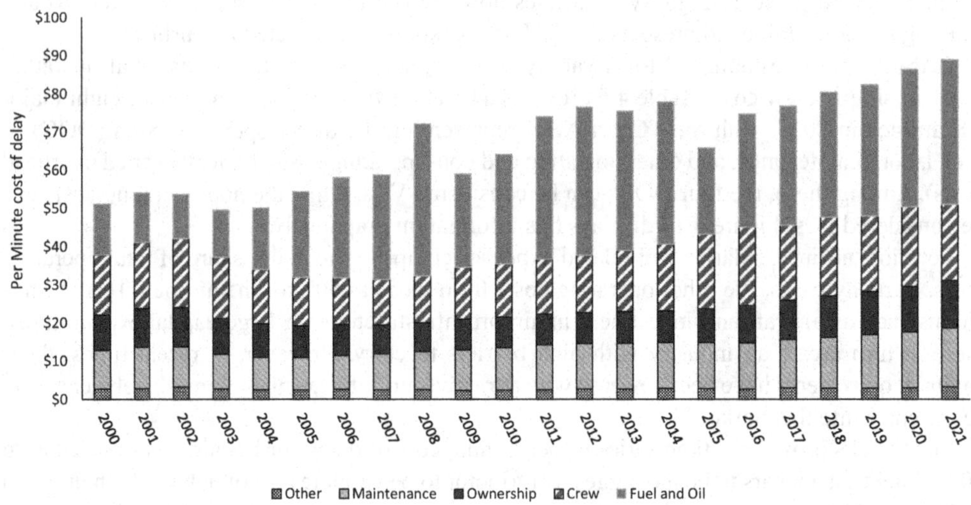

Figure 4.18 US Airlines Per-Minute Cost of Delay.

Source: Compiled by the authors from OAG Form 41 data, 2022

- General overhead and administrative expenses
- Ground expenses
- Passenger services
- Station cost

Non-Operating Costs (NOC)

A non-operating cost is an expenditure incurred by an airline that is not related to its core operations. Many airlines finance their capital expenditures with a combination of debt and equity. Interest payments are non-operating expenses because they do not arise during an airline's core operations. The most common types of non-operating expenses relate to:

- Depreciation
- Interest
- Insurance
- Losses from the retirement of property
- Losses from affiliated companies
- Other loss items, including those from foreign exchange transactions and sales of shares

Airline Economies of Scale, Scope, and Density

The airline industry is affected by the economies of scale, scope, and density as discussed earlier in the chapter. Economies of scale play a significant role in the industry due to considerable magnitude of FCs as we have observed. These high FCs and marketing requirements encourage expansion in the industry. This is a major reason why there are very few small airlines in the industry and why there is continual consolidation.

Economies of Scale (EOS)

Economy of scale is a fundamental concept in economics that relates a decrease in cost with an increase in production, and they are generally achieved through operational efficiencies. Economies of scope granted Boeing an advantage over Douglas and Lockheed, enabling the company to be the first success in the jet age as it could focus its developmental resources on incorporating jet technology rather than trying to figure out how to design a large aircraft. The same goes for airline manufacturers. Production for an airplane is divided among groups of specialists handling different parts of the process. This eliminates unnecessary training costs and results in a quicker, more efficient output.

> Economies of scale refer to the situation where the average costs per unit of output decrease with the increase in the level of production, whereas diseconomies of scale refer to the opposite.

From an operational standpoint, economies of scale also play a significant role. Due to pilot training and maintenance spare parts for aircraft, it is less costly to simplify aircraft fleets and to focus on just a few aircraft types. Airlines can often also negotiate cheaper aircraft prices by purchasing more of a single type, and underlying this are the economies of scale for aircraft manufacturers. Therefore, airlines generally prefer to operate a minimum number of aircraft type. The optimum number of aircraft required to achieve economies of scale is unknown, but JetBlue believes that it achieved all economies of scale from its 130-strong Airbus 320 fleet. The airline decided to order a fleet of 100 Embraer 190 aircraft in 2006, and it also took delivery of

A321s starting in 2016 (JetBlue, 2017). As of September 3, 2022, the airline possesses a fleet of 30 E190s and plans to fly them beyond 2026, with no firm retirement date as of now.[19] While the airline has decided to use more than one aircraft, it believes that its fleet is sufficient to maximize economies of scale.

In the realm of network carriers, the cost of adding one more flight to the network is relatively low, while the financial benefits are much higher. Within the airline industry, economies of scale are claimed as a justification for mergers and acquisitions among major airlines. The merger between United and Continental Airlines was expected to bring cost savings while at the same time increasing revenues by providing more routes and more effective competition against rivals. Joint operations have the potential to provide considerable cost savings. Economies of scale have the potential to provide larger airlines with a cost advantage over smaller airlines. After the Delta–Northwest merger in 2008, the accounting, revenue management, and other administrative departments of one airline are now smaller than the sum of each when they were under two separate airlines. This was also the case for the American Airlines–US Airways partnership and is expected of the current merger between Alaska and Virgin American.

Hub airports wield a substantial impact on the significance of economies of scale, in addition to the economies of density mentioned earlier. Hubs are extremely costly operations, and the costs that they generate, such as multiple labor shifts, terminal leases, and ground equipment, are FCs in the short term. Therefore, in order to spread the costs over more units of output (air seat miles), airlines have a strong incentive to use these assets as intensively as possible. While the majority of airlines operate banked hubs to provide shorter connection times for their passengers, airlines such as American and Delta have experimented with rolling hubs in order to better utilize hub assets. With banked hubs, assets sometimes remain unused for extended periods of time between banking periods. In contrast, the concept of rolling hubs uses hub assets throughout the day, making the airline's use of assets more efficient and thereby achieving greater economies of scale. In operations, economies of scale can be achieved by:

- Higher efficiency through labor specialization
- Less manufacturing startup cost
- Learning rate
- Quantity discounts
- Spreading FCs over more output units

Economies of Scope

Economies of scope play an important role in the aviation industry, referring to the practice of reducing the average cost of resources by spreading the use of productive resources over two or more different products. As mentioned earlier, aircraft manufacturers capitalize on economies of scope when producing aircraft. For example, economies of scope exist when the Boeing company decides to use its current equipment, facilities, technology, and labor to produce different classes of aircraft (i.e., B787, B777, B747, and B737) rather than just producing one type. Economies of scope rely on better utilization of the firm's limited productive resources.

Airlines achieve economies of scope by providing various ancillary products and services, such as cargo, maintenance activities, catering, and ground handling. Ultimately, the amount of outsourcing an airline depends on how many synergies exist between the organizations that are creating economies of scope. For example, FFPs are usually more effectively run by the airline itself, as an FFP's main cost is maintaining an inventory of reward seats. Economies of scope are achieved when this task is handled internally (because the airline already has a staff to schedule seats). An example is Air Canada's Aeroplan, which reversed this trend when it became its own publically traded loyalty program in 2005.[20] Airlines have also experimented with economies of scope by being directly involved in other related industries, such as cruise lines and hotels.

Airlines can achieve economies of density by establishing airport hubs, which the airports serve as transfer points for connecting flights. By concentrating their operations at a hub airport, airlines can reduce their costs by sharing facilities and services, such as gates, push trucks, and ground-handling services.

Another example of economies of scope can be observed in the case of Aer Lingus, which, in 1970, began to seek new sources of revenue by offering engineer training, maintenance services, computer consulting, and data-processing services to other airlines (Rivkin, 2005). Airlines around the world depend on ancillary revenue and are charging for services that were once included in the ticket price. Traditionally, airlines have earned ancillary revenue from catering, co-branded credit cards, duty-free shopping, ground handling, maintenance, and other activities. To increase on-board revenue, Ryan Air offers the cabin crew 10% commission on all on-board sales. Likewise, most major US carriers now charge for checked luggage and have adopted higher fees for overweight bags.

Economies of Density and Hub-and-Scope Network

Economies of density exist in the airline industry through the use of bigger aircraft or operating through a hub-and-spoke network. It has been argued that major airlines have an inherent cost advantage over smaller regional airlines due to economies of density. Moreover, aircraft size exhibits both economies of scale and density. Economies of scale become evident when airlines can place more seats into the aircraft to reduce unit costs. However, economies of density are also achieved by using larger aircraft. For example, suppose an airline could use a 100-seat aircraft or two 50-seat aircraft to service a route. On shorter domestic routes, a carrier may opt for a higher frequency of flights, while on longer domestic or international route, the airline will usually select the larger aircraft in order to capture the economies of density (the extra costs of pilots, gate agents, landing fees, baggage handling for the high-frequency decision). While airlines typically have moved toward smaller aircraft to provide increased frequency on a given route, if the aircraft depart in close proximity, a single larger aircraft will always be cheaper to operate than the two smaller ones. This is due to the various FCs required to operate a flight (pilots, gate agents, landing fees, baggage handling). This advantageous tradeoff is another example of economies of density and is common in the airline industry, especially on very long-range flights, where (due to time zones) most flights depart at around the same time.

Airline Breakeven Analysis

Understanding breakeven analysis is essential for an *y* type of financial planning. The breakeven point is the number of units or revenue required in order for the firm's costs to be recovered.

Operating at the breaking-even point means that an airline is not losing any money, but with the same token is not making any money.

Profit = total revenue − total cost

At Breakeven point:

Revenue = fixed costs + variable costs

P- = Contribution margin

$P \times Q = \text{FC} + \text{VC} \times Q$

$\text{FC} = (P - \text{VC}) \times Q$

$$Q_{B-E} = \frac{\text{FC}}{P - \text{VC}}$$

As the equation shows that the breakeven quantity, $Q_{B\text{-}E}$, depends directly on FC, and inversely, on the per-unit VC and per-unit revenue over the whole business. In manufacturing, the break-even point is represented in product units. For example, the breakeven forecast for the Airbus A380 program was 420 aircraft.[21] Thus, Airbus was required to sell 420 aircraft just to recoup the FCs related directly to the product. Assuming that the average list price of an A350 is about US $350 million, its VC of each aircraft produced is $314 million, and the total development cost is about $15 billion. Then we can calculate $Q_{B\text{-}E}$.

We can now calculate the breakeven level ($Q_{B\text{-}E}$) of sales for the Airbus Co (Figure 4.19) by applying the following breakeven formula:

$$Q_{B-E} = \frac{\text{Fixed costs}}{(Price - Variable\ costs)}$$

In the previous equation, the difference between the price and VCs of a good is called the contribution margin:

$$Q_{B-E} = \frac{\text{FC}}{P - V}$$

$$Q_{B-E} = \frac{\text{FC}}{\text{Contribution margin}}$$

$$Q_{B-E} = \frac{\$15{,}000}{\$350 - \$314}$$

$$Q_{B-E} = \frac{\text{FC}}{P - V}$$

$$Q_{B-E} = \frac{\text{FC}}{\text{Contribution margin}}$$

$$Q_{B-E} = \frac{\$15{,}000}{\$350 - \$314}$$

$$Q_{B-E} = 416 \text{ Aircraft}$$

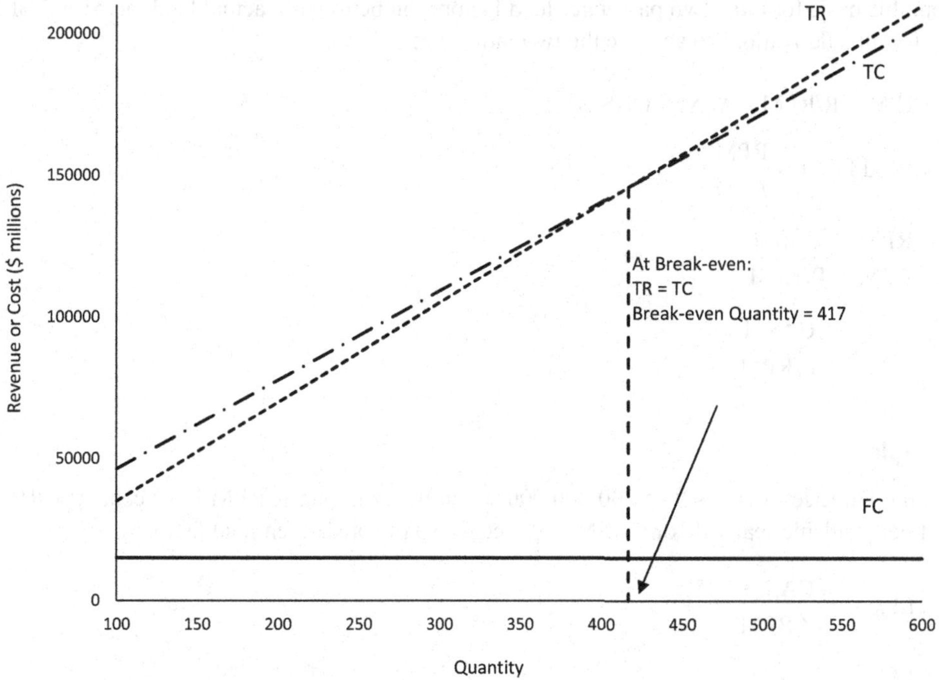

Figure 4.19 Breakeven Point (BEP).

In the airline industry, the concept of breakeven is usually expressed as a percentage of total ASMs. This yields the breakeven load factor (BLF), or a load factor which the airline must meet to recover all FCs. BLF is the percentage of seats that must be sold on an average flight at current average fares for the airline's passenger revenue to break even with the airline's operating expenses. The general formula for airline breakeven is the following:

$$\text{Profit} = \text{OP} - \text{OC}$$

$$\text{OP} = \text{RPM} \times \text{RRPM}$$

$$\text{OC} = \text{ASM} \times \text{CASM}$$

$$\text{Profit} = \text{O}$$

$$\text{RPM} \times \text{RRPM} - \text{ASM} \times \text{CASM} = 0$$

where:

RPM = Revenue Passenger Miles

R/RPM = Revenue per Revenue Passenger Mile

ASM = Available Seat Miles

CASM = Cost per Available Seat Mile

OP = Operating Profit

OC = Operating Costs

From this basic formula, two passenger load factors can be found—actual load factor and BLF. The formula derivations to achieve the two ratios are:

$$\text{RPM} \times \text{R/RPM} = \text{ASM} \times \text{CASM}$$

$$\text{Load factor} = \frac{\text{RPM}}{\text{ASM}}$$

$$\frac{\text{RPM}}{\text{ASM}} = \frac{\text{CASM}}{\text{R/RPM}}$$

$$\text{LF}_{B-E} = \frac{\text{CASM}}{\text{R/RPM}}$$

Example

Assume DirectJet Airlines flies 200,000,000 seat miles per year. R/RPM is 10 cents per RPM. Cost per available seat mile or CASM is 7.5 cents, so the breakeven load factor is:

$$\text{LF}_{B-E} = \frac{\text{CASM}}{\text{R/RPM}} = \frac{7.5}{10}$$

$$\text{LF}_{B-E} = 75\%$$

Obviously, if the actual load factor is greater than the BLF, the airline is generating adequate revenue to cover FCs. However, if the actual load factor is less than the BLF, then the airline is operating at a loss. Figure 4.20 shows the actual load factor and the BLF for eight major US airlines in 2022.

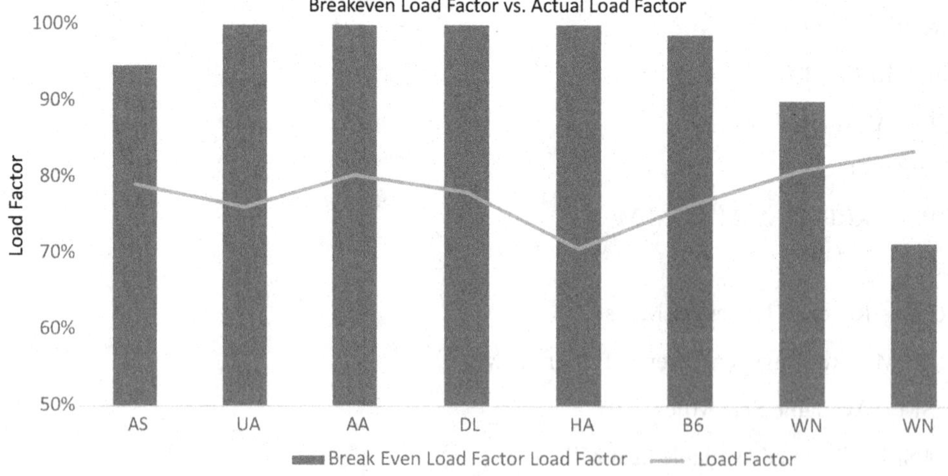

Figure 4.20 Comparison of Actual and Breakeven Load Factors for US Airlines, 2022.

Source: Compiled by the authors from OAG Form 41 data

Table 4.7 US Airline Operating Leverage, 2022

	AA	*AS*	*B6*	*DL*	*UA*	*HA*	*WN*
Operating revenues ($ millions)	29,882	6,176	6,037	29,899	24,634	1,371	15,790
Operating expenses ($ millions)	30,941	5,491	6,117	28,013	25,656	1,679	14,069
Contractual obligations ($ millions)[a]	43,634	3,720	4,447	32,897	36,364	2,331	11,828
Passengers (millions)	165	46	30	103	104	11	123
Degree of operating leverage	**0.024**	**−0.226**	**0.018**	**−0.061**	**0.027**	**0.117**	**−0.170**

Source: Compiled by the authors using SEC 10K filings.
[a]Current Maturities of Long-Term Debt and Capital Leases.

Airline Operating Leverage

As has been explained, operating leverage is the ratio between OP growth and sales growth. The DOL figures for various US airlines in 2021 are represented in Table 4.7. The contribution margin was found using operating revenues and expenses, while FCs were assumed to be contractual obligations for the airline in the next year. These contractual obligations include firm aircraft purchases, regional capacity purchase agreements, and long-term debt. A breakdown of these contractual obligations is a mandatory requirement in SEC 10K forms. Finally, the number of enplaned passenger serves as a reference for the scope of the airline's operation.

As demonstrated in Table 4.7, the DOL for US airlines does vary considerably among carriers. A positive DOL indicates that carriers' profits will increase at a greater rate than an increase in sales. Using American Airlines (AA) as an example, a DOL of 0.0241 means that for every 1% increase/decrease in sales, the airlines OPs will increase/decrease by 0.024%. An airline exhibiting an operating leverage value between 0 and 1 is an anomaly to the DOL equation because it can only exist when the firm is experiencing an operating loss, which suggests that it would be better off by selling fewer tickets (or ceasing operation). As mentioned earlier, a negative DOL indicates that a carrier would be experiencing an OP, but would also have incurred annual FCs that are greater than the OP, consequently incurring an annual net loss. This problem should be addressed by reducing FCs or increasing sales.

Summary

Accurate cost estimation is essential for project success, and cost estimation is intertwining both science and art. Cost efficiency remains a perennial challenge to the air transport industry, compelling businesses across the globe to reduce their costs for a return to profitability. The historical rise in fuel costs has spurred investment in new fuel-efficient aircraft. As a result, to curb fuel costs, airlines are placing orders for more cost-efficient aircraft like the Airbus A320neo, Boeing 737 MAX, and the Bombardier C-Series and also retiring older, more expensive airframes. This chapter delved into a range of cost classifications, all suited for different purposes, and this chapter discussed the following categorizations: Total Cost, Fixed Cost, Total Variable Cost, Marginal Cost, Average Total Cost, Average Fixed Cost, and Average Variable Cost. Marginal cost is the cost of producing additional unit of a product.

In economics, a variable cost is a corporate expense that changes in proportion to how much a company produces or sells. Examples of variable costs include fuel costs, air navigation charges, labor, utilities, commission, and distribution costs. Generally, between 30% and 35% of an airline's operating cost is variable. In contrast, fixed costs are expenses that remain the same regardless of production output. Examples of fixed costs are rent, power plant and equipment (PP&E), terminal charges, and aircraft lease contracts.

The use of costs for managerial decision-making is then discussed, and the intuitive rationale behind these decision rules is explained. Diverse cost aspects are compared across the spectrum of airlines. Finally, economies of scale, scope, and density are explained and discussed in detail.

Discussion Questions

1 Identify the reasons why airlines would want to take over other airlines.
2 What is impairment of asset with example?
3 What is the difference between economies of scale and economies of scope?
4 What is the difference between economies of scale and economies of density?
5 For many airlines in the short run, a major portion of the cost of production, such as aircraft and terminal space, is fixed. Should these very large FCs be ignored when the revenue managers are making output and pricing decisions? Why?
6 What is a sunk cost? Provide an example of a sunk cost in an airline. Should such costs be irrelevant in making future decisions?
7 Define and compare historical, replacement, and sunk costs.
8 Why is it important that an airline manager consider opportunity costs when making economic decisions regarding the airline?
9 Calculate BLF for the following airlines:

US Airlines, 2010

	Airlines	*Yield*	*CASM*	*BLF*
1	American	14.09	12.84	?
2	Continental	14.96	11.48	?
3	Delta	13.07	11.84	?
4	United Airlines	15.15	12.03	?
5	US Airways	11.68	11.73	?
6	Southwest Airlines	10.66	11.27	?
7	JetBlue	11.75	9.77	?
8	AirTran	9.71	10.35	?
9	Frontier	10.85	10.07	?
10	Virgin America	12.21	9.44	?
11	Alaska	12.38	10.93	?
12	Hawaiian	9.72	11.88	?
13	Allegiant	7.51	9.08	?

10 Suppose the total cost function is given by:

$$C = 50 + 4Q + 2Q^2$$

c What is the AFC of producing five units of output?
d What is the AVC of producing five units of output?
e What is the ATC of producing five units of output?
f What is the MC of producing five units of output?
g What is AFC function?
h What is AVC function?

11 At a certain manufacturer, the MC is:

MC = $3(Q-4)^2$ dollars per unit when the level of production is Q units.

a Express the total production cost in terms of the FCs and VCs.
b What is the TC of producing 14 units if the FC is $400?

12 Jet Services is a manufacturer of parts for the commercial aircraft. The company is established in Taiwan, and it's headquartered in Taipei City. Suppose that the cost function for a product is given by:

$TC(Q) = 4{,}000 - 9Q^2 + 0.002Q^3$

Find the production level that will lead to the minimum average cost per-unit AC (Q).

13 An aircraft manufacturer's estimates indicate that the variable cost of manufacturing a new aircraft will be $150 million. The fixed cost applicable to the new product is estimated to be $24 billion, and the selling price of an aircraft is $190 million.

a Compute the breakeven point in units as a percent of sales capacity in dollars.
b Determine the algebraic statements of the revenue and the cost functions.

14 Suppose that the cost of producing anti-icing liquid is given as (Q in hundred gallons):

$TC = 4{,}000 + 35\times Q - 0.01\times Q^2$

a What is the cost of producing $Q = 40$?
b What is the marginal cost when $Q = 40$?

15 Why might an airline choose direct flights rather than hub and spoke?

Airline Fixed and Variable Costs

FIXED COSTS

- Fixed salaries, benefits and training costs for flight crews, which do not vary according to aircraft usage
- Maintenance costs
  - Maintenance labor for maintenance scheduled on an annual basis
  - Maintenance contracts for maintenance scheduled on an annual basis
- Lease costs based on a length of time
- Depreciation
- Operations overhead
- Administrative overhead
- Self-insurance costs

VARIABLE COSTS

- Crew costs (travel expenses, overtime charges, wages of crew hired on an hourly or part-time basis)
- Maintenance costs scheduled on the basis of flying time or flight cycles
- Maintenance labor (includes all labor salaries, wages, benefits, travel, and training)
- Maintenance parts (cost of materials and parts consumed in aircraft maintenance and inspections)
- Maintenance contracts (all contracted costs for unscheduled maintenance, maintenance scheduled on flight-hour basis, on flight-cycle basis, or on condition)
- Engine overhaul, aircraft refurbishment, major component repairs
- Modifications
- Fuel and other fluids
- Lease costs (leasing costs based on flight hours)
- Landing fees, airport, and en route charges

Source: Foundations of Airline Finance, Methodology and Practice.

Appendix: Airline Cost Classification and Division

Airline Operating and Non-operating Costs

Operating Cost (OC)

Direct Operating Cost (DOC)
- Flight crew
- Aircraft fuel and oil
- Airport fees (landing fees: cost per aircraft ton landed)
- Navigation charges
- Direct maintenance: labor and materials
- Depreciation/rentals/insurance: flight equipment

Indirect Operating Cost (IOC)
- Marketing costs
- Ground property and equipment
- Depreciation, insurance, and maintenance
- Administration and sales
  - Servicing administration
  - Reservations and sales
  - Advertising and publicity
  - General
  - Servicing
- Passenger services
- Aircraft services
- Traffic services

Non-operating Cost (NOC)
- Depreciation
- Interest
- Insurance
- Losses from the retirement of property
- Losses from affiliated companies
- Other loss items, such as those from foreign exchange transactions and sales of shares

Source: Foundations of Airline Finance, Methodology and Practice.

Notes

1 *The Wall Street Journal*, January 6, 2016.
2 The term historical cost means the original cost at the time of a transaction.
3 Lessor Avolon records $304 million impairment over Russian aircraft, Reuters, May 3, 2022.
4 Assuming that the airline would fly these routes regardless of whether the seats are sold or not.
5 Formerly Air Transport Association (ATA).
6 Accountants are generally concerned with explicit costs for financial reporting purposes.
7 Economists are generally interested with economic costs for decision-making purposes.
8 Or, Cost per Available Seat-Kilometer (CASK).
9 In other countries (except the United States and Canada), available seat kilometer (ASK) is used as a measure of supply.
10 For this simple cost function, the average variable (bQ/Q) and marginal costs are equal.
11 Average cost remains unchanged as output varies.
12 The difference between price and the variable costs (P-VC) is called contribution margin.
13 Because of very high fixed costs, only a few companies can stay in market. As a result, there are at present only two aircraft manufacturing companies in the world (Boeing and Airbus) that manufacture large commercial aircraft.

14 *The Florida News Journal*, May 1, 2012.
15 Winglets have been installed by airlines on 727s, 757s, and 737Classics. Airlines such as Continental and Southwest heavily promoted the use of winglets, which resulted in decreased fuel costs per ASM.
16 Fuel efficiency is also affected by an airline's schedule as longer flights burn less fuel per ASM, where the takeoff and landing phases of flight burn the most fuel. On longer flights, these phases are spread out over greater distances, thereby making fuel costs per ASMs smaller for longer flights.
17 Boeing bags $5 billion deal with recovering Malaysia Airlines, $1 billion India patrol jet sale, *The Japan Times*, July 28, 2016.
18 Managing Maintenance Costs, Business Aviation Advisor, July 1, 2015.
19 JetBlue Delays Embraer E190 Retirement Plans to Support Growth, Simple Flying, July 27, 2021.
20 A similar situation would be catering companies, but with airlines largely ignoring food services on flights, this becomes an area where airlines can no longer achieve significant economies of scope.
21 The breakeven for the A380 was initially estimated at 270 units.

References

African Airlines Association (AFRAA). (2012). *Media Brief: AFFRA Launches Joint Fuel Purchase Project*, January 12, 2012. Retrieved February 9, 2017 from www.afraa.org/index

Airbus. (2017). *Commercial Aircraft, A320 Family: A320neo*. Retrieved on February 8, 2017 from http://www.airbus.com/aircraftfamilies

Aviation Partners Boeing. (2017). *Fuel Savings*. Retrieved on February 8, 2017 from http://www.aviationpartnersboeing.com.

Boeing. (2017). *Everett Production Facility*. Retrieved on February 8, 2017 from http://www.boeing.com/company/about-bca/.

JetBlue Airways. (2017). *Our Fleet*. Retrieved on February 10, 2017 from www.jetblue.com.

Rivkin, J. (2005). *Dogfight over Europe*. Harvard Business School. 9-106-033.

Stewart, M. (2008). A Risk and Cost-Benefit Assessment of United States Aviation Security Measures. *Journal of Transportation Security*, 1, 143–159.

5 Competitive Market Structure and Monopolistic Markets

The price of a product or service is determined by the forces of supply and demand in the relevant market. Markets in air transport are typically narrowly defined as city-pairs including indirect routes connecting the cities. For example, if you wish to fly from New York to London, an alternative flight from Tokyo to Beijing is not a substitute. Market structure refers to the degree of competition and the number of consumers and producers in that market. It is often described in terms of barriers to entry or exit, the numbers of buyers and sellers, number of competitors, extent of product substitutability, and the degree of mutual interdependence between firms. A significant change has undergone in the market structure of the US airline industry, alongside similar shifts in numerous liberalized air travel markets around the world. A series of bankruptcies and mergers over the last several years have taken what had been ten major U.S. airlines down to three large international carriers (American Airlines, Delta Air Lines, and United Airlines). Across the Atlantic, consolidation within the European airline market has moved at a much slower pace, despite the presence of large-scale legacy airlines and low-cost airlines. The most recent examples of consolidation include the acquisitions of Spanish airline Vueling and Ireland's Aer Lingus by International Airlines Group (IAG). Across the expanse of North Atlantic, the market has become concentrated, with around 70% of capacity provided by the three large anti-trust-immune alliances. In the United States, many airlines, including Aloha, Braniff, Eastern, Pan Am, TWA, and People Express, have all left the market. The commercial aircraft engine market is highly consolidated, with a few manufacturers dominating the market. Among these leading commercial aircraft engine manufacturers are CFM International (GE Aviation and Safran), Pratt & Whitney, and Rolls-Royce.

The subsequent two chapters of the text deal with market structure. In commercial aviation, the market for aircraft is typically divided into two product categories: narrow-body aircraft and wide-body aircraft. Moreover, the commercial jet market is dominated by two companies: Boeing and Airbus.

This chapter delves into the following topics:

- Introduction
- Perfect Competition
    - Conditions of Perfect Competition
        - Homogenous Product
        - Many Buyers and Sellers
        - Full Dissemination of Information
        - No Barriers to Entry
    - Perfect Competition in the Short Run

DOI: 10.4324/9781003388135-5

- Price and Output Determination
- Perfect Competition in the Long Run

- Monopoly
    - Economic Conditions of Monopoly
        - Only One Seller
        - Unique Product/No Close Substitute
        - Lack of Information
        - High Barriers to Entry
    - Common Barriers to Entry
    - Natural Monopoly
    - Price-Output Decision for Monopolies
    - Monopoly Pricing and Consumer Well-Being
- Monopoly Market Power in Aviation
    - Airports
        - Gate and Facility Availability
        - Slot Controls
        - Hub Airlines
    - Commercial Aircraft Manufacturing
    - Jet Engine Manufacturing
- Monopsony and Bilateral Monopoly
- Summary
- Discussion Questions

Introduction

Market structure is a reflection of both the number of firms in the market and the type of competition that is found in the relevant market. Table 5.1 is a depiction of the market continuum, displaying the four major market structures: perfect competition, monopolistic competition, oligopoly, and monopoly. Perfect competition occurs when there are many buyers and sellers who have minimal to no control over their price. At the other extreme of the continuum are monopolies. Here the market contains only one seller who essentially has complete control over the output or price. This chapter focuses on these two structures, while Chapter 6 addresses oligopolies and monopolistic competition.

The recent wave of consolidations among U.S. airlines has reduced the number of dominant carriers from ten to four namely, Delta Air Lines, American Airlines, United Airlines, and Southwest Airlines, collectively commanding the majority of the market share.

Emerging from Chapter 11 in late 2021, Avianca is diligently working to reinvent itself in Latin American aviation by forming a new mega-airline group in the region. The trend of airline consolidation in Latin American markets appears to be occurring at a rapid pace. Avianca continues to change Latin America's aviation market after reaching an agreement with GOL to establishing a powerhouse Latin American aviation group, Abra. The new entity will comprise the principal shareholders of Colombia's Avianca and the controlling shareholder of Brazil's GOL.[1]

Table 5.1 Market Continuum

	Perfect Competition	*Monopolistic Competition*	*Oligopoly*	*Monopoly*
Number of sellers	Large	Many	Few	One
Type of product	Homogenous	Differentiated	Homogenous or differentiated	Unique
Control over price	None	Very little	Strong	Very strong
Entry condition	Very easy	Easy	Difficult	Impossible
Example	Agriculture	Retail	Airlines	Public utilities

Perfect (Pure) Competition

> A perfectly competitive industry has many buyers and sellers, each with a relatively small market share. Buyers have complete information about the prices charged by each firm, and there are no barriers to entry or exit.
>
> As one moves from perfect competition to monopoly, concentration increases and competition declines.

A perfectly competitive industry is characterized by the presence of numerous small-scale buyers and sellers, who can enter and exit the industry with no restrictions. This dynamic creates a situation where the individual firm has little or no power on the price of its goods or services. The firm is then called a price taker as price is dictated by the market. In this situation, each firm must decide to either sell at the market-bearing rate or not sell at all. In the real world, perfectly competitive industries are a rare occurrence; the closest examples are agriculture and the stock market.

Conditions of Perfect Competition

In order for perfect competition to exist, four conditions must be met. Given the rarity of markets that precisely satisfy all four conditions, examples of perfectly competitive markets are

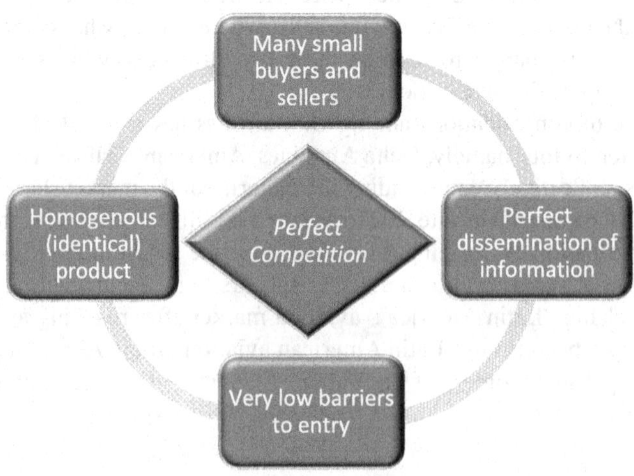

limited. Nonetheless, since many industries approximate these conditions, the idea of a perfectly competitive market is a useful construct when comparing market structures. The four essential conditions are as follows.

Homogenous Product

The first condition for perfect competition is that the product must exhibit homogeneity. Homogenous products are very similar in physical composition, as well as quality. A homogenous product is indistinguishable from other competing products, for instance, a single unit of any currency, like a 100 U.S. dollar bill, which are identical to each other. This condition flows naturally from the idea that buyers should feel that they are receiving essentially the same product, regardless of which seller they choose to purchase from. In contrast to homogenous products, heterogenous products are items that cannot be easily substituted or replaced by other products. The more heterogenous the product, the more opportunities sellers can exploit within their market position. Therefore, we should expect to see sellers attempting to differentiate their product offerings, regardless of the market. The availability of differentiated products allows firms to price them accordingly. For instance, consider agricultural commodities such as milk, corn, soybeans, and wheat. In such cases, sellers find it difficult to differentiate their products. Likewise, in the stock market, many individual stocks generally lack the capacity to influence the market by offering shares at significantly lower prices. Each share is identical, and pricing is based on supply and demand. This is a largely idealized form of basic competition theory, in which prices are created and kept down by the nature of the market.

Many Buyers and Sellers

The second condition of perfect competition is the existence of many buyers and sellers. The presence of multiple players enables the market to dictate the price of the product through competition. Again, agriculture is a good example; there are multiple individual producers and numerous buyers, preventing any single buyer or seller from controlling the market and artificially manipulate (raise or lower) the price of the commodity. In contrast, a counter-example of an industry where sellers have strong influence over price is the commercial aircraft manufacturing industry. Since Boeing and Airbus are the only two major sellers of large commercial aircraft, they have a strong influence on price. Thus, the commercial aircraft manufacturing industry is clearly not a perfectly competitive market.

Full Dissemination of Information

The third condition of perfectly competitive markets is the widespread availability and full dissemination of information. In order for markets to react efficiently, information needs to be accessible to all buyers and sellers. Without this information, distortions in price may occur within the market. Stock trading is a good example of perfect competition with full dissemination of information. Driven by investor demands and the requirements set by the US Securities Exchange Commission (SEC), companies disseminate information relating to the company's financial well-being. Using this information, investors buy or sell, thereby adjusting the stock price and making the market more efficient. Similar scenarios are observed in other perfectly competitive markets. Referring back to agriculture, commodity markets typically provide real-time, readily available information on prices. However, it is also observed that companies illegally withhold important information for the purposes of insider trading or personal gain. In summary, both sellers and buyers have complete market knowledge like costs, technological requirements, products' availability, features, quality, and prices. Hence, manipulating the market by either party is not possible.

No Barriers to Entry

The final condition for perfect competition is that barriers to enter the market must be low. In order for the market to act efficiently and adjust prices accordingly, firms must be able to easily enter and exit the industry. This enables many smaller sellers to enter the market or choose to leave. The nature of these entry barriers varies considerably by market, but common barriers include:

- Brand loyalty
- Capital requirements
- Economies of scale
- Government regulations
- Legal requirements (patents, licenses, and copy rights)

Given the massive capital requirements and the expertise to start and operate a commercial aircraft manufacturing company, the barriers to enter this industry are thought to be quite significant. The domain of aircraft manufacturing generally requires huge capital investments, economies of scale, economies of scope, and strong customer loyalty in order to be profitable. These hurdles are the primary reason why there are only a few companies, such as Boeing and Airbus, dominating the industry. We address these issues in more depth in the next chapter.

Perfect Competition in the Short Run

> The interaction between demand and supply determines the market clearing price. Business firms operating in this industry must charge this price and cannot deviate from it. A firm in a perfectly competitive market may generate a profit in the short run, but in the long run, it will have economic profits of zero.

In a perfectly competitive market, firms are the price takers and lack the ability to influence the price of their product. They are constrained to adhere to the market price, which is determined at a juncture where market demand equals market supply. This is displayed graphically in Figure 5.1, where the equilibrium point is the market clearing price.

While the equilibrium point determines the market clearing price, individual firms perceive this price as fixed for all quantities. The dynamic arises from the fact that the individual firms do not produce a sufficient quantity of the homogenous product to affect the market price. Therefore, Figure 5.2 displays price as a horizontal line, which equates to the equilibrium point determined in Figure 5.1. Additionally, since the price is constant for all quantities, price also equals average revenue and marginal revenue. Using a hypothetical example, Table 5.2 displays how price equals average revenue and marginal revenue for price takers.[2] In Figure 5.2, the horizontal line denoting price can be considered as the demand for a firm in a perfectly competitive industry.

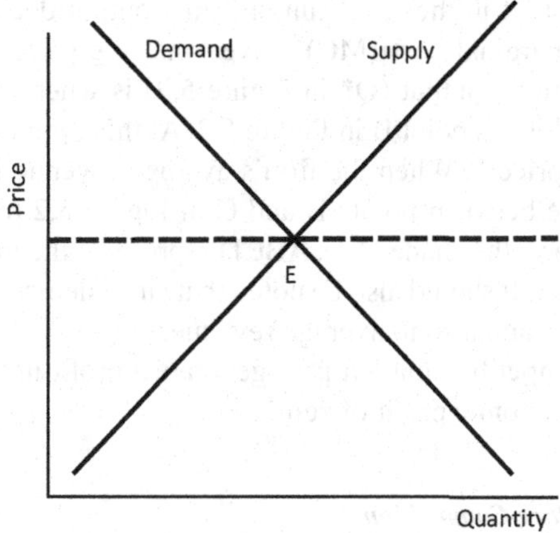

Figure 5.1 Market Equilibrium, Short Run.

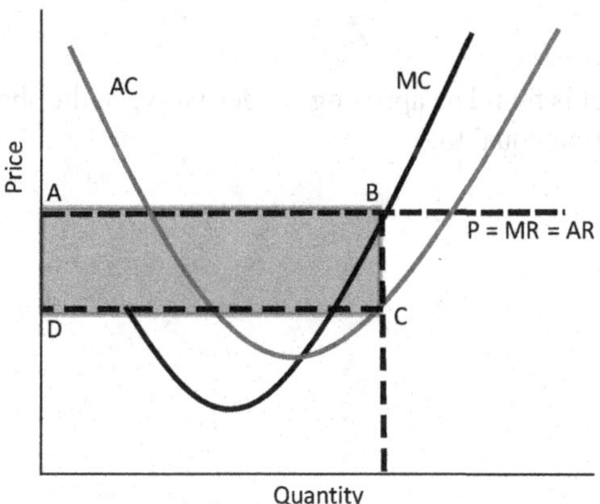

Figure 5.2 Market Equilibrium, Firm.

Table 5.2 Total Revenue, Average Revenue, and Marginal Revenue

Quantity	*Price*	*Total Revenue*	*AR*	*MR*	*MC*
0	$100	$0	$0	$0	$0
5	$100	$500	$100	$100	$80
10	$100	$1,000	$100	$100	$65
15	$100	$1,500	$100	$100	$60
20	$100	$2,000	$100	$100	$65
25	$100	$2,500	$100	$100	$80
30	$100	$3,000	$100	$100	$100
35	$100	$3,500	$100	$100	$120
40	$100	$4,000	$100	$100	$140
45	$100	$4,500	$100	$100	$160
50	$100	$5,000	$100	$100	$180

Since price is held constant in the short run, a firm's output decision is to produce where marginal revenue equals marginal cost (MC). Given that the price line is also the marginal revenue curve, a firm's optimal output (Q* in Figure 5.2) is where the marginal revenue line intersects the MC curve, which is point B in Figure 5.2. At this optimal level of output, the firm is producing Q* goods at price P. When the firm's average revenue is compared to the firm's average cost, the difference between points B and C in Figure 5.2 represents the contribution margin of the firm. Therefore, the shaded box ABCD represents the total profit for the firm in a perfectly competitive market. It should also be noted that since demand is perfectly elastic, price is equal to marginal revenue and also to average revenue.

A firm in a perfectly competitive market may generate a profit in the short run; however, in the long run, it will have economic profit of zero.

Price Determination under Pure Competition

The economic objective of any firm is to choose inputs and outputs that maximize economic profits. Profit is defined as the difference between the firm's total revenue and its total cost.

$$\text{Profit} = \text{TR} - \text{TC}$$

$$\pi = \text{TR} - \text{TC}$$

Profit maximization output is found by applying the derivative to the above function with respect to Q and setting the equation equal to 0:

$$\frac{d\pi}{dQ} = \frac{dTR}{dQ} - \frac{dTC}{dQ} = 0$$

$$\frac{dTR}{dQ} = \frac{dTC}{dQ}$$

As it is known, the derivative of total cost is marginal cost and the derivative of total revenue is marginal revenue. Therefore, to maximize profit, a pure competitive firm should produce up to the point where marginal revenue of the last unit is equal to the marginal cost of the last unit produced:

$$\text{MR} = \text{MC}$$

However, it's essential to note that the average cost curve may vary from firm to firm. For example, the firm in Figure 5.4 has a much higher cost structure, leading to incur losses rather than turning a profit, which is represented by the shaded region ABCD. Since the firm is a price taker, the firm has two options. It can either lower its cost structure to the point where it can actually make a profit, or it can simply shut down. A firm can only continue to produce if its revenues exceed its variable costs.

Envision a perfectly competitive firm operating in a market where the equilibrium price is $100. With the marginal cost figures given in Table 5.2, what level of output would the firm choose?

The profit optimizing level of output can be identified using marginal analysis. Profits are maximized when the production reaches 30 units of output. For the units of output up until the 30th, MR > MC; each of these units contributes more to marginal revenue (MR) than to marginal cost (MC).

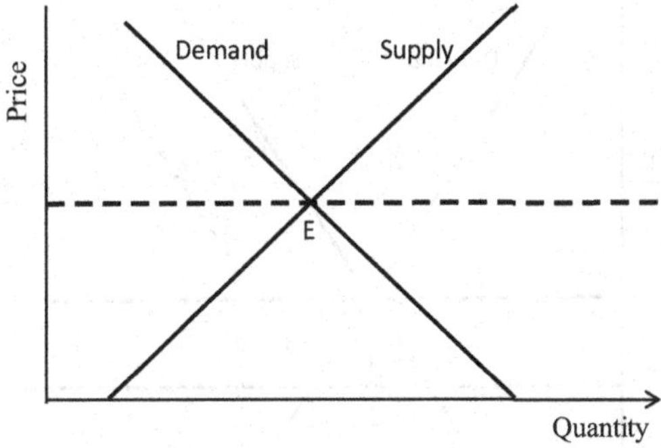

Figure 5.3 Market Equilibrium.

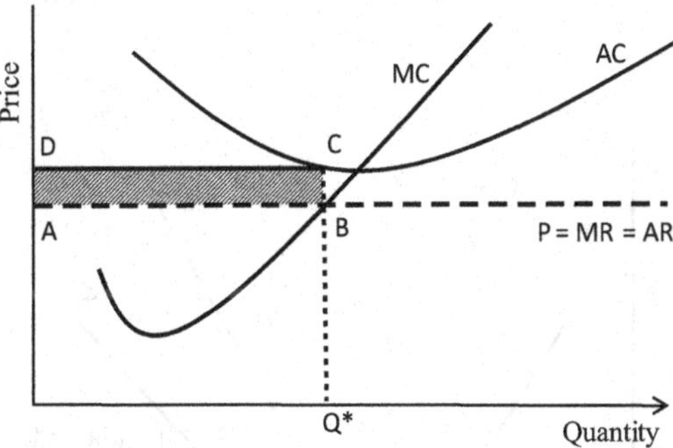

Figure 5.4 Short-Run Loss in Perfect Competition.

It follows that the production and sale of each of these units lead to higher profits. Beyond the 30th unit, MR < MC. Thus, production of units beyond the 30th unit would result in lower profits.

Perfect Competition in the Long Run

The aforementioned situations highlight the price-output decision for firms competing in a perfectly competitive market in the short run. However, markets are not static, but continually evolving. Given the low barriers to enter and exit in perfectly competitive markets, new firms will enter the market when the industry is profitable, and existing firms will exit the market when the industry is sustaining losses. Consequently, the key factor governing moderation of profits is not necessarily the high number of firms (although more firms encourage more competition) that keep profits low, but rather the entry of new firms.

To measure the effects that market entry and exit have on companies in a perfectly competitive market, consider the situation where the firm is making an economic profit, or one where the intersection between MR and MC is greater than average total cost.[3] Since the firms in this industry are making economic profits, these profits will entice new firms to enter the industry (due to low barriers to entry). These profits indicate that resources will earn more here than in alternative uses. The introduction of fresh participants ultimately increases supply in the market, causing a shift in the supply curve, which is represented in Figure 5.5. The shift in the supply curve also creates a new market clearing price, which all firms in the industry must accept (Figure 5.6).

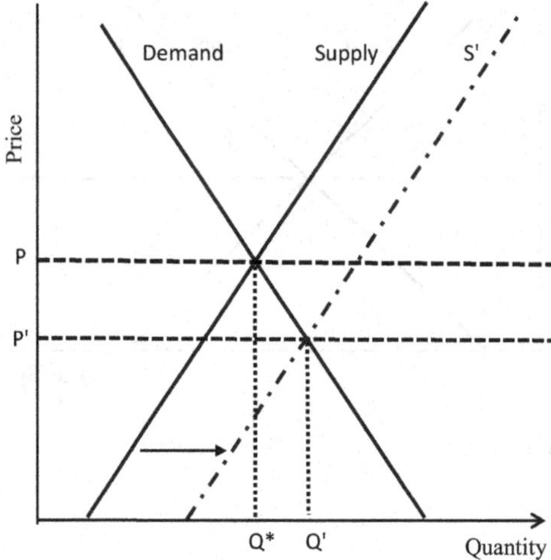

Figure 5.5 Industry.

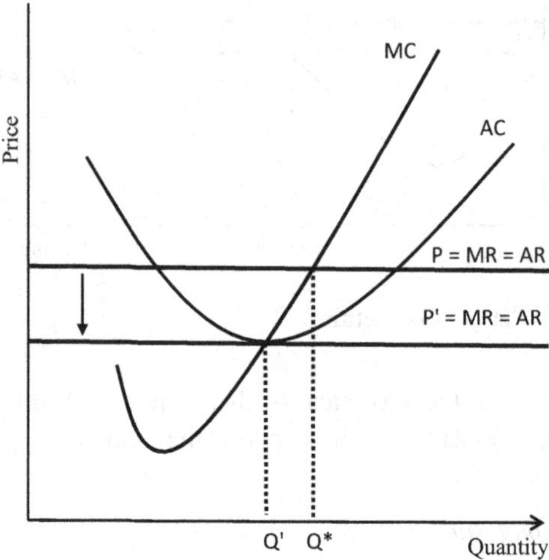

Figure 5.6 An Individual Firm.

In the short run, the firm will not cease operations as long as the loss from staying in business is less than the loss from leaving the market. The firm will shut down if it cannot cover average variable costs.

P = MR = MC

Short Run

- ATC>P>AVC Operate
- P<AVC Shutdown

Long Run

- P>ATC Operate
- P<ATC Shutdown

As time progresses, with a growing influx of firms into the market, the supply curve will continue shifting to the right. Every rightward movement increases market supply and resultantly decreases both the price and the quantity demanded for an individual firm. In order to maximize profits in the face of decreasing demand, the firm reduces output. These movements and market reactions occur until marginal revenue equals marginal and average costs for individual firms in the market. This juncture signifies the point at which the economic profit for the individual firm equals zero. Figure 5.5 displays the change in market output and individual firm output from a short-run scenario to a long-run scenario.

In the wake of these market adjustments, firms in perfectly competitive markets have zero economic profits in the long run. Since this is a long-run phenomenon, the market will continuously adjust in response to firms freely entering and exiting the market.

Market adjustments do not just occur in one direction. If some firms are grappling with financial losses, then these firms will exit the market causing a leftward shift in the market supply curve. This shift reduces the total quantity supplied by the market but increases the demand (and the price) for an individual firm. Over time, the individual firm will return to the point where marginal revenue equals marginal cost, and average cost and economic profit (or loss) both equal zero. Figures 5.7 and 5.8 display the market reaction when firms that are losing money exit a competitive industry.

In order to change this situation, firms try to differentiate their products so that they will gain some market influence. This endeavor underscores that there are very few markets where all the conditions of perfect competition hold, but there are numerous markets where the perfect competition model described above is a good approximation of reality.

Let's consider a hypothetical firm serving a market and the market demand curve is equal to P = \$105, and the total cost function is given by the equation

$$TC = 8{,}000 + 5Q + \tfrac{1}{2} Q^2$$

The MC can be found by calculating the first-order derivative of the TC function over the relevant range of production:

$$MC = 5 + Q.$$

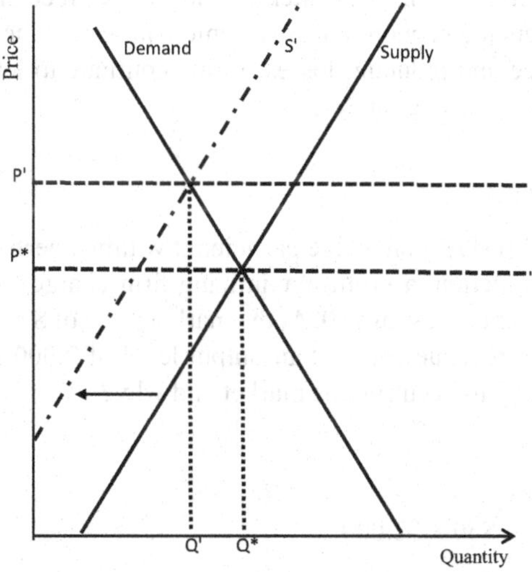

Figure 5.7 Industry Adjustment.

Given the market price, the purely competitive firm must decide what level of output to produce to maximize the profits. The profit is maximized when the market price is equal to MC.

$MC = P$
$5 + Q = 105$
$Q = 100$ units

Therefore, the total revenue is **\$10,500** (\$105 × 100), and the total cost is

$TC_{(Q=100)} = 4{,}000 + 5(100) + \frac{1}{2}(100)^2$
$TC_{(Q=100)} = \mathbf{\$9{,}500}$

This firm is enjoying a short-run profit = \$10,500 − \$9,500 = **\$1,000.**

If: MR = P = MC Normal profit
MR = P > MC, Profit
MR = P < MC, Loss
MR = P = MC
ATC > P >AVC,
Short-run loss (stay in business)
P < AVC, Loss (shutdown)

Since the typical firm in this industry is making abnormal profits (\$1,000) in the short run, there will be an expansion of the output of existing firms. Moreover, entry of new firms into the industry is expected. This phenomenon results in the market supply curve to the right and drives down the market price. Thus, the abnormal profit disappears. Perfect competition serves as a benchmark to compare with other market structures as it displays high levels of economic efficiency.

The existence of economic profits attracts new firms to the market and lowers price in the long run. With the influx of new firms in the market, the supply curve shifts to the right, which lowers price and profits. Firms continue to enter the industry until economic profits fall to zero. If typical firms are experiencing economic losses, some will leave. The supply curve then shifts to the left, increasing price and reducing losses. Firms continue to leave the market until the remaining firms are no longer losing money.

Example

General Tool International (GTI) is an active participant within a perfectly competitive market. At its current level of production, a profit-maximizing firm charges \$75 for each unit it produces. The firm faces an average cost of \$50. At the market price of \$75, the firm's marginal cost curve crosses the marginal revenue curve at an output level of 2,000 units. What is the firm's current profit? What is likely to occur in this market and why?

Profit = TC − TR
Profit = AC × Q − P × Q
Profit = \$75 × \$2,000 − \$50 × \$2,000
Profit = \$50,000

Since that the firm is earning positive economic profit, we should see new entry until economic profit is zero.

Monopoly

At the opposite end of the market spectrum lie monopolies. By definition, a monopoly is a market where there is only one seller. However, monopolies are all judged with respect to a certain market or geographical area. The rash of consolidation in the U.S. airline industry has distinctly reduced competition at many of the nation's major airports.[4] Notably, within 40 out of the 100 largest U.S. airports, a single airline controls a majority of the market.[5] Delta's market share over the last decade has increased from about 50% to 80% of the airport's passengers at the Atlanta airport in 2022.[6] In some cases, a single airline may hold a dominant position due to factors such as exclusive access to gates, control over distribution channels, or economies of scale that make it difficult for other airlines to enter the market.

> A **monopoly** is a market where there is only one firm producing a product for which there is no close substitute. As such, that firm is able to exert a significant degree of control over the price. In many cities, especially in small communities, a single airline controls the entire market.

For example, let's consider the case of a fixed-base operator (FBO) in a small airport to have a monopoly power with respect to the airport, yet when the geographical scope is widened to include other airports, the county, or state, there are invariably other FBOs competing in the market. In addition, airlines essentially have a monopoly over long-distance transportation.

This highlights the intricate dynamics at play. The market structure for providing aeronautical services such as fueling, tie-down and parking, aircraft rental, aircraft maintenance, and flight instruction would be considered a monopoly with respect to just the small airport. However, the market would be an oligopoly on a state level. At most commercial airports, car parks are monopolies and that is why people around the world complain about parking fees. Therefore, depending on the level of analysis, a monopoly can exist in many different ways. Since monopolies can potentilally exist in any industry, especially one that is narrowly defined, it is important to understand the economic principles.

Economic Conditions of Monopoly

1 **Sole seller:** The primary condition of a monopoly lies in the presence of a sole seller of the product. This is usually caused by significant increasing returns to scale, with the minimum efficient scale in the industry or geographical area allowing only one firm, or major barriers to entry and exit. Therefore, monopolies wield much pricing power compared to firms operating in a more competitive market condition.
2 **Unique product with no close substitute:** The second condition is the opposite of a homogenous product (a condition for a perfectly competitive market). A monopoly is defined by a single seller that offers a unique product for which there is no similar substitute. This scenario is common in the medical field. Imagine the revelation that a new medication is discovered to treat a previously untreatable illness; the company with this new-found medication has a

monopoly on the market. Although other treatments may exist, they are imperfect substitutes and cannot fully treat the illness.

3 **Lack of information:** When a seller's information is not disseminated throughout the market, an inherent advantage tilts towards the seller over the buyer. Because of this, the buyer's demand price is reflective of a different value placed on the product. The seller may very well be willing to accept a lower price for the good, but due to limited access to information, the buyer ends up paying more.
4 **High barriers to entry:** Finally, monopolies occur largely due to the existence of high barriers to entry in a given industry. As mentioned, a barrier to entry is any obstacle that makes it unprofitable or impossible for new firms to enter an industry. However, there is some disagreement as to which barriers are significant. Economists share concensus on the impact of government-erected barriers that seriously harm the economy. Foreign ownership restrictions are the most effective barriers to entry in the airline industry. In 2016, Brazil government relaxed the previous restrictions on foreign ownership of domestic airlines and increased to 49%, up from 20%.

> Eighth Freedom or cabotage is the right granted to a foreign airline to operate domestically. An example of this would be an airline like Lufthansa from German can operate a domestic route between two French cities, and a French airline can do the reverse.

Yet another barrier to entry is the right or privilege granted by one state to state to fly across its territory, with or without landing (Freedoms of the Air).[7] The common government prohibition of cabotage (Eighth Freedom) obviously eliminates foreign competition and allows domestic carriers to keep prices somewhat higher. Incumbent carriers benefit at the expense of consumers, and the industry is prevented from being as large and efficient as it would otherwise be.

Common Barriers to Entry

The issue with the fourth condition mentioned above is whether or not non-government barriers to entry can seriously harm the economy. This issue will be covered in detail in the next chapter. In this section, we discuss some of the more common barriers to entry, including:

- Brand loyalty,
- Capital requirements,
- Labor unions,
- Legal/government barriers,
- Project risks, and
- Technology.

Brand loyalty corresponds to the preference of consumers for a particular product from a well-recognized company. Illustratively, Singapore Airlines and Southwest Airlines stand as prime examples of established airlines with a loyal consumer base. In a competitive market, creating brand loyalty with existing customers plays an extremely important role for the survival of an airline.

Another major barrier, particularly in international markets, is **legal or government restriction**. Government regulations can prevent market access and create situations where an artificial monopoly may develop. A prevailing legal barrier to entry is a patent or copyright. The holder of the patent or copyright has exclusive legal right to sell the product. Initially, it might appear that these are inherently anti-competitive. When a company obtains a patent on, say, an aircraft design, this prevents anyone else from manufacturing the same aircraft. This, inturn, increases the likelihood that the firm will enjoy some degree of monopoly power and be able to keep prices higher. In the absence of the patent, another firm might well start producing the same aircraft and drive down the price. However, this simplistic, static analysis can be misleading. When examined from a dynamic, long-run perspective, this monopoly power serves to motivate far more research and development of new aircraft, thereby creating more competition and a wider variety of products.

For example, consider a scenario in which patent laws didn't exist during Boeing's contemplation of the 787's development. Boeing would have known that once the 787 was developed and had met necessary regulatory approval, a competitor could have purchased one, copied the design, and developed a similar product at a faction of the original development cost to Boeing. Knowing this, Boeing might well have abandoned the risky project, and the 787 wouldn't exist. Thus, in this case, the patent prevents too much competition in the short run, so that more new products can be developed over time. More monopoly power in the short run increases output and competition in the long run. The pharmaceutical industry also has extensive experience with monopolies, as new drugs receive legal protection and enable the company to have a monopoly over the drug. Yet, akin to the example above, however, an argument can be made that patent and copyright monopolies are justified as an incentive for research and development; that is, without patents, pharmaceutical companies would have much less incentive to spend significant resources on the development of new drugs.

The aviation industry has extensive experience with government restrictions. During US regulation of air transportation, the Civil Aeronautics Board (CAB) dictated which airlines were to fly specific routes, which in many cases created monopolies on many individual routes. Athough deregulation has alleviated some government barriers in the domestic sector, international markets are still heavily regulated. For example, a bilateral air service agreement may restrict access into a particular market, thereby creating a monopoly on a particular route. A more comprehensive exploration of aviation monopolies will be covered in more detail later in this chapter.

Another possible barrier to entry in any industry are **capital requirements**. The capital necessary to commence production may be sufficiently significant so that the potential profits do not justify the investment, the associated risk is too high, or the capital cannot be obtained. Firms only enter a market when they ascertain the viability of attaining a reasonable rate of return. Due to these factors, the larger the capital required to enter a new market, the smaller the number of firms. To illustrate, take the commercial aircraft manufacturing industry, which requires very large capital requirements for new entrants. A new aircraft manufacturing company would call for sizeable capital for production facilities, research and development, and general overhead expenses. Indeed, the magnitude of capital requirements are the major reason why very few firms enter aircraft manufacturing. Conversely, the capital requirements for a restaurant or small retail store are considerably less than aircraft manufacturing; restaurants are therefore far more numerous.

Standard capital requirements in aviation are project costs (Table 5.3). Airlines require a tremendous amount of capital and large physical assets to enter the commercial market. While start-up airlines and start-up general aviation manufacturers often complain about the difficulty of raising capital, it should be emphasized that this does not necessarily reflect any inefficiency in capital markets. Profits rarely come easy in any industry and seem to be particularly elusive for most airlines. At times "no" is the efficient answer to entrepreneurs high on enthusiasm but

Table 5.3 Airline and Airport Development Costs

Project			*Year*	*Cost (Billions)*
Aircraft Manufacturers:				
Boeing 707			1957	$1.3
Boeing 747			1970	$3.7
Boeing 777			1994	$7.0
Airbus A380			2005	$14.0
Airbus A350			2012	$15.0
Boeing 737-Max	2014	$2–$3	2014	$2-$3
Airbus NEO	2012	$3	2012	$3.0
Airports:				
JFK Terminal 8 (American)			2007	$1.3
JFK Terminal 5 (jetBlue)			2008	$0.8
Miami International Capital Improvement			2011	$6.5
JFK Terminal 4 (Delta)			2013	$1.2
Jet Engines:				
Pratt & Whitney PW1000G			2008	$10.0
General Electric GE9X			2016	$5.4

Sources: Compiled by the authors using airline and airport press releases.

short on viable business options. On the other hand, capital is clearly accessible to those who do have a persuasive business plan. For instance, JetBlue obtained $130 million in start-up investment, making the airline the most heavily financed start-up in US airline history.

Related to capital requirements are the prospects of profitability in the industry. If the industry has narrow profit margins in addition to large capital requirements, then it is even less likely that new firms will enter that industry. Naturally, in scenarios where profits are not high, there is no social need for new entry.

Technology can also be a substantial barrier, depending on the industry. Without a certain required level of technology, some firms may be unable to compete effectively in a market. For example, in the microprocessor industry, an entering firm requires a substantial level of technology to provide a product that might compete with Intel and AMD. Additionally, the required technology is not a one-time occurrence, but must be continually upgraded in order to keep up with the industry.

While technology gains do not create sustainable monopolies, they can create monopolies for a certain period of time. Boeing, for instance, held a monopoly in large commercial aircraft with its 747 model. This dominance was eventually punctuated by Airbus's introduction of the double-decker A380 aircraft for a span exceeding 30 years. While Boeing's monopoly was a result of several factors, the required level of technology played a significant role in preventing other companies from developing a similar product. Another case study pertains to Aerospatiale's Concorde, which remains the only supersonic passenger aircraft to undergo commercial production.[8] Before its demise, the Concorde held a monopoly, albeit not a very profitable one, over supersonic commercial aircraft through a technological advantage that other companies were unable to replicate or replicate efficiently. In this case, the technology for supersonic commercial aircraft represented a significant barrier to entry.[9] After almost 50 years, supersonic aircraft are returning. Boom Technology is designing a 65–88-passenger supersonic airliner. Branded as the Boom Overture, the airliner is planned to have a range of 4,250 nm to be introduced in 2029. According to Boom Supersonic, their Overture jets are expected to be rolled out in 2025 and enter commercial service sometime by the end of the decade.

Another barrier to entry, particularly within the aviation sector, are **labor unions**. Labor unions essentially band workers together to bargain as a monopolist of labor supply and can thereby raise members' wages above the competitive level.[10] A case in point, the Air Line Pilots Association, International (ALPA) represents and advocates for more than 67,000 pilots at 39 US and Canadian airlines, making it the world's largest airline pilot union. Founded in 1978, the Southwest Airlines Pilots Association (SWAPA) has been the sole bargaining unit for the almost 10,000 pilots of Southwest Airlines.

This monopoly power stems mainly from supportive government regulation, sometimes supplemented by direct government subsidy. For example, the US legislation prohibits employers from requiring new hires to contractually agree to not join a union and generally limits the efforts firms can make to avoid or expel unions. Labor unions can have significant power in bargaining relationships, and this can increase the barriers to entry or completely restrict entry into certain markets. Depending on the contract negotiations, conditions may be imposed that make it difficult or unprofitable for an airline to enter a specific market.

Labor unions can also increase the barriers to entry in airline markets through scope agreements. These contracts with labor groups dictate various requirements, such as the size of aircraft for the regional airlines. For example, a scope agreement may require all aircraft with more than 51 seats to be flown by mainline pilots, as opposed to cheaper regional affiliates. In this scenario, the barriers entering the 70-seat regional jet market are increased as a result of the agreement. Scope agreements can further weild a monopoly like power in terms of the number of aircraft that an affiliate can fly. For example, US Airways launched discount carrier MetroJet in 1998; however, the pilot contract limited MetroJet's operation to 25% of US Airways, thereby restricting the number of aircraft that MetroJet could use to roughly 100 (Daly, 1998). This operational restriction created an artificial barrier to entry.

In broader context, labor unions may restrict entry into new markets by indirectly restricting capital inflows. Although one can argue the benefits of unions, from an investor's perspective, unions tend to depress rates of return. Imagine, for example, the likely surge in stock prices and borrowing prospects for legacy carriers if laws were changed to make airline strikes and other union actions illegal. The fact that such a law does not exist makes it much harder for unionized firms to raise capital.

Finally, along with capital requirements is the overall risk of critical projects. At the beginning of 1960, the United States had 12 commercial aircraft manufacturers. However, by 1980, only three remained: McDonnell Douglas, Boeing, and Lockheed. Unfortunately, by the following year, Lockheed's L-1011 TriStar project had proven to be a dismal failure that cost the company $2.5 billion over the course of 13 years, thereby leading to Lockheed's exit as well. This left Boeing and McDonnell Douglas as the only two U.S. commercial aircraft manufacturers (Harrison, 2003).

The L-1011 TriStar project is a prime example of **project risk** involved with aircraft manufacturing. The project experienced considerable delays compared to the similar McDonnell Douglas DC10; these delays ultimately doomed the project. Although Lockheed remains a defense contractor, the financial failure of the L-1011 led the company to cease commercial aircraft production.

The final two competitors pursued separate strategic business paths. While Boeing embarked on the development of new aircraft types, McDonnell Douglas focused on redesigning existing aircraft types. The latter proved unsuccessful, and McDonnell Douglas's market share of the United States fell below 20% in 1993 (Harrison, 2003). In 1996, Boeing announced a $13 billion merger with McDonnell Douglas, leaving only one US commercial aircraft manufacturing firm. A similar story occurred in Europe with the market exits of BAE and Fokker. Ultimately, the end result was an international duopoly between Boeing and Airbus for large commercial aircraft (Harrison, 2003).

This global trend is largely due to the enormous cost of doing business in this market. There are substantial economies of scale, including the deep experience and institutional knowledge required on such complex engineering, which means the minimum efficient scale in the industry supports few firms. However, a major reason for Boeing's long-held monopoly was the high barriers to entry. The challenges were not only the financial requirements but also technological and operational hurdles. When Boeing decided to develop the 747 in 1965, the projected launch costs were $1.5 billion. In fact, the project was widely viewed as a "daring, bet-the-company gamble on an untested product." In addition to the large capital requirements, Boeing needed to create new technologies as well as an entirely new manufacturing complex in Everett, Washington. This level of risk was what made it difficult for new players to enter the market, especially after Boeing assumed the monopoly. However, a turning point arrived in 2000 when Airbus announced its intention to develop the A380, a large double-decker aircraft to compete with the Boeing 747. Initially, the project's estimated cost stood at $13 billion, but subsequent delays drove this figure to nearly $15 billion. Additionally, the original breakeven forecast of 270 aircraft climbed to 420. Nonetheless, the A380 undoubtedly increased competition with Boeing. Emirates, one of the world's fastest growing airlines, was operating 71 A380 aircraft by 2016. Other examples of competitive action in the aviation market include discount prices, attractive financing, and the purchase of older aircraft.

Expanding beyond aircraft manufacturing, the following list provides examples of other monopolistic industries and companies that have or continue to hold monopolies:

- Coal
- Major League Baseball
- Microsoft[11]
- Monsanto[12]
- Petroleum
- Public utilities (electricity, water, natural gas)
- Rail transportation
- US Postal Service
- US Steel

Natural Monopoly

Natural monopolies are a product of economies of scale. In industries with high fixed costs, significant economies of scale can be achieved as production increases. For example, constructing a hydroelectric power plant involves a very high fixed cost. However, once the plant is operational, the cost of generating electrical power is typically much lower. Therefore, if there is a competing hydroelectric power plant, then both plants can lower their prices down to the marginal cost of producing electricity. Neither plant can recover its fixed costs under this sort of a pricing arrangement, and one or both plants will eventually go out of business.

> A natural monopoly exists typically due to very high fixed costs or strong economies of scale. Hence, in a natural monopoly, one firm is much more efficient than multiple firms in providing the goods or services to the market.

In the late nineteenth century, railroads were subject to this sort of situation, which is sometimes referred to as a "ruinous competition." This predicament stemmed from the extremely high fixed costs in acquiring the land and constructing the railroad, but the costs of adding extra cars and engines to carry more freight were relatively low. Therefore, competing railroads could lower their prices to just cover their variable costs (so they could still operate) but could not cover the fixed costs that they had incurred in building the line. The result was a predictable bankruptcy for one of the railroads. In this situation, the bankrupt railroad was usually acquired by the competing line, and a monopoly was the final result. Any prospective new entrant would be faced with extensive capital costs and the high risk of failure.

Price-Output Decision for Monopolies

The initial point to note about a demand curve for a monopolist is that the market demand equals the firm's demand. This alignment is logical given that with only one firm competing in the market, the firm faces the entire market. The profit-maximizing output is the point where marginal revenue equals marginal cost. The reason for this is the fact that profit increases as long as the incremental revenue achieved from producing one additional unit is greater than the incremental production cost incurred to produce the additional unit. Figure 5.9 displays the profit maximization point for a monopolist.

In Figure 5.8, the monopolist would produce at Q*, which is the point where marginal revenue equals marginal cost. At a production level denoted by Q*, the firm would have profits equal to the shaded area between the demand curve and the average cost curve. Given that the new market entry is not possible (by definition) in a monopoly, these profits can be enjoyed in the long run, *ceteris paribus*. However, simply having a monopoly does not guarantee long-run profits, as a combination of shifts in the demand curve and changes in average cost could put the firm in a loss-making situation. This scenario is presented in Figure 5.10.

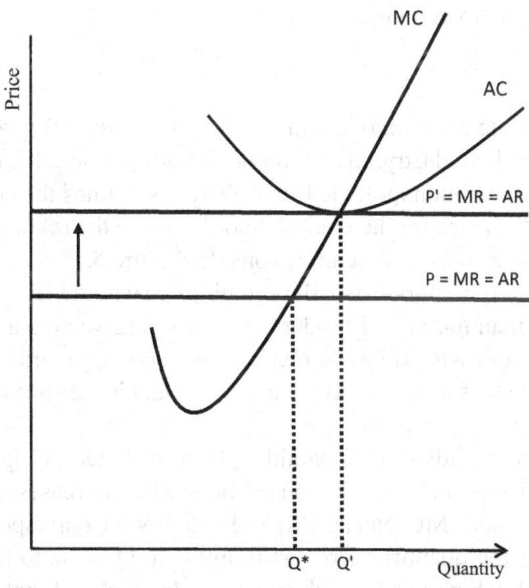

Figure 5.8 Firm Adjustment.

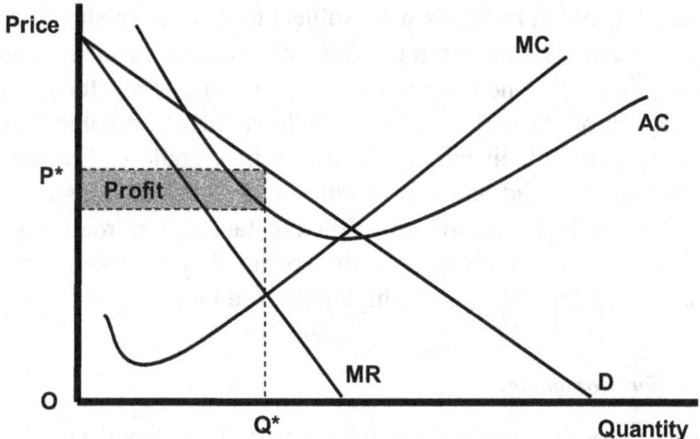

Figure 5.9 Profit Maximization for a Monopolist.

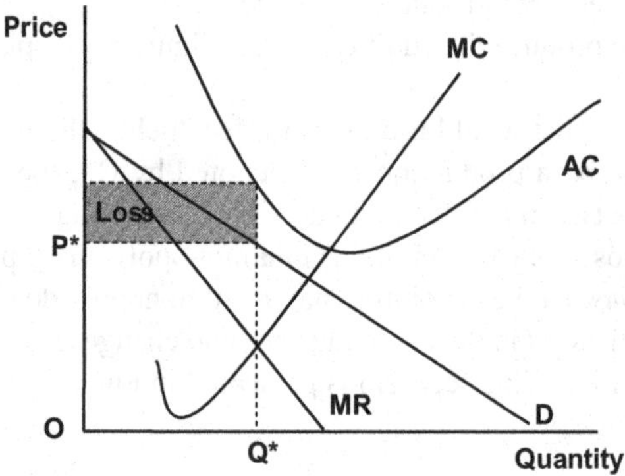

Figure 5.10 Loss Scenario for a Monopolist.

It is worth noting that the profit-maximizing (or loss-minimizing) quantity for the firm represents the total supply to the industry. In the absence of competition, the monopolist dominates the market, and therefore, the monopolistic firm effectively defines the supply side of the market, and this determines the price for the market. In order to see the relationship between pricing under monopolies and other market structures, consider Figure 5.10.

As mentioned previously, monopolists will set their price where MR = MC. When the MR of selling a good is greater than the MC of producing it, firms are making a profit on that product, and producing one more unit will add more revenues than costs, therefore increasing profits. If MR < MC, producing one less unit will save more costs than it sacrifices in revenues, resulting in enhanced profitability.

Consequently, the corresponding price would be P_m as depicted in Figure 5.11. When a monopoly is no longer available and competition in the market increases, the firm will move to a price/output decision where MC equals demand. This point corresponds to P_c, which lies below P_m.[13] Additionally, the quantity increases from Q_m to Q_c. Due to the increased competition, the price is lowered, which increases the quantity demanded. Finally, P_r corresponds to a price where government regulation requires cost-based pricing. Within cost-based pricing, the optimal output for the firm would be where average cost equals the demand curve. This point

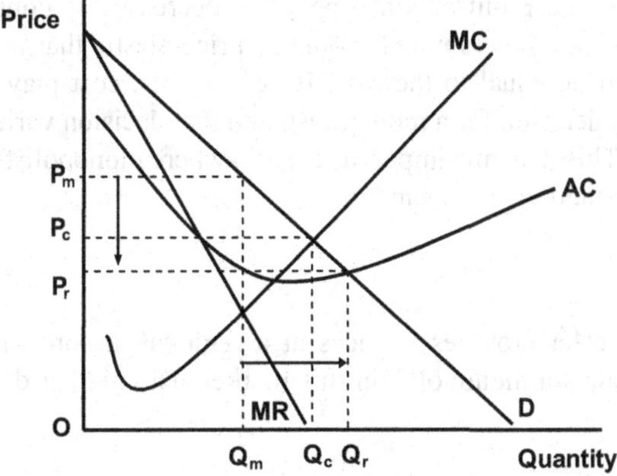

Figure 5.11 Equilibrium Price under Monopoly and Perfect Competition.

represents a further decrease in price and a further increase in the quantity demanded. Figure 5.10 graphically portrays the reason for price drop when new entrants enter a formerly held protective market.

In the realm of monopolies, after an optimal output is determined, the optimal price can be formulated as a function of MC and price elasticity (E_p). The formula below provides the optimal price for a monopolist to maximize total profit. Here, we simply state the formula which will be derived in the next section:

$$P = \frac{MC}{1 + \frac{1}{E_p}}$$

However, considering the price elasticity is rarely constant for all levels of output, the profit-maximizing profit will also vary by price elasticity. To illustrate this point, consider Table 5.4 which finds the profit-maximizing price for different price elasticities, assuming MC is held constant at $1,000.

Table 5.4 Profit-Maximizing Price for Various Price Elasticities

Marginal Cost	*Price Elasticity*	*P*
$1,000	−1.1	$11,000
$1,000	−1.2	$6,000
$1,000	−1.3	$4,333
$1,000	−1.4	$3,500
$1,000	−1.5	$3,000
$1,000	−2	$2,000
$1,000	−3	$1,500
$1,000	−4	$1,333
$1,000	−5	$1,250
$1,000	−6	$1,200
$1,000	−7	$1,167
$1,000	−8	$1,143
$1,000	−9	$1,125
$1,000	−10	$1,111
$1,000	−100	$1,010
$1,000	∞	$1,000

As Table 5.4 depicts, the profit-maximizing price decreases as consumers become more price elastic. Eventually, consumers may become so price-elastic that the monopolist's profit-maximizing price would be equal to the MC. Based on this, cost plays a significant role in shaping the price/output decision for a monopolist, and that decision varies because the elasticity of demand changes. This dynamic impels a scenario where monopolists must still be reactive to the market and understand their consumers.

Example

Let's imagine that DirectJet provides services at a regional airport with no other competition. Thus, carrier becomes a monopolist in this market. The market demand curve faced by DirectJet is:

$P = 2{,}400 - 5 \times Q$, and the cost is given by

$\mathrm{TC} = 1{,}500 + Q^2$

a What is the equation for the marginal revenue curve?

$\mathrm{TR} = P \times Q$

$\mathrm{TR} = 2{,}400 \times Q - 5 \times Q^2$

$$\mathrm{MR} = \frac{\mathrm{dTr}}{\mathrm{dQ}} = 2{,}400 - 10Q$$

b What is the profit-maximizing production quantity, and the price?

Set MR = MC

$2{,}400 - 10Q = 2Q$, and we can get

$Q = 200$

By plugging optimum units of $Q = 200$ into demand equation, we have

$\mathrm{PM} = 2{,}400 - 5 \times 200 = \$1{,}200$

The following section explains the derivation of the optimal pricing formula for a monopolist, as depicted here. Since profit is total revenue minus total costs, the optimal price for a monopolist can be determined mathematically. The total profit (π) can be stated as:

$$\pi = \mathrm{TR} - \mathrm{TC}$$
$$\pi = P(Q) \times Q - C(Q)$$

Since price is not constant for all levels of demand, the given formula represents price as a function of quantity, $P(Q)$. The price is then multiplied by Q to take into consideration the number of units sold by the firm. Similarly, cost is also represented as a function of quantity. However, it is not multiplied by Q since the function would be total cost. In order to determine an optimum price, the first-order derivative with respect to quantity leads to:

$$\frac{\mathrm{d}\pi}{\mathrm{dQ}} = P(Q) + \frac{\mathrm{dP}(Q)}{\mathrm{dQ}}Q - \frac{\mathrm{dC}(Q)}{d(Q)} \quad P(Q) + \frac{\mathrm{dP}(Q)}{\mathrm{dQ}}Q = \frac{\mathrm{dC}(Q)}{d(Q)}$$

Setting the above equation equal to zero yields:

$$P(Q)+\frac{\mathrm{d}P(Q)}{\mathrm{d}Q}Q-\frac{\mathrm{d}C(Q)}{d(Q)}=0$$

As price and cost per additional unit is the definition of marginal revenue and marginal cost, the equation could be restated in those terms. However, in order to explain things further, the cost function will only be rewritten in terms of MC. The resultant modified formula is:

$$P(Q)+\frac{\mathrm{d}P(Q)}{\mathrm{d}Q}Q=\mathrm{MC}$$

To help solve the equation, all terms are divided by *P*(*Q*):

$$\frac{P(Q)}{P(Q)}+\frac{\mathrm{d}P(Q)}{\mathrm{d}Q}\times\frac{Q}{P(Q)}=\frac{\mathrm{MC}}{P(Q)}$$

The term $\frac{\mathrm{d}P(Q)}{\mathrm{d}Q}\times\frac{Q}{P(Q)}$ is the mathematical definition of the inverse of price elasticity; therefore, the formula can be simplified into:

$$1+\frac{1}{E_p}=\frac{\mathrm{MC}}{P}$$

Solving for the optimal price at which a monopolist should price at provides:

$$P=\frac{\mathrm{MC}}{1+\frac{1}{E_p}}=\mathrm{MC}\times\left(\frac{E_p}{1+E_p}\right)$$

Example

Assume an airline is faced with a price elasticity of demand equaling −2 and the MC of providing additional seat is $100. Find the optimum markup and the ticket price:

$$\text{Markup}=\times\left(\frac{-2}{1-2}\right)=200\%$$

$$P=100\times\left(\frac{-2}{1-2}\right)$$

$$P=\$200$$

Example

Air Services International has a patent on a part on a general aviation aircraft. According to the estimates by the company business manager, the demand curve for this part is:

$P = 8{,}000 - 2Q$ and the total costs are

$\text{TC} = 50{,}000 - 6{,}000Q + 3Q^2$

a At what output level is average total variable costs at a minimum? To find the minimum of average total variable, we just need to set the derivative of TC to zero:

$$\text{TC} = 50{,}000 - 6{,}000Q + 3Q^2$$

$$\text{MC} = \frac{\text{dTC}}{\text{dQ}}$$

$$\text{MC} = -6{,}000 + 6Q$$

$$Q = 1{,}000$$

b At what price and output level does the ASI maximize profits? The optimum price will occur at the point which

$$\text{MC} = \text{MR}$$

$$\text{MR} = \frac{\text{dTC}}{\text{dQ}}$$

$$\text{MR} = 8{,}000 - 4Q$$

$$8{,}000 - 4Q = -6{,}000 + 6Q$$

$$10Q = 14{,}000$$

$$Q = 1{,}400 \text{ units}$$

$$P = 8{,}000 - 2(1{,}400)$$

$$P = \$5{,}200$$

c What are profits at this level?

$$\text{Profit} = \text{Total revenue} - \text{Total cost}$$

$$\text{Profit} = P \times Q - [\text{FC} + \text{AVC} \times Q]$$

$$\text{Profit} = (\$5{,}200 \times 1{,}400) - (50{,}000 - 6{,}000 \times 1{,}400 + 3 \times 1{,}400^2)$$

$$\text{Profit} = \$7{,}280{,}000 - 2{,}470{,}000$$

$$\text{Profit} = \$4{,}810{,}000$$

Monopoly Pricing and Consumer Well-Being

To many observers, the pricing decision for a monopolist might seem simple: charge the market as much as possible. A monopolist produces less output and sells it at a higher price than a perfectly competitive firm. However, while such a policy may provide extraordinary short-run profits, it tends to reduce profitability in the long run. Opting for maximum pricing will cause demand for the product to fall as consumers find ways to adapt to substitute goods or otherwise change their habits to buy less of the monopolized product. Even though no impeccable alternative might exist for airline travel over long distances, it is easy to notice how a monopoly airline could shift travelers over to corporate jets, chartered airlines, auto travel, train travel, or utilization of communication techniques such as video conferencing. Furthermore, an aggressive monopoly pricing will also cause other firms to invest more in overcoming barriers and entering the market. Monopoly pricing basically pits one firm against the rest of the world, and in that sort of contest, the world usually wins. Therefore, even a true monopolist protected by an iron-clad barrier, such as an effective patent, tends to moderate price somewhat in an attempt to discourage the consumer adjustments and market innovations that will eventually slash monopoly profits.

Economists point out another factor, often overlooked by most people, but which greatly mitigates the net harm of monopoly. If a monopolist restricts output and raises price in one market, it will simultaneously increase output and reduce price in other markets. If, for instance, a firm were to somehow monopolize the oil market and raise prices, the action would naturally lead to a reduction in the quantity of barrels being sold and therefore fewer resources employed in producing crude. Additional land, equipment, and other resources would now be available for solar energy resulting in a surge in production of solar panels. The harm done by monopoly in the oil market would be substantial but may be offset by cheaper, more environmentally friendly energy advancements in the future. Likewise, the imposition of any monopoly pricing in some air travel markets would shift aircraft and employees to other markets and reduce prices for consumers. There would still be some net harm as this reallocation of resources is triggered by monopoly manipulation rather than consumer preference, but the point is that the net cost of any monopoly is less than most people realize.

Monopoly Market Power in Aviation

The three industries under discussion are all sectors with firms that are capable of exerting substantial market power and, depending on the level of analysis, can easily be classified as monopolies. The airline industry is somewhat unique in that its major suppliers all have substantial market power. However, airlines compete in markets which more often resembles an oligopoly, which will be elaborated in the next chapter.

Airports

Another aspect of the aviation industry where market structure plays a significant role in shaping the industry is airports. An airport monopoly can arise due to a number of factors, such as slot availability, gate and facility availability, infrastructure, or government regulation.

The lack of competition at major airports may bestow pricing leverage upon the airport operator, which can result in higher costs for airlines and passengers. A case in point is London Heathrow, one of the most expensive airports in the world in terms of fees and charges for airlines and passengers. The airport charges some of the highest landing fees in the world for airlines, particularly during peak hours. Once again, the major issues concerning airports are the significant barriers to entry.

Slot Availability

The lack of available gates and slot controls at some airports acts to protect incumbent carriers and makes it difficult for new entry and, at some airports, can allow an airline to exert monopoly power.

In slot-controlled airports, demand for takeoff and landing slots exceeds the available capacity. This limitation on slots curbs the ability of new airlines to enter the market. For example, John F. Kennedy International has slot controls in place to manage demand, particularly during peak travel periods. In addition, London Heathrow Airport, Beijing Capital International Airport, Frankfurt Airport, and Frankfurt Airport have implemented slot controls to manage demand and ensure efficient use of its limited runway capacity. In 2016, Oman Air paid Kenya Airways $75 m for a single slot pair at LHR.

Gate and Facility Availability

For an airline aiming to establish a new airport, one of the first requirements is the availability of gates; schedule is limited by the availability of gates. Airlines are allocated with a specific count of gates in a particular airport, depending on the leasing agreements. While these requirements are universal, the ease of obtaining them varies considerably worldwide.

In the United States, the majority of gates and ticket counters are closely held by the individual airlines either through lease agreements with the airport or under full ownership. Leases provide the airline with exclusive control over a set number of gates, enabling the carrier to utilize the facilities as it deems fit. Practically, the airline acts as the owner of the gates and can update the facilities as needed. In return for this control over airport assets, airlines must make lease payments that are prescribed in a lease agreement with the airport authority. Depending on the terms, an airline may be stuck with the facilities until a suitable replacement is found. In some instances, airlines have found it profitable to sub-let these facilities to competing airlines. In some cases, airlines have even found success in terminating the lease agreements under Chapter 11 bankruptcy, although this is a rather drastic remedy.

At hub airports, airlines may own facilities. For example, Northwest Airlines (now Delta) invested heavily in their World Gateway hub at Detroit International Airport, while United Airlines has ownership over Terminal E at Houston Intercontinental Airport. In such scenarios, airlines may invest a large amount of capital into the airport to construct or revamp an entire terminal.

Regardless of the technical structure, airlines in the United States have significant control over airport facilities. This control represents a significant barrier to entry, as any new airline will have to acquire airport facilities in order to commence service. In cases where there are idle facilities at airports, this usually does not pose a significant problem. However, at airports with scarce resources, this can pose a significant problem to the new entrant. While the airport authority will attempt to work with all the airlines to accommodate the new entrant airline, this may not always work if the resources are all committed. Alternatively, the new entrant would be to enter an agreement with an incumbent airline to either use their facilities or sub-lease facilities. This option is usually costly, and there may be some instances where, in order to suppress competition, incumbent airlines may not be willing to allow a new entrant to the airport. This is particularly true at hub airports where the hub carrier may go to extensive lengths to obtain gates in order to block new entrants, particularly low-cost competitors.

Moreover, such a structure might not align with economic efficiency since airlines may sign gate leases to block competition, even if the airline does not require the gate. Even if leases contain minimum usage requirements, airlines can adjust their schedule or add extra flights to meet the minimum requirements. This creates a situation where the assets may not be used in the most efficient manner.

Another strategy is for airports to assign airlines access to common facilities. Under a common use system, airlines pay a fee per use for using the facilities. In theory, since the facilities are being utilized more intensely, the cost per use should be diminished. However, airlines are not fond of the common use approach as they have less control over their facilities and their operation. Common use facilities generally do not provide significant barriers to entry, since an airline can use the facilities when available. Even during peak periods, it is unlikely that an airline could not enter an airport using common facilities at some time of the day. Therefore, gates and other airport facilities do not generally provide a significant barrier to entry outside of the United States.

Slot Control

However, in Europe and other parts of the world, barriers to entry remain in the form of airport slots. A slot represents the right to land or takeoff from an airport at a given time. More formally, according to Article 1 of the European Council Regulation No. 95/93, the key regulation concerning airport slot allocation in Europe, define a slot as:

> … the entitlement established under this Regulation, of an air carrier to use the full range of airport infrastructure necessary to operate an air service at a coordinated airport on a specific date and time for the purpose of landing and take-off as allocated by a coordinator in accordance with this Regulation.
>
> (Commission of the European Communities, 2001)

Slots are allocated through a variety of mechanisms; however, according to EEC No. 95/93, there are two primary rules to slot allocation. The first rule, the "grandfather right," entitles an airline to the same slot in the future (if they are currently using it). While this rule was enacted to provide stability, in practice it provides the airline with quasi-ownership of the slot. Slot usage is determined by the "use-it or lose-it" rule, which stipulates that the airline must use the slot for at least 80% of the time during the scheduled period. If the airline fails to meet this requirement, then the grandfather right does not apply and the slot is lost. This provides an incentive for the airline to continue using the slot, even if it is not economically efficient. The remaining slots are then dispersed to applicants, with only 50% of the new slots are preserved for new entrants. Based on the grandfather right, the use-it or lose-it rule, and the new entrant slot limit, very few slots become available for new entrants. For example, in the summer of 2000, 97% of London Heathrow's slots were grandfathered, leaving only 3% of the total slots available, with only 1.5% available to new entrants (DotEcon, 2001). Moreover, the available slots were at inconvenient times. These slot controls represent a significant barrier to entry, but the grandfather right enables an airline to accumulate a significant number of slots over time.

> An airport slot provides an airline the right to land and take off at a particular day during a specified time period. Slots, once acquired by an airline, become valuable asset that can be worth millions of dollars. In 2020, Air New Zealand has sold its London Heathrow slot for a whopping NZ$42 million ($27 million). In the United States, John F. Kennedy International Airport (JFK), LaGuardia Airport (LGA), and Ronald Reagan Washington National Airport (DCA) are slot controlled. London Heathrow, Amsterdam Schiphol, Paris Charles De Gaulle, and Frankfurt are four of many slot-controlled airports in Europe.

Obtaining a slot at London Heathrow does not come easy. According to EC 95/93, the allocation of slots through the formal slot allocation process is the only legal method to obtain a slot in Europe. While swapping of slots is permitted, a 1999 UK court ruling opened the door to the "grey market," where slot swapping was permitted with monetary compensation. This ruling created a situation in the United Kingdom where slots could be traded, leased, and sold to other airlines; however, such practices are considered illegal in the rest of Europe. The grey market is widely rejected across the rest of Europe under the rationale that a private firm should not benefit financially from a public good (Mackay, 2006). However, this rationale certainly favors incumbent airlines over new entrants to the market. While the grey market does reduce the barriers to entry, it shifts the entry requirements from a legal/structural requirement to a financial requirement. From an economic point of view, financial barriers are more desirable than legal barriers since, under financial barriers, the slot is allocated to the firm that is willing to pay the highest price and therefore values the slot the most. With the recent Open Skies agreement signed between the EU and the United States, the grey market became more active, especially for slots at London Heathrow. In 2016, Oman Air made one of the most expensive deals, buying a pair of slots from Air France-KLM for $75 million. In pre-COVID times, airlines were required to operate 80% of their allocation or risk losing the slots. This regulation was temporarily suspended during the peak of the pandemic to help struggling airlines, but it has gradually come back.

The United States has limited experience with slot controls largely due to the fact that the United States has been successful at constructing additional runways (Mackay, 2006). However, the FAA implemented a slot system at the following airports[14]:

- LaGuardia Airport (LGA)
- John F. Kennedy International Airport (JFK)
- Washington National Airport (DCA).

In 1985, the FAA permitted a full secondary market for slots, similar to the United Kingdom's grey market, where slots could be sold, traded, or leased. However, secondary slot trading was not as successful as planned due to two major issues: market power, and uncertainty of duration and value.

Airlines decided to retain slots rather than sell or lease them in order to prevent new carriers from entering the market. The issue of market power also caused airlines to increase their slot ownership in order to become more dominant. This was especially true at Chicago O'Hare where United and American both increased their slot ownership, thereby making the airport less competitive. Finally, slots were only deemed temporary by the FAA, creating uncertainty over the lifetime and true value of the slot.

A lack of slot trading made the system relatively ineffective, and the slot mechanisms were eventually abolished at all four airports. As a result of the slot removal, airlines immediately increased service to the airports, especially at LaGuardia and O'Hare where tremendous delays were experienced (Mackay, 2006). This compelled the FAA to mediate with the airlines to reduce the number of flights to acceptable levels. The immediate increase in service to these airports illustrates that a slot system represents a barrier to entry, even with a buy/sell market for slots.

Due to either slots in Europe or airport facilities (gates, ticket counters) in the United States, new entrants face significant barriers to entry at the airport level. High gate utilization during peak periods is one of the major airport barriers. All these factors have allowed incumbent carriers to increase their market power at airports, and in particular, at hub airports. The near monopoly power that some airlines have acquired at hub airports has been a significant barrier to entry.

Hub Airlines

Numerous studies have investigated the hypothesis that airlines have exerted their strong market power at the hub airport in the form of hub premiums. The premise of hub premium hypothesis states that originating or terminating passengers are charged a higher fare than other passengers traveling throughout the carrier's system (Gordon and Jenkins, 1999).

The perspective of the actual existence of hub premiums remains divergent. Gordon and Jenkins (1999) used proprietary Northwest Airlines data to show that there was actually a hub discount at Minneapolis-St. Paul airport. Additionally, other studies have found that the hub premiums do not exist. Conversely, some studies have shown that hub premiums exist. Borenstein (1989) and Lijesen, Rietveld and Nijkamp (2004) claimed that a few carriers in Europe (Lufthansa, Swiss, and Air France) charged hub premiums. However, even if hub airlines do charge higher prices, this may simply reflect higher quality not adjusted for in such studies. For example, the dominant carrier may have more amenable airport facilities, may benefit from goodwill in the community where they are perceived as the "home-town company," holds a greater credibility on safety, or may have higher-valued frequent flier awards. The fact that most businesses and communities seem to like having a hub airline nearby supports this view.

Given the evidence for a hub premium is not conclusive and since hub airlines are frequently undergoing bankruptcy, if any actual premium exists, it may be small. Furthermore, even if there is some monopoly power at that airport, the positive network effects from hub-and-spoke systems also produce benefits that, as Economides (2004) shows, may be greater than the damage of higher prices at the hub. It implies that the efficiency gained from economies of scale, scope, and density in the hub network may help reduce prices and increase product availability in the overall network.

While specific studies appear to have differing conclusions on hub premiums, the actual case of Pittsburgh International Airport provides a good real-world example of what may happen when a hub airport is open to competition. In the autumn of 2004, US Airways announced that it was going to significantly scale back its Pittsburgh hub. The total number of flights at Pittsburgh was dramatically reduced and a greater number of gates became available. With the diminishing barriers to entry, low-cost carriers such as Southwest, JetBlue, and Independence Air all entered the market. Although the total number of passengers using the airport decreased, originating passengers increased by 12% (McCartney, 2005). Moreover, airfares dropped significantly, especially on a few dominated routes. For example, the average airfare between Pittsburgh and Philadelphia (a route between two US Airways hubs) fell from $680 to $180 (McCartney, 2005).

Commercial Aircraft Manufacturing

Presently, there are four major aircraft manufacturers, with two competing fairly evenly in each market. Boeing and Airbus compete in the large commercial aircraft (LCA) market. Until the late 1970s, the United States had a near monopoly in the LCA sector. Bombardier and Embraer compete in the regional jet market. A new entrant to the regional aircraft market in the 75- to 95-seat category, the Sukhoi Superjet, made its maiden flight in May 2008.[15] Both Commercial Aircraft Corporation of China (COMAC) and Bombardier have been trying to gain share in the commercial aircraft market dominated by Boeing and Airbus. Notably, Bombardier CS300 (rebranded the Airbus A220, after Airbus acquired a 50.1% stake in the Bombardier program in 2018) commercial aircraft is almost similar to Boeing 737 and Airbus A319neo, particularly in terms of specifications.

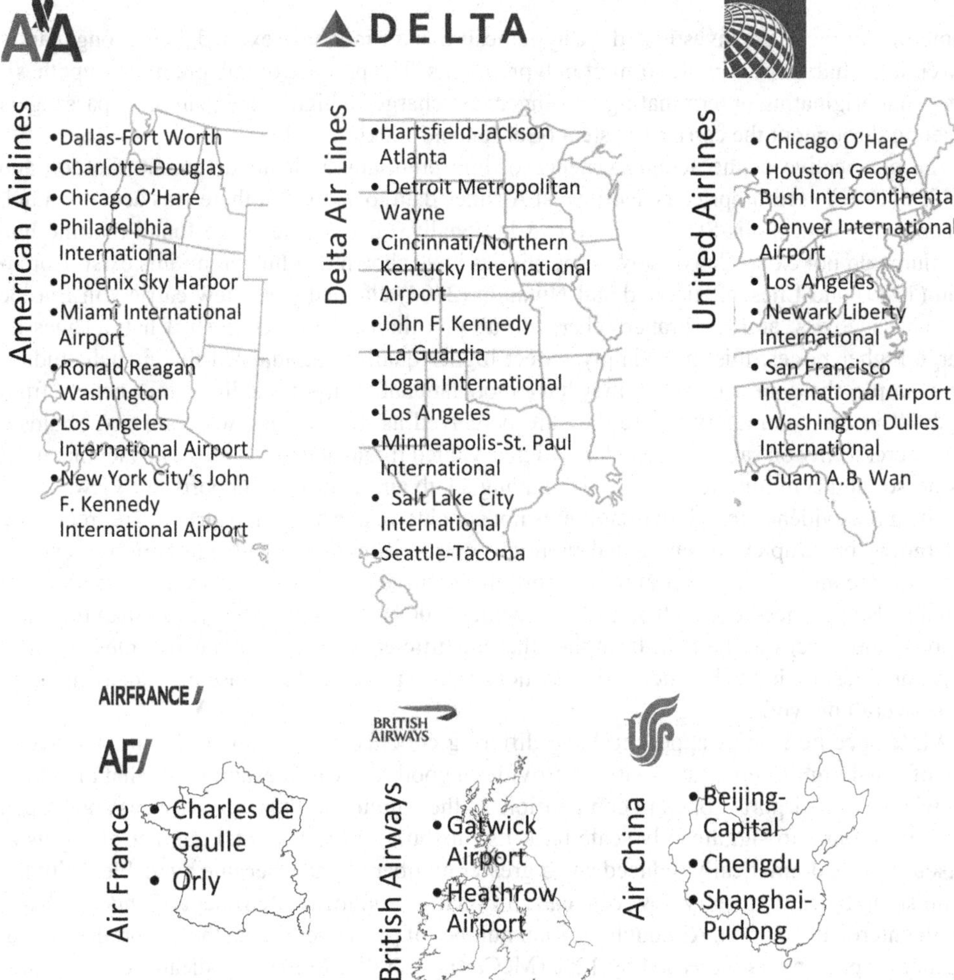

Boeing and Airbus compete aggressively with each other in almost all segments of their individual markets. Until recently, the biggest exception to this rule was the very large aircraft market, where Boeing had a monopoly with its 747. However, with the introduction of the Airbus A380, Boeing no longer enjoys this monopoly. Despite being an engineering marvel, the Airbus A380 did not achieve success in the air transport industry and the production stopped in February 2019. When the COVID-19 pandemic began, the Airbus A380 was the first wide-body aircraft to be grounded worldwide. However, the year 2022 has become a defining moment in the superjumbo's fortunes, and many A380s have returned to service, by airlines like British Airways, Qantas, and Lufthansa.

While the broad market for commercial aircraft is largely a duopoly, for some airlines, the market is more like a monopoly. Thus, while most carriers are able to play one manufacturer against the other in negotiations, some are more constrained by operational limitations. For example, consider Southwest Airlines, an all-Boeing 737 operator (before the acquisition of AirTran's 717s). Part of Southwest's success has been a common fleet type; this has increased crew flexibility, reduced crew training cost, and diminished spare part inventories. In this situation, switching to an Airbus aircraft would entail substantial costs. Such circumstances potentially put Boeing in a position to exert a degree of monopoly power over Southwest Airlines. However, this is greatly tempered by the resale market for aircraft; Southwest could even buy new aircraft indirectly through another airline that was better positioned to strike bargains with Boeing, then immediately resell to Southwest.

Furthermore, Boeing must also consider the possibly severe damage to its reputation if it ever were somehow able to exploit such situations. If the company is perceived to have betrayed one of its best and most loyal customers, then other airlines would be careful to avoid repeating Southwest's mistake. It is likely that any possible gain from exploiting Southwest would be far less than the loss from declining sales, as the global community witness a grave mistake to become too dependent on Boeing. Indeed, since anyone is likely to be hesitant about relying too much on a single supplier, it may be vital for Boeing to be able to point to a very satisfied, successful "dependent" in order to encourage other airlines to, as much as possible, follow Southwest's example.[16]

Modern aircraft manufacturing is a heavily capital-intensive industry requiring immense expenditures in research, development, and manufacturing. While technological advancements have increased and economies of scale benefits have become more important, the cost of designing and marketing an aircraft has become substantial, strengthening the barriers to entry into the industry. This trend has also seen the number of firms competing in the commercial aircraft industry drastically reduced. Therefore, there are now very few firms competing in the industry, creating a market structure that resembles an oligopoly, which will be discussed in greater detail in the next chapter.

Jet Engine Manufacturing

An industry with a market structure similar to the commercial aircraft manufacturing industry is the commercial aircraft jet engine manufacturing industry. Broadly speaking, the market has four major firms: General Electric (GE), CFM International, Pratt & Whitney (P&W), and Rolls-Royce. Actually, when considered with their joint ventures, General Electric, Pratt & Whitney, and Rolls-Royce control the largest share of the world's aircraft engine market at a combined percentage of around 98%. However, similar to the aircraft manufacturing industry, there may be certain situations where the market is in reality a duopoly or monopoly. For example, on the new Boeing 787, only two engines are being offered to customers: GE and Rolls-Royce. Therefore, the competitive actions of the firms will largely be based on duopoly competition theory. Taking a step further, all Boeing 737Max are powered by CFM LEAP-1B high bypass turbofans, meaning that CFM LEAP has a monopoly on the supply of engines for 737 aircraft. This dynamic interaction is intriguing, as an engine's success is highly tied to an aircraft's success. Moreover, if CFMI wants to enforce monopoly power by attempting to raise the engine's price, this would hurt the competitiveness of the 737. However, with CFMI also being one of the two suppliers for the rival Airbus 32X family, CFMI holds an extremely strong position in the narrow body jet engine manufacturing industry.

The capital requirements for engine manufacturing are quite large and, for the existing firms, have generally come from earlier military contracts. The "Big Three" all have roots tracing back to military applications. Rolls-Royce and P&W were deeply involved with engine manufacturing during the Second World War, while GE made the jump from military applications in the late 1960s (Smith, 1997). Without military applications and grants, the required technology would be extremely expensive for a new entrant. In the event that a new aircraft project looked profitable, then one of the "Big Three" would undoubtedly become involved, leaving new entrants the less desirable aircraft designs.

While some market power can be held by the engine manufacturers, airlines routinely play one engine manufacturer against the other in order to get the best deal. This practice signifies that engine manufacturers might have to provide deep discounts on engine purchases, but they are able to recover through maintenance agreements or "power by the hour" contracts. Therefore, engine manufacturers capitalize on economies of scope benefits wherever possible. This is especially true of GE, which leases aircraft with GE engines through GE Commercial Aircraft Services (GECAS). Economies of scope represent another barrier to entry into the industry, as it provides a competitive advantage to the incumbent firms.

Monopsony and Bilateral Monopoly

A *monopsony* is a market condition in which one buyer faces many sellers. Due to the presence of only one buyer, a common theoretical implication is that the price of the good is pushed down near the cost of production. Notably, Walmart generally exerts significant degree of monopsony power on suppliers and retailors. Similarly, the defense industry in the United States may also be a monopsony in which there is only one buyer (US government) and several sellers. For example, the Boeing B-1 Lancer bomber is a prime example of a monopsony structure, where the bomber is used exclusively by the United States Air Force (USAF) or Lockheed Martin F-22 Raptor. A single-payer health care system, in which the government is the only buyer of health care, is another example.

A market condition consisting of only one buyer and only one seller is called a bilateral monopoly. For example, in some countries, the national airline is the only employer of pilots, but there is only one supplier of pilot from the pilot union members.

A bilateral monopoly characterizes a market scenario in which a single seller is faced by a single buyer. The monopolist producer has an incentive to limit production to maximize profit, while the monopsonist buyer utilizes its market power to increase production to lower cost. The equilibrium price and quantity in such a market cannot be determined by the general tools of supply and demand.

		Numbers of buyers		
		One	*Few*	*Many*
Number of suppliers	*One*	*Bilateral monopoly*		*Monopoly*
	Few		*Oligopoly*	
	Many	*Monopsony*		*Perfect competition*

The determination of market price and output hinges factors such as the bargaining capability and market conditions. Examples may include:

- Professional athletes who are members of players unions, such as the National Basketball Association (NBA),[17] the National Football League (NFL), or the Major League Soccer (MLS). The player's union is the only source of labor for sports leagues, which makes it a monopoly. Similarly, the sports league is also the only major purchaser of the services of players, which makes it a monopsony.
- Pilot unions weild a labor-selling monopoly, and the monopsonist airline may be a single buyer of pilots.
- Certain classes of defense products such as the Lockheed Martin F-22 Raptor cannot be exported under U.S. federal law to protect its stealth technology and classified features.

In a bilateral monopoly, the outcome of negotiations between the buyer and seller will depend on their relative bargaining power and the market condition for the products produced.

Summary

This chapter introduced the reader to the concept of market structures. Markets in air transport are typically quite narrowly defined city-pairs, including indirect routings between the two cities. A market structure refers to the degree of competition and the number of consumers and producers in that market. This concept is often described in terms of entry or exit barriers, the number of buyers and sellers, the number of competitors, the extent of product substitutability, and the degree of mutual interdependence among firms. The chapter covered the more theoretical economic models of a competitive market and also those of a more monopolistic market. The competitive market model covers the conditions necessary for a competitive market to thrive, along with the overall determination of price within such a market, extending to the pricing challenges faced by an individual competitor or firm. It also outlines the long-term equilibrium solution within such a market. We also discussed the monopolistic market in a similar fashion to include the price output decision for the monopoly firm. The commercial aircraft market is fully dominated by Boeing and Airbus, which together hold 99% market share. Moreover, the chapter addressed some of the reasons that a monopoly might arise and some of the factors that might act to reduce monopoly power. While acknowledging that very few markets perfectly embody the ideals of competition or monopoly, the models are useful as benchmarks against which one can measure real-world market structures. The last part of this chapter contains a discussion of the market structure of the various parts of the aviation industry and how they may approximate monopolistic conditions under certain circumstances.

Discussion Questions

1 What is a real-life example of a monopsony?
2 What is normal profit?
3 What are the four basic market structures?
4 Consider a monopolist with $TC = 1{,}500 + 2Q$

   a If demand is given by $Q = 80 - P$, what is the monopoly price and quantity?
   b What are the profits?

5 State the four basic conditions that characterize a competitive market.
6 Does perfect competition exist in the real world?
7 Are perfectly competitive firms "price makers" or "price takers"? How is the profit-maximizing price and quantity decided upon by the perfectly competitive firm?
8 What happens when markets do not have enough competition?

9 What are the barriers to entry in the airline industry?
10 Is the aircraft industry an example of perfect competition?
11 Is it true that a monopoly can charge any price and that customers will still have to buy the product? Do you agree or disagree. Why?
12 You are the manager of a firm that sells its product in a competitive market at a price of \$50. Your firm's cost function is $TC = 40 + 5Q^2$.

   a Calculate the profit-maximizing output.
   b Calculate the total profit.

13 Explain how the price set by a perfectly competitive firm compares with the price under monopoly competition.
14 Assume a firm is operating under perfect competition with the following total cost and demand curves:

   $TC = 100 + 0.50 \times Q^2$
   $P = 50$

   a Find equilibrium price and quantity.
   b Is the firm making a profit or loss?
   c Is this a long-run or short-run equilibrium?

15 General Engine (GE) is the only producer of new jet engines for general aviation aircraft. Demand for a single engine is $P = 2{,}000{,}000 - Q$, while the MCs of producing an engine are $MC = 1{,}999Q$.

   a What would be the monopoly price and quantity of these engines?
   b What economic profit would GE earn on the sale of these engines?
   c What would happen to price and quantity if the market were competitive (assuming the same costs)?

16 Suppose you are the manager of NavGas, a major FBO, exclusively serving general aviation aircraft. Based on the estimates provided by a consultant, you know that the relevant demand and cost functions for your product are:

   $Q = 25 - 0.5P$
   $TC = 50 + 2Q$

   a What is the FBO's inverse demand function?
   b What is the FBO's marginal revenue when producing four units of output?
   c What are the levels of output and price when you are maximizing profits?
   d What will be the level of profits?

17 Explain what will happen in the long run in a competitive market when some of the firms are not covering their average total costs.
18 Is it true that a monopoly firm will always make a profit? Explain why or why not.

Notes

1 Avianca continues to shake up Latin America's aviation scene with creation of 'Abra'. CAPA, May 13, 2022.
2 Formulas and explanations for total, average, and marginal revenue are discussed in Chapter 4.
3 Recall that by definition, the average total cost curve contains a normal rate of return (profit) on investment. Anything above this is called an above average rate of return or economic profit.
4 *Denver Post*. Airline consolidation has created airport monopolies, increased fares. July 17, 2015.
5 Ibid.
6 Decade-after-landing-in-atlanta-southwest-still-distant-no-2-airline. *The Atlanta Journal of Constitution*, February 11, 2022.
7 ICAO, https://www.icao.int/pages/freedomsair.aspx
8 Tupolev manufactured the TU-144, a similar supersonic commercial aircraft, but it was not widely produced.
9 Many economists argue that the Concorde's time savings were not great enough to motivate enough travelers to pay the higher costs; regular jet service across the Atlantic turned out to be a very viable substitute. Perhaps Boeing and others could have readily mastered the technology but had the good business sense to stay out of this market.

10 Note that when unions succeed, at least temporarily, in forcing wages above the competitive level, the higher cost will ultimately reduce employment in the union sector. In turn, workers who can't get jobs in the union sector will enter non-union markets and depress wages there. Thus, unions push wages down in some sectors even as they raise them in others; the net impact on wages tends to hover around zero. Thus, it is a myth that unions are a significant cause of inflation.

11 It holds more than 75% market share and is the tech space's market leader and virtual monopolist.

12 Monsanto holds about 70%–100% of the market in commercial seed.

13 All this assumes that the production costs are the same for the tiny competitor and the huge monopolist – that no economies of scale exist. Alternatively, if there were major economies of scale, then it is very possible that the lower costs of the monopolist would translate into a price below the competitive level.

14 In addition, the FAA monitors traffic demand at other airports and has a formal schedule review and approval process. These airports are Chicago O'Hare International Airport, Los Angeles International Airport, Newark Liberty International Airport, and San Francisco International Airport

15 *ANTARA News*, May 11, 2012.

16 Also, if Boeing bargained too aggressively, Southwest could ultimately switch over. This scenario may have already occurred when easyJet placed a large order for Airbus aircraft after having been a consistent Boeing customer.

17 N.B.A. Owners and Players Ratify Labor Deal, *The Washington Times*, December 2011.

References

Borenstein, S. (1989). Hubs and High Fares: Dominance and Market Power in the US Airline Industry. *Rand Journal of Economics*, 20(3), 344–365.

Commission of the European Communities. (2001). *Proposal for a Regulation of the European Parliament and of the Council amending Council Regulation (EEC) No. 95/93 of 18 January 1993 on Common Rule for the Allocation of Slots at Community Airports*, June 20. Retrieved on April 4, 2007 from

Daly, K. (1998). Winds Rise in the East. *Airline Business*, September. Retrieved on March 12, 2007 from Air Transport Intelligence.

DotEcon. (2001). *Auctioning Airport Slots*. A Report for the HM Treasury and the Department of the Environment, Transport and the Regions.

Economides, N. (2004). *Competition Policy in Network Industries: An Introduction*. NET Institute Working Paper No. 04-24.

Emirates. (2015). *Emirates to Deploy A380 on More Routes in 2016*. Press Release, December 15, 2015. Retreived from https://www.emirates.com/media-centre/emirates-to-deploy-a380-on-more-routes-in-2016-to-be-distributed-in-30-minutes

Gordon, R. and Jenkins, D. (1999). *Hub and Network Pricing in the Northwest Airlines Domestic System*. Washington, DC: The George Washington University.

Harrison, M. (2003). *US Versus EU Competition Policy: The Boeing-McDonnell Douglas Merger*. American Consortium on European Union Studies on Transatlantic Relations Cases, 2.

Lijesen, M., Rietveld, P., and Nijkamp, P. (2004). Do European Carriers Charge Hub Premiums? *Networks and Spatial Economics*, 4(4), 347–360.

Mackay, L. (2006). *Overview of Mechanisms to Deal with Airport Congestion*. Unpublished work, Embry-Riddle Aeronautical University.

McCartney, S. (2005). The Middle Seat: Why Travelers Benefit When an Airline Hub Closes. *Wall Street Journal*, November 1.

Smith, D. (1997). Strategic Alliances in the Aerospace Industry: A Case of Europe Emerging or Converging? *European Business Review*, 9(4), 171–178.

6 Hybrid Market Structure and the Aviation Industry

While the previous chapter introduced the two extremes of the market structure continuum (Table 6.1), this chapter analyzes the two middle hybrid market structures: monopolistic competition and oligopoly. In contrast to perfect competition, which rarely exists in actuality, both oligopoly and monopolistic competition are prevalent in modern industry, with the airline industry heavily influenced by the characteristics of oligopolies. Air transportation serves as a highly concentrated industry where a small handful of firms—airlines, aircraft manufacturers, airports, and engine manufacturers—dominate the whole industry. Moreover, with the recent mergers of US Airways–American Airlines, Southwest–AirTran, and Alaska Airlines–Virgin America, the number of players in the United States industry is decreasing even further. Analogous trends toward airline industry concentration are evident in other liberalized markets, such as the North Atlantic and the European Union. Even more tightly concentrated is the aircraft manufacturing industry, which is dominated by two mega manufacturers, Boeing and Airbus. Similarly, among the leading four engine manufactures are CFM International, International Aero Engines (IAE),[1] General Electric, and Rolls-Royse. The combined grip of these firms hold more than 90% of the market share. This chapter explores both monopolistic competition and oligopoly, as well as demonstrates how each hybrid market structure impacts a company's productivity and profitability. The chapter is outlined as follows:

- Monopolistic Competition
  - Price–Output Decision
- Oligopolies
  - Characteristic and Condition
  - Differing Views of Oligopoly
  - Examples of Oligopoly
- Contestability Theory
- Kinked Demand Curve Theory
- Cournot Theory
- Profitability Issues
- Competition and Antitrust Issues
- Industry Consolidation
- Beyond Market Concentration Considerations
- Summary
- Discussion Questions

DOI: 10.4324/9781003388135-6

Monopolistic Competition

Monopolistic competition stands out perhaps as the most common market structure of the four types in the market continuum in Table 6.1. This configuration represents yet another form of market structure in which the firms produce similar, but not identical products. Therefore, each firm produces a small fraction of industry output. In other words, there exists limited market consolidation. Like perfect competition, it is relatively easy to enter the market, albeit not without associated entry costs. The key difference is that the ease of obtaining capital is considerably less in a monopolistically competitive market compared to an oligopoly market. Other barriers to entry may include customer loyalty or regulatory restrictions. A monopolistically competitive industry has the following characteristics:

> Monopolistic competition serves as a market situation in which many independent sellers produce differentiated products. In this market, each seller provides goods or services with some degree of product differentiation and some monopoly power.

- A large number of sellers
- Full dissemination of information
- Low barriers to entry
- Product differentiation

The key difference between perfect competition and monopolistic competition is that in perfect competition, companies mainly sell homogeneous products, while monopolistically competitive firms sell heterogenous products, facing numerous proximate substitutes. Firms in a monopolistic competitive environment sell products that are the same but not identical, and they have some power to set their own prices. The strategic use of product differentiation aims to encourage consumers to choose one brand more than another in a competitive market. Products are differentiated when customers perceive a sense of uniqueness, which leads them to pay more, despite the existence of close substitutes. That explains why customers pay about $30 for a bottle of Berg drinking water, while a bottle of Evian costs only $2 bottle.[2]

From a firm's point of view, this is a more desirable situation, since the more a product can be differentiated, the more control a firm has over its price. Since all the firms have the same profit incentive, there is still a good deal of price competition in monopolistically competitive markets. Companies in a monopolistic competition make economic profits in the short run, but in the long run, a result of the freedom of entry and exit in the industry, they make zero economic profit.

Table 6.1 Market Continuum

	Perfect Competition	*Monopolistic Competition*	*Oligopoly*	*Monopoly*
Number of sellers	Large	Many	Few	One
Type of product	Homogenous	Unique	Homogenous or differentiated	Unique
Control over price	None	Very little	Strong	Very strong
Entry condition	Very easy	Easy	Difficult	Impossible
Example	Agriculture	Retail	Airlines	Public utilities

Given the plethora of companies involved, each player keeps a small market share and is unable to influence the price. Monopolistic competition is extremely common in today's business environment. Examples include:

- Accounting firms
- Books
- Convenience stores
- Hairdressers
- Grocery stores
- Garment producers
- Hotels
- Jewelry shops
- Law firms
- Private music lessons
- Radio stations
- Restaurants

Hotels and restaurants stand as prime examples of monopolistic competition since they provide somewhat unique services, are fairly common in most markets, and exist in a market with relative ease of entry.

Price–Output Decision

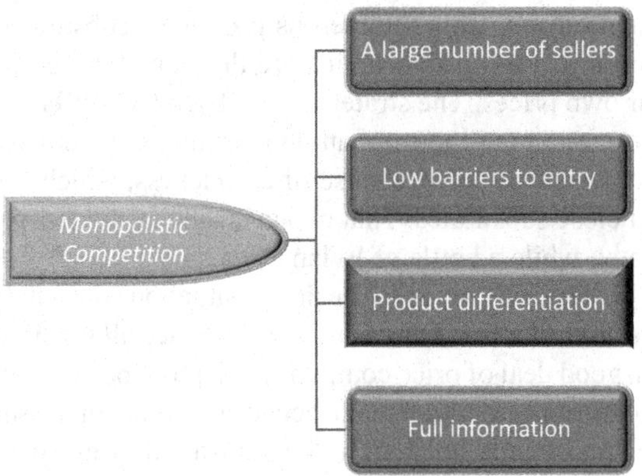

In perfectly competitive markets, the demand curve for a firm's product is essentially horizontal, as the firm is a price taker and has virtually no power to set prices. In this situation, demand is perfectly elastic. With the gradual escalation of product differentiation, the elasticity of demand decreases, which shifts the firm away from a perfectly competitive market and toward a more monopolistically competitive or oligopolistic market. As mentioned above, this increase in product differentiation creates the potential for a firm to have more control over the price that it charges. This situation is depicted in Figure 6.1.

The demand curve for a firm shifts from a horizontal line to a downward sloping line. As the firm progresses through the market structure continuum, the slope of the demand curve will become steeper until it eventually reaches a point where it encompasses the entire market, making a firm's transformation into a monopoly. In a manner analogous to a monopoly, in a

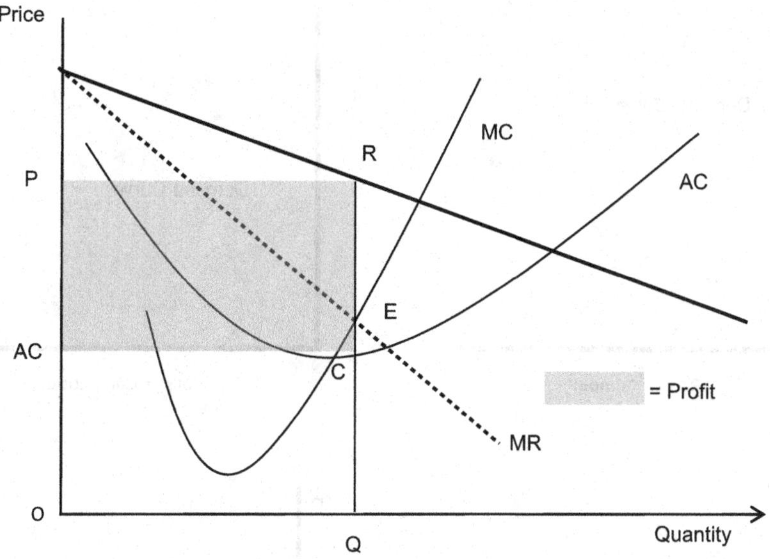

Figure 6.1 Short-Run Equilibrium: Monopolistic Competitive Market.

monopolistically competitive environment, firms produce the quantity (Q) where marginal cost (MC) equals marginal revenue (MR). MR measures the change in the revenue when one additional unit of a product is sold, while the MC refers to the additional cost to produce each additional unit. In monopolistic market, firms charge the highest price (P) that sells that quantity:

$$MR - MC$$
$$P > MR$$

The price the firm charges would be on the demand curve. As elucidated by the figure, the more elastic the demand curve facing the firm, the less control the individual firm has over its price. Figure 6.2 illustrates the typical demand curves across the various market structures. Oligopoly is an especially complex case in which the nature of demand can vary significantly given the dynamics of each industry. For instance, airlines often appear to have no more control over price than the typical monopolistic competitor does.

Example

Jet services operated in a monopolistic competitive industry with the following demand and cost functions:

$$P = 100 - 0.25 \times Q$$
$$AC = MC = 20$$

Find:

a Optimal output
b Market price
c Economic profit or loss
d Optimal markup

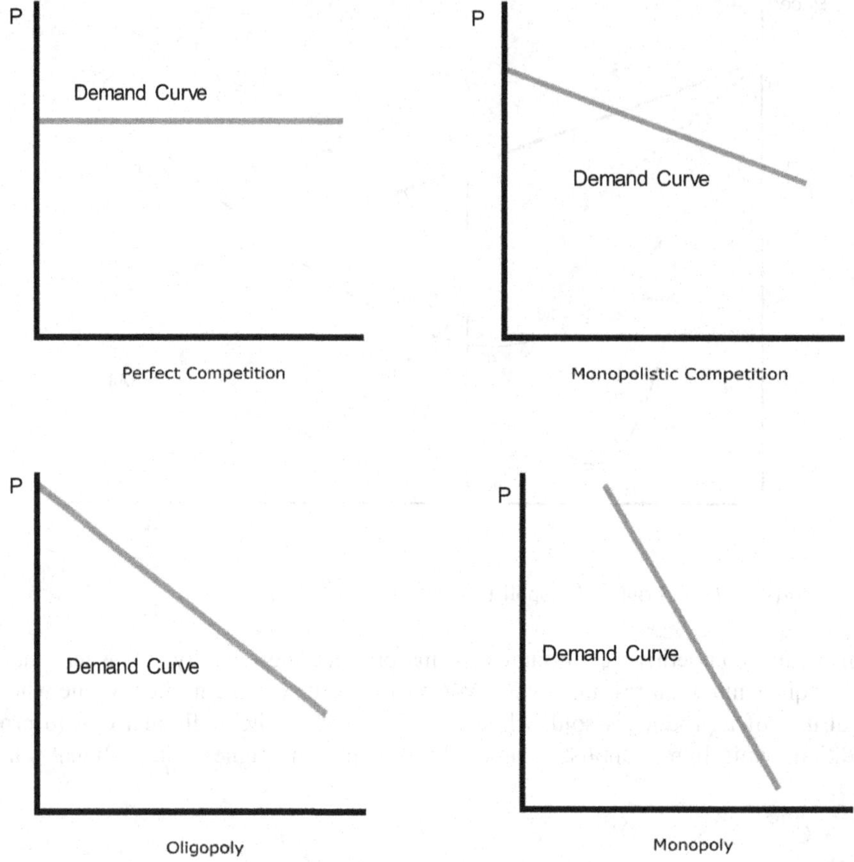

Figure 6.2 Progression of Demand Curve: Perfect Competition to Monopoly.

Solution:

a To find the optimal output, a monopolistic competitive firm sets MC = MR

$\text{TR} = P \times Q$
$\text{TR} = 100Q - 0.25Q^2$
$\text{MR} = 100 - 0.50Q$
$\text{MR} = \text{MC}$
$100 - 0.50Q = 20$
$Q = 160$ units

b To find market price, substitute the value of output.

$P = 100 - 0.25 \times Q$
$P = 100 - 0.25 \times Q$
$P = 100 - 0.25 \times 160$
$P = \$60$

c To find economic profit,

Profit = total revenue – total cost
TR = $P \times Q$ = \$60 × 160 = \$9,600

d To find optimal markup,

$$P = MC \times \left(1 - \frac{1}{E}\right)$$

$$P = \$20 \times \left(1 - \frac{1}{E}\right)$$

We substitute P = \$60 and Q = 160 in the point elasticity formula:

$$E_{\mathrm{D}} = \frac{\Delta \mathrm{Q}}{\Delta \mathrm{P}} \times \frac{\mathrm{P}}{\mathrm{Q}}$$

$$E_{\mathrm{D}} = -4 \times \frac{\$60}{160} = -1.5$$

$$P = \$20 \times \left(1 - \frac{1}{-1.5}\right) = \$33.33$$

Since it is relatively easy to enter a monopolistically competitive market, it can be expected that any above-normal profits that might be earned in the short run would ultimately erode in the longer term through the entry of new firms into the industry. Figure 6.3 exhibits the longer-term equilibrium in a monopolistic competitive industry where a typical firm earns zero economic profit.

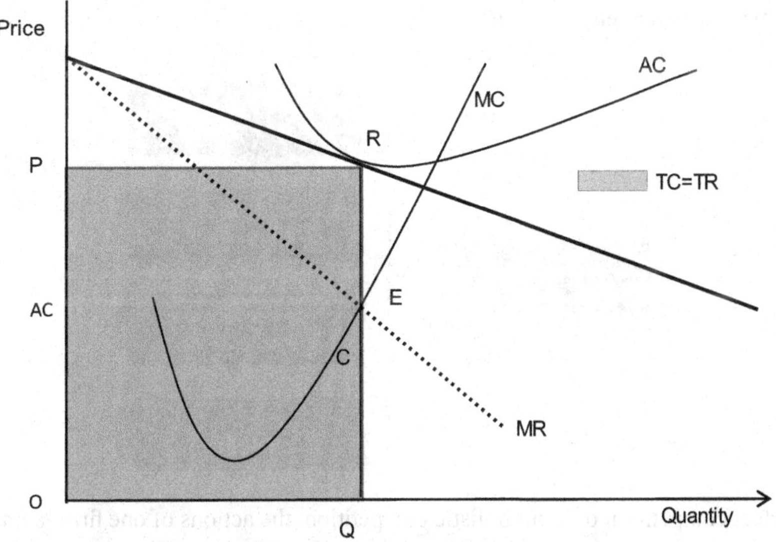

Figure 6.3 Long-Run Equilibrium: Monopolistic Competitive Market.

Oligopolies

An oligopoly is a market structure in which two or more firms dominate the market. In this market environment, oligopolists can effectively influence the price. The markets for aircraft, airports, airlines, jet engine manufactures, etc. are examples of oligopolistic markets.

The next step along the market continuum from monopolistic competition is oligopoly, which is characterized by the market dominance of a few firms. Oligopoly is the most relevant market structure with regard to aviation and is thus the focus of this chapter. Despite the large number of airlines that operate globally, individual routes are typically served by one or two dominant carriers and a handful of lesser competitors. Renowned airlines like Singapore Airlines, Cathay Pacific, British Airways, Air France, and United Airlines operate their routes with only a few close competitors, but they are also influenced by competition from smaller low-cost airlines. Similarly, the aircraft manufacturing industry is dominated by a handful of manufacturers (Boeing, Airbus, Embraer, Bombardier, and Sukhoi Superjet[3]). In July 2018, Airbus acquired a 50.01% stake in the CSeries (rebranded as the A220) and acquired an additional 25% in 2020 with an option to acquire the remaining interest by 2024. In addition, the CRJ program was sold to Mitsubishi Heavy Industries (MHI) in 2020.

Characteristic and Condition

In general terms, oligopolies are characterized by the following:

- A few firms dominating the market
- Heterogenous or differentiated products
- Restricted or asymmetric information
- Substantial barriers to entry or exit

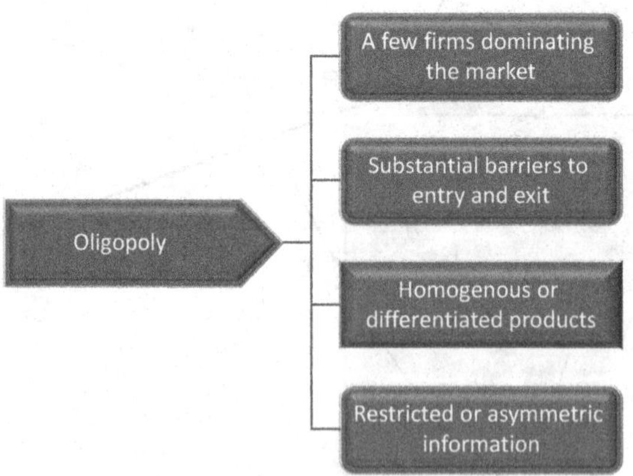

Unlike perfect competition or monopolistic competition, the actions of one firm in an oligopoly substantially affect the market and often the actions of competitors. This creates a complex interdependence among the firms; that is, each firm's decisions will be conditioned on how they believe the competition will react. For example, an airline might be more likely to reduce fares if it thought competitors would maintain their pricing, but it would prefer fares to remain constant if it believed competitors would instantly match price cuts. Thus, each airline's pricing strategy is rooted, to some extent, on what it believes its competitors' actions and reactions will be. Clearly, this is a complex problem and one that often presents no clear, optimal strategy.

Therefore, almost any short-run outcome is theoretically possible in oligopoly. In one conceivable scenario, a firm might adopt "tacit collusion" where it keeps prices relatively high. Put another way, it "goes along to get along" by avoiding any aggressive competitive act that would lead to a price war. On the other hand, oligopoly can, as frequently witnesses in the airline industry, produce aggressive "cut-throat" competition where the average firm is routinely operating in the red.

While monopolistic competition inherently leads to normal long-run profits, it is theoretically possible for long-run profits to be above normal in oligopoly if there is a sufficiently high barrier to entry. Numerous oligopolies, including such former paragons as General Motors, struggle just to earn normal long-run profits. In fact, majority of well-established airlines have consistently reported below-normal long-run profits. The barriers to entry in oligopoly markets keep the number of competitors relatively small and prevent new firms from coming into the market. These barriers include high startup fixed costs, the existence of sizeable economies of scale, control over scarce resources, and exclusive patent/legal rights.

Oligopoly is often viewed as inherently undesirable, better than monopoly but not nearly as desirable as perfect competition. While most economists would probably agree that there is a certain amount of truth to this perspective, there are some complications. In several instances, a few large firms can often enjoy economies of scale and produce at far lower costs and sell at far lower prices than could an industry composed of smaller, more numerous firms. It is far cheaper for Boeing or Airbus to develop and produce 1,000 aircraft than it would be for 100 small manufacturers to develop and produce ten comparable aircraft each. Boeing or Airbus can spread research and development costs over more units and ultimately price them lower. They can then benefit from the experience gained, becoming increasingly efficient with each additional aircraft produced. There is no doubt that airlines and air travelers are better served by having two manufacturers of large aircraft rather than having 200. The presence of economies of scale, scope, and density is also important in the airline industry, and therefore, it might be better to have an airline oligopoly than any feasible alternative.

However, this does not necessarily mean that a movement to fewer, larger firms is automatically more efficient and better for consumers. Such industry consolidation might be beneficial for efficiency, but it might also artificially suppress competition. So, how can we decide, say, if two competing airlines should be allowed to merge? Let us sketch two different views.

Differing Views of Oligopoly

One common perspective presumes that any substantial increase in market concentration is generally undesirable, and therefore, oligopolistic competitors should generally not be allowed to merge. Within the airline industry, the assumption is that airfares will increase as competition on routes is eliminated through industry consolidation. We will come back to this theory later in the chapter. A key exception is the situation where denying a merger cannot prevent increased market concentration because the weaker firm will simply liquidate if the merger is not approved. This was the rationale when Boeing acquired McDonnell Douglas in 1996. Rooted in this staunch anti-merger view is the perception that efficiency gains from economies of scale are likely to be less significant than the increased danger of oligopoly abuse through increased pricing power and artificially high profits.

An important foundation for this view is the high barriers to entry. The staunchest proponents of this view would even contend that elements such as advertising and brand name recognition are potentially enough in themselves to seriously impede new entry and, thereby, allow oligopolies to enjoy high profits even in the long run (see Galbraith, 1979). An alternative view called the market process view is that very few, if any, barriers to entry (other than legal barriers established by government) are significant. According to this theory, it is best to let the market evolve in whatever way firms choose. This approach is likely to yield efficiency gains, and it will likely be impossible for government regulators to estimate and predict, so it is best for them to merely stand aside and let the market process work. High profits, as in the perfect competition model, will always be short lived. New firms will enter and existing firms will increase capacity, thus driving down prices and profits. Government can improve efficiency only by getting its own house in order—eliminating international trade barriers and other government policies that seriously limit competition and harm the economy.

Capital Intensive

A capital-intensive industry is one whose greatest costs result from investments in infrastructure (land, buildings), intellectual properties, equipment, machinery, or other expensive capital assets. Many airlines choose to own aircraft or large computer systems, while other airlines choose to obtain the use of such assets through operating leases. Instances of capital-intensive industries include aircraft manufactures, airlines, major hub airports, jet engine manufactures, and automobiles. One advantage (for shareholders, but possibly not for consumers), inherent in capital-intensive industry, is less competition in light of the large capital necessity and on the negative side they have a high risk due to the large investment.

Let us compare and contrast these differing views by considering the difficulties posed by the capital-intensive and very complex technology requirements for a new entrant. To illustrate this, consider the field of aircraft manufacturing. Any entrepreneur intending to start a company that would compete with Boeing and Airbus would face quite a challenge. Most likely, the firm would need billions of dollars' worth of specialized capital equipment to begin production. Such funding would not be easy. According to the traditional view, this constitutes a serious barrier to entry.

The reality is that only a limited number of firms or countries have the resources to design and manufacture commercial aircraft, and this is the primary reason for the industry to become something of a global enterprise. Aircraft production stands as one of the most technologically complex and highly capital-intensive endeavors. For example, Boeing's 787 Dreamliner required development costs between $8 and $10 billion, and the company utilized partners from multiple countries, namely Japan (Kotha et al., 2005). The latest edition of the twin-engine, long-range, wide-body jetliners from Boeing Commercial Airplanes is the 777-X. They are known as the 777-9 and a larger version of the 777 wide-body jet. The 777-9 first flew on January 25, 2020; however, its development has also been interrupted with prolonged delays. The latest production delay has pushed its entry into service to 2025. Consequently, delivery of the first jet is scheduled for 2025, five years later than Boeing had planned when the jet was launched in 2013. In 2020, Boeing took a massive $6.5 billion charge for the previous delay on the 777X, with entry into service then pushed out to 2025.[4] Similarly, Beijing Daxing International Airport was completed on June 30, 2019, after almost five years of construction, with a massive cost of almost $11.4 billion.

However, the market process proponents would point out that modern capital markets have many trillions of dollars' worth of assets; billions can be readily mobilized by presenting persuasive business plan to investors. The example set by numerous Internet start-ups of the 1990s demonstrated just how easy it can be to quickly raise billions of dollars if investors are excited about your prospects. Presently, it seems that two producers, Airbus and Boeing, are enough. However, in the event that the industry grows sufficiently or Airbus and Boeing somehow otherwise manage to enjoy high prices and profits, then Lockheed Martin or some other firm will enter their market. In fact, on July 13, 2008, Bombardier Aerospace announced the launch of the CSeries, a family of narrow-body, twin-engine, medium-range jet airliners. The inaugural flight of the CS 100 transpired in 2013 and entered into service in July 2016. Later that year, Air Baltic took delivery of the larger version in the CSeries family, the CS300. The carrier announced that operational performance exceeded expectations, and it anticipates to put the CS300 on 10 more routes by June 2017.[5] The advent of CSeries was expected to bring more competition for Boeing and Airbus in the narrow-body market. The CSeries is a clean-sheet design purpose-built for the 100–150 seat market.

On October 16, 2017, Airbus and Bombardier announced that Airbus would acquire a 50.01% majority stake in the CSeries partnership. The Bombardier C Series was a great aircraft, but it encountered challenges in terms of sales. Sales increased significantly once Airbus took over the program.[6] Leveraging composite materials in A220 with a range of up to 3,450 nm, the A220 offers an exceptional ability to fly both short and longer ranges with one single aircraft type. The use of composites materials in the A220 contributes to reducing the fuel burn and overall maintenance costs. On February 14, 2020, Bombardier unloaded its remaining stake in the A220 program to Airbus, by getting out of the commercial aviation business to pay its massive debt.

High Exit Barriers

Another potentially serious entry barrier is high exit barriers. Therefore, investors must consider worst-case scenarios: what happens to their investment in a company that performs so poorly that it must be liquidated? Should our hypothetical aircraft manufacturer be forced into liquidation, it will face the problem of very limited resale market. Much of its equipment might have only two possible buyers (Airbus and Boeing). If neither is interested, the equipment will likely be sold as scrap metal. Thus, any major investment in illiquid assets faces unusually high risk. Theoretically, this risk might inhibit new entry and thereby allow Boeing and Airbus to enjoy higher than normal returns.

However, market process proponents argue based on the standard principle of finance: riskier investments must offer higher expected profits. In other words, if Boeing ever does earn unusually high long-run profits, it could be reasonably argued that such profits reflect merely the greater risk. In essence, the risk-adjusted rate of return would still be a normal rate of return. After all, their investors also face the risk of illiquid resale markets should Boeing ever fail. In a broader perspective, since economies of scale are so important in this industry and since the physical capital may be so specialized, it makes sense in terms of social welfare to be cautious before capital is plunged into aircraft production. In other words, because it is so hard to exit that industry, it is perfectly appropriate, in this view, to hesitate before plunging in. In terms of society's welfare, returns should be quite high before a new entry occurs.

Examples of Oligopoly

Oligopolies are very common in modern economies. For instance, when you rent a car in the United States, you find that almost all of the cars are provided by a relatively small number of rental companies: Alamo, Avis, Budget, and a few other smaller firms. This significant level of concentration means relatively high barriers to entry. Common examples of oligopolistic industries are:

- Aircraft manufacturers
- Airline industry
- Airports
- Automobiles industry
- Breakfast cereal
- Cable television companies
- Cigarettes
- Fixed-base operator (FBO)[7]
- Jet engine manufacturers
- Long-distance telephone service
- Soft drinks
- Supermarket chains

Oligopolistic markets are of particular interest, since most major aviation-related industries are oligopolies. The following sections will take a closer examination into three major forms of oligopolies that make up the greater part of the aviation industry: airlines, aircraft manufacturers, and jet engine manufacturers.

Airlines

The airline industry undoubtedly operates in an oligopolistic market structure, as it only has a few firms participating in a typical city-pair or route. The US airline industry is dominated by four mega carriers: Delta Air Lines, American Airlines, United Airlines, and Southwest Airlines. Collectively, these four airlines command about 70% market share.

While oligopoly market theory suggests that firms should compete by enhancing services, price cuts can be readily matched. As such, the US domestic airline industry has totally reversed this trend, as airlines have reduced costs and service amenities. This phenomenon is partially attributed to the fact that many non-price competitive aspects can be easily copied by competing airlines, such as frequent flier programs. Nonetheless, price remains a key driver of consumer behavior.

Airlines might prefer less price competition, but customer preferences demand the opposite. However, even an airline like Southwest Airlines, which has traditionally had a price leadership strategy, is also known for its friendly service and frequent flight schedule. Southwest's awareness of service quality is one of the reasons it has been successful. Similarly airlines, such as Emirates and Singapore, that pride themselves on their service quality have also been very successful by adopting this strategy.

Commercial Aircraft Manufacturing

A duopoly is a market structure in which two producers are competing for the same product.

Boeing and Airbus are the only two producers of commercial jet with about 99% of global large plane demand. Commercial Aircraft Corporation of China (COMAC) is planning to make waves in the aviation manufacturing industry, but not in the near future.

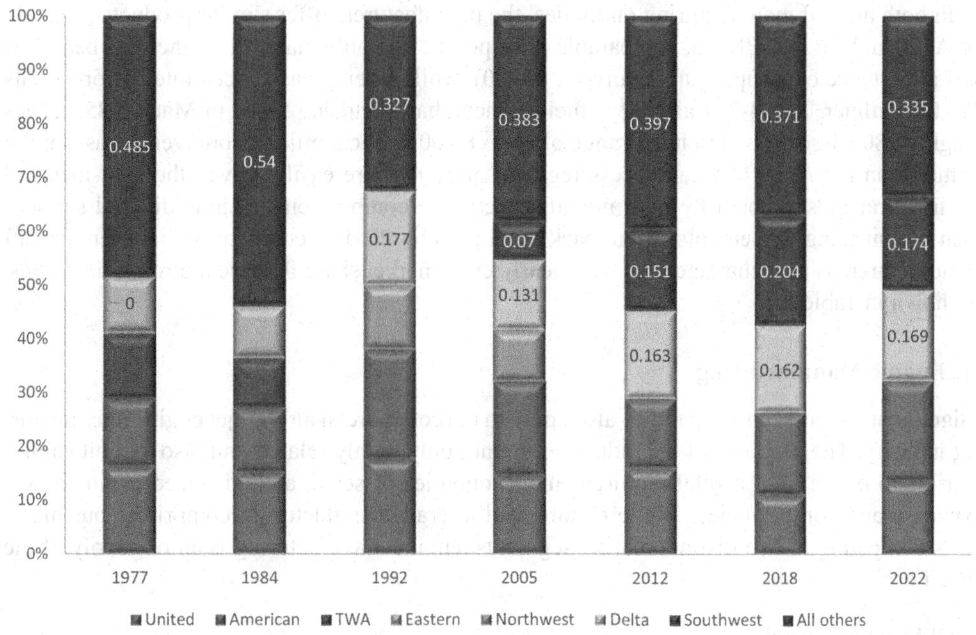

Figure 6.4 Market Share of the Top American Airlines, 1977–2022.

Source: Bureau of Transportation Statistics

The commercial aircraft manufacturing industry is largely a duopoly (an oligopoly with two firms). Airbus and Boeing compete in the 100-seat plus aircraft category, and Bombardier and Embraer compete in the regional aircraft market. This market is typically divided into two product categories: narrow-body and wide-body aircraft. Narrow-body aircraft are single aisle, short-range aircraft that typically carry between 100 and 200 passengers. Wide-body aircraft are double aisle, medium- to long-range aircraft that can carry between 200 and 450 passengers. A phase of consolidation transpired in aircraft manufacturing with the acquisition of McDonnell Douglas by Boeing and the exit of Lockheed from commercial aircraft manufacturing. Given the commercial aircraft manufacturing is extremely capital intensive, it is unlikely that another manufacturer will enter the market.

China plans to end the duopoly of Boeing and Airbus. China ranks second in the world, after the United States, for air passenger traffic and has the fastest-growing air passenger market. In 2007, however, China announced its intention to start making large commercial aircraft by 2020. The nation is expected to purchase 2,230 new aircraft before 2025. Indeed, the demand exists, but the technology proved to be a major barrier (AP, 2007). In an attempt to overcome this barrier, China reached an agreement with Airbus to open an A320 final assembly line (AP, 2007). The goal of this venture was to gain technical knowledge that would translate into success for China's own large aircraft program. The proof of this technological skill transfer was the launch and first flight of passenger jet, ARJ 21, in June 2016. This 90-seat jet was built entirely by the Commercial Aircraft Corporation of China (COMAC). A further development in the Chinese aircraft manufacturing sector came after the announcement of the larger COMAC C919, a narrow-body aircraft capable of carrying up to 268 passengers. This model is touted as competition to both the A320 and the B737. By January 2023, COMAC claimed it had more than 1,200 orders, mostly from Chinese carriers but also from GE Capital Aviation Services.

In both aircraft manufacturing duopolies, the manufacturers offer similar products (i.e., 737 vs. A320 and CRJ vs. ERJ) at comparable price points. The only major difference has been Airbus's insistence on a super-jumbo aircraft (A380), while Boeing has concentrated efforts on its 787 Dreamliner. The B-787 aircraft is fuel-efficient, has a cruising speed of Mach 0.85, carries roughly 280 passengers, and has a range of up to 8,500 nautical miles. Moreover, it has smaller stature than the A380 and can access regional airports more easily. Given the near-identical pricing strategies adopted by both manufacturers, the competition lies in additional services such as financing agreements or buyback of older aircraft. The competition between aircraft manufacturers is also characterized by a nearly even market share for recent aircraft deliveries, as shown in Table 6.2.

Jet Engine Manufacturing

Oligopolistic market characteristics also apply to the commercial aircraft jet engine manufacturing industry. The products of the industries are not only highly related, but also exhibit similar barriers to entry: high capital requirements, economies of scale, and advanced technological expertise and competencies. While commercial aircraft manufacturing comprises four major firms competing in two distinct market segments, engine manufacturing is an oligopoly of the "Big Four":

- CFM International
- Pratt & Whitney (P&W)
- General Electric Aircraft Engines (GEAE)
- Rolls-Royce

CFM International stands as the leading commercial aircraft engine manufacturer, with 39% of the engine market worldwide in 2020. In 2021, the global aircraft engine MRO market is expected to be worth 29.5 billion US dollars. Notably, General Electric has also partnered with Pratt & Whitney (a subsidiary of Raytheon Technologies) to form the Engine Alliance. This collaboration has given rise to the GP7000 engine for the A380.[8] They hold a near 100% market share of the commercial aircraft sector. In 2020, Pratt & Whitney came second with 35% of market share. The company is an American aerospace manufacturer and a subsidiary of Raytheon Technologies.

Table 6.2 Aircraft Manufacturers' Market Share (Deliveries)

Large Aircraft Manufacturers					*Regional Aircraft Manufacturers*				
Year	*2018*	*2019*	*2020*	*2021*	*Year*	*2018*	*2019*	*2020*	*2021*
Boeing	806	380	157	340	Embraer-commercial only[a]	90	89	43	41
Market share	50%	31%	22%	36%	Market share	62%	66%	44%	48%
Airbus	813	863	566	611	Bombardier – commercial	20	26	16	3
Market share	50%	69%	78%	64%	Market share	14%	23%		7%
					Others	35	19	39	41
					Market share	24%	14%	40%	48%

Source: Compiled by the authors using delivery reports from Boeing, Airbus, Embraer, and Bombardier.

General Electric Aviation occupies the third largest manufacturer of jet engine, with 14% of the North American market.

Additionally, two consortiums were formed to add more players to the engine market. CFM International (CFMI) was a partnership between GE and Snecma, the French state-owned engine manufacturer. CFM manufactures the CFM56 and LEAP engines, which can be found extensively on the A320 and 737 families of aircraft. Likewise, IAE was formed in 1983 between P&W, Rolls-Royce, Daimler-Benz, Fiat, and Japan Aero Engines. These consortiums pooled technological knowledge, reduced risk, and lowered production and development costs for individual manufacturers. This created an interesting situation where manufacturers could be both partners and competitors concurrently. In addition to the two consortiums, P&W formed an alliance with GE for the development of the GP7200 platform, an engine designed for very large commercial aircraft such as the A380 (Bowen and Purrington, 2006).

Figure 6.4 displays the worldwide market share for commercial jet engines in terms of deliveries over the past 45 years. P&W was the dominant jet engine manufacturer up until the early 1980s, at which point P&W made a strategic decision that shaped the market for many years. Notably, P&W, a principal McDonnell Douglas supplier, made the decision to focus on supplying engines for Boeing's new 757 instead of the 737, believing that the 757 was going to be the aircraft of the future (Bowen and Purrington, 2006). This choice led to a scenario in which CFMI became the sole jet supplier for 737s, while P&W and Rolls-Royce split orders for the 757s. Despite the commendable sale performance of the 757s, the 737s became the most successful commercial aircraft in history. P&W lost even more market share with the demise of McDonnell Douglas.

GE has been the main benefactor of P&W's declining market share. GE, a long-time military engine manufacturer, entered the commercial market with the backing of its large parent company, which encompasses aircraft leasing via GECAS. GE strengthened its position in commercial engine manufacturing with its CFMI joint venture with Snecma. In 2020, CFMI held a 39% market share, while Pratt & Whitney held 35%. The first is the Engine Alliance with GE that manufactures products for the Airbus A380. The second is the IAE Company of Rolls-Royce, MTU Aero Engines, and the Japanese Aero Engines Corporation that manufacture engines for the Airbus A320 and the McDonnell Douglas MD-90.

Figure 6.5 provides another comparison between the major commercial engine manufacturers in terms of in-service engines. Notably, Figure 6.5 is lagged, by roughly an engine's life,

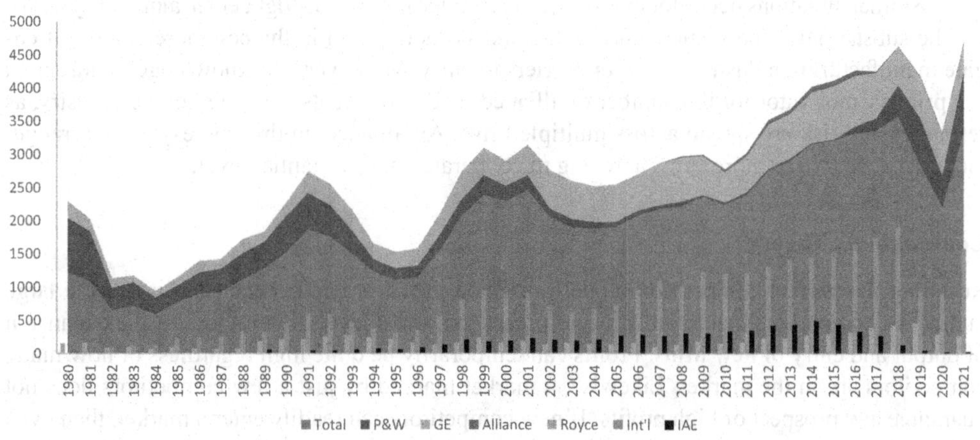

Figure 6.5 Commercial Jet Engine Manufacturing Market Share by Engine Deliveries.

Source: Compiled by the authors using the Airline Monitor (2015)

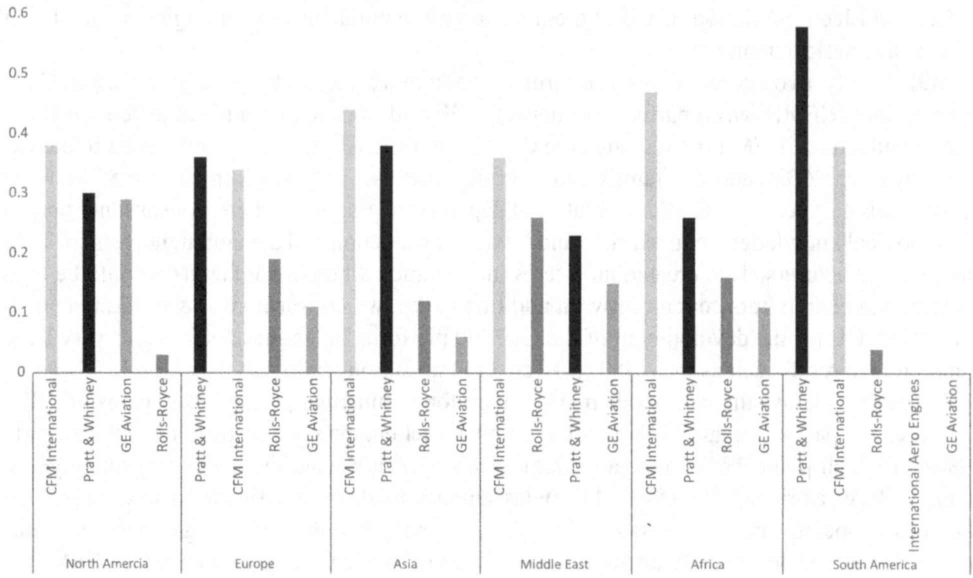

Figure 6.6 Commercial Jet Engine Manufacturing Market Share by In-Service Engines.

from Figure 6.4. This temporal offset serves as the major reason why P&W remains a market leader, as many of its older products are still being used on the Boeing 727 and MD-80 (Bowen and Purrington, 2006). Therefore, P&W can still turn substantial revenues through maintenance agreements and selling of spare part inventories. However, as the older aircraft are retired, P&W's market share has declined, while GE and CFMI have gained.

Engine manufacturers also compete in service categories by creating the most fuel-efficient engines and by providing the most attractive "power-by-the-hour" contracts. Within the framework of a power-by-the-hour arrangement, the engine manufacturers provide fixed-cost maintenance based on the number of hours flown each year. The airlines provide a fixed level of funding and expect to receive a given level of support by the engine manufacturers. The contractor expects to be provided a fixed level of funding, paving the way for a long-term support arrangement. Similar situations occur for avionics, aircraft interiors, and in-flight entertainment systems.

The substantial technological knowledge and skills required in the commercial aircraft engine manufacturing industry are major barriers to entry. Moreover, this knowledge requirement is a primary motivator for the number of alliances and agreements generated in the industry, as resources and risk are spread across multiple firms. An alliance, in this context, is an arrangement between two or more firms agreeing to cooperate on a substantial level.

Contestability Theory

Recalling the perfect competition model presented in the previous chapter, it is not the large number of competitors that reliably drives profits to normal levels, but rather, it's the expansion of output and entry of new firms. Profits can temporarily be quite high regardless of how many competitors are in the market. Likewise, a market marked by just a few competitors does not guarantee any prospect of high profits. If new competitors can readily enter a market, then even a single firm may be driven to behave in a competitive manner, earning only normal profits on average in order to discourage new entry.

The pure concept of "contestability theory" takes this idea one step further and posits that in the absence of significant entry barriers, the number of firms in an industry is completely irrelevant. The key element of contestability theory resides in the stipulation that the feasibility and profitability of entering the market must prevail, as pointed out in the given quotation.

Before deregulation, many economists speculated that pure contestability theory might well apply to the airline industry. Due to the inherent mobility of aircraft, the thinking was that they could, under certain conditions, readily be reallocated to whatever routes were commanding higher prices, thus driving those prices down. Since each airline knew this, they refrained from significantly raising prices. In other words, potential competition would have the same effect as actual competition. However, several studies examined the airline industry and found a positive relationship between airfares and the levels of market concentration. In essence, the fewer the airlines in a given market, the higher the fares on average, suggesting that airline markets are not perfectly contestable. One possible explanation is that economists underestimated the cost associated with entering a new market. Suppose, for example, that an airline had service to airport A and airport B but no nonstop service connecting A and B. It might appear that an aircraft could fly out of one market and be reassigned to a new A–B route almost instantly in pursuit of the greatest profit. But in reality, a new route must be planned and announced to consumers well ahead of time, normally at least three months. Moreover, there might be a need for dedicated advertising expenditures. These are not massive costs but perhaps create enough friction to the entry process to prevent pure contestability results.

One of the key elements of contestability theory is that entry and exit from markets must be free and easy (Bailey, 1981). The complete absence of barriers of entry would satisfy pure contestability theory. However, within the context of airline industry, there can be sizeable barriers to entry into a given airport. This is certainly the case at slot-controlled airports such as London Heathrow. Nevertheless, the existence of competing airports makes contestability theory apply to a certain extent even in this market. Ultimately, in oligopoly markets where there are low barriers to entry, the market power of any one carrier will considerably be much less compared to markets where there are high barriers to entry.

However, there is considerable doubt that these slight entry costs can fully explain observed price variances. Within the realm of intense competition, the influence of network effects may offer a better explanation. An airline network is more than the sum of its separate routes, particularly for the legacy carriers that aspire to offer seamless travel to "almost anywhere." Suppose, for instance, that such a carrier found it necessary to operate a nonstop route to Las Vegas because it is such a popular vacation destination. Additionally, a noteworthy portion of the airline's key customers preferred to redeem their frequent flier awards for a Las Vegas trip. In this case, the value of the Vegas route might far exceed the actual revenue garnered from paying customers on that particular flight. Thus, the airline would sensibly keep that route rather than reallocating the aircraft to another route, such as a nonstop to Minneapolis that would produce more direct revenue but less total value and revenue for the network as a whole. Thus, the price of a flight to Minneapolis could remain higher than the price to Las Vegas even if the market were purely contestable. The same thing happens in grocery stores when a particular item, a "loss leader," is sold at an especially low price in order to draw customers into the store to hopefully buy other items with higher markups.

To properly judge the contestability of the airline industry, it is imperative to examine the overall profits of the entire airline rather than at the prices of particular city pairs. Considering the extremely low long-run profits and return rates, it may well be that the industry is contestable in this broader sense. We will cover this in more detail later.

Naturally, it is possible to drown in a deep spot within a pond where *average* depth is only knee deep. Likewise, substantial discomfort can persist within particular cities and city pairs that face relatively high prices, even with the system-wide average fare being a consumer bargain, actually below the cost associated with a normal profit.

Fortunately, for consumers residing in those high-end markets, low-cost carriers (LCCs) with simpler point-to-point networks are entering with increasing frequency. Numerous instances abound wherein carriers abuse their market power and generate competition from other carriers. LCCs AirTran and Frontier created their own hubs in Atlanta and Denver, both of which were formerly dominated by oligopolistic legacy carriers. Meanwhile, Virgin Atlantic evolved to provide British Airways with legitimate competition on long-haul flights. While these examples provide an application of contestability theory on a widespread scale, the theory is arguably more relevant in small markets with only one or two airlines. In these situations, airfares typically remain somewhat high, but not high enough to encourage competition to enter that market.

Figure 6.6 displays a hypothetical demand curve for a firm in an oligopoly market. According to contestability theory, there are two components to the firm's demand curve. The initial aspect surfaces when the firm wants to increase the price. In a non-contestable market (dashed line above P), the firm can increase prices and not lose a substantial amount of demand, thus suggesting a gain in total revenue. However, in the presence of contestability (solid line above P), this increase in price will result in an even larger decrease in quantity demanded.[9] Here, the demand manifests relatively elastic since new competitors may enter and match the price increase.[10] The second component of the contestable demand curve is when a firm is pondering a price decrease, aiming to simulate a surge in the quantity demanded and thus increasing total revenue. This holds true in a non-contestable market, as demonstrated by the dashed demand curve below P. Alternatively, in a contestable market, new competitors may also see the benefit from a price decrease. They could strategically venture into the market by matching the price decrease, but the increase in the firm's quantity demanded from the decrease in price is unlikely to be as large as the firm had hoped. In this scenario, the demand is relatively inelastic since the potential competition is willing to follow the price decrease. This is demonstrated by the solid demand curve below P.

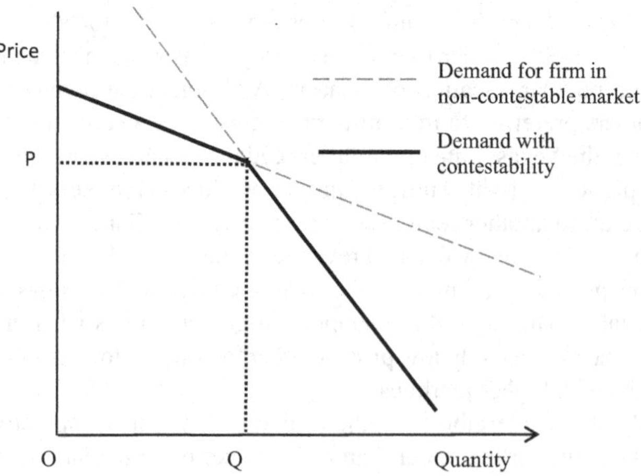

Figure 6.7 Price Competition and Market Reaction for Oligopoly.

Kinked Demand Curve Theory

The theory of the kinked demand curve predicts price stability in oligopolistic markets. The theory states that in this type of market, there exists a band of price stability. This band is the kinked portion of the demand curve.

Consider a duopoly with two firms having slightly different demand curves for their product. Illustrated in Figure 6.7 are these two demand curves for firms, D_1 and D_2. These two curves intersect at point A as shown in Figure 6.7; this point lies at price (*P*) and demand (*Q*). Both companies want to operate at a point where marginal revenue equals marginal cost. This particular point serves as the basis for determining the optimum price, traceable along the corresponding point along the demand curve. In a duopoly market, the firm with the lowest price sets the market price, which the other firm must then match in order to remain competitive.

Based on this information, we can outline the construction of the market demand curve. Up until point A in Figure 6.7, D_1's demand curve is less than that of D_2. Therefore, based on simple supply and demand, the first firm would charge a lower price than the second firm. However, the situation is reversed after point A where firm D_2's demand curve is significantly less than that of D_1. Therefore, the market demand curve will be from point E to point A and from point A to point G.

In order to construct the market's marginal revenue curve, firm D_1's marginal revenue curve should be used up to a demand level of *Q* units and firm D_2's marginal revenue curve should be used thereafter. This configuration yields a situation where the market marginal revenue curve contains a vertical portion, line B–C. Since the intersection of the marginal revenue and marginal cost curve will yield the optimum price for the industry, when the marginal cost curve intersects between points B and C, the market clearing price would be roughly Price (*P*) or the price at point A. Therefore, if the marginal cost curve's intersection shifts anywhere in between points

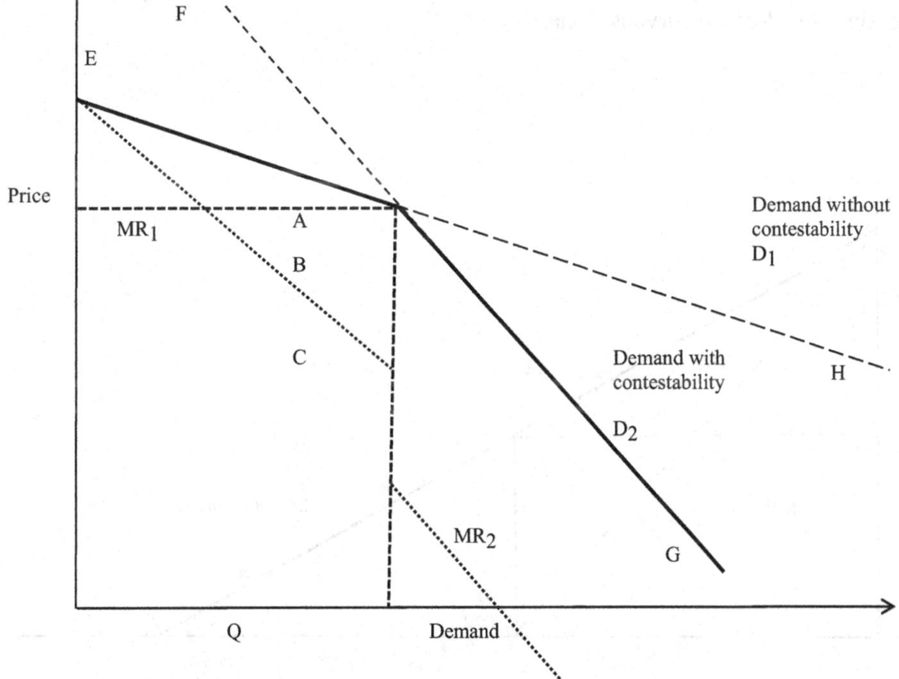

Figure 6.8 Kinked Demand Curve.

B and C, the market clearing price remains the same. At the market price, none of the individual oligopolistic firms would make any change in the prevailing price, even when there might be some slight changes in their production costs.

This creates a situation of long-run price stability in the market since there is a relatively wide range over which marginal cost can undergo alteration (B to C in Figure 6.8) without changing the profit-maximizing price (A in Figure 6.8).

The airline industry at times seems to provide some indication that this might be occurring. Notably, major shifts in the demand curves will create significant fluctuations in the market's marginal revenue curves, thus changing the market clearing price. A major shift occurred shortly after the terrorist attacks of September 11, 2001 which led to a downshift in demand and altered previously stable equilibriums.

Cournot Theory

The Cournot theory helps explain competition and market equilibrium based on firms competing through output decisions. This theory assumes that products are homogenous, market entry is difficult, firms have market power, and cost structures are similar. Furthermore, each firm assumes that its counterpart will remain unresponsive to changes. For instance, Boeing believes that Airbus will not respond to any changes in price and output initiated by Boeing. Likewise, Airbus assumes Boeing will be equally unresponsive. While this assumption is probably unrealistic, the model still offers some insight and, given that neither Airbus nor Boeing can definitely predict the response, the theory may at times approximate reality.

Consider a duopoly market where the firm's marginal costs are zero. The demand curve for the entire market is displayed in Figure 6.9, along with the total output in the industry being *Q*. We also observe the marginal revenue curve of the initial firm, which is exactly half the demand curve, since the demand curve is linear.

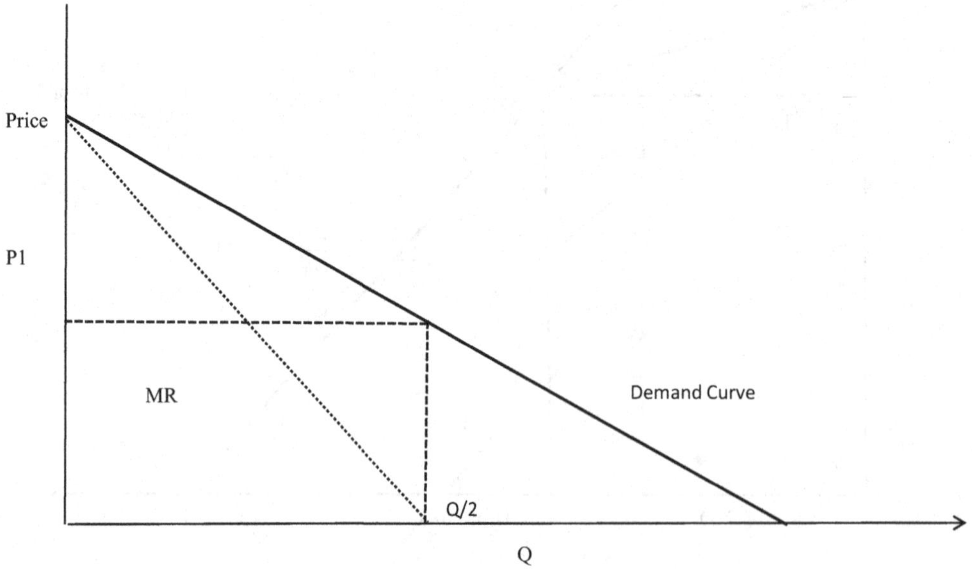

Figure 6.9 Initial Output Decision for the Dominant Firm.

The optimal output decision for the first firm occurs where marginal revenue equals marginal cost. Since marginal costs are assumed to be zero, the firm would want to produce at the point where the marginal revenue curve intersects x-axis. This point is exactly half of the total demand, denoted as point Q/2. The corresponding price for this level of output from the demand curve is P1. Since the first firm takes half of the market for itself, the second firm's maximum demand would be Q/2. Therefore, the demand curve for the second firm is shifted to the left and intersects the x-axis at point Q/2. This is displayed in Figure 6.10. Employing this calibrated new demand curve, the second firm's optimal output level is the point where the marginal revenue curve intersects the x-axis. This occurs exactly at Q/4, and the corresponding price point is P2. Consequently, based on this, the first firm would take half the market and the second firm would take a quarter of the market (3/4Q).

Remember that these firms are yet to achieve equilibrium, since the second firm's price is far below that of the first firm. With this disparity, most consumers would opt for the second firm's product, since the products are homogenous, and the price is significantly lower. The firms will ultimately readjust their output in an effort to obtain equilibrium. Moreover, as shown in Table 6.3, these readjustments will occur over various rounds rather than transpiring all at once.

The Cournot solution is where both firms are in equilibrium with the same price and output levels. Within a duopoly context, the Cournot solution would have each firm obtaining 1/3Q for a total market share of 2/3Q. It is worth noting that total market share declines as firms readjust to equilibrium; in this case, Firm 1's market share decreased, while Firm 2's market share increased. The Cournot theory predicts that firms will continue to readjust the level of output until they have achieved market equilibrium at the same price level.

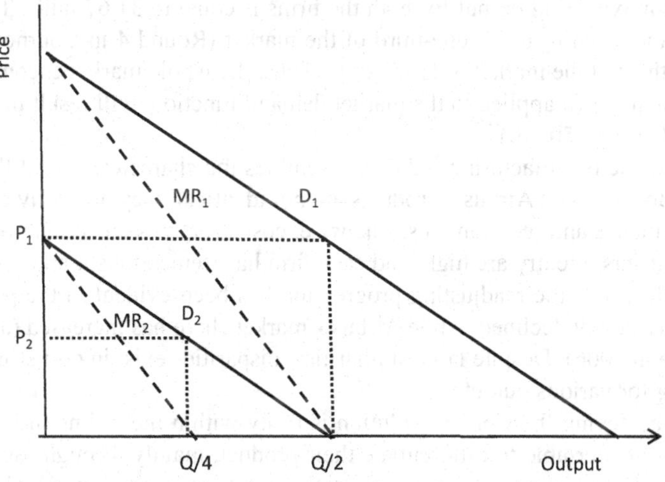

Figure 6.10 First-Round Cournot Theory.

Table 6.3 Cournot Market Share Theory

	Round 1	*Round 2*	*Round 3*	*Round 4*
Firm 1	1/2 Q	3/8 Q	11/32 Q	1/3 Q
Firm 2	1/4 Q	5/16 Q	21/64 Q	1/3 Q
Total Market	3/4 Q	11/16 Q	43/64 Q	2/3 Q

Example

Consider two Cournot competitors faced with the following inverse demand function:

$P = 1{,}000 - 10Q$

where P is the industry price and $Q = q1 + q2$ is the industry output. Both companies have constant marginal and average cost AC = MC = 50.

a Determine the Profit Maximization Output.

$$P = 1{,}000 - 10\,(q1 + q2)$$
$$P = 1{,}000 - 10\,q1 - 10\,q2$$
$$\text{MR1} = 1{,}000 - 20q1 - 10q2$$
$$\text{MR2} = 1{,}000 - 10q1 - 20q2$$

b Now set MR = MC,

$$\text{MR1} = 1{,}000 - 20q1 - 10q2 = 50$$
$$\text{MR2} = 1{,}000 - 10q1 - 20q2 = 50$$
$$20q1 + 10q2 = 950$$
$$10q1 + 20q2 = 950$$

c Solve the functions simultaneously.

$$20q1 + 10q2 = 950$$
$$-20q1 - 40q2 = -1{,}900$$
$$-30q2 = 950 \Rightarrow q2 = 31.67$$

Thus, the profit-maximizing output for both the firms is equal to 31.67 units. This equilibrium value signifies that each firm has one-third of the market (Round 4 in Cournot duopoly). The remaining one-third of the market is 31.67 units. Thus, the whole market encompasses 95 units (31.67 × 3), which, when applied to the market demand function, will result in the profit being zero (1,000 – 10 × 95 – 50 = 0).

Consider how the manufacturing industry resembles the characteristics of the Cournot theory. Although Boeing's and Airbus's products are not identical, they are fairly close in terms of technical performance and requirements. Likewise, cost structures are similar but not identical. Furthermore, barriers to entry are high, and each firm has tremendous market power and equal market share. However, the readjusting progression has been evident in the past, as Boeing's market share has slowly declined, while Airbus's market share has increased (although Boeing did regain share in 2006). Despite large similarities, disparities exist in cost structure and products, accounting for various outputs.

Conversely, achieving the Cournot solution is rarity within the airline industry. This is because airlines are better able to differentiate their product, mainly through route structure and flight frequency. Every airline has a different cost structure, and each individual carrier has little market power. Due to this, it is rarely seen that market share distributed evenly among multiple carriers. In fact, the development of the hub system has led to situations where one airline tends to dominate particular markets.

Price–Output Determination under Hybrid Market Structure

In order to understand the mathematics involved with determining the optimal price–output level for a firm within a hybrid market, let's examine a scenario of luxury airline DirectJet. The management at DirectJet has asked its financial managers to study short-run pricing and production policy. DirectJet's financial managers were able to determine the airline's price, fixed cost (FC), and variable cost functions to be:

$P = 10{,}000 - 8Q$
$\text{FC} = \$200{,}000$
$\text{VC} = 2{,}200\text{Q} + 5Q^2$

With the ultimate goal of pinpointing the optimal price–output decision for DirectJet, we need to find the marginal revenue and marginal cost curves. On the revenue side, the total revenue function (TR = $P \times Q$) can be found simply by multiplying the price function by quantity (Q). This yields the expression:

$\text{TR} = 10{,}000\text{Q} - 8Q^2$

The first-order derivative of the total revenue function will produce the marginal revenue function of:

$\text{MR} = 10{,}000 - 16Q$

On the cost side, the two cost components (fixed and variable) must be combined to create the total cost function:

$\text{TC} = 200{,}000 + 2{,}200Q + 5Q^2$

From this, the first-order derivative of the total cost function will yield the marginal cost function:

$\text{MC} = 2{,}200 + 10Q$

The final step in determining the optimal price–output combination for DirectJet is to set the marginal revenue and marginal cost curves equal to each other in order to determine the optimal quantity. This computation is demonstrated below and also displayed graphically in Figure 6.11.

$\text{MR} = \text{MC}$
$10{,}000 - 16Q = 2{,}200 + 10Q$
$7{,}800 = 26Q$
$\rightarrow Q = 300$

Based on this calculation, DirectJet's optimal output is 300 seats per day. At this level, average ticket price and the airline's total revenue are as follows:

$P = 10{,}000 - 8Q$
$P = 10{,}000 - 8(300)$
$P = \$7{,}600$
$\text{TR} = 10{,}000Q - 8Q2$
$\text{TR} = 10{,}000(300) - 8(300)2$
$\text{TR} = \$2{,}280{,}000$
or:
$\text{TR} = P \times Q \rightarrow \$7{,}600 \times 300 = \$2{,}280{,}000$

While total revenue is not maximized at this point, total firm profit is maximized at this value. In order to determine total profit at the optimal level, the total cost at the optimal output is:

$\text{TC} = 200{,}000 + 2{,}200Q + 5Q^2$
$\text{TC} = 200{,}000 + 2{,}200(300) + 5(300)2$
$\text{TC} = \$1{,}310{,}000$

Thus, total profit at the optimal output level is

TP = TR – TC
TP = $2,280,000 – $1,310,000
TP = $970,000

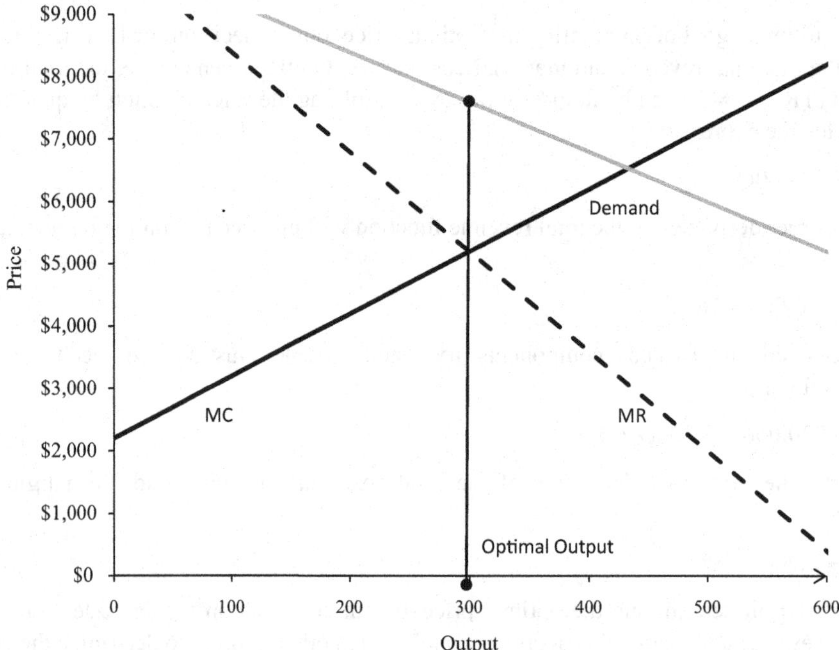

Figure 6.11 Marginal Revenue and Marginal Cost Curves.

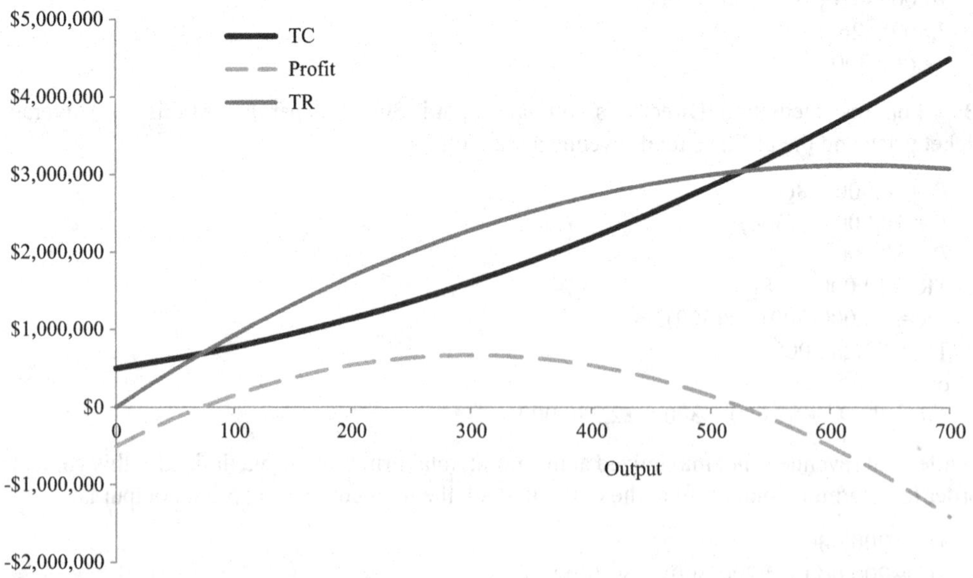

Figure 6.12 Total Revenue, Cost, and Profit.

No other combination of price and output, based on the cost functions provided by DirectJet's financial analysts, will yield the airline with a greater profit. This is displayed graphically in Figure 6.12, which shows the total revenue, total cost, and total profit functions. Since the total cost curve is an upward U-shape, the output level of 300 is the maximum for profit.

While the above scenario applies in the short term, it is much different in the long run. Similar to perfectly competitive markets, any super normal profits earned by monopolistic competitive firms in the short run will attract new firms to the market. These new firms will offer similar competing products, but with the increase in new firms and products entering the market, the degree of differentiation between products diminishes. As a result, the elasticity of the firm's demand decreases, inducing a progressive flattening in the firm's demand curve. This creates a situation similar to perfectly competitive markets, as monopolistic competitive firms tend to become price takers in the long run. This causes the super normal profits to diminish, and zero economic profits are earned. In essence, monopolistic competition acts like perfect competition in the long term. Hence, the principal differentiating characteristic between the two is the length of the short-run period where super normal profits are realized.

Profitability Issues

The existence of normal long-run profit levels might be explained by the industry being contestable in the manner already discussed. However, the mere attribute of contestability itself should not produce the below-normal returns observed in the airline industry. Rather, the explanation may relate to the industry's oligopolistic nature combined with very high fixed costs and very low marginal costs. Recall that an airline's schedule is usually set three months in advance and that most costs are essentially fixed for that period. The marginal cost of placing a passenger in an otherwise empty seat on an aircraft is extremely low—consisting mainly of the cost of ticket processing or travel agent commission. Thus, each individual airline finds itself in a position where even a very low price is better than nothing for an otherwise empty seat. As discussed in Chapter 11 on revenue management, each airline strives to make this low fare available only to those passengers who would not have chosen to fly at a higher price on *their own airline*. However, each airline is content to entice passengers away from a competitor. Suppose, for example, that Joe would have paid $200 to fly airline A, but is lured into flying airline B for $150. Likewise, Jane would have flown airline B for $200, but is lured over to airline A for $150. Each airline acts independently, but the collective result is that each receives $50 less, perhaps incurring a loss rather than making a profit.

If each could refrain from stealing the other's customers, they might both enjoy a normal profit rather than risk bankruptcy. This is a classic "prisoner's dilemma."[11] Regrettably, neither airline can trust the other enough to refrain from this cut-throat pricing, even though both would prefer to cooperate. In essence, if only one airline stops offering the $150 deal, that airline will lose both Jane and Joe to the competing carrier. Of course, any attempt to cooperate is complicated by the fact that government antitrust policy typically prohibits arranging such cooperation via a formal contract. Furthermore, another complication is that other airlines will tend to enter the market with aggressive price cuts even if the two airlines do somehow manage to cooperate. US airlines also argue that the bankruptcy laws exacerbate the problem by providing a subsidy[12] that keeps failed airlines from actually leaving the market. Thus, even in the long run, it is difficult for the industry to decrease capacity enough to keep prices high enough to support a normal profit.[13]

At first glance, the misery experienced by airline investors from pricing below costs appears to be a joyous gain for air travelers—as if most carriers were perpetually selling at "going out of business" bargain rates, and this might indeed be the prevailing scenario. Conventionally, most economists have viewed excessively low long-run returns as a problem that will eventually take care of itself as needed. In this regard, if many investors and lenders don't think it is worth investing in the airlines, then they can stop financing them until capacity decreases enough to raise prices, normalize profits, and thus warrant future investment. On the other hand, the strong performance by airlines like Ryanair and Southwest suggests that the business can be profitable if it is "done right." Therefore, a majority of economists are probably content to let the industry evolve as it will, even with rampant bankruptcies, until or unless there is clear evidence of a problem for consumers.

However, proponents of the "empty core" theory suggest there may already be a serious problem.[14] It is possible for the aforementioned cut-throat competition to be so severe that it actually does harm consumers by preventing airlines from offering some higher-priced products that consumers prefer. For example, suppose there is no available nonstop service on a given route and that two competing airlines offer service through their respective hubs for a price of $200. Suppose that the consumer demand is such that *one* airline could offer nonstop service on this route for $280 and, if the other carrier maintained its $200 service, both airlines would be financially viable in the market. In other words, the market possesses the capacity of supporting both airlines but only one with a nonstop flight. However, if competition leads either to duplicate such service and/or significantly cut their price, then the nonstop service becomes financially impossible to maintain. So, it is possible to offer consumers a chance to pay a premium and obtain the more desirable nonstop service only if there is no strong competitive response.

Consider a scenario in which every time one airline adds nonstop service, and the other either duplicates that service or substantially slashes prices on its stop and transfer service so that the nonstop service becomes a financial loser and is abandoned.[15] Moreover, since the two airlines compete in numerous markets, they each learn of this tendency and, therefore, choose never to start such nonstop service in similar markets. This problem might explain why airline customers complain so much about declining quality while at the same time making choices that drive airlines to reduce quality.[16] There is no practical way for an airline to contract with customers to get them to keep flying the new nonstop route after competitors respond, even though customers might be willing to do so if they understood that booking a bargain today would eventually result in poorer service/higher prices in the future. To illustrate, consider a situation where many customers' first choice is $150 with a stop and transfer. The second choice is nonstop service for $280, and the third choice is $200 with a stop and transfer. Suppose, airline a starts the nonstop $280 service, but then airline B offers the $150 service in response. This renders the nonstop service infeasible and it is abandoned, the market returns to $200 service by both airlines, and customers are left with their least preferred option. In such a case, consumers would be better served if the two airlines could freely negotiate a solution. This might involve one airline induced to not respond by receiving a small side payment, or the two airlines might take turns adding nonstop service in more marginal markets.

Additionally, a counter-intuitive situation is prevalent where consumers might actually be better served by an alliance that seems to closely resemble a cartel. However, this phenomenon is not actually as unique as it may appear. For appear, for example, in the realm of manufacturing, for firms that are normally competitors to occasionally team up on particular projects. Similarly, one airline will conduct maintenance or baggage handling for a competitor. One reason for this is that economies of scale for certain products may be such that only a single producer can be efficient enough to viably deliver the product to market. This relates to the fact mentioned earlier that reducing the number of competitors may sometimes increase efficiency and increase consumer well-being. If the airlines were permitted to collaborate, it is easy to perceive, for example, how two large aircraft with 95% load factors in a particular market might be more cost effective than three smaller aircraft with 75% load factors operated by separate airlines. Similar to how aircraft prices might be lower with two producers rather than three or four, reducing competition on some routes may benefit consumers in some cases.

It is probably reasonable to assert that most economists in the traditional vein would view airline cooperation as too radical of a step, primarily due to the contention that the risk of price collusion conspiracy would outweigh any potential gain. Conversely, there are those who contend that, given the financial plight of legacy carriers, the risk of them colluding to make "too much profit" is not significant. Also, strong proponents of market process would argue that new entry, and perhaps potential new entry (contestability), could effectively restrain any harmful anticompetitive impulses. In other words, price conspiracies are unlikely and, even if the airlines in a given market attempted collusion, a new entrant would undercut them; that is, the market is contestable, at least in a basic, practical sense.

Ironically, in this situation, staunch antitrust regulation may ultimately decrease the number of competitors. Since current regulation may prevent airlines from cooperating to improve efficiency in particular markets, the eventual outcome might be more airline failures and eventual liquidation and/or desperation mergers that antitrust enthusiasts have no choice but to accept. Although speculative, it is possible, for instance, that Lockheed or McDonnell Douglas might have remained as competitors to Boeing and Airbus had they been allowed to cooperate on some projects.

When regulatory preferences conflict with the economic reality of substantial economies of scale, scope, or density, economic reality will ultimately win. If more cooperative efforts between airlines are needed, they will eventually emerge, if not through approved alliances, then through bankruptcy, liquidation, or mergers that reduce the number of independent airlines. As regulators could not forestall the transformation of the aircraft manufacturing market into a duopoly, with each firm able to enjoy considerable economies of scale, it may be that a similar process is unfolding for airlines. Naturally, tremendous uncertainty persists in all of this. Nevertheless, given the financial disarray of many legacy carriers, major industry changes of some sort do seem likely.

Competition and Antitrust Issues

Antitrust policy has a basic and fundamental objective. The objective is to protect the process of competition for the benefit of consumers, ensuring strong motivations exist for businesses to operate efficiently, keep prices down, and maintain high quality. The Sherman Act (1890), the Federal Trade Commission Act (1914), and the Clayton Act (1914) are the three pivotal laws in the history of antitrust regulation in the United States. Similar legislation exists in Europe and many other jurisdictions. The ambit of antitrust policy restricts cartels and monopolies, thus eliminating price fixing and discrimination, and pricing practices. The Department of Justice's (DOJ) Antitrust Division is responsible for enforcing the federal antitrust laws in the United States and has the authority to review mergers to determine if they may lessen competition.

Antitrust regulation has evolved into a significant controversy. Some economists perceive problems with at least some aspect of antitrust regulation, and some even argue that such regulations should be completely abolished on the grounds that costs far exceed any benefit.[17]

One challenge is that the most problematic anticompetitive behaviors are completely exempt from antitrust oversight. Economists would generally be thrilled if it were possible, for instance, to address issues like international trade barriers under antitrust law, but all government policies are exempt from these laws. Since, as mentioned, there is also a question about the real power of any barrier to entry outside of government, there emerges a debate as to whether there is enough of a private monopoly problem to justify a government regulatory program. Even if there are some imperfections in market competition, as most economists would probably agree, it is not easy for regulators to make things better for consumers by imposing fines and escalating legal costs on firms. After all, such expenses typically get transferred to consumers in the form of higher prices. Also likely is substantial bias on the part of regulators.

Antitrust regulations are intended to prevent individual corporations from assuming too much market power such that they can limit their output and raise prices without concern for any significant competitive reaction. On September 21, 2021, the DOJ filed a civil antitrust suit against American Airlines and JetBlue, and the suit alleges a violation of the Sherman Act and seeks to enjoin an alliance formed between the two airlines.[18] Back in July 2020, American and JetBlue formed the Northeast Alliance. According to the DOJ's complaint, within this alliance the two rival airlines agreed to "share their revenues and coordinate which routes to fly, when to fly them, who will fly them, and what size planes to use for flights to and from four major airports."

Predatory Pricing

Predatory pricing is a strategy of selling a product below cost to force the competitions out of business. Predatory pricing is illegal under antitrust laws.

Predatory pricing, theoretically, occurs when a firm:

1 Slashes price below cost in order to drive competitors out of the market; then
2 Raises prices to a monopoly level once competition is gone. It is important to note that aggressive price cuts, even if they drive competitors out of business, are not in themselves predatory. Airlines often find themselves losing money, fighting over a market that isn't big enough to sustain all existing firms. In this case, they may fight it out until some firms leave the market and raise prices high enough to support normal profits. Therefore, aggressive price cuts and less-efficient firms going out of business are the routine results of healthy competition. The label 'predatory' solely applies if prices escalate to monopolistic heights. In many countries, including the United States, predatory pricing is considered an anticompetitive practice and is illegal under antitrust laws.

Also, question is raised as to whether predatory pricing is likely to occur at all. Undoubtedly, it is a high-risk strategy that would likely fail in many cases, even in the absence of any regulation. Assuming a firm survives Stage 1, that its competitors go bankrupt before it does, it is likely to face new entrants once price is increased at Stage 2. These potential newcomers would know that the predator could not easily afford another round of predatory cuts after already enduring losses in driving out the first group of competitors. If the predator did successfully repeat his/her predation, then a third round of new entrants would likely be drawn in by the knowledge that the predator would struggle to survive a third confrontation and so on. In other words, a successful predator must be so fierce that he/she completely frightens off the rest of the world. This is a possible, albeit uncommon, barrier to entry. A popular example of a failed alleged predatory pricing strategy comes from Delta and ValuJet. ValuJet began service hubbed out of Atlanta in 1994. By December 1994, Delta had matched ValuJet's cut-rate fares—as low as $29 one way—on flights between Atlanta and the 11 cities that both carriers served. On January 7, 1997, ValuJet suspended its low-fare service between Mobile and Atlanta. The next day, Delta raised its lowest fare for the route from $58 to $404—an increase of about 600%.

However, normal price competition is often mistaken for predatory behavior. If, for example, a competitor enters a market with a close substitute offered at a lower price, then clearly the incumbent firm must either match that price cut, at least approximately, or leave the market altogether. Airline A can't charge a price much above Airline B if B offers essentially the same product. If A was previously charging a much higher price before it matches the much lower price of B, then A will also likely increase output. Essentially, the presence of low-cost competitor B forces A to abandon its higher-price/lower-volume strategy and embrace a low-price/high-volume strategy. The only alternative for A is to abandon the market completely. In this scenario where B eventually pulls out of the market, A may find it optimal to return to the high-price/low-volume strategy. The standard business procedure of matching a competitor's price cuts when necessary is indistinguishable from predatory pricing. Does it truly make any sense to forbid legacy carriers from matching the lower prices of low-cost entrants?

US courts considering predatory pricing charges in recent decades have focused not on the price cuts but on the feasibility of a "predator" raising prices to monopoly levels. For example, in the case of *Frontier Airlines vs. American Airlines*, the judge summarily dismissed the case because, he maintained, the government really had no case at all; that is, no credible evidence of predation. American Airlines merely matched the prices of Frontier but, in the court's view, had no hope of gaining any monopoly power even if it destroyed Frontier, since there were numerous other competitors in the market. The fact that American, like all legacy airlines, struggled to earn even normal profits over the long run is supportive of the court's decision. Although some economists may disagree with this approach, the courts' deep skepticism combined with the fact that the legacy carriers have been, in recent years, struggling just to survive, seems to have dampened regulators' enthusiasm for bringing predatory pricing charges.

In 2000, Spirit Airlines initiated a lawsuit alleging that Northwest Airlines engaged in predatory pricing and other predatory tactics in the leisure passenger airline markets for the Detroit–Boston and Detroit–Philadelphia routes beginning in 1996. During this pricing competition, Spirit claimed that Northwest's fares were so low that these prices would force Spirit to exit the markets and consequently, Northwest would raise fares to monopoly levels and consumers would be harmed. Northwest responded by stating that the low fares in these two markets reflected head-to-head competition between the airlines. The district court awarded summary judgment to Northwest, but a panel of the Sixth Circuit unanimously reversed the district court's decision.[19]

Cartels and Collusion

> A cartel is another form of market structure created from a formal (or tacit) agreement between a group of producers to reduce the production and increase prices.

A cartel is another form of market structure created from a formal (or tacit) agreement between a group of producers to reduce the production and manipulate prices. This collusion enables the cartel to exert monopoly-like power in their pricing policies. While cartels and collusion are generally illegal in the United States, they are allowed in many foreign markets. In the United States under the Sherman Antitrust Act of 1890, the Clayton Antitrust Act of 1914, and the Federal Trade Commission Act of 1914, such collusive agreements are illegal. Nonetheless, there are several examples, particularly in the sports professions. The National Football League, Inc. (NFL), Major League Baseball, Inc. (MLB), the National Basketball Association (NBA), and the National Collegiate Athletic Association (NCAA) are often cited as examples of cartels.[20] Around the world, there have been famous cartels in oil and diamonds. Arguably, the most famous and most important cartel in the world economy is the Organization of the Petroleum Exporting Countries (OPEC).

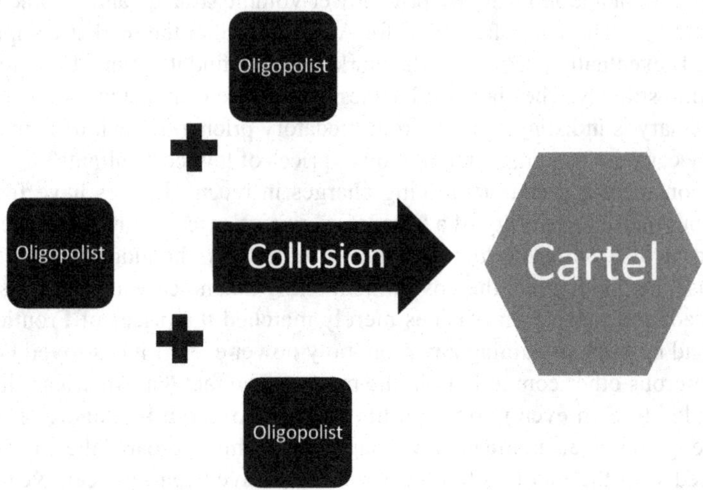

While OPEC cannot directly set the price of a barrel of oil, its control over much of the supply enables the cartel to dramatically impact the price by either increasing or decreasing output. According to US Energy Information Administration data, in 2022, OPEC members produce around 40% of the world's crude oil. However, OPEC members export about 60% of the total globally traded petroleum by volume.

Considering the international nature of and often extreme competition in air travel, there is strong potential for collusion in the airline industry. A notable instance of this occurred in 2006 when the British Airways became involved in a price-fixing scandal involving fuel surcharges on long-haul flights (Simpkins, 2006). Investigations by both British and American authorities uncovered the fact that calls were made to Virgin Atlantic concerning the timing and level of increases in fuel surcharges. British Airways admitted fixing cargo surcharges from 2002 to 2006 and passenger fuel surcharges from 2004 to 2006 (typical surcharges rose from £5 to £60 per ticket). In August 2007, the British Airways was charged $300 million by the Office of Fair Trading (OFT) and US Justice Department, but Virgin Atlantic was not fined as it was given immunity after reporting British Airways' actions.

An inherent problem arises when analyzing cartel and collusion issues in the airline industry—the fact that the prevalence of information in the industry makes it fairly simple for airlines to match the prices and output of competitors. This gives rise to the term "tacit collusion." Tacit collusion refers to coordination without express communication. A common example is price signaling. For instance, one airline raises its prices with the hope that the other airlines interpret this move as an invitation to collude and respond by matching the price increase. However, the fact that two airlines have price fluctuations that match exactly does not mean they are in collusion, but more likely that they are competing fiercely.

Airline alliances create interesting issues related to airline collusion. Ultimately, these airlines coordinate schedules and prices of flights. In order for alliances to be allowed, they must receive regulatory approval from the necessary bodies. However, limits may be placed on their coordination. For instance, American Airlines and British Airways have several stringent restrictions placed on them, while the KLM/Northwest relationship was given extensive antitrust immunity by US regulators. Antitrust immunity is given to potential alliances based on a variety of factors, including the level of consolidation that would exist in the industry.

Again, however, there is fierce debate as to whether government antitrust actions against alleged collusion have been appropriate and beneficial to society. The abysmal rate of return for legacy airline investment, perhaps the lowest for all industries, implies that competition is far from lacking. Even if collusion were attempted, it is difficult to orchestrate high prices for any length of time. For one thing, such high prices invite new competitors to enter the market and undercut the cartel. Even before new entry, there is always strong incentive for an individual firm to violate the collusive agreement as one can potentially earn far greater profits by slightly undercutting one's partners.

In fact, the behavior of US airlines in the age of regulation illustrates the strong tendency to break a cartel agreement. Historically, regulators have severely limited price cuts, much as a conventional cartel would do, and even prevented any new entry for nearly four decades. However, airlines struggled to earn even normal profits. They competed by improving quality—improving the food, giving away liquor, utilizing larger aircraft, providing roomier seating, and so on. Even though this quasi, government-aided cartel failed to suppress competition, it illustrates how difficult it is for firms to secretly suppress competition on their own.

Employing regulation to prevent price fixing is problematic because, as seen in the cases of alleged predatory pricing, there is often no clear way to distinguish innocent behavior from illegal collusion. For example, two airlines may constantly raise and lower their fares in tandem. This alignment might not result from collusion but because of logical, independent reactions to market conditions. One airline's product is normally a very close substitute for another's—in the leisure market, it may approach being a perfect substitute. Inherently, it is not possible for the prices of two close substitutes to vary greatly; most consumers would flock to the one that is substantially cheaper. Consequently, it is necessary to generally match any price cut by a competitor. The widespread availability of online information in the industry also makes it particularly easy for airlines to monitor and quickly match the prices and output of competitors. Likewise, any airline attempting to increase price because of, say, higher fuel costs, will retreat from the price increase unless competitors follow suit. This dynamic typically results in either a general increase in airline prices or no lasting price increase at all.

In the 1990s, US regulators took note of the fact that airlines seemed to be constantly signaling each other to raise prices. For instance, an airline would normally announce its intention to raise prices several weeks in advance. If, following the announcement but before the scheduled price increase, the competition eventually announced that they too would increase fares by similar amounts, then the announced price hikes would in fact materialize. On the other hand, if competitors left prices unchanged, then the airline would cancel the previously announced fare increase.

In their defense, airlines highlighted that the most announced increases were in fact canceled, that the overall long-run trend in inflation-adjusted fares was downward, and that the lack of industry profitability indicated that prices were not fixed but rather broken. Moreover, as already explained, it is understandable that prices for close substitutes will naturally either move in tandem or not move at all. It is also understandable that firms sustaining significant losses would make every effort to raise prices.

Nevertheless, antitrust regulators insisted on changes and, among other things, forced airlines to agree to no longer announce fare increases in advance. Numerous travel agents and consumer groups complained about the change since it seemed to make fare increases harder to predict and plan for. Airlines responded to the regulatory constraint by implementing fare increases on Saturdays, a time when relatively few people book flights. Thus, if competitors refused to join in the price increase, then the new prices could be canceled by the following Monday before they had significant impact.

Critics of antitrust regulation argued that the whole episode seemed absurd and that it was particularly ironic for regulators to force firms to actually raise prices as opposed to just announcing an intention to eventually raise prices. Still, it does seem at least theoretically possible that preventing airlines from signaling a desire to increase prices might ultimately benefit consumers. Regulators claimed that their actions and general vigilance would keep airline profits and prices from increasing too much.

Industry Consolidation

The level of concentration in the industry helps determine the market's structure. Industries that are highly concentrated may be more prone to exhibit characteristics of monopolies and oligopolies, while industries with multiple players may tend to exhibit characteristics of monopolistic competition. Table 6.4 presents the market share of US car rental companies over the past few years. Despite the relatively large number of players, the rental car industry is highly consolidated with the top three companies holding a combined 94.87% market share in 2016. Interestingly, this trend somewhat resembles the consolidation observed among the airlines. Although mergers within the car rental industry are less apparent to consumers, but according to Bloomberg, the industry is still in transition. Similar to the post-merger airlines, there could be potentially future increases in the stock prices for Enterprise, Hertz, and Avis.

There are two widely used methods for evaluating industry consolidation: the four-firm concentration ratio and the Herfindahl index.

Four-Firm Concentration Ratio

The concentration ratio is a measure of the total market share held by a certain number of firms in the industry. The formula for the concentration can be described as:

$$\mathrm{CR}_m = \frac{\sum_{m=1}^{n} Q_m}{n} \times 100$$

where n is the number of firms measured and Q is the output.

Table 6.4 Market Share of Car Rental Companies, 2022

Rental Companies	*Car in Service*	*Number of Locations*	*Market Share*
Enterprise Holdings	1,100,000	6,000	56.69%
Hertz	430,000	3,800	22.16%
Avis Budget Group	350,000	3,200	18.04%
Sixt	18,500	100	0.95%
Fox Rent A Car	18,200	21	0.94%
ACE Rent A Car	9,000	60	0.46%
NP Auto Group	7,500	100	0.39%
U-save Auto Rental System	5,500	124	0.28%
Rent-A-Wreck of America	1,750	71	0.09%

Source: Compiled by the authors from Auto Rental News Fact Book
https://www.statista.com/statistics/1022011/car-rental-companies-market-share-united-states/

The concentration ratio is simply the summed output of *n* airline companies divided by the total industry output. The most commonly used concentration ratio is the four-firm concentration ratio, which measures the output of the four largest firms in the industry. Consequently, the market can then be classified according to a continuum of the percentage share of the top four.

In this example, American, Delta, Southwest, and United would be grouped together as indicated using 2020 data from Figure 6.5. To calculate the four-firm concentration ratio of the US domestic airline industry in 2020, the four largest airlines in terms of output need to be grouped together and compared to the industry total. The combined output is 448,683 million available seat miles (ASMs). When this figure is divided by the total industry output, it produces a four-firm concentration ratio of 75.3%. The four largest airlines produce 75% of the industry's total output (Table 6.5).

Markets are separated into categories along the market continuum based on the four-firm concentration ratio:

- Perfect Competition: less than 20%
- Monopolistic competition: between 20% and 50%
- Oligopoly: between 50% and 80%
- Monopoly: above 80% four-firm measurement

As established earlier in this chapter, the airline industry is an example of an oligopoly market, and it appears that the four-firm concentration ratio that was calculated above does in fact support this claim with a 75.3% four-firm concentration ratio in 2021. In the context of the airline industry, the four-firm concentration ratios should be calculated on an airport or a

Table 6.5 Total US Airline Industry Output by Domestic ASM (Millions)

Airlines	*2014*	*2015*	*2016*	*2017*	*2018*	*2019*	*2020*
American	157,598	200,373	241,732	243,824	248,574	248,841	119,578
Delta	212,235	220,437	225,276	228,416	238,588	251,140	120,739
United	214,061	219,956	224,653	234,547	244,771	253,255	104,819
Southwest	122,753	140,671	148,658	153,966	159,920	157,297	103,547
JetBlue	45,028	49,347	53,705	56,039	60,412	63,832	32,710
Alaska	32,434	35,917	38,721	41,468	55,367	59,715	31,389
Hawaiian	17,078	17,701	18,351	18,978	20,147	20,564	7,547
Allegiant	8,806	10,365	12,125	13,310	14,581	15,863	12,924
Frontier	12,539	15,495	18,359	21,895	24,444	28,104	16,946
Spirit	16,401	21,351	25,641	29,585	36,270	41,817	27,938
Industry	838,934	933,630	981,580	1,012,444	1,066,803	1,098,611	550,198

Source: Compiled by the authors from US DOT Form 41

Airlines	*2017*	*2018*	*2019*	*2020*	*2021*
American	24,37,08,802	24,84,79,803	24,87,79,882	11,95,29,867	18,20,47,974
Delta	22,65,87,630	23,70,61,948	24,96,94,906	11,96,26,551	17,49,21,341
United	23,36,67,254	24,44,17,122	25,28,16,292	10,43,13,705	15,55,17,316
Southwest	15,38,14,165	15,97,98,408	15,72,58,128	10,34,61,328	13,20,10,033
JetBlue	5,60,30,468	60.407,120	6,38,28,029	3,26,90,655	5,40,68,585

Source: https://www.transtats.bts.gov/Data_Elements.aspx?Data=4

city-pair basis, which better reflects the relevant market. This reality remains for the majority of airports, merely a handful of major carriers, and this produces an oligopolistic market. Since consumers are ultimately impacted on an individual market basis, assessing the four-firm concentration ratio on an airport-by-airport basis provides a more realistic picture of the air transport industry.

Table 6.6 provides a synopsis of the four-firm concentration ratios when calculated on an airport-by-airport basis for six major airports in the United States. While the industry's concentration ratio was 75.3%, most of the airports analyzed had concentration ratios substantially above that. In the cases of Atlanta and Dallas, one dominant hub carrier receives near-monopoly power as it effectively controls the market. Chicago O'Hare, serving as a hub for both United and American, is essentially a duopoly. In similar vein, Los Angeles and Las Vegas both exhibit strong oligopolistic market tendencies with their four-firm concentration ratios equaling roughly 70%. Similar statistics would be found if the analysis were applied to other airports.

Using an airport-by-airport analysis of the domestic aviation market, it is clear that the industry resembles a strong oligopoly. While every market maintains its uniqueness, with varying levels of concentration, it is unlikely that any one airport would have a low four-firm concentration value. While the four-firm concentration ratio enables the analyst to get a quick look at the amount of concentration in the industry, it usually requires a more in-depth analysis to fully understand the specific market situation.

Herfindahl-Hirschman Index

Another method used to analyze the amount of concentration in an industry is the Herfindahl index (also known as the Herfindahl–Hirschman index, HHI).[21] This is a widely used measure, previously utilized in the first chapter to analyze the amount of consolidation that exists in the industry. HHI is obtained by squaring the market share of each of the players, and then adding up those squares:

$$\text{HHI} = \sum_{m=1}^{n} S_m^2$$

where:

S is the *m*-firms' market share
n is the number of firms

Table 6.6 Four-Firm Concentration Ratio

Airport	*2022*
Atlanta (ATL)	91.46%
Baltimore (BWI)	91.47%
Chicago (ORD)	73.37%
Dallas (DFW)	86.97%
New York (JFK)	88.09%
Los Angeles (LAX)	67.53%
Las Vegas (LAS)	70.10%
Phoenix (PHX)	82.70%
Seattle/Tacoma International (SEA)	81.67%
Washington (DCA)	57.83%

Source: Compiled using the Bureau of Transportation Statistics.

The Herfindahl–Hirschman index (HHI) is a frequently accepted measure of market concentration. The HHI approaches zero when a market is highly competitive with a large number of firms. The index approaches its maximum of 10,000 points when a market is controlled by a single firm.

The measure is simply the cumulative squared value of the market share for every firm in the industry. Therefore, the higher the index, the more the concentration (within limits), indicating a less competitive market. By squaring the market share values, firms with a large market share receive more weight in the calculation than do firms with a smaller market share. The US Department of Justice considers a market with a result of less than 1,500 to be a competitive marketplace. A result of 1,500–2,500 is a moderately concentrated marketplace, and a result of 2,500 or greater is a highly concentrated marketplace. It should also be noted that market share can be calculated in terms of different products; therefore, unique HHIs could potentially be created for the same market.

In a duopoly market for example, if each of the two firms has a market share of 50%, the HHI would be:

$$HHI = (50)^2 + (50)^2 = 2{,}500 + 2{,}500 = 5{,}000$$

Alternatively, if the two firms held 80% and 20%, respectively, then:

$$HHI = (80)^2 + (20)^2 = 6{,}800$$

Utilizing data sourced from Form 41, the industry HHI for the domestic US airline industry was calculated for the past several years. The respective market share for each airline was based on the number of passengers enplaned. Until 2010, the general trend in the US airline industry was de-concentration, as the HHI value had dropped over 200 points since 1998. In 2010, the HHI returned to its pre-1998 levels, a further indication of the cyclicality of the aviation industry. The current HHI value of around 1,782 is fairly typical of an oligopolistic market, as values greater than 2,500 generally indicate a high degree of concentration in the market. However, just as in the four-firm concentration ratio, a much higher degree of concentration exists at individual airports. The HHI for the top ten US airlines is presented in Table 6.7.

Table 6.7 US Domestic Airlines Herfindahl Index[a]

Year	*Index*	*Year*	*Index*
1995	1352	2009	1129
1996	1345	2010	1319
1997	1354	2011	1305
1998	1328	2012	1429
1999	1298	2013	1432
2000	1268	2014	1482
2001	1231	2015	1620
2002	1235	2016	1735
2003	1189	2017	1703
2004	1168	2018	1679
2005	1154	2019	1664
2006	1131	2020	1770
2007	1107	2021	1783
2008	1127	2022	1760

Source: Compiled by the authors using US DOT Form 41 via BTS, Schedule T1.

[a] Based on enplaned passengers.

The HHI is frequently used by the Department of Justice to determine whether or not a proposed merger is acceptable for antitrust reasons. Table 6.8 presents the pre-merger market share for the major carriers, while Table 6.9 provides the post-merger market share as well as the industry HHI.

Projected from the proposed mergers, the HHI would increase by nearly 300 points. The Department of Justice usually does not like mergers that raise the industry HHI above 1,000, as any point above that is deemed too monopolistic. In addition to these industry-wide HHI measures, certain markets, particularly in the Northeast, would experience far greater increases

Table 6.8 US Airlines, Pre-Merger Market Share

Carrier	*Market Share*
Delta	12.7%
Northwest	7.7%
American	16.0%
United	10.5%
Continental	**8.2%**
US Airways	9.5%
JetBlue	4.2%
AirTran	4.5%
Southwest	18.9%
Frontier	**1.8%**
Virgin America	0.7%
Alaska	2.9%
Hawaiian	1.6%
Allegiant	1.0%
HHI	**1,154**

Source: Compiled by the authors from Form 41.

Table 6.9 US Airlines, Post-Merger Market Share[a]

Airline	*Market Share*
American	19.00%
Southwest	18.30%
Delta	16.80%
United	14.50%
JetBlue	**5.50%**
Alaska	4.60%
Spirit	3.00%
SkyWest	2.40%
Frontier	2.30%
Hawaiian	**1.70%**
Other	11.90%
HHI	1,546

Source: Compiled by the authors from Form 41.

Tables 9.8 and 9.9 merely provide an overview of the major carriers' market share.

[a] HHI values included data from carriers not listed in the tables.

in the HHI. Given that the HHI is only one of many factors employed by the Department of Justice when evaluating mergers, mergers are often approved on other grounds. Markets are categorized based on their HHI[22]:

- Less than 1,500: competitive markets
- Between 1,500 and 2,500: moderately concentrated markets
- Higher than 2,500: concentrated markets

Beyond Market Concentration Considerations

Although the above calculations of market concentration lend a certain aura of rigor, it remains a very arbitrary decision criterion, partly because it completely ignores how mergers may increase efficiency and/or reduce prices through positive impacts of economies of scale, scope, and density. Of course, it is not possible for anyone, including the merging airlines themselves, to know with exact certainty how efficient the newly combined airline will be. The mix of corporate cultures, merging of separate labor unions, and/or other factors creates uncertainties that become clear, but long after the merger actually occurs. Proponents of strong anti-merger regulation argue that with no guaranteed gains in efficiency, it makes sense to keep the number of competitors as high as possible for as long as possible.

On the other hand, opponents of such vigorous regulation maintain that the dismal rate of return for the airline industry shows that there is more than enough competition, implying that firms should generally be free to combine as they choose. The struggling industry should be allowed to repair itself. For instance, Ben-Yosef (2005, 265–266) suggests that, had government regulators allowed them to merge, it is quite possible that United Airlines and US Airways might have avoided bankruptcy and been in a better position to keep fares low enough to profitably compete with the low-cost airlines. Thus, rather than focusing on concentration ratios, regulators might better serve the public interest by generally allowing troubled firms to merge as they see fit, and allowing the industry to evolve, as it will as long as there is no indication of higher than normal long-run profits being generated.

Up to this point, regulators have allowed such free choice in mergers only if it becomes obvious that one firm is on its way to shutting down anyway. However, airline alliances, which might be viewed as a sort of partial merger, have often been allowed considerably more freedom. For instance, the KLM/Northwest alliance is quite extensive, having received antitrust immunity from US regulators. At times, governments severely restrict the action of alliance partners, such as in the case of American Airlines and British Airways, but at least some cooperation is allowed. The greater degree of freedom allowed in alliances seems to represent some compromise; regulators may be implicitly admitting that rigid focus on concentration ratios is not appropriate in an industry largely floundering in bankruptcy. At the same time, from a pro-regulatory viewpoint, if alliances should prove to be anticompetitive, they can more readily be altered or even completely undone.

Antitrust, Market Evolution, and Cooperation

Antitrust law facilitates governmental agencies to restrict company behavior that creates monopolies or otherwise interferes with competitive markets.[23] As mentioned earlier, the US airline oligopoly is dominated by four firms: American, United, Delta, and Southwest, which together make up about 75% of the market. The US DOJ's antitrust jurisdiction originates from two industrialization-era rulings, namely, the Sherman Act and the Clayton Act.[24] The Sherman Act contains two main sections that provide a broad outline of antitrust law:

- Section 1 prohibits anticompetitive agreements and mergers.
- Section 2 prohibits anticompetitive behavior by a single company.

The Clayton Act provides mechanisms for enforcing the Sherman Act, including provisions for treble damages, prohibitions on stock acquisition, and regulatory review of mergers.

On September 21, 2021, the US Department of Justice sued to block an unprecedented series of agreements between American Airlines and JetBlue. These agreements entail the consolidation of their operations in Boston and New York City.

In 1965, the German and French governments started a framework about forming a consortium to build a European short-haul airliner. The outcome was Airbus Industrie, formed in 1970 as a Grouping of Mutual Economic Interest.

The rivalry between Airbus and Boeing may also illustrate how some cooperation can benefit consumers. Consider, for example, the problematic production of the jumbo aircraft, the A380. Suppose Boeing had decided to make its own version of the A380 and had then begun to encounter problems similar to those of Airbus. There was a possibility that both companies would have decided to simply abandon production. With each having to share demand with the other, the costs might have been prohibitive. Of course, it never came to this because Boeing chose not to enter the A380 market. Whether intentional or not, there was a sort of implicit cooperation when Boeing stepped aside to make the project viable for Airbus. Governments may unwittingly facilitate such cooperation through patent laws, which can have the effect of segmenting the market for different producers.

Implicit cooperation is less likely to take place, though, where the number of firms is greater. The airline industry may need explicit contracts to coordinate an efficient allocation of resources for consumers. Airlines might be able to offer more nonstop service or move to larger, more efficient, and comfortable jets on more routes if they were able to explicitly cooperate. Certain aspects of this might be arranged through mergers and some through more limited alliances that might sometimes resemble cartels but could be aimed at arranging efficient production rather than suppressing competition. The elimination of the restrictions on cabotage and international mergers would facilitate this and would also reduce entry barriers to help reduce the possibility of the cooperation taking an anticompetitive turn. The five years before COVID-19 hit, the industry saw US airlines generating significant above-normal profits and that does seem to have attracted new entrants into the US domestic market, with the launch of Avelo and Breeze Airways in 2021.

Naturally, current regulators and many economists would oppose such a move to allow cooperation. It's conceivable, for instance, that the lack of industry profitability reflects simple overcapacity rather than the need for complex cooperation. Eventually, bankruptcy, capacity cuts, and liquidation may decrease supply, increase price, and return the industry to normal profitability. In any case, many economists argue that airline consolidation in some form, both in Europe and in the United States, is inevitable. According to this view, the record shows that the industry cannot be profitable in its present state, either because there is simply too much capacity from too many airlines or due to a more complex lack of coordination. Since investors will ultimately require a reasonable rate of return to keep capital in the industry, some capital will be withdrawn. Consequently, the number of large airlines is probably bound to decline somewhat. While regulators might slow this decline in numbers but cannot prevent it and may, as outlined above, cause the adjustment to be less orderly and more severe than it would be had they simply gotten out of the way. Only time will offer definite insights.

Summary

As presented earlier, market structure refers to the number of firms involved in a market, typically a city-pair for airlines, and the degree of competition among them. The four types of market structures include perfect competition, monopolistic competition, oligopoly market, and monopoly. Some of the factors that determine a market structure include the extent of economies of scale, barriers of entering and exiting the market, the number of buyers and sellers, and the degree of product differentiation. Numerous industries contend with notable barriers to entry, such as high startup costs (as seen in the jet engine and aircraft manufacturing industries) or strict government regulations which limit the ability of firms to enter and exit such industries.

This chapter delves into the models of monopolistic competition and oligopoly, the so-called hybrid markets. A monopolistic competitive industry involves many firms producing differentiated products, and each firm has some degree of market power. An oligopoly market structure is characterized by a small number of large firms dominating the market. In an oligopoly market, the pricing decision by one firm can have a significant impact on the behavior of the other firms in the market (mutual independence). Most aviation industries fit the oligopoly model, but there are different views of what this implies. Some economists see oligopoly as inherently problematic, while others point to the lack of high profits in many oligopolies, particularly the airlines, and conclude that entry barriers are not so significant after all. This chapter then provided an overview of various theories of oligopoly, including contestability, kinked demand curve, and Cournot models. Empirical evidence indicates that the airline industry may be contestable, but only when viewed as a network. From this viewpoint, it may even be that increased concentration and cooperation through more alliances can benefit consumers, primarily through economies of density, and potentially restore the airline industry to reasonable long-run profitability. Finally, this chapter introduced various indices used to measure the amount of concentration in the industry.

Discussion Questions

1. What are the best examples of monopolistic competition in the real world?
2. How is price established in a pure competition?
3. How is price established in an oligopoly market?
4. The antitrust laws do not allow firms in the same industry to agree on what prices they will charge. Is that correct for the airline industry?
5. How is price established in a monopolistic competitive market?
6. If monopolies are socially undesirable, why do governments actually support having some?
7. Provide examples illustrating how markets change from one structure to another when technology or other market conditions change.
8. What are the implications for the regulatory authorities of the existence of contestable markets?
9. You are the manager for DirectJet and unable to determine whether any given passenger is a business or leisure traveler. Can you think of a self-correction mechanism that would permit you to identify business or leisure customers?
10. Graphically depict a shut-down case for a monopolistic competitive firm. When should any firm shut down in the short run?

11 Focus on the airline industry: why is the upper portion of the kinked demand curve elastic and the lower portion inelastic?
12 What are four distinguishing characteristics of monopolistic competition?
13 South Charleroi Airport is a regional airport serving the leisure travel market. The inverse demand curve for this airport is $P = 150 - Q$. Assume that there are only two airlines serving this airport, each with the identical marginal cost (MC) of $30.

  a Supposing they perform as Cournot oligopolists, determine the price and total firm productivity.
  b Compare this with the result under pure monopoly and perfect competition.

14 Suppose that a typical monopolistically competitive firm faces the following demand and total cost equations for its product:

  $Q = 50 - P$
  $TC = 375 - 25Q + 1.5Q^2$

  where P is the price of the product and Q is the number of units produced.

  a What is the firm's profit-maximizing price and output level?
  b What is the relationship between P and average total cost (ATC) at the profit-maximizing output level?
  d Is this firm earning an economic profit? Is this firm in short-run or long-run monopolistically competitive equilibrium? Will new firms enter into or exit from this industry?

15 Calculate the change in the HHI for the period of 2006–2017:

  a For the US airline industry
  b For US major airports
  c Have these industries become more or less concentrated over time?

16 Some students may think that university sweatshirts have a relatively high price when sold at the bookstore. Other than quality, can you think of a reason for the higher price of the sweatshirts in the bookstore?
17 There are a number of gas stations that are located near the lots of rental car companies around Orlando International Airport. These gas stations invariably charge a higher price than other gas stations that are located further away. Rental cars are normally rented with the proviso that the car be returned with a full tank of gas. Use these two facts to explain this phenomenon.
18 Suppose there are only two airlines that serve a certain route. Now suppose that one of the airlines institutes a sale on this route. What will be the effect on the other airline and what actions will the other airline take?
19 In the preceding example, suppose that one of the airlines opts out of the market entirely.
20 Will the other airline immediately adopt a monopoly pricing strategy? Why or why not?
21 Occasionally, an airline will ask passengers what the purpose of the trip is. Usually, the stated reason is to provide better service for the customer. In addition to this reason, what other information do you think the airline is trying to obtain with this type of questionnaire and why?
22 Suppose that two airlines, DirectJet and MyJet, with identical cost functions are serving a regional airport with following information:

  Market demand: $P = 1000 - 10Q$
  Cost functions: AC = MC= $50

  a Calculate the equilibrium output and price for each airline, assuming that each airline chooses the output level that maximizes profits taking its rival's output as given.
  b Calculate the profit level for each airline at equilibrium level.
  c Suppose that DirectJet's costs increased to AC = MC = 100 and MyJet's costs remained at the same level. Work out the equilibrium quantity and price for each airline.

Notes

1 IAE is a joint venture between Pratt & Whitney, Rolls-Royce, Aero Engine Corporation of Japan, and MTU Aero Engines of Germany.
2 Both drinking waters include two atoms of hydrogen (H) and one atom of oxygen (O).
3 The Sukhoi objective is to compete effectively with its Embraer and Bombardier counterparts by offering substantially lower operating costs.
4 *The Seattle Times*, April 27, 2022.
5 airBaltic.com press release, January 12, 2017.
6 *Simple Flying*, April 20, 2021.
7 An FBO is a company that has a permission to operate on airport grounds in order to provide services to the airports and the airlines. These services may include fueling services, hangar services for aircraft, and repair and maintenance services and facilities.
8 *Simple Flying*, June 22, 2022.
9 In October 2006, United raised fares in several markets, but when it became clear that airlines such as JetBlue and Northwest Airlines would not raise their fares, United rescinded fare increases.
10 Other airlines may not follow a price increase by one airline; therefore, demand will remain relatively elastic. Furthermore, an increase in price would not lead to an increase in the total revenue of the airline.
11 The term follows from the idea that two criminals might both go free if each lies to protect the other. But, under separate police questioning, each knows that he/she will face a very stiff sentence for lying should the other partner tell the truth. Unless each can somehow be certain that the other will also lie, they have an incentive to implicate each other in exchange for a lighter sentence.
12 For example, many airlines have effectively "dumped" the cost of their pension programs onto taxpayers via government assumption of these pension obligations, though with some cuts for wealthier pensioners.
13 Although this may be changing as of late, the much higher cost structure of the legacy carriers also leads to increased capacity from LCCs. Moreover, unusually powerful unions are also often cited as contributing to the legacy airlines' ongoing struggles.
14 See Raghavan and Raghavan (2005) for a discussion of an "empty core problem."
15 This situation explains, incidentally, the puzzling fact that an A–B–C flight is sometimes cheaper than an A–B flight.
16 Of course, it is also very possible that consumers really do just want lower prices and may enjoy complaining about quality because they unrealistically want extremely low prices *and* high quality!
17 See, for example, Crandall and Winston (2003) and Armentano (1986).
18 Complaint at 2, *United States v. American Airlines Group Inc. & JetBlue Airways Corp.* (filed September 21, 2021). https://www.justice.gov/opa/press-release/file/1434621/download.
19 *Spirit Airlines, Inc. v. Northwest Airlines, Inc.*, 431 F.3d 917 (6th Cir. 2005), cert. denied, 166 L. Ed. 12 (US 2006).
20 However, it might also be argued that these sports leagues are not really cartels at all since their product, entertainment, faces many substitutes. Cooperation among sports franchises might be of the same sort that exists among different franchises of a given restaurant chain.
21 *Herfindahl-Hirschman Index, United Stated Department of Justice, July 29, 2015.*
22 US Department of Justice and the Federal Trade Commission, Merger Guidelines § 1.51.
23 See Einer Elhauge, UNITED STATES ANTITRUST LAW AND ECONOMICS 1–4 (3d ed. 2018).
24 Federal Trade Commission. "The Antitrust Laws." https://www.ftc.gov/advice-guidance/competition-guidance/guide-antitrust-laws/antitrust-laws. Accessed September 2, 2022.

References

Bailey, E. (1981). Contestability and the Design of Regulatory and Antitrust Policy. *American Economic Review*, 71(2), 178–183.

Ben-Yosef, E. (2005). *The Evolution of the US Airline Industry Theory, Strategy and Policy Series: Studies in Industrial Organization*, Vol. 25. New York: Springer.

Bowen, K. and Purrington, C. (rev. 2006). Pratt & Whitney: Engineering Standard Work. Harvard Case, 9-604-084, March 27.

Crandall, R. and Winston, C. (2003). Does Antitrust Policy Improve Consumer Welfare? *Journal of Economic Perspectives*, October 19, 3–26.

Galbraith, J.K. (1979). *Age of Uncertainty*. Boston, MA: Houghton Mifflin.

International Herald Tribune, March 12. Retrieved on March 28, 2007 from http://www.iht.com/articles/ap/2007/03/12/business/AS-FIN-China-Homegrown-Jet.php.

Kotha, O., Nolan, D., and Condit, M. (rev. 2005). Boeing 787: The Dreamliner. Harvard Case, 9-305-101, June 21.

7 Forecasting in the Air Transport Industry

Virtually every important decision in management, as well as in life, is based on a forecast of future events. Before an airline decides to buy an aircraft, it would like to know what future revenues the aircraft will generate, along with all of its operating costs for the entire life of that asset. Operational and financial decisions are made based on current market conditions and predictions on how the future looks. Of course, no one can actually know these matters; yet, decisions must be made. Ultimately, forecasting is undertaken out of necessity and not because it is something that can be readily done with any precision. A good understanding of economics and forecasting techniques will not magically reveal the future in a crystal ball, but it will result in better decisions. Admittedly, there are some instances in management when forecasting is essentially guesswork, but an educated guess is better than an ignorant guess. Much of life is uncertain, but of all industries, aviation stands out as one of the most uncertain and unpredictable. Some manufacturers wait to receive customer orders before beginning production. Others maintain inventory; whatever is not sold today will be sold tomorrow. Scheduled airlines, however, cannot employ either of these techniques. They must commit to a schedule approximately three months in advance. Moreover, in order to maintain consumer goodwill, they cannot simply cancel a partially-filled flight. Finally, unlike manufacturers, airlines sell a perishable product; empty seats lose their value the instant the aircraft takes off.

This chapter examines the application of forecasting in the aviation industry and discusses numerous major methods used by airlines today. Even very marginal improvements to forecasting can produce major benefits in this industry. Thus, our discussion emphasizes quantitative tools, such as regression analysis, which is the most powerful method for forecasting passenger demand. The outline for this chapter is as follows:

- Introduction
- Qualitative Forecasting Methods
  - Focus Group
  - Market Survey
  - Market Experiments
  - Barometric Forecasting
  - Historical Analogy
  - Delphi Method
- Quantitative Methods
  - Time-Series Statistics
  - Cross-Section Statistics

DOI: 10.4324/9781003388135-7

- Descriptive Statistics
    - Mean
    - Variance
    - Standard Deviation
    - Time-Series Analysis
    - Trend Analysis
    - Seasonal Variations
    - Cyclical Variation
    - Random Effect
- Time-Series Forecasting
    - Moving Average
    - Weighted Moving Average
    - Exponential Smoothing
    - Trend Analysis
- Forecast Accuracy
- Regression Analysis
    - How to Estimate a Demand Function
    - Goodness of Fit
    - Performing Regression Analysis
    - Dummy or Binary Variables
    - Autocorrelation
    - Multicollinearity
- Data Sources
- Summary
- Discussion Questions

Introduction

The traditional purpose of a forecast is to accurately predict future events. Economic forecasting entails the process of attempting to predict the future value of a selected variable. Forecasting techniques range from simple qualitative methods to complex econometric techniques. Forecasting has many applications in the aviation industry, the chief among these being forecasting of demand. Since demand for air travel is not monolithic and varies for every flight, sophisticated forecasting tools need to be applied to assist in predicting the size and nature of demand. This process often involves determining the booking rate for each flight as well as identifying the mix between price-sensitive and time-sensitive travelers. Fleet planning, strategic revenue management, and strategic planning all depend on accurate demand forecasting.

However, over the years it has become evident that it is significantly challenging, sometimes impossible, to forecast accurately. An important distinction to clarify is between "conditional" forecasting or "what if" analysis and "future" forecasting. "Conditional" forecasting involves predicting, for example, the impact on demand for an airline's service if a competitor changes its fare or capacity. Econometric or "big data" techniques can be employed to successfully model and predict passenger behavior. But "future forecasting," such as estimating the demand to fly a particular route or market area over the next two or five years may be impossible. In practice, forecasts will be relatively successful during a stable period of trend growth, but turning points of upturns or downturns are usually impossible to predict with any accuracy.

A superficial difference between the two types of forecasting is that with "conditional" forecasts, the focus lies in the response to a single change, such as the demand shift following a competitor's fare adjustment. Conversely, a "future" forecast, like route demand, depends on numerous variables. In principle, sufficient data and computing power will allow successful modeling and produce an "accurate" forecasting equation. But the key difference between "conditional" and "future" forecasting is the difference between risk and uncertainty. When analyzing the response of passenger demand to fare changes, the dataset usually encompasses a wide range of points that provide a reasonably known probability distribution of demand responses to fare adjustment. Risk embodies a known probability distribution—in the words of Donald Rumsfeld,[1] it is a "known unknown"—and can, therefore, be confidently modeled using statistical techniques, with forecast outcomes confidently expected to fall within the probability distribution. With uncertain events, it is just not known. These events are often called "black swan," a concept stemming from the discovery of black swans in Australia, before which it was though all swans were white. Black swan events completely catch us by surprise, lacking probability distribution in the dataset to allow us to model or anticipate them. Although pandemics, recessions, and wars have happened in the past, the scale, timing, and causes of COVID-19 in 2020, the Great Recession in 2008 and 2009, and the war in Ukraine in 2022 were all unexpected—what Donald Rumsfeld would call "unknown unknowns." The economists John Kay[2] and Mervyn King point out that the economy and most markets are pervaded by what they call "radical uncertainty" (to be clear, this is not risk) and that makes accurate "future" forecasting difficult and sometimes impossible.

The pervasiveness of radical uncertainty does not mean that you should not try to forecast. It is known that "conditional" forecasting can be accurate, especially with the use of modern "big data" statistical techniques to estimate behavioral parameters from very large datasets. However, pervasive uncertainty does mean that the "future" forecasters should aim not so much for an accurate forecast, because that may be impossible, but for a well-specified narrative about the future that will add value to decision making.

Most business decision making does involve the future and therefore needs forecasts. However, the way forecasts are employed depends on the type of decisions. If it is to respond to, for example, a competitor's fare change, then an accurate "conditional" forecast of passenger response is critical. If it is to decide whether to open a new route or expand the fleet, then "future" forecasts will be required to develop the narrative, to describe a set of possible futures, and inform decisions that will also take into account other sources of information. When faced by radical uncertainty, as we often are, the best business response is usually to build in flexibility to a range of outcomes and pursue a modular or "trial and error" approach with clear criteria to stop if it is not working.

Forecasting is not just limited to demand. Planning of human resources, financial resources, route development, aircraft rotations, and infrastructure expansion are all based on some expectation of future events. While the forecasting methods employed can range from rudimentary to sophisticated, some types of forecasting are still applied. Airbus, for example, forecast 39,490 commercial aircraft required through the year 2041, valued at US$5.2 trillion.[3] Likewise, Boeing forecast demand for 39,620 commercial aircraft over the next 20 years, valued at US$5.9 trillion. Demand for pilots in the commercial airline industry is expected to increase over the next two decades, and Boeing's Pilot and Technician Outlook projects that 208,000 pilots are needed in North America.[4]

Forecasts concerning the amount of flying, crew requirements, training schedules, absenteeism, and employee turnover ratios are all important for the airlines. Additionally, project viability and profit projections are based on the expectation of future events. Since projects are analyzed over their lifespans, forecasts must include future expected cash flows. Based on these estimates, multi-million-dollar proposals are then either approved or rejected. For example, when considering the installation of an audio-visual on-demand (AVOD) in-flight entertainment system in a particular fleet, analysts would likely factor in installation schedules, future maintenance costs, and consumer opinions of the new in-flight amenity.

As the examples cited highlight, forecasting spans multiple functional areas. Therefore, it is critical to understand the numerous aspects of forecasting before attempting to apply it to aviation. In general, four critical skills are needed:

1 Knowledge of the airline industry
2 The ability to apply statistics and economic principles
3 Computer proficiency
4 Communication skills

This chapter focuses on the first two skills listed. We reintroduce airline concepts and basic economic principles, and continue with an introductory discussion of the various statistics applied in forecasting. As most forecasting is performed through software, emphasis is laid on various applications in Microsoft Excel and SPSS to show readers how to perform basic regression and statistical analysis. However, it is crucial to bear in mind that this text is not intended to replace a full statistics course; rather, it provides an overview of these concepts as they apply to aviation.

Forecasting analysis is generally categorized as either qualitative or quantitative. However, all forecasting models have distinct advantages and limitations. Selecting appropriate forecasting methods from numerous alternatives is a critical task. Quantitative forecasting involves a technique that uses past data to forecast future data especially with numerical data and continuous pattern. The quantitative forecasting approach can be broken up into trend analysis, moving average, exponential smoothing, and regression analysis. On the other hand, qualitative approaches are based on opinions from customers, experts, or what the potential customers would expect to see in a specific product or service. The qualitative forecasting approach can also be broken up into six different methods: focus group, market survey, market experiment, barometric forecasting, historical analogy, and Delphi method. As shown in Figure 7.1, these broad categories can be further divided into specific methods and techniques. We will detail each of these throughout this chapter.

Qualitative Forecasting Methods

Qualitative forecasting methods use subjective techniques. This approach does not typically involve statistical databases or provide measures of forecast accuracy, as each technique is based on opinions, surveys, or beliefs. A quantitative forecast, on the other hand, uses statistical relationships to help forecast future events. Although more mathematical in nature, quantitative forecasts are not always more accurate than qualitative forecasts.

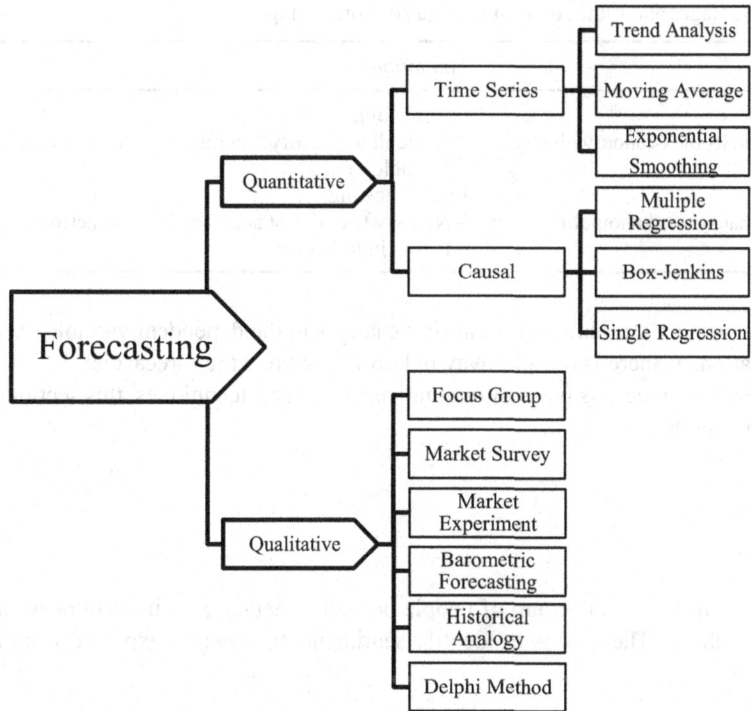

Figure 7.1 Forecasting Methods.

Table 7.1 outlines the key advantages and limitations of qualitative forecasting. One of the main benefits is flexibility. Qualitative forecast can easily be altered to reflect any changes in the economy or environment, thereby enabling early signals of change or anomalies in the data. On the other hand, qualitative forecasts can also be challenging to track, and it is not always possible

Table 7.1 Advantages and Limitations of Qualitative Forecasting

Advantages	*Limitations*
Flexibility: – Easily altered as the economy changes	Complexity: – Difficult to identify and track interactions between primary variables
Early signals: – Can catch changes and anomalies in data	Lack of testing: – No easy way to test accuracy in prior periods – Errors in judgment

to isolate the primary variable that is causing changes in the dependent variable. Accuracy is a further limitation, as there is no solid way to know how good the forecast is.

While there are numerous types of qualitative forecasting techniques, this section introduces six primary methods.

Focus Group

A **focus group** is a small group of people brought together by a moderator to discuss a particular subject. The goal is to identify sentiments that can be expected from a larger group.

A focus group is a relatively informal information gathering procedure, common in market research. It typically brings together 8–12 individuals to discuss a given subject. Focus group participants are usually brought into a room where a moderator asks questions to help move the discussion forward. Researchers observe the participants and their responses. This process provides quick and relatively inexpensive insight into a particular research problem. Focus groups can be quite effective when evaluating new product options, such as new aircraft seats or in-flight entertainment systems. An airline, for example, may gather external comments and feedback as a way to learn more about potential passengers. Airlines generally employ focus groups for planning and marketing and, particularly, when attempting to initiate new domestic or international service. Finally, a focus group can assist airline managers identify the optimal level of in-flight services and cabin crew. Following two fatal accidents involving 737 Max aircraft operated by Indonesia's Lion Air and Ethiopian Airlines, focus groups consisting of Federal Aviation Administration (FAA) employees were conducted. These groups revealed extensive apprehension among the agency's field employees in the wake of two fatal crashes of the Boeing 737 MAX.[5]

However, researchers should be aware of possible biases. For example, participants may not produce completely honest responses and may feel pressured into accepting what everyone else believes. Additionally, if the focus group is not a representative sample of the target population, then the responses are likely to be inaccurate.

Market Survey

A survey involves a simple method of acquiring information from external or internal participants. Unlike a focus group with open discussion, surveys are usually completed individually and consist of a fixed list of questions. Numerous ways to conduct survey exist, but the most common technique is a questionnaire. Depending on the nature of the questions, a questionnaire can provide the researcher with both quantitative and qualitative results. Key benefits of market surveys are their easy-to-use attribute and they do not require advanced theory or econometric analysis to interpret the results. A potential flaw with market surveys is that accuracy depends on the size and responsiveness of the sample. In the aviation industry, market surveys are often used to identify which services consumers value the most. An airline, for example, can use customer comment cards to improve in-flight service quality. This data can also be used to examine competitive performance, track performance, and measure the success of recent initiatives. Similarly, airports often survey passengers before and after a terminal renovation or when deciding which tenants to offer leases to.

Quantitative forecasting models relate air travel demand to factors such as Gross Domestic Product (GDP) and income per capita; however, they rarely account for passenger characteristics like household income. In fact, some economists argue that purely quantitative demand models fail to capture several key market-level characteristics that affect passengers' propensity to travel, including age, income, occupation, household composition, and various consumer preferences (Gosling, 2014). Using data obtained from a passenger survey conducted in the Bay area, Gosling found that household size and income can have a large effect on travel behavior.

Air travel surveys are usually administered to passengers in transit at the airport or by email or in-mail delivery following a recent trip. Both methods have limitations in terms of sampling, but the information obtained can still facilitate airport and airline managers further segment travelers and make more holistic forecasting decisions. Consider, for instance, the number of airports in or near the Los Angeles area. Figure 7.2 showcases a sample airport intercept survey questionnaire designed for passengers commencing their travel from Los Angeles International Airport (LAX).

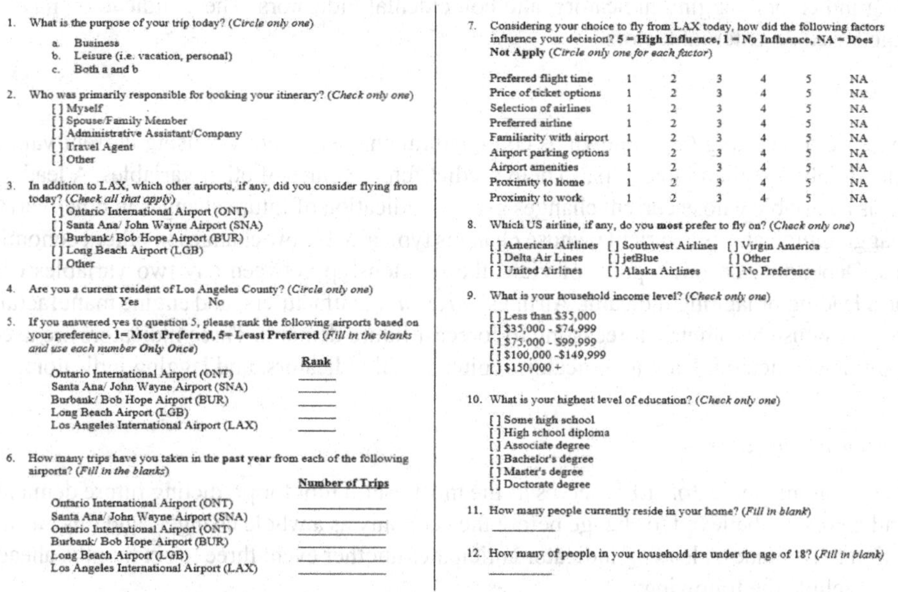

1. What is the purpose of your trip today? (*Circle only one*)
   a. Business
   b. Leisure (i.e. vacation, personal)
   c. Both a and b

2. Who was primarily responsible for booking your itinerary? (*Check only one*)
   [ ] Myself
   [ ] Spouse/Family Member
   [ ] Administrative Assistant/Company
   [ ] Travel Agent
   [ ] Other

3. In addition to LAX, which other airports, if any, did you consider flying from today? (*Check all that apply*)
   [ ] Ontario International Airport (ONT)
   [ ] Santa Ana/ John Wayne Airport (SNA)
   [ ] Burbank/ Bob Hope Airport (BUR)
   [ ] Long Beach Airport (LGB)
   [ ] Other

4. Are you a current resident of Los Angeles County? (*Circle only one*)
   Yes No

5. If you answered yes to question 5, please rank the following airports based on your preference. **1= Most Preferred, 5= Least Preferred** (*Fill in the blanks and use each number Only Once*)

	Rank
Ontario International Airport (ONT)	______
Santa Ana/ John Wayne Airport (SNA)	______
Burbank/ Bob Hope Airport (BUR)	______
Long Beach Airport (LGB)	______
Los Angeles International Airport (LAX)	______

6. How many trips have you taken in the **past year** from each of the following airports? (*Fill in the blanks*)

	Number of Trips
Ontario International Airport (ONT)	______
Santa Ana/ John Wayne Airport (SNA)	______
Ontario International Airport (ONT)	______
Burbank/ Bob Hope Airport (BUR)	______
Long Beach Airport (LGB)	______
Los Angeles International Airport (LAX)	______

7. Considering your choice to fly from LAX today, how did the following factors influence your decision? **5 = High Influence, 1 = No Influence, NA = Does Not Apply** (*Circle only one for each factor*)

Preferred flight time	1	2	3	4	5	NA
Price of ticket options	1	2	3	4	5	NA
Selection of airlines	1	2	3	4	5	NA
Preferred airline	1	2	3	4	5	NA
Familiarity with airport	1	2	3	4	5	NA
Airport parking options	1	2	3	4	5	NA
Airport amenities	1	2	3	4	5	NA
Proximity to home	1	2	3	4	5	NA
Proximity to work	1	2	3	4	5	NA

8. Which US airline, if any, do you **most** prefer to fly on? (*Check only one*)

[ ] American Airlines	[ ] Southwest Airlines	[ ] Virgin America
[ ] Delta Air Lines	[ ] jetBlue	[ ] Other
[ ] United Airlines	[ ] Alaska Airlines	[ ] No Preference

9. What is your household income level? (*Check only one*)
   [ ] Less than $35,000
   [ ] $35,000 - $74,999
   [ ] $75,000 - $99,999
   [ ] $100,000 -$149,999
   [ ] $150,000 +

10. What is your highest level of education? (*Check only one*)
    [ ] Some high school
    [ ] High school diploma
    [ ] Associate degree
    [ ] Bachelor's degree
    [ ] Master's degree
    [ ] Doctorate degree

11. How many people currently reside in your home? (*Fill in blank*)
    ______

12. How many of people in your household are under the age of 18? (*Fill in blank*)
    ______

Figure 7.2 Sample Market Survey, Airport Passenger Intercept Questionnaire.

Notice how the questionnaires center on various demand factors for a region with several international and domestic airports, whereas a mail-in survey from an airline might inquire more about quality-related aspects, such as amenities, in-flight service preferences, and so on.

Surveys like the one in discussion have been conducted in San Francisco, New York, and other highly-concentrated regions with multiple departure points for travelers. The purpose of Figure 7.2 is not to provide a comprehensive list of all potential questions; rather, it simply highlights several key factors that forecasters may consider. Additionally, notice the differences in the way the questions are structured. Depending on the goal, a surveyor may obtain responses through fixed multiple-choice, scale rating, fill-in-the-blank, or a more open-ended format.

Market Experiments

A more expensive method of qualitative forecasting entails a market experiment. This method involves testing new product factors, such as prices or packaging, in one or more selected test markets. Market experiments use real-life regions, which can be risky if the change is not accepted by consumers; this implies that the change may permanently alienate them from the company or product. Due to the costs involved, market experiments are rarely used for forecasting demand in the aviation industry. However, this method has been used to test new in-flight food and beverage options. For example, an airline may provide new meal options on a select number of flights to determine if there is in fact any demand for that particularly ancillary product.

Barometric Forecasting

> Barometric forecasting involves using current values of certain variables, called indicators, to forecast values of other variables. There are three types of economic indicators: leading indicators, lagging indicators, and coincidental indicators. These indicators may change based on external factors.

Barometric forecasting (also known as conjunctural analysis) involves using current values of certain variables, called indicators, to help predict future values of other variables. A leading indicator is a variable whose current changes give an indication of future changes in other variables. A lagging indicator is a variable whose changes typically follow changes in other economic variables. Depending on one's point of view, the relationship between any two variables can either be a leading or lagging indicator. Airlines, *aircraft* manufacturers, and engine manufacturers all regularly use barometric forecasting to forecast future demand. Three indicators are used in the barometric method: leading indicators, coincidental indicators, and lagging indicators.

Leading Economic Indictors

A leading economic indicator (LEI) serves as the most useful tool for predicting future demand. These indicators are believed to change before the economy as a whole changes, and this allows a prediction to be made. A leading indicator anticipates another event three to six months ahead. Examples include the following:

- Business and consumer confidence surveys
- Building permits

- Inventory levels
- Startups
- Stock markets

In aviation, business and consumer confidence indices are a useful leading indicator. Therefore, if confidence indices decline sharply over a period of time, airlines can expect a decline in demand shortly afterward.

Lagging Economic Indicators

A lagging economic indicator is one that follows the event. Its nature does not permit the prediction of events; instead, it confirms the occurrence or completion of the forecasted event or trend. The unemployment rate, for example, serves as a lagging indicator to the general economic condition. For an airline, profits and costs per unit of output are good lagging indicators of performance; these metrics are not useful for predictions, but they do confirm the airline's performance over a period of time. Examples include the following:

- Unemployment rate
- Business investment

Coincident Economic Indicators

A final type of indicator, known as a coincident indicator, while not notably advantageous for aviation forecasting, finds application in other context. Coincident indicators are variables that undergo changes that roughly coincide with changes in other economic variables. For example, an increase in GDP or international trade indicates the economy signifies a healthy economy. Or in another example, retail sales data provide information on consumer spending, which is an important impetus of economic growth. In aviation, for example, crude oil prices are a coincident indicator of jet fuel prices. Since changes in the price of crude oil roughly occur at the same time as changes in jet fuel prices, crude oil is a useful indicator at predicting future jet fuel prices. Crude oil is often used as a proxy variable in jet fuel hedging as it is traded much more heavily than jet fuel. Coincident economic indicators are often used to present a comprehensive view of the current state of the economy.

Historical Analogy

Historical analogy (or event analysis) comprises a simple forecasting technique where the future is forecasted based on historical events. While numerous quantitative forecasting methods use historical data to anticipate the future, historical analogy operates inherently on a qualitative level. Suppose an airline is considering adding a route from New York to Harrisburg, a city it has never previously offered service. The network planning department might examine the historical performance of similar routes in the East Coast region to determine whether or not the new service would be profitable.

Ultimately, the success of historical analogy is significantly dependent upon the depth of knowledge and history possessed by the forecaster. A forecaster with comprehensive experience across all facets of an industry over a long period is usually more adept at predicting the future compared to a relatively new employee. Therefore, historical analogy is only as good as the person making the forecast. Nevertheless, it is a useful step in developing knowledge for the process of modeling and forecasting.

Delphi Method

The Delphi method was originally developed by RAND Corporation in the 1950s to forecast the impact of technology on warfare. It is related to historical analogy in that the forecast is largely based on expert opinion. In fact, the name is derived from the Oracles of Delphi, which is said to have been a source of information about communal questions in ancient Greece. Today, the Delphi method collects forecasts and opinions from an independent panel of experts as an iterative process involving feedback through a series of stages or rounds. Each expert provides their analysis and opinion independently, and then a consensus forecast is created based on the analysis provided by each member of the panel. The primary critique of this method is that it is based on apparent consensus (Rowe and Wright, 1999). Moreover, there is no solid way to statistically analyze the results.

Nonetheless, the Delphi approach is commonly used in public transportation, public education, and other sectors where information is not always available as a tool for forecasting solutions to problems. Moreover, this technique has numerous applications in the business realm. One manufacturing company, for example, used the Delphi technique in the 1970s to forecast sales and ultimately reduce its forecast error to under 1% (Basu and Schroeder, 1977). In aviation, the Delphi method is used more for aggregate market forecasting than for route-level forecasting. International Air Transport Association (IATA), for example, based much of its early regional passenger and cargo reports on the opinion of industry experts.

By having members independently submit their opinions, the Delphi method benefits from not having steamroller or bandwagon problems. Likewise, it draws from the analysis of multiple experts instead of just one or two people in historical analogy. In theory, the accuracy of the forecast is based on the collective knowledge of the expert panel; however, because every opinion is equally weighted, the collective knowledge may not be as reliable as just a few experts.

Quantitative Methods (QMs)

In contrast to qualitative methods, the QMs use numerical values to analyze and forecast the future behavior of specific variables. QMs provide a relatively conclusive answer to the research questions (but note the earlier discussion about the distinction between risk and uncertainty). QM research means collecting and analyzing numerical data to explain functional relationship between variables, find correlations, or test hypotheses. Many airlines use quantitative data to forecast the number of passengers for a given flight, the number of no-shows, the number of go-shows, and the number of cancelations. Statistical information is broadly classified into time-series and cross-sectional data. Descriptive statistics, correlation, and regression analysis are popular quantitative analysis tools that are used to determine the relationship between two sets of related data.

Time-Series Statistics

Time-series analysis looks for patterns in data, while regression analysis assumes a causal relationship between two or more variables. The data is considered in three types:

- Time-series data
- Cross-sectional data
- Panel data (also known as longitudinal or cross-sectional time-series data)

Time-Series Data

Time-series data represents observations of certain variables over equal intervals and multiple points in time. Examples include the number of daily passengers at a given airport over the past three months, daily oil prices during quarter four, and monthly revenue during a particular year.

Cross-Section Statistics

Cross-sectional data is compiled for different variables at a single point in time, for example, the number of passengers over different geographically located airports or the total number of aviation accidents in each of 15 countries for one time period. While there are many methods of quantitative forecasting, this chapter covers only two broad categories: time-series analysis and regression analysis. Both methods will be analyzed in greater detail.

Panel Data

Panel data comprises data that contains observations about different cross sections over time. Examples of groups that may make up panel data series include airlines, aircraft type, passengers, and demographic groups. Panel data can detect and measure statistical effects that pure time series or cross-sectional data cannot.

In general, there exist several key advantages and limitations of quantitative forecasting. These are summarized in Table 7.2.

A key advantage of quantitative forecasting lies in the ease of conducting reliability test to determine the accuracy of the forecast. In time-series analysis, the most accurate forecasting method can be selected based on the test of reliability. Through regression analysis, forecasters are able to provide not only a probability of how accurate the overall forecast is, but also the reliability of the individual variables in the forecast. However, relying solely on quantitative forecasting has a significant drawback; historical data is not always a correct predictor of the future. Another chief drawback is the requirement of extensive data collection and processing for forecasts. However, the introduction of advanced statistical computer software has simplified data collection and processing, making quantitative forecasting much easier. Finally, the quality of a quantitative forecast is completely dependent upon the quality of the data that is used. Depending on how accurate and complete the data is, a quantitative forecast may distort reality, or it may model it perfectly.

Descriptive Statistics

Prior to analyzing various forecasting methods in detail, a fundamental understanding of elementary statistics is required. For most forecasting, the focus is on three basic statistics: the mean, the variance, and the standard deviation. Descriptive statistics are numerical estimates that organize, sum up, or present the data and provide simple summaries about the sample and

Table 7.2 Advantages and Limitations of Quantitative Forecasting

Advantages	*Limitations*
Organic relationships	Economic changes may distort results
Behavioral relationships	Extensive data mining of information
Tests of reliability determine forecast accuracy	Only a crude approximation of actuality

the measures. To meet that objective, a full range of indicators has been developed, and the definitions and applications of the most important ones are furnished. To illustrate descriptive statistics, the following scheduled revenue passenger miles (RPMs) data are utilized for the time period from Q1 2010 to Q3 2021.

Mean

The mean, probably the most common indicator of a dataset, is simply the average of the data. It should be noted that the mean may not be representative of an "average" if there are a few large numbers in the dataset, skewing the calculation. Sometimes the median, or the middle value in the ranked dataset, may be more useful as a representative "average." For the given data, the mean can be calculated by taking the sum of the RPMs and dividing by the number of years. In statistics, the mean is usually denoted with the Greek letter, μ. From this, the general form for the mean is:

$$\text{Mean} = \mu$$

$$\mu = \frac{\sum_{i=1}^{n} X_i}{n}$$

Based on this information, the average, or mean, RPMs between Q1 2017 and Q4 2022 can be calculated in a variety of ways (quarterly, yearly, or over a number of years). Over the time period as illustrated in Table 7.3, the average RPM is 212.42 billion.

In Microsoft Excel, the mean can simply be calculated by using the average function. This is depicted in Figure 7.3.

Table 7.3 Scheduled Revenue Passenger Miles, All US Airlines

Year	*RPM (Billions)*	*Year*	*RPM (Billions)*	*Year*	*RPM (Billions)*
2010 Q1	181.20	2014 Q1	197.45	2018 Q1	227.13
2010 Q2	208.28	2014 Q2	227.04	2018 Q2	264.89
2010 Q3	221.38	2014 Q3	235.37	2018 Q3	272.78
2010 Q4	198.20	2014 Q4	209.76	2018 Q4	246.57
2011 Q1	187.17	2015 Q1	203.07	2019 Q1	237.71
2011 Q2	215.44	2015 Q2	235.31	2019 Q2	276.55
2011 Q3	225.00	2015 Q3	247.77	2019 Q3	283.14
2011 Q4	198.26	2015 Q4	222.44	2019 Q4	258.11
2012 Q1	191.87	2016 Q1	213.89	2020 Q1	197.26
2012 Q2	217.31	2016 Q2	243.84	2020 Q2	248.51
2012 Q3	225.10	2016 Q3	253.60	2020 Q3	689.51
2012 Q4	198.41	2016 Q4	248.91	2020 Q4	866.56
2013 Q1	193.99	2017 Q1	216.50	2021 Q1	968.03
2013 Q2	220.49	2017 Q2	252.67	2021 Q2	174.00
2013 Q3	229.18	2017 Q3	259.16	2021 Q3	210.33
2013 Q4	204.30	2017 Q4	235.88	2021 Q4	206.74

Source: Compiled by the authors from OAG Form 41 data.

Table 7.4 Variance Calculation of RPM, 2017–2021

Year	*RPM (Billions)*	$x - \mu$	$(x - \mu)^2$
2013 Q1	193.99	−53.06	2,814.95
2013 Q2	220.49	−26.56	705.23
2013 Q3	229.18	−17.87	319.20
2013 Q4	204.30	−42.75	1,827.23
2014 Q1	197.45	−49.60	2,459.77
2014 Q2	227.04	−20.01	400.24
2014 Q3	235.37	−11.68	136.33
2014 Q4	209.76	−37.29	1,390.25
2015 Q1	203.07	−43.98	1,933.90
2015 Q2	235.31	−11.74	137.74
2015 Q3	247.77	0.72	0.52
2015 Q4	222.44	−24.61	605.46
2016 Q1	213.89	−33.16	1,099.33
2016 Q2	243.84	−3.21	10.28
2016 Q3	263.60	16.55	274.03
2016 Q4	253.60	6.55	42.95
2017 Q1	216.5	−30.55	933.06
2017 Q2	252.66	5.61	31.52
2017 Q3	259.16	12.11	146.75
2017 Q4	235.87	−11.18	124.91
2018 Q1	227.12	−19.93	397.05
2018 Q2	264.88	17.83	318.05
2018 Q3	272.78	25.73	662.23
2018 Q4	246.56	−0.49	0.24
2019 Q1	237.7	−9.35	87.35
2019 Q2	276.54	29.49	869.89
2019 Q3	283.14	36.09	1,302.77
2019 Q4	258.11	11.06	122.41
2020 Q1	197.25	−49.80	2,479.65
2020 Q2	248.51	1.46	2.14
2020 Q3	489.51	242.46	58,788.74
2020 Q4	366.56	119.51	14,283.57
2021 Q1	368.02	120.97	14,634.68
2021 Q2	174.63	−72.42	5,244.09
2021 Q3	210.33	−36.72	1,348.07
2021 Q4	206.73	−40.32	1,625.39
μ	247.05	Variance	57.15

Source: Form 41 DIIO Database.

Variance

The variance of a sample measures how the observations are dispersed around the mean. A large variance means the observations are widely scattered around the mean. The variance of variable x is calculated by summing the squared difference between the actual values of x and the mean of x. In statistics, the variance is denoted as σ^2, with the general form being:

$$\sigma^2 = \frac{\sum_{i=1}^{n}(x_i - \mu)^2}{n-1}$$

The variance of a dataset is important as it provides some insight into the accuracy of the mean. For example, the variance in the previous example is 380.57 as illustrated in Figure 7.4.[6] The computation assumes the dataset as a sample dataset. Thus, the variance can be computed using the Excel formula, VAR.S.

Table 7.4 depicts the calculation of mean and variance for the chosen dataset using the formulas provided.

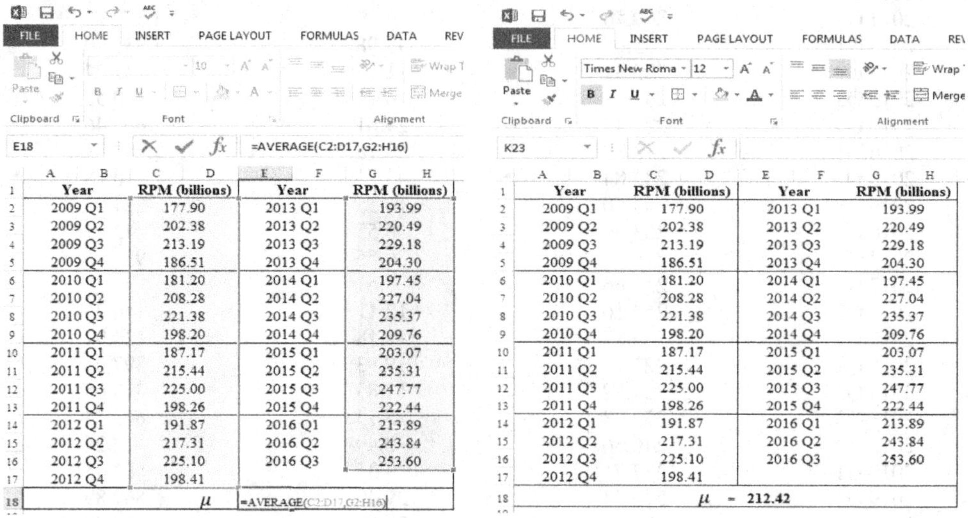

E18 =AVERAGE(C2:D17,G2:H16)

Year	RPM (billions)	Year	RPM (billions)
2009 Q1	177.90	2013 Q1	193.99
2009 Q2	202.38	2013 Q2	220.49
2009 Q3	213.19	2013 Q3	229.18
2009 Q4	186.51	2013 Q4	204.30
2010 Q1	181.20	2014 Q1	197.45
2010 Q2	208.28	2014 Q2	227.04
2010 Q3	221.38	2014 Q3	235.37
2010 Q4	198.20	2014 Q4	209.76
2011 Q1	187.17	2015 Q1	203.07
2011 Q2	215.44	2015 Q2	235.31
2011 Q3	225.00	2015 Q3	247.77
2011 Q4	198.26	2015 Q4	222.44
2012 Q1	191.87	2016 Q1	213.89
2012 Q2	217.31	2016 Q2	243.84
2012 Q3	225.10	2016 Q3	253.60
2012 Q4	198.41		
	μ	=AVERAGE(C2:D17,G2:H16)	

Year	RPM (billions)	Year	RPM (billions)
2009 Q1	177.90	2013 Q1	193.99
2009 Q2	202.38	2013 Q2	220.49
2009 Q3	213.19	2013 Q3	229.18
2009 Q4	186.51	2013 Q4	204.30
2010 Q1	181.20	2014 Q1	197.45
2010 Q2	208.28	2014 Q2	227.04
2010 Q3	221.38	2014 Q3	235.37
2010 Q4	198.20	2014 Q4	209.76
2011 Q1	187.17	2015 Q1	203.07
2011 Q2	215.44	2015 Q2	235.31
2011 Q3	225.00	2015 Q3	247.77
2011 Q4	198.26	2015 Q4	222.44
2012 Q1	191.87	2016 Q1	213.89
2012 Q2	217.31	2016 Q2	243.84
2012 Q3	225.10	2016 Q3	253.60
2012 Q4	198.41		

	μ = 212.42		

Figure 7.3 Computing Average in Excel.

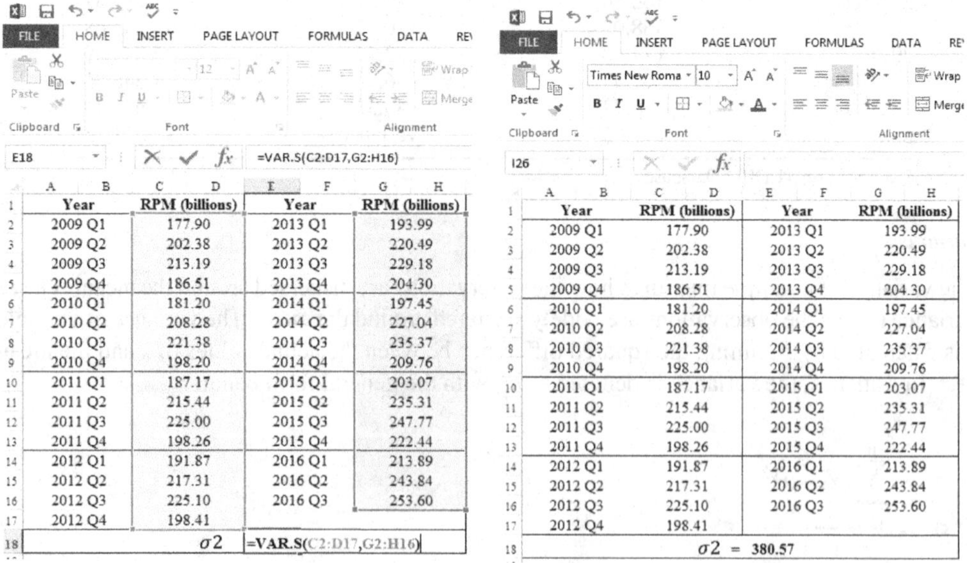

E18 =VAR.S(C2:D17,G2:H16)

Year	RPM (billions)	Year	RPM (billions)
2009 Q1	177.90	2013 Q1	193.99
2009 Q2	202.38	2013 Q2	220.49
2009 Q3	213.19	2013 Q3	229.18
2009 Q4	186.51	2013 Q4	204.30
2010 Q1	181.20	2014 Q1	197.45
2010 Q2	208.28	2014 Q2	227.04
2010 Q3	221.38	2014 Q3	235.37
2010 Q4	198.20	2014 Q4	209.76
2011 Q1	187.17	2015 Q1	203.07
2011 Q2	215.44	2015 Q2	235.31
2011 Q3	225.00	2015 Q3	247.77
2011 Q4	198.26	2015 Q4	222.44
2012 Q1	191.87	2016 Q1	213.89
2012 Q2	217.31	2016 Q2	243.84
2012 Q3	225.10	2016 Q3	253.60
2012 Q4	198.41		

	$\sigma 2$	=VAR.S(C2:D17,G2:H16)	

Year	RPM (billions)	Year	RPM (billions)
2009 Q1	177.90	2013 Q1	193.99
2009 Q2	202.38	2013 Q2	220.49
2009 Q3	213.19	2013 Q3	229.18
2009 Q4	186.51	2013 Q4	204.30
2010 Q1	181.20	2014 Q1	197.45
2010 Q2	208.28	2014 Q2	227.04
2010 Q3	221.38	2014 Q3	235.37
2010 Q4	198.20	2014 Q4	209.76
2011 Q1	187.17	2015 Q1	203.07
2011 Q2	215.44	2015 Q2	235.31
2011 Q3	225.00	2015 Q3	247.77
2011 Q4	198.26	2015 Q4	222.44
2012 Q1	191.87	2016 Q1	213.89
2012 Q2	217.31	2016 Q2	243.84
2012 Q3	225.10	2016 Q3	253.60
2012 Q4	198.41		

	$\sigma 2$ = 380.57		

Figure 7.4 Computing Variance in Excel.

Standard Deviation (SD)

Standard deviation is directly related to variance as it is the positive square root of the variance. The standard deviation is a statistic that depicts how tightly all the observations are clustered around the mean in a set of data. When the observations are spread around the mean, it indicates a relatively large standard deviation. In order to avoid problems with the negative signs of some deviations from the mean (note that the sum of the values of the deviations from the mean in the given example is zero and this will always be true by definition), the values of the deviations are displayed in squared terms. By calculating the square root of the variance, the standard deviation, denoted as σ, returns the variance to a more easily interpretable number:

$$\sigma = \sqrt{\frac{\sum_{i=1}^{n}(x_i - \mu)^2}{n}}$$

Standard deviation (SD) is a commonly used measure of dispersion. SD denotes a statistic that measures the dispersion of a dataset around its mean and is calculated as the square root of the variance. A large standard deviation indicates a great dispersion in the data around the mean.

However, it should be noted that while the squaring procedure eliminates the problem of negative deviations canceling out positive ones, it also provides much greater weight to outlying observations. This implies that the further an observation deviates from the mean, the greater the difference between the observation and the mean. Therefore, the greater is the squared value of this observation.

From the RPM data used above, the standard deviation is simply obtained to be 19.51, which can be calculated using the STDEV.S formula in Excel as shown in Figure 7.5.

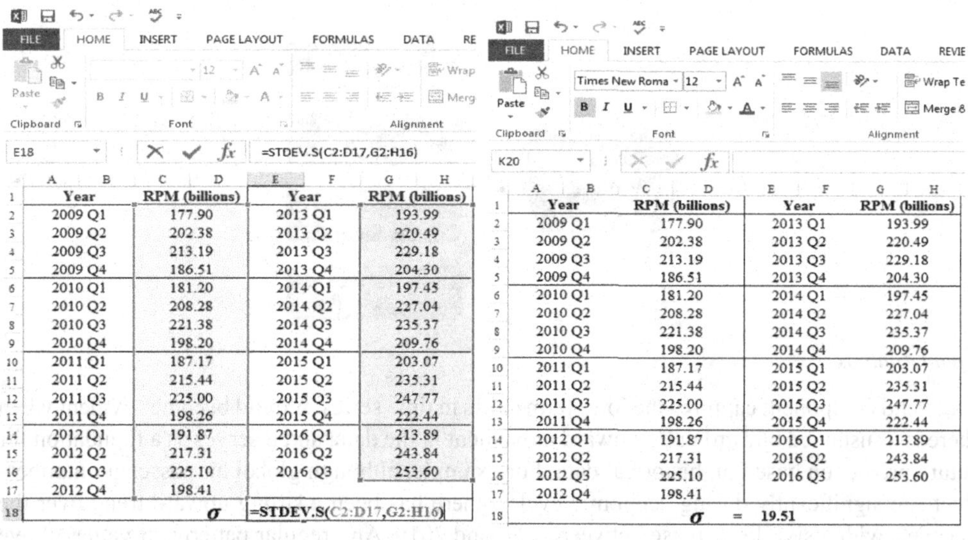

E18 =STDEV.S(C2:D17,G2:H16)

	Year	RPM (billions)	Year	RPM (billions)
1	Year	RPM (billions)	Year	RPM (billions)
2	2009 Q1	177.90	2013 Q1	193.99
3	2009 Q2	202.38	2013 Q2	220.49
4	2009 Q3	213.19	2013 Q3	229.18
5	2009 Q4	186.51	2013 Q4	204.30
6	2010 Q1	181.20	2014 Q1	197.45
7	2010 Q2	208.28	2014 Q2	227.04
8	2010 Q3	221.38	2014 Q3	235.37
9	2010 Q4	198.20	2014 Q4	209.76
10	2011 Q1	187.17	2015 Q1	203.07
11	2011 Q2	215.44	2015 Q2	235.31
12	2011 Q3	225.00	2015 Q3	247.77
13	2011 Q4	198.26	2015 Q4	222.44
14	2012 Q1	191.87	2016 Q1	213.89
15	2012 Q2	217.31	2016 Q2	243.84
16	2012 Q3	225.10	2016 Q3	253.60
17	2012 Q4	198.41		
18		σ	=STDEV.S(C2:D17,G2:H16)	

K20

	Year	RPM (billions)	Year	RPM (billions)
1	Year	RPM (billions)	Year	RPM (billions)
2	2009 Q1	177.90	2013 Q1	193.99
3	2009 Q2	202.38	2013 Q2	220.49
4	2009 Q3	213.19	2013 Q3	229.18
5	2009 Q4	186.51	2013 Q4	204.30
6	2010 Q1	181.20	2014 Q1	197.45
7	2010 Q2	208.28	2014 Q2	227.04
8	2010 Q3	221.38	2014 Q3	235.37
9	2010 Q4	198.20	2014 Q4	209.76
10	2011 Q1	187.17	2015 Q1	203.07
11	2011 Q2	215.44	2015 Q2	235.31
12	2011 Q3	225.00	2015 Q3	247.77
13	2011 Q4	198.26	2015 Q4	222.44
14	2012 Q1	191.87	2016 Q1	213.89
15	2012 Q2	217.31	2016 Q2	243.84
16	2012 Q3	225.10	2016 Q3	253.60
17	2012 Q4	198.41		
18		σ	=	19.51

Figure 7.5 Computing Standard Deviation in Excel.

The concept of standard deviation is not difficult to understand. Assume we have collected one month of ticket prices, for example, from New York to London, about 1,250 observations, and entered them into a spreadsheet to calculate the average. Suppose the average price is calculated as $870. This number, by itself, is of limited significance. By measuring the standard deviation of the ticket price, however, we can gain an idea of how volatile the ticket price really was; the larger the standard deviation, the more volatile the ticket price. For a perfectly normal distribution, 68.4% of all the observations fall within plus or minus one standard deviation of the average, 95.4% fall within plus or minus two standard deviations of the average, and 99.7% of the observations fall within plus or minus three standard deviations of the average.[7] To summarize:

- About 68.4% of the data will be within: $X \pm 1\sigma$
- About 95.4% of the data will be within: $X \pm 2\sigma$
- About 99.7% of the data will be within: $X \pm 3\sigma$

If the standard deviation in the given example was obtained to be $13.52, then the spread for this scenario is illustrated here:

- About 68.4% of passengers paid within: $\$870 \pm 1 \times \$13.52$
- About 95.4% of passengers paid within: $\$870 \pm 2 \times \$13.52$
- About 99.7% of passengers paid within: $\$870 \pm 3 \times \$13.52$

Time-Series Analysis

As previously mentioned, time-series analysis measures the status of some activity, such as aviation accidents, number of aircraft operations, or number of enplanements over a period of time. A time-series analysis records the activity with measurements taken at equally spaced intervals with a consistency in the activity and the method of measurement. Observations may be carried out annually, quarterly, monthly, weekly, daily, or even hourly. Every the time-series dataset contains four components.

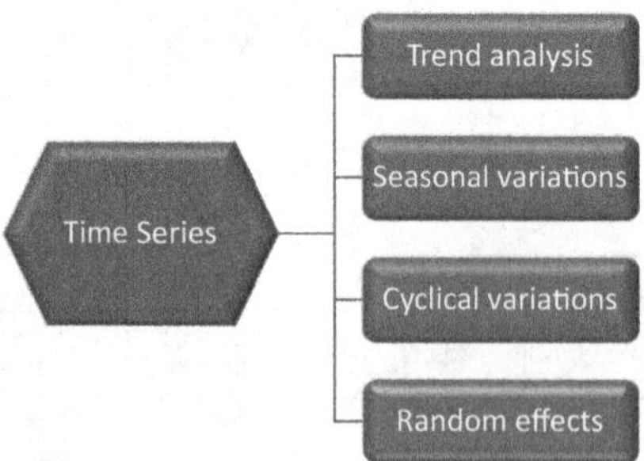

Trend Analysis

The trend component captures the long-term shifts in time series. A trend becomes evident when there is a sustained upward or downward movement in the data, and it serves as a foundation for future prediction based on historical data. For example, although global air passenger numbers fluctuate significantly during economic cycles, there has been a strong upward trend over the decades, with a sixfold increase between 1980 and 2019. Any regular patterns of values above and below the trend component are likely attributable to the cyclical component of a time series.

For the air transport industry, this shift or trend is usually attributed to factors such as liberalization, deregulation, change in disposable income, introduction of new technology, population growth, and/or privatization. The overall trend of demand has been consistently increasing (Figure 7.6). The volume of US traffic during the 1991–2022 period grew at a healthy rate of 2.92% on average per year.[8]

In Excel, trend analysis can be conducted using the robust "trendline" tool in charts. Upon selecting the data series and right-clicking, a menu of options appears, from which you can choose "Add trendline." Figure 7.7 depicts a trendline for RPMs for all US carriers from 1991

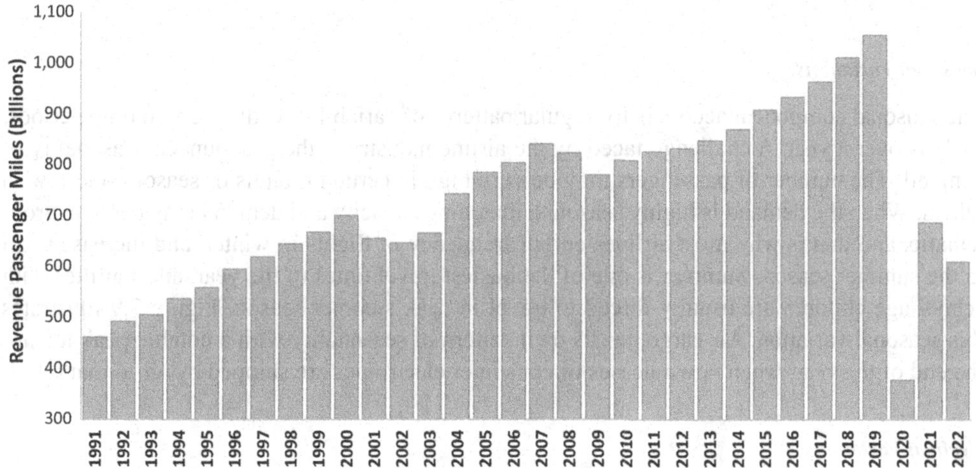

Figure 7.6 Scheduled Revenue Passenger Miles, 2009–2022.

Source: Compiled by the authors from Diio Mi Form 41 data

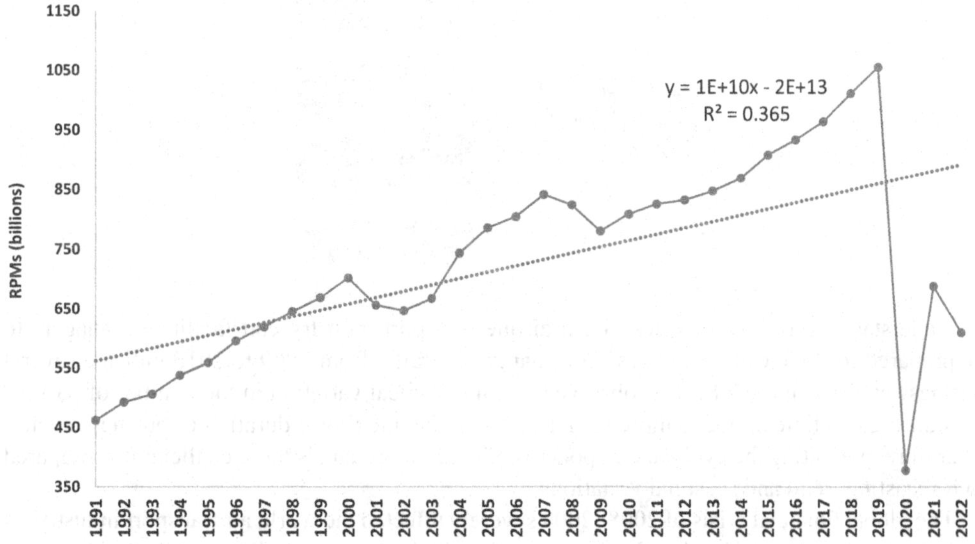

Figure 7.7 Trendline for RPM: All US Airlines, 2009–2022.

Source: Compiled by the authors from Diio Mi Form 41 data

through Q4 2022. By using years instead of quarters, we can achieve a smoother representation of our time series, facilitating a better visual of the year-by-year growth over time.

Choosing the different options, namely, Exponential, Linear, Logarithmic, Polynomial, Power, and Moving Average, would change the fit of the trendline and its accuracy. The accuracy of the chosen trendline can be seen by the closeness of the R-squared value to 1. This can be done by selecting the check boxes at the bottom of the set of options. The R-squared value for the "Linear" trendline in the example is demonstrated in Figure 7.7.

The explanation for the R-squared value is discussed under the regression analysis section of this chapter. In this example, an R-squared of 0.9467 means that 94.67% of the variation of the dependent variable is "explained" by the independent variable.

Seasonal Variations

The seasonal component accounts for regular patterns of variability within certain time periods, such as over a year. A challenge faced by the airline industry is the pronounced seasonality of demand. The number of passengers may be very high in certain months or seasons and low in others. When the demand is highly seasonal, matching capacity and demand may become problematic, and that is why most airlines curtail frequency of flights in winter, and increase them in the summer season. Summer is one of the busiest travel times of the year, and families with school-age children are usually forced to travel in peak summer season. Figure 7.9 illustrates this seasonal variation. Air cargo has its own pattern of seasonality with a notable peak toward the end of the year, when new releases of consumer electronics are shipped by air to market.

Cyclical Variations

The cyclical component refers to long-term fluctuation of time-series statistics. A business cycle consists of four stages: expansion, peak, contraction, and trough.

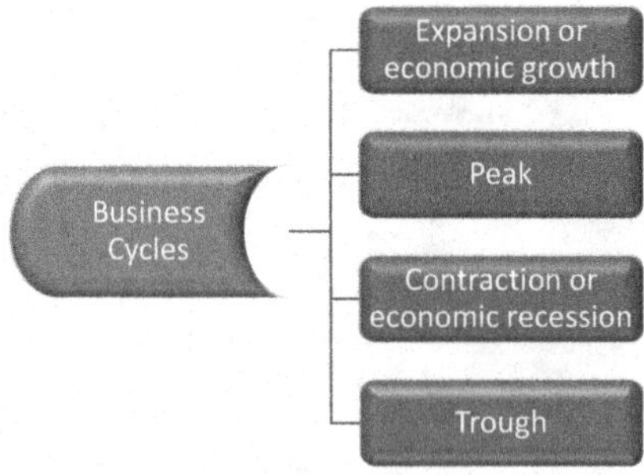

Understanding business cycles in the airline transport industry can facilitate managers to be prepared for financial challenges. The changes in traffic from 2009 to 2016 indicate several business cycles (Figure 7.8). It is observed that the cyclical variation in the number of passengers during this time period is more irregular due to the ununiform duration of business cycles. Therefore, predicting the cyclical components of time-series data is more challenging compared to forecasting trend and seasonal variations.

The global financial crisis of 2008–2009 severely affected the world air transport industry, as passenger volumes continued to decline, even though the price of fuel plummeted. US carriers posted combined 2008 losses of about $4.5 billion due to the economic recession, and many of the small airlines as well as mega carriers filed for bankruptcy or were forced to liquidation.[9]

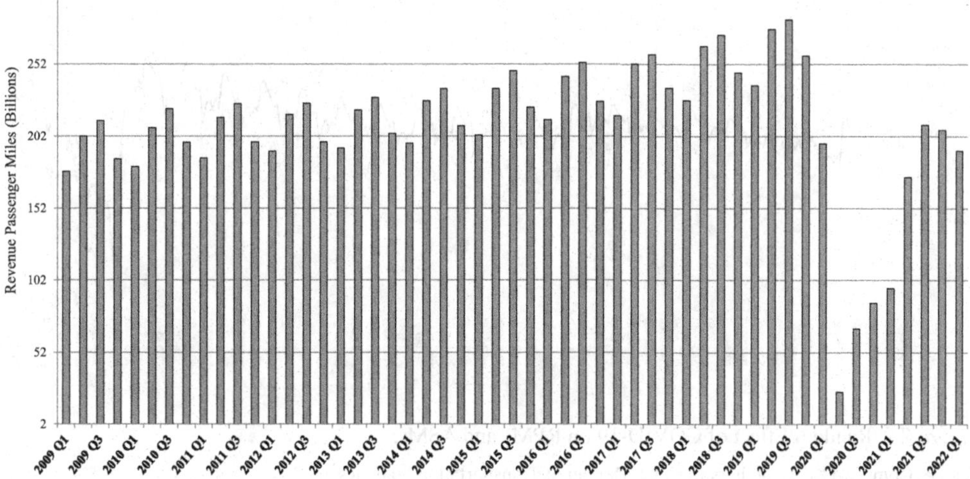

Figure 7.8 Scheduled Revenue Passenger Miles, Q1 2009–Q1 2022.

The COVID-19 pandemic had a profound impact on the world aviation industry, and demand for air travel plummeted and remained significantly below 2019. According to Department of Transportation (DOT) statistics, passenger traffic remained 60% below 2019 traffic levels throughout 2020. According to IATA's latest industry report, worldwide passenger demand is projected to reach 85.5% of 2019 levels over the course of 2023.[10]

Random Effect

> Shares in US airlines were battered yesterday as a monthly report from Delta Air Lines and a travel warning related to the Zika virus in Miami raised concerns about air carriers' revenue at a time when they typically benefit from summer travel… Airlines with the greatest exposure to South Florida include American Airlines, JetBlue Airways and Spirit Airlines.[11]
>
> *The Australian*

Expansion is a part of a business cycle when the economy moves from a trough to a peak, and this results in higher employment. Contraction results in a slowdown in the level of economic activity and is accompanied with higher unemployment.

Finally, random factors of a series are short-term, unanticipated, and non-recurring factors that affect the values of the series. These factors are part of the natural variability present in all measurements. Or, it can be argued that the random component is what remains when all the other components of the series (trend, seasonal, and cyclical) have been accounted for. For example, events such as September 11, 2001 are impossible to predict (Figure 7.9). Likewise, the COVID-19 pandemic severely affected the aviation and aerospace sectors that depend on commercial passenger travel. Due to travel restrictions and a collapse in demand among travelers, several airlines filed for bankruptcy. The Italian airline Ernest Airlines collapsed on April 5, 2020. The Ecuadorian government liquidated TAME and ceased all operations on May 20, 2020.[12] LATAM Airlines Group filed for Chapter 11 bankruptcy and its subsidiaries in Chile, the United States, Ecuador, Colombia, and Peru on May 26, 2020.[13]

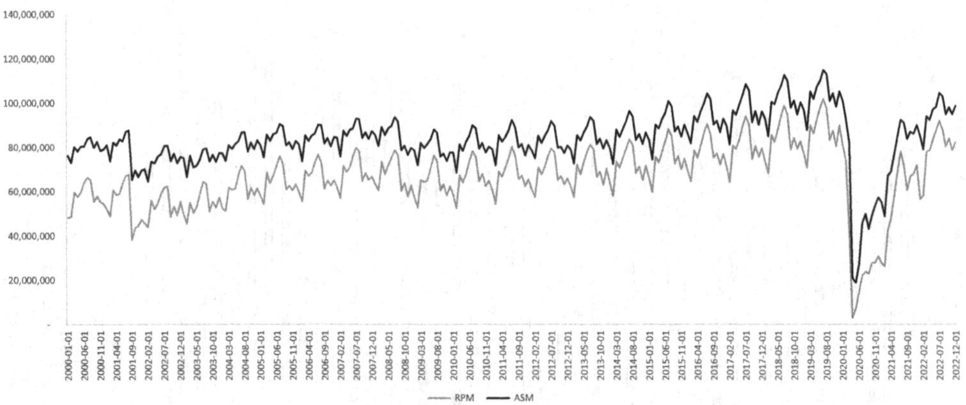

Figure 7.9 Random Effect of COVID-19 on RPMs and ASMs.

Source: Compiled by the authors from US Bureau of Transportation Statistics

Even if an airline could perfectly predict cyclical operating costs and revenues, the costs (and benefits) of random effects or uncertainty remain unfeasible to accurately forecast. Other random effects may stem from aviation accidents, airline mergers, and bankruptcies. The trend component analyzes the data over a long period of time, the cyclical component occurs over a medium term, and seasonal variations occur in the short term (under one year).

Moving average is a technique that smooths out fluctuations in data, making it easier to find trends and patterns. For example, a five-day SMA would be calculated by taking the sum of the last five days of data points and dividing it by 5. Another type of moving average is weighted moving average (WMA) that assigns different weights to each data point in the calculation.

Time-Series Forecasting

Time-series forecasting stands as one of the most frequently used quantitative techniques in economics, business, finance, and inventory planning. These forecasts inform all kinds of business decisions. Illustratively, they aid in forecasting demand for pilots, predicting the number of no-shows in an aircraft, and estimating equipment failures and maintenance requirements to uphold safety standards. While several different methods exist for forecasting time series, our focus will center on four major methods:

- Moving average
- Weighted moving average
- Exponential smoothing
- Trend analysis

Moving Average (MA)

Moving average serves as a smoothing technique that employs the average of the most recent data values to assist in forecasting the upcoming period. Moving average is a very simple technique that contains the underlying assumption that the most recent values are the best representation of the future. Mathematically, the formula for calculating the moving average is:

$$MA = \frac{\sum_{i=1}^{n} X_i}{n}$$

In order to understand the applicability of moving averages, consider the following data which display the historical bookings for the last ten days of a DirectJet flight (Table 7.5).

If the goal is to forecast the number of bookings on the eleventh day with a moving average, the first step is to determine *n*, which represents the number of recent data values to include in the forecast. Since every value is given equal weight in the moving average, the larger the *n*, the more the weight historical values given. Assuming that a three-day moving average is desired, the three most recent data values (days 8, 9, and 10) are used to help forecast DirectJet's bookings on day 11. The forecast for the eleventh day is:

$$F(11) = \frac{(150+130+160)}{3}$$
$$F(11) = \frac{440}{3}$$
$$F(11) = 146.67$$

Using the last three data values, the forecast number of bookings on the eleventh day is 146.67 (rounded to 147). If it is believed that a three-day moving average provides too much emphasis on the most recent days, we can calculate a five-day moving average using the same logic. The five-day moving average provides a forecast for the eleventh day of:

$$F(11) = \frac{(130+145+150+130+160)}{5}$$
$$F(11) = \frac{715}{5}$$
$$F(11) = 143$$

Table 7.5 Time-Series Data of Bookings for a DirectJet Flight

Day	*Bookings*
1	115
2	100
3	105
4	120
5	135
6	130
7	145
8	150
9	130
10	160
11	?

Based on the five-day forecast, the forecasted value of 143 is less than the three-day forecast value of 146.67. While results will vary depending on the dataset, any moving average attempts to smooth out any distortions in the data; this can be extremely useful, especially with highly variable data.

Moving average can easily be calculated in Microsoft Excel using the moving average function in the "Data Analysis Toolpack," found under the "Data Tab." With the aid of Microsoft Excel, the three-day and five-day moving average forecasts were created for multiple days to compare the forecasted values and the actual values.

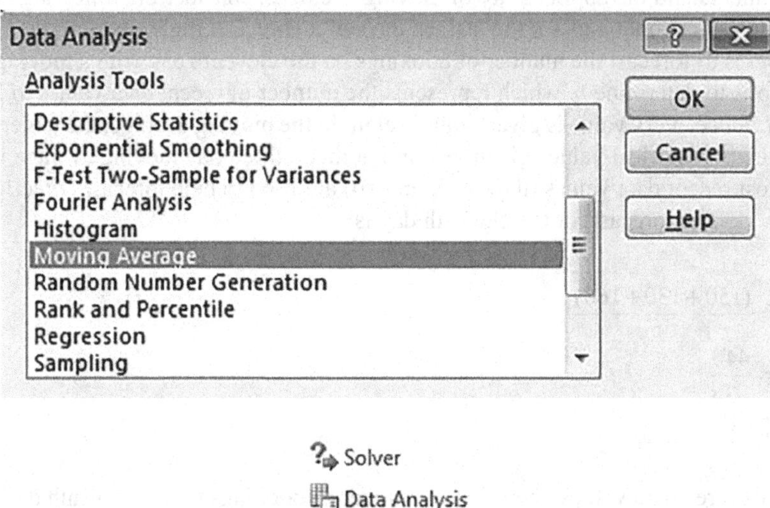

Once Moving Average is selected, the following window appears, where the input range or the data for which the moving average is to be determined is selected. Another important input is the "Interval," which signifies whether we are using a three-day or a five-day moving average. The output range is the set of cells where the result appears.

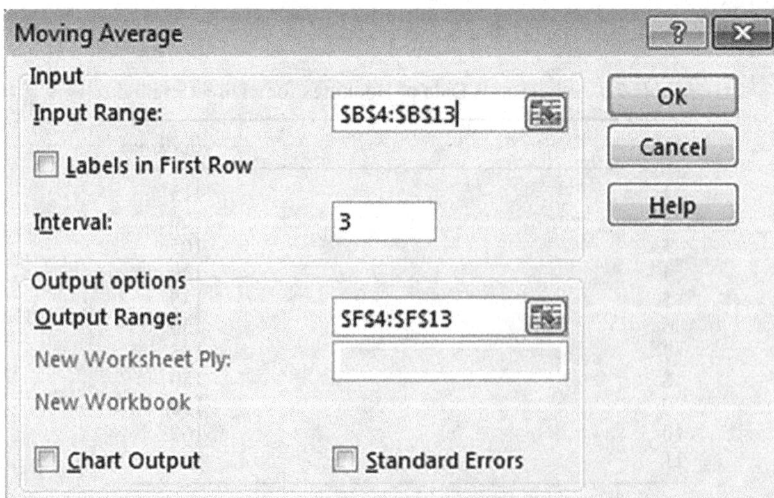

Note the fact that the three-day moving average forecasts cannot be computed for the first three days and likewise the five-day average for the first five days, as these are needed to start the series. Table 7.6 presents these data. The accuracy of the forecasts can be determined by comparing the difference between the actual and forecasted values. These techniques will be discussed in more detail later in this chapter.

Weighted Moving Average

Weighted moving average (WMA) is similar to moving average. It also employs historical data to provide a forecasted value; however, instead of each value receiving equal weighting, as in moving average, values receive different weightings. For example, in a three-period moving average, each value receives an equal weighting of 1/3. However, weighted moving average enables the forecaster to weight the values as desired. Mathematically, the formula for WMA is presented as:

$$\text{WMA} = \sum_{i=1}^{n} W_i \times X_i$$

Using the same data contained in Table 7.5, a weighted moving average for day 11 can be created assuming that the most recent value receives a 50% weighting, the next most recent value receives a 30% weighting, and the third value receiving 20%. This is shown in Table 7.7. Based on this, the forecasted value is:

$$F(11) = 0.5(160) + 0.3(130) + 0.2(150)$$

$$F(11) = 80 + 39 + 30 = 149$$

Using the designated weights, the forecast value for day 11 is 149. However, the forecast value can change based on the assigned weightings. Assuming that the most recent value receives an 80% weighting, the second value a 15% weighting, and the final value a 5% weighting, the forecast value for the eleventh day would be:

$$F(11) = 0.8(160) + 0.15(130) + 0.05(150)$$

$$F(11) = 128 + 19.5 + 7.5 = 155$$

Table 7.6 Three-Day and Five-Day Moving Average Forecasts

Day	*Bookings*	*Three-Day Moving Average*	*Five-Day Moving Average*
1	115		
2	100		
3	105		
4	120	107	
5	135	108	
6	130	120	115
7	145	128	118
8	150	137	127
9	130	142	136
10	160	142	138
11	?	147	143

Table 7.7 Three-Day Weighted Moving Average Forecast

Day	*Bookings*	*Weights*	
1	115		
2	100		
3	105		
4	120		
5	135		
6	130		
7	145		
8	150	50%	80%
9	130	30%	15%
10	160	20%	5%
11	?	149	155

With this new weighting scheme, the forecast value for the eleventh day is considerably higher, as in this circumstance, the most recent value received a high weighting. Ultimately, the weightings assigned are based on the forecaster's judgment. Therefore, the more experience and expertise the forecaster has, the more likely that the assigned weightings will be accurate. Weightings can be assigned for any number of periods, as long as the total sum of the weightings equal 100% or 1.

Exponential Smoothing

A third smoothing technique that can be used to forecast time-series data is exponential smoothing. Unlike a moving average which uses multiple historical values to help forecast, exponential smoothing only uses data from the previous period. Exponential smoothing indirectly takes into consideration previous periods by using the previous period's forecast value to determine the forecasted value. This creates a situation where the weighting for a value gets exponentially smaller as time moves on. The general formula for exponential smoothing is:

$$F_{i+1} = a \times Y_t + (1-a) \times F_t$$

where:

- F_{t+1} is the forecast value in the next period.
- Y_t is the actual value in the previous period.
- F_t is the forecasted value in the previous period.
- α is a smoothing constant with values between 0 and 1.

The smoothing constant plays a crucial role in determining the weight attributed to the forecast value. It is based upon the actual value from the previous period and the forecast value. The higher the smoothing constant, the greater the weighting the actual value receives. Like the two previous forecasting methods, the forecaster must make a judgment in assigning the value for the smoothing constant. While higher smoothing constants usually provide more accurate forecasts, the overall objective of the forecast is to be as accurate as possible. Since the formula contains a term on the right-hand side that depicts a previously forecast value, the question arises as to where that value will come from for the first observation. The answer to this is that value comes from the actual value of the first period. This means that no matter what value is picked for the constant, the first value of the forecast will equal the first period of the series. Subsequent values will of course differ between constants because the actual and forecast values will differ.

Using the exponential smoothing function in the "Data Analysis Toolpack" from Microsoft Excel, forecasts can be created for DirectJet. Table 7.8 provides forecasts with two different smoothing constants (α): 0.3 and 0.8.

From Table 7.8, it is evident that a smaller smoothing constant provides greater fluctuation in the forecast value, while a larger constant provides less variability in the forecasts.

The Exponential Smoothing dialogue box (selected from the Data Analysis Toolpack) is depicted in the image given. The input range is the "Bookings" column in Table 7.8, the Damping factor is α, and the output range displays the results in those cells.

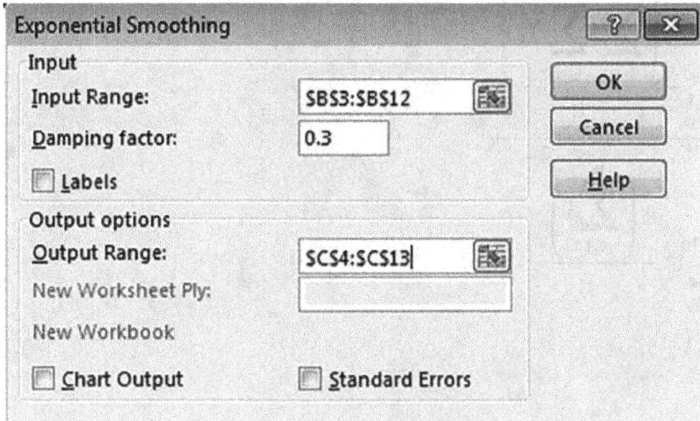

Trend Analysis

The fourth and final time-series method to be investigated is trend analysis. Scatter diagrams and line graphs provide a good first approximation in identifying the existence of a trendline between independent and dependent variables. Depending on how closely the points group together, a discernable trend might emerge. Unfortunately, trends are not always easy to see graphically, and there may also be a problem with units. A more quantitative method to identify a trendline is regression analysis. Regression analysis attempts to create a linear trend equation to describe the data. Such equations can then be used to provide a forecast for a future value. The general form for these equations follows:

$$F_t = b_0 + b_1 t$$

Table 7.8 Exponential Smoothing Forecasts with Two Different Smoothing Constants

Day	*Bookings*	$\alpha = 0.3$	$\alpha = 0.8$
1	115		
2	100	115	115
3	105	105	112
4	120	105	111
5	135	115	112
6	130	129	117
7	145	130	120
8	150	140	125
9	130	147	130
10	160	135	130
11	?	153	136

where:

- F_t is the forecast value in period t.
- b_0 is the intercept of the trendline.
- b_1 is the slope of the trendline.

In order to calculate the forecast value, the parameters b_0 and b_1 must first be calculated. The formulas for these values are:

$$b_1 = \frac{\sum_{t=1}^{n} tY_t - \frac{\left(\sum_{t=1}^{n} t \sum_{t=1}^{n} Y_t\right)}{n}}{\sum_{t=1}^{n} t^2 - \frac{\left(\sum_{t=1}^{n} t\right)^2}{n}}$$

$$b_0 = \bar{Y} - b_1 \bar{t}$$

where:

- Y_t is the actual value in period t.
- n is the number of periods.
- $\bar{Y}$ is the average value of the time series.
- $\bar{t}$ is the average value of t.

Based on these formulae, the linear trendline can be constructed. To complete the calculation, however, some additional information is required. Therefore, the original DirectJet problem is expanded in Table 7.9.

Table 7.9 Expanded Dataset for DirectJet

Day	*Bookings*	*Day × Bookings*	*Day Squared*
1	115	115	1
2	100	200	4
3	105	315	9
4	120	480	16
5	135	675	25
6	130	780	36
7	145	1,015	49
8	150	1,200	64
9	130	1,170	81
10	160	1,600	100
55	1,290	7,550	385

From the expanded dataset, the values required to determine the slope and the intercept can be found as follows:

$$\sum_{t=1}^{10} tY = 7{,}550$$

$$\sum_{t=1}^{10} t = 55$$

$$\sum_{t=1}^{10} Y_t = 1{,}290$$

$$n = 10$$

$$\sum_{t=1}^{10} t^2 = 385$$

$$\bar{Y} = \frac{\sum_{t=1}^{10} Y_t}{n} = \frac{1{,}290}{10} = 129$$

$$\bar{t} = \frac{\sum_{t=1}^{10} t}{n} = \frac{55}{10} = 5.5$$

$$b_1 = \frac{\sum_{t=1}^{n} tY_t - \frac{\left(\sum_{t=1}^{n} t \sum_{t=1}^{n} Y_t\right)}{n}}{\sum_{t=1}^{n} t^2 - \frac{\left(\sum_{t=1}^{n} t\right)^2}{n}}$$

$$b_1 = \frac{7{,}550 - \frac{(55*1{,}290)}{10}}{385 - \frac{(55)^2}{10}}$$

$$b_1 = \frac{7{,}550 - 7{,}095}{385 - 302.5} = \frac{455}{82.5} = 5.52$$

$$b_o = 129 - 5.52(5.5)$$

$$b_o = 129 - 30.33 = 98.67$$

Using the values of the slope and intercept, the trendline is:

$$F_t = 98.67 + 5.52t$$

Based on this formula, forecasts for the number of bookings for DirectJet can be formulated by solving the equation. It is important to recognize that trend analysis only forecasts the trend portion of a time series. Cyclicality, seasonality, and random factors can cause distortions from the trendline. Using the provided equation, the forecast for the number of bookings on the eleventh day is:

$$F(11) = 98.67 + 5.52(11)$$

$$F(11) = 98.67 + 60.72 = 159.39$$

Trend analysis can be performed more quickly through computer programs such as Microsoft Excel and SPSS.[14] By graphing the time-series data, a trendline can be fitted to the data, and the equation can also be provided. Figure 7.10 displays the trendline, with the computer producing the exact same formula as was calculated.

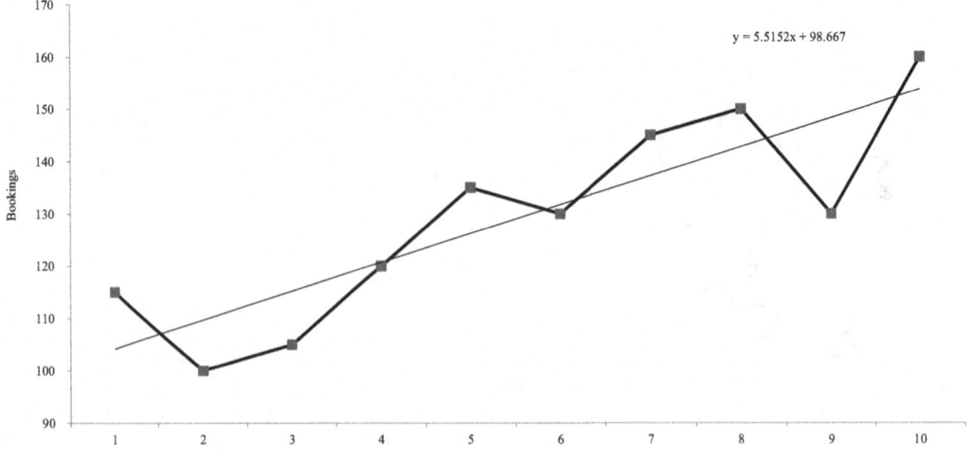

Figure 7.10 Graphical Representation of Trendline for the Time Series

Forecast Accuracy

Forecasting is ultimately useful only if the forecasts are reasonably accurate. While the actual accuracy of the forecast is not known until the event has occurred, historical time-series data can be analyzed to provide an indication of how well the technique works. Numerous examples of forecasting errors are prevalent in the aviation industry, leading to significant losses for the company involved. For example, in 2006, the Airbus's parent company EADS announced that the company needed to sell 420 A380s to break even, up from its initial announced prediction of 270 aircraft. The two major methods of analyzing forecast accuracy are mean squared error (MSE) and mean absolute deviation (MAD):

Forecast error = Actual − Forecast

MSE averages the squared difference between the actual value and the forecast value. The values are squared to eliminate the effect of negative errors canceling out positive errors (similar to the squaring of the deviations from the mean that was used to calculate the variance) and also to give greater weight to larger errors. The basic formula for MSE can be written as:

$$\text{MSE} = \frac{\sum_{t=1}^{n} (Y_t - F_t)^2}{n}$$

Tables 7.10–7.12 demonstrate the MSE calculation for the different forecasting methods employed in the DirectJet example. Table 7.10 provides the MSE calculation for both the three-day and five-day moving averages. Based on the results, the three-day moving average appears more accurate as its MSE value is less than the five-day MSE.

Table 7.11 illustrates the MSE for the weighted average forecasts used in the DirectJet example. Both were three-day moving averages; however, the first forecast used a 50/30/20 weighting, while the second forecast used an 80/15/5 weighting. Based on the MSE, the more evenly distributed forecast provides the most accurate forecast for this particular time series.

Table 7.12 exhibits MSE for exponential smoothing forecasts with smoothing constants of both 0.3 and 0.8. Based on all these calculations, the exponential smoothing forecast with a smoothing constant of 0.3 provided the most accurate forecast, since it had the lowest MSE.

Table 7.10 Mean Squared Error Calculation for Moving Average Forecasts

Day	*Bookings*	*3-Day M.A.*	*Forecast Error*	*Squared Forecast Error*	*5-Day M.A.*	*Forecast Error*	*Squared Forecast Error*
1	115						
2	100						
3	105						
4	120	107	13	169			
5	135	108	27	729			
6	130	120	10	100	115	15	225
7	145	128	17	289	118	27	729
8	150	137	13	169	127	23	529
9	130	142	−12	144	136	−6	36
10	160	142	18	324	138	22	484
			MSE	274		MSE	401

Table 7.11 Mean Squared Error Calculation for Weighted Moving Average Forecasts

Day	*Bookings*	*Forecast*	*Forecast Error*	*Squared Forecast Error*	*weighted moving average*	*Forecast Error*	*Squared Forecast Error*
1	115						
2	100						
3	105						
4	120	109	11	121	112	8	64
5	135	106	29	841	102	33	1,089
6	130	116	14	196	109	21	441
7	145	127	18	324	123	22	484
8	150	136	14	196	135	15	225
9	130	139	(9)	81	133	(3)	9
10	160	144	16	256	145	15	225
			MSE	301		MSE	369

Table 7.12 Mean Squared Error Calculation for Exponential Smoothing

Day	*Bookings*	*α = 0.3*	*Forecast Error*	*Squared Forecast Error*	*α = 0.8*	*Forecast Error*	*Squared Forecast Error*
1	115						
2	100	115	−15	225	115	−15	225
3	105	105	0	0	112	−7	49
4	120	105	15	225	111	9	81
5	135	115	20	400	112	23	529
6	130	129	1	1	117	13	169
7	145	130	15	225	120	25	625
8	150	140	10	100	125	25	625
9	130	147	−17	289	130	0	0
10	160	135	25	625	130	30	900
			MSE	230		MSE	369

Another measure of forecasting accuracy is MAD. MAD finds the average of the absolute value of the deviations. Since the deviations are not squared, larger deviations do not carry additional weight. The general formula for MAD is:

$$MAD = \frac{\sum_{t=1}^{n} |Y_t - F_t|}{n}$$

MAD can also be calculated for the various time-series forecasts in the DirectJet example. The absolute value of the forecast error is found in Microsoft Excel by using the “abs ()” function. Table 7.13 displays the MAD for the moving average forecasts, Table 7.14 for the weighted moving average forecasts, and Table 7.15 for the exponential smoothing forecasts.

Table 7.13 MAD Calculation for Moving Average Forecasts

Day	*Bookings*	*3-Day M.A.*	*Forecast Error*	*Squared Forecast Error*	*5-Day M.A.*	*Forecast Error*	*Absolute Forecast Error*
1	115						
2	100						
3	105						
4	120	107	13	13			
5	135	108	27	27			
6	130	120	10	10	115	15	15
7	145	128	17	17	118	27	27
8	150	137	13	13	127	23	23
9	130	142	(12)	12	136	(6)	6
10	160	142	18	18	138	22	22
			MAD	16		MAD	19

Table 7.14 MAD Calculation for Weighted Moving Average Forecasts

Day	*Bookings*	*Forecast*	*Forecast Error*	*Squared Forecast Error*	*weighted moving average*	*Forecast Error*	*Squared Forecast Error*
1	*115*						
2	100						
3	105						
4	120	109	11	11	112	8	8
5	135	106	29	29	102	33	33
6	130	116	14	14	109	21	21
7	145	127	18	18	123	22	22
8	150	136	14	14	135	15	15
9	130	139	(9)	9	133	(3)	3
10	160	144	16	16	145	15	15
			MAD	16		MAD	17

Table 7.15 MAD Calculation for Exponential Smoothing Forecasts

Day	*Bookings*	*α = 0.3*	*Forecast Error*	*Squared Forecast Error*	*α = 0.8*	*Forecast Error*	*Squared Forecast Error*
1	115						
2	100	115	(15)	15	115	(15)	15
3	105	105	–	–	112	(7)	7
4	120	105	15	15	111	9	9
5	135	115	20	20	112	23	23
6	130	129	1	1	117	13	13
7	145	130	15	15	120	25	25
8	150	140	10	10	125	25	25
9	130	147	(17)	17	130	–	–
10	160	135	25	25	130	30	30
			MAD	13		MAD	16

From the exponential smoothing calculations, the forecast with a smoothing constant of 0.3 appears once again to be the most accurate forecasting method for this particular time-series data. In this situation, both MSE and MAD picked the same forecasting method as the most accurate; however, this will not always hold true, as it will depend on the observed data. Both are commonly used in practice. The MSE assigns more weight to significant errors, while the MAD is easier to interpret. Based on the measures of accuracy, an appropriate forecasting method can be chosen. Using this method, forecasts can be generated for future periods. While the measures of accuracy highlight the most precise forecasting method based on historical information, the data serve as an ongoing repository of continually growing measurements that can be refined and updated. During this process, new forecasting methods may be substituted for the original selection. Therefore, the forecaster must exercise some judgment in choosing which measure of accuracy to employ, the extent of data to be incorporated, and the frequency of its utilization. Regardless of the choices, the ultimate goal of the forecaster is to furnish the most accurate forecasts available.

Regression Analysis

The other major quantitative forecasting method is regression analysis, which involves a statistical process for estimating the relationships between dependent and independent variables. Regression analysis finds applicability across diverse industries and fields. For example, regression analysis could be employed to identify the relationship between airline accidents (dependent variable) and pilot experience, aircraft age, weather condition, maintenance, and preflight plan (independent variables). The specific two-variable linear regression model is:

$$Y_i = \beta_0 + \beta_1 \times X_i + \varepsilon_i$$

where:

- Y_i is the dependent variable.
- β_0 and β_1 are the coefficients of the regression line (the intercept and slope).
- X_i is the independent variable.
- ε_i is the predictor error or so-called residual.

> Regression analysis constitutes a statistical process for estimating the relationships between a dependent variable and one or more independent variables. It is applied to assess the strength of the relationship between variables and for exhibiting the future relationship between them.

A dependent variable relies on other factors and variables, while an independent variable has a value which does not rely on any other factor. For example, in a market, airline managers might examine how changes in the ticket price cause changes in the dependent variable (Demand). The number of tickets sold depends on the passenger's income and average ticket price. In this case, the independent variables are the passenger's income and average ticket price.

In order to understand the applicability of regression analysis, consider the following dataset, Table 7.16, with consumption (*C*) and income (*Y*) values, as well as the regression graph displayed in Figure 7.11.

Table 7.16 Dataset for Perfect Relationship between Consumption and Income

Consumption (C)	*Income (Y)*
$100	–
$195	$100
$290	$200
$385	$300
$480	$400
$575	$500
$670	$600
$765	$700
$860	$800
$955	$900
$1,050	$1,000
$1,145	$1,100
$1,240	$1,200
?	$1,300

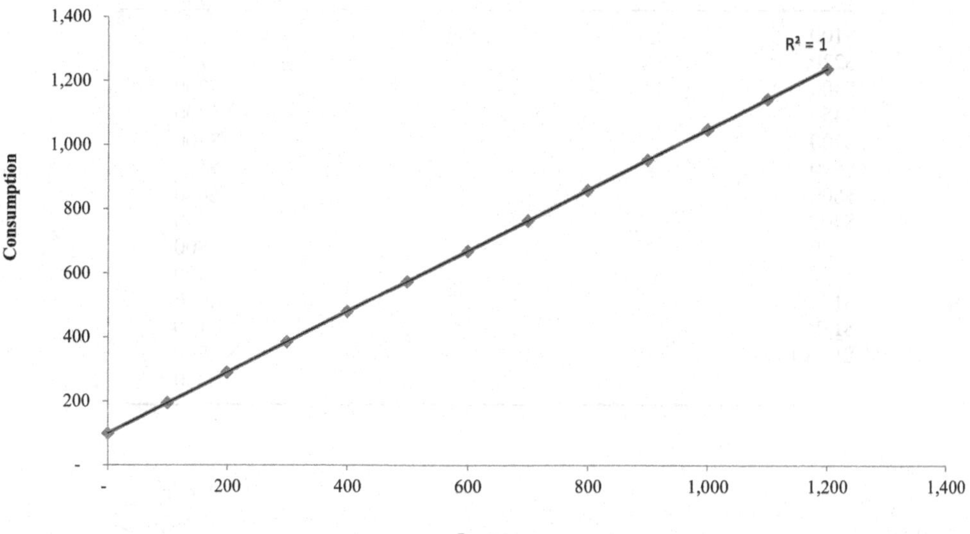

Figure 7.11 Graphical Perfect Relationship between Consumption and Income.

Using both the dataset and the graph, a simple linear relationship between consumption and income becomes evident. Since consumption is dependent upon income, consumption is the dependent variable and income the independent variable. Forecasting in this situation is fairly easy, as the pattern is obvious from the graph. In this case, for every 100 unit increase in income, consumption increases by 95 units. Based on the linear relationship, predicting the level of consumption for an income level of 1,300 becomes easy. For this example, and using the graph provided, consumption would be 1,335 for an income level of 1,300. Applying the formulas from the trend analysis to calculate the slope and the intercept (the best fit formulas are the same for both techniques because they both assume a linear relationship between the variables), it can be easily determined that the slope of the function is 0.95 (95/100) and the y-intercept value is 100. This leads to the formation of the function, $C = 100 + 0.95Y$, which can be used for future forecasts.

In this example, the relationship between consumption and income is very straightforward as they form a perfect linear relationship. However, real-world data are never perfectly correlated, since random events and other factors cause distortions in the relationship. Consider the same relationship where the values are slightly modified.

In this situation, a clear linear relationship between consumption and income is absent. However, when the data from Table 7.17 are plotted in Figure 7.12, the points lie in a somewhat random nature but with a general upward trend. Since the previous trend analysis method would not provide an accurate forecast, regression analysis needs to be employed. As displayed in Figure 7.13, regression analysis fits a trendline for the data points. In simple terms, regression analysis calculates a quantifiable linear relationship for the various data points. It should be noted that regression analysis can also estimate exponential, quadratic, or other relationships, depending on the general trend of the data points. However, such estimating techniques require a functional form transformation that is linear in the parameters.

Table 7.17 Dataset for Strong Relationship between Consumption and Income

Consumption (C)	*Income (Y)*
$100	–
$220	$100
$300	$200
$450	$300
$700	$400
$590	$500
$800	$600
$400	$700
$950	$800
$700	$900
$1,020	$1,000
$1,200	$1,100
$1,240	$1,200
?	$1,300

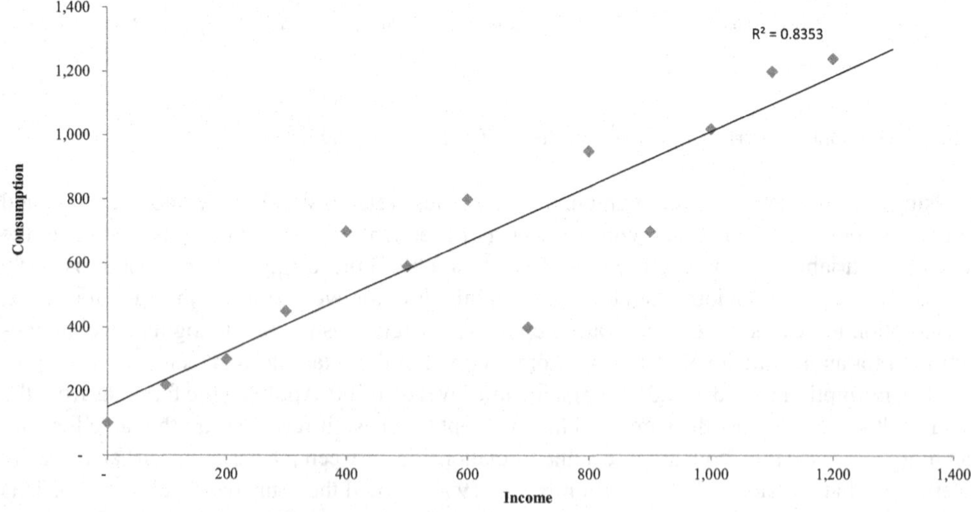

Figure 7.12 Graphical Strong Relationship between Consumption and Income.

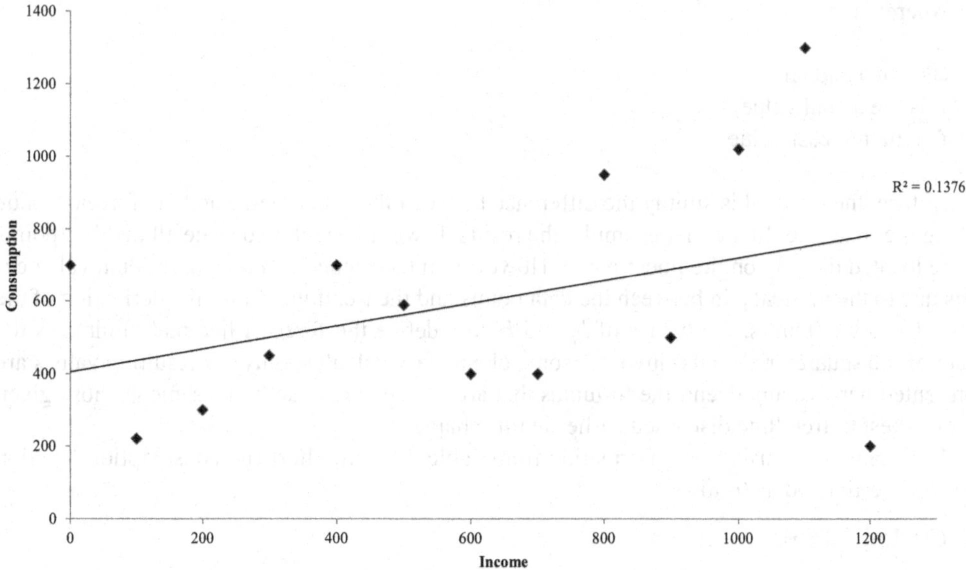

Figure 7.13 Weak Relationship between Consumption and Income, with Trendline.

In this example, the data points have a general linear trend, and therefore, linear regression analysis should be chosen. However, the linear trendline is not perfectly accurate as all the values do not lie directly on the trendline. Figure 7.13 represents an example of a scatter diagram, which essentially plots the points on a Cartesian plane with the dependent variable plotted on the y-axis and the independent variable plotted on the x-axis. Prior to performing regression analysis, a scatter plot should be created to grasp the nature of the data points. From this, the appropriate regression analysis (linear, exponential, and so on) can be chosen to provide the most accurate forecast of the dependent variable.

While all types of regression analysis perform the same function, different methods are available for creating the trendline. The most common method is Ordinary Least Squares (OLS), which minimizes the squared value of the residuals. OLS is a method that assists in estimating the unknown parameters in the linear regression model. OLS evaluates the parameters by minimizing the sum of squared residuals. Although it would appear more natural to minimize the sum of the errors, the same problem that was observed earlier with the variance is encountered; significant positive errors (deviations above the line) tend to cancel out very significant negative errors (deviations below the line). Therefore, the errors are squared to eliminate this problem. This, of course, implies that the significant errors carry more weight in the procedure. Thus, the formula for OLS regression can be stated as:

$$\text{OLS} = \text{Min}\sum_{i=1}^{n}\left(y_i - \hat{y}_i\right)^2$$

$$\text{OLS} = \text{Min}\sum_{i=1}^{n}\left(e_i\right)^2$$

where:

- e_i^2 is the residual
- y_i is the actual value
- $\hat{y}_i$ s the forecast value

Therefore, the residual is simply the difference between the actual value and the forecast value along the trendline. In the first example, the residuals would equal zero since all the data points were located directly on the linear curve. However, in the second example, a residual value exists due to the vertical gap between the data points and the trendline. Since the derivation of the OLS trendline (that is, the values of b_0 and b_1 that define the forecast line that minimizes the sum of the squared residuals) involves some elementary calculus, only the resulting values are presented here. In any event, the formulas that are derived are exactly the same as those given for the best fit trendline discussed earlier in this chapter.

For example, by using the information from Table 7.18, the short-run consumption function has been estimated as follows:

$$C = 150 + 0.8615Y$$

where:

- $b_0 = 150$ and $b_1 = 0.8615$
- C = Consumption
- Y = Income

Given the basic formula for a residual involves the difference between the actual and forecast values, we can calculate the difference for each observation as follows:

$$\text{Residual } e_i^2 = (C_i - \hat{C}_i)^2$$

These values are documented in Table 7.18.

As OLS regression minimizes the sum of the residuals, no other linear trendline would produce a sum of the residuals smaller than 266,385. The accuracy of the forecast is ultimately determined by the magnitude of the residuals. Forecasts with extremely large residuals imply

Table 7.18 Residual Values for Forecasts of Consumption

C	*Y*	$\hat{C}$	*e* $(C - \hat{C})$	*e^2*
\$100	\$0	\$150	(50)	2,500
\$220	\$100	\$236	(16)	256
\$300	\$200	\$322	(22)	484
\$450	\$300	\$408	42	1,764
\$700	\$400	\$495	205	42,025
\$590	\$500	\$581	9	81
\$800	\$600	\$667	133	17,689
\$400	\$700	\$753	(353)	124,609
\$950	\$800	\$839	111	12,321
\$700	\$900	\$925	(225)	50,625
\$1,020	\$1,000	\$1,012	8	64
\$1,200	\$1,100	\$1,098	102	10,404
\$1,240	\$1,200	\$1,184	56	3,136
			Σe2	266,385

that the spread between the forecast value and the actual value is wide, and therefore, indicating a less accurate forecast. However, depending on the nature of the data, any trendline may be extremely accurate or not accurate at all. Measures of accuracy are discussed in the subsequent section.

How to Estimate a Demand Function

1 Collect available data regarding the number of tickets sold at different ticket prices.
2 Plot these data points on a graph, positioning price on the vertical axis and quantity sold on the horizontal axis.
3 Draw a line of best fit through the data points.
4 Measure the slope, *m* (which must be negative), and the vertical intercept, *b*.
5 Formulate a demand function utilizing the parameters measured: price = $mQ + b$.

Goodness of Fit

> The coefficient of determination or R-squared serves as a statistical tool to measure how close the data are scattered around the regression line. This correlation, known as the "goodness of fit," is represented as a value between 0.0 and 1.0. A value of 1.0 indicates a perfect fit, whereas a value of 0.0 suggests that the model fails to accurately model the data at all.

The "goodness of fit" of the regression model evaluates the strength of the proposed relationship between the dependent and independent variables, and can be measured in several ways. The test that is most often used for the accuracy of any given regression is the coefficient of determination or R-squared. The coefficient of determination measures the percentage of variability in the dependent variable that the independent variable(s) explains. It usually aids in expressing the degree of confidence one has in the forecast. The coefficient of determination ranges from 0 to 1, with 1 being a perfectly accurate forecast (like the first example provided) and 0 being a completely inaccurate forecast. Using the following formula for the coefficient of determination, the R-square value is computed in Table 7.19.

$$R^2 = \frac{\sum_{i=1}^{n}\left(C_i - \overline{Y}C_\mu\right)^2}{\sum_{i=1}^{n}\left(C_i - C_\mu\right)^2}$$

where:

- R^2 = coefficient of determination
- $\hat{C}_i$ = forecast value
- C_i = actual value
- $\overline{Y}C_\mu$ = mean of the actual values

Table 7.19 Coefficient of Determination Calculation

C	Y	$\hat{C}$	$e\ (C - \hat{C})$	e^2	$(\hat{C} - C\mu)$	$(\hat{C} - C\mu)$^2	$C - C\mu$	$(C - C\mu)$^2
$100	$0	$150	(50)	2,500	(517)	267,289	−567	321,489
$220	$100	$236	(16)	256	(431)	185,761	−447	199,809
$300	$200	$322	(22)	484	(345)	119,025	−367	134,689
$450	$300	$408	42	1,764	(258)	66,564	−217	47,089
$700	$400	$495	205	42,025	(172)	29,584	33	1,089
$590	$500	$581	9	81	(86)	7,396	−77	5,929
$800	$600	$667	133	17,689	–	–	133	17,689
$400	$700	$753	(353)	124,609	86	7,396	−267	71,289
$950	$800	$839	111	12,321	172	29,584	283	80,089
$700	$900	$925	(225)	50,625	258	66,564	33	1,089
$1,020	$1,000	$1,012	8	64	345	119,025	353	124,609
$1,200	$1,100	$1,098	102	10,404	431	185,761	533	284,089
$1,240	$1,200	$1,184	56	3,136	517	267,289	573	328,329
$667	C_μ		$\Sigma e2$	266,385	Σ $(C - C\mu)$^2	1,351,238	Σ $(C - C\mu)$^2	1,617,277

Table 7.20 Dataset for Weak Relation between Consumption and Income

Consumption (C)	*Income (Y)*
$700	$0
$220	$100
$300	$200
$450	$300
$700	$400
$590	$500
$400	$600
$400	$700
$950	$800
$500	$900
$1,020	$1,000
$1,300	$1,100
$200	$1,200
?	$1,300

From the calculation in Table 7.19, the coefficient of determination for the linear regression model is 0.8352. This shows that 83.52% of the variability of the dependent variable, *C*, is explained by the independent variable, *Y*. Or, in simpler terms, the model is roughly 84% accurate. While the process of calculating the coefficient of determination is lengthy, almost all statistical programs display the R-square value in the regression output.

To better understand the accuracy of regression analysis, consider the same example, but with modified values of consumption. Table 7.20 provides the new dataset, and Figure 7.7 displays the new scatter plot with the trendline.

In this new scenario, the data points have less of a linear relationship, increasing the summation of the squares of the residual values. While OLS regression provides the best possible trendline for the data points, the increase in the size of the residuals over the previous example indicates that this trendline is not as accurate as the previous one. This is confirmed through a coefficient of determination value of 0.1376, which is significantly lesser than the previous value of 0.8352. The forecast for this third dataset yields an R-square value of only 0.1376, which means this forecast is not very powerful and may have limited use. While the coefficient of determination establishes the accuracy of the overall regression, it is also possible to decide the statistical relevance of separate independent variables in the regression. This topic is discussed in the subsequent few sections.

Regression can be a very useful tool for finding patterns in datasets.

For ease of exposition, the previous examples contained only one independent variable; however, most regressions will include multiple independent variables as the dependent variable can rarely be explained by one factor. For example, demand for airline services includes a host of factors, such as ticket price, income, competitor's price, seasonality, and customer service. Performing OLS regression by hand for multiple independent variables is highly challenging, computer programs such as Microsoft Excel and SPSS enable regressions to be performed quickly and easily.

In order to gain a more comprehensive understanding of applied regression analysis and to identify the important factors to analyze when interpreting regression results, a concrete example is presented. Let's consider the demand for air travel between Orlando and Los Angeles, using four independent variables to determine demand: average ticket price, income, seasonality, and the presence of a random one-time event, such as September 11, 2001. Prior to any forecasting, a hypothesis should be created to help identify the expected relationship between the dependent and independent variables. This hypothesis can then be employed to ascertain the accuracy of the regression analysis outcomes. In this example, ticket price should have a negative coefficient, income should have a positive coefficient, seasonality could potentially have either a positive or negative (depending on the season), and economic shocks such as 9/11 or COVID-19 should yield a negative value. The dataset used in the regression analysis is exhibited in Table 7.21.

In order to forecast demand, historical data on the number of passengers flying between Orlando and Los Angeles needs to be found. Origin and Destination (O&D)[15] data employs a 10% sample of total bookings to quantify the total number of passengers flying the city-pair, regardless of whether they are flying on a non-stop flight or on connecting flights. Since determining the specific income to be measured is challenging, GDP serves as a reasonable proxy for income. Finally, the average ticket price for all travelers is determined through O&D data for each quarter. Quarterly data were used in order to provide a sufficient number of observations. In order for regression analysis to be accurate, an appropriate number of observations is required. When there is significant variance in dependent and independent variables, fewer observations are required for efficient and unbiased parameter estimates. Conversely, when variance is lower, an extensive dataset is needed. However, a minimum of 30 observations is generally considered sufficient.

Dummy or Binary Variables

A binary or dummy variable is an artificial variable created in regression analysis to represent an attribute with two or more distinct categories of qualitative events. It takes only the value 0 or 1 to indicate the absence or presence of some categorical effect that may be expected to shift the outcome.

A dummy variable or binary number is a variable that can only take the values 1 or 0. For example, to capture the effects of a random event such as September 11, 2001, or the impacts of qualitative events such as seasonality, we can apply dummy variables in a regression analysis. Dummy variables, also called categorical variables, require no additional economic data

Table 7.21 Dataset for Forecasting Demand for Orlando to Los Angeles Flight

Quarter	*Demand (# of Passengers)*	*Income (GDP in Billions)*	*Ticket Price (Average)*	*Q1*	*Q2*	*Q3*	*COVID-19*
2012 Q1	66,985	$16,068.82	$244.00	1	0	0	0
2012 Q2	69,160	$16,207.13	$229.00	0	1	0	0
2012 Q3	65,777	$16,319.54	$214.00	0	0	1	0
2012 Q4	69,297	$16,420.39	$213.00	0	0	0	0
2013 Q1	71,283	$16,629.05	$217.00	1	0	0	0
2013 Q2	75,827	$16,699.55	$212.00	0	1	0	0
2013 Q3	73,609	$16,911.07	$220.00	0	0	1	0
2013 Q4	70,021	$17,133.11	$231.00	0	0	0	0
2014 Q1	69,454	$17,144.28	$250.00	1	0	0	0
2014 Q2	76,769	$17,462.70	$245.00	0	1	0	0
2014 Q3	71,942	$17,743.23	$231.00	0	0	1	0
2014 Q4	72,541	$17,852.54	$253.00	0	0	0	0
2015 Q1	71,895	$17,991.35	$252.00	1	0	0	0
2015 Q2	81,701	$18,193.71	$237.00	0	1	0	0
2015 Q3	82,631	$18,306.96	$216.00	0	0	1	0
2015 Q4	96,247	$18,332.08	$200.00	0	0	0	0
2016 Q1	1,01,913	$18,425.31	$184.00	1	0	0	0
2016 Q2	1,12,796	$18,611.62	$179.00	0	1	0	0
2016 Q3	1,08,054	$18,775.46	$173.00	0	0	1	0
2016 Q4	1,06,104	$18,968.04	$185.00	0	0	0	0
2017 Q1	1,15,786	$19,148.19	$168.00	1	0	0	0
2017 Q2	1,30,747	$19,304.51	$175.00	0	1	0	0
2017 Q3	1,20,516	$19,561.90	$150.00	0	0	1	0
2017 Q4	1,24,410	$19,894.75	$173.00	0	0	0	0
2018 Q1	1,37,285	$20,155.49	$159.00	1	0	0	0
2018 Q2	1,36,146	$20,470.20	$169.00	0	1	0	0
2018 Q3	1,30,326	$20,687.28	$159.00	0	0	1	0
2018 Q4	1,16,055	$20,819.27	$192.00	0	0	0	0
2019 Q1	1,15,915	$21,013.09	$183.00	1	0	0	0
2019 Q2	1,23,496	$21,272.45	$197.00	0	1	0	0
2019 Q3	1,14,148	$21,531.84	$183.00	0	0	1	0
2019 Q4	1,09,739	$21,706.53	$244.00	0	0	0	0
2020 Q1	95,773	$21,538.03	$181.00	1	0	0	1
2020 Q2	11,211	$19,636.73	$170.00	0	1	0	1
2020 Q3	46,372	$21,362.43	$124.00	0	0	1	1
2020 Q4	70,006	$21,704.71	$108.00	0	0	0	1
2021 Q1	74,450	$22,313.85	$98.00	1	0	0	1
2021 Q2	1,07,842	$23,046.93	$140.00	0	1	0	1
2021 Q3	1,12,466	$23,550.42	$145.00	0	0	1	1
2021 Q4	1,16,074	$24,349.12	$172.00	0	0	0	1

Source: DIIO O&D, https://fred.stlouisfed.org/series/GDP

(Barreto and Howland 2006). Suppose we are interested in the gender pay gap between female pilots and male pilots. The variable DUM_{MALE} might indicate whether an individual in our dataset is male, in which case $DUM_{MALE} = 1$, or female, in which case $DUM_{MALE} = 0$.

The solution is to use a dummy variable called "Gender" whereby we assign a 1 if this variable is a female pilot and a 0 if the pilot is male.

Numerous economists incorporate dummy variables in regression models to capture the impact of qualitative variables on the dependent variable (exogenous). These variables solely determine in the presence or absence of a factor. In the case of seasonality, three unique independent variables can be generated. The Q1 dummy variable assumes a value of one during the first quarter of every year and the value of zero for every other quarter. Similar dummy variables were generated for the second and third quarters. A fourth seasonal dummy variable is not needed since the fourth quarter is acting as the reference for all the other quarters. For example, the coefficient in the regression equation for the first quarter would measure the additional (or smaller) quantity demanded over the fourth quarter.[16] With this setup, the first three quarters are being compared to the fourth quarter. Of course, any of the four quarters could have been excluded, resulting in the regression coefficients of the remaining three quarters being compared to the quarter excluded, yielding the same outcomes.

The other dummy variable used takes into consideration the one-time shift in demand caused by the events of September 11, 2001. Since these events impacted the demand for air travel, all quarters following and including the third quarter of 2001 received a value of 1 to identify the impact of 9/11. In this case, the excluded variables are the quarters not affected by the events; that is, all prior quarters.

Once the data has been collected and placed in a statistical computer program, the program will return the values for the regression. Most programs require the user to identify the dependent variables and the independent variables. In this example, the number of passengers is the dependent variable, and the remaining variables are all independent. The regression is then run, and the output is displayed. While the output varies from program to program, they all contain the same basic characteristics. For our example, all regression output is from SPSS.

The first major chart displayed in all regression output is a summary of the model. The model summary from SPSS for the regression is contained in Table 7.22. One of the most important statistics contained in any model summary is the R-square value. As mentioned previously, the R-square value, or coefficient of determination, determines the percentage of variation in the dependent variable that is explained by the independent variables. In this model, approximately 88% of the demand for travel between Orlando and Los Angeles is explained by the independent variables.

The adjusted R-square value is akin to the R-square value; however, it factors in the degrees of freedom of the model. By way of definition, the degrees of freedom are the number of observations beyond the minimum needed to calculate a regression statistic. The degrees of freedom are determined by taking the total number of observations minus the number of independent variables. Higher degrees of freedom are created through more observations or fewer independent variables. In this example, the degree of freedom is 28.[17] As forecasts tend to be more accurate with an increased number of observations or with a smaller number of independent variables, the adjusted R-square value considers this. Therefore, the ordinary R-square value is adjusted downward to account for the degrees of freedom in the particular model. Models with low degrees of freedom exhibit a greater difference between the ordinary R-squared and the adjusted R-squared values. Due to a relatively high degree of freedom (28) in this model,

Table 7.22 SPSS Model Summary of Demand Forecast MCO-LAX

Model	*R*	*R-Square*	*Adjusted R-Square*	*Std. Error of the Estimate*	*Durbin-Watson*
1	0.940	0.883	0.858	3,702.89391	1.885

Predictors: (Constant), 9/11 Dummy Variable, Q2 Seasonality, Q3 Seasonality, Q1 Seasonality, Average Ticket Price, GDP.

Dependent Variable: Number of Passengers.

the difference between the adjusted R-square and the ordinary R-square is not significant. Additionally, it is worth noting that temperatures on different days in a month are autocorrelated.

Assumptions and Performing Regression Analysis

Regression analysis is a very useful tool for finding patterns in datasets. Nevertheless, before conducting linear regression, it requires to be ensured that the following assumptions are met. If one or more of the following assumptions are violated, then the results of our linear regression may be unreliable or even misleading:

- No heteroscedasticity
- No autocorrelation
- No multicollinearity

Heteroscedasticity

Heteroscedasticity refers to a situation where the variance of errors or residuals in a regression model is not constant across the range of independent variables. In other words, the variability of the errors or residuals changes systematically as the values of the independent variable(s) change. Heteroscedasticity is a problem because ordinary least squares regression assumes that all residuals are drawn from a population that has a constant variance. In forecasting, an error is how far a point deviates from the regression line. Ideally, the data should be homoscedastic or constant variance.

Heteroscedasticity presents a distinctive cone shape in residual plots. If there is an unequal scatter of residuals, the population used in the regression contains unequal variance, and therefore, the analysis results may be invalid.

One common example of heteroscedasticity is presented by the relationship between education and income. The plot reveals that the mean of the distribution of earnings increases with the level of education. As the level of education increases, individuals tend to choose different jobs with different workloads and different salaries. Therefore, there is a greater variance in the salary of individuals with post-graduate education relative to individuals with high school degree. Another example is the collection of data on house prices and size, followed by a regression analysis. However, we notice that the difference between the predicted and actual prices increases as the size of the house increases.

Autocorrelation

Autocorrelation refers to the degree of correlation between the values of the same variables across different observations in the data. Another major statistic to analyze in the model summary output is the "Durbin-Watson statistic."[18] The Durbin-Watson statistic measures autocorrelation, which can severely distort the accuracy and significance of the regression model. Autocorrelation occurs when the residuals are not independent and involve an underlying trend, which violates one of the major underlying assumptions used in performing regression analysis. In the derivation of the parameters of OLS, it is assumed that the error terms or residuals are independent of each other. While the Durbin-Watson statistic detects autocorrelation, the residuals can also be plotted against time to detect if any patterns exist in the residuals. Potential patterns that could exist include linear lines, fanning, or cyclical movements where the residual alternates from positive to negative. Figure 7.14 presents the residual plot for the Orlando to Los Angeles regression.

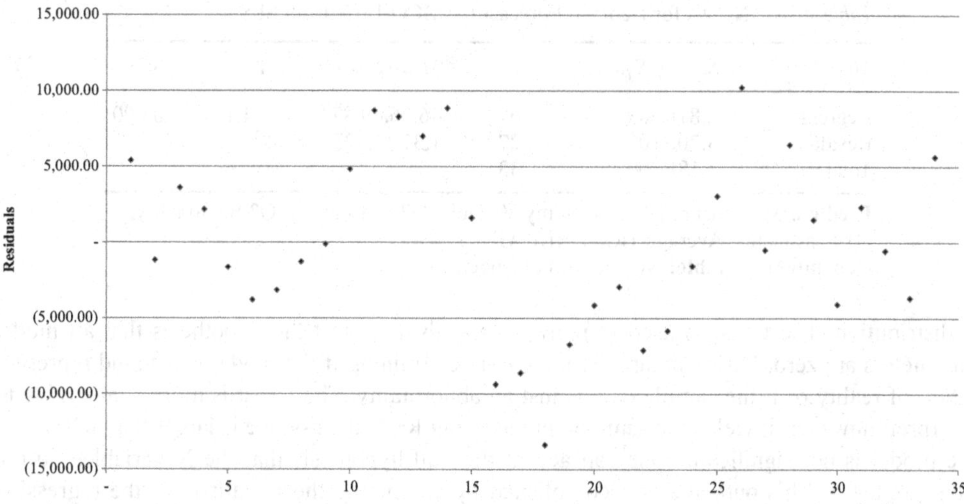

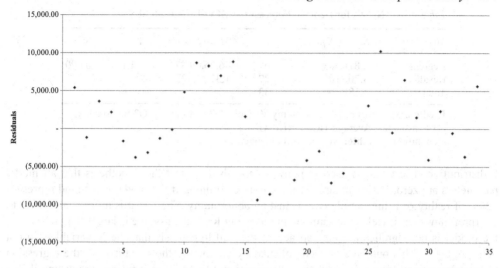

Figure 7.14 Residuals of the Regression Plotted against Time from Microsoft Excel.

Autocorrelation is an attribute of data highlighting the degree of similarity between the values of the same variables over successive time intervals. For example, autocorrelation between the number of intensive care unit beds during COVID-19 pandemic, or the temperatures on different days in a month are autocorrelated.

Since Figure 7.14 does not display any trend in the residuals, it can be safe to say that autocorrelation does not exist in the regression. This is confirmed by a Durbin-Watson statistic of 1.885. Durbin-Watson statistics can range from 0 to 4. An outcome closer to 0 suggests a stronger positive autocorrelation, and an outcome closer to 4 suggests a stronger negative autocorrelation. However, only values less than 1.5 or greater than 2.5 suggest that autocorrelation may exist in the regression. An outcome closely around 2 means a very low level of autocorrelation. Therefore, the Durbin-Watson statistic of 1.885 falls within the acceptable range.

F-Statistic

The F-test is used in regression analysis to test the hypothesis that all model parameters are zero. The F-test is more difficult to interpret; however, it always yields the same result as using R^2. If the p-value is larger than 0.05, then the model is not significant; one can accept the null hypothesis that the X variables do not help predict Y.

The second major table contained in all regression outputs is an ANOVA table.[19] The ANOVA table for the Orlando to Los Angeles demand forecast is depicted in Table 7.23. The ANOVA table presents the overall significance of the regression equation. As might be expected, a direct mathematical relationship exists between R-squared and the ANOVA F value for the overall significance of the regression.[20] The difference between them is the fact that the F-statistic allows us to pick a level of significance for the overall equation and compare this to a predetermined

Table 7.23 ANOVA for Demand Forecast for MCO-LAX from SPSS

Model	*Sum of Squares*	*Df*	*Mean Square*	*F*	*Sig.*
Regression	2.81E+09	6	46,76,49,874	34.11	0.000[a]
Residual	3.70E+08	27	1,37,11,423		
Total	3.18E+09	33			

Predictors: (Constant), 9/11 Dummy Variable, Q2 Seasonality, Q3 Seasonality, Q1 Seasonality, Average Ticket Price, GDP
Dependent Variable: Number of Passengers.

F distribution. The F-test is used in regression analysis to test the hypothesis that all model parameters are zero. Put more simply, it aids in determining if the model is a sound representation of reality or if the sample data is just an abnormality. The F-test is more challenging to interpret; however, it yields the same output as using R^2. If the p-value is larger than 0.05, then the model is not significant. One can accept the null hypothesis that the X variables do not help predict Y. This outcome is accomplished by comparing the F-statistic of the regression to a predetermined level of significance. Conventional levels of significance are ordinarily set at 0.90, 0.95, and 0.99, and these mean, respectively, that we can be 90%, 95%, and 99% sure that our regression results are due to a true relationship between the independent and dependent variables and not due to random chance. Most statistics textbooks contain complete tables of F distributions against which the regression F value can be compared; however, it is also true that most computer programs for regression contain (as part of the output) the level of significance of the independent variables for the given number of observations and degrees of freedom of the specific regression, such that, for example, the level of significance might be reported at 0.001 or 0.02. This means, respectively, that we can be 99.9% and 98% sure that our results are not due to chance.

The third major table contained in all regression output is the table of coefficients. This is displayed for the demand forecast from Orlando to Los Angeles in Table 7.24. The coefficients table allows the researcher to construct a linear equation used for forecasting. It also determines if the individual variables are statistically significant. The first column of the coefficients table lists all the independent variables used in the analysis plus the constant. The constant term is usually interpreted as the value of the dependent variable when all the other independent variables are set to zero. Columns two and four both display values for the coefficients. The standardized values (column four) are generally used to compare the respective size of the impacts of the independent variables on the dependent variable. This is derived by calculating them in standardized units; that is, the standardized coefficient is the unstandardized value of the coefficient multiplied by the ratio of the standard deviation of the independent variable to the standard deviation of the dependent variable. Therefore, a standardized coefficient of 1.14, as the one for GDP, means that a 1 standard deviation change in the independent variable will lead to a 1.14 standard deviation change in the dependent variable. Similar interpretations apply to the other standardized coefficients. However, since the unstandardized values are the coefficients directly applicable to forecasting actual values, the unstandardized beta values are the coefficients that are used in the forecast equation. Nevertheless, as a final step prior to forming a demand equation, each independent variable needs to be tested to verify if it is statistically significant.

The *t-statistic* is similar to the F-statistic discussed earlier except that it applies to a single individual variable rather than to the whole (or some subset) of the independent variables. The t-statistic is a measure of how accurate a statistical estimate is. More specifically, a t-value is calculated for each independent variable, and this value is compared to

Table 7.24 SPSS Coefficients Significance for Demand Forecast, MCO-LAX

Model	*Unstandardized Coefficients*		*Standardized Coefficients*			*Collinearity Statistics*	
	B	Std. Error	Beta	t	Sig.	Tolerance	VIF
Constant	23409	6123.16		1.45	0.16		
GDP	9	0.87	1.15	9.88	0.00	0.32	3.13
Average Ticket Price	−212	52.47	−0.46	−4.04	0.00	0.34	2.95
Q1 Seasonality	779	2,032.16	0.04	0.38	0.71	0.50	1.99
Q2 Seasonality	5,219	1,857.77	0.24	2.81	0.01	0.60	1.67
Q3 Seasonality	3,841	1,869.17	0.17	2.06	0.05	0.64	1.56
9/11 Dummy Variable	(19,972)	2,216.17	−1.02	−9.01	0.00	0.34	2.95

Dependent Variable: Number of Passengers.

a standardized t distribution. At this point, a probability statement can be made about the significance (at some predetermined level of confidence) of the independent variable, so that, for example, if the predetermined level of significance is 0.90 or 0.95 and the t-value for the independent variable selected exceeds the t-value for the standardized table (at the degrees of freedom for the specific regression), we can say that we are 90% or 95% sure that the relationship between the individual variable and the dependent variable is not due to chance. Therefore, a significant t-value indicates that the variable in question influences the dependent variable while controlling other explanatory variables. Quantitatively, the t-statistic contained in column five is simply the unstandardized coefficient divided by the standard error of the coefficient. For example, the t-statistic for the independent variable GDP is determined by dividing the beta value of 8.586 by the standard error of 0.869. This produces a t-statistic of 9.880.

$$t_i = \frac{b_i}{S_{b_i}} = \frac{8.586}{0.869} = 9.88$$

Generally speaking, if an independent variable passes the predetermined t-test, then it should be included in the model. However, if the variable fails the t-test, then it should be considered for exclusion from the model unless there are strong theoretical reasons to include the variable or there is a clear problem of multicollinearity (discussed in the next section). As a rule of thumb, if the value of a parameter is more than twice the size of its corresponding standard deviation (error), we can conclude, under a two-tailed test, that the estimated coefficient is significantly different from 0 at a 95% confidence level. Furthermore, if the estimated coefficient surpasses three times the estimated standard error, we can conclude the estimated value is significantly different from 0 at a 99% level of significance.

Multicollinearity

Multicollinearity occurs when two or more independent variables are highly correlated with each other. Examples: including the same information twice (ASM and RPM, or years of education and income).

Another critical assumption of multiple linear regression is the absence of significant multicollinearity in the data. Such a situation can arise when the independent variables are too highly correlated with each other, such as the case of ASM and RPM. Multicollinearity occurs when two or more independent variables exhibit high correlation. If two independent variables are perfectly correlated, then the estimates of the coefficients cannot be computed. Intuitively, the problem arises since regression cannot separate the effects of the perfectly correlated independent variables. Quantitatively, it arises because there is a term in the denominator for the variance of the individual independent variables that contains the correlation factor between the independent variables. As this term approaches unity (perfect correlation), the variances of both of the independent variables approach infinity. As established earlier, the t-statistic is calculated by dividing the numerical value of the coefficient by its standard deviation. Since the standard deviation is simply the square root of the variance, the larger the variance, the larger the standard deviation and the smaller the t-value. Thus, a high degree of multicollinearity between independent variables can cause a low level of significance for either one or both of the independent variables.

Two different methods can be employed to identify multicollinearity. In SPSS, collinearity diagnostics are available within the coefficients table, appearing in the last two columns in Table 7.24.

The Variance Inflation Factors (VIF) statistic detects multicollinearity and, while the threshold of an acceptable VIF values varies (similar to confidence levels discussed earlier), a conventionally accepted level is that a VIF statistic above five indicates the presence of high multicollinearity.[21] A VIF equal to one signifies the noncorrelation of variables and the absence of multicollinearity in the regression model. The tolerance statistic is simply the inverse of the VIF score (1/VIF); therefore, smaller tolerance values indicate higher degrees of multicollinearity.

The other method for detecting a high degree of correlation between independent variables is to simply create a correlation matrix. Table 7.25 displays a correlation matrix for all the hypothesized independent variables in the example regression.

Generally

- VIF equal to 1 = variables are not correlated
- VIF between 1 and 5 = variables are moderately correlated
- VIF greater than 5 = variables are highly correlated

A VIF equal to one means variables are not correlated, and multicollinearity does not exist in the regression model.

From Table 7.25, the correlations between all the independent variables are presented. The key statistic is the Pearson correlation statistic, and any correlations greater than 0.90 are of concern. While the correlation between GDP and the 9/11 dummy variable is sizeable at 0.783, both variables are still highly significant from their independent t-tests (see Table 7.23). Therefore, it is clearly not enough to eliminate either variable from the regression analysis. Based on both

Table 7.25 Correlation Matrix for Independent Variables from SPSS

		GDP	*Average Ticket Price*	*Q1 Seasonality*	*Q2 Seasonality*	*Q3 Seasonality*	*9/11 Dummy Variable*
GDP	Pearson correlation	1	−0.659[a]	−0.023	0.042	−0.039	0.783[a]
	Sig. (2-tailed)	.	0	0.895	0.811	0.828	0
	N	34	34	34	34	34	34
Average ticket price	Pearson correlation	−0.659[a]	1	0.370[b]	0.062	−0.272	−0.668[a]
	Sig. (2-tailed)	0	.	0.031	0.729	0.119	0
	N	34	34	34	34	34	34
Q1 Seasonality	Pearson correlation	−0.023	0.370[b]	1	−0.360[b]	−0.333	−0.04
	Sig. (2-tailed)	0.895	0.031	.	0.036	0.054	0.823
	N	34	34	34	34	34	34
Q2 Seasonality	Pearson correlation	0.042	0.062	−0.360[b]	1	−0.333	−0.04
	Sig. (2-tailed)	0.811	0.729	0.036	.	0.054	0.823
	N	34	34	34	34	34	34
Q3 Seasonality	Pearson correlation	−0.039	−0.272	−0.333	−0.333	1	0.041
	Sig. (2-tailed)	0.828	0.119	0.054	0.054	.	0.816
	N	34	34	34	34	34	34
Dummy variable	Pearson correlation	0.783[a]	−0.668[a]	−0.04	−0.04	0.041	1
	Sig. (2-tailed)	0	0	0.823	0.823	0.816	.
	N	34	34	34	34	34	34

[a] Correlation is significant at the 0.01 level (2-tailed).
[b] Correlation is significant at the 0.05 level (2-tailed).

the collinearity diagnostics and the correlation matrix, multicollinearity does not appear to be a problem in this particular demand forecast.

If multicollinearity is found to be a problem in a particular regression, then conventional methods for dealing with the problem are acquiring more data or eliminating one or more of the highly collinear independent variables. Since it is rarely possible to acquire more data for a given regression (time constraints and so on), attention shifts to elimination of variables. If all of the variables are still significant at conventional levels of significance, then it is generally advisable to retain the original model, as it was our best initial theoretical formulation of the relationship. If, on the other hand, one or more of the collinear variables are not significant at conventional levels, then consideration should be given to dropping the non-significant variable and rerunning the regression. In this case, the researcher is implicitly assuming that the two highly collinear variables are providing the same information with respect to the dependent variable.

Once all the regression issues have been checked, the last step is to quantify the demand function so that forecasts can be formulated. While computer statistical packages provide a wide array of regression results, the default regression performed is the linear OLS regression discussed earlier in this chapter. Therefore, the predicted demand function is a typical linear equation. Using the unstandardized coefficients for statistically significant variables, the forecasted demand function for air travel between Orlando and Los Angeles is:

$$D_{MCO\text{-}LAX} = 23{,}409 + 8.59(GDP) - 211(P) + 778.91\ DUM_{Q1} + 5{,}218\ DUM_{Q2} + 3{,}840\ DUM_{Q3} - 19{,}971 DUM_{9\text{-}11}$$

Based on this equation, the demand for Orlando to Los Angeles air transportation can be estimated. Moreover, the forecast demand function also displays the impact that a change in one of the independent variables has on the demand. For example, a one-dollar increase/decrease in the average ticket price will cause demand to decrease/increase by over 200 seats. As we might expect, this kind of information is extremely useful to aviation managers of all types. The seasonality dummy variables also have a large impact on demand. For example, if the flight is in the second quarter, then the demand for the flight will increase by over 5,200 passengers as compared to the fourth quarter. Again, this information is critically important to successful fleet mix planning. The other variables in this equation can be analyzed in a similar fashion.

Therefore, and by way of summary, air transportation industry demand forecasting is critical to strategic planning and the ultimate success of the airline. Regression analysis is a powerful tool that can be extremely useful in forecasting and other strategic decisions. While this chapter has merely provided an overview of various methods for forecasting, and a somewhat more detailed presentation of regression analysis, in-depth discussions of all the topics can be found in the reading list provided at the end of this chapter.

Sources of Data

In order to perform successful forecasting in the aviation industry, various data are required. This section outlines some of the data sources commonly employed in aviation applications. It also indicates whether the data is freely accessible or can only be obtained through subscription fees. Where appropriate, the web addresses are provided.[22] While the majority of data sources described are from the United States, data sources for international aviation are also provided.

US Department of Transportation (DOT)/DIIO Database

The US Department of Transportation (DOT) stands as one of the best sources for aviation-specific data for US aviation activity. Within the DOT, multiple databases offer a wealth of information for the airline industry.

One database that is used throughout this book is Form 41, which provides information concerning US airlines. Information ranges from general airline financial data, specific airline cost data, general traffic data, to airport activity statistics. All US-registered airlines are required to provide the data to the DOT. Form 41 is useful when evaluating airlines.

Another useful database is O&D, which stands for Origin and Destination. Using a 10% sample of actual tickets, various statistics are provided for individual US domestic city pairs. The O&D database shows on what airline the passengers traveled, the average ticket price, and a large amount of other data. As might be expected, O&D data is very useful for demand estimation. The T100 database is akin to O&D, but for international city pairs. However, the data is presented in a slightly differently format and is not as extensive.

In addition to these three major databases, the DOT also provides additional databases, such as schedules, fleet, and commuter.[23] While DOT statistics are technically public information and can be obtained for free, unless the user has advanced Excel and Access skills, the data is very difficult to access. Therefore, in order to use most of the DOT data, airline database packages such as Back Aviation are required. Unfortunately, these products require a paid subscription.

Federal Aviation Administration (FAA)

The Federal Aviation Administration (FAA) is another good source for US data, particularly, information concerning aviation accidents and safety. The FAA also offers data concerning aviation forecasts and other issues, such as terminal space usage, passenger facility charges, airline service indexes, and aircraft registration and certifications. It provides data across a range of categories:

- Aircraft: Aircraft certification, aviation safety, general aviation and recreational aircraft, repair stations, etc.
- Air Traffic: Numbers, environmental reviews, flight information, National Airspace System, international aviation, technology and weather
- Airports: Safety and certification, pilot regulations
- Accident and incident data, aviation forecasts, commercial space data, passengers and cargo
- Airspace integration, legislation and policies, regulations and guidance
- Drones: Advanced operations, public safety, government and regulations for certificated remote pilots including commercial operators

All data can be obtained without charge through the FAA website, www.faa.gov.

Another resource, Future & Active Pilot Advisors (FAPA.aero), aims to assist every professional pilot in landing a successful cockpit career. The team assists in guiding with career decisions, offers Pilot Job fairs, provides interview preparation, and many more. The website has information about Major Airline Pilot Hiring by Year (2000–Present) and monthly data for the years 2007–2022 of all US carriers such as American, Delta, Southwest, JetBlue, FedEx, UPS, Alaska, Spirit, Continental, AirTran, Atlas Air, Northwest, America West, ATA, Frontier, and Allegiant Air.

Federal Reserve Economic Data (FRED)

FRED is a database maintained by the Research division of the Federal Reserve Bank of St. Louis. The database has more than 816,000 economic time series from various sources, and covers banking, business transactions, consumer price indexes, employment and population, exchange rates, GDP, interest rates, monetary aggregates, and producer price indexes. Categories of data include money, banking, and finance (interest rates, exchange rates, monetary data, financial indicators, banking, business lending, foreign exchange intervention); population, employment, and labor markets (current population survey, employment statistics, ADP employment, education, income distribution, job openings and labor turnover, labor market condition indexes, population, productivity, and costs). All data can be obtained without charge through the FRED website, https://fred.stlouisfed.org/.

International Air Transport Association (IATA)

The International Air Transport Association (IATA) provides information concerning issues affecting airlines globally. The economic analysis section offers free access to industry outlook, cost comparisons, traffic analysis, and fuel prices. It provides key insights on the latest best practices, trends, and aviation issues. Data spans a variety of areas including airlines–safety auditing, airports–infrastructure, security, ground handling safety, cargo handling, air traffic management, and freight forwarders. Government regulations can be obtained through IATA's website, www.iata.org. Subscription data services on air passenger and cargo flows worldwide, ticketing data, such as the MarketIS database, and flight operational data such as the FDX database. These resources are available at www.iata.org/en/service/statistics.

International Civil Aviation Organization (ICAO)

The International Civil Aviation Organization (ICAO), an arm of the United Nations, serves as the source for pertinent legal issues, particularly international air service agreements. ICAO is responsible for development and review of international technical standards for aircraft operations and design, crash investigations, personnel licensing, telecommunications, meteorology, air navigation equipment, ground facilities for air transport, and search and rescue missions. Perhaps the most valuable resource is ICAO data. This subscription database provides international data, including origin and destination passenger statistics, airline financial data, and airport activity statistics. ICAO data is a useful backup source to fill in any data not covered by DOT O&D and T100. Information concerning ICAO and ICAO data can be obtained through the website, www.icao.int.

Official Airline Guide (OAG)

The Official Airline Guide (OAG) is a compilation of over 1,000 airline schedules, creating the definitive source on airline schedules and flight datasets. Air Traffic Data provide necessary information to understand sales locations by country and region.

OAG provides data on Global Airline Schedules, Flight status, historical flight, flight seats, emissions data, minimum connection times, Passenger booking data, global flight connections data, and airfare data. Users can access date-specific schedule information through www.oag.com without charge. However, for airlines, a complete historical OAG database is more useful. Through this database, researchers can determine ASMs for a large number of city pairs

Airports Council International (ACI)

Airports Council International (ACI) is a community of international airports that collectively lobbies on various issues concerning airports. Through ACI's website, www.aci.aero, readers can obtain data and rankings, such as the number of passengers handled by various airports, the cargo movements through the airports, the number of international passengers, and more. Also information on Total Aircraft Movements (Passenger and Combi Aircraft, All-Cargo Aircraft, Total Air Transport Movements, General Aviation, and other aircraft movements), Total Commercial Passengers (International & Domestic Passengers (enplaned and deplaned), Total terminal passengers, direct transit passengers), Total Cargo (Freight & Mail) International Freight,

Domestic Freight, Total Freight, and Mail (Loaded +Unloaded) ACI help collate information concerning airports worldwide.

Cirium (Formerly Air Transport Intelligence)

Flightglobal currently publishes articles and data provided by Cirium under a mutual content partnership agreement. The website provides a wealth of industry-related information, as well as database of aviation-specific journal articles from such publications as *Airline Business* and *Flight International.* These journals can be quite helpful in any qualitative analysis. Flight global also provides searchable databases on information concerning airlines, airports, aircraft, suppliers, and schedules. While Flightglobal does not provide quantitative data, it is a valuable resource when initially researching specific areas. The platform is only available to subscribers, and more information can be gathered at www.flightglobal.com.

The Airline Monitor

Another subscription database is The Airline Monitor, which reviews trends in the airline and commercial jet aircraft industries. Airline Monitor provides a variety of reports in a variety of formats and discusses issues such as block hour operating costs, airline financial results, and commercial aircraft production. The platform also provides historical data, which is especially helpful in constructing time-series data with numerous observations. Historical aircraft data on production, retirement forecast, and time frame includes aircraft manufacturers and macro drivers utilized in aircraft production forecast.

Engine forecast may include items such as:

- Total installed engines delivered by manufacturer, with market share
- Number of aircraft delivered powered by engine manufacturer with market share
- Installed engine in service at the end of each year by engine manufacturer, with market shares
- Estimated engine prices and dollar value of deliveries from 1990 onward for each engine model
- Engine manufacturer, engine deliveries, other instated equipment.

More information concerning the products offered by The Airline Monitor can be found at www.airlinemonitor.com.

The Airline Analyst

This subscription database hosted by the *Air Finance Journal* is a valuable and unique collection of financial accounts data for more than 300 airlines, from around the world. Data from many years of annual and quarterly reports on individual airline profit and loss, cash flow and balance sheet accounts are provided in a consistent, comparable form. More information can be found at www.airfinancejournal.com/Home/TheAirlineanAlyst.

UK Civil Aviation Authority (CAA)

The UK Civil Aviation Authority (CAA) provides a function similar to the FAA, and researchers can find information on passengers such as Commercial industry-Pilot Licenses, Aircraft

Airworthiness, dangerous goods, leasing, operations, Airspace-Traffic management, navigational services, communication navigation/surveillance and aviation security overview in terms of compliance and regulation, general aviation policies, international raising aviation standards worldwide, space, safety initiatives, and resources covering the entire UK aviation industry. Moreover, a wealth of statistical data is available in the economic regulation and statistics portion of the CAA's website, www.caa.co.uk.

Transport Canada (TC)

Transport Canada (TC) is the governing body for all transportation-related activities in Canada. Statistics, information on air travel, drone safety, aviation security, registering and leasing aircraft, operating airports and aerodromes, licensing for pilots and personnel, licensing for aircraft maintenance engineers (AME), medical fitness for aviation, aircraft airworthiness, general operating and flight rules, commercial air services, aviation accidents and investigations, transportation of dangerous goods on aircraft, air navigation services, data, and regulations concerning the commercial aviation industry can all be obtained through Transport Canada and StatsCan. More information can be found at www.tc.gc.ca.

Eurocontrol

The European Organization for the Safety of Air Navigation (Eurocontrol) is the primary provider of air traffic control services throughout Europe. While specific data can be difficult to obtain from Eurocontrol directly, the website does provide a variety of resources concerning the aviation industry in Europe. More specifically, Eurocontrol can provide detailed information pertaining to airport traffic, delays, and capacity management initiatives, data snapshot on rise of LCC in Europe, on-time performance in the United States and Europe, the daily utilization of aircraft by type, COVID-19's impact on the passenger fleet, market share of cargo flights, and manufacturer share of flights in Europe (www.eurocontrol.int).

The Aircraft Owners and Pilots Association (AOPA)

The Aircraft Owners and Pilots Association (AOPA) is a membership community works to improve aviation safety, maintain and improve community airports, and promote and advocate for the general aviation industry. Recently, AOPA has been involved in the fight over fuel surcharges and restrictions concerning the use of general aviation aircraft in congested airspace. The AOPA website, www.aopa.org, is split into two sections: public and members. While the general public can receive basic information, members can obtain a more thorough investigation of issues facing the general aviation community. Members also receive information pertaining to weather and flight planning.

Bureau of Economic Analysis (BEA)

The US Bureau of Economic Analysis (BEA) is an essential source when forecasting demand for air transportation services, etc. BEA provides official macroeconomic and industry statistics, most notably reports about the GDP of the United States and its various units: states, cities, town, townships, and metropolitan areas. These data are used extensively by academicians, policymakers, and businesses to understand industry interactions, productivity, and the changing structure of the US economy. Data can be freely obtained at www.bea.gov.

Bureau of Labor Statistics (BLS)

The US Department of Labor's Bureau of Labor Statistics (BLS) is the definitive source concerning the labor force in the United States. BLS provides data on labor market activity, working conditions such factors as unemployment, consumer price indices, wages, and labor demographics. Charts and applications such as CPI inflation calculator, injury and illness calculator, pay measure comparison, demographic data sources, COVID-19 economic trends, and employment and wages data viewer. The level of data can be quite detailed, with the various statistics broken down into industries and regions. For any analysis involving labor, www.bls.gov should be consulted.

Organization for Economic Cooperation and Development (OECD)

The Organization for Economic Cooperation and Development (OECD) is comprised of 30 member countries which have active relationships with over 70 countries and multiple nongovernmental organizations (NGOs). OECD is primarily concerned with social and macroeconomic issues; therefore, the selection of data encompasses these categories. Statistics are sorted into various industries and enable comparisons between countries. Unfortunately, OECD does not publish any reports concerning the aviation industry; therefore, much of the useful data from the OECD will be general macroeconomic data such as population, education, GDP, tax, income equality, CO_2 emissions, and debt, usually displayed on a monthly or quarterly basis. Topics like agriculture, development, economy, education, energy, environment, finance, government, health, innovation, and technology are available on the website (www.oecd.org).

Summary

Forecasting is a technique that uses past information as inputs to make estimates that are predictive in determining the future values. It has many applications in the aviation industry, one of which being forecasting of demand for air travel. The future demand for global air transport industry will undoubtedly be subject to unanticipated external shocks. Since demand for air travel is not monolithic and varies for every destination, region, and time, sophisticated forecasting tools need to be applied to help predict the size and nature of demand. Since demand is not deterministic and varies with time, forecasting tools need to be developed to help researchers estimate future demand. In order to run an airline efficiently, it is very important to generate and maintain an accurate demand forecast, based on a combination of historic data and statistical modeling. Naturally, the most accurate estimate possible is desired, which means continually updating the forecasting process and techniques. Forecasting has many applications in the aviation industry, the chief among these is the forecasting of demand. Aircraft manufacturers can use both qualitative and quantitative tools in forecasting. The Boeing Commercial Market Outlook (CMO) is a long-term forecast of commercial air traffic and airplane demand, including global and regional analysis. Similarly, Airbus' Global Market Forecast (GMF) provides an in-depth overview of the global commercial aviation services market. Perhaps most useful for air transport businesses are "conditional" or "what if" forecasts, such as estimating the demand response to a change in a competitor's fare or the establishment of a new route. These will be less vulnerable to the uncertainty or "black swan" events that often confound the accuracy of "future" forecasts.

Two techniques are used in business forecasting: qualitative and quantitative. Qualitative forecasts do not use econometrics tools and do not provide measures of forecast accuracy, as they are based on opinions, surveys, and beliefs. Quantitative forecasts, on the other hand, use statistical relationships to help forecast future events, while they are more mathematical in nature, they may or may not be any more accurate than qualitative forecasts. It is important to realize that while "conditional" forecasts can be used with confidence, "future" forecasts need to be used with care. During periods of stability, the latter may well be accurate, but pervasive uncertainty about the timing and scale of future shocks mean that major turning points are likely to be missed, which is when forecasts really matter. However, forecasts are still useful for decision making, allowing a consistent narrative about alternative futures to be developed, enabling businesses to take decisions that build in flexibility and robustness to the radical uncertainty in markets.

Discussion Questions

1. Explain the differences between qualitative forecasting and quantitative forecasting, and provide an advantage and disadvantage of each.
2. Imagine that you are an airline attempting to forecast the demand for seats over the next two to three years. What do you think could be used as leading indicators?
3. What is multicollinearity in a regression model?
4. What is autocorrelation in a regression model?
5. What is the difference between seasonal and cyclical variations? Give an example of how airlines respond to seasonal variations.
6. Describe the four different components of a time-series statistics.
7. If a regression analysis had an R^2 of 0.89, what does this mean?
8. In a regression analysis, how would you incorporate seasonal variations and other important events (shock) like September 11?
9. Formulate a multiple regression model showing how the quantity demanded of an airline depends on the ticket price, the income of passengers, and the ticket price of other airlines operating in the same market. What are the anticipated signs of the coefficients?

   $$PAX = \pi r^2$$

10. In a simple regression model, is it possible that all the actual Y values would lie above or below the true regression line? Explain.
11. List ten questions you would ask a group of passengers in order to estimate their demand function for a specific airline and a specific route.
12. Discuss the different methods of obtaining a trend projection from past observations to estimate the future demand.
13. Write the demand equation, in general form, for an airline and identify the following terms:

    a. Dependent variable
    b. Independent variables
    c. Y-intercept
    d. Slope

Logically, one can often expect a multicollinearity effect between the independent variables in a regression model. Which variables in this regression are expected to be highly correlated among each other?

14 EZjET, a small regional airline, wishes to predict sales for its business travelers between two cities for 2017. It has recorded data for its past 14 years' demand and has obtained information on the number of businesses within its market area. This information is listed in the table:

Year	*Number of Seats Sold*	*Number of Businesses*
2003	74,970	4,664
2004	76,500	4,759
2005	78,795	5,480
2006	83,000	6,100
2007	80,000	6,940
2008	92,000	8,300
2009	94,760	9,850
2010	101,000	10,800
2011	103,000	12,100
2012	106,000	13,300
2013	104,880	13,034
2014	115,256	13,890
2015	118,713	14,307
2016	122,274	14,736
2017	119,829	14,442

a Plot the annual sales data against the number of businesses in the market area and draw in the "line of best fit" that seems to be visually appropriate.
b Measure the intercept and slope of the above line of best fit, and state the approximate function relationship between the two variables.
c Suppose the number of businesses is projected to increase to 14,500 in 2017. Use the above functional relationship to forecast the demand for the number of seats sold in business class in 2017.
d Comment on the probable accuracy of your forecast.

15 Quantico Australian Airlines faces the following annual demand function for its Los Angeles–Sydney route: $Q(p) = 38{,}658 - 8.67P$, where Q is the number of tickets sold and P is the average ticket price. The regression analysis also produced the following statistics: coefficient of determination, 0.73; and standard error of the estimate, 4,200. Quantico's marginal cost per seat is $150 for all foreseeable levels of output.

a What is the profit-maximizing price for this route (assume single pricing)?
b What is the sales revenue-maximizing price?
c Calculate the price elasticity of demand at the profit-maximizing price and comment on the value obtained.
d At the profit-maximizing price, what is the 95% confidence interval for sales?
e What other qualifications and assumptions underlie your prediction?

16 DirectJet is a small regional airline based in northern Europe. It operates a small number of jet aircraft and could initially produce only 400,000 ASMs per day. However, the output rate picked up as soon as management learned to schedule their flights more efficiently, save turnaround time on the ground, decrease fuel consumption, and so on. Suppose that the average cost per seat mile during the first year was as shown below and that the variable factors will continue to become more productive as total output measured in ASM continues to increase.

ASM	*CASM*
400,000	15.82
350,000	16.85
500,000	12.15
450,000	10.25
400,000	10.95
500,000	10.01
490,000	9.75
530,000	9.00
580,000	9.65
380,000	12.89
480,000	9.25
380,000	15.00
340,000	16.00

- a Obtain the estimated regression function. Does a linear regression function appear to give a good fit?
- b Test the overall significance of the regression parameters.
- c Write the estimated equation for this relationship.
- d Based on the above statistics, forecast the average cost per seat mile when total output reaches 1 and 1.2 million ASM.
- e Interpret slope and intercept in your estimated regression function. Do they provide any relevant information? Explain.
- f Calculate MSE and MAD for the independent variable.
- g Perform an F-test to determine whether or not there is a lack of fit of a linear regression function.

17 Why would one want to use the standard deviation instead of the variance to describe a distribution?

18 Explain in an intuitive way why the F-statistic and the R-squared statistics provide essentially the same information.

19 What is the difference between the T-statistic and the F-statistic?

20 Use the following regression analysis to answer the questions below. The dependent variable is the number of tickets sold per week, and the independent variables are the price of the flight (X1) measured in dollars; the price of the competitor's ticket (X2) measured in dollars; GDP (X3) measured in thousands of dollars; the general season of the year (X4) measured as a 0 for summer and a 1 for winter; the price of automotive gasoline (X5) measured in cents per gallon (consider driving as a substitute for flying in this regression); and the local population in thousands (X6). The "t" statistic is given in parenthesis below the independent variable (use a "t" value of 2 for a 95% confidence level and consider this significant).

$Y = 300 - 15\ X1 + 2\ X2 + 25\ X3 - 150\ X4 + 30\ X5 + 5X6$ R-squared = 0.85

"t" value= (3) (2) (4) (2.5) (1.0) (2)

- a What is the most statistically significant independent variable in the regression?
- b According to this equation, how does winter affect the number of tickets sold?
- c Does the price of gasoline in the equation have the correct sign?
- d Suppose that competitors reduce their price by $20 and there is a population growth of 2000 at the same time. What will happen to the number of tickets sold?

21 A small regional airline wishes to predict sales for its business class between two cities for the year 2019. The airline has recorded the following data for its past ten years: ticket sold and the number of businesses within its market area.

Year	*Tickets Sold*	*Number of Businesses*
2009	70,000	3,500
2010	76,500	4,620
2011	71,500	5,480
2012	83,000	6,100
2013	80,000	6,940
2014	92,000	8,300
2015	90,500	9,850
2016	101,000	10,800
2017	103,000	12,100
2018	106,000	13,300

a Plot the annual sales data (PAX) against the number of businesses (BUS) in the market area and draw in the "line of best fit" that seems to be visually appropriate.
b Measure the intercept and slope of the above line of best fit, and state the approximate function relationship between the two variables.
c Suppose the number of businesses is projected as increasing to 16,500 in 2019. Use the above function relationship to forecast the demand.
d Comment on the probable accuracy of your forecast.

22 Explain how a dummy variable can improve the accuracy of a forecast model.

Notes

1 Quote by Donald Rumsfeld: "There are known knowns, things we know that we ..." (goodreads.com).
2 Radical Uncertainty – John Kay.
3 *Australian Aviation.* July 12, 2016.
4 Boeing. Pilot and Technician Outlook 2022–2041.
5 FAA workers in survey say top managers have pro-Boeing bias. *The Seattle Times*, April 7, 2020.
6 The population standard deviation is represented by the Greek letter sigma "σ", and the sample standard deviation is represented by S.
7 A normal distribution is a distribution where the area to each side of the mean under the distribution curve is equal to 0.5.
8 The growth rate in each period is the ratio of the absolute change in RPM to an earlier value.
9 Impact of global financial crisis on the aviation industry. *UK Essays*. March 23, 2015.
10 CNN, Global air traffic may return to pre-Covid levels in June, with China leading the way, January 16, 2023.
11 Zika virus, Delta Air Lines unit revenue hit airline shares. *The Wall Street Journal*, August 4, 2016.
12 Ecuador Puts TAME In Liquidation. *Simply Flying*. May 19, 2020.
13 Chile's LATAM Airlines files for U.S. Chapter 11 bankruptcy protection. *Reuters*. 26 May 2020
14 A software program for statistical analysis, originally called *Statistical Package for the Social Sciences*.
15 O&D is a data tool operated by OAG Aviation; www.oagaviation.com.
16 In fact, if all the classes for a binary variable are included in a regression equation that includes a constant, the regression cannot be estimated since a linear dependence exists between the independent variables. This is the so-called dummy variable trap. See Hanushek and Jackson (1977).
17 Degrees of Freedom = Number of Observations – Number of Independent Variables = 34 – 6 = 28.
18 It should be noted that the Durbin-Watson statistic is not displayed in the regression output obtained through Microsoft Excel.
19 ANOVA stands for *analysis of variance*.
20 $F = R^2/k - 1/(1 - R^2)/N - k$, where k stands for the number of independent variables and N stands for the number of observations. See Hanushek and Jackson (1977), pages 127 and 128.

21 Variance Inflation Factors (VIF) is a statistic used to measuring the possible collinearity of the explanatory variables.
22 Website addresses were current as of May 2017.
23 It should be noted that additional aviation data is provided through the Department of Transportation (http://www.dot.gov) and the Bureau of Transportation Statistics (http://www.bts.gov) websites.

References

Anderson, E. and Mittal, V. (2000). Strengthening the Satisfaction-Profit Chain. *Journal of Service Research*, 2(3), 107–120.

Anderson, D., Sweeney, D., and Williams, T. (2019). *Statistics for Business & Economics* (14th Edition). Boston, MA: Cengage.

Barreto, H. and Howland, F. (2006). *Introductory Econometrics: Using Monte Carlo Simulation with Microsoft Excel*. New York: Cambridge University Press.

Basu, S. and Schroeder, R. (1977). Incorporating Judgments in Sales Forecasts: Application of the Delphi Method at American Hoist & Derrick. *Interfaces*, 7(3), 18–27.

Durbin, J. and Watson, G. (1951). Testing for Serial Correlation in Least Squares Regression, II. *Biometrika*, 8(1–2), 159–179.

Gosling, Geoffrey D. (2014). Use of Air Passenger Survey Data in Forecasting Air Travel Demand. *Journal of the Transportation Research Board*, 2449, 79–87.

Hanushek, E. and Jackson, J. (1977). *Statistical Methods for Social Scientists*. New York: Academic Press.

8 Dynamic Pricing Policy and Revenue Management

This chapter will introduce the reader to the concepts of airline pricing policy and revenue management. Revenue management is essentially the combination of methods, analysis, and techniques which an airline applies to the types of services it offers in order to maximize aircraft revenue. Airlines employ revenue management not only to sell as many high-priced seats as efficiently as possible, but also to keep airplanes full. The chapter begins with a short section on airlines' past pricing practices, followed by the current pricing structure. Further, it demonstrates how segmenting the market or "price discrimination" based on the elasticity of demand for different types of passengers can increase revenues. The second part of the chapter discusses revenue management and the strategies an airline can use to segment its market directly and indirectly, including advanced purchase restrictions and other ticket requirements. Historically, last-minute purchasers have faced higher fares. For instance, many airlines impose steep fees if a passenger tries to purchase on the same day at the departure airport, rather than in advance. A fare booked 45 days in advance might be $175 round trip; a 21-day fare may be $290; a 14-day fare may be $425; a 7-day fare may be $550; and a 3-day fare might be $672.

This chapter will delve into the following topics in detail:

- Dynamic Pricing Policy
- Cost-Based Pricing
- Markup and Price Elasticity of Demand
- Bundling
- Unbundling and Airline Ancillary Revenue
- Market Skimming and Penetration Pricing
- Peak-Load Pricing
- Price Discrimination in the Airline Industry
- Consumer Surplus
- Necessary Conditions for Price Discrimination
- Degrees of Price Discrimination
- Uniform Pricing versus Price Discrimination
- Uniform versus Multiple Pricing
- Airline Revenue Management
- Revenue Management "Fences"
- Revenue Management Control Types
- Spoilage and Spillage
- Leg-Based Expected Marginal Seat Revenue Model

DOI: 10.4324/9781003388135-8

- Overbooking
  - Forecasting Overbooking Levels
- Other Issues Associated with Revenue Management
- Summary
- Discussion Questions
- Appendix: Derivation of Overbooking Probability Equation

Dynamic Pricing Policy

Pricing policy and practices in the airline industry refer to how an airline sets its ticket prices based on demand, cost, and market competition. In the airline industry, pricing policies are often dynamic; prices change daily and vary from airline to airline. Moreover, it is not always an exact science. Low-cost and startup carriers offer services at lower prices to increase market share and stay in business in response to retaliation by incumbents. Today, airline ticket prices are highly volatile. For any one flight, more than ten different fares are available, from the lowest discounted ticket to first class. A passenger who buys his or her ticket at the right time can pay considerably less compared to other passengers on the same flight. According to Yapta's study on airfare volatility, the Dallas (DFW) to Washington (DCA) route had the highest degree of price fluctuation in 2016 (Yapta, 2016). Results shown in Table 8.1 were placed on an index, with 100% representing relatively stable prices. The top five city pairs fell between 200% and 250%, while the remaining entries were all above 150%.

In the airline industry, pricing policies are often dynamic; prices change daily and vary from airline to airline. If seats are sold faster than expected, then prices are raised. If the seats are not sold as expected, then prices are lowered. The lower price then encourages an increase in the quantity demanded.

Table 8.1 Top Domestic City Pairs for Volatile Airfare Prices

Rank	*Route*	*Passengers*	*Year-on-Year Change*	*Number of Flights*	*Average Base Fare*	*Distance (km)*
1	Jeju – Seoul Gimpo	1,34,60,306	9.4%	65,967	$94.39	449
2	Melbourne – Sydney	90,90,941	2.2%	54,209	$148.04	705
3	Sapporo – Tokyo Haneda	87,26,502	4.4%	38,717	$135.63	835
4	Fukuoka – Tokyo Haneda	78,64,000	5.0%	40,106	$201.53	889
5	Mumbai – Delhi	71,29,943	4.4%	47,017	$81.53	1,150
6	Beijing Capital – Shanghai	68,33,684	2.0%	30,201	$183.19	1,081
7	Hanoi – Ho Chi Minh City	67,69,823	1.1%	39,791	$109.10	1,171
8	Hong Kong – Taiwan	67,19,030	−0.1%	28,881	$172.15	802
9	Jakarta – Juanda Surabaya	52,71,304	−6.3%	37,214	$103.56	700
10	Tokyo Haneda – Okinawa	52,69,481	4.3%	22,271	$319.22	1,573
11	Tokyo Haneda – Osaka	51,06,584	3.4%	21,900	$146.63	407
12	Jeddah – Riyadh	50,91,629	13.9%	36,353	$152.92	857
13	Jakarta – Denpasar	49,52,852	9.4%	32,496	$128.74	991
14	Chengdu – Beijing	49,51,620	−0.7%	24,285	$206.87	1,559
15	Guangzhou – Beijing	48,64,177	5.8%	20,823	$173.77	1,898

The Civil Aeronautics Act of 1938 established a policy of economic regulation of the domestic US airline industry (Brown, 1987). This act was created by the Civil Aeronautics Board (CAB), which had authority over the level and structure of airfares within the United States. Prices were set by the CAB according to industry average costs, which disbarred low-cost airlines from offering lower prices, as it was deemed unhealthy for the industry.[1] Even though airfares were regulated, the policy of setting airfares above average costs is a dynamic pricing policy; in this case, cost-based pricing. The only exceptions to this rule were in California and Texas where airlines were able to set their own prices on intra-state routes where the CAB did not have authority. This led to the rise of low-cost carriers (LCCs)—AirCal in California and Southwest Airlines in Texas.[2] Within the regulated environment, airlines were provided a protected route structure and guaranteed revenues that exceeded costs. This meant that they rarely failed in the domestic marketplace, and in the event that an airline incurred losses, federal subsidies were available to bail them out (Spiller, 1981). Hence, airline ticket pricing was simple and fixed. A small range of available fares for a route existed, and every so often there might be a sale fare.

The Airline Deregulation Act of 1978 abolished the CAB's authority over airlines, thereby permitting the market to decide airline fares and routes. After the deregulation, airlines were allowed fly any domestic route without legal restrictions and could offer any fare on any flight.[3] Deregulation also allowed LLCs like Southwest to expand outside of its Texas market and encouraged the creation of new discount carriers like People Express. Shortly after deregulation, about 50% of total traffic traveled on a discount fare, yet by 1990, nearly 90% of traffic was on discounts. The increased competition and liberalized pricing structure led industry analysts to claim that today's air fares are 20%–30% below what they would have been had regulation remained in place.

Cost-Based Pricing

Cost-based pricing is one of the simpler approaches to pricing. It refers to the process in which prices are determined on the basis of costs plus an additional profit expressed as a percentage of the cost. This approach was utilized during the period of airline regulation when the CAB set prices based on the average costs of the route with an added percentage. This pricing method does not consider the elasticity of demand or the extent of competition. For example, in the case of an urgent business trip, ticket prices should be evaluated by the consumer (and set by the airline) based on the benefits of the trip, which would factor in demand in addition to cost.

Markup Pricing

Markup is the amount that a business firm charges over and above the total cost of producing its product or service. Firms employ this strategy to ensure a certain profit, and it is generally expressed as a percentage. In industries characterized by a multitude of products with varying values, including wholesale and retail, firms adopt this pricing model as a guideline for determining sale prices. This approach allows the company to cover all expenses associated with the production and sale of the products and still make a profit. For example, if the total cost of producing a product is $200, but it's sold for $250, and then the extra $50 is the markup and can be expressed as 25%. The following equation illustrates the relationship between price, cost, and markup:

$$P = \text{AC} + \text{Markup}$$

$$P = \text{AC} + \text{MU} \times \text{AC}$$

$$P = \text{AC} \times (1 + \text{MU})$$

where:

- P = price
- AC = may include direct, indirect, and fixed costs of a product or service
- MU = markup percentage.

Example

A product costs $1,300 per unit. Therefore, if you want a markup of 10% (a profit equal to 10% of total cost), the selling price must be set at $1,430.

$$P = \$1{,}300 \times (1 + 0.10)$$

$$P = \$1{,}430$$

Higher elasticity leads to a price closer to the competitive price. Conversely, lower elasticity leads to a price closer to the monopolistic price. The price sensitivity of airline passengers makes it difficult for airlines to charge more for ancillary services and build brand loyalty, two goals in place at many carriers.

If demand is elastic, a rise in price reduces total revenue, and if demand is inelastic, a rise in price increases total revenue.

Markup pricing offers both advantages and disadvantages. On the positive side, its strength stems from its simplicity and relatively straightforward application. Moreover, it can benefit the buyer if there is enough information about the supplier's costs. By working backward through the equation, the buyer can determine what the markup is on a particular product as a percentage of the costs. However, the simplicity of markup pricing also leads to its disadvantages; if the elasticity of demand is ignored, then a firm may increase the price in an elastic market. This decreases total revenue, and vice versa in an inelastic market. Markup pricing also does not reflect the cost of replacing a product, which often is lower than the initial cost of acquiring/manufacturing it (Table 8.2).

Markup and Price Elasticity of Demand

When demand is elastic, applying a high markup to the cost of a product may result in a decrease in income, as consumers may switch to cheaper substitutes. In this case, a lower markup may be necessary to maintain sales volume and revenue. On the other hand, when demand is inelastic, applying a high markup may not significantly affect demand, allowing for a higher revenue.

Table 8.2 Advantages and Disadvantages of Markup Pricing

Advantages	*Disadvantages*
Easy to calculate	Ignores elasticity of demand
Relatively quick and simple to apply	Based on historical costs
Useful if buyer has information about supplier's costs	May ignore opportunity costs
	A lack of incentive for efficiency

Depending on the industry and product, the preferred markup amount varies significantly and depends on several factors. The key is identifying and utilizing the specific relationship that exists between price elasticity and markups. If demand is relatively inelastic, then a company can set a high price. At the other extreme, if demand is perfectly elastic, then a firm has no choice but to accept the market price. This is the reason why markup pricing is not optimal if market structure and demand sensitivity are not considered. If the elasticity of demand is taken into account, then markups can vary significantly from industry to industry. With elastic demand, businesses may not recognize that a higher markup may not lead to higher revenue or greater profits. However, in some industries, such as health care, the markup may be a large percentage of the total cost of the product or service because the demand for these services is inelastic.

Optimum Markup

Every business faces two questions: how much to produce and what price can be charged to maximize profit. The profit-maximizing rule is to increase quantity as long as marginal revenue (MR) is greater than marginal cost (MC). Conversely, profit will decline if MC exceeds MR; hence, the profit-maximizing level of output is found by equating its MC with its MR.

Therefore, since the objective of markup policy is to maximize profit by charging the optimum price (not too high, and not too low), a product's price elasticity is a key element in setting its markup and price. The following formula describes the relationship between optimal markup, price, and maximum profit. It should be noted that the formula only works when *E* is greater than 1 since it is already assumed that the firm is pricing beyond the inelastic portion of the demand curve.

The profit-maximizing condition is:

$$MC = MR$$

where:

$$MR = P \times \left(1 + \frac{1}{E_P}\right)$$

Rearranging the above, we obtain:

$$MC = P \times \left(1 + \frac{1}{E_P}\right)$$

$$P = MC \times \frac{1}{\left(1 + \frac{1}{E_P}\right)}$$

$$P = MC \times \left\{\frac{E_P}{1 + E_P}\right\}$$

$$\text{Optimal markup} = \left\{\frac{E_P}{1 + E_P}\right\}$$

Example

Jet Services provide jet fuel to general aviation aircraft. Suppose that the marginal cost of jet fuel is \$2.50 per gallon, and the price elasticity of demand is $E_p = -1.5$. In this case, the multiplier is:

Table 8.3 Effect of Elasticity on Optimum Markup and Price

Case	*Elasticity*	*Optimal Markup*	*Marginal Cost (MC)*	*Price (P)*
1	−10	1.11	100	$111
2	−9	1.13	100	$113
3	−8	1.14	100	$114
4	−7	1.17	100	$117
5	−6	1.20	100	$120
6	−5	1.25	100	$125
7	−4	1.33	100	$133
8	−3	1.50	100	$150
9	−2	2.00	100	$200
10	−1.5	3.00	100	$300
11	−1.4	3.50	100	$350
12	−1.3	4.33	100	$433
13	−1.2	6.00	100	$600
14	−1.1	11.00	100	$1,100
15	−1.01	101.00	100	$10,100

$$\text{Optimal markup} = \frac{-1.5}{1-1.5} = 3$$

and this item would sell for:

$$P = \$2.50 \times 3 = \$7.50$$

Thus, the profit-maximizing markup is $5.00 or 300% on cost.

According to the above formula, as long as the price elasticity demand is very low, it is advantageous to increase the price; that is, the seller receives more money for fewer goods sold. Conversely, if the price elasticity of demand is very high (elastic), it is beneficial to reduce the price; the seller gets more money from selling even more goods. Hence, assuming that $E = -5$, it can be seen from the given formula that the price is equal to 1.25 times the MC.

Table 8.3 presents a variety of elasticities along with the resulting optimum markup and effect on selling prices of a particular good where the MC is $100. From this table, it is observed that the higher the elasticity of demand, the smaller the optimum markup and, consequently, the lower the selling price. Products with relatively inelastic demand will be optimally priced with higher markups.

Bundling

A product bundling strategy is used extensively in the airline industry where multiple products or services are packaged into one bundled solution. For example, items such as priority boarding, luggage, and drinks can be sold together. An effective product bundling strategy can significantly increase revenue on individual sales.

On many occasions the pricing arrangement includes purchasing groups of complimentary products. Bundling represents the combination of services offered within the cost of the ticket. The products are bundled or sold as a block, which has become common practice for airlines, fast-food restaurants, banks, cable companies, and theatrical or sporting events. Bundling often results in greater revenue for the producers across industries. Virgin Atlantic bundles door-to-door limousine service, in-flight massage, and drive-through check-in with its transatlantic flights (Ovans, 1997). Bundling can be good for consumers and may provide the following advantages:

- Reduced transaction costs
- Simplified billing
- Lower prices
- Integration of products and services

Airlines routinely bundle vacation packages, combining air travel and life insurance, with car rentals and lodging. For example, United Airlines bundled hotel reservation, car rental, and airline services with the coordination of Allegis Corporation but eventually had to abandon the practice. In fact, the US Department of Justice sued Microsoft in 1998 alleging that it attempted to monopolize the market by bundling its Internet Explorer web browser software with its Windows operating system (Washington Post, 2000). Some common examples of bundling in other industries include computer hardware and software (Microsoft Office) and utility companies.

Unbundling and Airline Ancillary Revenue

Numerous airlines have been busy unbundling services that traditionally came with a seat, such as bag check, carry-on luggage, pillows, fuel surcharges, overhead bins, food, seat reservations, and even the ability to pay by credit card. The unbundled revenue from these fees is considered airline ancillary revenue; that is, any revenues generated beyond the direct sale of airline tickets. The list of commission-based selling is growing with the inclusion of any duty-free items and products purchased on board. Airline ancillary revenue can be separated into three primary categories:

- *A la carte features*: pillows, overhead bins, baggage, seat selection, and so on.
- *Commission-based*: hotels, rental cars, and travel insurance.
- *Frequent flier activities*: sale of miles to program partners including hotel chains and co-branded credit cards.

Today, businesses focus on ancillary revenue, a revenue derived from goods or services other than a company's primary product offering. For instance, the cruise industry has been enjoying ancillary revenue for years by selling tours, photos, on-board activities, and services like restaurants, nightlife, casino, special events, and car parking. United Airlines was the first US airline to start charging separate fees for checked bags, and low-cost Spirit Airlines was the first US airline to begin charging passengers for carry-on bags that didn't fit under a seat. As of January 20, 2016, the standard per bag fee ranged from $35 online to $100 at the gate.[4] Some airlines have even started charging additional fees for the window, aisle, or emergency-exit row seats. Ryanair and AirAsia sell the external surface of their aircraft as advertising space. Other airlines engage in commission-based selling for third parties with products and services that are relevant to fliers, including hotel rooms, rental cars, and travel insurance (Airline Weekly, 2015). Unbundling may also be a forced event in the wake of anti-trust violations. For example, in 2004, the European Court of First Instance ruled that to prevent a possible monopoly, Microsoft must provide the European market with a version of Windows operating system without their media player (The Economist, 2004).

Penetration Pricing and Market Skimming

Upon entering a market, an initial pricing strategy is selected. This strategy depends on the nature of demand for the product/service and takes the form of either market skimming or penetration pricing. One of the prime examples of penetration pricing comes from the Irish-based carrier Ryanair. In 1991, Ryanair transformed into a LCC with an aggressive market penetration strategy and rapid expansion. In new markets, Ryanair frequently employs penetration pricing, a technique where a new entrant into a market sets its initial prices relatively low in order to attract new customers and gain market share. This is evident through fares as low as £1 and €1 in new markets, with prices increasing following the entry period. Penetration pricing is based on the principle that leisure travelers are price-sensitive (demand is elastic) and will switch over to the new brand solely based on the cost. In 2007, JetBlue Airways launched a new service from New York to San Francisco and Los Angeles. To compete with United Airlines and American Airlines, JetBlue used a penetration pricing strategy by offering low introductory fares of $99 each way. This price was significantly lower than the average fare of around $600 at the time. JetBlue hoped that the low introductory fares would attract customers away from its competitors and allow it to gain market share in these new routes.

Market skimming takes the opposite approach; that is, a relatively high price is set for a new product or service, and the price is lowered over time. Market skimming, as the name implies, "skims" the maximum that the consumer is willing to pay for the product before competition and other market forces decrease the price. This is successful when demand is inelastic. This approach has been largely utilized in technological and high-end markets where a relatively high price is charged for the product initially. As the product approaches maturity, the price is decreased to appeal to a larger number of consumers. Price skimming usually doesn't yield long-term success. Before long, competitors will flood the marketplace with lower-priced alternatives to your product. In 2007, when Emirates Airlines introduced its Airbus A380 aircraft, it employed a market skimming pricing strategy by offering premium fares to early adopters and customers willing to pay a premium for a unique travel experience.

Peak-Load Pricing

Peak-load pricing has been employed by companies in various industries for many years. It involves charging higher prices when demand for a service or product is at its peak.[5] Airlines deal with peak-load pricing through revenue management. Demand for transatlantic airline travel is much higher in the summer compared to the rest of the year. At commercial airports, if most of the air traffic is concentrated around the peak times, it can exceed the airport capacity, resulting in significant delays. The basis for peak-load pricing is that it reflects the supplier's cost to meet demand at peak times. Implementing higher landing fees during peak hours or lower fees during off-peak hours can provide incentives to more efficient utilization of existing runway capacity. This pricing policy has also been adopted by several airports around the world, applying peak-load pricing for landing fees where, during peak hours, the charges increase significantly. Uniform pricing is not generally effective for landing charges as it does not reflect the willingness to pay higher prices for peak-load landing slots.

Penetration pricing is a pricing strategy used by many startup airlines to gain a significant market share through an introductory low-fare offer to entice passengers to fly their airline.

Peak-load pricing involves charging higher prices when demand for a service or product is at its peak. The technique is an attempt to shift demand to accommodate supply.

Several commercial airports charge higher landing fee during peak time and lower prices off-peak. To minimize capacity shortage, airports could price at marginal costs during off-peak times and at marginal plus capacity costs during peak times.

Uniform pricing also neglects the cost of increasing capacity to meet peak demand periods that may be under-utilized during off-peak times. The British Airports Authority (BAA) employs different landing charges for peak, shoulder, and off-peak times at London Heathrow (LHR) and Gatwick Airport (LGW). For instance, at Heathrow, peak fees exceed off-peak charges by 230%, while at Gatwick, this difference goes up to 300% (Ewers, 2001). Peak-load pricing of landing slots presents the following advantages to airports:

- Shifts demand to off-peak periods, thereby making better use of facilities and resources and reducing over- and under-utilization.
- Distributes expansion costs to the airlines that utilize the airport during that period and require the additional capacity.
- Better reflects cost-based pricing by focusing solely on peak times instead of utilizing average costs across all periods.

Price Discrimination in the Airline Industry

Price discrimination refers to the practice of charging different prices for the same product to different customers based on elasticities. Last-minute travelers may have a lower price elasticity because they have an urgent trip.

Price discrimination is generally lawful; however, a price discrimination is illegal if it's done on the basis of religion, nationality, race, or gender.

Price discrimination refers to the practice of charging different prices to different customers for the same product. The difference is based on the different price elasticities of demand between consumers. While the practice of price discrimination may seem unfair on the surface, it is legal and very common in modern business. For example, grocery stores practice price discrimination by offering coupon discounts to consumers who are not time-sensitive but price-sensitive, and who are willing to search out and bring the coupons to the store. Universities, especially state institutions, practice price discrimination by offering different tuition levels for international, out-of-state, and in-state students. The practice of discounted calling rates on evenings and weekends by telephone companies is also price discrimination. In many flea markets, no set prices are defined for the goods offered; however, customers bargain with the merchants. In fact, bargaining is the oldest form of price discrimination and has existed since commerce began.

Price discrimination is essentially the complementary aspect of yield management and is a requirement for its practice in the airline industry. And, as is now commonly appreciated, every flight has numerous fare classes for essentially the same seats and service. The airline industry stands as one of the several sectors that expend great effort on price discrimination.

As an example, imagine that DirectJet only offers seats priced at $500, but some passengers are willing to pay up to $700. The airline is losing the opportunity to make $200 more for some of the seats sold. Other passengers are more price-sensitive and are only willing to pay $500, while still others will only purchase at a still lower price. With price segmentation, more revenue can be generated by offering more prices.

Price discrimination is common in many different types of markets and even among firms with no market power. Industries that widely adopt price discrimination include:

- Airlines and other travel industries
- Car dealers
- Cinemas and theaters
- Colleges and universities
- Happy hour in bars and restaurants
- Movie theaters
- Nightclubs (Ladies' night)
- Railroads
- Senior citizen discount
- Student discounts
- Supermarkets (discount coupons)

The firm must be able to identify different market segments and separate the markets.

Consumer Surplus

> The reservation price signifies the highest price a buyer is willing to pay for goods or a service. Similarly, it represents the lowest price that a seller is willing to accept for a good or service.
>
> Consumer surplus stands as the difference between the maximum price a consumer is willing to pay for a good or service and the actual price they pay.

Consumer surplus is the disparity between the highest amount the passenger is willing to pay and the amount they actually pay. In essence, consumer surplus is the perceived "deal" that consumers receive when they purchase a good or service. The goal of price discrimination and, therefore, yield management is to reduce the amount of consumer surplus.

Consider a flight with six passengers who are all willing to pay various prices for the same flight (Table 8.4). Based on this data, a demand curve can be formulated for this flight, which is demonstrated in Figure 8.1. If an airline charges a single fare of $250, consumer surplus, or the difference between the maximum willingness to pay and the actual ticket price, would exist for five of the six passengers. Only passenger F would receive no consumer surplus. The ultimate goal of price discrimination and revenue management is to minimize consumer surplus; therefore, six individual fare categories would have to be created to maximize airline revenue

Table 8.4 Consumer Surplus under Uniform Pricing

Passenger	*Demand*	*Ticket Price*	*Maximum Ticket Price Willing to Pay*	*Consumer Surplus*
A	1	250	500	250
B	2	250	450	200
C	3	250	400	150
D	4	250	350	100
E	5	250	300	50
F	6	250	250	0

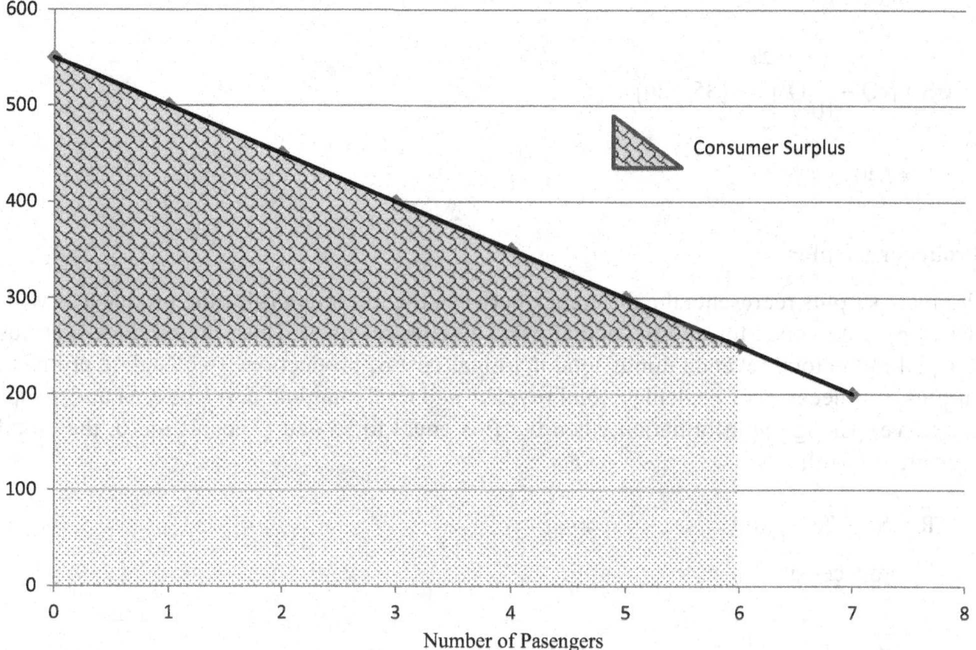

Figure 8.1 Consumer Surpluses under Uniform Pricing.

and minimize consumer surplus. The catch for the airlines is knowing every passenger's willingness to pay. Therefore, achieving the flight's exact demand curve can be challenging (if not impossible) in reality.

Example

Suppose the market demand and supply function for a given company are given as:

$P = 9 - (1/5) \times Q_d$

$P = 1 + (1/5) \times Q_s$

Solve for the equilibrium quantity, price, and the consumer surplus.

Set supply equal to the demand

$Q_d = 45 - 5P$

$Q_s = -5 + 5P$

$45 - 5P = -5 + 5P$

$P = \$5$ and $Q_s = Q_d = 20$ units

$$CS = \int_0^{20} = \left[9 - \frac{1}{5}Q_d\right]dq - (P \times Q)]$$

$$CS = \left|9Q - \frac{1}{10}Q^2\right|_0^{20} - (\$5 \times 20)$$

$CS = \$40$

Producer Surplus

Producer surplus represents the difference between the minimum price the producer is willing to provide goods for and the actual price a seller receives. Thus, the producer surplus is equal to the total revenue minus total marginal cost of production. To calculate producer surplus, it is necessary to calculate total revenue and total marginal cost (the area under supply curve). Using the information when the P is equal to \$5 and Q equals to 20, then total revenue is equal:

$TR = \$5 \times 20 = \$100$

The producer surplus is:

$$PS = \int_0^{20} = (P \times Q) - \left[1 + \frac{1}{5}Q_d\right]dq$$

$$PS = (\$5 \times 20) - \left|5Q + \frac{1}{10}Q^2\right|_0^{20}$$

$PS = \$40$

Example

Assume the market for a product has the supply and demand curves given by:

$P = 9{,}000 - 0.8Q_d$
$P = 1{,}000 + 0.2Q_s$

where P is in dollars and Q is in hundreds of pounds.

Using the above information,

a Find the equilibrium price and quantity in the market.
b Calculate the consumer surplus at equilibrium.
c Calculate the producer surplus at equilibrium.

Answer:

a $Q_d = Q_s$

$9{,}000 - 0.8Q_d = 1{,}000 + 0.2Q_s$

$8{,}000 = 0.8Q + 0.2Q$

$8{,}000 = Q$

$P = 9{,}000 - 0.8 \times (8{,}000)$

$P = 9{,}000 - 6{,}400$

$P = \$2{,}600$

b @ $P = \$9{,}000$, $Q_d = 0$

$$CS = \frac{(9{,}000 - 2{,}600)}{2} \times 8{,}000 = 25{,}600{,}000$$

c @ $P = \$1{,}200$, $Q_s = 0$

d $$PS = \frac{(9{,}000 - 1{,}200)}{2} \times 8{,}000 = 31{,}200{,}000$$

Necessary Conditions for Price Discrimination

In practice, a number of ways exist for a business to institute at least some form of price discrimination. However, in order for it to be effective, three necessary conditions are needed to be applied to the market.

Market Segmentation

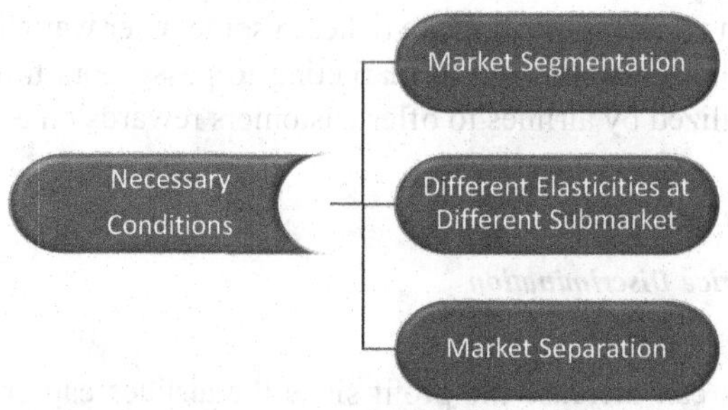

The first requirement for price discrimination to exist is that the markets must be segmented. This requires different groups of consumers who do not have the same interests should exist.

In the aviation industry, a common method of market segmentation lies between leisure and business travelers. However, due to extensive overlap in these categories, a more accurate segmentation emerges between time-sensitive and price-sensitive travelers. Time-sensitive travelers are typically business travelers who demand to travel on certain days and at certain times. These passengers will typically ignore the ticket price in order to satisfy their scheduling needs. Additionally, certain types of leisure travelers may be contained in this category, particularly vacationers who may be leaving and returning on a set schedule. Conversely, price-sensitive travelers lean toward selecting flights based on the ticket price. These travelers are willing to travel at inconvenient times and via longer routes if it results in lower fares.

Different Elasticities in Submarkets

The second requirement for price discrimination is the existence of different elasticities for different submarkets. This requirement is closely related to the first one as the market segmentation can be based on price elasticity. However, the first requirement deals with how the passengers can be grouped, while this requirement deals with the passengers' willingness to pay. If all passengers had the same price elasticity, then the airline would not be able to charge different prices. In the air travel industry, both requirements are easily met, since every market contains a variety of people who are willing to fly at different times and at different prices. Time-sensitive passengers generally have inelastic demand for airline tickets, while vacation/price-sensitive travelers have more elastic demand.

Market Separation

> Market segmentation refers to the division of the market into different submarkets having similar needs and interest. The most identified passenger segments are minimum stay conditions, maximum stay conditions, advance purchase, time of day, day of week, and pricing response to competitors pricing.

The third requirement for price discrimination is the airline's ability to effectively isolate the market and successfully apply different prices to different passengers. Market segmentation involves dividing the total passengers into different groups to be able to charge different prices according to their price sensitivity. Airlines achieve market separation through pricing "fences" (this practice will be covered in detail in a subsequent section). Briefly, some examples of fences are the non-transferability of tickets and minimum stay requirements. These allow the airline to keep the customer from reselling or using the ticket in some other way than for the flight, hence the term "fences." Airlines also engage in marketing to passengers through a "frequent flyer scheme," a program utilized by airlines to offer customers rewards on a given flight.

Degrees of Price Discrimination

First-Degree (Perfect) Price Discrimination

> Price discrimination can increase the profit since the airlines can charge a higher price to those passengers with less elastic demand, and a lower price to those passengers with more elastic demand. First-degree price discrimination is the situation where a producer charges consumers their reservation value for each unit consumed.

First-degree price discrimination, also called perfect price discrimination, involves charging the maximum amount each customer is willing and able to pay. In economic terms, this maximum price is called the reservation price. A consumer surplus occurs when the consumer is willing to pay more for a given product than the current market price. For example, if a passenger is willing to spend up to EUR 5,400 on a round-trip first-class flight from LHR–JFK, but they are able to purchase the ticket for just EUR 4,700, the consumer surplus from the transaction is EUR 700.

Bartering is the classic case of perfect price discrimination. Consider a car dealership where consumers are paying different prices for the same product. Another example is an auction where consumers will keep bidding up the price until they reach their maximum willingness to pay. In the airline industry, perfect price discrimination is practically non-existent for reasons mentioned earlier.

Example

In May 2015, Iberia introduced a Spanish-language online auction to sell off some of its domestic flights.[6] Below is a depiction of the website where passengers can bid for specific flight tickets.

Auctions originating madrid

Flight to Milan

Ida: Friday November 18, 2016

Return: Monday November 21, 2016

Quedan 9h 29 min 33 seq

Current bid **52** €

Flight to Brussels

Ida: Friday November 18, 2016

Return: Monday November 21, 2016

Quedan 33h 29 min 33 seq

Current bid **61** €

Second-Degree (Quantity Discounts) Price Discrimination

Second-degree price discrimination is simply the existence of quantity discounts. The practice is common in industrial sales where large quantities of a product are purchased at once. The commercial airline industry has had limited experience with second-degree price discrimination, with the exception of charter flights and corporate travel deals. In these situations, the companies secure discounted prices by agreeing to buy a large proportion of seats on a flight. Airlines find this advantageous as it ensures a certain amount of guaranteed revenue for a flight, albeit at a reduced rate.

Example

Airline consolidators are companies that buy large quantities of tickets from airlines at bulk prices and resell them at attractive discounts. Consolidator fares are typically cheaper than the lowest published airfares from the airlines. The main purpose for airlines to sell to wholesalers at reduced prices is to ensure the sale of tickets that might not otherwise be sold. Wholesale consolidators in turn resell these consolidated tickets to retail consolidators and approved travel agencies.

Third-Degree (Multi-Market) Price Discrimination

Third-degree price discrimination is the kind most typically practiced within the airline industry. It involves dividing consumers into different groups based on a set of characteristics, and estimating their respective demand curves. At this point, each group is charged a different price. The group with the most inelastic demand (typically the most time-sensitive group) is charged the highest price. This price discrimination is identifiable by the different fare classes observed in the market. With third-degree price discrimination, a certain amount of consumer surplus will exist since the prices are not set for every individual but for the group as a whole. However, introducing additional fare classes diminishes the amount of consumer surplus and ultimately increases revenues for the airline. The general pricing rule for third-degree price discrimination is (Baumol and Bradford, 1970):

$$\frac{\frac{P_1 - MC_1}{MC_1}}{\frac{P_2 - MC_2}{MC_2}} = \frac{\varepsilon_2}{\varepsilon_1}$$

Every airline practices third-degree price discrimination by means of different fare. The major and most common fare classes include Cabin/Economy and Business/First. Fare classes and their implications are discussed in more detail in the revenue management section further in the chapter.

Example

DirectJet Airlines' leisure travelers account for 80% of airlines' passengers, but they are typically three times more price elastic. If Direct Jet Airlines charge $500 business travelers, given the following table, how much should it charge its leisure travelers?

	Elasticity	*Marginal Cost*
Business Travelers	−1.5	$250
Leisure Travelers	−4.5	$50

$$\frac{\frac{\$500-\$250}{\$250}}{\frac{P_2-\$50}{\$50}}=\frac{-4.5}{-1.5}=3$$

Solving the above questions leads to the following answer:

$$P_2=\$200$$

Example

A manufacturer jet engine produces an engine at a constant marginal cost of $6,000,000. The price elasticity of demand for the good is –4.0. To determine the profit-maximizing price, the company should charge:

$$P=MC\times\left(\frac{\varepsilon}{1+\varepsilon_1}\right)$$

$$P=\$6{,}000{,}000\times\left(\frac{-4}{1-4}\right)$$

$$P=\$8{,}000{,}000$$

Example

Suppose marginal cost of gasoline at a general aviation airport in Florida with a price elasticity of demand for gasoline of −2 is $2.25. What will the station charge for gasoline?

$$P=MC\times\left(\frac{\varepsilon}{1+\varepsilon_1}\right)$$

$$P=\$2.25\times\left(\frac{-2}{1-2}\right)$$

$$P=\$4..50$$

Uniform Pricing versus Price Discrimination

Despite the negative connotation, price discrimination follows a common and generally efficient procedure. Consider the impact of a uniform-pricing policy as shown in Figure 8.2. With the typical cost structure of imperfect competition, we see long-run equilibrium where P* = ATC at output Q*. Note that this leaves a huge segment of demand unsatisfied and results in a great

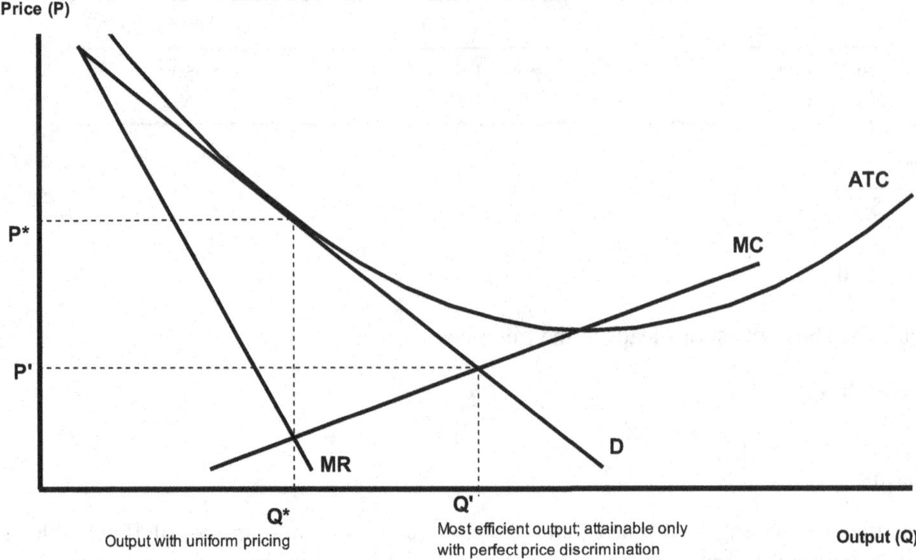

Figure 8.2 Pricing Policy and Price Discrimination.

degree of wasted capacity (that is, an awful lot of empty airline seats). Many consumers would be willing to pay a price higher than the MC for serving them, though lower than P*. However, with uniform pricing, the price cannot be set below average total cost (ATC) in the long run since the airline is barely breaking even at a price equal to ATC. The only option available to airlines to increase their revenues is selective price cuts. If it were possible to read consumers' minds, price could have been reduced just enough below P* to induce them to buy a ticket. In this case, each consumer pays exactly the highest price they are willing to pay; MR is now equal to this personalized price so that every customer willing to pay a price greater than MC can be served. Under this "perfect price discrimination" regime, output can be increased to Q.[7]

For airlines, perfect price discrimination is not possible, but sophisticated third-degree price discrimination can allow airlines to move closer to the efficient output level of Q' as they fill otherwise empty seats with selective price cuts. For instance, if most students are on the demand segment below P*, then a discount for students will bring in new revenues. Similarly, demographically based price cuts for senior citizens or families can also achieve the desired effect. The airlines can also keep the price cuts limited through the use of the revenue management "fences" mentioned earlier and discussed in a later section.

Naturally, transitioning from uniform pricing to the more tailored approach of price discrimination might entail some demand segments facing a price higher than P*. An interesting question arises whether price discrimination leads to an average fare lower than P*, the theoretical uniform price. Most economists concur that price discrimination typically does lead to a lower average price, producing fewer empty airline seats and greater economic efficiency. The key reason for this is the presence of competition. It is always easier to cut prices than it is to raise them because of the threat of being undercut by a competitor.

Even if price discrimination reduces average price, it may still raise price for particular consumers in the upper portion of the demand curve. A commonly asserted complaint is that certain business travelers end up paying high fares to "subsidize" consumers receiving discounts. However, problems persist with this theory. As already explained, a uniform price would drive many discount customers completely out of the scheduled airline market. This would reduce airline revenues and ultimately lead to price increases and reductions in available seat miles (ASMs), both of which would be unpleasant to business travelers. Thus, in a sense, one could just as easily argue that discount fliers "subsidize" business travelers. In order to continue the present service standards, airlines need every penny of revenue they can get, just as a restaurant may be financially viable only with revenues from regular, full-paying customers combined with revenues from patrons that dine there only occasionally when they have a discount coupon. Each set of consumers benefits from the other since only their combined revenues are enough to sustain the product they both enjoy.

Some studies examine price discrimination based on other characteristics, such as when firms offer policies at a fixed price or when they charge according to some consumption variable that is correlated to costs. For instance, consider an airline serving only leisure vacationers (no business or time-sensitive travelers). This airline would have a very different product design compared to other carriers. Its consumers care little about the exact time of departure, are willing to commit to a schedule way in advance, and are very price-sensitive. This type of airline would resemble today's charter airlines quite closely: it would operate with infrequent service, employ large aircraft in a high-density seating configuration with very high load factors (probably over 90%), and routinely cancel any flight well in advance if it was substantially undersubscribed. Under such conditions, costs and average prices could be kept very low. However, if the airline wanted to accommodate business travelers, it would have to offer multiple flights with varying departure times and adhere to a schedule published a few months in advance. The airline would also keep some seats open for late, even last-minute, travelers. Since business travelers require the design of a more expensive product, it appears reasonable to argue, as Frank (1983) does, that it is philosophically appropriate to charge them more. In essence, the appearance that business and leisure travelers are sometimes paying very different prices for the same service is an illusion. In reality, the typical time-sensitive travelers demand a very different and much more expensive sort of service than price-sensitive travelers.

Uniform versus Multiple Pricing

People Express was founded by Donald Burr in 1980. By unbundling the different components of air travel services, People Express allowed the passengers to pay for what they needed, not pay for what they did not need.

The example of the People Express[8] highlights that revenue management in the airline industry was first introduced in 1985 by American Airlines through its "Ultimate Super Saver" fares. People Express's simplified pricing strategy, which was based on a single class of service and a simplified fare structure, was initially successful in attracting price-sensitive customers and gaining market share in the highly competitive airline industry. However, over time, this pricing strategy contributed to the downfall of the airline. Since then, almost every airline in the world has adopted a revenue management scheme to some degree. The benefits of doing so are immense, as Delta Air Lines attributed $300 million in profits to revenue management when it first started implementing it. To highlight the benefits and provide a better understanding of revenue management, here's a quantitative example. Assume that DirectJet Airlines operates a short-haul route where the maximum daily demand for the flight is 100 passengers and the maximum any passenger is willing to pay for the flight is $250. This information helps us construct a demand curve for the flight, which in this case is assumed to be linear (Figure 8.3).

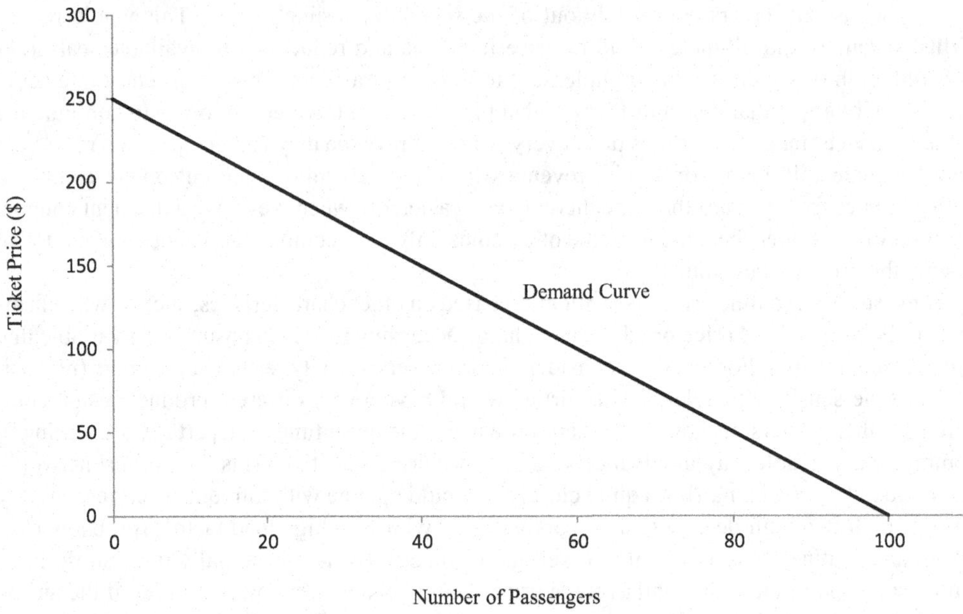

Figure 8.3 Linear Demand Curve.

Under a uniform-pricing strategy, DirectJet sets one single price for all passengers on a single flight. Recall that People Express was an airline operating with a uniform-pricing strategy. In our example, let's assume that DirectJet charges a uniform price of $100 for this particular short-haul flight. Based on the estimated demand function and at $100 airfare, 60 passengers are willing to buy tickets from the airline. This would generate $6,000 in total daily revenue for DirectJet. This is graphically represented in Figure 8.4 with the shaded area under the curve representing total daily revenue for the flight.

The second pricing scenario available to DirectJet is a multiple-pricing strategy where the airline uses segmented (differential) pricing to maximize revenue. In our example, DirectJet decides to adopt a new four-tier pricing structure where it offers fares ranging from $200 to $50. Based on the estimated demand function for this particular flight, 20 passengers are willing to pay the $200 fare, 40 passengers are willing to pay the $150 fare, 60 passengers the $100 fare, and 80 passengers the $50 fare. Figure 8.5 graphically displays the revenue potential for the DirectJet flight using a multiple-pricing strategy. It is immediately apparent that the shaded area under the multiple-pricing policy is greater than the shaded area in Figure 8.4 under the uniform-pricing policy. This is confirmed numerically where the four-tier pricing structure generates $10,000 in total daily revenue:

$$\text{New Aircraft Revenue} = 20 \times (\$200) + 40 \times (\$150) + 60 \times (\$100) + 80 \times (\$50) = \$10{,}000$$

This is greater than the uniform-pricing policy of $6,000. Therefore, the major benefit of multiple-pricing policy is to increase total flight revenues; however, it also enables DirectJet to offer cheap, discounted airfares that could undercut the competition. Assuming that DirectJet is operating a 100-seat aircraft, price-sensitive passengers would simply be occupying an otherwise empty seat. This is exactly what American Airlines accomplished with its "Ultimate Super Saver" fares. The end result of a multiple-pricing strategy is the likelihood of both elevated total revenue and an increased number of passengers. In this example, revenues increased from $6,000 to $10,000.

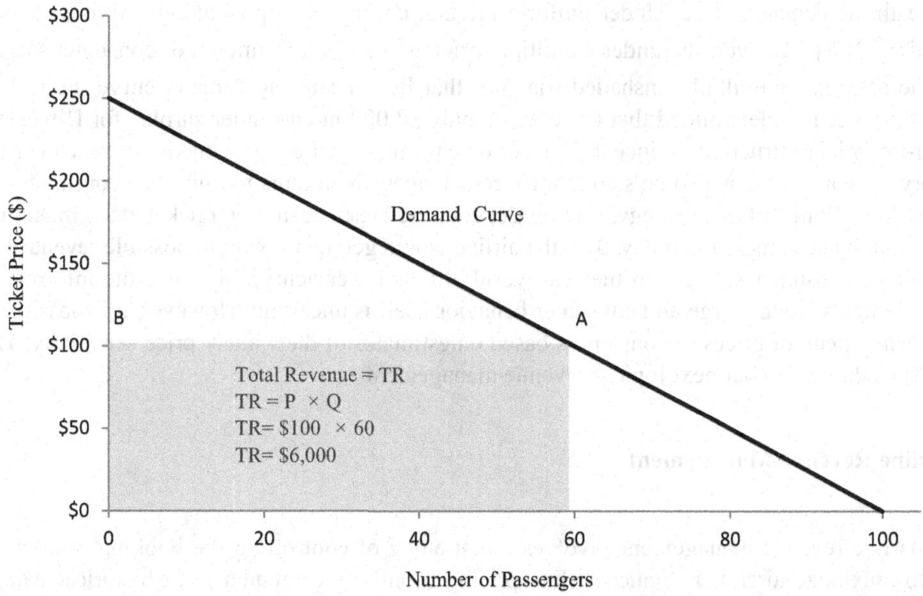

Figure 8.4 Uniform Pricing for DirectJet Flight.

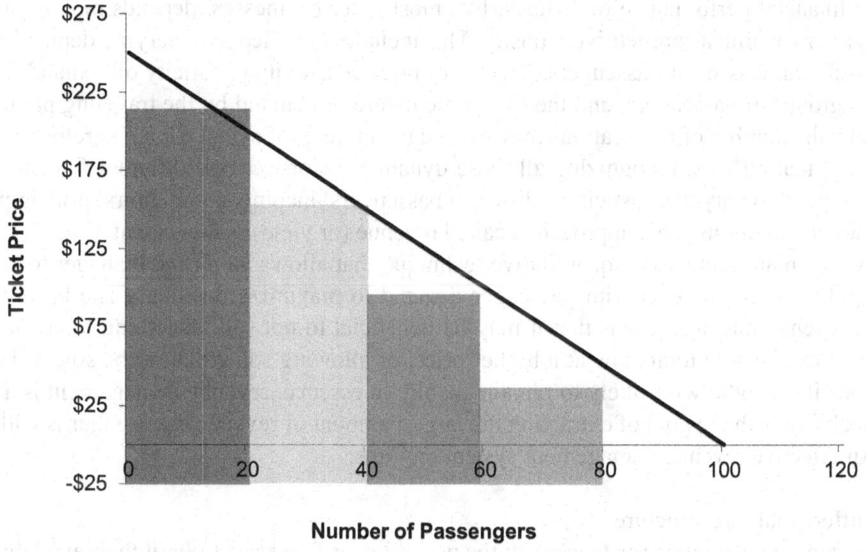

Figure 8.5 Multiple Pricing for DirectJet Flight.

Another perspective on uniform versus multiple pricing involves considering the passengers' viewpoint. In our example, under uniform pricing, many passengers who purchased the $100 airfare were willing to pay more than that. Several passengers were willing to pay over $200, but ended up only having to pay $100. As mentioned, this difference between what a passenger is willing to pay and what the passenger actually paid is called consumer surplus. Consumer surplus can also be easily calculated by finding the area of the unshaded triangle region that lies beneath the demand curve. Under uniform pricing, consumer surplus amounted to $4,500 or $[\frac{60 \text{ seats} \times \$150}{2}]$.[9] Conversely, under a multiple-pricing strategy, the amount of consumer surplus is the area of the multiple unshaded triangles that lie beneath the demand curve. From Figure 8.5, it can be determined that there exists only $2,000 in consumer surplus for DirectJet's four-tier pricing structure.[10] Since the goal of revenue management is to maximize revenue from every passenger, it can also be said that revenue management aims to minimize consumer surplus. At the limits of this strategy, if DirectJet could sell each customer a ticket at the maximum fare that the customer would pay, then the airline would get the maximum possible revenue and eliminate consumer surplus. In the real world, this is never achievable since the information requirements are too large and consumer behavior itself is uncertain. However, it is possible to present a menu of prices to consumers based on estimates of their likely price sensitivity. This leads us directly to our next topic—revenue management.

Airline Revenue Management

> Airline revenue management involves the strategy of controlling the booking requests to maximize aircraft revenue. Airline pricing usually is estimated from historical data including booking trends.

The financial performance of airlines, like most other businesses, depends mainly on their sales strategy within a competitive industry. This includes knowledge of varying demand conditions, different classes of passengers, degrees of price sensitivity (elasticity of demand) among various groups of passengers, and the stochastic nature of demand by the traveling public. For example, the number of reservations may exceed the number of actual trips. Therefore, it is not surprising that airlines, recognizing all these dynamic factors, charge different fares to effectively respond to varying elasticities, different passengers' income, competitors' pricing policy, and market conditions. This approach is called revenue (or yield) management.

Revenue management is a quantitative technique that allows an airline manager to balance the supply of aircraft seats with passenger demand to maximize revenues. The basic theory behind revenue management is that it may be beneficial to not sell something today at a low price if it can be sold tomorrow at a higher price, or allowing something to be sold today at a low price if it is otherwise likely to remain unsold. In essence, revenue management is a game of probability with the goal of extracting the largest amount of revenue a passenger is willing to pay. An effective revenue management system requires:

- A differential fare structure
- A system of constraints (or fences) on the use of lower-fare seats to limit their availability to passengers who might otherwise be willing to a pay a higher fare
- A system for seat allocation that maximizes expected revenue in the face of stochastic demand
- A reliable forecast of demand, no-shows, cancelations, overbooking, and inventory limit

Revenue management is critical for airlines. A case in point is People Express in the 1980s.

This was a fledgling discount airline that was born out of deregulation. Initially, People Express flew niche markets that competed mostly with buses and cars. With a cost structure that was $1 billion below other airlines, such as American Airlines, the carrier started competing

Table 8.5 People Express' Breakeven Load Factor, 1984–1986

	1981	*1982*	*1983*	*1984*	*1985*	*1986*
Load factor	58%	61%	75%	70%	61%	57%
Breakeven load factor	71%	60%	72%	70%	62%	72%

Source: OAG Form 41 data.

on major routes, operating with a 75% load factor and a 72% breakeven load factor (BLF). As such, the discount airline, with its simple pricing structure and extensive cost advantage, seemed unstoppable, yet it had one significant disadvantage: a reservations system that was simple and unable to employ revenue management. People Express's information technology system could offer peak and off-peak fares, but each flight had to be either one or the other (peak or off-peak). This meant that on each flight, the carrier was able to offer only one fare. The system did not have the capability of offering multiple fares on a single flight (Cross, 1995).

On January 17, 1985, American Airlines became the first airline to implement revenue management, and it did so by exploiting a competitor's flaw. The carrier launched "Ultimate Super Saver" fares that were priced at People Express's lowest prices (Cross, 1995). Their strategy also included 21-day advance purchase restrictions on the saver fares in order to draw in only the most price-sensitive travelers (Cross, 1995). Additionally, American controlled the number of "Ultimate Super Saver" fares available on each flight in order to save space for high-revenue passengers. In essence, the airline was able to generate profit from both low-revenue and high-revenue passengers, while People Express could only accommodate low-revenue passengers with its single fare class reservations system. As a result, People Express's load factor dropped from 70% in 1984 to 57% in 1986 (Table 8.5). Conversely, its BLF jumped 10% from 1985 to 1986, and because it was well above the actual load factor, the airline lost money.

The example of People Express not only displays the importance of revenue management for an airline but also its application in any business. Plagued by a persistent overcapacity (low load factor) despite consistent growth in passenger traffic, the airline suffered a $14.2 million operating loss for the final quarter of 1984, and by June 1985, People Express had lost $5.8 million on an operating income of $18.7 million.[11] While modern revenue management has its roots in the airline industry, it is widely used in the car rental companies, hotels, and cruise ships, to name a few. The same theory and practice of revenue management applies to all these industries, therefore making it an important management tool.

Revenue Management "Fences"

One of the most important factors of a revenue management system is the effective use of "fences," or barriers that limit the use of discounted seats to only passengers who are price-sensitive, rather than to passengers who might be willing to pay a much higher fare. For example, many business travelers are willing to pay full fares, and the airlines don't want these customers obtaining deeply discounted tickets. They avoid this through the use of "fences." In practical airline pricing policy, there are seven major fences[12]:

- Advance purchase requirements (APR)
- Frequent flier mileage
- Ticket refundability

- Change fees
- Airline schedule
- Minimum stay

Advance Purchase Restrictions

Advance purchase restrictions are some of the oldest "fences" implemented in the airline industry. These restrictions simply limit the period before the day of departure within which a ticket can be purchased. American Airlines' "Ultimate Super Saver" fare, for example, had a 21-day advance purchase restriction. Likewise, Delta Air Lines' "deeply discounted fares" may require advance purchases of 3, 7, 14, or 21 days. Advance purchase restrictions were implemented under the belief that passengers who were more price-sensitive (and less time-sensitive) would book further out. Conversely, if passengers show up at the airport and wish to travel on the next flight, they are clearly extremely time-sensitive and price-insensitive and would therefore be willing to pay a much higher price. A typical fare class structure relating to advance purchase restrictions is illustrated in Table 8.6. Although there is no industry standard for fare codes, Y is generally considered to be unrestricted economy travel. Major carriers may employ as many as 15 different fare codes, while LCCs tend to use only a few.

For example, an airline with 75 seats in economy class may show it in a reservation system as:

Y21, K15, M12, T18, and E9.

Some codes cannot be sold by agents but may be reserved for code-shared airlines, international connections, airline staff relocation, or frequent travelers.

Table 8.6 Fare Class Restrictions

Fare Type	*Fare Code*	*Restrictions*
Economy	B	Coach, but is able to be upgradable
Economy	E	Coach discounted
Economy	G	Coach discounted
Economy	H	Coach discounted, is able to be upgraded
Economy	K	Coach discounted
Economy	L	Coach discounted
Economy	M	Coach discounted
Economy	N	Coach discounted
Economy	O	Coach discounted
Economy	Q	Coach discounted
Economy	V	Coach discounted
Economy	W	Coach discounted
Economy	X	Coach discounted/award
Economy	Y	Economy
Business class	C	Full fare
Business class	D	Discounted
Business class	I	Discounted
Business class	J	Full fare
Business class	Z	Discounted
First class	A	Class discounted
First class	F	Full fare first class
First class	R	Suites

Source: Compiled by the authors from Delta Air Lines' Fare and Ticket Rules, 2023.

Frequent Flier Mileage

While frequent flier programs have been around for quite some time, only recently have they begun to be employed as a revenue management fence. Frequent flier programs are successful at attracting and retaining loyal customers, and the number of miles earned for a flight can be an important factor for passengers. For instance, a passenger may be willing to pass up a fare if the next fare class offers more frequent flier miles. However, in order for this fence to be effective, full transparency of the fare classes/options is required; that is, if only one fare option appears when a passenger wishes to purchase, then this fence will not be effective since the passenger will not know about other options. The most effective marketing use of frequent flier mileage as a yield management fence is a matrix approach with various fare types available to the passenger. Alaska Airlines and Air Canada are both good examples of this strategy. Another related frequent flier benefit is a first-class upgrade. Depending on the fare class booked, a passenger may be entitled to a complimentary upgrade or to pay for one using miles. For most airlines, the passenger must be booked above a certain fare class level to be eligible for these perks.

Prior to 2015, passengers typically earned miles based on the distance flown. Now, most major US airlines offer miles based on the ticket price (excluding government charges) and program tier, with some exceptions for specialty fairs, certain memberships, and codeshare flights. Table 8.7 presents the current mileage earned from two US carriers.

Refundability

Ticket refundability is another major fence used by airlines worldwide to help segment the market. The general rule is that higher-fare classes will have full ticket refundability, which enables a passenger to cancel a reservation without penalty. Thus, the refundable ticket provides the passenger with greater flexibility, which appeals primarily to time-sensitive travelers. Lower-fare classes usually do not provide a refund unless there are extenuating circumstances.

Change Fees

Similar to ticket refundability, change fees are used to differentiate travelers based on their time sensitivity. Travelers who require more flexibility generally like the option to change flights for

Table 8.7 Fare Class Frequent Flyer Mileage Credit

Delta Air Lines	
Skymiles Program Tier	Miles Earned per $1
General Member	5
Silver Medallion	7
Gold Medallion	8
Platinum Medallion	9
Diamond Medallion	11
United Airlines	
Mileage Plus Program Tier	Miles Earned
Member	1
Premier Silver	1
Premier Gold	1
Premier Platinum	2
Premier 1K	2

Source: Compiled by the authors using published ticket rules on Delta.com and United.com.

free or for a nominal fee. Usually, the highest-fare class allows full flexibility and is popular among business passengers with schedules changing on short notice. On the other side of the spectrum, some of the lowest-fare classes may not even allow schedule changes. However, most fare classes require a change fee to be paid in addition to the difference in fare. While the change fee may be minimal, the difference in fare could be drastic, especially from lower-fare classes. In essence, the difference in fare charge is the difference between the fare class paid by the passenger and the lowest available fare class on the flight the passenger wants to change to. Since higher-fare passengers have fewer classes above them, any difference in charge is usually small. International carriers like Delta have adopted a multi-pronged approach to change fees. Specifically, if all fare and ticket rules are met and seats are available, there won't be a change fee for a refundable ticket. However, based on the particular fare class rules, a service fee and/or a difference in fare may be applicable.

Airline Schedule

The final fence relates to the timing of an airline's schedule. Since different types of passengers have different traveling patterns, airlines can more profitably allocate high- and low-fare seating if they are aware of the likely composition of the passengers for a flight. For instance, time-sensitive travelers might desire an early morning departure and an evening return so that they can conduct a full day's business. Therefore, the airline will choose to limit the number of low-fare flights for a same-day round trip. Leisure passengers, on the other hand, exhibit different travel patterns that might include the ability to be flexible with departure and return dates. Hence, we observe midweek sale promotions and last-minute discounts to various locations.

Minimum Stay

A minimum stay rule is another type of fence instrumental in airline revenue management. The use of minimum stay rules is common in the airline industry, particularly for discounted fares or promotional offers. For example, airlines may offer lower prices for passengers who stay for a certain number of days or require a Saturday night stay, while charging higher prices for customers who stay for shorter periods of time. This fence ensures that the airline is able to sell the same seat multiple times, while also preventing customers from taking advantage of lower fares by booking a longer stay.

Revenue Management Control Types

Before the various fare class allocation methods (or control types) are presented, two key terms need to be explained. Booking limit is the maximum number of seats that can be purchased for each fare class, and protection level is the number of seats that are left unsold so that they may be purchased at a higher-fare class. Depending on the control type implemented, there may be only a few protected seats for Y fares, or there may be many. Booking limits and protection levels are critical concepts for yield management analysts as they attempt to maximize revenue for every flight.

Two main types of control limits are adopted in yield management: distinct and nested. In distinct control, a fixed number of seats are allocated to each fare class, and the fare can only be purchased if there remains inventory in the fare bucket. Under distinct control, protection level and booking level are equal since there is no provision for shifting fare classes, as shown in Figure 8.6. From the airline's point of view, this is obviously an inefficient scheme as it amounts

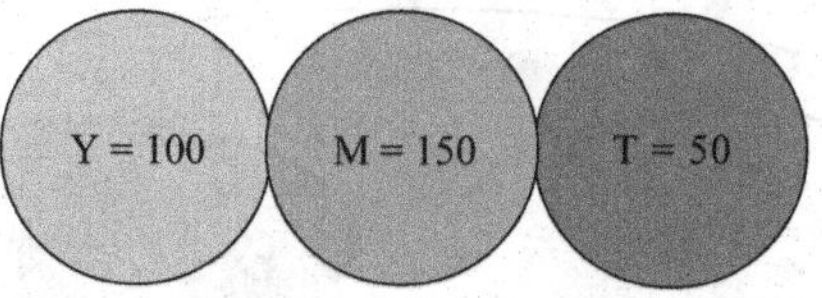

Figure 8.6 Distinct Fare Control.

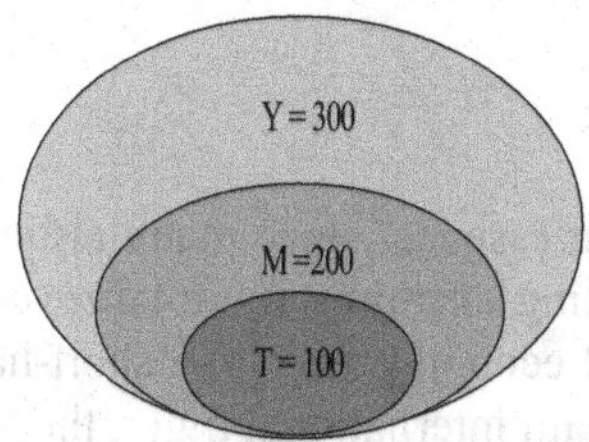

Figure 8.7 Serial Nesting.

to a rather inflexible form of price discrimination. For example, there may be numerous price-sensitive passengers who would purchase a lower-priced fare if it were available. If the airline guesses wrong on the number of seats allocated at the lower fare, and if the passengers are unwilling to pay the next highest fare, then there are likely to be unsold seats on the flight. This, of course, results in lower overall revenue. Due to these inefficiencies, distinct control is very rarely implemented in airline yield management.

The predominant scheme utilized in yield management is some derivation of nested control. These nested control schemes can be customized to suit the individual characteristics of the flight, but the basic principle lies in embedding lower-fare classes within higher-fare classes. Therefore, under a pure (or serial) nested control scheme, a higher-fare bucket will never be closed out prior to a lower-fare bucket. Figure 8.7 highlights a serial nesting scheme for the same 300-seat aircraft, with the number representing the booking limit for each class. Under this scenario, the total aircraft capacity could be booked in Y class, but only 100 seats are reserved for Y class. In this case, the protection level is calculated by simply finding the difference between each of the fare classes. Another example of a nested control structure is a parallel nesting scheme as presented in Figure 8.8. While similar to serial nesting, a parallel structure allows for the M class fare to be closed prior to the T class, while still ensuring the entire aircraft to be booked in full Y class. Such a structure, or derivation thereof, may be used to provide a set inventory reserved for frequent flier mileage redemption or corporate travel arrangements (Vinod, 1995).

Spoilage refers to the empty seats on a given flight, leading to loss of revenue due to high airfare and the lack of demand. Conversely, spillage transpires when the average fares are set too low for the flight and the passengers are turned away for lack of seats.

A major type of nested control is virtual nesting. Virtual nesting is best understood from a total revenue and total network perspective as it helps determine if selling a seat in a high-fare class on a single sector might be sub-optimal relative to selling that same seat to a connecting

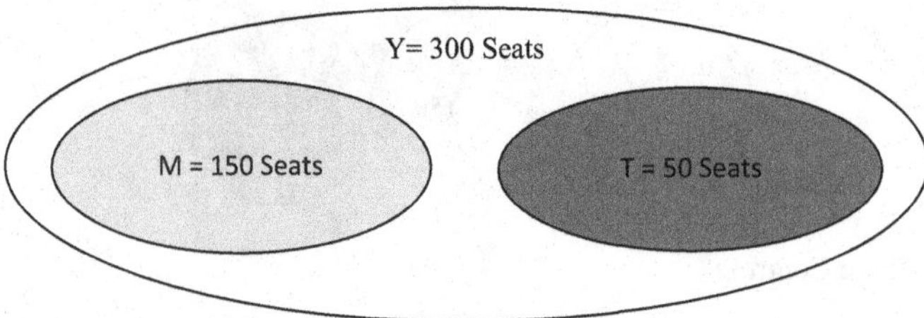

Figure 8.8 Parallel Nesting.

passenger in a lower-fare class. In essence, since many airline itineraries involve a change of planes through a hub, virtual nesting examines the total revenue the booking would generate. For instance, if a full unrestricted economy fare on a short-haul sector generates less revenue than a discounted fare on a long-haul international flight, the longer itinerary would have priority. This is accomplished by "clustering" the various itinerary fare classes that flow over a flight leg into a manageable number of buckets, based on customer value (Vinod, 1995). Thousands of potential itineraries can be grouped into a few virtual buckets, but the variance in each of these buckets can be considerable (Vinod, 1995).

Spoilage and Spillage

Using various control types, revenue management analysts can effectively manipulate the opening and closing of fare buckets to adjust to the demand for the flight. Prices for flights are adjusted with respect to the normal booking curve for the flight, which is based on historical demand. A normal booking curve is generated by assuming that ticket purchases follow a normal historical distribution and that the last seat of the aircraft is purchased just before the time of departure.[13] If such a situation were to occur, this would represent complete revenue management effectiveness and maximize the airlines' revenues (Littlewood, 2005). Figures 8.9–8.11 display different situations that may occur with respect to the normal booking curve.

In Figure 8.9, the actual booking curve results in the number of bookings at the date of departure being less than the capacity of the flight. This difference between capacity and actual bookings is called "spoilage." Spoilage is visually represented as empty seats on an aircraft. Airlines want to reduce spoilage since an empty seat does not provide any additional revenue for the airline, and in all likelihood, that seat could have been sold if the price was right. Spoilage is a result of prices that are too high for the market for the given fare class. When this occurs, the booking rate is less than the normal booking curve for the flight, as shown by points C and D in Figure 8.9. At this point, the revenue analyst can lower the average ticket price or open lower-fare classes to reduce potential spoilage. Conversely, points B and F represent situations where the analyst would want to increase the price of the ticket.

Figure 8.10 depicts the reverse situation of spoilage, occurring when all the seats are purchased prior to the flight's departure. This situation, referred to as "spillage, or rejected demand," poses a problem because the airline generally sells seats at very low prices and passengers are turned away for lack of seats. By already having the flight fully booked, the airline is incurring a potential loss of revenue for the flight. Spillage is the result of average fares that are too low for the flight, which may lead to a booking curve that lies above the normal booking curve. Both spillage and spoilage are of concern for revenue analysts, and they must balance the fine line between both problems to reach an ideal normal booking curve.

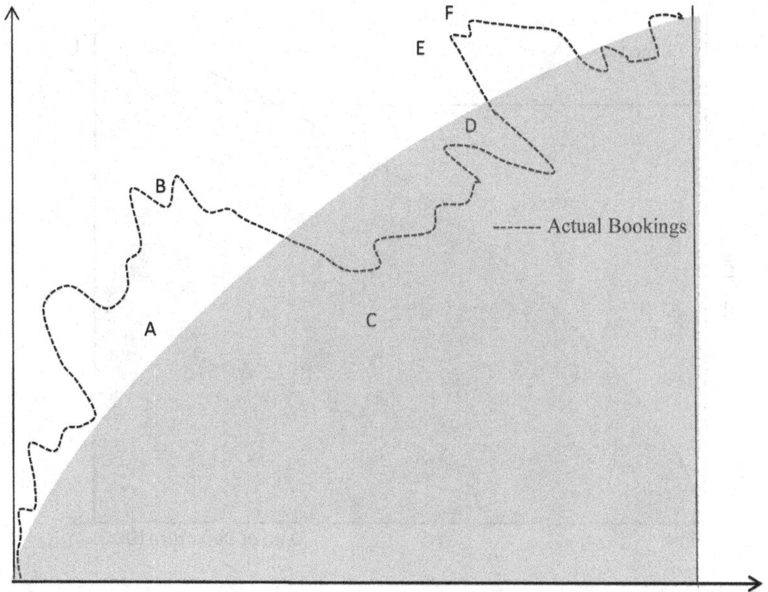

Figure 8.9 Actual Booking.

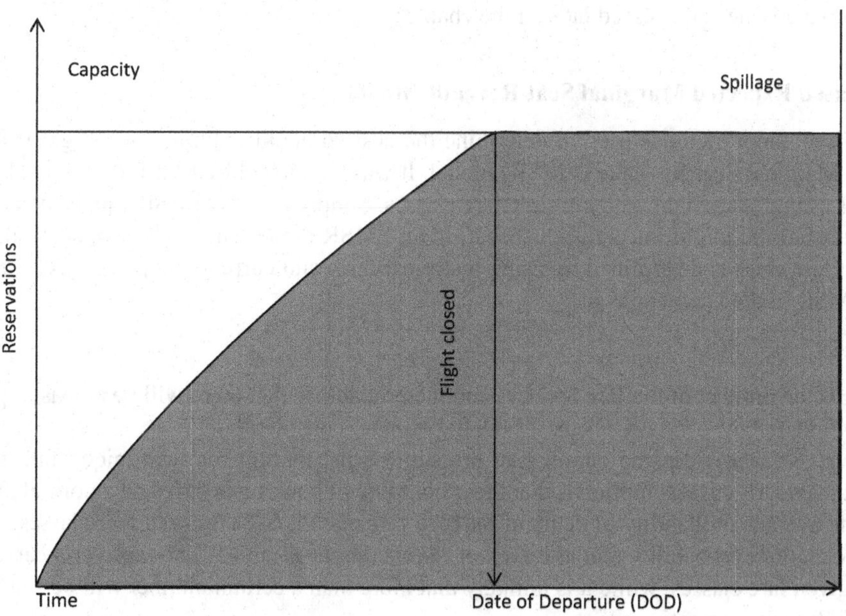

Figure 8.10 Spillage (Rejected Demand).

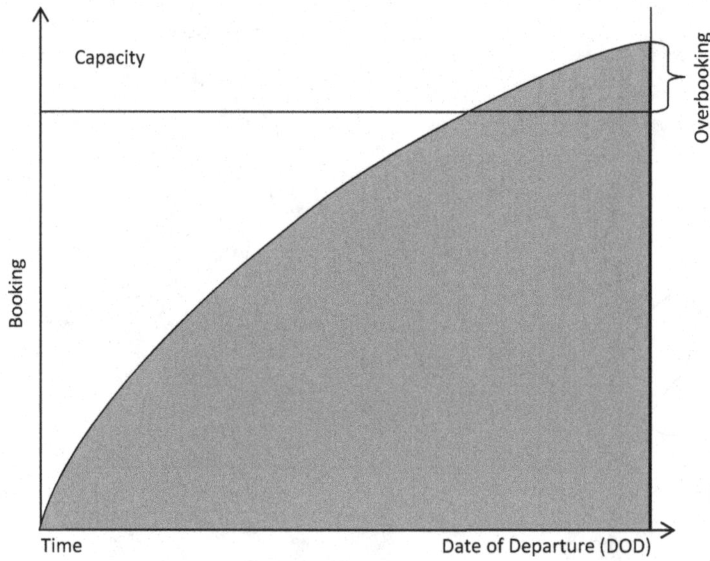

Figure 8.11 Overbooking.

Figure 8.11 depicts a situation similar to spillage when the airline books more passengers for the flight than capacity. This situation, called "overbooking," is a normal occurrence, since a probabilistic percentage of passengers usually do not show up for their flights. Airlines routinely set booking limits that exceed the capacity of the aircraft in order to maximize revenue. The overbooking issue is discussed later in the chapter.

Leg-Based Expected Marginal Seat Revenue Model

One of the major methods used to determine the desired booking limits for a flight is the Expected Marginal Seat Revenue (EMSR) model. It was developed by Ken Littlewood (1972) to address a single-leg flight with multiple fare classes. Simply put, the EMSR equals the expected revenue contribution of one additional seat. In an EMSR model, the number of seats allocated to each fare class is determined by using historical fares and current and past booking figures. The EMSR of the ith seat sold is:

$$\text{EMSR}_i = f_i \times P(S_i)$$

EMSR is the product of the fare level, f_i, and the probability that there will be at least n passengers willing to buy "i" class tickets for the flight under consideration.[14]

Figure 8.12 provides the cumulative probability distribution for two unique fare classes. Since the underlying assumption is that the probability of booking is based on a normal distribution, the average probability of demand for each fare class is 50%. In both fare classes, there is close to a 100% probability that at least some seats (about 15 and 12, respectively) can be sold at the given fare classes, while it is unlikely that more than a certain number will be sold (about 25 and 50 seats, respectively).

Using the formula, the EMSR for every seat can be calculated by simply multiplying the ticket fare by the cumulative probability of demand for that seat. For instance, assuming that a ticket costs $500 and the cumulative probability of demand for that seat is 50% (or 0.5), the EMSR for that seat is $250. This formula is applied to every seat for every fare class, so that it is

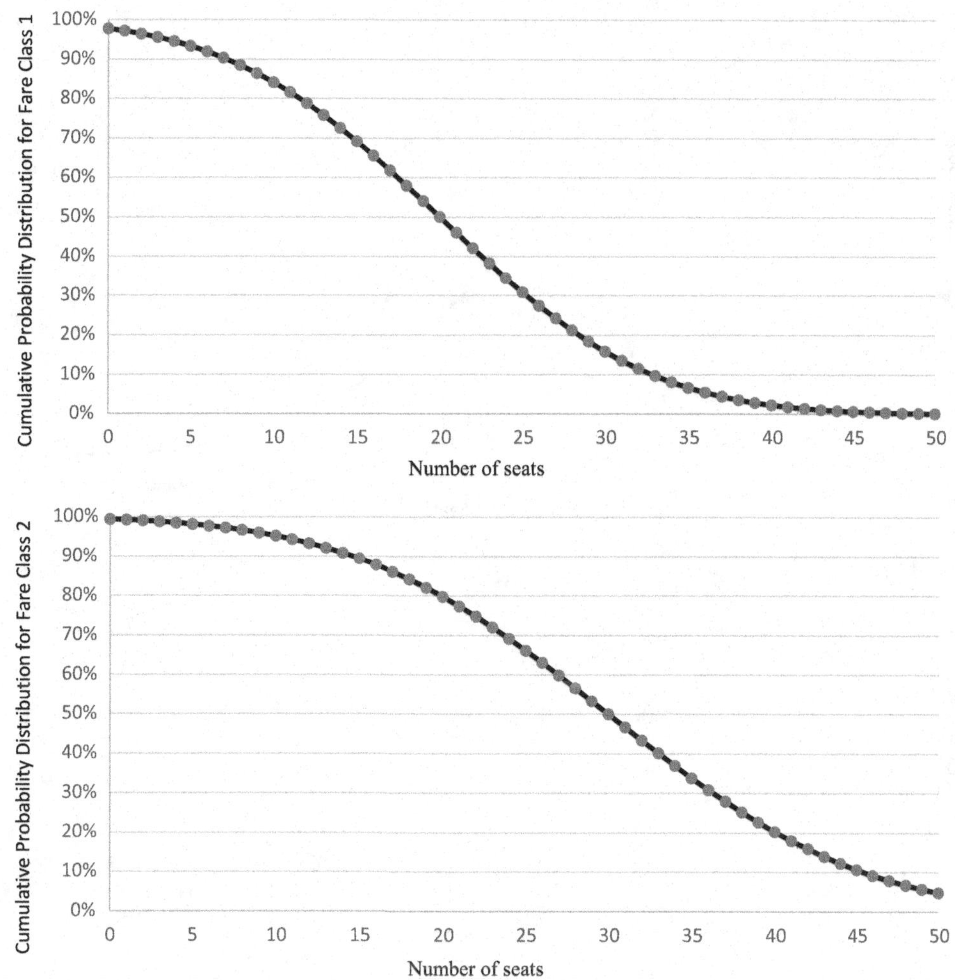

Figure 8.12 Cumulative Probability Distribution for Fare Classes 1 and 2.

now possible to graph the EMSR curve. This has been done for the two cumulative probability distributions that were presented above, assuming the fare in the first fare class is $500, and the fare in the second fare class is $400.

As exhibited in Figure 8.13, the EMSR curves for both fare classes are similar to the cumulative probability distributions, except that the vertical axis is no longer probabilities, but actual dollars. The average EMSR for fare class 1 occurs at $250 and roughly 20 seats, while in fare class 2, the average EMSR is $200 at 31 seats.

The final step in the analysis involves merging the two EMSR curves to determine the protection level and booking limits for the fare classes. In Figure 8.14, the two EMSR curves intersect at a point close to 19 seats. This point represents the protection level for fare class 1 over fare class 2. Assuming these are the only two fare classes for the flight, the booking limit for the higher-fare class would be the capacity of the aircraft. If all the seats can be sold at the highest fare, the airline would, of course, be happy with this outcome. However, for this example, the

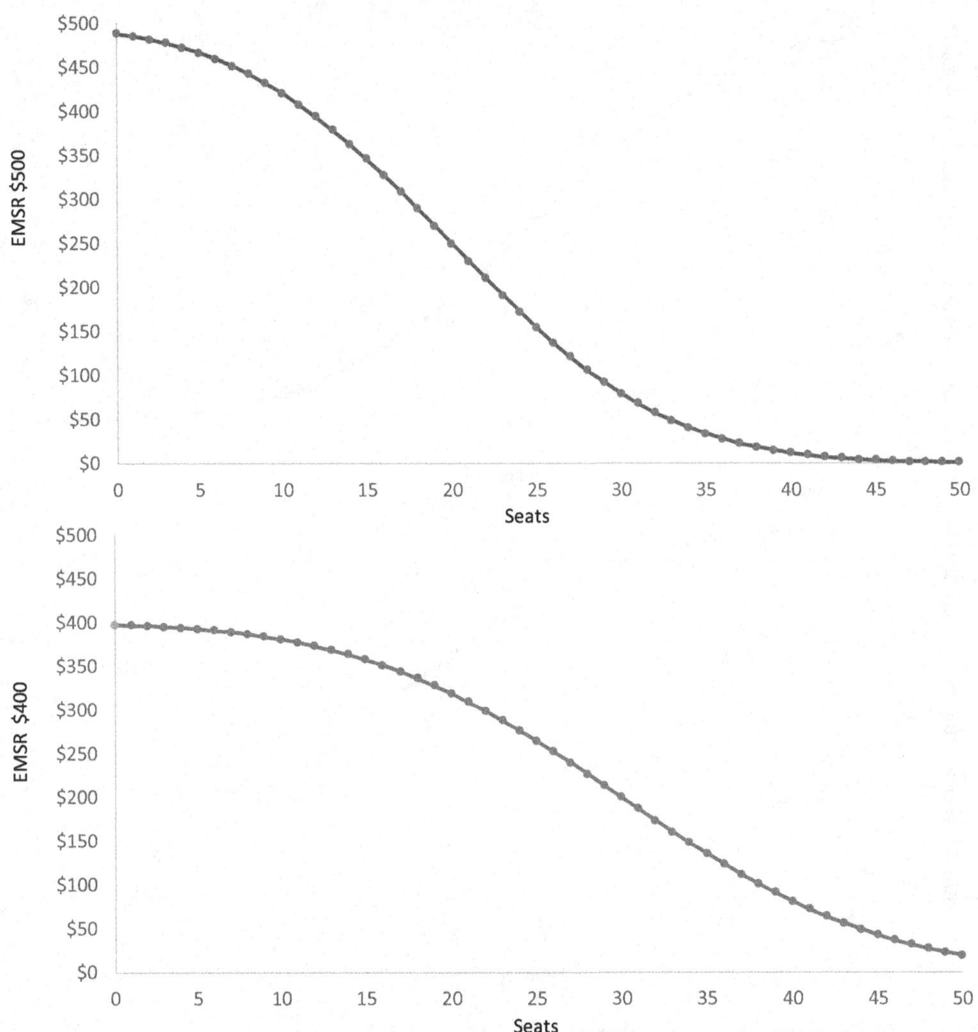

Figure 8.13 Expected Marginal Seat Revenue ($500 and $400).

actual protection level would be 19 seats for the first fare class. It is at this point that the expected revenue of the second class exceeds that of the first class. Thus, the airline should begin selling tickets in the second class. As Figure 8.14 clearly shows, this pattern should continue until all seats are sold, since the expected revenue of the second class exceeds that of the first class for the remaining seats.

The application of the EMSR to revenue management can be presented through the use of a decision tree, as shown in Figure 8.15. In essence, every seat has some probability of being booked, and an airline revenue management analyst must choose the option that provides the airline with the greatest expected seat revenue. Since demand is not deterministic, revenue management analysts must use probability to foresee the future and be able to reserve some number of seats for higher-paying customers. This protecting of seats is in addition to the "fences" described earlier.

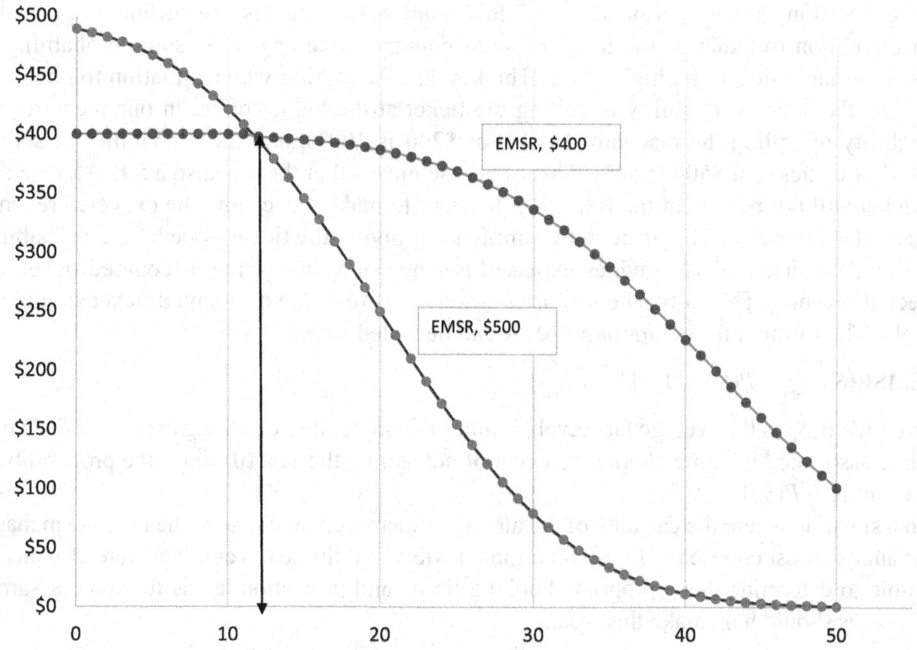

Figure 8.14 Optimal Booking Limit and Protection Level in Two Nested Fare Classes.

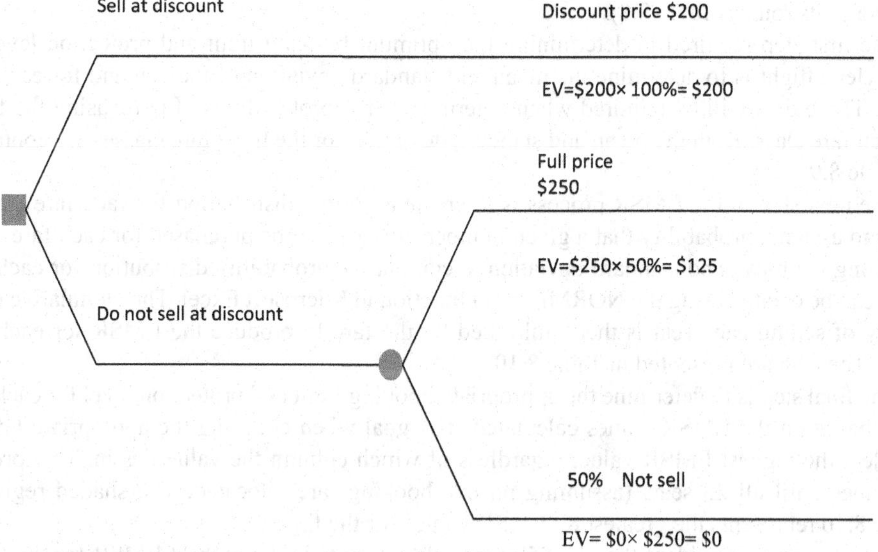

Figure 8.15 Decision Tree.

The decision tree scenario presented in Figure 8.15 assumes the airline is presented with the option to either sell a ticket at the discounted price or rest on some probability of selling the same ticket at a higher fare. The key in determining which situation to choose is based on the actual probability of selling the ticket at the higher price. In our scenario, the probability of selling the discounted ticket at $200 is 100%, and the probability of selling the full price ticket at $500 is 50%. This of course means that there is also a 50% chance that the ticket will not be sold at the full price. In order to make a decision, the expected revenue needs to be computed. This is done by simply multiplying the ticket price by the probability of selling the ticket. This provides expected revenue of $200 for the discounted ticket and expected revenue of $250 for the full price ticket; therefore, the discounted ticket should not be sold. The formula for computing EMSR can be stated as:

$$\text{EMSR}(S_i) = f_i \times P(S_i) + 0 \times [1 - P(S_i)]$$

where $\text{EMSR}(S_i)$ is the average fare level (f_i) times the probability of selling the ith seat $P(S_i)$ plus the fare associated with the alternative event of not selling the seat (0) times the probability of that event $[1 - P(S_i)]$.

In a situation where the capacity of the aircraft is increased by one seat, the revenue management analyst must choose the highest marginal EMSR that the seat would generate. A concrete example to determine the appropriate booking limits and protection levels for some assumed fare classes should help make this clear.

Example

Assume that DirectJet is a new airline that operates a 25-seat regional jet aircraft. The airline utilizes a nested three-tier fare structure ($250, $400, $500), and demand for all three fare classes is assumed to be normally distributed. The airline has historical demand data for the past 30 days for one of its routes (Table 8.8).

The first step required in determining the optimum booking limit and protection level for DirectJet's flight is to determine the mean and standard deviation of the demand for each fare class. These data will be required when determining the probabilities of purchasing the ticket in each fare class. Both the mean and standard deviation for the three fare classes are contained in Table 8.9.

The next step in the EMSR process is to create a normal distribution for each fare class in order to assign a probability that a given number of seats will be purchased for each fare class. Knowing the mean and standard deviation, a cumulative probability distribution for each fare class can be created using the NORMDIST() function in Microsoft Excel. The cumulative probability of selling each seat is then multiplied by the fare to produce the EMSR for each fare class. The data are presented in Table 8.10.

The final step is to determine the appropriate booking limit and protection level for each fare class based on the EMSR values calculated. The goal when choosing the appropriate level is to select the highest EMSR value, regardless of which column the value lies in. This process continues until all 25 seats (assuming no overbooking) are allocated. The shaded region of Table 8.10 represents the greatest 80 EMSR values for the flight.

In this case, it is evident that the $500 fare class results in the highest EMSR for the first 7 seats. Continuing down the table, we see the initial intersection point between the $500 fare EMSR and the $400 fare EMSR, occurring roughly between seats 7 and 8. Seats in the $400 fare class then have the highest EMSR, up to 13, whereupon the next highest EMSR once again belongs to the $500 fare class. As such, the next seat is once again allocated back to the $500

Table 8.8 Historical Demand for DirectJet's Three Fare Classes

Flight History (Day)	*$500 Fare*	*$400 Fare*	*$250 Fare*
1	10	13	30
2	8	17	20
3	12	20	25
4	14	10	25
5	6	12	20
6	10	18	30
7	11	15	25
8	9	14	30
9	10	16	27
10	13	12	23
11	7	12	23
12	4	18	27
13	8	18	26
14	14	15	22
15	15	14	22
16	13	14	25
17	12	16	25
18	11	16	23
19	9	18	25
20	7	12	24
21	7	15	25
22	12	16	25
23	8	14	22
24	11	13	23
25	10	17	22

Table 8.9 Mean and Standard Deviation

	$500 Fare	*$400 Fare*	*$250 Fare*
Mean	20	30	40
Standard deviation	2.76	2.47	2.75

fare class. Continuing on, the $400 fare now has the highest EMSR for the next six seats until the $300 fare takes over for 14. We then switch back and forth in sequence until all seats have been allocated among the fare classes.

For DirectJet, the appropriate protection levels for the flight would be 8 $500 fares (7 seats against $400 and 9 seat against $250), 17 $400 fares, and 0 $250 fares. The appropriate booking limits for each class would be 25 for the $500 fare, 13 for the $400 fares, and 4 for the $250 fares. These values are expressed in Table 8.11. As expected, the booking limit always includes the protection level for the class under consideration plus all classes below that class—another example of the fact that the airline is always prepared to sell all seats at a higher fare.

The EMSR curves can also be graphed, as displayed in Figure 8.16. Graphing provides a visual method of determining the protection level and booking limit for each fare class. Note that the points of intersection between the EMSR curves correspond to the values in Table 8.10 where the EMSR for one fare exceeds that of another. This is an example of serial nesting which, is also displayed in Figure 8.16.

The example of DirectJet highlights how booking limits and protection levels are determined in revenue management. Of course, airlines utilize many more fare classes, making the process

Table 8.10 Optimal Booking Limit for DirectJet's Three Fare Classes

Seat	*Probability*	*EMSR ($500)*	*Probability*	*EMSR ($400)*	*Probability*	*EMSR ($250)*
1	0.999444644	$499.72	0.999999993	$400.00	1	$300.00
2	0.998125542	$499.06	0.999999932	$400.00	1	$300.00
3	0.994397375	$497.20	0.999999431	$400.00	1	$300.00
4	0.985144167	$492.57	0.999995915	$400.00	1	$300.00
5	0.964975539	$482.49	0.999974949	$399.99	1	$300.00
6	0.926369651	$463.18	0.999868693	$399.95	1	$300.00
7	0.861471987	$430.74	0.99941093	$399.76	1	$300.00
8	0.765662832	$382.83	0.99773444	$399.09	1	$300.00
9	0.64144311	$320.72	0.992514711	$397.01	0.999999997	$300.00
10	0.5	$250.00	0.97869818	$391.48	0.999999975	$300.00
11	0.35855689	$179.28	0.947604751	$379.04	0.999999822	$300.00
12	0.234337168	$117.17	0.888111312	$355.24	0.999998862	$300.00
13	0.138528013	$69.26	0.791325781	$316.53	0.999993604	$300.00
14	0.073630349	$36.82	0.657450504	$262.98	0.999968329	$299.99
15	0.035024461	$17.51	0.5	$200.00	0.999861743	$299.96
16	0.014855833	$7.43	0.342549496	$137.02	0.999467424	$299.84
17	0.005602625	$2.80	0.208674219	$83.47	0.998187593	$299.46
18	0.001874458	$0.94	0.111888688	$44.76	0.994543221	$298.36
19	0.000555356	$0.28	0.052395249	$20.96	0.985438523	$295.63
20	0.000145497	$0.07	0.02130182	$8.52	0.965481826	$289.64
21	3.36681E-05	$0.02	0.007485289	$2.99	0.92710243	$278.13
22	6.87468E-06	$0.00	0.00226556	$0.91	0.862343557	$258.70
23	1.2377E-06	$0.00	0.00058907	$0.24	0.766470549	$229.94
24	1.96349E-07	$0.00	0.000131307	$0.05	0.641935216	$192.58
25	2.74316E-08	$0.00	2.50511E-05	$0.01	0.5	$150.00
26	3.37354E-09	$0.00	4.08529E-06	$0.00	0.358064784	$107.42
27	3.65059E-10	$0.00	5.68879E-07	$0.00	0.233529451	$70.06
28	3.47484E-11	$0.00	6.75848E-08	$0.00	0.137656443	$41.30
29	2.90856E-12	$0.00	6.84547E-09	$0.00	0.07289757	$21.87
30	2.14051E-13	$0.00	5.90784E-10	$0.00	0.034518174	$10.36
31	1.38778E-14	$0.00	4.34224E-11	$0.00	0.014561477	$4.37
32	1.39E-15	$0.00	4.34224E-11	$0.00	0.014561991	$3.64
33	1.69E-15	$0.00	4.34224E-11	$0.00	0.015561477	$3.89

all the more complicated. Nonetheless, the principles are exactly the same. The one glaring omission from the DirectJet example is the presence of overbooking. This is a real issue revenue management analysts face and is usually taken into account when setting the appropriate protection levels for a flight. Overbooking is explored in the next section where the DirectJet example is expanded.

Overbooking

Overbooking is the practice of selling more tickets on the plane than there are seats. Many airlines routinely overbook their flights so as to fill their planes even if there are last-minute cancellations.

Bumping is a practice of denying seats to passengers with confirmed tickets for an overbooked flight. Getting bumped from a given flight could be voluntarily or involuntarily.

The disturbing incident happened in United Airlines flight 3411 in 2017. A passenger was forcibly dragged off overbooked flight after refusing to give up seat.

Table 8.11 Optimal Booking Limit and Protection Level in Three Nested Fare Classes

Fare	*$500*	*$400*	*$250*
Protection level (PL)	8	17	0
Booking limit	25	13	4

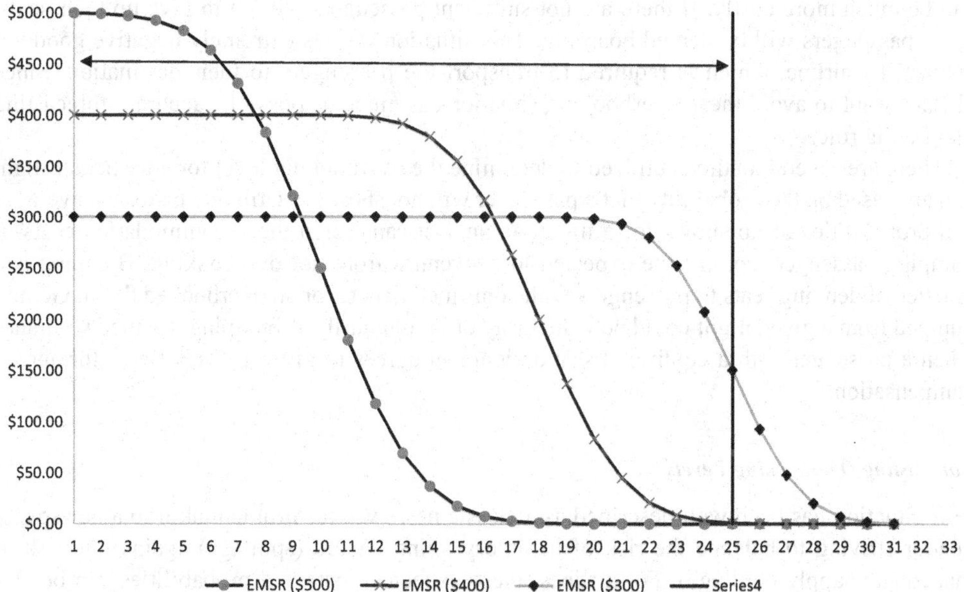

Figure 8.16 Optimal Booking Limit and Protection Level in Three Nested Fare Classes.

Overbooking is practiced by airlines to combat spoilage, since invariably some passengers miss flights or connections, especially when departing from hubs. While overbooking may cause headaches for a few passengers, the benefits to the airline include increased seat availability, more access to the flight of first choice, and the reduced overall cost of travel through more efficient use of airline seats (Dunleavy, 1995). Additionally, overbooking is practiced in other industries such as car rentals and hotels (Netessine and Shumsky, 2002).

Airlines are able to predict to some degree the "no-show" level, or percentage of passengers who will fail to show for the flight, based on the probabilistic nature of the situation. Additionally, passengers themselves have differing patterns of not showing up for a flight. Typically, business passengers have a higher probability of missing their flight than do leisure passengers. Therefore, it is not surprising that flights to leisure markets have lower authorization levels for overbooking than flights to business-heavy markets. Additionally, revenue managers must also take into consideration the probability of passengers canceling itineraries close to departure, misconnecting, or showing up for a flight without a confirmed reservations. These ticket issues are coined "go-show" in the airline industry (Dunleavy, 1995).

While the benefits of overbooking for the airline is reducing spoilage and increasing potential revenue, the tradeoff is that overbooking can be costly. Costs include meal and hotel vouchers, flight coupons for future flights, departure delays, passengers being rolled over to other flights, staffing issues, and loss of goodwill. The amounts vary from flight to flight. For instance, costs associated with a daily (or less frequent) international flight are invariably higher than a short-haul flight where the airline offers ten daily flights.

In a situation where more passengers show up for a flight than there are seats, the airline will ask for volunteers to give up a seat. In order to entice passengers to do so, the airline will usually offer some form of compensation package that may include future travel discounts, meal vouchers, hotel accommodation, or first-class upgrades. Ideally, airlines want to solve their overbooking problem by asking for volunteers, as the next step, involuntary denied boarding, can be much more costly. If there are not sufficient passengers willing to give up their seats, some passengers will be denied boarding. This situation creates extremely negative goodwill against the airline, which is required to transport the passengers to their destination. Since airlines want to avoid these overbooking situations as much as possible, accurate forecasting plays a big role.

There are several methods utilized to determine the overbooking level for a particular flight and are based on the probability that a passenger will not show up. Utilizing historical averages and probabilities of no-shows for a flight, an analyst can weigh the accommodation costs of bumping passengers against the expected lost revenues from not overbooking. Bumping is a practice of denying seats to passengers with confirmed tickets for an overbooked flight. Getting bumped from a given flight could be voluntarily or involuntarily. A bumping is called voluntary when a passenger with a confirmed seat assignment agrees to give up his/her seat for agreed compensation.

Forecasting Overbooking Levels

This situation has been well described as a classic news vendor problem akin to a newspaper vendor striving to balance the risk of inventory going unsold (spoilage) against the risk of inadequate supply (spillage). For airlines, these expected costs and probabilities can be manipulated to calculate the optimal number of seats to overbook. The following ratio of these expected costs offers the probability that the opportunity cost of underselling is equal to the cost of overbooking. The optimal overbooking level corresponds to the smallest value of Q such that[15]:

$$\Pr(Q \leq X) = \frac{C_U}{C_U + C_O}$$

where:

- C_U = opportunity cost of flying an empty seat
- C_o = Negative goodwill and penalties of denying a passenger boarding
- Q = actual number of seats overbooked
- X = optimum number of seats to overbook

The probability determined from this ratio can then be expressed as a z-score which takes the probability percentage and translates it into terms of standard deviations under the area of a normal distribution. Along with the historical mean and standard deviation from the sample, the resulting z-score can then be substituted into the following equation to determine the optimal overbooking limit.

$$Q_{\text{overbooking}} = \mu + Z \times \sigma$$

Excel functions can also be used as demonstrated in this next example. Suppose that DirectJet has been able to determine the following data for one of its flights: the average number of no-shows for the flight is normally distributed with a mean of five and a standard deviation of three. Moreover, DirectJet estimates that it costs $200 to "bump" a passenger (the airline receives no revenue from the passenger and $200 is the cost of accommodating the passenger for his/her next flight). If the seat is not sold then the airline loses revenue equal to the price of a ticket at the discounted rate. In this example, the lowest discounted air fare is $80.

- Standard Deviation, σ 3
- Mean, μ 5
- Overbooking Cost, C $200
- Under booking Cost, B $80

Applying the formula previously identified to DirectJet's analysis, the corresponding optimum number of seats to overbook can be determined.

$$\Pr(Q \geq X) = \frac{80}{80+200} = 0.2857$$

From the normal distribution table (or using the NORMSINV() function in Excel) the z-score associated with a probability of 0.2857 is approximately −0.566. Plugging the z-score into the second equation yields an optimal overbooking limit of 3.30. Rounding down, we determine that the number of seats to be overbooked is three.

$$Q_{\text{overbooking}} = 5 + -0.566 \times 3 = 3.30$$

The other, and simpler option, is to use the NORMINV() function in Microsoft Excel (Netessine and Shumsky, 2002) which returns the value of seats to be overbooked after the probability, mean, and standard deviation are input. For the above scenario, the NORMINV() function would be as follows:

= NORMINV (probability, mean, standard deviation)
= NORMINV (0.2857, 5, 3)
= 3.302

Regardless of the method utilized, the optimum number of seats for DirectJet to overbook is equal to three. This solution computes the tradeoff between overbooking passengers and the additional revenue that would be generated against the costs associated with overbooking. We can also determine the additional revenue that overbooking would generate. Overbooking by three additional seats would generate additional revenue of $240 (fare × number of seats). The following figures illustrate the overbooking costs and spoilage costs as the number of aircraft seats sold increases (aircraft capacity is 150 seats). Figure 8.18 shows the overbooking costs as the number of seats sold begins to exceed the capacity of the aircraft. The spoilage costs in Figure 8.17 reflect the opportunity cost associated with not selling an aircraft seat; the fewer the seats sold, the higher the costs.

Figure 8.19 combines the previously mentioned two figures to show that the minimum difference in costs is obtained for three seats, which, according to the previous calculation, represents the optimum number of seats to be overbooked.

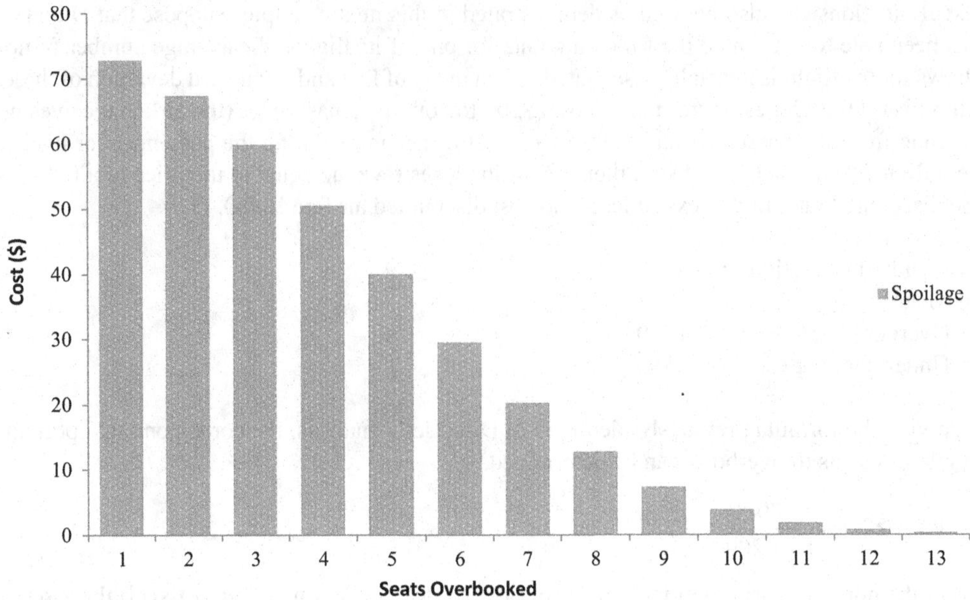

Figure 8.17 Spoilage Costs.

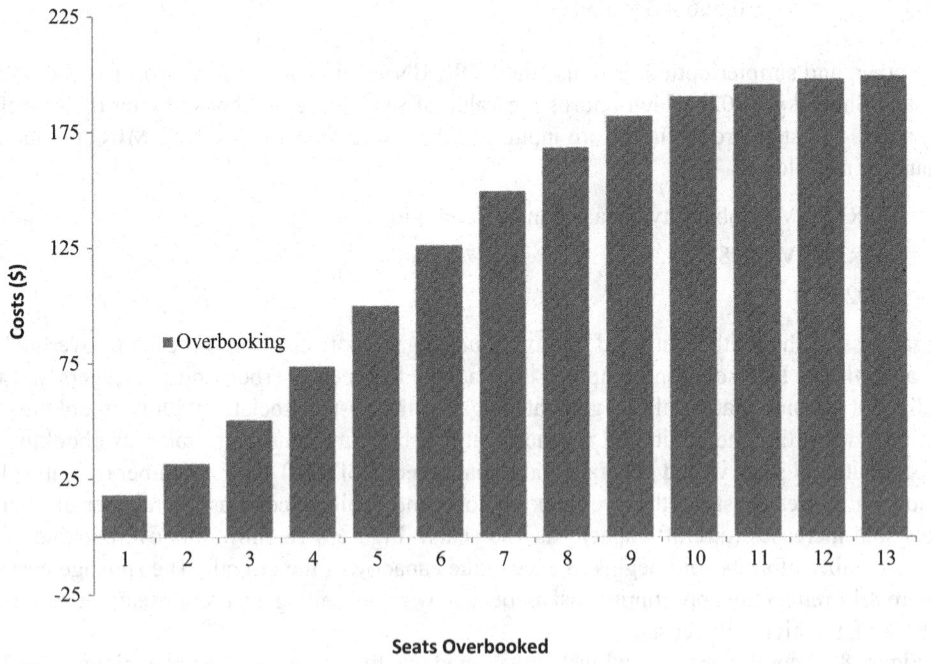

Figure 8.18 Overbooking Costs.

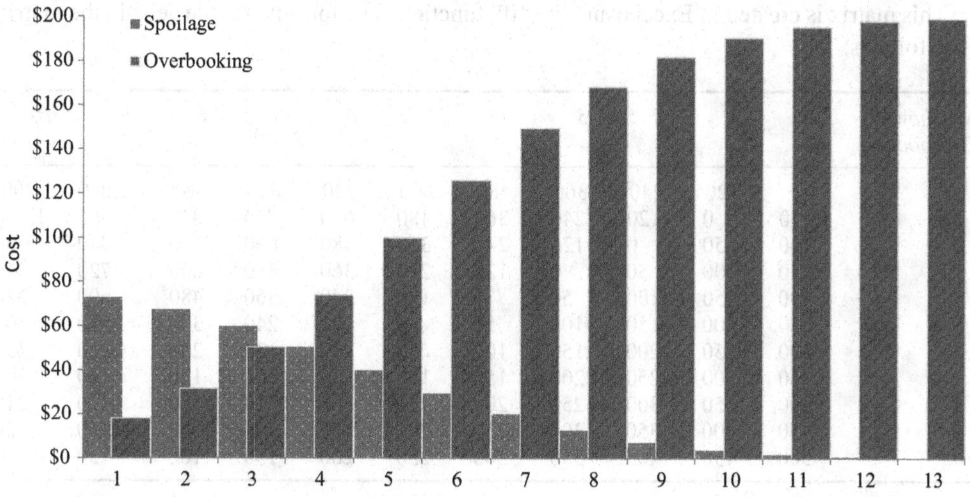

Figure 8.19 Combined Overbooking and Spoilage Costs.

Example

Consider an example where the historical probabilities for a set number of no-shows are provided, as in the given table:

Number of No Shows	*Probability*
0	0.05
1	0.1
2	0.2
3	0.15
4	0.15
5	0.1
6	0.05
7	0.05
8	0.05
9	0.05
10	0.05

In this scenario, the cost of overbooking is given to be $120 and the cost of no-shows is given to be $50. What would be the optimal overbooking level?

Since the normal distribution is not provided for the probability of no-shows, a slightly different approach must be followed to determine the optimal overbooking level. A cost matrix can be created, combining the cost of overbooking with the cost of no-shows. The minimum cost of overbooking among the number of overbookings possible is chosen as the optimal level. The matrix is formed as follows:

This matrix is created in Excel using the "if" function. The formula for the cells in the matrix is as follows:

No-Shows/ Overbooking	*0*	*1*	*2*	*3*	*4*	*5*	*6*	*7*	*8*	*9*	*10*
0	0	120	240	360	480	600	720	840	960	1,080	1,200
1	50	0	120	240	360	480	600	720	840	960	1,080
2	100	50	0	120	240	360	480	600	720	840	960
3	150	100	50	0	120	240	360	480	600	720	840
4	200	150	100	50	0	120	240	360	480	600	720
5	250	200	150	100	50	0	120	240	360	480	600
6	300	250	200	150	100	50	0	120	240	360	480
7	350	300	250	200	150	100	50	0	120	240	360
8	400	350	300	250	200	150	100	50	0	120	240
9	450	400	350	300	250	200	150	100	50	0	120
10	500	450	400	350	300	250	200	150	100	50	0

= IF (No. of overbooking) > No. of no-shows
(No. of OB – No. of NS) × Cost of overbooking,
(No. of NS – No. of OB) × Cost of no-shows

For example, for 4 No-Shows and 6 Overbookings, the cost is calculated as:

= ($6 – $4) × 120

= $240

To determine the total expected cost of each possible number of overbookings, a sum product of the probabilities of no-shows and the cost of no-shows for a given overbooking number is found. For example, the calculation for one overbooked seat is shown below.

The expected cost for all possible number of overbooked seats is as follows:

Since the least cost is obtained for two seats overbooked, the optimal overbooking level is two seats.

No-Shows/ Overbooking	*0*	*1*	*2*	*3*	*4*	*5*	*6*	*7*	*8*	*9*	*10*
0	0	120	240	360	480	600	720	840	960	1,080	1,200
1	50	0	120	240	360	480	600	720	840	960	1,080
2	100	50	0	120	240	360	480	600	720	840	960
3	150	100	50	0	120	240	360	480	600	720	840
4	200	150	100	50	0	120	240	360	480	600	720
5	250	200	150	100	50	0	120	240	360	480	600
6	300	250	200	150	100	50	0	120	240	360	480
7	350	300	250	200	150	100	50	0	120	240	360
8	400	350	300	250	200	150	100	50	0	120	240
9	450	400	350	300	250	200	150	100	50	0	120
10	500	450	400	350	300	250	200	150	100	50	0
Expected cost	202.5	161.0	**136.5**	146.0	181.0	241.5	319.0	405.0	499.5	602.5	714.0

FILE HOME INSERT PAGE LAYOUT FORMULAS

Paste B I U 11 A A

Clipboard Font Alig

	A	B	C
1	No of No shows	Probability	Cost of Overbooking 1 seat
2	0	0.05	120
3	1	0.1	0
4	2	0.2	50
5	3	0.15	100
6	4	0.15	150
7	5	0.1	200
8	6	0.05	250
9	7	0.05	300
10	8	0.05	350
11	9	0.05	400
12	10	0.05	450
13			
14		Total Cost	=SUMPRODUCT(B2:B12,C2:C12)

	A	B	C
1	No of No shows	Probability	Cost of Overbooking 1 seat
2	0	0.05	120
3	1	0.1	0
4	2	0.2	50
5	3	0.15	100
6	4	0.15	150
7	5	0.1	200
8	6	0.05	250
9	7	0.05	300
10	8	0.05	350
11	9	0.05	400
12	10	0.05	450
13			
14		Total Cost	161

Other Issues Associated with Revenue Management

Since its first introduction by American Airlines in 1985, revenue management has become more complex to better minimize consumer surplus. While current revenue management practices have been effective in enhancing airlines' profits, revenue management is still largely based on historical, probabilistic demand. While this is not an ideal situation, it is arguably the best way to forecast demand for revenue management purposes. Additionally, the creation of fare classes is done by grouping customers together based on their price elasticity, but even with multiple fare classes, customers are still going to be grouped into classes that they may not be part of. This can increase consumer surplus, which reduces revenue for the airline.

A potential solution to both of these problems is dynamic pricing, with which seats are priced based on existing (ongoing) passenger demand and other factors, such as competitors' revenue management strategy (Burger and Fuchs, 2005). In essence, dynamic pricing is timelier since it allows a carrier to more closely match its normal booking curve. It allows the airline to change fares based on whether ongoing bookings are above or below the normal booking curve before the actual takeoff time. A few airlines, mostly LLCs, have implemented dynamic pricing into their revenue management models.

Another recent trend in airline revenue management that began with LLCs is to reduce the complexity of fare structures. Instead of having a seemingly infinite number of booking classes and fares for a particular flight, airlines are reducing the number of booking classes for marketing reasons. To curb customer confusion about different booking classes and restrictions, airlines like Delta and Air Canada have introduced simplified fare structures. These new structures, termed restriction-free pricing, compel revenue management to employ a form of "weak" market segmentation through active management of fare availability, as opposed to "strong" market segmentation, such as fences (Ratliff and Vinod, 2005). It remains to be seen whether or not the increase in consumer surplus from simpler fare structures can be offset by any incremental increase in bookings. Additionally, the move by legacy carriers to allow one-way tickets has added further complexities to revenue management systems.

Revenue management is one of the most important business units in an airline organization, Department analysts, more than almost any other employee, directly impact the company's bottom line on a daily basis. Ever since the theory was introduced by American Airlines, it has been a key tool for maximizing profits.

Summary

The primary objective of dynamic pricing policy and revenue management is selling the same product to the right customer at the right time for the right price to maximize revenue. Dynamic pricing is a common practice in several industries such as airline industry, tourism, entertainment, retail, electricity, and public transport. This chapter covers the topics of pricing policy and revenue management. Various pricing models are discussed, and the crucial underlying assumptions of price discrimination are explained together with the conditions necessary to implement a policy. A quantitative example is presented to show how price discrimination can be used to increase revenues and sales. We also discuss how to use price discrimination for revenue management. The topics of spoilage and spillage are explained with a graphical presentation, while the more sophisticated EMSR model is explored using concrete quantitative examples and graphs to show nesting fare structures and the probabilistic normal booking curve. We also introduce dynamic pricing and further explain seat allocation using appropriate protection and booking levels for the example classes. Finally, the important topic of overbooking is covered with a numerical example showing how an overbooking amount can be determined in practice.

Discussion Questions

1 Define peak-load pricing and provide at least two examples.
2 Explain markup pricing and why it may not be a good tool to apply in the airline industry.
3 If a Fixed Based Operator (FBO) charges $5 per gallon for jet fuel with a marginal cost of $4, what is the markup on cost? When $Ep = -2$, the optimal markup on cost is:

4 What is meant by the terms "reservation price" and "consumer surplus" and how are these concepts related to price discrimination?

5 A major hotel offers 20% discounts for renting a room for more than three days. Therefore, in this case, the price paid by a traveler will be much lower than that of another traveler who stays less than three days. Is this an example of price discrimination? Why or why not?

6 How do airlines use price discrimination to maximize revenue based on elasticity of demand?

7 Calculate the optimal markup on cost for each service, based on the following estimates of point price elasticity of demand:

Passenger Type	*Cost*	*Elasticity*
First Class	\$400	−1.25
Business Travelers	350	−1.1
Leisure	150	−3.5
Holiday	150	−2.5

8 Why is price discrimination more widely used in service industries than in product industries?

9 What is the main issue with average cost pricing?

10 What is the basic idea behind EMSR models?

11 How are seats allocated using the EMSR model?

12 What are the merits of using peak-load pricing at commercial airports?

13 The demand function for a given company is given as:

$P = 100 - Q^2$

where P is the price per unit and Q is the quantity demanded. Find the consumer surplus if the company charges $P = \$75$.

14 Can every firm with monopoly power discriminate?

15 List three revenue management fences that airlines typically use to practice price discrimination and briefly explain how each one works.

16 Discuss the advantages and disadvantages of price discrimination for airlines and passengers.

17 Suppose that DirectJet Airlines has divided their passengers into economy class and business class. The price elasticity of demand for the business class is −1.5, and for the economy class is −3. If the marginal cost of a seat on a flight from London to Paris is EUR 150, what are the optimal prices for each group?

18 List the conditions that are needed for successful price discrimination.

19 Explain how the Expected Marginal Seat Revenue model is constructed and what assumptions are used to build the model.

20 Airlines generally charge lower fares to travelers willing to purchase tickets well ahead of time. Explain what assumptions the airlines are making when they engage in this type of pricing.

21 From time to time, when purchasing certain items such as jewelry, the salesperson will ask the customer what price the customer has in mind. What do you suppose is the purpose of this question?

22 Assume that the probability of selling a seat in first class is 50% and the fare for that class is \$500. The probability of selling tickets in the next class is 90%, and the fare is \$300. The

probability of selling the ticket in the final class is 100% at a fair of $220. Where should the seat be allocated and why?

23 Define spillage and spoilage as they are used in the airline industry and what steps might an airline take to avoid either of these problems.

24 DirectJet has a daily flight between two regional airports. Historical data shows on the average 12% of ticketed passengers fail to show up for their flight. Assume that DirectJet consistently sells 50 tickets for this route. Calculate the average number of passengers on each fight if the aircraft has capacity for 45 passengers.

25 MyJet Airlines provides daily services between London and Rome with a 300 seater A320 aircraft. Assume that the airline charges an average of $450 per seat and the number of passengers who reserve a seat but do not show up for departure is normally distributed with mean 40 and standard deviation 15. Calculate the maximum number of booking in this market if the cost of overbooking is $800.

MINI Case:

DirectJet (DJ), Inc. is an ultra-low-cost carrier headquartered in Pittsburg, Pennsylvania, which operates scheduled services throughout the United States as well as the Caribbean, Mexico, and Latin America. Founded in 1993, DJ first began service on October 26 of the same year. DirectJet employs over 1,600 people including more than 900 cabin crew and some 400 pilots, and operates an Airbus fleet of over 40 aircraft.

DJ runs daily flights from Boston to San Francisco, facing a fixed cost of $75,000 for each flight (basically independent of the actual number of passengers). The planes offer 200 seats available on its planes. One-way tickets generate revenues of $600 a piece when used; however, they are fully refundable if not used. On the typical Thursday flight, the number of no-show falls within the range of 5–75, with all intermediate values are equally likely. DJ overbooks its flights, but must give compensation of $250 to all ticketed passengers who are not allowed to board, and must provide those passengers with alternative transportation on another carrier (the cost of providing the alternative transportation just wipes out the $600 revenue).

How many tickets should DJ be willing to sell for the Thursday flight?

Mini Case 2:

MyJet is a regional airline providing shuttle service between Inchon International Airport (ICN) and Jeju International Airport (CJU). As a new revenue management analyst, you should attempt to determine the appropriate number of seats to allocate between 3 fare classes on a 50-seat aircraft. As a first step in your analysis, you collected data for the flight over the last 30 days. This information is provided in the following table. Demand for all fare classes is estimated to be normally distributed.

Questions:

a In the past, DirectJet used a uniform pricing. If all of the seats were priced at $150, what was the expected total revenue?

b The airline has decided to hire a revenue management team and to use a different pricing system. How is the new strategy going to impact the profitability?

c Calculate and graph EMSR for each group of airfare, and then by using the Expected Marginal Revenue approach with a nested model, determine the appropriate number of seats to allocate to each fare class.

d Calculate the protection level and the booking limit for each fare classes.

e The airline has found that the number of people who purchased tickets and did not show up for a flight is normally distributed with a mean of 20 and a standard deviation of 10.

The airline estimates that the penalty costs associated with not being able to board a passenger holding confirmed reservation are estimated to be $600. Assume that the opportunity cost of flying an empty seat is $100 (price that discount passenger would pay). How much should airline overbook the flight?

f What recommendations would you give to the airline to improve its pricing?

Appendix: Derivation of Overbooking Probability Equation

The expected payoff of overbooking, assuming the following:

- For each ticket sold as an overbooking, there is an incremental profit of $80.
- For each bumped passenger, there is an incremental loss of $200.
- A historical no-show mean of 5 with a standard deviation of 3.

The incremental profits associated with selling *X* overbooked seats if the quantity demanded (*Q*) is *greater than or equal* to *X* is:

$$\pi_{\text{Incr}}\cdot = IP_s X = 80X$$

The incremental profits associated with selling X overbooked seats if the quantity demanded (Q) is *less* than X is:

$$\pi_{\text{Incr}}\cdot = IP_s Q - IC\pi(X - Q)$$

$$\pi_{\text{Incr}}\cdot = 800Q - 200(X - Q)$$

Expected incremental profit of selling *X* overbooked seats is:

$$\text{E}_{\Pi\text{Incr}}\cdot = Pr(Q \geq X) \cdot 80X + (1 - Pr(Q \geq X)) \cdot (80Q - 200(X - Q))$$

To determine the optimal number of high-fare tickets to hold, take the derivative with respect to *X* and set it equal to zero:

$$E_{\Pi\text{Incr}}\cdot = 80X \cdot Pr(Q \geq X) - 200 \cdot (1 - Pr(Q \geq X)) = 0$$

$$\Rightarrow 80\text{X}\ \Pr\left(\text{Q} \geq \text{X}\right) = 200 - 200\left(\Pr\left(\text{Q–X}\right)\right)$$

$$\Rightarrow \Pr\left(\text{Q} \geq \text{X}\right) = \frac{80}{80 + 200} = 0.2857$$

This probability can then be translated into a z-score, multiplied by the standard deviation, and added to the mean in order to calculate optimal overbooking as shown in the text.

Notes

1 Civil Aeronautics Act of 1938, P.L. 75-706, 52 Stat. 973. Approved 1938-06-23.
2 AirCal was a California-based airline and was eventually bought out by American Airlines.
3 *Business Week*, Airline Deregulation, Revisited, January 20, 2000.
4 Spirit Airlines: www.spirit.com
5 Consumption of these services is high during peak periods and lower in off-peak periods.
6 The bidding website for Iberia is https://subastas.iberia.com/.
7 Beyond Q', MC is greater than the price that could be charged so that segment of demand will not be serviced.

8 People Express was a low-cost airline that operated in the United States from 1981 to 1987. People Express offered a single class of service with no assigned seating and no in-flight meals or amenities.
9 The area within Triangle ABC in Figure 8.4.
10 Consumer surplus = 0.5(20 × 50) + 0.5(20 × 50) + 0.5(20 × 50) + 0.5(20 × 50) = $2,000.
11 People Express to Begin New York-Brussels Flight with $99 Introductory Fare. Associated Press. August 2, 1985.
12 Additional fences include the minimum stay rule and one-way fares that are priced higher than round-trip fares. To overcome these restrictions, a passenger could purchase a discounted round trip ticket and use only the outbound leg.
13 If there is no overbooking.
14 The probability for a passenger's willingness to buy is assumed to be a normal distribution. Values for a cumulative normal distribution can be calculated by using the "NORMDIST()" function in Microsoft Excel or similar functions in other spreadsheet packages.
15 The derivation of this formula can be found in the Appendix.

References

Airline Weekly. (2015, February). *Ancillary Revenue: It's Not Non-Core Anymore*. Retrieved on March 23, 2011 from http://www.airlineweekly.com/AWSR1.pdf.

Baumol, J. and Bradford, F. (1970). Optimal Departures from Marginal Cost Pricing. *American Economic Review*, 60(3), 265–283.

Brown, A. (1987). *The Politics of Airline Deregulation*. Knoxville: University of Tennessee Press.

Burger, B. and Fuchs, M. (2005). Dynamic Pricing—A Future Airline Business Model. *Journal of Revenue and Pricing Management*, 4(1), 39–53.

Cross, G. (1995). An Introduction to Revenue Management, in Jenkins, D. (Ed.), *Handbook of Airline Economics*. New York: McGraw-Hill, pp. 443–458.

Dunleavy, N. (1995). Airline Passenger Overbooking, in Jenkins, D. (Ed.), *Handbook of Airline Economics*. New York: McGraw-Hill, pp. 469–476.

The Economist (2004, December 29). Unbundled. Retrieved on April 2006 from http://www.economist.com/node/3523035.

Ewers, H.J. (2001). *Possibilities for the Better Use of Airport Slots in Germany and in the EU – A Practical Approach*. Berlin: Wirtschafts and Infrastruktur Politik.

Frank, R. (1983). When Are Price Differentials Discriminatory? *Journal of Policy Analysis and Management*, 2(2), 238–255.

Littlewood, K. (1972). Forecasting and Control of Passenger Bookings. *12th AGIFORS Symposium Proceedings*, Nathanya, Israel, pp. 103–105.

Littlewood, K. (2005). Forecasting and Control of Passenger Bookings. *Journal of Revenue and Pricing Management*, 4(2), 111–123. (Note: Originally written in 1972.)

Netessine, S. and Shumsky, R. (2002). Introduction to the Theory and Practice of Revenue Management. *INFORMS Transactions on Education*, 3(1), 34–44.

Ovans, A. (1997). Make a Bundle Bundling. *Harvard Business Review*, 75(6), 18–20.

Ratliff, R. and Vinod, B. (2005). Airline Pricing and Revenue Management: A Future Outlook. *Journal of Revenue and Pricing Management*, 4(3), 302–307.

Spiller, T. (1981). The Differential Impact of Airline Regulation on Industry, Firms, and Market. *Journal of Law and Economics*, 26(3), 655–689.

Vinod, B. (1995). Origin-and-Destination Revenue Management, in Jenkins, D. (Ed.), *Handbook of Airline Economics*. New York: McGraw-Hill, pp. 459–468.

Washington Post (2000). US v. Microsoft Timeline. Retrieved on November 12, 2011 from http://www.washingtonpost.com/wp-srv/business/longterm/microsoft/timeline.htm.

Yapta for Business (2016). *Airfare and Hotel Rate Volatility: Dynamic Pricing in the Corporate Travel Market*. Inside The Travel Industry White Paper, July 2016.

9 Ultra-Low-Cost and Low-Cost Airlines
Paradigm Shifts

Low-cost airlines have been around since the 1970s, with the first one being Southwest Airlines in the United States. Another example of successful low-cost airlines in the United States is the People Express Airlines. Ryanair and easyJet were the first airlines that followed the low-cost carrier model of Southwest in the United States. Founded in 1984, Ryanair did not become a low-cost carrier until the mid-1990s. Low-cost carriers (LCC) have transformed the traditional airline business model and have significantly changed the competitive nature of the industry. LCCs specialize in providing point-to-point services, eliminating the costs and complications of mainline airlines operating hub-and-spoke networks, connecting passengers through large hub airports, and mostly use smaller secondary airports that are often closer to the city served. The secondary airports are usually less crowded and easier to access from downtowns. Moreover, these airports are cheaper to rent gates and operate. The growth of LCC carriers has been aggressive in Europe, Asia, Latin America, and North America, carving out a significant proportion of market share. The emergence of the LCCs in Europe is mainly attributed to liberalization and deregulations in the air transport sector which encouraged the creation of new airlines. Airline Deregulation and Liberalization has shifted control over air travel from the government to the private sector. In the United States (1967), Herb Kelleher, Rollin King, and Lamar Muse examined what Pacific Southwest Airline (PSA) was doing and believed it could work within the state of Texas. Major airlines protested and fought the potential upstart, spending nearly three years in court before earning Southwest the right to fly.[1] On June 18, 1971, Southwest took its inaugural flight. While there have been many failures in the low-cost sector, there has also been tremendous success. It must be pointed out that many of the failures did not retain the major characteristics of LCCs. Thus, many defunct carriers were not truly cost leaders. The clear message is that the successful LCCs had focused solely on reducing costs and being efficient. Throughout history, air travel has been a highly regulated industry. Even where private companies operated airlines, government regulation was so pervasive that it defined the industry. An airline that sees all its prices and routes set by politicians and their appointed bureaucrats is in no meaningful sense "private." These quasi-government legacy airlines were anything but low cost, having no incentive to be so since government price controls were based on a cost-plus formula. In such a distorted environment, unusually powerful labor unions developed among the legacy carriers. Although far less powerful than they once were, these organizations continue to influence industry today. The advent of deregulation finally opened the door to operations by truly private airlines, and the age of the low-cost carriers (LCCs) began. Airlines such as Laker Airways and People Express were among the wave of budget airlines that emerged following deregulation. Moreover, after a period of stabilization, a subsequent wave of LCCs emerged. Europe's experience of low-cost scheduled operators began in 1991, when Irish carrier Ryanair

DOI: 10.4324/9781003388135-9

transformed itself from a conventional regional airline into a carbon copy of the US low-cost pioneer Southwest Airlines.

Allegiant, Frontier Airlines, and Spirit Airlines pioneered a new business model that now represents a new category of airline known as the Ultra-Low-Cost Carrier (ULCC). This innovation has paved the way for other Ultra-Low-Cost Airlines worldwide. Notable names include VivaAerobus, Volaris, Sun Country, easyJet, Norwegian Air, Ryanair, Vueling and Air Asia/Air Asia X. AirAsia X is the long-haul subsidiary of Malaysia's low-cost mega airline AirAsia. The airline's fleet of Airbus A330-300 jets are equipped with both premium and economy cabins.

Essentially, ULCCs focus on bare-bone fares and unbundle nearly every element of their product.[2] While full-service carriers usually offer cabin amenities such as in-flight entertainment, drinks or meals, free carry-on bag, free checked bag, or snacks, ULCCs offer none of these.

To keep their cost structure low, these airlines charge fees for everything from carry-on baggage and in-flight beverages to seat selection and ticket printing.

ULCCs are becoming key players in the commercial market, bringing heavy competition to both LCCs and full-service carriers. In this chapter, as outlined here, we will discuss the evolution of the low-cost business model and how it impacts the industry today.

- Introduction
- Evolution of Low-Cost Business Model
- Characteristics of Low-Cost Carriers
- Cost Structure Comparison
- Incumbent Carriers' Response to Low-Cost Carriers
- Ultra-Low-Cost Carriers
- Summary
- Discussion Questions
- Appendix: Select Airline Two-Letter Codes

Introduction

Air travel was a relatively luxurious event until the late 1970s. However, with the imminent emergence of low-cost carriers due to deregulation, legacy carriers had some obvious competitive advantages: elevated service standards, well recognized brand names, and massive initial market shares. These legacy airlines had dominance with business travelers who were somewhat less sensitive to price. Nonetheless, legacy airlines had a swollen cost structure driven by all the inefficiencies of their past quasi-government state. Most significantly, the legacy carriers found themselves with militant labor unions that often pushed for inefficient work rules and sometimes damaging strikes. The newcomers entering the market were typically either union free or, as in the Southwest case, had unions that were decidedly less hostile, no inefficient work rules and rare or non-existent strike activity. The nimble LCCs, though small at first, soon began to remake the industry, forcing legacy carriers to cut cabin amenities and service level and moving them toward a more operational lower cost structure. These airlines focus on price-conscious travelers. Rather than offering cabin amenities, low-cost carriers provided low fares to those passengers who were looking to save money. Today, while legacy carriers still retain the bulk of the market, the major growth is with the LCCs. There is a strong evidence that price-sensitive travelers are using LCCs, and time-sensitive passengers with higher disposable income fly with full-service carriers. The remarkable success of Southwest, easyJet, and Ryanair point to a possible future of LCC dominance that legacy carriers are desperately fighting to stave off.

On the one hand, the line between an LCC and a legacy carrier is blurry. LCCs such as JetBlue are providing free live television entertainment, and some legacy carriers may have no audio/visual entertainment. Several LCCs have adopted leather seats and increased legroom to provide additional amenities for their passengers. Moreover, airlines such as Southwest have loyalty programs just like their legacy competitors. From a passenger standpoint, the differences are becoming hard to distinguish. On the other hand, LCCs face tremendous competition from both legacy carriers and ULCCs. As a significant portion of the low-cost strategy is based on growth, LCCs must continually develop new markets, particularly in emerging economies full of first-time fliers. However, they are also facing rising customer expectations and will, therefore, need to balance their cost advantage with their investment in service quality. Even the rising LCCs in China and Southeast Asia are beginning to experiment with a more hybrid model (Bohlman, Kletzel, and Terry, 2017).

The legacy carriers have focused their capacity into international markets, since this is where profits are being made. Moreover, it is also the only area where the majors do not face fierce competition from LCCs. This is principally a result of international air treaty regulations and the fact that international flying diverges from the low-cost model (since it generally requires different and larger aircraft types). Although Southwest Airlines recently built a new $156 million international terminal at Houston Hobby airport, which started service in October 2015, the success of such a model is unknown (although the example of People Express shows that it is possible). The question is whether LCCs can successfully use and sustain the low-cost model on international flights. At present, low-cost giant AirAsia is aggressively expanding its budget service into long-haul markets in Asia. Thus, we may, in fact, be seeing an industry shift that will continue in the twenty-first century.

Evolution of Low-Cost Business Model

Since the 1978 Airline Deregulation Act completely liberalized the US market, a substantial number of new carriers have emerged, particularly those following a low-cost business model. In Europe, the liberalization occurred in a decade-long process, in the wake of the Single European Act of 1986.[3] The liberalization process occurred in several different stages, initially from granting airlines the freedom to change fares and then finally allowing any EU carrier to fly within the borders of any other EU country.[4] The European liberalization laid the foundation for the emergence of low fares airlines.[5] The evolution of LCCs is an interesting example of competitive market forces in action. At present, there exists no part of the world which is not served by at least one low-cost airline. Across Australia, New Zealand, Latin America, and Asia, many low-fare, low-cost airlines are available. While only the last decade has seen tremendous growth in this sector of the industry, the roots of the budget model can be traced back to 1971 when founder Herb Kelleher mapped out the route and cost structure for Southwest Airlines. Since the US aviation industry was still regulated at the time, Southwest Airlines was able to only fly intra-Texas routes where the Civil Aeronautics Board (CAB) did not have authority. Stemming from these humble beginnings, and based on its simple low-cost strategy, Southwest was able to grow into one of the most successful airlines in the United States.

In the aftermath of deregulation, many new airlines entered the market. This caused airfares to plummet 40% in real terms between 1978 and 1997, while the number of passengers more than doubled. Airlines like Southwest were able to successfully expand, while new LCCs like America West, Reno Air, and People Express emerged, each with varying degrees of success.

Today, many successful LCCs emerged in the United States, including Frontier Airlines, JetBlue, Spirit Airlines (now merged with JetBlue), and Las Vegas-based Allegiant, all of which have taken share from the traditional legacy carriers. On the other hand, many LCCs have failed despite the huge demand for low-cost travel. As expected, the remaining LCCs have been those with the lowest cost base. For example, an airline like Southwest has been tremendously successful at retaining a low-cost structure while still expanding aggressively.

The low-cost carrier business model has grown tremendously over the past three decades. Moreover, it is not just a North American phenomenon, but rather a global industry trend. Today, almost all markets contain at least some low-fare carriers. While Southwest is the founder of the LCC model, the idea spread to the United Kingdom in the early 1970s when Sir Freddie Laker was able to secure the necessary route authorizations to launch cheap transatlantic flights between Gatwick and New York. With North America experiencing a wave of LCC start-ups following US airline deregulation, Europe experienced a "second-wave" of LCCs following the liberalization of European airspace. This rapid entry of LCCs quickly became a key growth area for air traffic in Europe.

David Neeleman co-founded Morris Air, a low-fare charter airline in 1984, and in 1993, Morris Air was acquired by Southwest Airlines. In 1998, JetBlue was incorporated in Delaware and officially founded in February 1999 under the leadership of Neeleman. But in 2008, Neeleman was replaced as chairman of the board by Joel Peterson.

LLCs are also gaining substantial traction in Latin America. After stepping down as JetBlue's chief executive officer and founder, David Neeleman started a new low-cost airline (Azul) in Brazil in 2008. David Neeleman launched Breeze Airways in May 2021, making it his fifth commercial airline low cost and startup along with Morris Air, WestJet, JetBlue, and Azul.[6]

By the year 2022, Azul was Brazil's second largest carrier after LATAM in South America.[7] Similarly, EasySky[8] began low-cost operations in Honduras in September, 2011. In Mexico, many LCCs including Interjet, Volaris, and Viva Aerobus provide services to domestic markets as well as international destinations. Azul's dominance in the domestic market is evident from its substantial market share; between January and December 2020, Azul had 23.5% of the domestic and 5.0% of the international market share.

As shown in Table 9.1, low-cost carriers have been successfully earning market share in every region around the world for the last ten years. To illustrate, in Asia, the number of airport

Table 9.1 Low-Cost Carrier Capacity Share by Total Seats and Region, 2007–2021

	World	*North America*	*Europe*	*Asia-Pacific*	*Africa*	*Latin America*
2007	17.50%	26.30%	29.50%	11.30%	7.00%	20.70%
2008	19.20%	27.80%	32.00%	13.60%	8.90%	24.90%
2009	20.30%	28.10%	34.00%	16.10%	7.80%	25.20%
2010	21.40%	28.70%	35.00%	18.00%	8.00%	28.40%
2011	22.90%	29.80%	35.80%	20.50%	9.30%	33.50%
2012	23.40%	30.00%	38.10%	21.10%	8.70%	32.40%
2013	25.00%	30.00%	39.60%	23.60%	10.30%	37.10%
2014	25.90%	30.10%	41.00%	25.70%	10.50%	38.00%
2015	25.40%	31.00%	39.00%	25.10%	9.40%	36.10%
2016	25.50%	31.80%	38.90%	25.80%	8.90%	33.50%
2017	30.00%	32.70%	39.00%	26.80%	10.80%	34.30%
2018	31.00%	32.00%	41.00%	29.00%	N/A	36.00%
2019	31.00%	30.00%	33.00%	27.50%	N/A	37.00%
2020	35.00%	34.90%	44.50%	32.50%	N/A	45.00%
2021	35.02%	35.00%	44.80%	32.40%	N/A	46.00%

Source: Compiled by the authors from CAPA Centre for Aviation data.

pairs flown by LCCs doubled from 2009 to 2014, and according to Airbus, LLCs are expected to have a 34% global share of traffic by 2030.[9] Adding to their achievements, they have also been profitable, and many are consistently reporting load factors above 90%.[10]

To illustrate this trend, Figure 9.1 displays the LCC global market share in terms of seats from 2007 to 2016. Furthermore, Figure 9.2 depicts the increasing global share of low-cost carriers compared with the corresponding decreasing global share of full-service network carriers.

The LCC industry in Asia has witnessed explosive growth since 2000. This is a heavily populated region, and the less-developed nations have millions of first-time fliers who have welcomed a reasonably-priced alternative to slower modes of transportation. As an exemplar of this trend, Indigo, the New Delhi-based airlines, with more than 291 Airbus jets on order is one of the quickest growing airlines in the region. Indigo started in 2006 and quickly became one of the best low-cost carriers in Asia.

Malaysia's AirAsia has rapidly expanded to become the major carrier in the region and the largest by fleet size.[11] AirAsia's rivals, notably Singapore's Tiger Airways and Australia's Qantas-owned Jetstar compete aggressively on Asia-Australia routes as well the domestic Australian market. The Melbourne-based airline operates a fleet of Airbus A320 and Boeing 787 Dreamliners. Moreover, both AirAsia and Cebu Pacific have effectively expanded the low-cost model to include long-haul budget service.

The growth in this region is also evident by the number of aircraft orders. For example, Asia-Pacific will require up to 3,190 regional jets with up to 150 seats.[12] In 2022, three Chinese state airlines placed an order for nearly 300 Airbus jets, the biggest order from Chinese airlines in approximately five years.[13]

While the market in North America and Europe exhibits a slightly higher level of maturity, the large Asia-Pacific LCCs have expanded at rates exceeding 20% per annum. As the region's economy (at 4.1% per year for the next 20 years) is expected to significantly outpace the world's

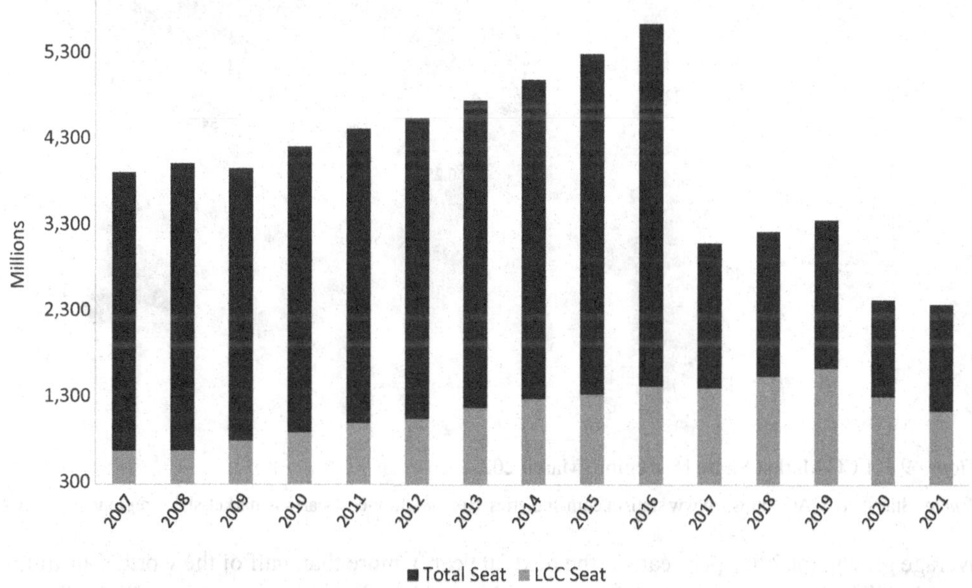

Figure 9.1 LCC Seats to Total Seats, Worldwide.

Source: Compiled by the authors using CAPA Centre for Aviation data through October 2022, https://centreforaviation.com/data

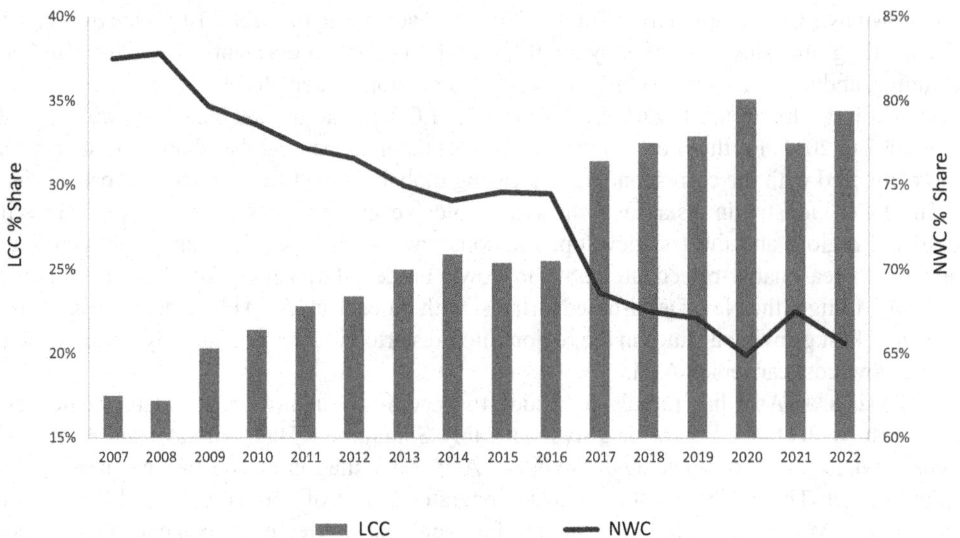

Figure 9.2 LCC Share vs NWC Share, Worldwide.

Source: Compiled by the authors using CAPA Centre for Aviation data

* Through October 2022

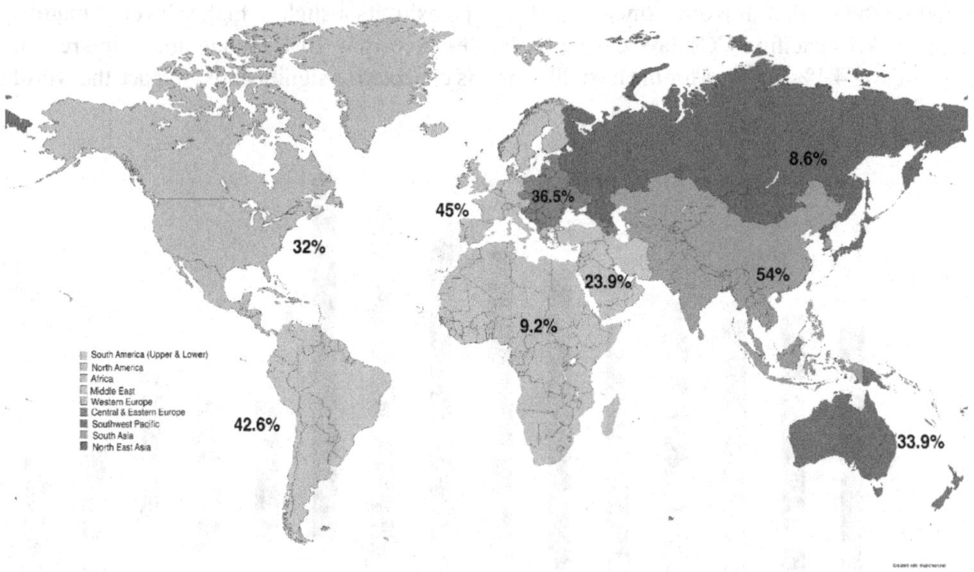

Figure 9.3 LCC Market Share by Region, March 2022.

Source: Statista & OAG, https://www.statista.com/statistics/1088686/low-cost-carrier-market-share-region/

average growth (at 2.9% per year for the next 20 years), more than half of the world's air traffic growth will be driven by travel to, from, or within the Asia-Pacific region.[14] Over the forthcoming two decades, a majority of the demand for new airplanes will come from outside North America, with about 40% of deliveries going to the Asia-Pacific region.[15]

Table 9.2 Low-Cost Carrier Operating Revenue and Passenger Numbers, 2021

Rank	*Airline*	*USD (Million)*	*Passengers (Million)*
1	Southwest Airlines	$15,790	123.30
2	Ryanair[a]	$1,921	72.40
3	easyJet[a]	$1,458	20.40
4	JetBlue Airways	$6,037	30.10
5	WestJet[a] (2020)	$1,300	8.00
6	Gol	$1,305	18.97
7	Jetstar[a]	$1,140	NA
8	Norwegian[a]	$469	6.20
9	IndiGo[a]	$1,794	48.40
10	Spirit Airlines	$3,230	30.77

Source: Company annual reports.

[a] Year ended 31 March, 30 September, or 30 June.

Table 9.2 provides a brief synopsis of the financial situation of some of the world's major LCCs. As the table displays, the founding airline, Southwest, is still the largest airline in the low-cost category in terms of operating revenue and passengers enplaned. In fact, in 1991, Ryanair went to the Southwest Airline headquarters to study the low-cost business model. Armed with confidence about implementing the strategy in Europe, Ryanair eventually restructured its business as a low-cost carrier. Subsequently, in 1995, easyJet was established following a model very similar to that of Ryanair.

While many LCCs have been successful, the list of failed LCCs is long. In North America, four major legacy carriers launched their own LCC brands between 1998 and 2004, and all four failed within five years: MetroJet by US Airways (1998–2001); Tango by Air Canada (2001–2003); Song by Delta Air Lines (2003–2006)[16]; and Ted by United Airlines (2004–2009) (Shannon, 2011). In Europe, Snowflake,[17] a low-cost airline subsidiary of Scandinavian Airlines System (SAS), ceased operations partially in 2004. KLM divested itself of Buzz, while British Airways did the same with its budget subsidiary, Go. Moreover, not only have the major carriers struggled to replicate the success of LCCs, but we have also seen the failure of independent LCCs like Reno Air, People Express, and Independence Air. In Europe, additional instances include Airlib Express (France: 1987–2003), Berline (Germany 1991–1994), LTU (Austria: 2004–2008), Fresh Aer, and Air Finland (Finland: 2002–2012). This raises the obvious question of why some LCCs were successful while others failed.

UK-based airline Flybe went into administration on March 4, 2020, and the Flybe company was renamed FBE Realizations 2021 Limited. In 2020, many low-cost airlines such as Aigle Azur (France), Avianca Brazil (Brazil), Germania (Germany), Jet Airways (India), Thomas Cook Airlines (UK), WOW Air (Iceland), and XL Airways (France) filed for bankruptcy.[18] The rapid expansion of low-cost carriers in the global air travel market over the last decade is noteworthy. In 2020, low-cost carriers accounted for 35% of the world's total seat capacity.

Part of these problems stems from the fact that many airlines (particularly major carriers) that have tried to imitate the low-cost model were never truly on target. In the absence of healthy financial resources and strong liquidity, competing in this industry is very close to impossible. In essence, those defunct carriers that tried to brand themselves as low cost were unable to actually change their existing cost structure. Additionally, regardless of the type of carrier, any new airline entrant faces tremendous competition from the incumbent airlines, making it very difficult to successfully launch a startup rival.

While every carrier is unique, there are certain common characteristics that have enabled some LCCs to succeed where others have failed. Broadly speaking, these characteristics allowed successful carriers to maintain a low-cost structure, and these specific characteristics will be elaborated in the following sections.

Characteristics of Low-Cost Carriers

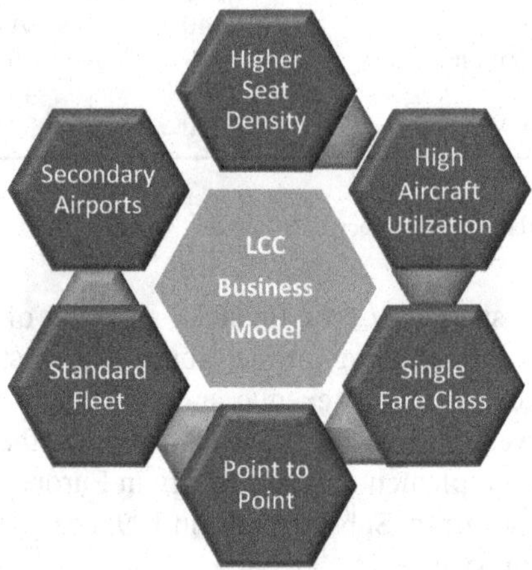

The concept of LCCs isn't novel. When Herb Kelleher and Rollin King founded Southwest Airlines in 1967, the airline was based on a business model that offered low fares by combining low cost and high productivity.[19] Moreover, in 1977, Laker Airways became one of the first carriers to offer long-haul, no-frills flights between London and New York. With the advent of Airline Deregulation Act in 1978, a multitude budget carriers entered the scene, including People Express in North America and Ryanair in Europe. In spite of the fact that LCCs operate all over the globe in different environments, they all exhibit a few basic general characteristics.

Lower Labor Costs and Higher Labor Productivity

The cost advantages enjoyed by low-cost carriers are remarkable. Since labor accounts for one of the largest costs for any airline, it is imperative for LCCs to keep an eye on labor productivity. While numerous LCCs simply pay below-average wages, Southwest has proved that LCCs can pay competitive rates, yet still have low labor costs per hour of productivity. Through attaining high employee productivity, Southwest has been able to pay high salaries yet remain very competitive on a per block hour basis. For example, Southwest pilots are some of the highest paid in the industry. However, they significantly log more flying hours per month than their counterparts at other airlines, and they also pitch in to help in other areas, such as baggage loading and aircraft cleaning.

While employee productivity accounts for a portion of the narrative, the importance of low labor costs cannot be overstated. An airline boasting high labor rates and moderate to low productivity will ultimately be unsuccessful. Both Air Canada and Delta launched LCCs that utilized employees from the mainline carrier. Essentially, the new carrier was supposed to be low cost, yet they operated with the same employee group as the high-cost airline. Since these new

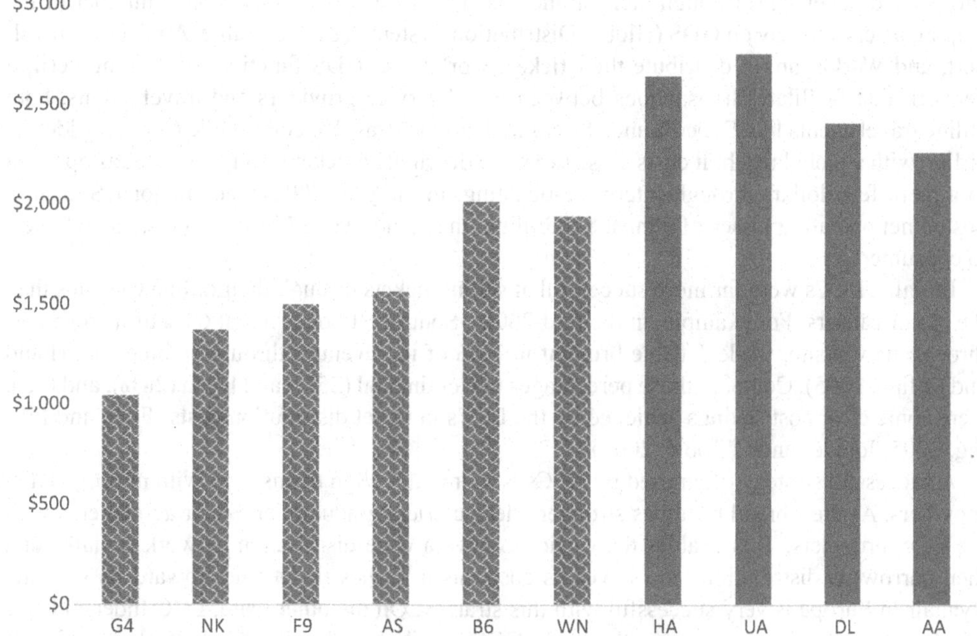

Figure 9.4 Cockpit Costs per Block Hour, 2022.
Source: Compiled by the authors

LCCs were uncompetitive on the labor front and had no new productivity increases, their swift disappearance shortly after launching is no surprise. According to Southwest Airlines, Average Southwest Airlines Pilot yearly pay in the United States is approximately $245,145, which is 339% above the national average.[20]

Figure 9.4 provides a comparison of cockpit costs per block hour for various US airlines, which include both legacy carriers and LCCs. While LCCs Allegiant and Spirit are the two leading carriers in terms of cockpit cost per block hour, Southwest Airlines is in the middle of the pack.[21] The relatively low cockpit costs for the first two airlines represent a significant competitive advantage, whereas Southwest Airlines, an airline with a more established presence, must focus on employee efficiency to help offset the relatively higher cockpit costs per block hour. As anticipated, the legacy carriers, such as American Airlines, Delta Airline, and United Airlines, had the highest cockpit costs in 2022.[22]

> Low-cost airlines are characterized by a simple fare structure, one aircraft type, direct ticket sales, a focus on secondary airports, no frequent flier programs, no complimentary food or beverages, and fast aircraft turnaround times.

Lower Ticket Distribution Costs

Ticket distribution costs are another major area where the entire airline industry is attempting to reduce costs. The initial step airlines took to reduce ticket distribution costs was to cut travel agent commissions. Subsequently, through the Internet, airlines moved to electronic ticketing and pushed ticket sales through their online websites. However, a considerable number of the major carriers still rely on GDS (Global Distribution Systems), such as Sabre, Amadeus, Travelport, and Worldspan, to distribute their tickets worldwide. GDS functions as a computerized network that facilitates transactions between travel service providers and travel agents, both online travel agents like Expedia and "bricks and mortar" travel agents. While GDS provides an airline with a global reach, it costs close to $13 to distribute a ticket through a GDS, as opposed to a mere few dollars through Internet e-ticketing. In the year 2002, when major US airlines posted net operating losses of almost $10 billion, they paid over $7 billion to distribute tickets to consumers.

Initially, LCCs were far more successful at selling tickets through their online websites than the major carriers. For example, in the mid-2000s, Southwest books about 60% of its revenues through its website, while JetBlue brought in 75% of its revenues through jetblue.com (Field and Pilling, 2005). Compare those percentages to Continental (25%) and Delta (28%), and there were some clear cost savings achieved by the LCCs in ticket distribution costs (Field and Pilling, 2005; Ionides and O'Toole, 2005).

A successful strategy often used by LCCs is to initially align themselves with multiple GDS providers. As their brand becomes stronger, these carriers gradually end their agreements with the GDS providers. This enables the carrier to have a wide distribution network initially, and then narrow its distribution (and lower its costs) as it pushes ticket sales toward its website. Ryanair in Europe is very successful with this strategy. On the other hand, LCC Independence Air decided to begin operations without any GDS distribution, but its website lacked sufficient brand recognition, and ultimately the airline went out of business (Field and Pilling, 2005).

It is worth noting that a universal push toward online ticket distribution by LCCs was not typical for all LCCs. However, as a general trend, LCCs indeed had been the catalyst in the e-ticketing/website distribution world, and this had provided them with a significant ticket distribution cost advantage. By 2008, the International Air Transport Association (IATA) required all member airlines to issue e-tickets to passengers and have now largely replaced the older multi-layered paper ticketing systems.[23] An e-ticket, essentially, provides the same information as a paper ticket. The main difference lies in the fact that an e-ticket is located in an airline's computer database, instead of the passengers.

Minimum Cabin Services

Historically, one of the clearest examples of the difference between LCCs and legacy airlines for consumers was a "no-frills" service. On a US legacy carrier's flight, passengers used to receive a complimentary hot meal with extensive beverage service, whereas a Southwest flight only offered peanuts and soda. However, with the cost-cutting measures implemented by legacy carriers, all economy-class service in North America has turned into "no-frills." In Europe, LCCs have gone one step further where everything, including beverages, is on a buy-on-board basis. Therefore, the in-flight food service that used to easily distinguish low-cost airlines from "full-service" carriers is no longer applicable. However, the concept of no-frills does not just pertain to in-flight service. Many LCCs also do not have frequent flier programs or expensive business lounges. This is another way for carriers to cut costs. Similarly, LCCs also restrict luggage allowances. Especially in Europe, LCCs have strict rules concerning luggage allowance weights per passenger, a practice that not only conserves fuel but also generates extra marginal revenue.

The underlying premise behind the LCCs' no-frills service strategy is ultimately a "pay as you go" approach, wherein the ticket price only entitles you to a seat on the aircraft. This strategic approach empowers LCCs to furnish attractive airfares. While these service cuts may seem minimal, when they are compounded over multiple flights, it can actually make the difference between profitability and loss.

Common Fleet Type

Another major characteristic of successful LCCs is the use of a common fleet type. Southwest Airlines was the pioneer of this strategy, structuring its entire fleet around the Boeing 737. As of April 2022, Southwest Airlines currently operates a fleet of 726 Boeing 737Max. Ryanair operates a majority Boeing 737 fleet, although the Airbus A320 has been added through acquisition of Lauda Europe.[24] Employing a single fleet type provides many advantages for an airline, including reduced spare parts inventories, reduced flight crew training expenses, and increased operational flexibility. Additionally, bulk purchase discounts from suppliers (including aircraft manufacturers) can be negotiated when using a single fleet type. However, it is economies of scale that are the most important cost reduction elements underlying the common fleet type strategy. In essence, the airline is required to spend fixed fleet costs only once. For example, all the specialized equipment that might be needed for a 737 only needs to be purchased once.

In addition to savings from economies of scale, adopting a single fleet provides increased operational flexibility. In the event of irregular operations, a single fleet type makes it easier to find a replacement aircraft and, more importantly, replacement flight crew. Since airlines usually have a reserve pilot pool for each fleet type, limiting the number of fleet types limits the number of reserve pilots the airline requires.

Using one fleet can also have advantages and disadvantages with regard to the markets served. Depending on aircraft choice, the planes used by the airline may not be the optimal aircraft for different markets. Thus, if the aircraft has a relatively short range, many intercontinental markets will not be feasible. The former AirTran, for example, had this problem with the 717s and therefore had to purchase another fleet of 737s.[25] Conversely, a single fleet contains aircraft that have the same pilot requirements and maintenance standards. In the case of LCCs, the two most widely used generic aircraft types are the 737 (NG or Max) and the A320X. Both aircraft types enable a carrier to have planes with as few as 120 seats and as many as 200 seats. This adaptability allows them to change aircraft seating capacity to better meet demand on any given day.

Although majority of the LCCs operate a single-aircraft fleet, both JetBlue and easyJet bucked the trend by creating fleets with two aircraft types. In doing so, both airlines felt that the economies of scale benefits on their initial fleet had reached a threshold. This phenomenon arises when the benefits of the first large fleet type are outweighed by the benefits of a second large fleet type. Based on these examples, it appears that the minimum number of aircraft needed to achieve full economies of scale benefits is probably slightly under 100.

Table 9.3 clearly shows that LCCs in North America have less diverse fleets than the legacy carriers. A contributing factor of legacy carrier's more complex fleets is that international flying requires larger aircraft, and legacy carriers have undergone more mergers, thereby combining fleets. LCCs are also generally younger companies and have emphasized a single fleet strategy. And while Southwest Airlines is shown as having two fleets (B737NG and B737Max), the airline still operates only one aircraft type since these are two different generations of the same aircraft.

Irrespective of aircraft type, low-cost operators configure their aircraft in a high-density, all-economy configuration. In some cases, closets and washrooms are removed in order to squeeze more passengers onto the flight. Moreover, the seats on easyJet and Ryanair are all non-reclining

Table 9.3 Select Airline Fleets as of September 2022

Carrier	*Fleet Types*	*# of Aircraft Types*
Low Cost		
Southwest	B737-CL/NG/700/800	1
Frontier	A320-200/neo, A321-200/neo (A320 Family)	1
JetBlue	A220, A320-200, A321-200/neo/LR/XLR (A320 Family), ERJ 190 AR	2
Ryanair	B737-700/800	1
Spirit	A319-100/neo, A320-200/neo, A321-200/neo (A320 Family)	1
WestJet	B737-600/700/800/MAX, B787	2
easyJet	A319, A320, A321 (A320 Family)	1
Germanwings	A319, A320 (A320 Family) (Ceased Operation 2020)	1
IndiGo	A320-200/neo, A321-neo (A320 Family), ATR 72-600	2
Legacy		
AeroMexico	737 NG/MAX/800/9, 787-8/9	2
Air Canada	A220-300, A319, A320-200, A321-200/neoXLR (A320 Family), A330-300E/300X, B737-8, B787-8/9, B767-300ER/300ER(F), B777-200LR/300ER/F	7
Lufthansa	A319-100, A320-200/neo, A321-100/200/neoACF (A320 Family), A330-300E/300X, A340-300X/600/600HGW, A350-900XWB, B747-400/8, B777-9X, B787-9	7
American	B737-8/800, B777-200ER/300ER, B787-8/9, A319-100, A320-200, A321-200/neo ACF/neo XLR (A320 Family), Embraer ERJ175 LE	5
Delta	A220-100/300, A319-100, A320-200, A321-200/neo ACF (A320 Family), A330-200/300E/900neo, A350-900XWB, B717-200, B737-10/800/900ER, B757-200/300, B767-300ER/400ER	8
United	A319-100, A320-200, A321-neo ACF/neo XLR (A320 Family), A350-900XWB, B737-MAX/10/700/8/800/9/900/900ER, B757-200/300, B767-300ER/400ER, B777-200/200ER/300ER, B787-8/9/10	7

Source: CAPA Centre for Aviation, includes aircraft on order.

in order to accommodate more passengers. Clearly, since every flight is largely a fixed cost (once it has been launched), the greater the number of passengers on board, the greater the revenue the airline can obtain. This in turn enables the airline to offer a few seats at highly discounted prices. In the context of the North American market, LCCs have pursued different marketing practices, as both JetBlue and WestJet removed seats from their aircraft to provide additional legroom in an effort to attract more business clientele. WestJet operates two variants of the Boeing 737 Next Generation family, the Boeing 737 MAX, as well as a Boeing 787 aircraft, dedicated to specific long-haul routes. Today, WestJet operates a variety of jet and turboprop aircraft to support our expanded existing destinations.

Also, very few discount carriers operate any sort of premium cabin, believing that additional economy revenue would exceed any premium cabin revenue. All the LCCs adopt a strategy of installing more seats in their aircraft than the industry average, thereby spreading costs per seat over a greater number of seats.

Seat Pitch signifies the measurement between the same positions on two identical seats, one behind the other. Reducing seat pitch would mean reduced leg room, and this is precisely how airlines increase the number of seats on an aircraft. Notably, the international airlines with the most legroom in economy are:

- Japan Airlines: 33–34 inches
- ANA, Emirates, EVA Airways, and Singapore Airlines: 32–34 inches
- Air China, Air France, Ethiopian Airlines, and Korean Air: 32–33 inches

- Cathay Pacific, SWISS, and Vietnam Airlines: 32 inches
- Aer Lingus, Aerolineas Argentinas, Eurowings, Turkish Airlines, Virgin Australia, and many others: 30–32

Among all the prominent global airlines, Spirit Airlines has the lowest seat pitch of 28.5, in the A320 aircraft. Following closely behind are Frontier, Iberia, and other low-cost carriers. Lufthansa, for example, has an average seat pitch of 30 on the same A320.

Hub-and-Spoke and Point-to-Point Services

Hub-and-spoke is taking one airport as a hub and connecting all other airports (spoke) through the hub. For example, with an eight-airport network, one as the hub, we can have full connectivity with only eight flights, while point-to-pint requires 20 flights.

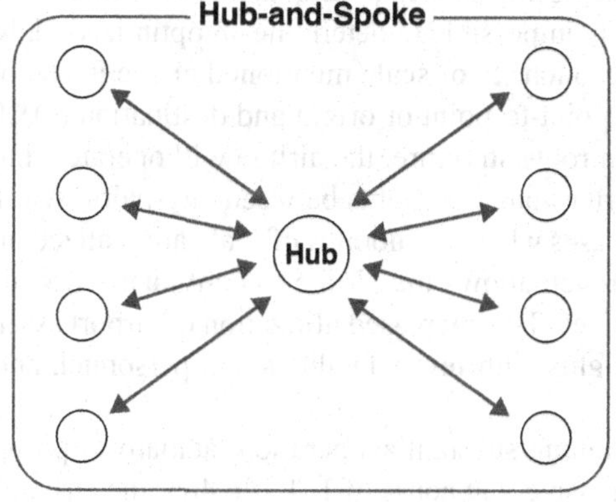

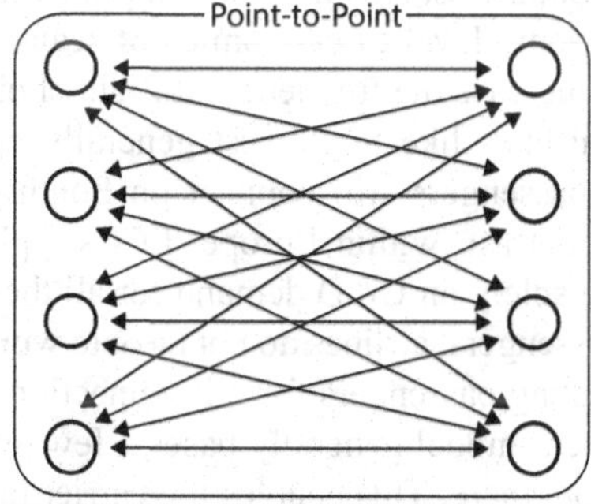

Following deregulation, the legacy carriers have adopted a hub-and-spoke route structure, whereby all flights from spoke come into one hub airport and this airport provides the connecting feed for the spoke flights that depart shortly thereafter. While the hub-and-spoke system has been effective for legacy carriers in providing a large number of city pair connections, a hub is also an extremely expensive operation. Hubs invariably experience peak periods to minimize passenger transfer time, but this also means that the hub will have downtimes where it is not fully utilizing many of its facilities. This is extremely costly as employees may be idle for extended periods of time and assets (such as gates and ground equipment) may be left unused.

Since employees and gates must be paid over the full working day (and not only when flights are arriving and/or departing), this represents some level of inefficiency. Moreover, the converse aspect of this is equally true, and that is that the hub carrier must also have adequate staffing for its peak number of flights, thereby further increasing the cost of unproductive time.

In addition to the undoubted revenue advantage of many city pair choices and the ability to increase load factors by consolidating passengers at the hub, a pivotal cost benefit underlying a hub is the ability to realize certain economies of scale. The concentration of operations in one place reduces fixed overhead costs such as required reserve labor pools, maintenance operations, and terminal-related expenses. However, the problem arises from the fact that the peak flight scheduling necessary for passenger convenience also leads to situation where these economies of scale are not always achieved. Moreover, once the number of flights reaches a critical level, diseconomies of scale will set in. To elaborate, any additional flight will actually increase average costs instead of reducing them. This arises due to the fact that the added congestion increases costs. For example, as the airport becomes busier and busier, aircraft have to wait longer to land and takeoff, and this is reflected in higher fuel and labor costs. Arguably, numerous hubs in the United States have surpassed the critical inflection point where economies of scale have turned into diseconomies of scale. Unfortunately, since there are numerous different and interactive decision makers, it is nearly impossible to determine an optimized flight level for a hub airport.

The prevalence of diseconomies of scale mentioned above is one of the major reasons why LCCs typically operate a point-to-point or origin and destination (O&D) route structure. In the context of a point-to-point route structure, the airline will operate a more spread-out route network and typically will offer non-stop flights between city-pairs. Within such a route structure, airlines will still operate bases where economies of scale are realized but will not have any peak level of flights. This approach allows the airline to continually use airport facilities and more evenly use employee services. This increased utilization of airport assets allows a point-to-point airline to operate more flights with fewer facilities and personnel, and this ultimately reduces costs.

Southwest Airlines maintains substantial operations at many airports across the United States. In 2021, boasting an impressive seat count of 151,146,489, the airline became the world's largest carrier in terms of seats.[26] Southwest Airlines generally operates at least eight to ten flights out of any city to experience some level of economies of scale, spreading fixed costs over a greater number of flights, and increase the frequency of flight choice for the passengers.

In North America, while airlines like Southwest generally operate a point-to-point route structure, a good number of passengers still connect on Southwest flights through some of Southwest's larger bases. In contrast, within Europe, LCCs typically do not allow any connecting flights, thereby relying solely on O&D demand for all their flights. By abstaining from accommodating connecting passengers, airlines do not have to worry about transferring luggage between aircraft and compensating passengers for misconnections and this further reduces operating costs. The European LCC model generally bases a few aircraft at one airport and then flies to various destinations from there. This enables the carrier to receive some of the benefits of economies of scale at these bases. Thus, European LCCs operate a base-and-spoke network with no connections or synergies with the airline's other bases. Both Ryanair and easyJet have been successful using this strategy.

Use of Secondary Airports

Analogous to adopting a point-to-point route structure, the use of secondary airports is another characteristic of LCCs. A secondary airport is usually under-utilized and further from a city center, like Malmo Airport compared to Copenhagen. Congested primary airports usually mean more time on the ground and higher airport fees, so LCCs avoid them where possible. For example, Southwest historically used secondary airports in cities where the primary airports had high costs. Nevertheless, in the recent years, the airline has been expanding into primary airports and crowded airspace such as Los Angeles, LaGuardia Airport, Atlanta, and George Bush Intercontinental Airport. While Southwest was the pioneer of utilizing secondary airports (saving costs by being able to turn aircraft around quicker), Ryanair has been the most aggressive in serving secondary airports. Examples of Ryanair using secondary airports include Hahn airport for Frankfurt, Charleroi Airport for Brussels, Beauvais airport for Paris, and Weeze airport for Dusseldorf. Opting for secondary airports allows lower landing fees, less congestion, and quicker aircraft turnaround. Hence, at these secondary airports low-cost airlines are able to operate more efficiently and more cost effectively. For passengers, these secondary airports offer a relaxed atmosphere with quick access to parking and gates.

The benefits an airport garners in terms of passenger numbers from an LCC starting service are immense. Therefore, airports have become very aggressive in attracting new LCC service. The classic example of this is an agreement Charleroi Airport made with Ryanair[27] whereby Ryanair received a reduction in airport charges of around €2 per passenger, a reduction in ground handling charges to €1 per passenger, one-time incentive bonuses for starting new routes, and marketing promotion. Additionally, airports have begun to design airports that cater specifically to the needs of a LCC (that is, low operating costs). Marseille Airport has designed a dedicated low-cost terminal with cheaper passenger service charges, while Geneva airport has opened a terminal for "simplified aviation" (Buyck, 2005). These strategic initiatives inherently lead to lower overall costs, and these can in turn be passed to passengers in the form of lower fares.

High Aircraft Utilization

Another central focus contributing to the success of low-cost airlines is a high level of aircraft utilization. Since an aircraft is not earning money while sitting on the ground, the more an aircraft is flying, the more passengers the airline can carry. There are two central ways an airline can increase its daily average aircraft utilization: turn the aircraft around quicker or fly longer routes. Figure 9.5 provides a comparison of average daily block hours per aircraft between LCCs and network carriers, wherein Spirit, Frontier, JetBlue, and Alaska Airlines all enjoyed higher block hours than the average. Aircraft utilization in the fourth quarter of 2022 was 10.8 hours, down 7.7% compared to the 11.7 hours in the same period of 2019 and a sequential improvement from the third quarter 2022 of 1.9%.[28] The Mexican airlines Volaris is another industry leader in aircraft utilization. In 2021, its average aircraft utilization was about 12.4 hours per day, significantly more than any other airlines.

Given that high aircraft utilization rates are one of the major strategies for any LCC and ULCC, it is not surprising that the top airlines in terms of aircraft utilization are Spirit, Frontier, and JetBlue. Airlines like JetBlue are able to achieve high aircraft utilization rates since they focus on having quick turnarounds. Through the implementation of an open seating policy, passengers tend to enplane and deplane faster, and by having considerably fewer hub-and-spoke operations, the ground baggage handling situation is less complex. Additionally, the use of secondary, less-congested airports allows the airlines to schedule more flights since there is less delay in the schedule. These operational efficiencies enable LCCs to operate more flights, thereby providing more revenue. The downside to increased utilization is that maintenance costs will increase since the aircraft are being flown more often, yet this is a tradeoff most airlines are willing to make.

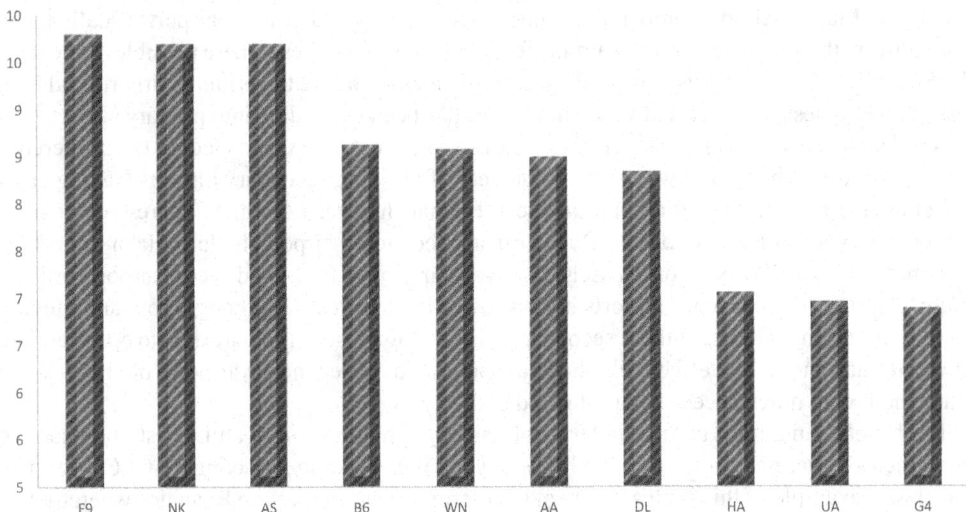

Figure 9.5 Aircraft Utilization (Block Hours per Day), 2021.

Source: Compiled by authors using Form 41

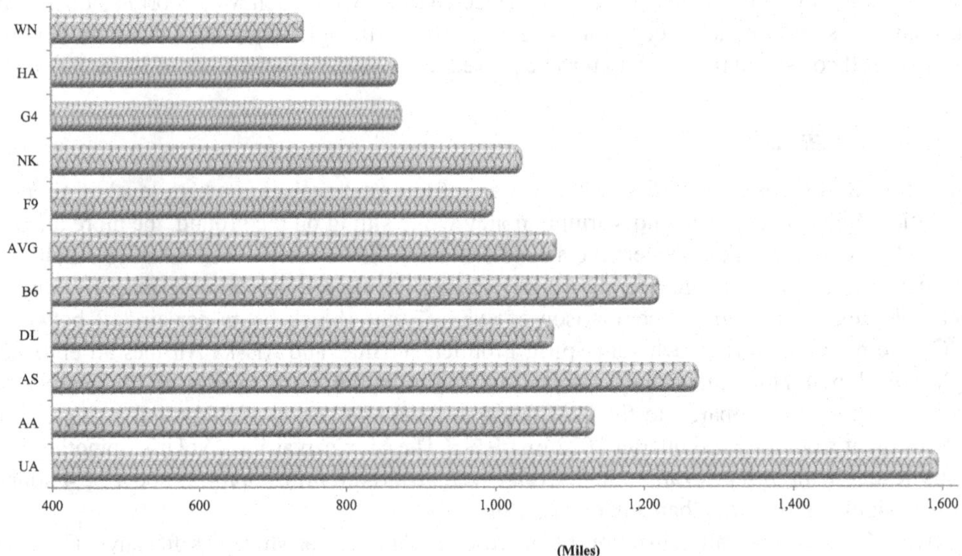

Figure 9.6 Average Aircraft Stage Length in Miles, 2022.

Source: Compiled by the authors from MIT

The other method of increasing aircraft utilization is by flying longer routes. As illustrated in Figure 9.6, it provides a comparison of the average domestic stage length for major US carriers. JetBlue accomplishes high aircraft utilization rates by flying transcontinental and Florida flights from its New York JFK base, while Southwest obtains high aircraft utilization by operating short flights with quick turnarounds (like intra-Texas flying). Since a Southwest aircraft will be landing and departing more frequently in a day than a JetBlue aircraft, this highlights Southwest's

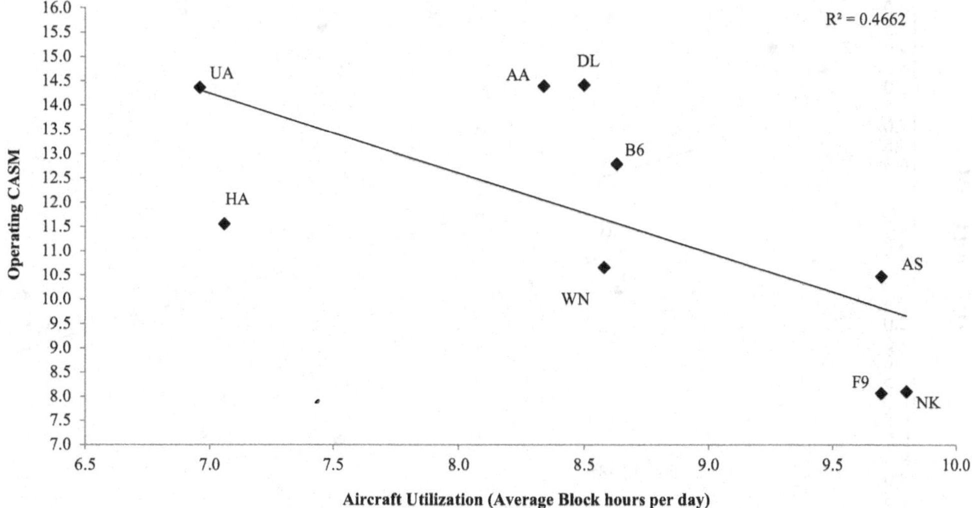

Figure 9.7 Correlations between Operating CASM and Aircraft Utilization, 2021.

Source: Compiled by authors using Form 41 data and annual filings

tremendous efficiency in its ground handling operations. Only recently has Southwest ventured into the transcontinental flying market in an effort to increase its average stage length and increase aircraft utilization.

Presented in Figure 9.7 are the results of a correlation analysis between operating Cost per Available Seat Mile (CASM) and aircraft utilization. CASM is expressed in cents to operate each seat mile offered and is calculated by dividing operating costs by Available Seat Miles (ASM). The regression line is plotted in the figure, and it is evident that a strong negative relationship exists between increased aircraft utilization and reduced operating costs. This metric is calculated by having a significant R-squared value of 0.8405. Airlines that lie below the trendline have a lower operating CASM for their level of aircraft utilization than the industry trend. As anticipated, ULCCs and LCCs such as Frontier, Spirit, and Southwest lie below the trendline, while legacy carriers are generally at the top. More specifically, Figure 9.7 shows clearly that legacy airlines need to reduce their operating CASM for their level of aircraft utilization as they lie significantly above the trendline.

The number of aircraft departures per day is also directly related to aircraft utilization; that is, the more departures per day per aircraft, the higher the utilization and the lower the CASM. This phenomenon is graphically depicted in Figure 9.8, which shows the negative relationship between operating CASM and departures per aircraft per day. This relationship has an R-squared value of 0.3018. Notably, the majority of the legacy carriers are all grouped in the upper-left quadrant. Alaska Airlines, although a full-service carrier, has lower operating CASM relative to number of departures per day. The positioning of Southwest in this graph shows that although the number of departures for Southwest are greater compared to all the other airlines, the operating costs are higher due to the competitive salaries and wages offered by Southwest.

A third correlation to operating CASM is fuel efficiency. Fuel efficiency is the number of seat miles flown with one gallon of fuel. As expected, the general relationship between operating CASM and fuel efficiency is downward sloping, since the more fuel efficient an airline is, the lower its operating costs. Figure 9.9 displays the relationship, which contains an R-square

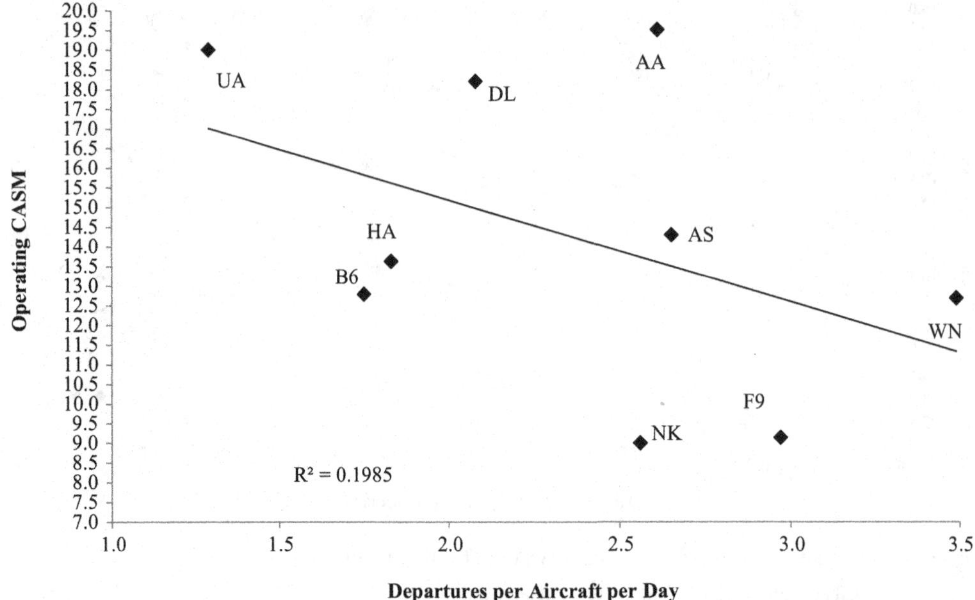

Figure 9.8 Correlation between Operating CASM and Departures per Aircraft per Day, 2020.

Source: MIT

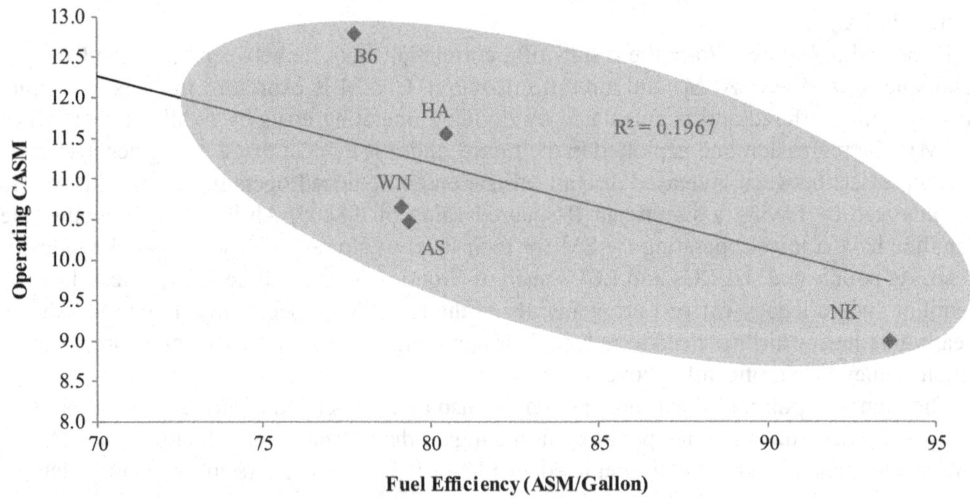

Figure 9.9 Correlation between Operating CASM and Fuel Efficiency, 2021.

Source: Compiled by the authors using Form 41 data and annual filings

value of roughly 0.1985. Based on the trendline, the legacy carriers are the least fuel-efficient airlines. Conversely, LCCs generally outperform the market in terms of fuel efficiency as many of these observations fall below the trendline, with Southwest being the slight exception due to a greater number of takeoffs and landings.

Cost Structure Comparison

In the modern competitive aviation world, the most successful airlines are those with the lowest cost structure. A prime illustration is the Southwest, which has a long record of continually maintaining low operating costs, so that it can offer attractive air fares.

The cost analysis of CASM (Figure 9.10) for the A320 aircraft shows LCC JetBlue as the cost leader, until ULCC Spirit began operation in 2010. Remarkably, the airline has on average been a whole cent lower than the competition, and this could easily be the difference between profitability and non-profitability in any given quarter. This highlights the fact that the scheduling and operating procedures for individual carriers can have a significant impact on the CASM for any given aircraft. United's statistics for this figure include numbers for both mainline A320 flights and Ted[29] flights so it appears (from the figure) that the introduction of Ted has not impacted United's CASM figures dramatically.

Except for the exceptions noted here, the general trend of comparisons by individual aircraft type shows that LCCs have been able to achieve lower operating costs. This trend is further reinforced in Figure 9.11. This visualization contrasts the average domestic CASM as compared between LCCs and legacy carriers since 2000. In this figure the LCCs include US airlines such as Southwest, JetBlue, Frontier and Spirit, while the legacy carriers include American, United, and Delta.

As the figure clearly shows, the cost structure difference between LCCs and legacy carriers was sizeable. Fortunately for them, the legacy carriers were still able to obtain high revenues during a boom period in the economy. However, following the tragic events of September 11, 2001 and the subsequent dramatic drop in air traffic, the LCCs responded more quickly to the

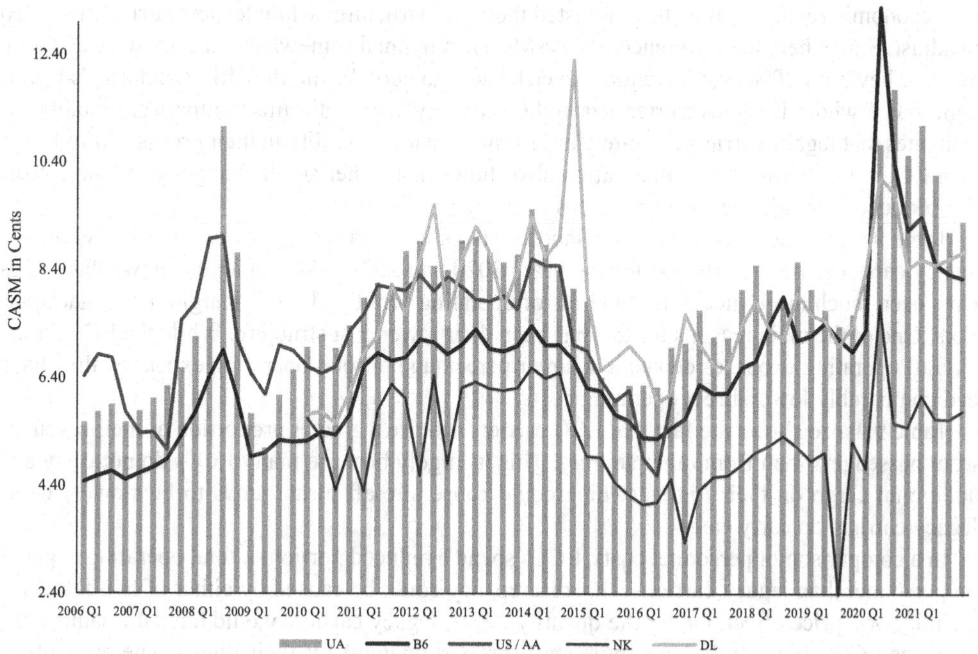

Figure 9.10 CASM, Airbus A320-200 Operators in the United States, 2006–2022.
Source: Compiled by the authors using Diio Mi Form 41

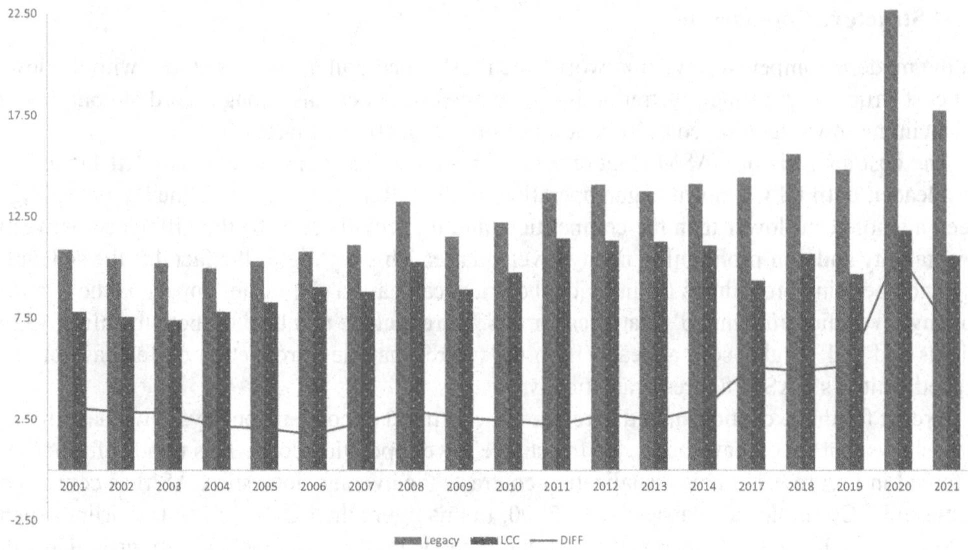

Figure 9.11 CASM Comparison between LCCs and Legacy Carriers.*
Source: Compiled by the authors using Diio Mi Form4, 2021
* Through Q3 2016.

new economic reality; that is, they adjusted their cost structures while legacy carriers struggled to adjust. Since then, the difference in CASMs has remained somewhat constant, with LCCs on average having a 20% cost advantage over legacy carriers. While the airline industry's profitability as a whole is highly correlated to the economy's strength, this comparison notably accentuates that legacy carriers definitely experience greater volatility in their profits and/or losses than LCCs. Furthermore, the illustration also shows that rather small changes in average costs can produce dramatic returns in revenues.

Table 9.4 provides a common-size income statement[30] that compares an LCC (easyJet) to a legacy carrier (British Airways) for the years 2020 and 2021. This depiction shows that LCCs have been much more successful in terms of operating profit and profit margin than legacy carriers. One of the main reasons for this has been their lower cost structure. While the LCCs' total aircraft operating expenses consume a larger percentage of total operating expenses, they have had comparably lower direct operating costs.

Table 9.4 also shows the fact that LCC carriers acquire a greater proportion of their revenues from passengers than from other sources. This is largely because many LCCs do not carry any additional cargo on their flights (which could cause aircraft turnarounds to be slower) while legacy carriers do carry cargo.

In a comparison of personnel costs, LCCs spend a reduced portion of total operating expense on personnel than legacy carriers. This discrepancy could be caused by either of two factors: a quantity or a price effect. Under the quantity effect, legacy carriers would have the same wage levels as LCCs, but simply have more staff (proportionately) for their flights. The price effect would be the opposite pattern—where the proportionate staffing levels are the same, but LCCs simply pay their employees less. In all probability, the difference in personnel expense proportions is probably caused by a mixture of the two effects.

Finally, LCCs spend a greater proportion of their operating expenses on fuel as compared to legacy carriers. A possible explanation for these higher cost proportions is that Southwest and

Table 9.4 Common-Size Income Statement Comparison, LCC vs Legacy Carrier

Revenues	*2021*		*2020*	
	easyJet	*British Airways*	*easyJet*	*British Airways*
Passenger revenues	68.6%	89.2%	76.5%	93.0%
Other revenue	31.4%	10.8%	23.5%	7.0%
Total operating revenues	100.0%	100.0%	100.0%	100.0%
Expenses				
Labor	25.9%	26.4%	20.3%	27.2%
Fuel	19.4%	16.7%	23.3%	18.4%
Maintenance	11.6%	6.7%	9.0%	7.1%
Airports/Handling	23.3%	14.7%	30.3%	13.6%
Selling	3.1%	2.5%	3.5%	2.0%
Other expenses	16.7%	32.9%	13.7%	31.8%
Total operating expense	100%	100%	100%	100%

Source: Compiled by the authors from annual filings.

Spirit have shorter average stage lengths. Since takeoff consumes the largest amount of fuel for any stage of flight and most maintenance programs revolve around the number of takeoffs, the more departures per aircraft there are, the higher the expected proportion of fuel costs. This theory is supported in Figure 9.12. The figure shows the average number of departures per aircraft in 2020 for major US airlines. Notably, Southwest and Spirit lead this list, indicating that this could be the driving factors behind the slight rise in the LCC's percentage of fuel costs compared to the legacy carriers.

Ancillary Revenue

Ancillary (non-ticket) revenue has been a mainstay in the low-cost business model and is becoming the key driver for the emerging ultra-low-cost strategy. In fact, several ULCCs today generate more than one-third of their revenue from non-ticket sources. Again, budget airlines typically unbundle their products and services in order to offer lower ticket prices. Potential sources of ancillary revenue include:

- Baggage fees
- Credit or debit card surcharges
- Flight changes
- Group/family seating
- Overhead bin space
- Snacks, meals, drinks, pillows, blankets, TV, and Internet
- Seat selection, change, and upgrade
- Ticket printing

The share of total revenue that is ancillary increased in 2021 to 22.2% for major US carriers from 16.1% in 2019, and to 36.3% for low-cost airlines versus 27% two years prior.[31]

Incumbent Carriers' Response to Low-Cost Carriers

Legacy airlines are incrementally chipping away at amenities that passengers have long taken for granted, and they are beginning to charge for some of these services, such as ticket changes

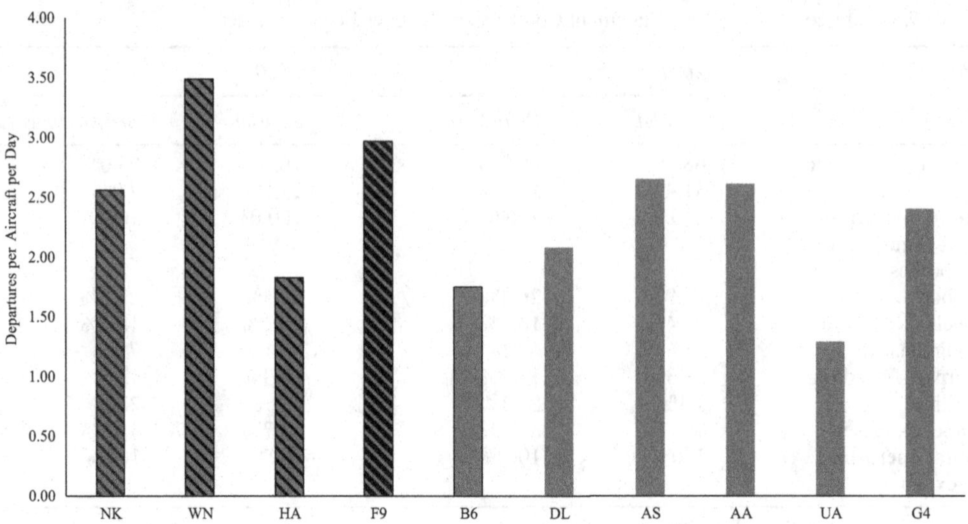

Figure 9.12 Average Departures per Aircraft per Day, 2020.

Source: MIT, http://web.mit.edu/airlinedata/www/2020%2012%20Month%20Documents/Aircraft%20and%20Related/Total%20Fleet/Departure%20per%20Aircraft%20Day%20-%20ALL%20AIRCRAFT.htm

and cancelations. Additionally, they have also implemented two major strategies to combat LCCs: creation of their own LCCs and unilateral cost cutting.

Low-Cost Carrier Creation

Most major carriers in both North America and Europe have experimented with creating their own LCCs, although few have been successful. In the early 1990s, Continental launched its own LCC, Continental Lite, which was configured with all economy seats, the absence of on-board dining, and operated flights under 2.5 hours (Bethune, 1998). Continental committed over 100 aircraft to the subsidiary, but it ceased operations shortly after launching (Bethune, 1998). "There was only one problem: People said, 'I don't want to buy that. That is not what I want'" (Bethune, 1998). Ultimately, it was not a competitive product. Additionally, Continental lost passengers on its mainline due to brand confusion (Bethune, 1998). Continental's experiment with Lite was one of the first of a long list of failed attempts by legacy carriers to develop their own LCCs.

Delta Air Lines, in a similar vein, made two attempts at introducing its own LCC. Delta Express began operations in 1996 utilizing 737-200's in a high-density layout (O'Toole, 1999). The budget airline was based out of Orlando International and operated flights principally along the north-east corridor. This strategic motivation was to compete with Southwest, Air Tran, and eventually JetBlue (O'Toole, 1999). A study conducted in 1999 put Delta Express's CASM at 10.86 cents, which was considerably lower than Delta mainline, but still well above Southwest's CASM of 7.75 cents (O'Toole, 1999). In the aftermath of 9/11, Delta Express's operations were significantly reduced as leisure travel declined sharply (Johnston, 2001). Express ceased operations in November of 2003, shortly before Delta started its second LCC, Song. Song launched services in April 2003 amid much fanfare. The carrier attempted to obtain a hip, style-conscious brand by operating larger 757-200's in an all-economy configuration with leather seats and an excellent in-flight entertainment system. The airline largely served leisure routes from Florida and transcontinental flights from the Northeast. However, prior to restructuring under bankruptcy protection, Delta shut down the Song operations in April 2006, only three years after its launch.

Similarly, former US Airways launched MetroJet in 1998[32] to respond to low-cost competition from Southwest and Delta Express (Henry, 1998). The airline's base was Baltimore/Washington International (BWI) where Southwest also had a large operation. MetroJet operated at a fleet of 737-200's in an all-economy configuration, and the operation received labor concessions from the unions (Henry, 1998). MetroJet's main focus was on Northeast and Florida flights, but MetroJet mostly reduced its own mainline passengers, and it faced fierce competition from Southwest. The majority of the cost savings achieved by MetroJet were the result of lower pay rates for employees and economies of density achieved through all-economy seating. However, while MetroJet did have lower costs than mainline US Airways, its cost structure was still high. This was as a direct result of the fact that it was embedded within the mainline carrier. Following the events of 9/11, MetroJet's operations were shut down and much of US Airways presence at BWI was never restored (Johnston, 2001).

United Airlines is another carrier that has operated two LCCs. The first, Shuttle by United, was an all-economy service utilizing 737-300/500's out of San Francisco International Airport (SFO) (Flint, 1996). During the late 1990s, the Shuttle operation appeared quite successful for United, but actual statistics and data for Shuttle were never publicly released (Flint, 1996). The Shuttle service lasted for several years and provided United an avenue to emphasize on operational efficiencies, but like other first-generation legacy LCCs, United ended Shuttle in 2001 with the aircraft being folded back into mainline service.

In 2004, United relaunched its low-cost model in the form of Ted (standing for the last three letters in United), which operates all-economy A320's from Denver. The airline served leisure-oriented markets such as Orlando and Phoenix, replacing mainline service to such cities. All Ted flights were operated by United Airlines crew since it did not have its own operating certificate. As a result of spiking fuel prices, TED's operations were folded back into the mainline brand on January 6, 2009.

In 2001, Air Canada launched Tango utilizing A320s that were configured in an all-economy layout. Although Tango was operated by Air Canada crews, the airline was totally autonomous from Air Canada mainline flights. This arrangement posed as a predicament as Tango's flights relied solely on O&D demand. Tango was created to respond to LCCs such as Canada 3000. However, shortly after Tango's launch, Canada 3000 fell into bankruptcy.

Air Canada's second discount carrier, Zip, was launched in 2002 and operated as a totally separate airline with its own operating certificate, labor force, and management. It engaged in code-sharing on all its flights with Air Canada. The carrier was based in Calgary to compete heavily against Calgary-based LCC WestJet. The airline operated 737-200's in an all-economy layout, but following Air Canada's entry into bankruptcy in 2004, both Zip and Tango disappeared.

Among the LCCs spun off by US legacy carriers, none are currently operating. In Canada, Air Canada holds the dubious distinction of operating two LCCs at the same time, neither of which has survived.

In Europe, a similar phenomenon occurred with both British Airways and KLM setting up their own LCCs. In 1997, British Airways launched Go Fly using Boeing 737s that were based at London Stansted Airport (Goldsmith, 1998). The airline highlighted its ties with British Airways and posted a profit in 2000. However, with new management taking over British Airways, Go became a liability, as it was reducing the airline's core business (Goldsmith, 1998). In a move that is not in the business model for LCCs in the United States, easyJet bought Go in May 2002 (Clark, 2002). Go's network was subsequently integrated into easyJet's.

KLM launched Buzz in 2000 to compete with other low-cost operators, such as easyJet, Ryanair, and Go (Dunn, 1999). Unlike most LCCs, Buzz operated two small fleets of Bae 146s and 737-300s. As such, no economies of scale could be realized, and operating costs were not truly "low cost." Additionally, from Buzz's base in London Stansted, the airline flew into busy airports such as Amsterdam and Paris Charles de Gaulle (Dunn, 1999). In a similar manner to the easyJet deal, Ryanair bought Buzz in 2003 for £15.1 million, but with Buzz having close to £11 million of cash on hand, the true cost of the purchase was much less (BBC News, 2003). Ryanair operated Buzz as a separate unit for a year, but eventually dissolved the operation and had Ryanair take over all operations. Therefore, KLM's experience with a low-cost carrier was short-lived and, like most other legacy carriers, ultimately unsuccessful. In 1997, Deutsche Lufthansa set up a low-cost department, which became a separate company under the name Germanwings on October 27, 2002. However, Germanwings was closed in April 2020 as part of a broad restructuring.[33]

In both Europe and North America, legacy carriers' experiments in creating their own LCCs have largely failed. Part of the problem lies in the operation never truly being low cost, especially with regard to labor costs. The legacy carriers have also been very concerned about the new operator reducing its own core business. An approach that has been more promising is the "platform" approach of International Airlines Group (IAG), which has effectively bought and operates LCC airlines, like Vueling, alongside legacy airlines, like British Airways, by allowing them to operate independently but allocating capital and coordinating support based on their relative financial performance. As evidenced in the earlier discussion, the earlier legacy carrier strategy of creating LCCs of their own has been a complete failure (at least to date).

Cost Cutting

While under Chapter 11 bankruptcy, United Airlines reached an agreement with pilots, which saved the company $1.1 billion. In 2007, Finnair and the Finnish Flight Attendants' Association concluded negotiations by cutting the cost and improving the work productivity of cabin staff. The other major response by legacy carriers has involved unilateral cost cutting of mainline service. In the United States, on-board food service has been reduced to the point where almost no food is served in economy on any domestic flight. US Airways, by removing in-flight entertainment systems on domestic flights, managed to save about $10 million annually in fuel and other costs (Cassels, 2008).

Legacy carriers have also begun to charge for such amenities as pillows, blankets, and in-flight entertainment. While these measures enable legacy airlines to reduce costs, it also introduces the problem of lack of product differentiation. When legacy carriers reduce their service product to equal LCCs, they are essentially engaging in a competition centered primarily on cost. However, as demonstrated, competing solely on cost is risky, since LCCs have much lower cost structures than legacy carriers.

Legacy carriers have also attempted to reduce their cost structure by retiring older aircraft, receiving labor concessions, and reconfiguring aircraft seating layouts. In general, however, the legacy carriers' response to LCCs has largely been ineffective. Many carriers have attempted to avoid LCCs by focusing on international flying where they have definite competitive advantages due to legal restrictions.

Other methods of cost cutting involve the usage of e-kiosks in the airport and efficient e-ticketing, which reduces labor and thereby costs. In the contemporary aviation landscape, airlines have also shifted focus to new and more fuel-efficient engines to reduce fuel costs, which are one of the biggest contributors to operating expense. This is also mainly why LCCs are moving toward acquiring more of the A320 neo and 737 Max lines.

Ultra-Low-Cost Carriers

The future of low-cost carriers appears to be steady, although a further modification to the low-cost model was the introduction of ULCCs. The main idea of an Ultra-Low-Cost Carrier is the extremely low base fare over which all the fringe fares or ancillary revenues are added. ULCCs, characterized by their deeply discounted fares, stimulate demand and drive continuing growth. The pioneers of this business model were Spirit Airlines and Allegiant Air. Subsequently, Frontier Airlines assumed the same strategy, making it the third airline in the United States which claims to be following this business model. In early 2022, Frontier attempted to acquire Spirit Airlines for $2.8 billion cash-and-stock deal, soon after announcing the proposal, JetBlue made a competing offer to acquire Spirit for $3.6 billion in cash. On July 27, 2022, Spirit announced that its shareholders had rejected Frontier's offer. Spirit was the eighth largest passenger carrier in North America as of 2021, as well as the largest Ultra-Low-Cost Carrier in North America.

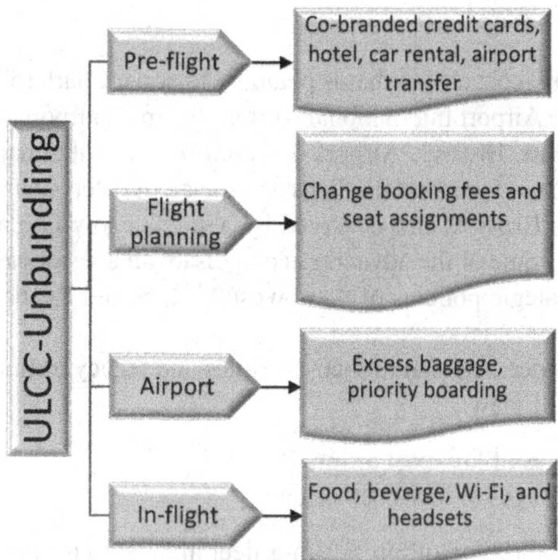

The ULCC business model is not exclusive to the United States. It extends globally, with ULCCs even offering international flights. A prominent illustration was, Icelandic Ultra-Low-Cost Carrier, WOW Air. This airline flew to six destinations in the United States, the latest addition being flights between Miami and Reykjavik, Iceland. The airline, in line with the ULCC business model, earned the majority of its profits by selling ultra-low-cost base fares and then adding supplemental fees over the course of the travel experience. WOW Air initiated flights from Chicago's O'Hare in 2017 and rolled out sale fares of $99 one-way to Iceland and $149 to connecting destinations elsewhere in Europe.[34] While it charged for checked bags and flight changes like traditional airlines, for example, there was also a fee for in-flight meals and seat selection, something atypical for international carriers. Despite these inconveniences, budget travelers have found low fares on international flights hard to pass up. But many of the cost advantages of the ULCC model, such as rapid turnaround times and other lower airport costs, are less relevant on long-haul flights and WOW failed in 2019. Another initially successful transatlantic ULCC, Norwegian Air, also failed in early 2020.

Copa Airlines is another airline seeking to diversify its business model by launching a Columbia-based ULCC in late 2016, in Colombia. Wingo will operate as a sub-fleet of its existing subsidiary, Copa Airlines Colombia. If proven to be successful, the Panama-based company seeks to export the model to other countries in which it operates.

Summary

This chapter introduces the history of LCCs, the various strategies used by low-cost airlines to gain competitive advantages over legacy airlines, and how the low-cost models have evolved over time. A low-cost airline has many characteristics that differentiate it from the legacy airlines, and these characteristics are discussed and analyzed in some detail in the chapter. The growth and evolution of LCCs outside of the United States, particularly in the Asia-Pacific region, is discussed and compared to the more mature markets of Europe and North America. The response of legacy carriers, from creating many failed low-cost competitive brands to a more calculated response of matching some of the offerings of the LCC carriers is also covered in depth. Finally, we discuss the emergence of ULCC airlines and, in particular, their prominence in international markets.

Discussion Questions

1 You are a manager at a low-cost airline that is planning to serve Charleroi Airport. Your airline has the option of serving Brussels Airport International Airport, the main airport serving Belgium, or Charleroi Airport, a secondary airport. Brussels Airport is served by all of the major legacy, international, and LCCs, and is the closest to governmental offices and the city center. Charleroi Airport is located about 29 miles south of central Brussels and is served by a smaller low-fare airline and several European charter airlines. What are some of the advantages and disadvantages of each airport for your airline?
2 What are some of the strategic policies of Southwest Airlines and Ryanair that have allowed them to be so successful?
3 What's the biggest difference between low-cost airlines and legacy airlines?
4 From a passenger points of view:

   a What are the advantages of low-cost airlines?
   b What are the disadvantages of low-cost airlines?

5 Explain how having a single type of aircraft in a fleet affects an airline's ability to recover from irregular operations, such as diversion recovery or an extended airport shutdown due to bad weather?
6 Describe some of the differences of basic no-frills service between LCC carriers in the United States and those in Europe.
7 What are the challenges and problems faced by LCCs to expand into international markets?
8 How can legacy airlines compete effectively and efficiently with low-cost competitors?
9 In the last 30 years, there has been a surge in the low-cost market. Do you see any possibility for creation of airline alliances among LCCs? Explain you answer.
10 Many legacy airlines have attempted to create a low-cost airline that is separate from the legacy carriers. Without exception, almost all of these attempts have failed. Can you explain why legacy airlines have been unable to enter this market?
11 Explain the relationship between the bankruptcy proceedings that many legacy airlines have entered into with respect to competition from the low-cost carriers.
12 What are some of the major reasons why a low-cost airline might be reluctant to locate at a major hub?
13 List some of the major technological advancements that have enabled low-cost airlines to succeed in the highly competitive domestic airline market.
14 Which model tends to have lower fuel costs—LCC or Legacy? Why?

Appendix: Select Airline Two-Letter Codes

Airline	*Code*
Air Canada	AC
AirTran Airways	FL
Air Transat A.T.	TS
Alaska Airlines	AS
American Airlines	AA
America West Airlines	HP
Continental Airlines	CO
Delta Air Lines	DL
easyJet	U2
Frontier Airlines	F9
JetBlue Airways	B6
Northwest Airlines	NW
Ryanair	FR
Southwest Airlines	WN
United Airlines	UA
US Airways	US
WestJet	WS

Notes

1 Southwest Airlines Media, 1966–1971.
2 Million Mile Secrets, A Guide to Surviving Ultra-Low-Cost Carriers. June 15, 2019.
3 European Parliament. *Fact sheet on European Union. June* 2016.
4 Europe Completes Airline Deregulation the Process Has Been Deliberately Slow, But Competition Has Taken Off on Some Routes. *The Inquirer*, April 7, 1997.
5 European Low Fares Airline Association. The Benefits of Low Fares Airline, 2004.
6 Focus Wire. In the Big Chair, February 8, 2022.
7 Center for Aviation (CAPA), Rankings by seat capacity, April 2017.
8 EasySky Aerolinea de Bajo Costo.
9 Airbus Long Term Passenger Aircraft Forecast 2011–2030.
10 "Mapping Demand," Airbus Global Market Forecast, 2016–2035.
11 Subsidiaries include Thai AirAsia, Thai AirAsia X, AirAsia X, Indonesia AirAsia, Indonesia AirAsia X, and Philippines AirAsia.
12 Simple Flying, Why North America & Asia-Pacific Will Dominate Future Embraer's Deliveries, July 31, 2022.
13 *Reuters*, September 22, 2022.
14 Boeing Current Market Outlook 2016–2035.
15 Airbus Global Market Forecast 2016–2035.
16 Delta to Close Song, Its Low-Fare Airline. *The New York Times*, October 29, 2005.
17 SAS now has a new budget airline: Snowflake. Fodors Travel, April 13, 2003.
18 Simple Flying, These Airlines All Went Bankrupt, December 31, 2019.
19 We Weren't Just Airborne Yesterday, Southwest Airlines. Retrieved October 28, 2016, Air Southwest Co.
20 https://www.indeed.com/cmp/Southwest-Airlines/salaries/Pilot, November 1, 2022.
21 The Appendix contains the two letter airline identification codes for various airlines.
22 Note that Southwest Airlines is considered a legacy airline since it was established prior to deregulation. However, because it has the business model of a low-cost carrier, it is classified under LCCs.
23 How Do Electronic Airline Tickets Work? *USA Today*. June 8, 2008.
24 Since June 2020, all Lauda flights were operated as wet leases with Ryanair flight numbers.
25 After being acquired by Southwest, the 88 Boeing 717s formerly operated by AirTran were agreed to be sub-leased to Delta in May 2012, as part of Delta's plan to remove older DC-9-50s and smaller regional jets from its fleet.

26 *Insider*, August 14, 2022.
27 Ryanair launched a new base of operation in Charleroi Airport in 2001.
28 Spirit Airlines, February 6, 2023.
29 Ted was a United LCC subsidiary from 2004 to 2009.
30 A common-size income statement essentially displays the income statement in percentage terms. All revenue categories are stated as a percentage of total revenue. Conversely, all expense categories are stated as a percentage of total operating expenses. The benefit of a common-size income statement is that it enables a better comparison of cost structures and helps recognize where money is being spent.
31 *Business Travel News (BTN)*. Ancillary airline revenue on the rise. September 27, 2022.
32 In 2013, American Airlines and US Airways merged, and the US Airways brand was retired.
33 *Reuters*. Lufthansa to discontinue Germanwings in sweeping restructuring. April 7, 2020.
34 *USA Today*, March 27, 2017.

References

BBC News. (2003). *Q&A: Ryanair Wwoops on Buzz.* Retrieved on September 19, 2006 from http://news.bbc.co.uk

Bethune, G. (1998). *From Worst to First: Behind the Scenes of Continental's Remarkable Comeback.* New York: John Wiley & Sons.

Bohlman, J., Kletzel, J., and Terry, B. (2017). 2017 Commercial Aviation Trends. *Strategy&.* PwC.

Buyck, C. (2005). Wooing Europe's New Breed. *Air Transport World*, 42(9), 32–35.

Cassels, K. (2008, July 10). *US Airways to Shut Down In-Flight Movies.* The Associated Press, Retrieved on November 3, 2010 from http://www.travelagentcentral.com/airline-policies/us-airways-shutdown-flight-movies.

Clark, A. (2002). easyJet Lines Up Merger with Go: Shake-Up of Budget Airlines Could Mean Higher Fares. *The Guardian*, May 4, 2.

Dunn, G. (1999). KLM Launches Low Cost Airline—Named "Buzz". *Air Transport Intelligence News*, September 22.

Field, D. and Pilling, M. (2005). The Last Legacy. *Airline Business*, 21(3), 48–51.

Flint, P. (1996). The Leopard Changes Its Spots. *Air Transport World*, 33(11), 51, 54.

Goldsmith, C. (1998). British Airways Launches No-Frills Unit—Move May Risk Diluting Brand Name, Some Say. *Wall Street Journal*, May 22, 5.

Henry, K. (1998). Aiming High with Lower Fares; US Airways' MetroJet Set to Debut, Battle Southwest, Boost BWI. *The Sun,* May 31, 1.

Ionides, N. and O'Toole, K. (2005). Points of Sale. *Airline Business*, 21(3), 42–45.

Johnston, D.C. (2001). Airlines Are Cutting Their Discount Services. *New York Times*, November 18, 5.

O'Toole, K. (1999). Express Yourself. *Airline Business*, January 28. Retrieved on November 28, 2006 from Air Transport Intelligence.

Shannon, D. (2011). North American Legacies Take Another look at LCC Concept, *Aviation Week*, November 23.

10 Economics of Aviation Safety and Security

Today's commercial airlines provide the safest mode of transportation, and according to a report issued by the International Air Transport Association (IATA), airlines have enjoyed their lowest rate of major accidents in recent years. The global average jet hull loss rate declined slightly in 2021 when compared to the five-year average (2017–2021). The mortality rate, measuring at 0.07 fatalities per billion passenger miles, is significantly lower as compared to 7.28 fatalities per billion passenger miles for automobile travel. These statistics imply that it is over 100 times more hazardous to drive than fly on a per-mile basis. In 2015, there were four accidents, resulting in 136 passenger fatalities, all of which involved turboprop aircraft. This represents a 30% improvement over the previous five-year period, which had an average of 17.6 fatal accidents and 504 fatalities per year.[1] The fatality rate on commercial airlines worldwide jumped in 2018 after airlines recorded zero accident deaths in the prior year. Despite this increase, 2018 was the third safest year ever in terms of the number of fatal accidents. There was one fatal accident involving jet aircraft last year and the jet fatality risk in 2021 was 0.04 per million sectors, an improvement over the five-year average of 0.06.[2] The overall fatality risk of 0.23[3] means that on average, a person would need to take a flight every day for 10,078 years to be involved in an accident with at least one fatality. However, this enviable record still needs to be put into perspective when the topic of safety is considered. The term "safety" is often used incorrectly as an absolute value; that is, one is either safe or unsafe. Moreover, safety is never absolute since there is always some probability of an accident. Therefore, the level of safety depends on the given situation and the risks that are part of that situation. However, a considerable number of individuals claim that safety should be maximized regardless of the cost. The line of reasoning follows a certain logic: if human life is deemed sacred then it may seem reasonable to consider human safety to be sacred—shouldn't our goal be to achieve as much safety as possible? However, if this proportion is true, then we should outlaw any activity where fatalities are even remotely possible. A ban needs to be imposed on swimming, skiing, fishing, flying, pregnancy, social gatherings (where disease may spread), driving more than 15 mile per hour, and virtually everything else that people enjoy doing!

The benefits of safety are undeniable, encompassing not solely from a moral standpoint, but also from an economic standpoint. Some of the potential economic benefits of aviation safety include strengthened passenger demand, strengthened labor supply, reduced insurance costs, lower cost of capital, lower liability risk, and reduced costs associated with government fines or penalties. While this chapter predominantly analyzes aviation safety from an economic

DOI: 10.4324/9781003388135-10

standpoint, it also provides some more specific facts and figures on aviation safety. The general outline is as follows:

- The Basics of Aviation Safety
- The History of Aviation Safety
- Incentives for Aviation Safety
    - Passengers' Reaction
    - Labor Reaction
    - Financial Concerns
    - Insurance Costs and Liability Risks
    - Government Enforcement
- Causes of Aviation Accidents
    - Flight Crew Error
    - Aircraft Malfunction
    - Weather Related
    - Airport/Air Traffic Control
    - Maintenance
    - Miscellaneous/Other
- Classification of Accidents by Phase of Flight
- Classification of Accidents by Regions
- Basic Economics of Safety
- Politics and Safety Regulation
- Accident Prevention
- Summary
- Discussion Questions

The Basics of Aviation Safety

The economics of airline safety is concerned with the costs and benefits of investing in safety measures to minimize the risk of aviation accidents. The benefits derived from investing in airline safety can be significant, including reducing the likelihood of accidents and incidents that can result in loss of life, property damage, and reputational damage to the airline. In the United States, the Federal Aviation Administration (FAA), and in Europe the European Union Aviation Safety Agency (EASA) have the responsibility for the safety of civil aviation. These agencies are in charge of pilot certification, supervision of the air traffic control system, and also the conduction of investigative and monitoring activities. Increases in safety are optimal only when the benefits of safety justify the costs. Thus, even minor increases in safety that impose major costs are never cost-efficient. This rationale elucidates why some people refuse to wear seatbelts or why the government does not establish a national speed limit of 15 mph, even though both of these actions would minimize the risk of injury and accidents. However, airlines cannot select their level of safety by balancing the benefits of reducing accidents with the cost of investing in safety improvements. The trade-off between safety and operational freedom affects all, so must be a decision made in the public interest by the governmental bodies. No airline or airport should be able to benefit from a competitive advantage by operating with airworthiness standards below acceptable levels—the "moral hazard" problem. The aviation industry is as a result subject to significant regulation and oversight. The FAA issues and enforces safety regulations covering manufacturing, operating, and maintaining aircraft, and also certifies airmen and airports that serve air carriers. In spite of the fact that expressions like "safety must be preserved at any price" are commonly used, safety still needs to be judged within the economic context of a simple cost-benefit analysis.

Prior to discussing the topic of aviation safety, it is useful to understand some basic aviation safety terminology, since several terms are used synonymously but may contain different meanings. The National Transportation Safety Board (NTSB) defines an aviation *accident* as:

> An occurrence associated with the operation of an aircraft which takes place between the time any person boards the aircraft with the intention of flight until all such persons have disembarked, and in which any person suffers death or serious injury as a result of being in or upon the aircraft or by direct contact with the aircraft or anything attached thereto, or in which the aircraft receives substantial damage.

On the other hand, the NTSB defines an aviation *incident* as "an occurrence other than an accident, associated with the operation of an aircraft, which affects or could affect the safety of operations" (Vasigh and Helmkay, 2002). In reality, the difference between an accident and an incident is largely based on the severity of the situation. If an aircraft sustains damage, then the situation would likely be deemed as an accident. However, instances like an aircraft landing on a parallel taxiway or a runway incursion may not provide aircraft damage and therefore be classified as an incident, but it may actually represent a more serious threat to safety.

A fatal aviation accident is one that results in fatalities, or deaths. The fatalities could involve passengers, crewmembers, or people on the ground. A hull loss occurs when an aircraft is a complete write-off from an accident and is deemed unfit for further flight. Generally, aviation safety is measured in terms of accidents, fatal accidents, fatalities, and hull losses. Despite improvements in five regions, the global average hull loss rate rose slightly in 2020 compared to the five-year average (2016–2020).

In aviation safety literature, terms that may have common reference include a near midair collision (NMAC), a pilot deviation, and a runway incursion. While a midair collision involves two aircraft making contact while in flight, a NMAC is an incident associated with an aircraft flying within 500 feet of another airborne aircraft (Vasigh and Helmkay, 2002).

Pilot deviation refers to the actions of a pilot that result in the violation of a Federal Regulation or a North American Aerospace Defense Command (NORAD) Air Defense Identification Zone (ADIZ) Directive (Vasigh and Helmkay, 2002). Essentially, pilot deviation means that the aircraft goes into airspace that is either totally restricted or the aircraft has entered the airspace without taking the appropriate procedural steps. Such deviations may be a result of equipment malfunctions, weather conditions, operational factors, and/or pilot experience (Vasigh and Helmkay, 2002).

Finally, a runway incursion refers to any occurrence on an airport runway involving an aircraft and any object or person on the ground that creates a collision hazard or results in a loss of separation with an aircraft taking off, intending to takeoff, landing, or intending to land. Despite the decreasing trend in aviation accidents over the past few years, runway incursions continue to occur (Table 10.1). Runway incursions are further classified into four categories: A, B, C, and D, where A and B are considered serious. These categories are based on available reaction time,

Table 10.1 Number of "Serious" Runway Incursions, 2017–2022

Year	*OE/D*	*OI*	*Other*	*PD*	*V/PD*	*Total*
2017	57	306	7	1,142	293	1,748
2018		345	10	1,142	335	1,832
2019		324	16	1,118	295	1,753
2020		164	15	841	241	1,261
2021		226	30	1,033	285	1,574
2022		294	26	997	293	1,610

Source: FAA Runway Safety Fact Sheet, 2017–2022. https://www.faa.gov/airports/runway_safety/statistics/

evasive or corrective action, environmental conditions, speed of the aircraft and/or vehicle, and proximity of aircraft/vehicle.[4] Furthermore, the FAA classifies runway incursions into three error types:

a *Operational Errors/Deviations*: an event of the air traffic system where an aircraft, vehicle, equipment, or personnel encroaches upon a landing area that was delegated to another position of operation without prior approval or coordination.
b *Pilot Deviation*: action of a pilot that violates Federal Aviation Regulation.
c *Vehicle/Pedestrian Deviations (V/PD)*: involves pedestrians, vehicles, and other objects interfering with aircraft operations. These incursions are not to be misunderstood as causative but are the nature of incursion occurrence.

The History of Aviation Safety

In 1903, the Wright Brothers achieved the historic milestone by conducting the very first controlled and sustained heavier-than-air flight. Today, more than a century later, tens of thousands of airplanes are in the air at any one time. These aircraft span all shapes and sizes. As aviation technology has developed at a tremendous rate, so too has aviation safety. Once a highly risky method of transportation, aviation has developed into the safest mode of transportation available to the public. In fact, in terms of fatalities per passenger miles (0.0068) in the United States from 2000 to 2020(?), air transportation was 100 times safer than passenger autos. Furthermore, the air transport industry produced zero fatalities for years 2010–2017 and 2020. This achievement is vividly represented in Figure 10.1 and Table 10.2, which compare fatalities from airlines to those fatalities that occur from other forms of transportation.

Note that Figure 10.1 represents the average of fatalities during 2010–2020. For example, less than a percentage of transportation fatalities are due to airline accidents.

These statistics support the fact that one is more likely to be involved in a fatal accident while driving than while flying. While there may be grievances voiced regarding the service provided by airlines, the one thing consumers have little to complain about is safety. Over time, airlines have effectively proven that they successfully meet their primary objective of safety. In the wake of the September 11, 2001, terrorist attacks, many Americans started driving more due to a fear of flying, air traffic decreased causing an indirect increase in automobile accidents. In the 12 succeeding attacks, there were approximately 1,600 more accident-related deaths on American roads than would have been expected statistically.[5]

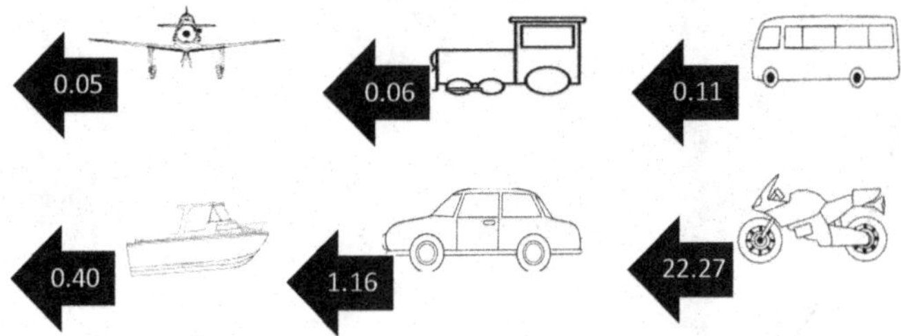

Figure 10.1 US Fatalities per Billion Miles Traveled, 2022.

Source: Airline Profiler

Table 10.2 US Fatality Rates by Mode of Transportation, 2022[a]

Passenger, Auto	33%
Light Truck	25%
Motorcycle	14%
Bicycle	2%
Rail, Passenger	0.573%
Rail, Freight	2%
Rail, Transit	0.431%
Water, Vessel	0.027%
Bus	0.039%
Airline	**0.000%**
Other	2.74%
Total Fatalities 2020	80%

Source: Compiled by the authors using Bureau of Transportation Statistics.

[a] Figures are rounded and not normalized for distance traveled.

At the beginning of the jet age, 40 fatal accidents per million flights were recorded. The accident rate fell rapidly and a decade ago was down to less than one fatal accident per million flights.

The increase in aviation safety has its most striking progress over the past few decades. The Second World War was a significant event in aviation history as aircraft technology advanced rapidly to cope with wartime demand. Following the conclusion of war, the industry took off as the new technologies and aircraft developed during the war were applied commercially. An excellent example of this technology transfer was the German Messerschmitt 262, which was the world's first operational jet-powered fighter aircraft. Subsequently, its technology was

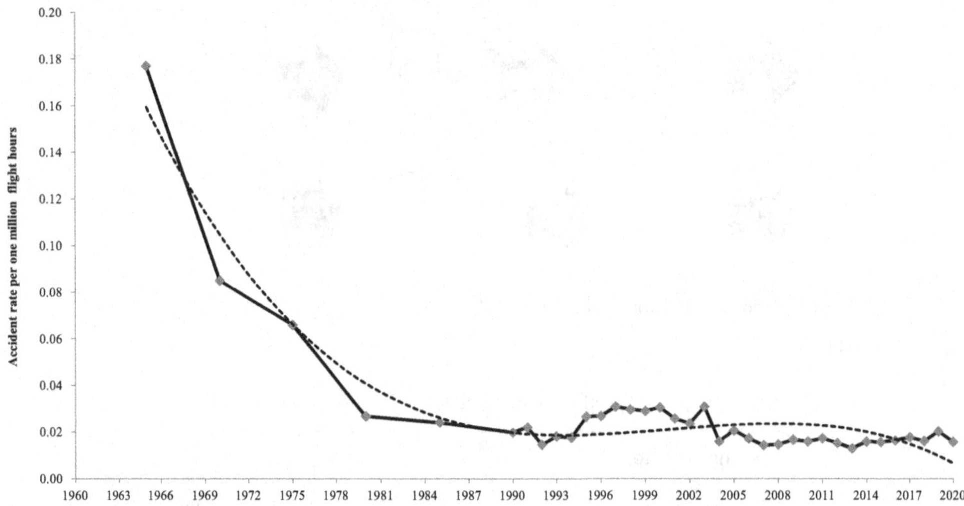

Figure 10.2 Commercial Aircraft Accidents per Million Flight Hours in the United States.

Source: Compiled by the author using Air Transport Association (ATA) data

subsequently used as a basis for future jet aircraft. Although it took some time for jet aircraft to power the majority of commercial aircraft, the development of the jet engine marked a significant event in commercial aviation safety. By allowing aircraft to fly further, faster, and higher, the jet engine proved to be more reliable than the piston engine, thereby increasing safety. Thus, the increase in safety is evident in Figure 10.2, which depicts the number of accidents per million flight hours for commercial aircraft in the United States. The evolution of the jet engine through the 1960s resulted in an accident rate that was decreasing in an exponential fashion, signaling a dramatic change in aviation safety. Among the groundbreaking technologies, Terrain Awareness and Warning Systems (TAWS) alert pilots when they're flying too close to terrain. It's one of the technologies that has virtually eliminated the risk of controlled-flight-into-terrain accidents in US commercial passenger operations.

Like many other new technologies, such as fly-by wire, additional advancements have also made commercial aviation safer. One emerging technology is machine learning technology (ML), and Artificial Intelligence (AI) has been improving the operations of the aviation industry during the pandemic. For example, AI has been used to gather flight data for route optimization and provide detailed weather forecasting.[6] While all of these factors have played a role in improving safety, they have also been accompanied by improvements in pilot training. The integration of advanced simulation training and research into crew resource management has reduced the number one cause of aviation accidents—pilot error. Due to these remarkable advancements, aviation has continually become safer. However, as shown in the graph above, safety somewhat plateaued for the last 20 years; the accident rate has hovered between 0.02 and 0.04 accidents per million flight hours since the mid-1980s. This phenomenon can be attributed in part to fewer advancements in aviation technology, but it also may well be that aviation safety has reached an economic equilibrium. This implies that accidents could conceivably be further reduced, but the costs of doing so may be excessively expensive.[7] Therefore, aviation safety appears to be approaching a point where the benefits of safety are approximately equal to the costs (the cost-benefit analysis of commercial aviation will be discussed in more detail later in this chapter). The plateau effect mentioned is also shown in Figures 10.3 and 10.4, which display

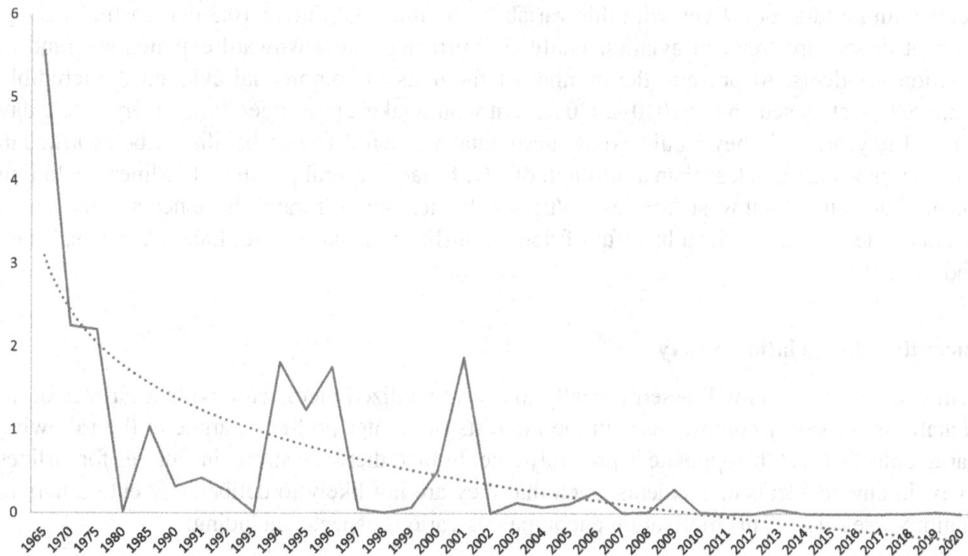

Figure 10.3 Number of Fatalities per 100 Million Aircraft-Miles.

Source: BTS National Transportation Statistics, Table 2.9: U.S. Carrier Safety Data

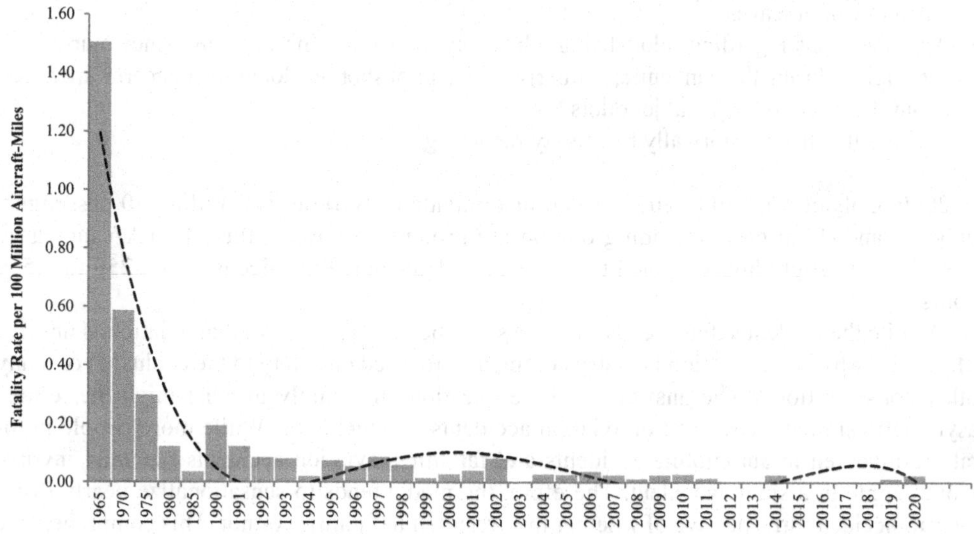

Figure 10.4 Commercial Aviation Fatality Rate per Million Aircraft Miles in the United States with Five-Year Moving Average.

Source: BTS National Transportation statistics, Table 2.9: US Carrier Safety Data

the number of fatal aviation accidents and total fatalities per 100 million aircraft miles in the United States.

As depicted in Figures 10.3 and 10.4 (in comparison with Figure 10.2), fatalities and fatal accidents are more random than generic accidents, with significant fatality years followed by years with no fatalities. Even with this variability in the data, Figure 10.3 demonstrates a significant downward trend in aviation fatalities, mirroring the downward exponential trend in aviation accidents. At present, the number of fatalities in commercial aviation is incredibly minute. In fact, based on the 2010–2020 data, it would take a passenger flying every single day for 39,139 years until they would experience a fatal accident.[8] The probability of being killed in an aviation accident is less than a billionth of 1%. In fact, several prominent airlines, including Qantas,[9] JetBlue, Southwest Airlines,[10] Virgin Atlantic,[11] and Emirates, have never had a single fatality. The same goes for a handful of defunct airlines, including Go, Laker Airways, Song, and MetroJet.

Incentives for Aviation Safety

While some observers will assert (usually in sensationalized media stories) that airlines occasionally make safety compromises in the interests of greater profit, we argue in the following paragraphs that just the opposite is probably true. In fact, there are strong incentives for airlines to avoid any accidents or incidents, such that they are not likely to deliberately cut corners to compromise safety. This motivation encompasses various aspects, including:

- The maintenance practices
- Pilot training, pilot experience, and pilot fatigue
- The corporate cultures, where pilots fear punishment if they report safety issues
- Pilot mental health, especially at airlines that don't have a second person go into the cockpit when one pilot leaves
- Apprehensions regarding pilots being a bit rusty after returning to flying, since many were furloughed during the pandemic; similarly, with a pilot shortage looming, concerns are raised about the future of regional jet pilots
- Airlines that have historically bad safety recordings

In 2009, Colgan Air flight 3407 crashed just outside of Buffalo, NY, killing 50 passengers onboard and flight crew including one on the ground. Following this, the FAA increased the minimum flight hours needed to earn an Air Transport Pilot license from 250 to 1,500 hours.

Despite the evident safety trends, why do some people still believe that aviation is unsafe? Moreover, why is the aviation industry continually focused on safety to the exclusion of many other considerations? The answers to these questions lie mainly in what might be termed asymmetrical media coverage of aviation accidents and incidents. While more people in total are involved in automobile accidents and fatalities, aviation accidents typically involve more people in a single accident. Therefore, the media tends to sensationalize nearly every aircraft accident, irrespective of whether they resulted in fatalities or not. This comprehensive media coverage creates a situation where, if an airline has an accident, their logo may be emblazoned into the minds of consumers across the world for all the wrong reasons. While the media does not document the thousands of routine safe flights taking place each day, nor the incredibly small probability of an aviation accident, even a slight minor safety slip by an airline will draw extensive media coverage. This dynamic creates a climate where airlines have a very strong incentive to further ensure safe operations. However, media coverage is just one of many incentives. Further incentives for aviation safety can be grouped into five broad categories:

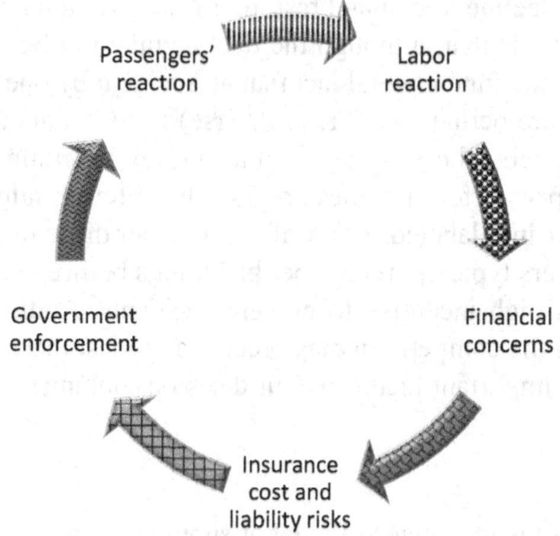

Passengers' Reaction

A majority of passengers place a high value on airline safety and expect airlines to take all necessary measures to ensure the safety of their onboard passengers. This includes adhering to strict safety protocols, maintaining well-trained and competent staff, and investing in the latest safety equipment and technology. Given that consumers can choose among firms in the market, they can decide how important safety is to them. Therefore, an airline garners a perception of being less secure, as a result of an accident or investigation, is likely to see a decrease in demand compared to "safer" airlines. For passengers, the decision factor is based on the perception of safety rather than on the actual level of safety, since passengers usually know very little about the actual level of safety of their flight (Squalli and Saad, 2006). Perceptions of aviation safety primarily stem from accidents, particularly those accidents that receive extensive media attention. Additionally, altering these perceptions are challenging and may last for an extended period of time; this creates a situation where a single aviation accident may have a long-term impact on an airline's demand (Squalli and Saad, 2006). The ValuJet Flight 592 fatal accident had a significant impact on ValuJet Airlines, which ultimately merged with AirTran Airways in 1997. The ValuJet name faced such substantial tarnishing from this single accident that it was forced to merge with AirTran Airways in 1997.

Although economic logic would imply that the demand for a particular airline should be reduced after it experiences an accident, researchers have found it difficult to empirically prove this decrease in demand. Borenstein and Zimmerman (1988) conducted an extensive study of 74 accidents in the United States from 1960 to 1985, only to find out that there was no statistically significant decrease in demand for the airline's services as a result of the accident.[12] Squalli and Saad (2006), on the other hand, did find a minor decrease in demand resulting from aviation accidents in the United States, while Wong and Yeh (2003) estimated a 22.11% decline in monthly traffic lasting for 2.54 months resulting from an aircraft accident in Taiwan. Part of the difficulty in statistically showing a decrease in demand is that following an aviation accident, airlines tend to undertake competitive action to help offset a shift in the demand curve, such as lowering ticket prices. While their study shows no statistical significance, Borenstein and Zimmerman (1988) did find that consumers responded more adversely to aviation accidents post-deregulation than they did during regulation.

While quantifying the decline in demand resulting from aviation accidents has proven intricate, economic logic suggests that, although the decline may not be large, it definitely exists. This assertion is rooted in the fundamental fact that an accident by one carrier will undoubtedly cause some people (who are perhaps very risk adverse) to fly on another carrier. This may be particularly true of consumers who view aviation as unsafe in certain regions of the world, as there exists a prevailing perception that these regions have lower safety standards. While this may or may not be true, airlines labeled as "unsafe" encounter difficulties in changing the public perceptions since consumers typically remember bad things before good things.

Again, airlines have a high incentive to prevent accidents. Additionally, an airline that is perceived to be safer than the competition may receive a modest increase in demand if the passengers view safety as an important factor in their decision-making.

Labor Reaction

Much like the response of the passengers, the labor supply may also react adversely to an aviation accident. Employees do not want to work in an environment which they consider unsafe. Therefore, an airline may experience two labor issues as a result of an accident: increased turnover and/or increased wage demands.

Due to the perception or the reality of reduced safety, employees, particularly members of the flight crew, may feel that the airline is engaging in questionable safety practices. This could cause employees to leave the company or have the union enforce new safety measures. Moreover, an accident or a series of incidents could make it more difficult for an airline to attract quality employees.

The other labor supply outcome of decreased safety would be increased wages. For instance, employees may demand better compensation for having to work in a less safe environment. In essence, this would be a form of "combat pay," wherein employees are compensated for working under uncertain or dangerous conditions. While such demands might be difficult for employee groups to obtain in the short term, an airline's safety could become a bargaining issue in the long term.

These impacts represent both explicit and implicit costs to the airline, and therefore provide strong incentives to avoid accidents and incidents. As a result, the airline has an economic incentive to continue operating safely in order to avoid the costs imposed by the market forces resulting from an accident.

Financial Concerns

The stock market will always react negatively toward an airline that experiences an accident, particularly one that involves fatalities. The reason for this is the prevailing and rather evident belief that such an accident will cause great uncertainty over the future of the airline. Borenstein and Zimmerman (1988) found that on average, aviation accidents caused a 0.94% equity loss for the firm on the first day of trading, which was statistically significant at the 1% level. This value is slightly lower than two other studies that determined equity losses amounting to 1.18% and 1.19% on the first day of trading (Borenstein and Zimmerman, 1988). Mitchell and Maloney (1989) went one step further in analyzing the impact of an aviation accident on the firm's equity value in the long term. If the findings revealed that accident was proved to be the airline's fault, then equity value dropped by 2.2% (Mitchell and Maloney, 1989). However, if the accident was not deemed to be the airline's fault, equity value dropped by only 1.2% (Mitchell and Maloney, 1989). Irrespective of the fault attribution, the airline's equity will decline, which is another incentive to avoid aviation accidents and promote safety. Notably, Boeing's stock dropped following reports that one of its planes operated by China Eastern Airlines has crashed with 132 passengers on board. The Boeing 737-800 passenger jet was crashed on March 21, 2022 when it plunged into a mountainous area in Guangxi, China.[13]

The erosion of equity value for an airline will have additional, and possibly greater, negative financial effects, namely, a large increase in the cost of capital. Due to this greater risk and uncertainty associated with the decline in equity value, the airline will find it more expensive to raise capital. This can pose a serious concern, since airlines are highly capital intensive. While a loss of equity through a decline in the stock price is not an explicit cost against the airline, an increase in the cost of capital directly impacts the airline's finances, providing another major incentive to avoid accidents and incidents.

Insurance Costs and Liability Risks

When an aviation accident occurs, airlines are usually fully indemnified from the losses through insurance coverage. Insurance companies will pay out various liability and damage claims for the airlines, causing airlines little direct financial loss from an accident. Notably, the aircraft hull insurance is very costly. The explicit risk exclusions section under insurance policy, may not cover damages for events such as war, terrorism risk, or force majeure.

However, as a result of an airline accident, particularly when the airline is determined to be liable to any extent, the airline's insurance premiums are poised to experience a sharp increase dramatically in the future. Similar to the dynamics of automobile insurance premiums, airlines will see insurance hikes if they experience an accident or incident. Moreover, the insurance rate hike does not just occur for one year but lasts for several years. These elevation increases can have a significant effect on an airline's profit margins. Not only do airlines currently pay substantial insurance premiums, but it has been estimated that increases in insurance rates explain about 34% of equity loss (Wong and Yeh, 2003). In relation to insurance premiums, airlines will find that their liability risks will increase substantially as a result of an accident. Therefore, the threat of increased liability risks provides airlines with one more economic incentive (from increased insurance premiums) to promote safety and avoid aviation accidents.

Government Enforcement

The ultimate and concluding incentive for aviation safety is not a true market incentive; however, the threat of government penalties provides another real incentive. In response to two deadly crashes (the Ethiopian Airlines Flight 302, and Lion Air Flight 610) the FAA grounded 737 MAX jets in the United States, on March 13, 2019. A worldwide ban was in effect by March 18, 2019. Unlike traffic penalties, safety fines levied by the FAA can be substantial. Boeing settled to pay over $2.5 billion after being charged with fraud over the company's hiding of information from safety regulators: $1.77 billion of damages to airline customers, a criminal monetary penalty of $244 million, and a $500 million victim beneficiaries' fund.[14] As another example, the FAA levied more than $10 million in fines against Southwest Airlines for not inspecting cracks on dozens of its planes (Levin, 2008). The FAA argued that the carrier flew more than 60,000 flights with these planes without their required inspections. In another instance, in 2010, the FAA imposed a $24.2 million penalty on American Airlines on the grounds that the airline made 14,278 flights on 286 MD-80 jets without making required upgrades to wiring during 2008 (Levin, 2010). Likewise, United Airlines was hit with an $805,000 fine in 2002 for improper maintenance techniques (FAA, 2002). Clearly, fines levied by the FAA are substantial and provide an incentive for safety. However, the greatest threat posed to an airline would be the threat of a complete shutdown due to a severe violation in safety practices. The FAA holds the authority to order an airline to cease operations; this would effectively cut off revenue while imposing sizeable costs and penalties. The apprehension of a shutdown is one of the greatest threats to an airline and, while the FAA has rarely used its authority to temporarily shut down an airline, the mere presence of this threat provides a tremendous incentive to adhere to FAA with safety protocols. For example, ValuJet, Kiwi Airlines, and Nation's Air all were shut down by the FAA for safety violations. Similarly, the French authorities grounded Point Air Mulhouse back in 1988 subsequent to numerous and recurrent maintenance problems with the B-707 and DC-8. Therefore, the presence of the FAA and other aviation regulators provide airlines with a strong financial incentive to promote safe air travel.

Causes of Aviation Accidents

Aviation accidents occur for a variety of reasons, and every accident undergoes a thorough investigation to help prevent future accidents. Accidents are rarely attributed to just one cause, as a variety of factors must go wrong for the accident to occur. Understanding the nature of the accidents and how they occur is important to continually improve aviation safety and to help understand the economic principles of safety. The six major categories by which airline accidents can be categorized are:

Table 10.3 displays the number of worldwide fatalities resulting from aviation accidents between 2000 and 2020. These fatalities are classified by the Commercial Aviation Safety Team (CAST) and the International Civil Aviation Organization (ICAO), utilizing primary classification based on principal categories agreed upon by air carriers, aircraft manufacturers, engine manufacturers, pilot associations, regulatory authorities, transportation safety boards, as well as members from Canada, the European Union, France, Italy, the Netherlands, the UK, and the United States. Due to the existence of varying definitions, the cause of an aviation accident could be embedded among the different categories.

For example, flight crew errors could be categorized as CFIT (Controlled Flight into Terrain) or LOC (Loss of Control), depending on the nature of accident. On May 9, a Sukhoi SSJ-100-95 crashed into Mount Salak in Indonesia during a demonstration flight with 45 people onboard.[15] Regardless of such cross-classifications, the ICAO taxonomy provides a standardized worldwide definition of aviation accidents that can be of use in safety research. Given that CFIT and

Table 10.3 Safety Record of US Air Carriers

Year	*Total Accidents*	*Fatal Accidents*
2000	49	2
2001	41	6
2002	34	0
2003	51	2
2004	23	1
2005	34	3
2006	26	2
2007	26	0
2008	20	0
2009	26	1
2010	28	0
2011	29	0
2012	26	0
2013	19	0
2014	28	0
2015	27	0
2016	29	0
2017	30	0
2018	28	1
2019	36	1
2020	11	0

Source: Compiled by the author using Air Transport Association (ATA) data

LOC are generally caused by crew mistakes, the table underscores the fact that the vast majority of aviation accidents are still caused by human mistakes. As is evident by Boeing and shown in Table 10.4, LOC is the number one category of fatalities in aviation. LOC accidents are the result of a variety of factors. CFIT can result from numerous issues but is usually caused by pilot error. While the ICAO classification is different, the major cause of aviation accidents remains roughly the same—human error.

Flight Crew Error

Undoubtedly, safety is increased with automation; however, automation may lend complacency and a false sense of security, particularly among flight crew (pilots and copilots) or air traffic controllers. Misjudgments from the flight crew is the leading cause of airline accidents globally. While Table 10.4 does not specifically distinguish which accidents were caused by human error, it is evident that flight crew error has consistently occupied the top spot as the primary cause of aviation accidents worldwide. New technologies have indeed played a role in making aviation safer, but it still cannot compensate for errors made by humans. Considerable research has been conducted into reasons why flight crews make errors, and while areas such as crew resource management have helped reduce human error, the fact is that as long as humans are in control of the aircraft, flight errors are likely to transpire.

While aviation accidents may result from several contributory factors, most accidents could have been avoided had the crew done something differently. For example, one of the worst aviation accidents in history resulted from human error. The 1977 PanAm/KLM accident in Tenerife occurred when the pilot starting his takeoff prior to receiving air traffic control clearance. The subsequent collision with a PanAm 747 killed 583 passengers in total. Likewise, in

Table 10.4 Fatalities by Occurrence Categories, Worldwide 2012–2022

Cause	*Number of Fatal Accidents*	*Fatalities*
Loss of control—in flight	9	757
Unknown or undertermined	1	239
Controlled flight into terrain	4	170
System/component failure or malfunction (powerplant)	2	164
System/component failure or malfunction (non-powerplant)	2	158
Runway excursion (takeoff or landing)	7	146
Fuel related	1	71
Icing	1	12
Ground handling	4	10
Midair/near midair collision	2	9
Collision with obstacle(s) during takeoff & landing	1	5
Runway incursion – vehicle, aircraft, or person	1	1

Source: Boeing Statistical Summary of Commercial Airplane Accidents, Worldwide Operations, https://www.boeing.com/resources/boeingdotcom/company/about_bca/pdf/statsum.pdf, p. 13.

2009, Colgan Air Flight 3407 crashed into a home in upstate state New York, killing all 49 people on board. After a thorough investigation, the National Transportation Safety Board found the probable cause to be the pilot's incorrect reaction to a stall warning (NTSB, 2010).

Having said that, many other fatal aviation accidents have been avoided due to exemplary efforts by the flight crew. For example, an Aloha Airlines 737-200 was able to land safely (with only one fatality) despite a portion of their fuselage was torn apart by a sudden decompression. Similarly, US Airways Flight 1549 lost engine thrust after being struck by a flock of geese. The crew successfully executed an emergency water landing in the Hudson River, ultimately sparing all lives on board. Therefore, while human errors have caused accidents, flight crews have also saved numerous lives.

The development of realistic flight simulators has made it possible for pilots to experience a variety of problems without ever taking to the sky. Thus, while technology has successfully made aviation safer, future effort aimed at refining crew training and management which may result in fewer flight crew errors.

Aircraft Malfunction

Recall the category divisions from Table 10.4. The second major determinant of an aviation accident is an airplane-related malfunction. Contemporary aircrafts are meticulously designed with safety in mind, showcasing considerably greater sophistication than previous models. However, systems can still malfunction and ultimately cause a serious accident. Components ranging from multi-million-dollar engines to trivial items have all been the cause of serious aviation accidents. The Aloha Airlines flight highlighted above is an example of an airplane-related accident. In this case, metal fatigue caused part of the fuselage to deteriorate and the aircraft experienced rapid decompression. Another example would be United Airlines Flight 232. This flight crash landed in Sioux City, Iowa, after one of the engines failed and thereby disabled the aircraft's hydraulic systems. While fatal aircraft malfunction accidents usually occur when the engines experience a problem, malfunctions can still stem from other systems.

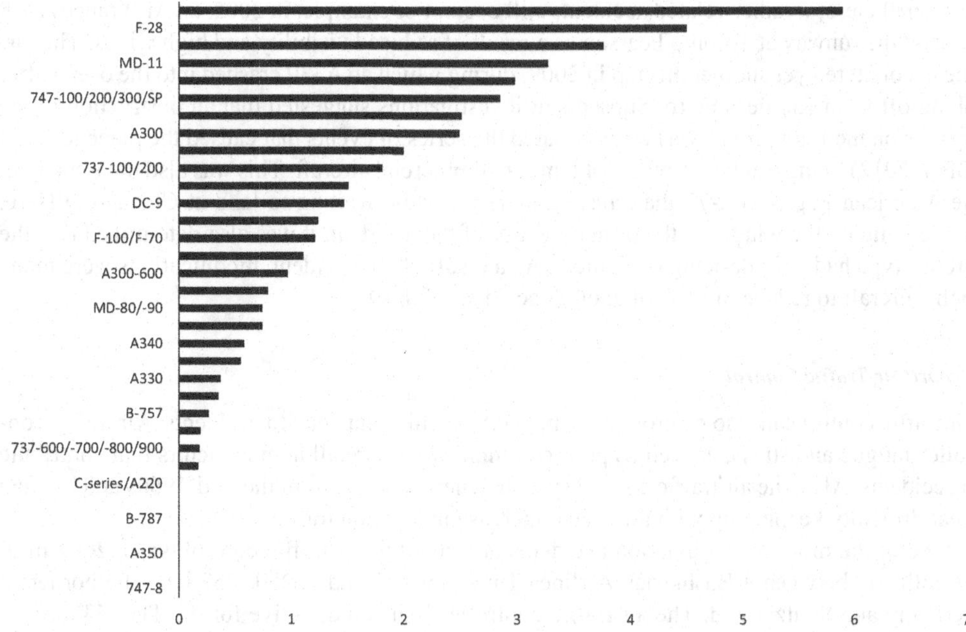

Figure 10.5 Commercial Aircraft Hull Loss by Aircraft per Million Departures between 1959 and 2022.

Source: Compiled by the author using Boeing data

Two separate Boeing 737 Max 8 crashes, one involving Lion Air and the other Ethiopian Airlines, killed 346 people in a span of less than five months. Investigations into the accidents revealed that they were caused by a combination of factors, including technical issues with the aircraft's Maneuvering Characteristics Augmentation System (MCAS).

Figure 10.5 displays a ratio of aircraft hull losses resulting from accidents per 1 million departures for the major aircraft manufacturers since 1959. The underlying data encapsulates a variety of reasons for the accidents, but a trend could possibly be extrapolated if it was assumed that the probability of an accident due to pilot error, weather, maintenance, or air traffic control is approximately the same for all manufacturers (this may not be a good assumption for the smaller companies that do not have their aircraft spread throughout the world). This vantage point reveals that aircraft have become significantly safer as newer models are developed. For example, Boeing's 707 had an 8.87 hull loss rate per million departures, whereas its latest model (which data was available), the 777, had a hull loss rate of only 0.15 per million departures.

Weather

The third major cause of aviation accidents is weather. Through the development of the jet engine, weather-related accidents have become less of a concern since jet engines enable aircraft to fly higher and avoid troublesome atmospheric conditions. Additionally, the development of instrument landing systems allows aircraft to auto-land in adverse weather, which greatly reduces the chance of error during final decent.

Nonetheless, weather-related accidents still occur. For example, in 2005, an Air France A340 overran the runway at Toronto Pearson as a result of reduced visibility and high winds. The airline encountered yet another mishap in 2009, during which an A330 crashed into the ocean after taking off from Rio de Janeiro. Subsequent investigations suggested that an obstruction of ice crystals on the Pitot probes was what initiated the series of events that caused the plane to crash (BEA, 2012). Icing can be a major problem for commercial aircraft. This was also the issue with the American Eagle ATR-72 that crashed in 1994, while waiting to land at Chicago O'Hare. While icing on the wing was the primary cause of the accident, it was also determined that the aircraft type had poor de-icing equipment. As a result of the accident, modifications were made to the aircraft to reduce the risk of another accident of this type.

Airport/Air Traffic Control

Air traffic control can also be prone to human error, which can lead to accidents. Air traffic controller fatigue and stress, as well as poor communication, are all human factors that contribute to accidents. Also, the air traffic control system generally dates from the mid-1960s and has had great difficulty keeping up with the recent increase in aviation traffic.

One of the more recent aviation accidents attributed to air traffic control was a 2002 midair collision between a Bashkirian Airlines Tupolpev 154 and a DHL 757 near the border of Germany and Switzerland. The air traffic controller issued a directive for the TU-154 aircraft to disregard TCAS (Traffic Collision Avoidance System) warning, resulting in both aircraft descending and making contact. In this tragic accident, a series of events led to the air traffic control system failing, resulting in the fatal crash. Heartbreakingly, about 50 of the victims of the midair plane crash over Germany were Russian children going on holiday to Spain.[16]

Air traffic controller fatigue has also been blamed for several aviation accidents in the United States.[17] For example, although the 2007 Comair accident in Lexington, Kentucky was a result of several factors, the investigation found that the controller was working on just two hours of rest (Ahlers, 2007). Had the controller been more adequately rested, it is possible that he might have noticed the CRJ aircraft beginning to take off on the wrong runway. Several other incidents may have resulted from air traffic controller fatigue, and regulations have been amended in order to help minimize human error by air traffic controllers (Ahlers, 2007).

The Tenerife airport disaster was a deadly aviation accident that occurred on March 27, 1977, at Los Rodeos Airport in Tenerife in the Canary Islands, Spain. The accident involved two Boeing 747s, KLM and Pan Am Airlines, which collided on the runway, resulting in the deaths of 583 people. The accident was caused by a miscommunication between the air traffic controllers and the pilots of two planes which led to a collision on the runway.

Maintenance

Human errors are the largest contributor to aircraft accidents. Undoubtedly, the maintenance department of any airline is critical to ensuring that the airline operates safely. Aviation accidents sometimes occur as a result of maintenance being performed either incorrectly or not thoroughly. However, maintenance has accounted for only 4% of hull loss accidents worldwide from 1996 to 2005. This statistic, in itself, serves as a strong testament to the generally high quality of work maintenance personnel do on a worldwide basis. Guided by both domestic and international regulations and inspections, maintenance is usually performed to strict standards; unfortunately, there have been exceptions to this rule.

In 1985, a tragic incident unfolded as Japan Airlines 747 crashed outside of Tokyo killing 520 passengers and crew. The accident resulted from the aircraft losing its rear stabilizer and hydraulic systems due to an explosive decompression. The accident investigation determined that repairs performed by Boeing on an earlier tail strike of the aircraft were inadequate. Over time, the repairs began to fatigue, and the fuselage eventually cracked, causing a massive depressurization in the rear of the aircraft.

Unfortunately, a similar accident occurred in 2002 when a China Airlines 747 on its voyage from Taipei to Hong Kong crashed into the ocean killing all aboard. Once again, the investigation uncovered the fact that the aircraft had experienced a tail strike over 20 years earlier, and the repairs were not carried out according to standards. Eventually, metal fatigue led to rapid depressurization, which ultimately caused the accident.

On May 11, 1996, a ValuJet aircraft crashed in the Florida Everglades and killed 110 passengers and crew. According to the NTSB, the ValuJet crash was the result of failures by the airline, its maintenance contractor, and the FAA. Consequently, prompted by this catastrophe, the Department of Transportation's Inspector General required that the FAA be more proactive in monitoring airline maintenance work performed by non-certified contractors. The aftermath of ValuJet crash has led to changes at the FAA, including closer scrutiny of new carriers and more monitoring of their growth. In 1997, a year after the crash, ValuJet bought Florida-based AirTran Airways and took its name. This metamorphosis later was acquired by Southwest. The airline industry needs to focus on improving maintenance by implementing the following:

- Continuous re-training for aircraft maintenance technicians
- Introduce better mechanisms for reporting, investigating reports, and provide legal protections to the whistle blowers
- Human factors training for airline management and aircraft engineers

Miscellaneous/Other

The final category of aviation accidents is miscellaneous/other, which can include a variety of events, although hijackings represent the largest share. Unfortunately, commercial aircraft are still used for ulterior (usually political) motives, as the terrorist attacks of September 11, 2001 showed. The imperative of increased screening and security will assist in helping to prevent further terrorist attacks. However, more restrictive, and labor-intensive security regulations can rapidly become more detrimental to the traveling public than can any small increase in safety that they generate.

Finally, the cause of some aviation accidents remains unknown due to a lack of evidence or unusual issues. Recalling the ocean crash of Air France Flight 447, the investigation into the accident was hindered by the lack of evidence and the difficulty finding the aircraft's black boxes. Eventually, these crucial components were located and recovered from the ocean floor in May 2011, almost two years after the incident.[18] On April 28, 2012, another mishap took place when a Somali Antonov 24-passenger plane sustained substantial damage in a landing because its tires blew out at Galkayo Airport (GLK).[19] Arguably one of the most perplexing mystery in aviation occurred in 2014, with the disappearance of Malaysia Airlines Flight 370 en route from Kuala Lumpur to Beijing. After losing contact with ATC, the B777-200ER went down somewhere in the ocean, and while the crash sparked an extensive and expensive investigation, the plane has yet to be found.[20]

Classification of Accidents by Phase of Flight

Aviation accidents are typically classified by the phase of flight during which the accident occurred. Figure 10.6 displays the time proportions of each flight phase of a commercial jet, based on Boeing's recent estimates for a 1.5-hour flight.

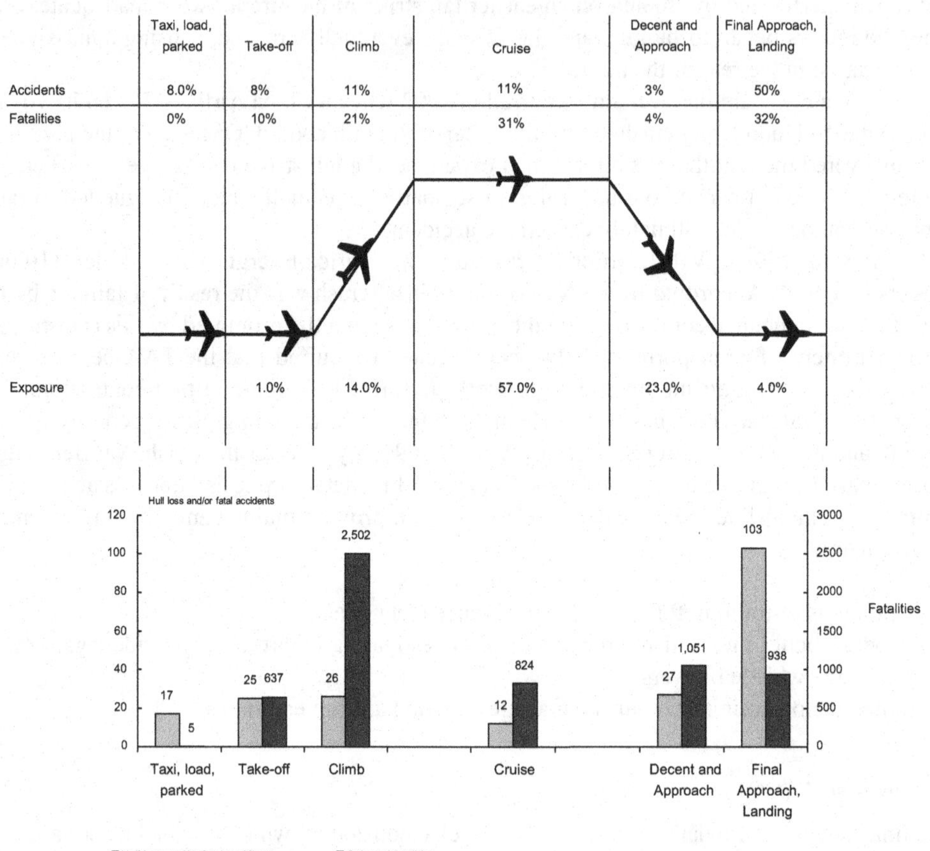

Figure 10.6 Commercial Jet Flight Exposure by Phase of Flight.

Source: Adapted by the authors using Boeing Statistical Summary

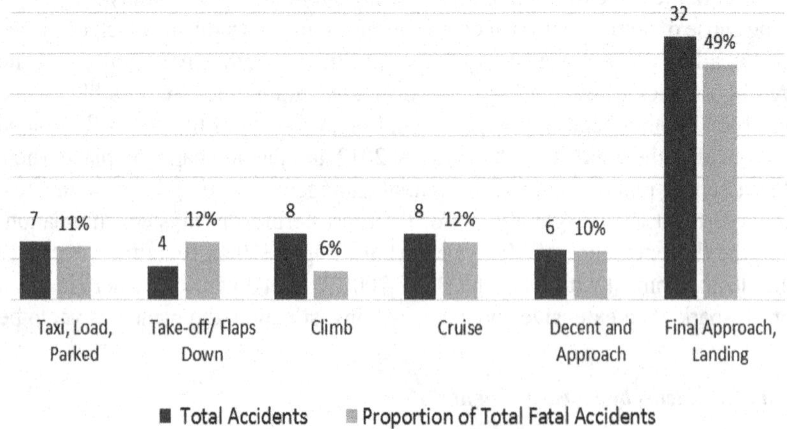

Figure 10.7 Worldwide Commercial Accidents and Fatalities Categorized by Phase of Flight.

Source: Adapted by the authors using Boeing Statistical Summary, 2021

Moreover, Figure 10.7 displays the number and proportion of worldwide fatal accidents that occurred during each flight phase for the period of 2012–2022. Concurrently, Figure 10.7 shows the number and proportion of total fatalities that occurred during each phase of flight for the same period. Notice that nearly half (49%) of all fatal accidents and half (47%) of all fatalities occur during landing/final approach. On the other hand, the takeoff and initial climb accounts for only 12% accidents and 8% of fatalities. Despite constituting approximately 57% of a flight's duration, the cruise phase emerges as the safest flight phase. While accidents and fatalities have occurred at cruise, pilots generally have more time to react and to avoid more serious consequences during this phase. An example of a cruise incident that ended safely was the Air Transat A330 which ran out of fuel and glided to safety in the Azores in 2001. Had the aircraft run out of fuel at a lower altitude or during climb or approach, the result could have been catastrophic.

Classification of Accidents by Region

Industry analysts often classify aviation accidents by their geographical regions. Figure 10.9, for example, displays hull loss rates per million flights for various regions worldwide in 2013–2021 (Figure 10.8). This visual representation shows that aviation safety varies widely by region, with Africa experiencing the highest number aircraft accidents. Regional differences can be attributed to a variety of reasons; however, overall economic prosperity appears correlated with aviation safety. Impoverished regions like Africa have neither the same level of safety regulation nor the same degree of infrastructure as do wealthier nations. Particularly, air traffic control coverage can be sporadic across Africa, and the general lack of instrument systems can make rough weather landings even more dangerous. Moreover, since the number one cause of aviation accidents is human error, training standards are extremely important, and it is difficult to gauge the overall training standards in less-developed countries. Finally, numerous airlines in developing nations operate older aircraft that may be more prone to accidents. Consequently, it stands to reason that the number of accidents in developing nations to be higher than developed nations; however, probably not to the extent that currently exists. It is crucial to emphasize that older airplanes have to meet strict safety requirements, and proper maintenance and supervision are essential to safe flight.

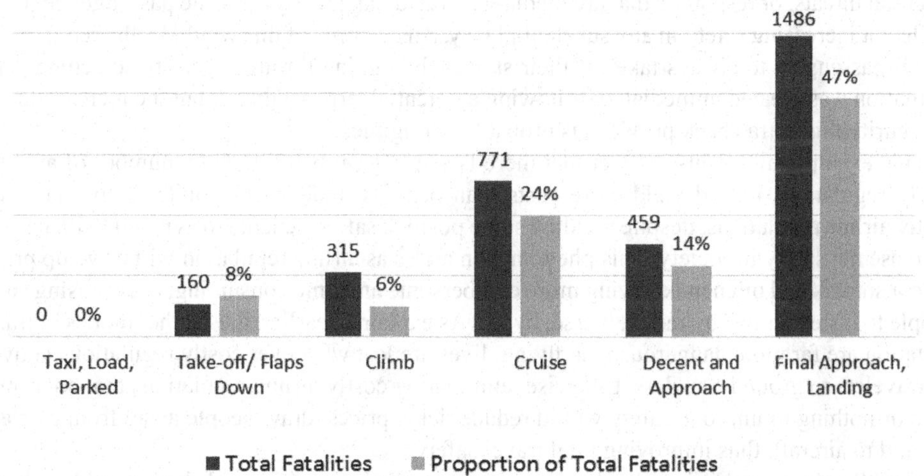

Figure 10.8 Fatality Rate.

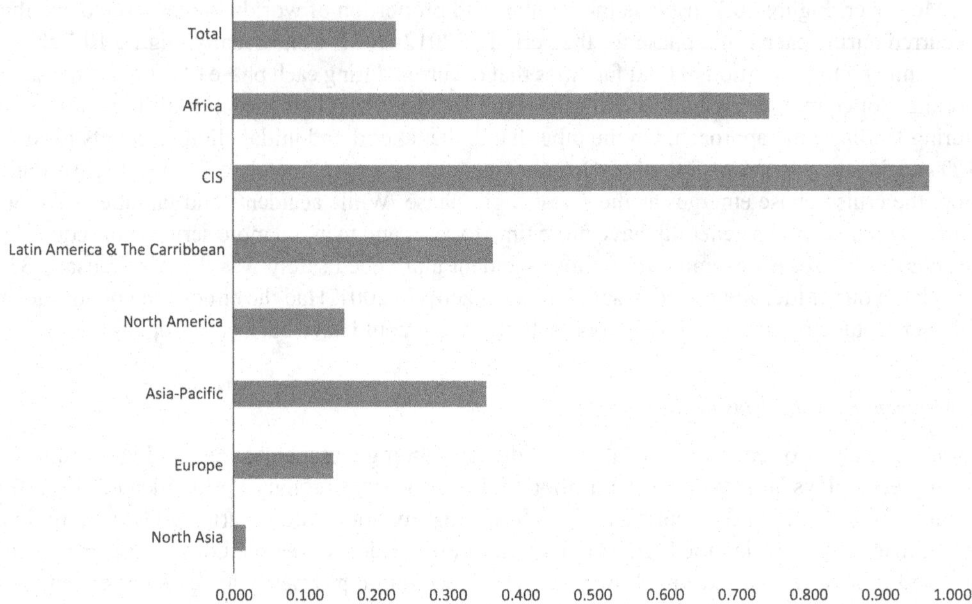

Figure 10.9 Average Hull Losses per Million Flight by Region, 2013–2021.

Source: Compiled by the author using IATA data

Basic Economics of Safety

To understand the economics of aviation safety, one must adopt a macro-level perspective, wherein the benefits of safety regulations to consumers and companies are weighed against the costs of imposing the regulations. Since the costs and benefits of safety are both explicit and implicit, it is sometimes difficult to fairly evaluate a regulation. This intricacy is one of the main reasons why many aviation safety regulations put into place by the government do not always make sound economic rationale.

More specifically, some safety regulations enacted by governments are blanket responses to potential threats, or responses that are media-generated that merely alleviate passenger concerns while not increasing safety in any substantial way. An example of this would be the requirement for all passengers to always take off their shoes while going through security screening. This regulation was created immediately following a potential terrorist threat, but the increased level of security this extra check provides is probably negligible.

This example highlights the fact that there is a strong probability that a number of aviation safety regulations indeed yield more costs than benefits. Indeed, it is quite likely that some costly airline regulations, despite yielding some positive safety benefits to aviation, will actually decrease net safety in society. This phenomenon arises as airline regulation will drive up prices for consumers and often make flying more cumbersome and time consuming, thus causing some people to instead travel by rail or, worse, by car. As explained earlier, these other modes of transportation are far more dangerous than flying, lives are lost whenever costly regulations convert air travelers to ground travelers. Likewise, eliminating costly airline regulations that contribute little or nothing to improve safety would reduce ticket prices, draw people away from cars and rail and to aircraft, thus improving total travel safety.

The "Southwest rule" is a good example of a regulation that, if abolished, would probably increase total safety. In fact, it is likely the benefit of this regulation is about zero, since in all the years prior to the rule there were no injuries caused by the aircraft slowly taxiing toward takeoff position as passengers continued to settle into their seats. Ben-Yosef (2005, Ch. 6) argues that the FAA's eventual 1996 decision to ground ValuJet Airlines, the low-cost leader in the eastern United States at the time, also cost far more in increased highway fatalities than any conceivable benefit. Ben-Yosef also documents the general public's misperception that aircraft maintenance failures cause the most accidents, and, more broadly, the huge disconnect between public perception regarding the causes of airline crashes versus the reports of safety regulators and other industry experts. Breyer (1994) maintains that the interaction of public misperceptions and the political process produces an essentially random agenda. Naturally, for politicians, to rise above the politics of safety and make decisions based on costs and benefits proves to be a challenging endeavor. The notion that airlines may well be too safe, forcing travelers into riskier transportation modes, appears to be too sophisticated to be effectively dealt with through the political process. This prospect will change in time with continued efforts to educate the public in this regard; however, such efforts have so far been remarkably ineffective and probably will not succeed in the future.

The fundamental analysis provided serves as an example of a simple economic cost-benefit analysis for aviation safety. Such an analysis could be conducted for almost all safety regulations to determine if any one regulation is economically efficient. However, since it may be difficult to quantify all the benefits from improved safety, such analysis is rarely undertaken. Therefore, and as pointed out earlier, the political and bureaucratic process usually assumes, especially where aviation safety is concerned, that the benefits of almost any safety or security regulation outweigh their corresponding costs. Moreover, as mentioned earlier in the chapter, the reasons for this are easy to identify. Commercial aviation is a critical sector of the economy; however, the vast majority of people who fly do so only a few times a year. Therefore, the actual number of people who fly on a regular basis is only a small proportion of the population.[21] In addition to these consideration, the media's tendency to sensationalize all aviation-related accidents or incidents, and the natural inclination of regulators to avoid even the remote appearance of not being vigilant on safety, and one can readily see that even elementary cost-benefit analysis would be difficult to implement in this culture.

Moreover, it is also probably true that, if one were to perform the economic cost-benefit analysis for all safety regulations, many would pass due to the substantial benefits from improved safety. However, some regulations would also fail, largely because they were enacted in response to political pressure. Primarily due to their focus on safety, some decisions do not receive economic scrutiny because other competitive factors are in play. For example, the regulation banning aircraft push-back until everyone is seated was created in part as a response to other airlines lobbying against Southwest's practices. Therefore, it is worth noting that aviation safety and security exceed the levels that might be considered economically efficient.[22]

Politics and Safety Regulation

Certain economists have argued that airline safety regulation can be effectively privatized and is thus driven by economic analysis rather than regulations. They envision a system where private insurers essentially replace politicians as the ultimate safety authorities. In this envisioned system, insurers have a vested interest in assuring that airlines do not take imprudent risks given their obligation to shoulder the financial burden caused by an accident. However, insurers do not have to explain their decisions to uninformed voters. Thus, insurance companies are unlikely to have any interest in continuing the "Southwest rule" or any other regulation that doesn't truly improve safety. Likewise, insurers would allow airlines to cancel safety programs that produce more costs than benefits; that is, an airline would be allowed to slightly increase risk as long as a higher insurance premium was paid to cover the slightly higher risk. Presently this pattern of conduct is observable now in that consumers can buy personal injury insurance, at a higher price, for a motorcycle or sub-compact car even though such vehicles are substantially less safe than standard size automobiles. Insurers, know better than to try to eliminate all risk—any movement in that direction would result in customers leaving them for a more reasonable insurer. The fact is that insurers ban only imprudent risks and insist that customers pay more for any increase in prudent risks. In this setting, the role of government could merely require that airlines purchase legitimate insurance, and then let insurers handle the details. Regulatory bodies like the FAA and comparable regulators in other countries could continue their same basic mission but be converted into a private organization, paid by insurers rather than by taxpayers. The head of the FAA would, of course, no longer be a political appointee, evolving instead to a private manager appointed by a board of stockholders, just like any other corporate CEO. Ideally, this rejuvenated FAA, would be driven by economic analysis and would be able to maintain a more long-term focus on true accident risks, rather than being driven by the latest headlines and the whims of politics.

Although there is currently no private regulator of airline safety, Poole points to a number of examples of private safety regulation in other areas. Underwriters Laboratories, for example, sets safety standards for a number of electronic components. It seems that many people have assumed that the company is some sort of public agency since its function is so commonly associated with the government. In a parallel vein, the fire departments in the United States, though usually government bureaucracies themselves, are, in effect, regulated by a private insurance organization, the National Board of Fire Underwriters (NBFU). NBFU conducts inspections of fire departments, to rate their response time, quality of equipment, staffing, and so on. Naturally, NBFU does not have authority to demand corrections at problem fire departments. However, if a local fire department is poorly rated then fire insurance premiums in the area are raised, immediately exposing inadequacies. Therefore, fire departments generally work with NBFU to correct problems and improve themselves as needed. NBFU embarked upon this role in 1890, stepping in to deal with the problem of widely varying quality in firefighting, and, after more than a century of experience, continues to operate without incident. The standards set by NBFU do not appear to have anything comparable to the Southwest rule or other inappropriate regulation.

In a broader context, any independent private agency that provides product information and ratings is performing a function similar to the private airline regulation envisioned by Poole and other supporters. Just as consumers have difficulty judging if an airline is appropriately safe, they may have trouble judging the safety and general quality of many products. Government agencies sometimes provide such judgments to some extent and do not charge consumers for this service. However, the government does not do this extensively enough to satisfy consumers' demands. Therefore, private companies like Consumer Digest and Consumer Reports inspect products and make recommendations to consumers. Likewise, when investors want to know more about a company, they turn, not to the Securities and Exchange Commission, but to Moody's or Standard and Poor's.

Naturally, many people would question whether private regulation can really perform better than government. A constructive exercise entails a comparison of the incentives and operational nature of private and public entities in this area. Poole and other privatization proponents argue that private regulators have superior incentives and better flexibility to deal with problems. If the FAA were private, working under contract for insurers, it could be replaced, in part or in full, by another organization if it performed poorly. Basically, any entrepreneur, perhaps even a former FAA employee, could approach an insurer and make a case that he or she could provide inspection in a given area more efficiently. Recognizing the possibility of dismissal, the private FAA would seem to have a strong incentive to operate efficiently, appropriately monitor the competence and integrity of its workers, and so on. Likewise, being private would enable the

FAA to more freely adjust policies or fire employees who weren't performing and more quickly promote those who excel.

The important part of the aforementioned discussion is that there should be more and better benefit-cost analysis of regulations, preventing measures that bring only marginal safety benefits at excessive cost. Nonetheless, the evidence on whether market mechanisms, such as reputation, can deliver levels of safety acceptable to the public appears to suggest otherwise. This assertion gains credence judging from the failed self-regulation behind the 2018 and 2019 crashes of Boeing 737MAX aircraft, noted at the start of this chapter.

Accident Prevention

Accident prevention program (APP) comprises all measures taken in an effort to improve; safety, minimize accidents, save lives, lessen the severity of injury, avoid damage to property, and prevent the loss of productive time and resources.

The main reasons for the rapidly decreasing aviation accident rate since the 1950s are the various safety programs/inventions adopted by safety regulators, airlines, and aircraft manufacturers. The collaborative synergy among these three groups have combined resources to make aviation the safest mode of transportation. This increase in safety has ultimately helped stabilize the industry and make it a more attractive transportation option for consumers. Based on the incentives described previously, methods to increase safety have sizeable economic benefits. Some illustrative instances are poor product design, aging aircraft regulations, collision avoidance systems, wind-shear detection, de-icing, and human factors. Notably, in February 2023, and for the third time in three years, Boeing halted deliveries of its 787 Dreamliner jets over fuselage issue related forward pressure bulkhead.

As mentioned previously, aging aircraft can compromise aviation safety in some specific cases. In order to help minimize this problem, the FAA and the former Joint Aviation Authorities (JAA) require specific component overhauls at specified intervals (well ahead of the time the components would be expected to fail). The JAA was an associated body of the European Civil Aviation Conference (ECAC), an intergovernmental organization which was established by the ICAO and the Council of Europe (it was in existence from 1970 until disbanded in 2009). In 2002, the European Aviation Safety Agency (EASA) was created with the power to regulate civilian aviation safety and, in 2008, also took over the functions of the JAA. In line with the resolution of ECAC's Director Generals in adopting the FUJA[23] II Report, it was decided to disband the JAA system, as of 30 June, 2009. However, the JAA Training Organization remained operational. In certain countries, the regulation of aircraft aging is taken to an extreme by not allowing airlines to operate commercial aircraft over a certain age. As pointed out in the previous section, this type of rather arbitrary safety regulation might improve safety somewhat, but it will also impose significant extra costs on the industry; these, of course, will ultimately be passed down to the passengers. From an economic standpoint, passengers may not be better off from such stringent aircraft age regulations (with no decrease in overall safety levels).

While midair collisions have never been the number one cause of aviation accidents, collaborative research by governments and industry resulted in the development and deployment of TCAS.[24] This remarkable system of TCAS alerts pilots of a possible midair collision and provides instructions to help avoid a serious accident. This advent of TCAS has reduced the number of midair collisions; however, the system has not eliminated midair collisions all together, as in the case of the fatal accident involving the DHL and Bashkirian Airlines aircraft over Europe in 2002. Additionally, TCAS is not immune to human error, as pilots and air traffic controllers can still make mistakes and disobey TCAS warnings that may result in tragedy.

Wind-shear represents another significant threat to aircraft since it can cause an aircraft to become uncontrollable. Previously, wind shear was undetectable; however, through government and industry research, warning devices have been created to alert pilots of possible wind-shear conditions. In response to these wind-shear warnings, regulations have been developed to help ensure aircraft do not fly during dangerous wind-shear conditions. While the American Eagle ATR-72 de-icing accident highlights the fact that fatal accidents still occur due to ice forming on the wings, advancements in anti-icing have significantly reduced the number of icing accidents. Aircraft manufacturers have designed aircraft with anti-icing boots, while chemical compositions have enabled de-icing to occur on the ground.

Summary

Measuring airline safety involves a comprehensive and systematic approach that considers a variety of factors. Safety performance indicators are quantitative measures of safety that are used to assess an airline's safety performance over time. Accident and incident rates, usually computed as the occurrences per million flights or per number of hours flown, stand out as prominent metrics. More precisely, these rates refer to the number of accidents or incidents per flight hours, per takeoff, or per million passengers carried. Remarkably, the airline accident rates have dropped significantly every decade since the 1950s. The increase in airline safety is attributed to a combination of several factors such as the introduction of the jet engine in the 1950s as a significant milestone, improvement in navigation equipment and air traffic control technology, more effective safety management systems, and the advent of fly-by-wire technology in the 1980s. In fact, we have more chance of being killed riding a bicycle, driving a car, sailing a boat, or strike by lightning. This chapter provides an overview of the state of aviation safety and security. The European Union Aviation Safety Agency (EASA) and the US Federal Aviation Administration are agencies with responsibility for civil aviation safety.

The notion that there exists a perfectly safe aviation environment is discussed and critiqued from a more realistic economic benefit and cost approach. The very strong and ongoing economic incentives to pursue safety within the industry are discussed and contrasted with the sometimes-responsible media coverage that is prevalent about this subject. The chapter analyzes the accident record of the aviation industry versus other modes of transportation. The various causes of aircraft accidents are then discussed and analyzed in some depth. In addition, this chapter points out that safety and security in aviation underscore the remarkable efficacy from an economic point of view, although there are arguably numerous rules and regulations that could be relaxed with no decrease in overall safety. In fact, the stringent regulations for the introduction of new technologies and procedures probably act to decrease rather than increase overall safety in the industry. Future developments in this field will have to center on replacing human judgment with automated technologies. However, these developments have been and continue to be extremely difficult to implement due to bureaucratic and political inertia.

Discussion Questions

1 What are some of the incentives for airlines to continuously improve safety?
2 What are the most common causes of airline accidents?

3 Over the past several decades, both the fatalities per million aircraft miles and accidents per million aircraft departures have decreased. Briefly explain some of the reasons for these improvements in aviation safety.
4 Explain how safety regulations may increase overall safety for travelers.
5 Explain how passengers and employees are able to influence the safety practices of an airline.
6 From an economic cost-benefit perspective, evaluate the often-heard statement that "airline safety must be preserved at any cost."
7 Who regulates the airline industry? What is the difference between the FAA and the EASA?
8 Which is the safest airline to fly?
9 Has the Airline Deregulation Act of 1978 improved airline safety?
10 What impact does the use of modern technologies such as jet engines, fly-by-wire programs, and flight simulators have on commercial aviation?
11 How do aircraft manufacturers ensure that their planes meet safety standards and requirements?

Notes

1 International; Air Transport Association (IATA). Press Release No. 6, February 16, 2016.
2 International; Air Transport Association (IATA). Press Release No. 11, February 16, 2022.
3 One accident every 0.23 million flights.
4 FAA Adopts ICAO Definition for Runway Incursions, FAA news release, October 1, 2007.
5 More traffic deaths in wake of 9/11. Science News, September 11, 2012.
6 DTN. How Today's Aviation Technology Boosts Safety and Efficiency, November 16, 2021.
7 A good analogy here might be automobile safety. It would be possible to reduce automobile fatalities if every abutment on the interstate highway system was surrounded by crash-absorbing material. However, it is clear that the cost of doing so outweighs the benefit of the few fatalities that it might prevent.
8 In a similar study, Barnett (2000) examined the mortality risk of air travel and found it to be extremely small. He estimated a death risk per flight of 1 in 13 million for aircraft operated by countries that have a well-developed aviation industry. At this level of mortality risk, a passenger would have to take one flight per day for 36,000 years before having a fatal plane crash.
9 Flying since 1921.
10 On December 8, 2005, the airplane slid off a runway at Chicago-Midway Airport. The aircraft struck at least two vehicles, killing a six-year-old boy.
11 Flying since 1984.
12 Results displayed a 4.3% reduction in consumer demand resulting from an accident during regulation and a 15.3% reduction in demand post-deregulation. However, neither value was statistically significant.
13 China Eastern Black Box Points to Intentional Nosedive, *The Wall Street Journal*, March 17, 2022.
14 Boeing Charged with 737 Max Fraud Conspiracy and Agrees to Pay over $2.5 Billion (Press release). January 8, 2021.
15 *Tass News Agency*, September 19, 2012.
16 *CNN*, Children's Holiday Party on Doomed Plane, July 2, 2002.
17 According to the National Transportation Safety Board (NTSB), four aviation mishaps between 2001 and 2007 were attributed to air traffic controller fatigue.
18 Flight AF 447 on 1 June, 2009. Bureau d'Enquêtes et d'Analyses (BEA), July 25, 2011.
19 Flight Safety Foundation, Aviation Safety Network, May 1, 2012.
20 Factual information safety investigation for MH370, March 2015, Malaysian ICAO Annex 10.
21 Again, this can be contrasted to the automobile where the ill-fated safety regulation tying the ignition of the car to a fastened seatbelt was quickly abandoned when a major proportion of the population (automobile drivers and voters) discovered what a nuisance this particular regulation would be in practice.
22 The opposite is probably true of automobile safety.
23 The Future of JAA (FUJA).
24 FAA Advisory Circular AC 20-151A (2009). Airworthiness Approval of Traffic Alert and Collision Avoidance Systems (TCAS II), Versions 7.0 and 7.1 and Associated Mode S Transponders.

References

Ahlers, M.M. (2007). NTSB: Air Controller Fatigue Contributed to 4 Mishaps. *CNN*, April 10.

Barnett, A. (2000). Air Safety: End of the Golden Age? *Blackett Memorial Lecture Presented*, November 27, 2000, Royal Aeronautical Society. London, UK.

Ben-Yosef, E. (2005). *Evolution of the US Airline Industry*. The Netherlands: Springer.

Borenstein, S. and Zimmerman, M.B. (1988). Market Incentives for Safe Commercial Airline Operation. *The American Economic Review*, 78(5), 913–935.

Breyer, S. (1994). Breaking the Vicious Circle: Toward Effective Risk Regulation, *Harvard University Press*, 8(1), 127.

Bureau of Enquiry and Analysis for Civil Aviation (BEA). (2012). Final Report on the Accident on 1st June 2009 to the Airbus A330-203 registered F-GZCP Operated by Air France flight AF 447 Rio de Janeiro. Published July, 2012. Retrieved April 11, 2017 from www.bea.aero.

Federal Aviation Administration (FAA). (2002). FAA Proposes $805,000 Fine against United Airlines, December 3.

Levin, A. (2008, March 7). FAA Levels Record $10.2M Fine against Southwest. *USA Today*.

Levin, A. (2010, August 27). American Airlines Tilts at Record $24M fine. *USA Today*.

Mitchell, G. and Maloney, M.T. (1989). Crisis in the Cockpit? The Role of Market Forces in Promoting Air Travel Safety. *The Journal of Law and Economics*, 32(6), 329–356.

National Transportation Safety Board (NTSB). (2010). Aircraft Accident Report: Loss of Control on Approach Colgan Air, Inc. Operating as Continental Connection Flight 3407 Bombardier DHC-8-400, N200WQ Clarence Center, New York, February 12, 2009.

O'Brien, B. (2006). *IOSA: IATA Operational Safety Audit*. Retrieved on August 23, 2012, from http://www.iata.org/SiteCollectionDocuments/Documents/ISMEd2Rev2.pdf.

Squalli, J. and Saad, M. (2006). Accidents, Airline Safety Perceptions and Consumer Demand. *Journal of Economics and Finance*, 30(3), 297–305.

Vasigh, B. and Helmkay, S. (2002). Airline Safety: An Application of Empirical Methods to Determine Fatality Risk, in Jenkins, D. (Ed.), *Handbook of Airline Economics*. New York: McGraw-Hill, pp. 501–511.

Wong, J.T. and Yeh, W.C. (2003). Impact of Flight Accident on Passenger Traffic Volume of the Airlines in Taiwan. *Journal of the Eastern Asia Society for Transportation Studies*, 5(5), 471–483.

11 International Economics and Aviation

The ultimate purpose of an economy is to maintain full employment, improve the level of economic activities, ensure price stability, and achieve economic growth. There are variety of labor-saving techniques, which are widely used in different industries that range from agriculture to automobile manufacturing and other fields. The majority comprehends that replacing people with machines raises our standard of living, despite the need for assistance in transitioning displaced workers. Indeed, without the integration of technology which replaced most farm workers, we would find ourselves engrossed in agricultural toil leaving little room to produce aircraft. The replacement of workers with technology is not fundamentally different from replacing workers with other workers. Competition constantly drives private firms to shift production techniques to bring costs lower or improve quality for consumers. In essence, if importing a good is more efficient than making it ourselves, this affects the economy like any other advance in technology, making some jobs obsolete but indirectly creating new jobs with higher productivity. The extra labor and resources become liberated for the production of new products. Aviation is not an exception to this rule, although it has some special complications. This chapter addresses international aviation agreements, industry alliances, and the fallacies behind anti-trade arguments. Allowing international competition in aviation, as well as other domains, produces a net gain to the economy rather than a destructive "concession," as often propagated by politicians. While acknowledging other viewpoints, the crux of this chapter is to explain why most economists agree that increased competition through international trade is generally a net benefit to any economy. This chapter will cover the following topics in order:

- Trade Globalization
  - World Trade Organization (WTO)
  - Trans-Pacific Partnership (TPP)
- International Balance of Payments
- Current Account
- Capital and Financial Accounts
- International Economics and Trade
  - Arguments for Free Trade
  - Arguments against Free Trade
  - Job Losses
  - National Security Concerns
  - Infant Industry
  - Trade Deficit and Surplus

DOI: 10.4324/9781003388135-11

- Why Nations Trade
  - o Production Possibility Curve
  - o Absolute Advantage
  - o Comparative Advantage
  - o Trade Protections and Trade Barriers
    - Tariffs
    - Quotas
    - Other Forms of Trade Protection
- Aircraft Manufacturing and Governmental Subsidies
  - o Boeing Versus Airbus
  - o Recent World Trade Organization Rulings Against Airbus
- International Trade Policy in Air Travel–Optimality Versus Political Realities
- Foreign Currency and Exchange Markets
  - o Exchange Rate Quotes
  - o Exchange Rate Regimes
  - o Fixed (Pegged) Exchange Rate
  - o Floating (Adjustable) Rates
- Summary
- Discussion Questions
- Appendix: International Free Trade Agreements

Trade Globalization

International economics and trade play a significant role in the air transport industry, affecting exchange rates, trade policies, and economic growth. Airlines must navigate these economic factors to remain competitive and profitable in an increasingly globalized market. The sphere of international trade remains an important engine of world economic growth. The economic prosperity of all countries, regardless of size, depends partly on trade with other countries. The transportation of internationally traded goods by air is a critical business for many firms in air transport. The importance of this aviation business to airlines and the supply chains they support became apparent during the COVID-19 pandemic, when most borders were closed to passengers. The ramifications of COVID-19 pandemic have disrupted global supply chains in numerous industries. The shortage of semiconductors impaired the automotive industry, according to some estimates, the average modern car has between 1,400 and 1,500 semiconductor chips.[1]

Free trade agreements, such as the North American Free Trade Agreement (NAFTA) and the Trans-Pacific Partnership (TPP), are examples of economic globalization. Following the assumption of office by the US President Donald Trump in January 2017, he decided to withdraw or replace NAFTA with a new agreement. In September 2018, the United States, Mexico, and Canada reached an agreement to replace NAFTA with the United States–Mexico–Canada Agreement (USMCA), and all three countries had ratified it by March 2020. NAFTA remained in force until USMCA was implemented. Subsequently, in April 2020, Canada and Mexico notified the United States that they were ready to implement the agreement.[2]

Globalization has taken root nearly in every nation, fostering the emergence of numerous regional trade agreements. Trade improves global efficiency in resource allocation. A barrel of oil may have little value to someone living in Kuwait where energy is plentiful, but it is very important to people living in Singapore or Switzerland, with few natural resources. Furthermore, trade has allowed China, the United States, Japan, and Vietnam to transform themselves into the world's largest producers of solar panels, cars, steel, and fiber products. However, international trade agreements are not without criticism and pushbacks, as critics claim that the issues of labor, intellectual property, and environment have been ignored.

World Trade Organization (WTO)

The World Trade Organization (WTO) stands as an international organization dealing with the rules of trade between nations. Established in 1994, the WTO succeeded to the General Agreement on Tariffs and Trade (GATT). The major objective of WTO is to discourage unfair trade practices, such as import taxes, export subsidies and dumping products at below normal value to gain market share, and to ensure that trade flows as smoothly, predictably, and freely as possible. At the core of the WTO multilateral trading system are agreements that are negotiated among and ratified by the majority of the world's trading nations. The WTO's primary functions include:

- Acting as a forum for trade negotiations
- Administering trade agreements
- Assisting developing countries in trade policy issues, through technical assistance and training programs
- Cooperating with other international organizations
- Reviewing national trade policies
- Settling trade disputes

The WTO comprises 164 members and accounts for approximately 95% of global trade, which takes place under rules (agreements) are the result of negotiation between members. The original GATT rules of 1948 were revised during the Uruguay Round, the first round of negations, which took place from 1986 to 1994. This event also established the WTO. The 30,000-page revision consists of 30 agreements and separate commitments (schedules) made by individual members.[3] However, these rules are often disputed. For example, complaints against Airbus brought forth to the WTO by the US government on behalf of Boeing continue to argue that Airbus has outgrown an infant industry's need for the aid it receives from EU governments. Nevertheless, many countries are queuing up to join the WTO, believing that future economic prosperity lies in the WTO system. With this in mind, we will now move into key aspects of the WTO, with a particular emphasis on the methods used for settling trade disputes.

The Trans-Pacific Partnership (TPP)

The Trans-Pacific Partnership is a trade agreement originally among 12 Pacific Rim countries, collectively representing about 36% of the world's economic output. This trade pact may create the largest trade zone in the world, covering four continents and 800 million people. At February

4, 2017, partners included Australia, Brunei, Canada, Chile, Japan, Malaysia, Mexico, New Zealand, Peru, Singapore, the United States, and Vietnam. However, on January 30, 2017, the United States formally withdrew from the agreement.[4] Furthermore, China is not a member of TPP, but it may have the propensity to create its own trade initiatives in Asia.

Proponents of free trade argue that reductions in trade barriers facilitated by the TPP will enable firms and industries to take advantage of free trade to export goods and services (Velk, Gong, and Zuckerbrot, 2015). Others, however, argue against what they believe to be the underlying motive. A prominent critic, Senator Bernie Sanders, for example, has been a major opponent of the TPP, claiming that it was enacted as a way to boost profits on Wall Street. In this vein, the argument claims that the TPP has outsourced jobs, undercut worker rights, and allowed companies to challenge basic laws regarding the labor, health, finance, and the environment. Nonetheless, the agreement will continue unless all remaining countries decide to withdraw. TPP opponents worry that foreign companies could argue that the way America regulates banks, the minimum wage, or the environment constitutes an unjust taking of their property.

International Balance of Payments

The Balance of Payments (BOP) method is used by countries to benchmark local economic activity against the global economy. It serves as a system of recording all of a country's economic transactions, exports, and imports, with the rest of the world during a given period of time and is divided into two main categories: current accounts and capital accounts. As per the rules of the WTO, any trade restriction taken by a member must be consistent, or in compliance, with the rules of the international trading system.[5] The balance of payments serves as a metric that gauges all payments and obligations to other countries against all payments and obligations received from all other countries. For example, if the value of imported items to the United States equaled \$2 trillion in 2017, but the value of exported items from the United States equaled \$2.75 trillion in the same year, then the United States would have a negative \$750 billion BOP. In the United States, the trade deficit, as a percentage of gross domestic product (GDP), increased dramatically in the 1980s and again in the late 1990s. During the 2000s, imports continued to rise as a percentage of GDP, but exports fell. In instances when a country is experiencing persistent BOP current account deficits, it may signal that the country's industries lack productivity and efficiency. Alternatively, it may be the inevitable result of persistent inflows of direct and portfolio investment attracted by strong economic prospects, creating a surplus on the capital account. In such cases, a current account deficit is inevitable as the BOP have to balance.

Current Account

The current account is the sum of the trade balance (difference between a nation's total exports and its total imports), net factor income (dividends and so on), and net transfer payments (i.e. foreign aid). Thus, the current account balance can therefore be either a surplus or a deficit, emerging as one of the broadest measures of international trade.

The main parts of the current account are:

- Trade in goods and services
- Investment incomes such as interest income and stock dividends
- International aid

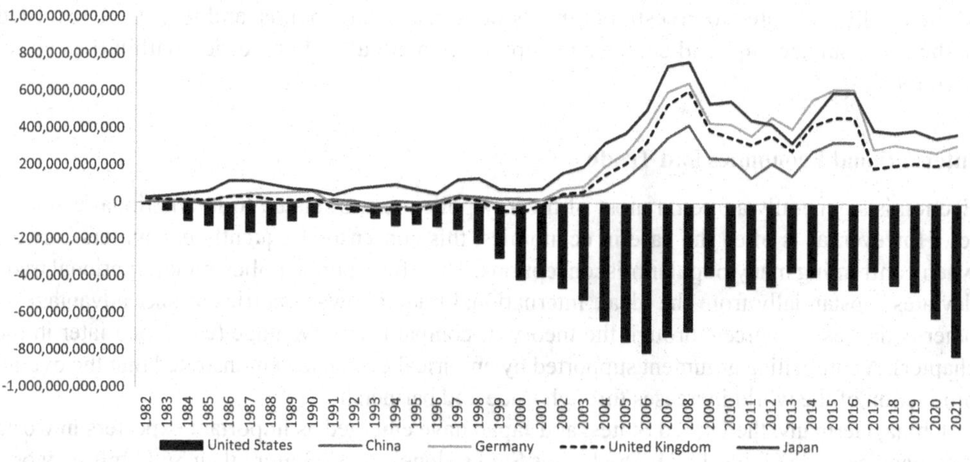

Figure 11.1 Current Account Balances, 1982–2021.

Source: The World Bank, Economic Policy, and External debt data

The balance of payments displays all payments and obligations to other countries against all payments and obligations received from all other countries.

Current account may be in a deficit if the value of imports is greater than the value of exports. Thus, a deficit in the current account occurs if the value of imports is greater than the value of exports.

In straightforward terms, if the current account balance is positive, the country is a net lender to the world and vice versa for a deficit. The United States' current account has been in a deficit since 1992. This trend continued into 2021 when the nation recorded a current account deficit of $821.6 billion (see Figure 11.1).[6] When a country runs a current account deficit, its purchases of goods and services from abroad exceed its sales of goods and services to foreign buyers. Contrary to the United States, Japan continues to realize a current account surplus. In this situation, the value of goods and services sold to foreign buyers exceeds the purchases of goods and services from other countries.

In the aftermath of China's accession to the WTO in 2001, its exports surged and generated tremendous growth in its trade surplus in the 2000s. In 2021, China's current account recorded a surplus of $317.3 billion, including a surplus of $562.7 billion under trade in goods.

Capital and Financial Accounts

The capital account is the net result of public and private investment flowing into and out of a country. It includes changes in foreign direct investment, stocks, bonds, loans, bank accounts, and currencies. The major components of the capital account are capital transfers and acquisition/disposal of non-produced, non-financial assets. In synergy with the current account, this forms the BOP framework. The current account reflects net income while the capital account reflects net change in national ownership of assets. The International Monetary Fund (IMF) divides the capital account into financial and capital components.

Monetary flows related to investment in business, real estate, bonds, and stocks are recorded in the financial account, and changes in capital are meticulously recorded within the capital account.

International Economics and Trade

Economists generally agree on most of the key policy issues related to international economics. However, as is often the case in economics, this consensus frequently encounters barriers when confronting many popular misconceptions. Therefore, public policy on international trade deviates substantially from the ideal. International trade allows countries to take advantage of other countries' resources through the theory of comparative advantage (explained later in the chapter). A compelling argument supported by empirical evidence demonstrated that the overall production of the world increases through trade and partnership.

China, Germany, the United States, and Japan have emerged as important exporters in world merchandise trade (Table 11.1). The Unites States alone exported more than $684 billion worth of products, which accounted for 13.9% of total global exports. Among the ten leading exporters, the five most dynamic economies are China, the United States, Germany, Japan, and the Netherlands.

In terms of imports, the United States ranked number one in 2020, bringing in $436 billion worth of merchandise (Table 11.2). China came in second with $1,682 billion (10.1%), followed by Germany with $307 billion during the same period. The top five spots for importing comprise the same leading exporters with the exception of the Netherlands, which is replaced by the United Kingdom.[7]

World trade can also be broken down according to region as shown in Tables 11.3 and 11.4. It's evident that the level of merchandise exports originating in Europe remained fairly stable between 1948 and 2020, with Europe maintaining a dominant position throughout. Moreover, the runner-up in percentages of global merchandise exports by region has shifted from North America to the Asian region. In 1948, North American exports comprised 28.1% of global exports, while Asia accounted for only 14.0%. In 2020, we see near exact numbers in reverse: 13.1% for North America and 36.1% for Asia.

Figure 11.2 categorizes the world merchandise by its region. Noting that Asia and Europe make up the largest collective exporters/importers, both in absolute terms and the exposure of

Table 11.1 Top 10 Exporters in World Merchandise Trade, 2020

Rank	*Exporters*	*Value ($billions)*	*Percentage Share*	*Annual Percentage Change*
1	China	684	13.9	−20.0
2	United States	339	6.9	−16.0
3	Germany	305	6.2	−11.0
4	Japan	278	5.7	−1.0
5	Netherlands	262	5.3	6.0
6	Republic of Korea	245	5	−17.0
7	Hong Kong, China	203	4.1	−5.0
8	France	187	3.8	−14.0
9	United Kingdom	186	3.8	−32.0
10	Italy	156	3.2	−23.0

Source: World Trade Organization—International trade statistics 2020, https://www.wto.org/english/res_e/statis_e/wts2021_e/wts2021_e.pdf

Table 11.2 Top 10 Importers in World Merchandise Trade, 2020

Rank	*Importers*	*Value ($billions)*	*Percentage Share*	*Annual Percentage Change*
1	United States	436	9.5	−23.0
2	China	378	8.2	−24.0
3	Germany	307	6.7	−17.0
4	Japan	296	6.4	−11.0
5	United Kingdom	232	5	−14.0
6	France	201	4.4	−26.0
7	Hong Kong, China	183	4	−11.0
8	Netherlands	172	3.8	−17.0
9	Republic of Korea	169	3.7	−36.0
10	Canada	153	3.3	−14.0

Source: World Trade Organization—International trade statistics 2020.

Table 11.3 World Merchandise Exports by Region (Percentage), 1948–2020

	1948	*1953*	*1963*	*1973*	*1983*	*1993*	*2003*	*2015*	*2020*
North America	28.1	24.8	19.9	17.3	16.8	17.9	15.8	14.4	13.1
South and Central America	11.3	9.7	6.4	4.3	4.4	3.0	3.0	3.4	3.1
Europe	35.1	39.4	47.8	50.9	43.5	45.4	45.9	37.3	38.2
Commonwealth of Independent States (CIS)	–	–	–	–	–	1.5	2.6	3.1	2.7
Africa	7.3	6.5	5.7	4.8	4.5	2.5	2.4	2.4	2.2
Middle East	2.0	2.7	3.2	4.1	6.8	3.5	4.1	5.3	4.5
Asia	14.0	13.4	12.5	14.9	19.1	26.0	26.1	34.2	36.1

Source: World Trade Organization—International trade statistics 2020.

Table 11.4 World Merchandise Imports by Region (Percentage), 1948–2020

	1948	*1953*	*1963*	*1973*	*1983*	*1993*	*2003*	*2015*	*2020*
North America	18.5	20.5	16.1	17.2	18.5	21.3	22.4	19.3	18.5
South and Central America	10.4	8.3	6	4.4	3.8	3.3	2.5	3.8	3
Europe	45.3	43.7	52	53.3	44.1	44.5	45.0	36.2	37.3
Commonwealth of Independent States (CIS)	–	–	–	–	–	1.5	1.7	2.1	2.1
Africa	8.1	7	5.2	3.9	4.6	2.6	2.2	3.4	2.9
Middle East	1.8	2.1	2.3	2.7	6.2	3.3	2.8	4.3	3.7
Asia	13.9	15.1	14.1	14.9	18.5	23.5	23.5	30.8	32.4

Source: World Trade Organization—International trade statistics 2014.

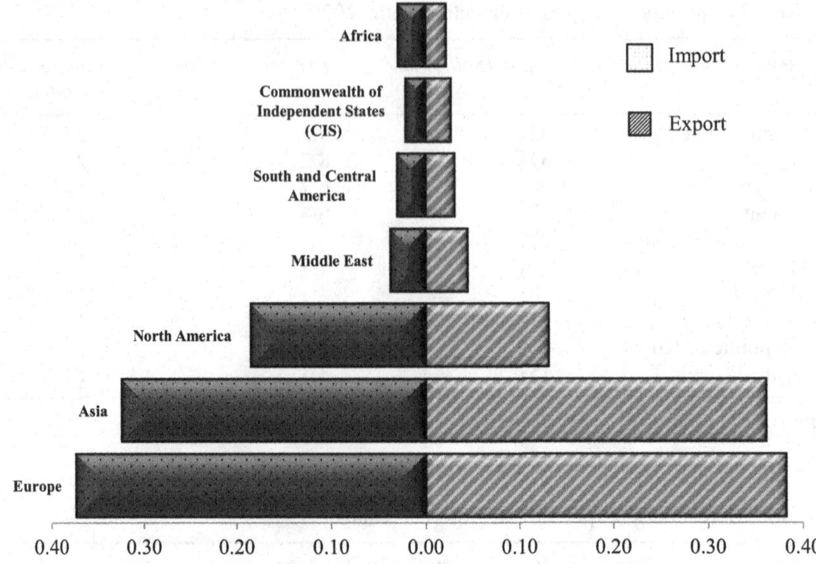

Figure 11.2 World Merchandise Trade by Region (Percentage), 2022.

Source: World Trade Organization—International trade statistics

Table 11.5 Top 15 US Trading Partners in 2021 ($Billions)

Rank	*Country*	*Exports (Year-to-Date)*	*Imports (Year-to-Date)*	*Total Trade (Year-to-Date)*	*Percent of Total Trade*
1	Canada	307.60	357.20	664.80	14.5%
2	Mexico	276.50	384.70	661.20	14.4%
3	China	151.10	506.40	657.40	14.3%
4	Japan	75.00	135.10	210.10	4.6%
5	Germany	65.20	135.20	200.40	4.4%
6	South Korea	65.80	95.00	160.70	3.5%
7	United Kingdom	61.50	56.40	117.80	2.6%
8	Taiwan	36.90	77.10	114.14	2.5%
9	India	40.10	73.30	113.40	2.5%
10	Vietnam	10.90	101.90	112.90	2.5%
11	Netherlands	53.60	35.30	88.90	1.9%
12	Ireland	13.60	73.30	87.30	1.9%
13	Switzerland	24.00	63.00	87.00	1.9%
14	Italy	21.70	61.00	82.70	1.8%
15	France	30.00	50.30	80.30	1.8%
Total, top 15 countries		1,233.30	2,205.60	3,438.90	75.0%
Total, all countries		1,754.60	2,832.90	4,587.50	100%

Source: US Census Bureau: Foreign Trade Division—Foreign Trade Statistics 2021.

their economies to fluctuations in international trade. Conversely, economies in North America by contrast are less exposed with a smaller share of GDP taken by international trade.

Further analysis can be conducted to determine the largest trade partnerships. Table 11.5 shows the top ten trading partners with the United States in 2020.

Arguments for Free Trade

For more than a hundred years, economists have engaged in a debate over whether global trade yields positive or negative outcomes. But the economies around the world have become more open to international trade. Proponents claim that free trade:

- Reduces the price of every item sold in the market,
- Increases the supply of products in other markets,
- Encourages open trade partnerships, which help the global economy,
- Increases the number and variety of products for consumers to choose from, and
- Stands as a driving force behind a high standard of living.

The majority of economists argue that the world at large benefits from free trade and that trade liberalization promotes development. Similarly, proponents of free traders claim that trade protection always harms all trading partners. The main political objections to free trade center on the fear that cheaper imports will destroy jobs and reduce income. Labor unions and managers may be against free trade if they believe that the competition will result in job losses and/or bankruptcy of a firm or industry. However, the simple "two-good" case illustrated later on in the chapter shows that this fear has no basis in reality. Although some jobs may indeed be made obsolete by free trade, other jobs are created. Moreover, these new jobs are more productive. Thus, average wages and overall income rises, although there may be a distributional impact with both winners and losers in the economy.

This comparative advantage principle is not always obvious. Suppose, for instance, that a country dramatically increases purchases of imported automobiles. Everyone will be able to see the downside which would be the resulting layoffs in the domestic auto sector. However, the new jobs created by this trade are widely dispersed and not at all apparent. When consumers buy cheaper cars, they will then be able to spend more on computers, air travel, new clothing, restaurants, new homes, and so on. As a result, the availability of cheap auto imports allows us to produce more of other products while creating new jobs. However, once again, the job gains will be widely dispersed throughout many seemingly unrelated industries. The individual who obtains an airline job made possible by the availability of cheaper cars in the economy is unlikely to see the interconnection. In other words, even though the benefits of trade far outweigh the costs, free trade is often controversial because the costs are concentrated. These costs are conspicuous and visible to the least discerning citizens, and therefore easy to politically exploit.

Arguments Against Free Trade

In the present day, most countries around the world impose some form of trade restriction, such as tariffs, taxes, and subsidies. The most common arguments against free trade aim to:

- Keep jobs within the country,
- Limit imports to keep wealth within the country,
- Avoid trading with nations that treat their workers unfairly,
- Reduce national security concerns,
- Avoid trading with nations that do not respect the environment,
- Prevent the country from becoming too specialized and dependent on other nations.

Job Losses

Preserving jobs within the domestic market is important, yet prioritizing jobs in industries in which we operate efficiently is paramount. Economically speaking, the way to protect jobs is not by limiting imports, other nations will retaliate against protectionist policies anyway. Returning back to the issue of job losses, even though free trade increases average wealth, some individuals may be made worse off. Many American workers have been negatively impacted by liberalized trade with China, because goods that China exports to the United States have substituted for comparable American-made products. This effect has particularly pronounced with technological advances. For example, discovering a cure for cancer would eliminate many jobs in health care. While most people would be able to adapt to new positions, some individuals may require substantial assistance to survive and adjust to a new economy. However, technology increases overall wealth, which makes such assistance more readily affordable. Low trade barriers inherently create hundreds of billions of dollars more in benefits than they impose in costs (Pugel, 2007). Hufbauer and Elliott (1994) state that preserving an average job costs an economy $170,000. So, rather than using trade barriers to "protect jobs," it would be cheaper for consumers to allow free trade and then, as taxpayers, compensate all workers who have lost jobs to more efficient foreign competition.

National Security Concerns

In very few instances, it may be true that national security justifies a particular trade barrier. For instance, it would not be prudent, for a country to allow aircraft from hostile nations to have open skies access to its airspace. In most cases, however, national security is purely a cover for more traditional economic protection of domestic industries. Contrarily, the reality is that free international trade actually enhances national security by raising income and promoting friendly relations. This is particularly true in aviation since free trade in air travel inherently makes the world smaller and promotes more economic integration and social interaction between nations. In tightly integrated economies, individual citizens assume larger stakes in other countries and therefore have a strong motivation to avoid the destruction and loss of wealth associated with war. This explains the rarity of conflicts between major trading partners throughout history. Indeed, it was the desire to promote peaceful interaction, even more so than economic development, which initially motivated European leaders to form the European Union (EU). The impact of uncertain geopolitical dynamics, spurred by the Russian invasion into Ukraine, will change this thinking.

Some individuals argue that allowing foreign airlines, even those from friendly nations who are staunch allies, to compete freely in domestic markets somehow jeopardizes national security. They insist that airlines must be domestically owned just in case the government needs to use civilian aircraft in some emergencies, like moving military troops within the country. Most economists are very skeptical of such claims. All governments reserve the right, for example, to confiscate private property (hopefully with just compensation being paid at the appropriate time) in emergencies, regardless of who owns the needed property. Instances necessitating a government would confiscate or utilize commandeer civilian aircraft are rare, possibly even non-existent. However, if such a situation ever arises, the government has the power to take what it needs.

In the United States, the federal government has a contract in place with some airlines to provide troop transportation if ever needed (US Air Force: Air Mobility Command, 2006). Given the relative efficiency of US airlines and the availability of military transport aircraft, it is unlikely that the presence of foreign carriers would ever result in an insufficient number of US commercial aircraft available to the military. Even if foreign carriers do begin to achieve such dominance, there seems to be no reason that the United States would not arrange the same sort of contract with external airlines. In fact, such an agreement might even be required as a condition for the right to use US airspace. Other countries could do the same. National security does not provide a reasonable argument against free international trade and competition in air travel.

Infant Industry

Infant industries (emerging domestic industries) are usually offered some limited and temporary protection by their governments through tariffs, quotas, and duty taxes from international trade competitors. This safeguarding allows the infant industry sufficient time to take advantage of the learning curve and mature enough to sustain itself amid global competition, without the need for continued protection. Noteworthy instances that highlight the success of the Japanese and Korean car and steel industries are often touted as successful infant industries. In aviation, this protection is also often labeled under "launch aid." This temporary protection stems from the learning curve that all industries experience. In the early development stage, costs are usually higher compared to those in foreign companies that have already passed the learning curve necessary to reduce unit costs. Consider a country that traditionally reliant on aircraft imports from overseas and has no domestic aircraft production facilities. The creation of a domestic automotive industry would be an example of an infant industry. Japan, for example, acted as an entrepreneur of sorts when it attempted to reduce barriers for the budding auto industry in the mid-1900s. This proactive stance paved the way for Mitsubishi and others to acquire the trade skills necessary to grow and diversity.

Nonetheless, the provision of launch aid and infant industry protection, particularly in aviation, has long been argued as unfair trade practices, generally by the direct foreign competitor.

Trade Deficit and Surplus

A trade surplus occurs when a country's exports (goods and services) exceed its imports. When the opposite is true, the country is said to have a trade deficit. The United States has the largest trade deficit in the world. The largest exports of the United States were commercial and military aircraft, and cars. In 2020, China was the country with the highest trade surplus with approximately $535.37 billion.

The term "trade deficit" is completely arbitrary and might just as easily be called a "trade surplus", if we consider the value of the goods to the consumer, rather than solely focusing on just the net flow of payments. When imports are greater than exports, more goods and services flow into a country than flow out. This creates a deficit in payments. Contrarily, if the difference in the value of a nation's exports over imports is positive, the country enjoys a trade surplus.

Is it harmful when money "leaves the economy?"

To begin, it is crucial to recognize that the world's leading currencies are no longer backed by gold or any other real assets. Dollars, yen, and euros are pieces of paper, valuable in exchange, but very inexpensive to print in virtually limitless quantities. Naturally, printing too much currency results in devaluation of that currency, or inflation, but printing up currency to simply replace that which leaves the country will not be inflationary at all (as long as foreigners just hold the dollars). Suppose that the United States were to experience the ultimate trade deficit—foreigners acquiring dollars but refusing to buy anything from the United States. If the government did nothing to offset the effect of dollars pouring out of the country, the result would be deflation with pervasive falling prices. Therefore, to keep the value of the currency stable, the government needs to create and put into circulation new currency as a replacement.

To infuse currency into the system, authorities (Federal Reserve System in the United States) buy existing US treasury debt. Since interest is paid on this debt, the government is now paying interest to itself; in effect, this debt is retired and no longer a burden to taxpayers. Thus, the more money that leaves the country the better.[8] The United States is able to trade paper currency for real goods while retiring substantial portions of debt. Hence, governments generally encourage other countries to use their currency. Another perspective is that the United States is the principal place where dollars can be spent. This naturally amplifies the demand for US goods and services or, more likely, investment in productive resources within the country. The United States welcomes the fact that there are currently more dollars circulating outside the country than within.

However, what if those outside dollars are suddenly returned and spent in the United States? Although not catastrophic, it would be somewhat costly. Consumption levels would have to fall as foreigners traded their dollars for goods and services. To prevent price inflation, some currency would have to be removed from circulation. In other words, some US treasury debt would be resold, and taxpayers would be charged the cost to make interest payments to the outside buyers. The currency gained from reselling that debt would be held out of circulation.

Of course, foreigners willingly hold dollars because they believe that it is in their interest to do so. Thus, a mass influx of dollars into the United States is highly unlikely. However, it is reassuring to acknowledge that even if such a thing should somehow happen, the negative impact would not be overwhelming.

As indicated in Figure 11.3, the United States has generally experienced a perpetual, growing trade deficit since about 1980. While a few trade surpluses have occurred, but only when the economy weakened in recessions. Despite a portion of currency did flow out of the country,

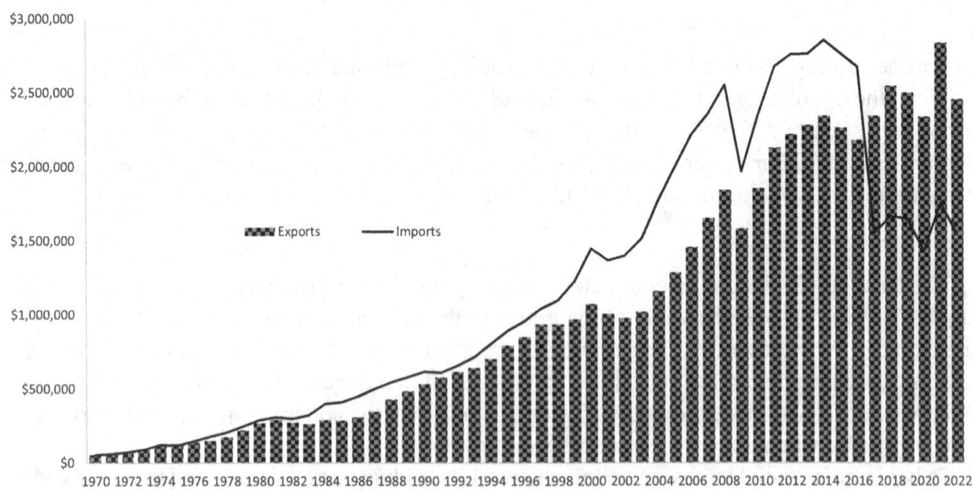

Figure 11.3 Imports and Exports in the United States (in Million), 1970–2022.

Source: US Department of Commerce—Bureau of Economic Analysis

the trade deficit is basically balanced by a surplus of capital inflows. The surplus in the capital account (capital inflow minus outflow) is essentially the mirror image of the trade deficit. In other words, foreigners who wish to invest in the United States have largely outbid foreigners who wish to consume American goods. When the nation "sends dollars out of the country" they "come back" in the form of capital flows. For instance, foreigners build factories in the United States or buy stocks and bonds from American companies (US Department of Commerce, Bureau of Economic Analysis, 2007). The United States is seen as a favorable place to invest, as it boasts the world's largest economy, strongest political stability, and a substantial degree of economic freedom. As long as this remains the case, we will likely continue to see US capital surpluses/trade deficits for the foreseeable future.[9]

Why Nations Trade

In this section, we begin to explore the reasons why nations choose to engage in international trade as well as the advantages of doing so. The fundamental reasoning behind international trade is the fact that nations are not equally able to produce all goods. Consider a nation that is particularly abundant in fossil fuels, might not have the wherewithal to capitalize on those resources. Before delving further, it is crucial to explain the concept of a production possibility curve (PPC).

Production Possibility Curve

A production possibilities curve or frontier (PPC or PPF) is a graph that shows all different combinations of goods and services an economy can produce with fixed resources. The production possibilities curve measures the tradeoff between producing one good versus another.

A PPC can be used to represent a number of different economic concepts, such as the term of trade, opportunity cost, and economies of scale. Opportunity cost is the value of the next best alternative that must be given up in order to produce a good or service.

Whenever one delves into the structure of production within an economy of any scale, understanding the concept of a PPC is beneficial. A PPC shows all different combinations of output that an economy can produce using all available resources. The production possibilities curve measures the tradeoff between producing one good versus another. The curve is plotted along a two-dimensional graph, on which the y and x axes each signify a quantity of a good, making it a "two-good" analysis. The curve itself is seen as a frontier outside of which production of the two goods is impossible. Any output combination within the curve would prove to be inefficient; maximum efficiency lies only along the curve. Therefore, any point within the PPC represents inefficiency and any point outside the PPC represents something unattainable, given available technology and other resources. The PPC illustrated in Figure 11.4 shows the tradeoff in production between, such as food and clothing. Any combination of these two products (A, B, C, or other) could be chosen. For instance, at point A, 600 units of food can be produced with 300 units of clothing. Alternatively, at point B, 200 units of food can be produced along with 700 units of clothing. Hence, the opportunity cost to create 400 more units of food at point B can be said to be the 400 units of clothing that must be given up moving from B to A. Point M represents a level of production that cannot be achieved with the current

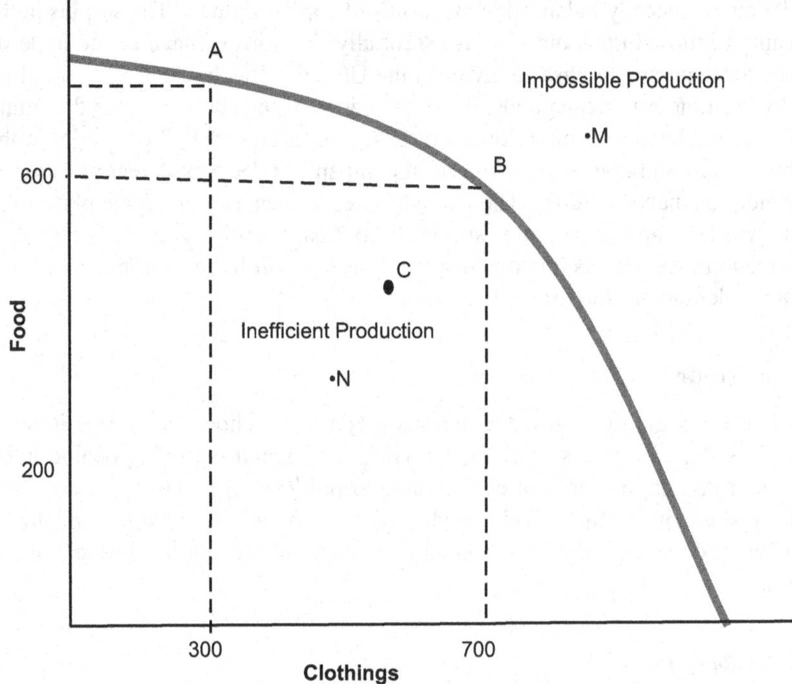

Figure 11.4 Production Possibility Curve.

level of resources. It lies outside the production possibilities curve, while point N represents a level of inefficient production.

> Absolute advantage denotes a country's ability to produce a good or deliver a service at a lower cost. Absolute advantage describes a scenario in which one country can manufacture a product at a higher quality, a lower cost for a greater profit than another country.
>
> An economy is said to have a comparative advantage in whichever good has the lowest opportunity cost. Hence, comparative advantage implies an opportunity cost associated with the production of one good compared to another. David Ricardo built on Smith's concepts by introducing comparative advantage, saying countries can benefit from trade even when they have absolute advantage in producing everything.

The slope at any given point on the curve describes the marginal rate of substitution or how much of one good must be sacrificed to produce one more unit of the other. For example, if the slope at point C is 0.75, then that is equal to the opportunity cost at point C; that is, to produce one more unit of clothing, 0.75 units of food will be taken out of the production schedule. Inversely, to produce one more unit of food, 1.33 units of clothing will not be produced.

Absolute Advantage

A country is said to have an absolute advantage over another in the production of a good if it can create the good using fewer resources (Das, 2008). Adam Smith, a Scottish social

Table 11.6 Production Possibilities

	Aircraft per Unit of Input	*Cars per Unit of Input*
China	100	100,000
United States	160	80,000

Table 11.7 Opportunity Cost

	Opportunity Cost of Producing	*Opportunity Cost of Producing*
	One Aircraft	*One Car*
China	1,000 Cars	0.001 Aircraft
United States	500 Cars	0.002 Aircraft

philosopher, first described the principle of absolute advantage in the context of international trade, using labor as the only input. Absolute advantage is determined by a simple comparison of labor productivities, so it is possible for a country to have no absolute advantage in any domain. If a country can achieve more output per unit of productive resources than its trading partner, then that country is said to have an absolute advantage in terms of trade. Through specialization, different countries can produce and export goods for which they have a natural or acquired absolute advantage, subsequently importing other goods in which they do not specialize. Table 11.6 shows an absolute advantage situation for the United States and China in terms of aircraft and automobile production. Let's assume that China can produce 100 aircraft or 100,000 cars per unit of productive resources, while the United States can produce 160 aircraft or 80,000 cars per unit of productive resources. Evidently, the United States has an absolute advantage in aircraft production while China has an absolute advantage in car production.

Based on this information, we can calculate the opportunity cost of producing each product in each country as demonstrated in Table 11.7. To produce one aircraft, China must forego 1,000 cars, giving an opportunity cost of 1,000 cars. Similarly, to produce one aircraft, the United States must forego 500 cars, giving an opportunity cost of 500 cars.

With an absolute advantage, a country can charge a lower price compared to trading country since more of the good with the absolute advantage can be produced with fewer resources. In the absence of free trade, one unit of aircraft in China will exchange for 1,000 cars and one unit of aircraft in the United States will exchange for 500 cars. Upon the introduction of free trade, both the United States and China stand to benefit. If the United States can get more than 500 cars per unit of aircraft, then the country will be better off than if would without the trade. On the other hand, China has been giving up 1,000 cars to get one aircraft, so if it can get an aircraft for fewer than 1,000 cars, then it will be in a more advantageous position. Therefore, the terms of trade should fall somewhere between 500 and 1,000 cars per unit of aircraft. Let's suppose that the terms of trade are 750 cars per unit of aircraft. In this case, we arrive at the possibilities shown in Figures 11.5 and 11.6.

In relation to the previously introduced PPC, trade has effectively moved the curve to the right, thereby making available more of both goods. Clearly, this simple example shows that there are significant gains to trade when each country has an absolute advantage in the production of one of the goods. However, what happens when one country has an absolute advantage in the production of both goods? This situation is discussed in the next section.

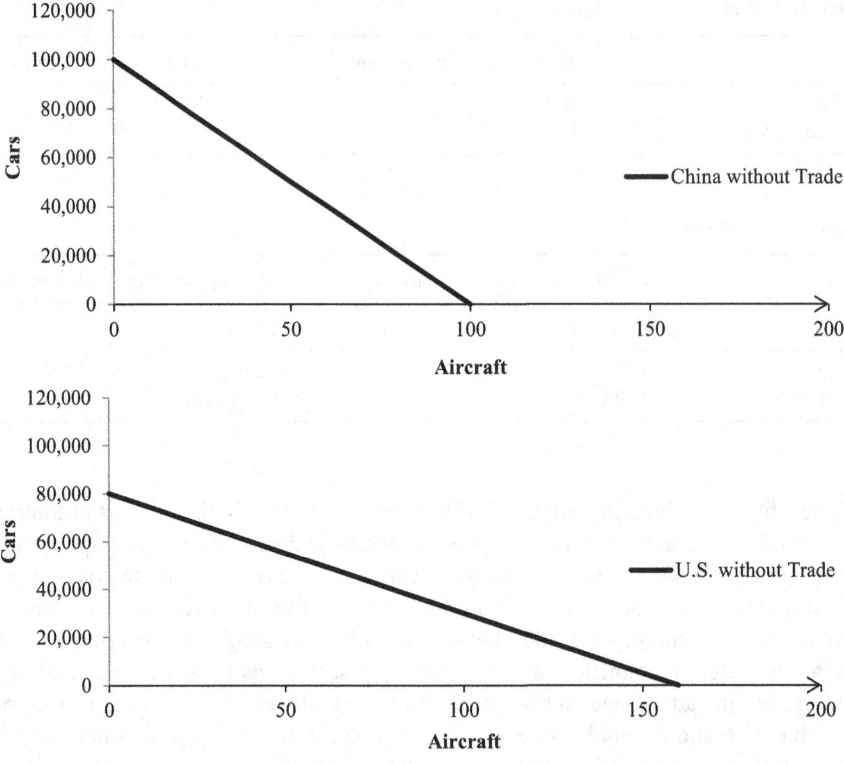

Figure 11.5 China/US Production Capabilities without Trade.

Comparative Advantage

Comparative advantage exists when a country can produce a particular good or service at a lower opportunity cost, in terms of the amount of other goods and services that must be given up producing it, than another country.

In the following example, United States has an absolute advantage in both car and aircraft production. However, if Country United focuses on producing aircraft and China focuses on producing cars, and they trade with each other, both countries will be able to consume more of both goods than they could have produced on their own.

In 1817, David Ricardo outlined the theory of comparative advantage, which shows how the gains from trade can still come about even if one country has an absolute advantage in the production of both goods. A country has a comparative advantage in the product with the lowest opportunity cost of production, thus implying that China should specialize in cars and the United States should specialize in aircraft. To illustrate, let's alter the numbers in the example we presented earlier to provide a simple proof of the benefits of international trade when one country as an absolute advantage in both goods.

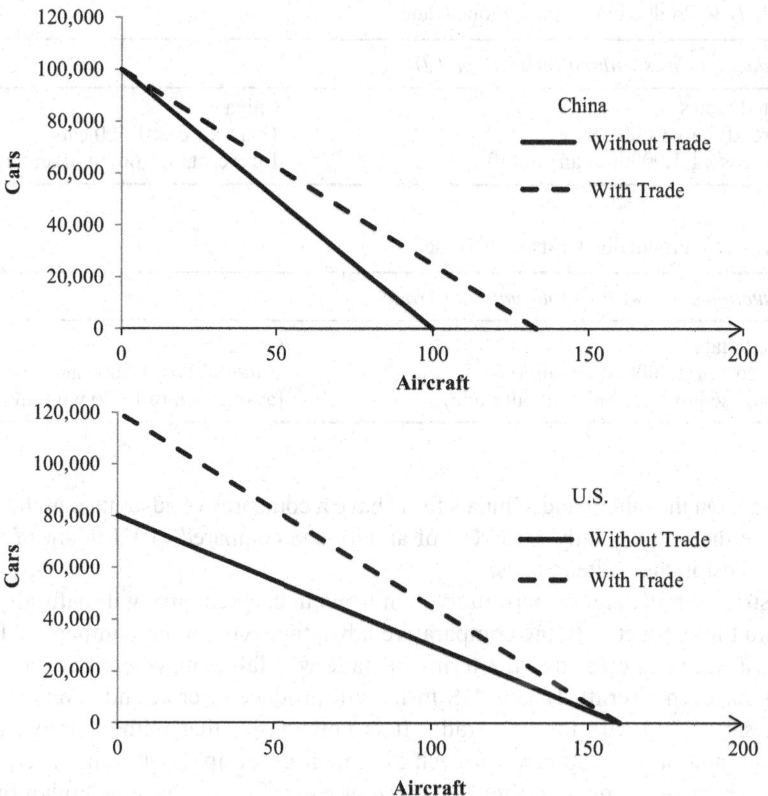

Figure 11.6 China/US Production Capabilities with/without Trade.

Table 11.8 China/US Comparative Production Possibilities

	Aircraft per Unit of Input	*Cars per Unit of Input*
China	50	80,000
United States	100	100,000

Table 11.8 assumes that the United States has an absolute advantage in both cars and aircraft. Nonetheless, Ricardo argued that both countries can still derive benefit from trade. In the United States, the opportunity cost of 1,000 cars is one aircraft. This includes the comprehensive opportunity cost of production. In other words, if energy, material, and other resources are reallocated away from car production to aircraft production, then US firms can produce another aircraft, but the country's output will decrease by 1,000 cars. Likewise, if we reverse the reallocation and devote more resources to making cars, then US firms can produce another car but will have to sacrifice 1/1,000th of an aircraft.

Meanwhile, in China, the opportunity cost of an aircraft is 1,600 cars, with the opportunity cost of a car equal to 1/1,600th of an airplane. Thus, even though the United States boasts an absolute advantage in the production of both cars and aircraft, it has a comparative advantage only in the production of airplanes, since each plane costs 1,000 cars compared to a cost of 1,600

Table 11.9 Production Costs without Trade

Production Costs without International Trade	
United States	China
1 aircraft cost 1,000 cars	1 aircraft cost 1,600 cars
1 car costs 1/1,000th of an aircraft	1 car costs 1/1,600th of an aircraft

Table 11.10 Production Costs with Trade

Production Costs without International Trade	
United States	China
1 car costs 1/1,300th of an aircraft	1 aircraft cost 1,300 cars
(as opposed to 1/1,000th without trade)	(as opposed to 1,600 without trade)

cars in China. On the other hand, China's firms have a comparative advantage in the production of cars since their cost is only 1/1,600th of an airplane compared to 1/1,000th of an airplane opportunity cost in the United States.

If unrestricted trade is now permitted, then firms in each country will naturally shift production into the product with the comparative advantage. Given the numbers in Tables 11.9 and 11.10, it becomes clear that the terms of trade will fall somewhere between 1,000 and 1,600 cars for each aircraft. Hence, US firms will produce aircraft and "convert" each aircraft into, say, 1,300 cars through trade. It is noteworthy that without trade, the United States could gain only 1,000 cars for each aircraft it gives up. By trading aircraft for cars, the country can acquire more cars and US citizens can afford to consume both more cars and more aircraft.

China's wealth also grows since they can now trade 1,300 cars for an aircraft, instead of being compelled to give up 1,600 cars for each aircraft they directly produce. This simple mathematical proof confirms the intuitive notion that when a society produces goods at the lowest possible cost of resources, it is possible to produce more. Allowing free international trade unambiguously increases overall wealth. Likewise, it follows that international trade barriers reduce wealth. Such barriers include tariffs (special taxes on imports), import quotas, discriminatory regulation, and other import bans.

Trade Protections and Trade Barriers

Trade barriers are attempts by the government to regulate or restrict international trade. They all work on the same common principle of imposing an additional cost on the imported goods, leading to an increased price for that good. A country can protect domestic industry by imposing tariffs, subsidies, quotas, and currency manipulation. Critics contend that such a policy would only result in an inefficient allocation of resources at the local and global level.

Tariffs

A tariff is an additional tax on imported goods. Some tariffs are intended to protect local industries from cheaper foreign goods, while others are instituted by governments to generate revenue from the imported good. Tariffs are the easiest trade barrier to impose and can successfully

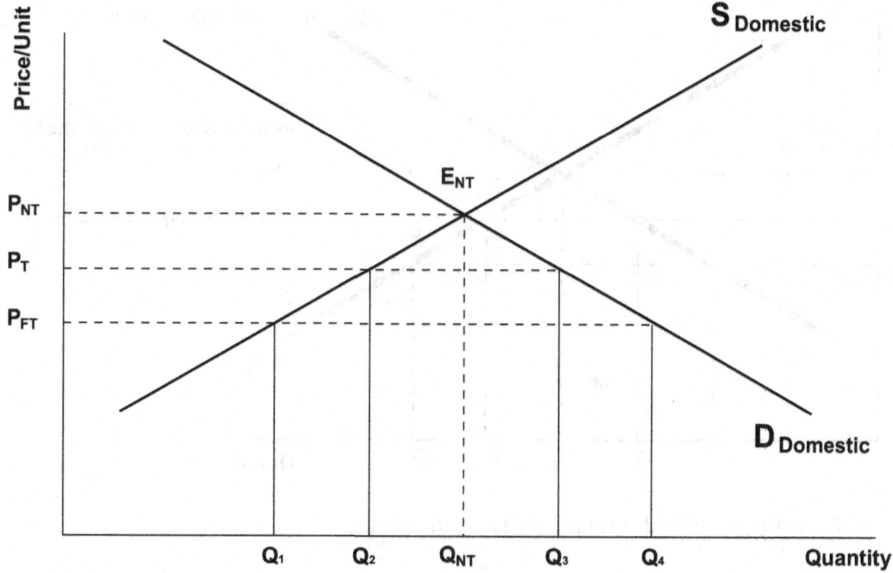

Figure 11.7 The Effects of International Trade Barriers on a Domestic Market.

reduce free trade. Let's assume that Figure 11.7 represents supply (S) and demand (D) for automobiles in the United States. In the absence of trade restrictions, cars will be imported at the prevailing market price of (PFT). In this example:

Q_4 = Total consumption in United States

Q_1 = Total domestic production

$Q_4 - Q_1$ = Total import

$Q_4 = Q_1 + (Q_4 - Q_1)$

P_{NT} and Q_{NT} represent the unit price and quantity available under no international trade and hence no international competition. P_{FT} and Q_4 are the unit price and quantity available under free international trade and no international trade barriers.

Suppose the United States imposes a tariff on imported cars. As a result, the price of cars will rise by the amount of the tariff, to P_T. Without any retaliatory actions from other countries, the increase in price reduces consumption and increases domestic production. This would change the values to:

Q_3 = Total consumption in United States

Q_2 = Total domestic production

$(Q_3 - Q_2)$ = Total import

$Q_3 = Q_2 + (Q_3 - Q_2)$

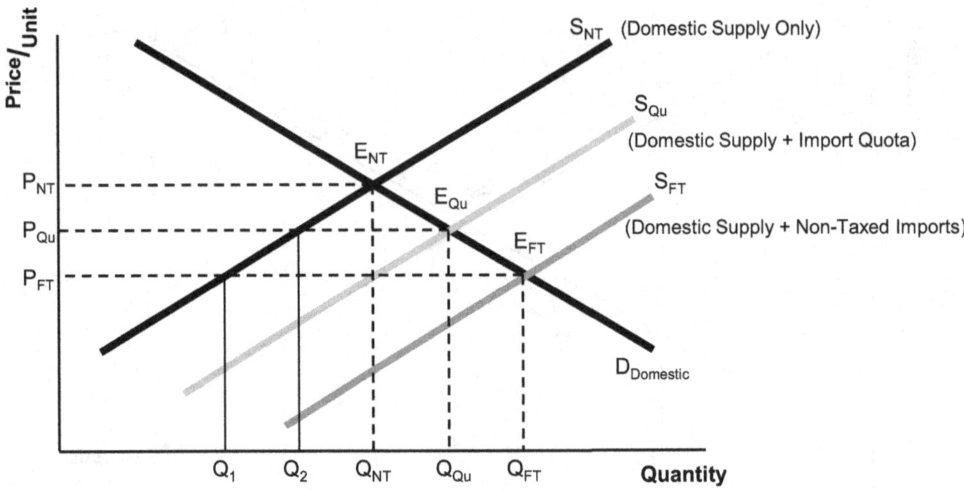

Figure 11.8 The Effects of Trade Quotas on a Domestic Market.

Quotas

The objective of an import quota is to protect domestic producers from outside competition. Import quotas limit the quantity of various commodities that can be imported into a country during a specified period of time. In Figure 11.8, the imposition of import quotas on cars will induce domestic manufacturers to expand production from Q_1 to Q_2, with Q_{QU} being the total supply counting both domestic production as well as the quota. Dairy products in the United States are a good example, as they are subject to annual import quotas administered by the Department of Agriculture. The common reason is often leaning toward protecting newer or inefficient domestic industries that are seen as important to the domestic economy and the protecting of jobs. Other forms of trade protection include:

In the concept of international trade, a quota is a government-imposed trade restriction that limits the volume of goods that a country can import or export during a particular year.

A tariff is a tax imposed by a country on the goods and services imported from another country.

Recently, there have been numerous examples of tariff trade wars, including the ongoing trade dispute between the United States and China. In 2018, the US government-imposed tariffs on billions of dollars' worth of Chinese goods and services. As the result, the Chinese government imposed similar retaliatory measures on US products.

Dumping

Another trade practice that stirs controversy is so-called "dumping." Dumping supposedly occurs when a manufacturer in one country exports their product and sells it at an unreasonably low price, usually claimed to be below the cost of production, in another country. It is then usually alleged that workers in the second country may become unemployed because of this "unfair competition." However, free market advocates see dumping, if it actually occurs, as beneficial to consumers since it obviously lowers the price of the product in question. According to The World Trade Organization (WTO) regulations, a government may act against dumping in cases where material injury to the domestic industry has occurred. This directive is intentionally vague so as to allow each government to decide on its own to what extent dumping will be permissible.

Currency Manipulation

Currency manipulation is a deliberate attempt by a country to lower the value of its currency. By buying foreign currency in the market, a country can artificially change the price of its imports and its exports. Manipulating currency to gain an unfair competitive advantage is already prohibited for members of the International Monetary Fund and WTO, but the prohibitions lack enforcement.

In the past several years, many countries have been accused of currency manipulation including China, Japan, Germany, Switzerland, and South Korea, among others.

In the 1980s, Japan implemented a policy of "Yen (¥) intervention," in which it would buy large amounts of US dollars and other foreign currencies in order to keep the value of the Yen at a lower level. Starting from ¥221 per US$ in 1981, the average value of the yen actually dropped to ¥239 per US$ in 1985. China, too, has been accused of manipulating its currency, the Yuan, by keeping its value artificially low in order to make Chinese exports more competitive in global markets. Likewise, Switzerland had been accused of manipulating its currency, the Swiss franc, by setting a minimum exchange rate against the euro.

Another common practice is a subsidy, which entails government-provided aid to help a company produce or purchase a product. Subsidies have been used to help new and failing industries and even companies that have failed to generate enough revenue to maintain operation and public interest (Carbaugh, 2007). For instance, Amtrak has received government subsidies in the form of loans to keep its service running. In 2007, the Bush Administration agreed to pay $900 million of Amtrak's estimated $3.1 billion budget. Among the array of subsidies, one of the more controversial subsidies is that which allegedly exists between Airbus and its associated countries. We will cover this topic in a subsequent section. In 2019, the United States won the largest arbitration award in WTO history in its dispute with the European Union over illegal subsidies to Airbus. The ruling from the WTO stipulated that the United States could target $7.5 billion of imports from the European Union over illegal subsidies for Airbus.[10]

Aircraft Manufacturing and Governmental Subsidies

Much of the discussion of government subsidies as it pertains to aircraft manufacturing tends to focus on Large Commercial Aircraft (LCA) production by Airbus and Boeing. However, it is important to recognize that even smaller regional jet manufacturers are also recipients of government aid and subsidies. Embraer in Brazil and Bombardier in Canada have both been engaged in their own battles over unfair subsidies since the 1990s. Several WTO rulings between 1999 and 2002 found that both countries ran illegal subsidy programs for their aircraft manufacturing companies. Specifically, a 2000 ruling charged Embraer for receiving illegal subsidies and ordered Brazil to modify its Proex export subsidies program. Similarly, in 2001, Bombardier and Canada faced similar charges due to low-interest government loans designed to increase market share.

Boeing Versus Airbus

It is commonly alleged that Airbus and Boeing are unfairly subsidized by their respective governments, allowing them to charge less than full price for their aircraft, thereby disadvantaging other manufacturers. These disputes originate from the first Airbus aircraft manufactured in the 1970s, the A300. In the case of Boeing, partisans argue that the US government should impose some sort of tariff on Airbus, thereby counterbalancing the subsidy and affording Boeing a level playing field. While Airbus disputes this analysis, economists point out that even if the subsidy exists as alleged, it would be harmful to the United States to impose a tariff. Throughout the history of aircraft manufacturing, a number of truces and agreements have been signed between Boeing, Airbus, and their respective governments. Among these, there is a bilateral agreement from 1992 that established limits on the direct and indirect subsidies used for financing new aircraft. In the wake of a 2004 complaint against the EU citing a breach of the agreement, the governments of the United States and the EU agreed (again) to stop subsidizing Boeing and Airbus for a short period of time in order to resolve the decades-old dispute over billions in subsidies to the aircraft makers outside of the WTO.

If people in the United States can buy aircraft at a lower price locally, then they will have more resources to produce and consume additional aircraft and whatever else they might desire. Thus, in return, total wealth clearly increases. The impact would generally be the same if the European taxpayers mailed checks directly to US consumers, rather than giving money to Airbus. In this situation, if there were a party that incurs a loss, it is the European taxpayers who see some of their wealth being transferred to the United States.

Boeing does suffer some lost sales from the subsidy. However, the extent of Boeing's loss is less than the combined gain to airlines, air travelers, and the economy in general. It is worth noting that the general effects of trade are not affected by the existence or lack of a subsidy. Boeing loses less than the general economic gains if Airbus provides a better aircraft for the price. Whether this favorable pricing comes from a subsidy, hard work, luck, or better technology, the impact is the same.

Recent World Trade Organization Rulings against Airbus/Boeing

The WTO requires proof of damage (measurable injury to competitors) before any government assistance can be termed a subsidy. The initial WTO report, released in 2010, stems from the 2004 complaint brought forth against Airbus, that includes rulings on over 300 separate instances of alleged subsidization over a period of nearly 40 years. The subsidies under scrutiny pertain to the comprehensive spectrum of Airbus products (A200 through A380) and fall under five general categories:

1 *Launch aid or "member state financing"*: This encompasses the provision of financing by the Governments of France, Germany, Spain, and the UK (hereinafter, the "member States") to Airbus for the purpose of developing the A300, A310, A320, A330/A340, A350, and A380.
2 *Loans from the European Investment Bank (EIB)*: This pertains to a series of 12 loans provided by the EIB to Airbus companies between 1988 and 2002 for aircraft design, development, and other purposes.
3 *Infrastructure and infrastructure-related grants:* This encompasses the allocation of resources, involving provision of goods and services, as well as grants, to develop and upgrade Airbus manufacturing sites.

4 *Corporate restructuring measures:* This consists of the provision to Airbus by Germany[11] and France of equity infusions, debt forgiveness, and grants through government-owned and government-controlled banks.
5 *Research and technological development funding:* This consists of the provision of grants and loans undertaken by Airbus.

These WTO rulings were appealed by the EU. On May 18, 2011, the Appellate Body upheld the Panel's finding that certain subsidies provided by the EU caused serious prejudice to the interests of the United States. The principal subsidies covered by the ruling include financing arrangements (as launch aid or member state financing) provided by France, Germany, Spain, and the UK for the development of the A300 through to the A380 aircraft. The Appellate Body found that the effect of the subsidies was to displace exports of Boeing single-aisle and twin-aisle aircraft from the EU, Chinese, and Korean markets and Boeing single-aisle aircraft from the Australian market. The Appellate Body determined the number of illegal subsidies and aid to be $18 billion. Boeing has also received subsidies considered illegal by the WTO. In 2011, the WTO found that Boeing received $5.3 billion in illegal subsidies between 1989 and 2006.[12] Furthermore in 2019, a ruling established that the United States had continued to subsidize Boeing illegally through a Washington State tax break and business incentives from South Carolina.

And as we said it earlier, the United States and the European Union then reached to an agreement in their epic 17-year-old transatlantic battle over aircraft subsidies, and ending the world's largest corporate trade dispute.

International Trade Policy in Air Travel: Optimality versus Political Realities

Economists generally agree that free trade is the best policy in aviation and most other industries. Ideally, foreign airlines from friendly nations should be allowed to freely compete, and there is no reason for government policy to favor domestic carriers over foreign carriers. Implementing such a policy would maximize competition and efficiency in air travel—prices would be lower and there would be more variety in services. Moreover, this approach would bolster wealth because air travel would be more efficient in its use of resources, which would effectively increase transportation efficiency for all industries. Streamlined air travel has impacts analogous to a more efficient road system—it allows firms to expand into more output markets, to gather resources from more input markets, and to take advantage of economies of scale in production.

We mentioned earlier that establishing free international trade in 2004 likely would have increased annual world income by about a half trillion dollars. Formal estimates for the impact of free competition in air travel alone are not available, but income would certainly increase by the billions.

Considering the huge benefits of free trade in air travel, why have politicians in most nations failed to implement it? Think back to the public choice principles discussed in Chapter 2. Most citizens are "rationally ignorant" and unaware of the benefits of free international trade; there is no strong consumer movement clamoring for free trade in air travel or anything else. However, all firms, including airlines, want to avoid increased competition as much as possible. As a result, governments have a tendency to act in the interests of airlines rather than in the interests of the nation as a whole. In other words, in the absence of a well-informed public, politicians tend to give into the special interests of the domestic airline industry.

This is reflected in the typical language of trade politics. Politicians frequently use the term "trade concession" to refer to the participation of foreign firms which are allowed to compete in a market. However, a point of contention that politicians are reluctant to agree upon is the exchange rights in trade concession. The entire attitude is that increasing import competition is an awful result that must be tolerated in order to negotiate export rights for domestic firms. This is the perspective of the domestic firms these politicians seek to please—access to more markets is welcomed but competition and lower prices are not. Despite the fact that the overall national wealth and consumer welfare increase, the wealth of companies facing more competition does not usually increase. Ironically, politicians who increase national well-being by reducing trade barriers feel compelled to cloak these good steps by calling them concessions.

From an economists perspective, the optimal policy would be for a country to unilaterally open its own market to foreign competition. The ideal outcome would involve swift augmentation in competition and lower prices as soon as possible, with no negotiations necessary.

It is useful to summarize the likely results of such a policy in the US market. If the United States allowed *cabotage*, foreign carriers handling domestic traffic within the country, the immediate results, though beneficial, are unlikely to be spectacular. US airlines have been deregulated for a long time and are quite efficient by world standards. Achieving profitability within this market is not easy. Thus, foreign airlines would not be anxiously pouring into the United States. While a few carriers, such as Virgin America, Inc., might enter in a major way, others might enter a few markets to which they are already linked. For example, a number of foreign carriers are already flying a few *blind routes* where domestic traffic is prohibited. For example, an airline might travel from London to New York to Los Angeles but is currently prohibited from picking up passengers in New York and dropping them off in Los Angeles. If this prohibition were lifted, they could freely market that segment.

For U.S. domestic carriers, the disadvantage of increased competition would be at least partially offset by the injection of foreign capital. In abolishing the laws prohibiting cabotage, the United States would inherently also be abolishing the laws prohibiting foreign controlling investment in US airlines. Some financially strained carriers would welcome some sort of partnership, perhaps even a formal merger, with a wealthier foreign airline. Likewise, the best strategy for a foreign airline looking to break into the US market might often be to team up with a US partner. The current airline alliances achieve only small degree of this type of cooperation.

Since there would be lower prices and greater efficiency, more people would fly, and therefore create a higher demand for labor in the airline industry. Some of the new jobs might go to foreign workers brought in by foreign-based airlines, but net airline employment for US workers is still likely to rise since airlines, like most service industries, prefer to hire locally in order to promote better customer relations.[13]

The impact on average wages in the airlines is more complex. In competitive labor markets, rising labor demand would normally bid up the wages. However, the US airline industry is dominated by unusually powerful labor unions. These unions unite workers together to bargain as a labor monopoly and thereby raise wages above competitive levels. With the introduction of cabotage, increased competition tends to erode union monopoly power of these unions and subsequently average wages. That means that while rising labor demand tends to increase wages, rising competition tends to reduce union power and union wages so that the overall wage effects of cabotage are not immediately clear.

In 2022, the US domestic aviation market has reach to pre-pandemic levels, according to data IATA reported, and airlines are offering significant pay increases to pilots as flight crew shortages continues. The effect of increased labor demand swamped the effect of eroded union monopoly power, and wages generally rose after deregulation.

Since the move from regulation to deregulation probably impacted airline competition far more dramatically than cabotage would, it seems reasonable to conclude that airline wages would not be driven down following the opening of the US market. Of course, while the effects on the US economy overall are clearly beneficial, these effects are unlikely to be dramatic (at least in the short run) given the relative efficiency of the US airline industry.

The same general impact would naturally occur in any country that opened its airline market, although the effects might be more intense. It is possible that efficient foreign carriers would drive prices so low that flag carriers would not survive. Most economists would not consider this loss would to be tragic. The broader gains for the economy in a more efficient air transport system would easily exceed the sentimental regret at the loss of an inefficient flag carrier. There is no more reason to insist that air travel be supplied internally than there is to insist on locally grown pickles.

But does "national pride" justify preserving an inefficient flag carrier? One response is to acknowledge that in an open market, the flag carrier is free to market itself to travelers on the basis of national pride. If consumers believe in supporting the flag carrier significantly, they are free to do so. Naturally, there are likely to be limits on how much consumers would be willing to pay, and a flag carrier that is vastly less efficient than the competition is probably doomed. If that is true, then people do not necessarily value "national pride" when it comes to travel. Without free consumer support, the argument for flag carriers is flawed. It may also be possible to compromise and overcome the politics of protectionism by requiring foreign carriers to exclusively employ native-born employees and perhaps use aircraft adorned in the home country's colors. This would preserve much of the feel of having a flag carrier while still enjoying at least some of the benefits of open competition.

Ironically, government interference has rendered air travel, an industry that should naturally be more global than most, far less global in its operations than virtually any other major industry. Foreign ownership of US airlines is another restriction that prevents a full open market. US law limits foreign control in its domestic airlines to 49%, with a maximum of 25%. Other countries have similar protection of their domestic markets.

The pace of government reform is typically very slow, but the current trend is at least somewhat encouraging. Deregulation of air travel within the EU has been impressive, and the United States and Europe are working toward establishing a Transatlantic Common Aviation Area (European Commission, Directorate General, Energy and Transport, 2004). A significant step in this direction transpired in 2004 when the EU–US Open Skies Agreement took effect. Perhaps open skies, in lieu of cabotage, will eventually become routine and allow the industry to truly flourish and the world to become truly small.

Foreign Currency and Exchange Rates

International trade (imports and exports) requires foreign currency in order to complete the transactions. When goods and services are purchased in a country, they are purchased using that country's currency. An exchange rate is the value of one country's currency expressed in terms of another country's currency, and they are determined by supply and demand in the foreign exchange market. To obtain foreign currency, Trading in the local currency via the currency exchange rate is required. Exchange rates are influenced by a wide range of different factors, and the importance of each differs from country to country. For example, one factor affecting the exchange rate between currencies is the rate of inflation. As a general rule, the currency from countries with lower inflation rates rise in value, while the currency from countries with higher inflation rates fall in value. Therefore, the products from countries with high inflation rates become more attractive compared to the products from countries with lower inflation rates due to the relative increase in purchasing power of the lower inflating currency.

Exchange rates have a significant impact on the air transport industry due to the effect on the cost of aircraft, jet engine air travel, and the competitiveness of companies. When a country's currency appreciates relative to another currency, products and services from that country becomes more expensive for foreign customers. Exchange rates can have a significant impact on Airbus, which is a multinational aerospace company that manufactures and sells commercial and military aircraft, satellites, and other related products. In addition, exchange rates can impact Airbus's competitiveness in the global market.

Another factor affecting the exchange rate is interest rate. Everything being equal, a higher interest on US securities compared to, say, Canadian securities would make an investment in US securities more attractive. Therefore, an increase in the US interest rate raises the flow of Canadian dollars into US securities and decreases the outflow of American dollars to Canadian securities. This increased flow of funds into the US economy would increase the value of the US dollar and decrease the value of the Canadian dollar. Hence, the ratio of US dollar to Canadian dollar, as it is represented in the foreign exchange market, would decrease. Finally, the balances of payments of a country with the rest of the world influence the country's exchange rate. Demand for foreign currency arises from the import of foreign merchandise, the payment for foreign services, or from the redemption of foreign capital obligations. The supply of foreign currency, on the other hand, comes from the export of goods and services, or from an inflow of foreign capital.

Exchange Rate Quotes

An exchange rate quotation denotes the value of one currency in terms of another. For example, a quotation of 1.35 CAD/USD signifies that 1 Canadian dollar will be needed to acquire 0.74 US[14] Dollars. In this quotation, the price currency is CAD (Canadian Dollars) and the unit or base currency is US dollars. Additionally, a quotation of 1.08 Euro/USD signifies that 1 Euro will be needed to acquire 1.08 US dollars. When the base currency is the home currency, it is known as a direct quotation. Using direct quotation, the exchange rate decreases when the home currency appreciates and increases when the home currency depreciates.

Exports generally increase the exchange rate of the domestic currency (appreciation) due to the influx of foreign currency into the domestic country. For example, if Japan Airlines were to make significant purchases of wide-body aircraft from the US-based Boeing Company, it would have to convert its Japanese yen to US dollars to complete the transaction. This would result in US banks receiving the Japanese yen and exchanging them for the requisite amount of US paper dollars at the current exchange rate. This increased demand for US dollars acts like any increase in demand, causing the price of dollars in yen rise. This increase in price is depicted in Figure 11.9.

Imports reduce foreign currency reserves, causing a decrease in the foreign currency supply (leftward), driving up the value of foreign currency relative to the local currency (depreciation), and decreasing the exchange rate. For example, suppose Wal-Mart buys consumer electronics from the Sony Corporation of Japan. To complete the transaction, Wal-Mart must convert its US dollars to Japanese yen. The Bank of Japan would take the US dollars and issue the requisite number of Japanese yen to Wal-Mart at the current exchange rate. The supply of yen relative to the dollar would be depleted so that the supply curve for yen would shift to the left. Alternatively, this would cause a relative increase in the supply curve for the dollar, depreciating the dollar and increasing the dollar price for yen as shown in Figure 11.10.

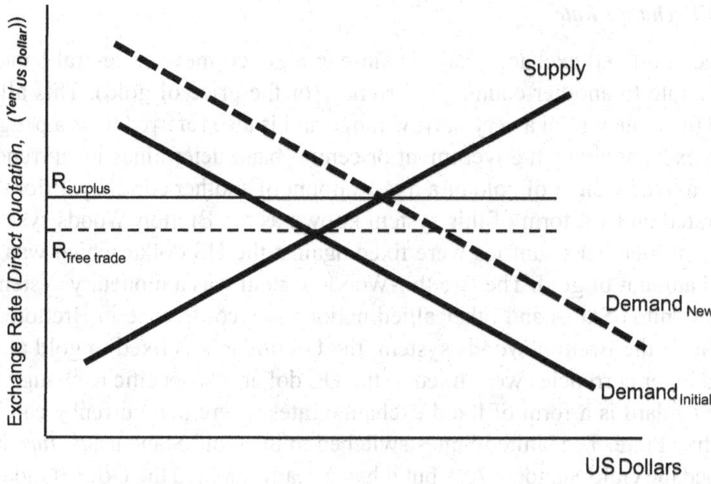

Figure 11.9 Demand for Dollars Causes the Value of US Dollar to Rise, Exchange Rate Increases.

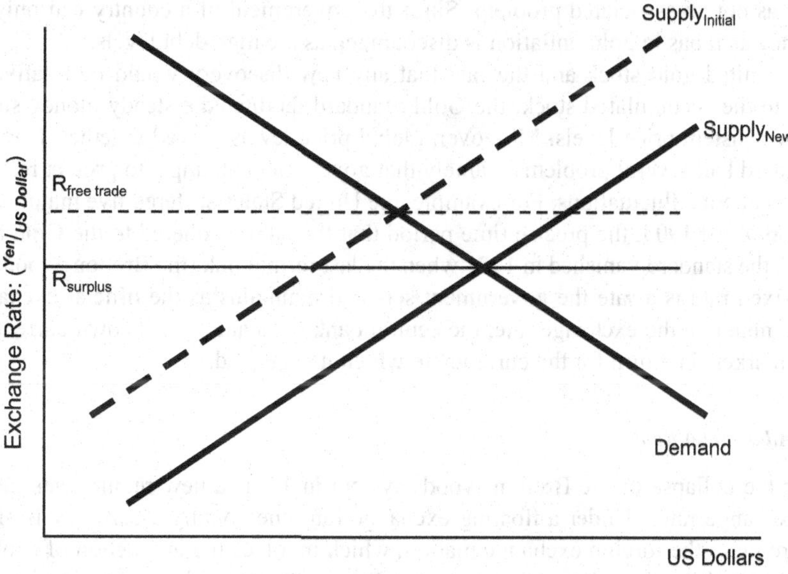

Figure 11.10 Surplus in Dollars Causes the Value of US Dollar to Drop, Exchange Rate Decreases.

Exchange Rate Regimes

An exchange rate regime is how a country manages its currency in relation to other currencies. There exists a spectrum across which the price of a currency can be determined against another: fixed exchange rates are situated at one extreme end of the spectrum, while floating (adjustable) rates are at the other.

Fixed (Pegged) Exchange Rate

The concept behind fixed exchange rates is simple: a government or central bank links its official exchange rate to another country's currency (or the price of gold). This allows the currency value to fluctuate within a very narrow range and is also referred to as a pegged exchange rate. With this exchange rate, a government or central bank determines its currency's worth in terms of either a fixed weight of gold or a fixed amount of another currency. Prior to 1971, most countries operated under a form of this system known as the Bretton-Woods system where the exchange rates of member countries were fixed against the US dollar which was in turn fixed against a fixed amount of gold. The Bretton-Woods system was a monetary system established in 1944 by the United States and other allied nations at a conference in Bretton Woods, New Hampshire. Under the Bretton-Woods system, the US dollar was fixed to gold at a rate of $35 per ounce, and other currencies were fixed to the US dollar at a specific exchange rate.

The Gold Standard is a form of fixed exchange rates where that currency can be converted into gold at a fixed rate. The United States switched to the Gold Standard *de jure* in 1900 when Congress passed the Gold Standard Act, but it had already adopted the Gold Standard de facto in 1834. Between 1880 and 1914, the majority of countries stuck to the Gold Standard as a means of valuing their currency. The trend broke down during World War I, but dissatisfaction with high inflation rates in the 1970s and 1980s renewed moderate interest in the Gold Standard, as inflation was not an associated problem. Since the government of a country can only print as much money as it has in gold, inflation is discouraged as are high debt levels.

Due to limited gold stock and the fact that any new discovery would be relatively small compared to the accumulated stock, the Gold Standard facilitated a steady money supply and relatively consistent price levels. Moreover, global price levels moved together. However, the Gold Standard had several problems, namely that government attempts to protect reserves created large economic fluctuations. For example, the United States suffered five major recessions between 1890 and 1905, the precise time period that the nation adhered to the Gold Standard. Ultimately, the standard vanished in 1971 when the last formal link (the Bretton-Woods system) ended. A fixed rate is a rate the government sets and maintains as the official exchange rate. In order to maintain the exchange rate, the central bank buys and sells its own currency on the exchange markets in return for the currency to which it is pegged.

Floating (Adjustable) Rates

Following the collapse of the Bretton-Woods system in 1971, a new regime was introduced: floating exchange rates. Under a floating exchange rate, the country's currency is allowed to vary according to the foreign exchange market, which involves the interaction of banks, firms, and other institutions that sell and buy currency. Despite the transition to floating rate systems, only a few of the world's currencies are classified as true floating exchange rates. This includes the United States, Canada, Australia, Britain, and the European Monetary Union. In a floating system, the central bank may also intervene when it is necessary to ensure stability and avoid recession or inflation. Floating exchange rates may lead to uncertainty and volatility in the foreign exchange market, which can make it more difficult for businesses and investors to plan and operate across borders. Under this system, the exchange rate can appreciate or depreciate in response to changes in economic fundamentals such as inflation, interest rates, and trade balances. In addition, a floating exchange rate system provides greater independence for a country's monetary policy, allowing the monetary authorities to adjust interest rates to achieve macroeconomic objectives.

Several advantages of a floating exchange rate include:

- A floating exchange rate system allows for automatic stabilization of a country's economy in response to changes in global economic conditions,
- Allowing greater flexibility in implementing internal policy,
- Reducing the influence of central banks as changes occur automatically, and
- Dispensing with the need for large reserves.

The disadvantages of a floating exchange rate system may include:

- A floating exchange rate system allows for automatic stabilization of a country's economy in response to changes in global economic conditions,
- Day-to-day uncertainty,
- Highly volatile,
- Difficulty for the government to maintain export-oriented growth strategies.

Finally, a floating exchange rate can make it more challenging for countries to continue stable economic policies, particularly in the areas of international trade and finance.

Summary

International economics and trade play a significant role in the air transport industry, affecting exchange rates, trade policies, and economic growth. Airlines must navigate these economic factors to remain competitive and profitable in an increasingly globalized market. International trade can lead to increased economic growth by generating more opportunities for businesses to access new markets and expand their customer base. Furthermore, it can lead to increased standard of living, better employment, higher income, and increased consumer spending. This chapter discusses the international aspect of the airline industry, which is shown to be particularly relevant given the characteristics of air travel and the role of air cargo as a key transport mode for international trade in goods. In other words, aircraft can cross international borders much easier and quicker than any other mode of transportation. Economists generally argue that the world at large will benefit from free trade and that trade liberalization can promote development. Trade protectionists claim that trade protection in most cases benefits all the domestic economies, whereas the majority of economists argue that trade protection only benefits individual industries and is probably not sustainable in the long run. Comparative advantage and absolute advantage, the two important concepts in international trade are discussed in this chapter. Absolute advantage refers to a country's ability to produce a good or service more efficiently than any other country, while comparative advantage refers to a country's ability to produce a good or service at a lower opportunity cost than any other country.

This chapter has examined the arguments for and against free trade, with a presentation of the theories of absolute and comparative advantage. These theories are illustrated with quantitative examples. Moreover, the determination of foreign exchange rates is analyzed using standard supply and demand models along with historical methods for controlling exchange rates. A fixed rate is a rate the government sets as the official exchange rate. Unlike the fixed rate, a floating exchange rate is determined by the private market through supply and demand. The chapter concludes with a discussion on free trade agreements.

Discussion Questions

1 Explain why it is particularly important to understand the international aspects of the aviation industry.
2 Consider the following situation: Country A takes 50 hours to produce ten aircraft or five jet engines. Country B takes 50 hours to produce five aircraft or ten jet engines. Which country has an absolute advantage in which product? What are the domestic terms of trade for each country? Draw the production possibilities frontier for each country if they do not engage in trade. Draw the production possibilities frontier if the two countries do engage in trade.
3 Now assume that Country A takes 100 hours to produce 20 aircraft, or 10 jet engines and Country B takes 100 hours to produce 15 aircraft or five jet engines. Which country has an absolute advantage in which product? Does either country have a comparative advantage in one of the products? If so, which product is it? Can trade take place between the two countries? What would be the limits of the terms of trade if it were to take place?
4 Why do nations trade? Briefly explain the arguments for and against free trade.
5 Name and describe the rationale behind the three types of barriers to trade that a country may impose.
6 How have the effects of free trade impacted the aviation industry?
7 Generally speaking, what happens to the value of a country's currency when imports exceed exports and how, in terms of supply and demand, does this take place?
8 Explain why it is often said that trade is always good, but not always good for everybody.
9 Assume that the domestic demand for a certain product is equal to $P = 1{,}000 - 5Q$. Assume further that the domestic supply for the same product is equal to $P = 500 + 5Q$. With free trade, the supply curve is horizontal at a price equal to \$700.

   a Find the equilibrium quantity with free trade.
   b Now, assume that the domestic government imposes a tariff of \$25 per unit of the product. Find the new equilibrium price and quantity.

10 Using the numbers given in the preceding problem, how much does the domestic government gain from the tariff? How much do the domestic suppliers gain because of the tariff? How much do domestic consumers lose because of the tariff?
11 What do you conclude about the gains from trade when you compare the sum of producer surplus and government gain to the loss of consumer surplus?
12 Now suppose that instead of the tariff, an import quota is imposed on the product. Assume that the original supply and demand curves with free trade are $P= 1{,}000 - 5Q$ for demand and $400 + 5Q$ for supply.

   a Find the price and quantity with the new free trade supply curve.
   b Calculate the new price and quantity with the quota.
   c Now calculate the increase in producer surplus and the decrease in consumer surplus. Is there any difference between the two situations? Why or why not?
   d Why does the production possibilities curve have a negative slope?

13 What is the difference between a production possibilities curve that has a convex shape versus a production possibilities curve that is a straight line?
14 What is the difference between a free-floating currency and a pegged exchange rate?
15 What are the different types of barriers to international trade, and how do they affect global trade patterns?
16 If United States can produce 500 aircraft with 1,000 units of cars, while Japan can produce 600 aircraft with 1,500 units cars, which country has an absolute advantage in the production of aircraft?

Appendix: International Free Trade Agreements

Regional Trade Agreements (RTA) among different countries are the framework by which most of the world's economy is organized. Over the last few years, the number of RTAs has significantly increased, but their actual effectiveness is controversial. While the main purpose of many RTAs is to reduce trade barriers and encourage free trade, an increasing number of agreements also deal with other trade-related issues, such as the environment and labor. This section reviews and discusses several current regional trade agreements.

- **Dominican Republic-Central America Free Trade Agreement (CAFTA-DR)**
  It was signed on August 5, 2004 and came into effect in 2006. The United States signed the CAFTA-DR along with Costa Rica, El Salvador, Guatemala, Honduras, and Nicaragua, and the Dominican Republic. The CAFTA-DR is the first free trade agreement between the United States and a group of smaller developing economies. CAFTA aims to create a trade free zone among its member nations like that of NAFTA. Eighty percent of tariffs on US exports were eliminated immediately, with the remaining 20% to be phased out over time.
- **North American Free Trade Agreement (NAFTA)**
  NAFTA was originally signed on January 1, 1994, to link Canada, the United States, and Mexico. NAFTA essentially eliminated almost all tariffs among the participating nations, allowing for the smooth flow of goods and supplies across borders. As a result of NAFTA, imports and exports from the United States to Canada and Mexico increased from one-quarter to one-third. NAFTA was controversial when first proposed, mostly because it was the first free trade agreement involving developed countries and a developing country.[15] One of the major fears of the implementation of NAFTA was the potential loss of jobs in the United States. And, while manufacturing jobs in the United States did decrease, this loss was compensated for by the creation of over 2 million jobs a year in other industries from 1994 to 2000. Mexico has become part of North American supply chains, which provide US businesses access to lower-cost inputs. In 2018, the United States, Canada, and Mexico reached a new agreement to replace NAFTA with the United States–Mexico–Canada Agreement (USMCA), which includes revised clauses on labor and environmental policy, intellectual property rights, and digital trade. The USMCA went into effect on July 1, 2020.
- **The US–Jordan Free Trade Agreement (USJFTA)**
  The agreement between the United States and Jordan was fully implemented on January 1, 2010. This is the third agreement implemented by the United States, but the first trade agreement between the United States and an Arab nation. The goal is to eliminate tariff and non-tariff barriers on industrial goods and agricultural products over 10 years. In addition, the Qualifying Industrial Zones (QIZs), established by Congress in 1996, allow products to enter the United States duty-free if manufactured in Israel, Jordan, Egypt, or the West Bank and Gaza.
- **US–Australia Free Trade Agreement (AUSFTA)**
  FTA is an agreement (modeled after NAFTA) between Australia and the United States that was implemented on January 1, 2005. The agreement, like others, sought to reduce barriers to trade; however, following its inception, trade from Australia to the United States declined, while trade from the United States to Australia has continued to increase. The agreement created new opportunities for businesses in both countries, particularly in sectors such as agriculture, manufacturing, and services. Nevertheless, there has also been some criticism of the agreement, specifically from environmental groups and labor unions who argue that it has weakened environmental and labor standards in both countries.

- **European Union (EU)**
  The EU was established in 1993 by the Treaty on European Union (The Maastricht Treaty) and is the successor to the six-member European Economic Community (EEC). The EEC was an organization established by the Treaty of Rome in 1957 between Belgium, France, Italy, Luxembourg, the Netherlands, and West Germany. These countries are informally known as the Common Market or The Six. The EU is a confederation run by 27 member nations, most of which are located in continental Europe. Representatives make decisions partly by unanimity, partly by majority vote, and partly by delegation to lesser bodies. It has its own flag, anthem, central bank, currency, elected parliament, Supreme Court, and common foreign and security policy.[16]

Citizens belonging to EU member states are also EU citizens. They are allowed to invest, live, travel, and work in all member states except for temporary restrictions on newly inducted member states. With a few exceptions, systematic border controls were mostly abolished by the Schengen Agreement in 1985. The EU economy relies on a complex web of multilateral trade agreements, international rules, and standards that cover products, markets, investment, health, and environmental issues. There are still concerns about the nature of the union being intergovernmental (unanimous voting only) or supra nationalist (majority votes imposed on all members). However, the EU has proved to be a mix of both. In the last five decades, the EU has shown remarkable success in achieving economic prosperity and stability on a continental scale. It now accounts for about 30% of global GDP and 20% of global trade flows, and the euro has become an important international currency. The EU was considered a working model for regional integration.

The UK held a referendum on EU membership on June 23, 2016, and Britons stunned the world in 2016 by voting to leave the European Union. Consequently, many fear that Brexit could trigger a domino effect as the EU without Britain becomes less attractive to the other EU members. Later on, the UK and the EU agreed on a trade deal on December 24, 2020, which went into effect on January 1, 2021.

- **Union of South American Nations (UNASUL)**
  Loosely modeled on the EU, the Union of South American Nations combine the free trade organizations of MERCOSUR (Southern Common Market) and the Andean Community, in addition to Chile, Guyana, and Suriname by the end of 2007. The Union's headquarters is located in Quito, the capital of Ecuador. Formerly known as the South American Community of Nations, it was renamed at the First South American Energy Summit on April 16, 2007. The foundation of the Union was formally announced at the Third South American Summit, on December 8, 2004. Representatives from 12 South American nations signed the Cuzco Declaration, a two-page statement of intent.[17] An important operating condition is the use of institutions belonging to the pre-existing trade blocs (MERCOSUR and Andean Communities) to establish the union. So far, most of the countries within the union have waived visa requirements for travel, and there is an established consensus for a single South American currency.

- **AFTA (ASEAN Free Trade Area)**
  The Association of Southeast Asian Nations (ASEAN) is an organization of ten countries located in Southeast Asia. The AFTA agreement was signed on January 28, 1992, in Singapore by the member nations. At this time, ASEAN had six members: Brunei, Indonesia, Malaysia, the Philippines, Singapore, and Thailand. Subsequent members were required to sign the agreement upon entry into ASEAN and were given timeframes in which to meet AFTA's tariff reduction obligations. Beginning in 1997, ASEAN began creating organizations within its frame-

work with the intention of accelerating Southeast Asian integration to include the People's Republic of China, Japan, South Korea, India, Australia, and New Zealand.[18]

- **African Union (AU)**
  The African Union (AU) is an organization of 54 African states created in 2001 from the amalgamation of various pre-existing regional blocs. It is composed of 55 member states in Africa, with its headquarters located in Addis Ababa, Ethiopia. The AU preserved the free trade areas established by these pre-existing blocs and will be combining and expanding them under the banner of the African Economic Community. The AU aims to have a single currency and a sustainable economy by bringing an end to intra-African conflict and creating an effective common market. The AU has played an important role in resolving political and trade conflicts among its member, including Libya, Mali, and Sudan.

- **Greater Arab Free Trade Area (GAFTA)**
  GAFTA came into existence in January 2005. Similar to ASEAN, this agreement was initially signed by 17 Arab League members and aimed to decrease the customs on local production and the creation of an Arab Free Zone for exports and imports between members. The GAFTA rules involve member nations coordinating their tariff programs, maintaining common standards for specifications and restrictions on goods, promoting the private sector across all member countries, maintaining a base of communication, and decreasing customs duties. The members participate in 96% of the total internal Arab trade, and 95% with the rest of the world.[19] The agreement has been credited to the elimination of tariffs and non-tariff barriers, provisions on investment, services, and intellectual property.

- **South Asian Free Trade Area (SAFTA)**
  Born out of the efforts of the South Asian Association for Regional Cooperation (SAARC), the South Asian Free Trade Area was an agreement reached on January 6, 2004 for the creation of a free trade area involving India, Pakistan, Nepal, Sri Lanka, Bangladesh, Bhutan, Maldives, and Afghanistan. Its influence is the largest of any regional organization in terms of population, with almost 1.5 billion people. The SAARC members have frequently expressed their unwillingness to sign free trade agreements. Though India has several trade pacts with Maldives, Nepal, Bhutan, and Sri Lanka, similar trade agreements with Pakistan and Bangladesh have been stalled due to political and economic concerns on both sides. However, even with this slow progress, the foreign ministers of the member countries signed a framework agreement to initially bring their duties down to 20% and eventually down to zero.

- **Trans-Pacific Strategic Economic Partnership (TPP)**
  TP-SEP is a free trade agreement between Brunei, Chile, New Zealand, and Singapore and was signed on June 3, 2005. The TP-SEP was previously known as the Pacific Three Closer Economic Partnership (P3-CEP). Despite cultural and geographical differences, the four member countries share the similarities of being relatively small in size. Furthermore, all are members of the Asia-Pacific Economic Cooperation (APEC). TP-SEP attempted to reduce all trade tariffs by 90% by January 2006 and to completely eliminate them by 2015. Because of an accession clause within the agreement, it has the potential to include other nations as well. Countries belonging to the 21 member APEC have shown some interest in this agreement. The TPP was expected to promote economic growth and development among the participating countries, as well as to increase trade and investment flows. President Trump instructed US officials to withdraw forever from the Trans-Pacific Partnership in 2017.[20] But other countries such as Japan want to bring the trade pact back and revive the agreement.

- **Pacific Regional Trade Agreement (PARTA)**
The Pacific Regional Trade Agreement (PARTA) was established in 2001 and is aimed at increasing trade between the island nations of the Pacific. Prominent members include Australia and New Zealand, but other member island nations are much smaller and quite poor.[21] Australia's population is nearly twice that of the other 15 members combined, and its economy is five times larger. Due to their position, the poorer countries are awarded concessional tariff deals to ease their exports. PARTA has been effective in promoting trade and economic integration among its member countries.

- **Caribbean Community (CARICOM)**
The Caribbean Community was originally called the Caribbean Community and Common Market and was established in 1973. Membership has grown to a total of 20 countries (15 members and five associate members), the majority of which have joined the CARICOM Single Market and Economy (CSME) and the CARICOM Common Passport. Moreover, CARICOM is representing all its members as one single entity for bilateral agreements with the EU, members of NAFTA, and members of UNASUL.[22] Twelve of the CARICOM countries have signed an oil alliance with Venezuela (Petrocaribe) which permits them to purchase oil on conditions of preferential payment.[23] Under the agreement, the member countries have committed to reducing trade barriers, to promoting the free trade, services, and people within the region.

- **Central American Common Market (CACM)**
The Central American Common Market (CACM) is an economic trade organization that was established in 1960 between the nations of Guatemala, El Salvador, Honduras, and Nicaragua. Costa Rica joined the CACM in 1963. The organization collapsed in 1969 due to a war between Honduras and El Salvador but was reinstated in 1991. Because of its inability to settle trade disputes, the CACM has not been able to achieve all of its original goals. However, despite its shortcomings, the CACM has succeeded in removing duties on most products traded between its members, unifying external tariffs, and increasing trade between member nations.

*Results do not reflect any one country's specific trade.

Notes

1 Auto Media. The Semiconductor Shortage's Wide-Reaching Impact. March 2022.
2 *CBC News*, Mexico joins Canada, notifies U.S. it's ready to implement new NAFTA. April 6, 2020.
3 World Trade Organization, 2012.
4 How Trump killed Obama's vaunted trade deal and why it could affect the United States for decades. *Business Insider*, February 8, 2017.
5 World Trade Organization, Balance of Payments: Technical Information.
6 The World Bank Economic Policy and External Debt data, 2012.
7 World Trade Organization, *International Trade Statistics*, 2011.
8 Recall the original assumption that foreigners prefer to hold the dollars.
9 Even though the so-called trade deficit is not harmful, there are occasional negative reactions from the financial markets. This happens because investors fear that rising trade deficits/capital surpluses may eventually trigger trade barriers that will harm the economy. Also, under certain circumstances, a rising trade deficit/capital surplus can be an early indicator of currency depreciation, which can also spook investors.
10 *Reuters*. WTO awards U.S. right to hit 7.5 billion of EU goods over Airbus subsidies, October 2, 2019.

11 Panel Report, para. 2.5(e). The United States challenged specific transactions arising from the German Government's restructuring of Deutsche Airbus in the late 1980s, including the 1989 acquisition by the German Government, through the development bank Kreditanstalt für Wiederaufbau ("KfW"), of a 20% equity interest in Deutsche Airbus (ibid., paras. 2.5(e) and 7.1250), the 1992 sale by KfW of that interest to Messerschmitt-Bölkow-Blohm GmbH ("MBB"), the parent company of Deutsche Airbus (ibid., paras. 2.5(e) and 7.1253), and the forgiveness by the German Government, in 1998, of debt owed by Deutsche Airbus in the amount of DM 7.7 billion (ibid., paras. 2.5(d) and 7.1308).
12 WTO Report of the Appellate Body Measures Affecting Trade in Large Civil Aircraft, May 18, 2011.
13 Although most economists would prefer to avoid added regulations, if employment politics are an obstacle to establishing cabotage, then government regulation could stipulate a certain level of "native employment."
14 As of April 6, 2023, within the 52-week range of 0.7158–0.8064.
15 Congressional; Research Services, February 22, 2017.
16 As of today, the EU has 27 members, including Austria, Belgium, Bulgaria, Cyprus, Czech Republic, Denmark, Estonia, Finland, France, Germany, Greece, Hungary, Ireland, Italy, Latvia, Lithuania, Luxembourg, Malta, Netherlands, Poland, Portugal, Romania, Slovakia, Slovenia, Spain, Sweden, and the United Kingdom.
17 The member countries of UNASUL are Argentina, Bolivia, Brazil, Chile, Colombia, Ecuador, Guyana, Paraguay, Peru, Suriname, Uruguay, and Venezuela.
18 The member countries of AFTA are Brunei Darussalam, Cambodia, Indonesia, Laos, Malaysia, Myanmar, the Philippines, Singapore, Thailand, and Vietnam.
19 The member countries of GAFTA include Algeria, Bahrain, Egypt, Iraq, Jordan, Kuwait, Lebanon, Libya, Mauritania, Morocco, Oman, Palestine, Qatar, Saudi Arabia, Sudan, Syria, Tunisia, the United Arab Emirates, and Yemen.
20 *Financial Times*, March 3, 2017.
21 PARTA's member countries are Cook Islands, Kiribati, Niue, Samoa, Solomon Islands, Tonga, and Tuvalu.
22 Caribbean Community (CARICOM) Secretariat, 2012.
23 The member countries included are Antigua and Barbuda, Bahamas, Barbados, Belize, Dominica, Grenada, Guyana, Haiti, Jamaica, Montserrat, Saint Kitts and Nevis, Saint Lucia, Saint Vincent and the Grenadines, Suriname, and Trinidad and Tobago.

References

Carbaugh, R. (2007). *International Economics* (11th ed.). Mason, OH: South-Western.

Das, M. (2008). Absolute and Comparative Advantage, in Darity, W. (Ed.), *International Encyclopedia of the Social Sciences*. Detroit: Macmillan Reference USA, pp. 1–2.

European Commission–Directorate General, Energy and Transport. (2004). *International Aviation Agreements: Opening the Market for Efficient Air Travel.* Luxembourg: Office for Official Publications of the European Communities.

Hufbauer, C. and Elliott, A. (1994). *Measuring the Costs of Protection in the United States*. Washington, DC: Peter G. Peterson Institute for International Economics.

Pugel, T. (2007). *International Economics* (13th ed.). New York: McGraw Hill.

US Air Force–Air Mobility Command. (2006). *US Air Force Fact Sheet: Civil Reserve Air Fleet.* Retrieved June 13, 2007, from US Air Force, Air Mobility Command Library. http://www.amc.af.mil/library/factsheets/factsheet.asp?id=234.

US Department of Commerce–Bureau of Economic Analysis. (2007). *US International Transactions.* Retrieved June 13, 2007, from Bureau of Economic Analysis: International Economic Accounts.

Velk, T., Gong, O., and Zuckerbrot, A.S. (2015). A Trans-Pacific Partnership. *The Antitrust Bulletin*, 60(1), 4–13.

12 Air Traffic Liberalization and Global Alliances

Air traffic liberalization refers to the process of removing government restrictions on airlines, allowing them to operate freely between countries. This includes Open Skies agreements, global alliances which remove restrictions on the number of flights, routes, and pricing. Nevertheless, liberalization can also amplify apprehensions concerning monopolies, safety standards, and environmental impact, which necessitate meticulous evaluation by regulators and other stakeholders. Right from its inception, politicians, often appealing to "national pride," have prohibited or significantly limited access of foreign carriers to their markets. Thus, an industry that would inherently have been exceptionally international and global was instead rendered remarkably parochial and malfunctioning. With competition being stifled, the artificially high prices for air travel prevented the streamlined movement that was originally envisioned. Over the past four decades, the air transport industry has freed itself from some boundaries, with significant benefits to society. However, the liberalization of air transport has also raised many questions with regard to labor rights and the preservation of equitable competition. Progress toward making international markets more efficient was slow until the emergence of alliances in the early 1990s, when carriers finally began to find ways around political obstacles. Preceding this, regulations prevented a traveler from flying a single, efficient airline to anywhere in the world, but alliances brought this concept closer to reality. In industries, when economies of scale, scope, and density are present, mergers can create a larger, more efficient business with enhanced services and, in some circumstances, lower prices. In international air travel, this is often prohibited by government, but alliances can effectively accomplish similar outcomes. Naturally, concerns arise that alliances, like mergers, could also reduce competition, though true Open Skies with a wide-open global market mitigates this possibility.

This chapter explores these two major themes in international aviation: the goal of Open Skies and the current state of global alliances. It includes the following specific topics:

- Chronology of International Air Transport Agreements
- Bilateral and Multilateral Air Service Agreements
    - Freedoms of Air Transportation
    - Bermuda Agreement
    - Open Skies Agreement
        - Characteristics of Open Skies
        - Benefits of Open Skies

DOI: 10.4324/9781003388135-12

- Open Skies in Europe
- Open Skies in Asia and the Pacific
- Global Airline Strategic Alliances
  - History of Global Airline Alliances
  - Global Alliances and Competitiveness
  - Benefits of Global Alliances
  - Disadvantages of Global Alliances
  - Future for Global Alliances
- Summary
- Discussion Questions

Chronology of International Air Transport Agreements

The impediment of government over-regulation has prohibited the fulfillment of the vision expressed in air traffic liberalization, despite notable advancements. It is interesting to note the stark historical contrast between shipping and aviation. Freedom for one country's ships to travel to another country through its waterways has generally been the norm between friendly countries. Tragically, this has not at all been the case for air travel.

In 1919, the first international agreement concerning air transportation occurred shortly after the First World War in Paris. With the tremendous leap in aviation witnessed during the First World War, delegates from 26 countries drew up the Convention relating to the Regulation of Air Navigation (US Centennial of Flight Commission (USCOF), 2006). The Convention voted to give each nation, "complete and exclusive sovereignty over the airspace above its territory" (USCOF, 2006). This marked the first instance where countries were provided with an internationally recognized legal authority over their airspace, which enabled them to allow or disallow airplane access into their country. In the end, neither Russia nor the United States signed the Paris Convention of 1919 (USCOF, 2006).

A decade later, in 1928, the United States signed its first international aviation agreement at the Havana Convention on Civil Aviation. This agreement guaranteed the fundamental right of passage as well as the formulation of rules concerning such issues as aircraft navigation, landing facilities, and pilot standards. The Havana Convention also provided the right for each country to set the route to be flown over its territory. Drawing inspiration from the Paris Convention, it applied exclusively to private aircraft and laid down basic principles and rules for aerial traffic. This pivotal agreement recognized that every state had complete and exclusive sovereignty over the airspace above its territory and adjacent territorial waters.[1]

The Convention for the Unification of Certain Rules Relating to International Carriage by Air was convened on October 12, 1929, in Warsaw, Poland. This pivotal agreement was further amended in 1955 at the Hague Convention and in 1975 at the Montreal Conventions. The major objectives of the Warsaw Convention were as follows:

- To define the liability of the carrier in case of loss, damage, injury, or death due to accident on international flights.
- To lay down the requirements for format and content of air transport documents, passenger tickets, luggage tickets, and air consignment notes.
- To spell out procedures for claims and restitution.

One of the major results of the Warsaw Convention was a formal definition of "international carriage." Article 1 of the agreement states:

> International carriage means any carriage in which, according to the contract made by the parties, the place of departure and the place of destination whether or not there be a break in the carriage or a transshipment, are situated either within the territories of two High Contracting Parties, or within the territory of a single High Contracting Party, if there is an agreed stopping place within a territory subject to the sovereignty, suzerainty, mandate or authority of another Power, even though that Power is not a party to this Convention. A carriage without such an agreed stopping place between territories subject to the sovereignty, suzerainty, mandate or authority of the same High Contracting Party is not deemed to be international for the purposes of this Convention.
>
> (Warsaw Convention (WC), 2006)

The Convention additionally laid down a general set of guidelines for the operation of the commercial air transportation industry for international flights. For example, Article 3 describes the requirements for a passenger ticket, while Article 4 outlines what needs to be incorporated within a luggage tag (WC, 2006). One of the more practical outcomes of the Warsaw Convention concerned air carrier liability. Article 17 states that the air carrier is liable for:

> …damage sustained in case of death or bodily injury of a passenger upon condition only that the accident which caused the death or injury took place on board the aircraft or in the course of any of the operations of embarking or disembarking.
>
> (WC, 2006)

This article states that an air carrier bears responsibility for any death or bodily injury suffered by a passenger on an air carrier's flight. However, Articles 20 and 21 provide escape clauses for the airlines if it is determined that they took all measures necessary to avoid the loss or there was some contributory negligence on the part of the individual involved (WC, 2006). Such issues are less pressing in contemporary times due to the safety of aviation, but it was important at the time of this convention.

Eventually, the Warsaw Convention was completely overhauled by the Montreal Convention of 1999, now serving as the current convention that governs international carriage liability. According to Article 21 of the Montreal Convention, an air carrier has unlimited liability; that is, there is no maximum cap on the payment, and that in the event of death, the minimum the airline must compensate is 100,000 Special Drawings Rights (SDRs) (Montreal Convention, 2006),[2] equivalent to almost $150,000.

The next major international agreement concerning air transportation was the Chicago Convention of 1944. This landmark event took place near the end of the Second World War and was hosted by US President Franklin D. Roosevelt. Roosevelt's goal for this convention was revolutionary—to craft an agreement that would allow any airliner from any country to fly to any other country with little or no restriction. His pursuit was directed toward a true Open Skies agreement, wherein the restrictions on international flying would be notably sparse, if exist at all. Unfortunately, only a handful of the 54 attending delegates actually backed him on his goal for Open Skies (Phillips, 2006). Instead, Article 6 of the Chicago Convention created a system of bilateral air service agreements between countries for all scheduled international flights. The article states:

> No scheduled international air service may be operated over or into the territory of a contracting State, except with the special permission or other authorization of that State, and in accordance with the terms of such permission or authorization.
>
> (Chicago Convention (CC), 2006)

A major outcome of the Chicago Convention was the creation of the International Civil Aviation Organization (ICAO), with the purpose of formulating the principles and techniques of international air navigation, while also fostering the planning and development of international air transport (CC, 2006). The Chicago Convention superseded the Paris Convention and remains the primary basis for all international aviation law.

Bilateral and Multilateral Air Service Agreements

The operation of international scheduled airlines depends on the approval of the states to or through the territory of which they fly. Bilateral and multilateral air services agreements allow designated airlines of participating countries to operate commercial flights, and legally cover the transport of passengers and cargo between their countries. After the Chicago Convention, bilateral air service agreements became the predominant method of regulating international air travel. These agreements governed aspects such as market access, market entry, and, in many cases market pricing. While granting market access, countries allow various levels of flexibility. Bilateral air service agreements can encompass up to nine degrees of freedoms that may be granted (Figure 12.1).

Freedoms of the Air Transportation

> The freedoms of the air are a set of regulations and rights granting a country's airlines the privilege to enter and land in another country's airspace.
>
> The first freedom provides the right for an airline to fly over another country without landing. While the second freedom is the right to make a landing for technical reasons in another country without picking up or setting down revenue passengers.
>
> The third freedom grants the right to carry revenue traffic from your own country to another country, while the fourth freedom provides the right to carry revenue traffic from the other country back to your own country.

The *first freedom* entails the privilege for an airline to conduct flights over another country without landing (ICAO, 2004). An illustrative scenario involves an international nonstop flight from Los Angeles to London that overflies Canada on the way to England. In order for this to occur, Canada must grant the United States first freedom rights. Presently with a few exceptions, virtually all countries grant unilateral first freedom rights. Moreover, countries may impose charges upon airlines for the permission to fly over their country, essentially placing economic barriers around the first freedom. For example, the overflight fee for the United States is $61.75

Freedoms of Air Transportation

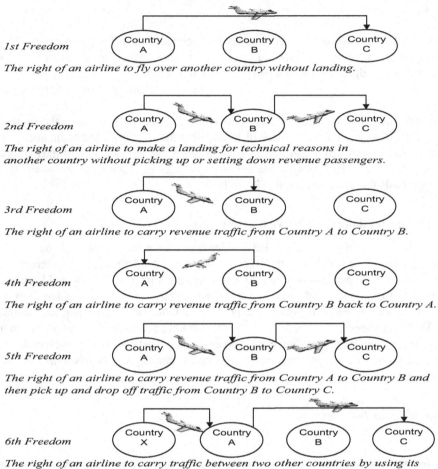

1st Freedom

Country A Country B Country C

The right of an airline to fly over another country without landing.

2nd Freedom

Country A Country B Country C

The right of an airline to make a landing for technical reasons in another country without picking up or setting down revenue passengers.

3rd Freedom

Country A Country B Country C

The right of an airline to carry revenue traffic from Country A to Country B.

4th Freedom

Country A Country B Country C

The right of an airline to carry revenue traffic from Country B back to Country A.

5th Freedom

Country A Country B Country C

The right of an airline to carry revenue traffic from Country A to Country B and then pick up and drop off traffic from Country B to Country C.

6th Freedom

Country X Country A Country B Country C

The right of an airline to carry traffic between two other countries by using its home base as a transit point.

7th Freedom

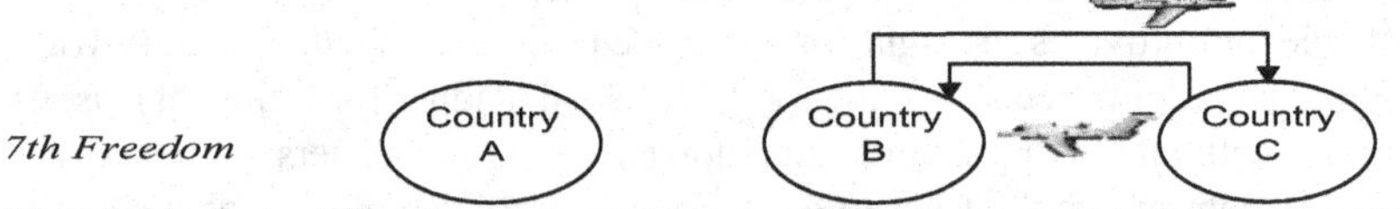

The right of an airline to carry revenue traffic between points in two countries on services which lie entirely outside its own home country.

8th Freedom

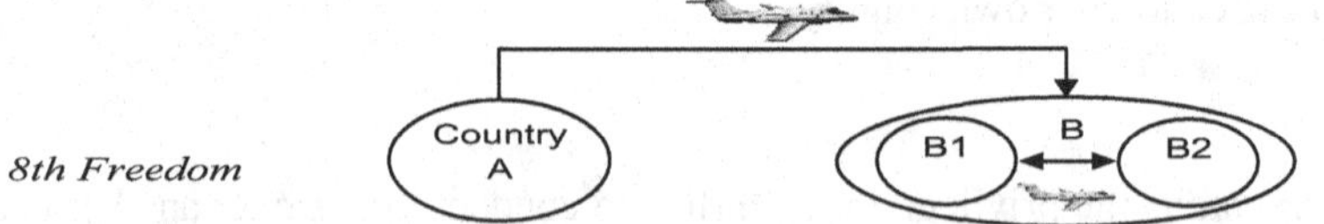

The right of a foreign airline to transport passengers, freight, and mail within Country B on flights originating in the (home) Country A (aka Cabotage).

Figure 12.1 Freedom of Air Passage.

per 100 nautical miles over the continental United States or $26.51 over Oceanic per 100 nautical miles (FAA, 2017). On the other hand, China requires an overflight permit costing roughly $500, along with a separate charge for overflight navigational services amounting to $0.44 per kilometer. This provides an economic hindrance for airlines flying such routes.

The *second freedom* of the air encompasses the right to make a landing in another country for technical reasons (i.e., refueling) without picking up or setting down revenue passengers (ICAO, 2004). An example of a flight requiring the second freedom would be Cathay Pacific's flight from Hong Kong to Toronto, Canada with a refueling layover in Anchorage, Alaska. In order for this flight to proceed, the United States would have to grant second freedom rights to Hong Kong. Generally, the second freedom right is granted because the airline provides revenue to host country through landing fees and fuel purchase and does not compete with the domestic airlines. While the second freedom has been important for many airlines, with recent improvements to modern aircraft, fewer flights are requiring refueling stops. Cargo carriers, on the other hand, continue to fully leverage this prerogative.

The *third and fourth freedoms* of the air essentially constitute two sides of the same coin. The third freedom grants the right to carry revenue traffic from one's nation to another, while the fourth freedom provides the right to carry revenue generating traffic back to one's homeland (ICAO, 2004). These rights are usually granted together in order to allow an airline to operate a return air service. However, the allocation of third and fourth freedoms may only be granted to certain city pairs in air service agreements, imposing limitations on air travel. Consequently, any international flight that carries passengers between two countries requires the granting of third and fourth freedoms for that particular flight.

The *fifth freedom* enables an airline to carry revenue traffic from its own country to a foreign nation, and then, pick up and drop off traffic originating from the intermediate country to a third country. For these rights to be useable, the third country must also agree to the right. A prime example of fifth freedom rights is observed in Cathay Pacific's flight from Hong Kong to Vancouver, continuing onward to New York. On this flight, Cathay Pacific is allowed to carry traffic from Hong Kong to Vancouver and also from Vancouver to New York. In order for Cathay Pacific to operate this flight, both Canada and the United States must grant Hong Kong fifth freedom rights for the route. Such rights are rarely granted, since the foreign airline would essentially be competing with domestic airlines for the same traffic. Nonetheless, other examples include Emirates' transatlantic flight from New York to Milan, as well as EVA Airways' operation of a Taipei–Bangkok–London flight, with full traffic rights from Bangkok to London. Airlines place high value on fifth freedom rights, as they are highly desirable to airlines, as segments can be tagged on to an existing flight, thereby increasing profitability.

The *sixth freedom* of the air allows an airline to carry traffic between two other countries via its home base, as a transit point. A prime illustration of this concept involves an airline that flies a passenger from Europe to North America and then transfers that passenger onto a flight to Mexico or Central America. Sixth freedoms are not usually granted explicitly, but are implied when third and fourth freedoms are granted. A slightly modified form of the sixth freedom, often referred to as "modified sixths", would allow an airline to transfer a passenger through its hub from two points within the same foreign country (Field, 2005). One of the primary reasons that low-cost carriers have not joined global alliances is that they are not flying to major international hubs. Ryanair and easyJet fly out of London Gatwick, Luton, and Stansted, all of which are situated quite far from central London, requiring time-consuming transport to the major hubs. In Brussels, the low-cost carriers (Ryanair) fly to Charleroi Airport (CRL) Airport is 55 km to Brussels Airport (BRU).

An example would be a Canadian airline flight from Boston to Seattle on which a passenger uses Toronto, Canada as a transfer point. Currently "modified sixths" are not allowed, but there is movement in North America to possibly allow this to happen (Field, 2005).

The *seventh freedom* enables an airline to carry revenue traffic between points in two countries on services which lie entirely outside its own home country. The relaxation of regulations governing European airspace has granted seventh freedom rights, enabling airlines to fly throughout Europe. For instance, Ireland-based Ryanair can operate flights from Germany to Portugal. The tremendous access provided by seventh freedom rights has led to increased competition, resulting in reduced airfares and an increased quantity of air travel demand. Nonetheless, Europe stands as one of the few exceptions, as other countries rarely grant seventh freedom rights.

The *eighth freedom,* also referred to as cabotage, allows a foreign airline to fly between two domestic points in a country, but having initiated the flight in the home country.

The ninth freedom allows a foreign airline to fly between two domestic points in a country, without having originated the flight in the home country.

The *eighth freedom* (consecutive cabotage) is probably the most controversial freedom. Also referred to as cabotage, the eighth freedom allows a foreign airline to fly between two domestic points in a country but having initiated the flight in the home country. For instance, the acquisition of cabotage rights would be necessary if Qantas wanted to continue its Los Angeles flight onto New York with local traffic between Los Angeles and New York. The topic of cabotage stirs controversy because it allows foreign competition within domestic routes. Few countries have granted cabotage rights, but they are actively sought during negotiation process. Achieving a true Open Skies agreement between two countries would require cabotage rights from both countries. Once again, Europe's liberalization of air transportation has granted cabotage, since the entire European community is considered one domestic air transport market.

The concept of the *ninth freedom* ("stand-alone" cabotage) is an extension of the eight freedom. Also referred to as "stand-alone" cabotage, the ninth freedom enables a foreign airline to fly between two domestic points in a country without having originated the flight in the home country.

Bermuda Agreement

Soon after the Chicago Convention, the first bilateral air service agreement was signed between the United States and the United Kingdom on February 11, 1946, in Bermuda (DOT, 1978). While this agreement holds the distinction of being the first bilateral air service agreement to be signed, it is also one of the longest standings and most important treaties in aviation (Cooper, 1946). This agreement, which was overhauled in 1977, has undergone multiple updates, resulting in the creation of the Bermuda II Agreement. This was the standing body of airline regulation between the United Kingdom and the United States until the EU–US Open Skies agreement was finalized in 2000. Nevertheless, the Bermuda II Agreement is a good example of bilateral air transport treaties between countries; therefore, it is instructive to take a closer look at some of its important provisions.

One major theme of most bilateral agreements is regulatory approval on airfares. It is imperative that both countries must approve the pricing of tickets for all carriers operating between the two countries. This process of "double approval" of tariffs is usually related to a cost-plus profit formula, ensuring a profitable operation while keeping airfares artificially high. There are other possibilities for tariff regulation, including dual disapproval, zone pricing, or free pricing, which is also known as no pricing regulation.

The tariff approval system in the Bermuda II Agreement was based on Article 11, which states that, "the designated airlines of one Contracting Party shall have a fair and equal opportunity to compete with the designated airlines of the other Contracting Party"[3] (DOT, 1978). This stipulation governed all actions undertaken by the airlines, including tariffs, and therefore acted to create some level of price fixing. The article contains specific stipulations against capacity dumping, which could severely impact the profits of other operators. In the contemporary landscape, with greater liberalization of competition laws, the tariff approval mechanism largely rubber stamps airlines' requests for changes in fares.

The Bermuda II Agreement also dealt with other issues concerning security, airworthiness, dispute resolution, and customs. However, when scrutinized both from an economic standpoint and from an airline standpoint, the greatest impact of the Bermuda II Agreement was the granting of air freedoms and route authorizations. The rights granted by the Bermuda II Agreement were considered quite liberal at the time; however, today they are considered very bureaucratic. The treaty placed numerous restrictions on air transportation, which are discussed in the consecutive section.

Article 2 of the Bermuda II Agreement granted the United Kingdom and United States the following rights regarding the use of one another's airspace:

a The right to fly across its territory without landing; and
b The right to make stops in its territory for non-traffic purposes (DOT, 1978).

Part (a) provided the first freedom to airlines from both countries, while part (b) granted second freedom rights to all airlines. Furthermore, Article 2 goes on to grant fourth and fifth freedom rights, as long as they were a part of the agreed upon routes (DOT, 1978). One of the major restrictions instituted within the framework of Bermuda II Agreement was that only two airlines from each country were allowed to operate scheduled passenger services from London Heathrow to the United States (Competition Commission, 1999). Under this agreement, only British Airways, Virgin Atlantic, American Airlines, and United Airlines were permitted to fly from Heathrow to the United States. This arrangement effectively created a government-enforced cartel that severely limited competition, especially considering the fact that Heathrow is London's most desirable airport for passengers. Notably, American and United received these rights from Trans-World and Pan Am, respectively, and in doing so, also received considerable windfall profits. Given that Heathrow was the only airport that had such restrictions, all other carriers operating between the United States and London were forced to do so from secondary UK airports, such as London Gatwick. With the advent of Open Skies agreement, any airline can now legally operate from Heathrow to the United States; granted of course that there are slots available.

Within the framework of Bermuda II Agreement, there were only certain cities that could be served by the US and UK airlines. For example, US airlines could only access Gatwick and Heathrow from a select number of US cities. Likewise, UK airlines had a list of US cities that they were permitted to serve from London. Although some of these cities on these lists were switchable, the archaic system impacted not only airlines, but communities as well. Like many other bilateral air service agreements, Bermuda II placed tremendous restrictions on international travel.

The general essence of bilateral air service has revolved around safeguarding national interests and providing support for national airlines. While such protection helps carriers who receive the benefits, it is frustrating for airlines looking from the outside yearning for a place within. Inherently, bilateral agreements curtail a market solution for international air travel and replace it with government regulation. Generally speaking, the artificial restrictions that are imposed actually raise costs, create inefficiencies in the market, and allow rent-seeking behavior on the part of the favored airlines. Opening up of international skies would be similar to the deregulation movement that occurred domestically in the United States in 1978. Open skies would not only benefit consumers and the economy, but it would also reduce costs and increase the airlines' profits.

Open Skies Agreements

Open Skies are multilateral agreements between states to liberalize the airline industry and minimize governmental regulations.

Open Skies Agreements promote competition and provide choices on international commercial air routes. These agreements are bilateral or multilateral in nature.

Open Skies Agreements stand as bilateral or multilateral agreements between states to liberalize the airline industry and minimize governmental regulations. These agreements promote competition, improve flexibility for airline operations, and stimulate travel and tourism. The United States and the Netherlands signed the first Open Skies agreement in 1993. Under the agreement, the Department of Transportation granted antitrust immunity to Northwest Airlines and KLM.[4] This agreement, thereby, gave both countries unrestricted access to each other's airports and bestowed carriers with the freedom to set international fares, without governmental intervention.

This agreement was followed by similar Open Skies agreements between the United States and Canada in 1995 (Field, 2005). The core objective of the Open Skies agreements is to increase travel, trade, productivity, and economic growth by removing government interference in air carrier decisions about routes, pricing, and capacity (DOS, 2021).

In March 2007, the United States finalized Open Skies with the EU.[5] The subsequent phase of this accord, Phase 2, was signed in June 2010 and further eliminates the restrictions on air service between the United States and EU nations. Airlines hailing from both sides can now fly any route without limitations on the number of carriers that can fly or the number of flights that can operate.

As of 2022, the United States has signed 130 open skies agreements with nations around the world. Over 70% of international departures originating from the United States now fly to Open Skies partners. Recent partnerships include Azerbaijan, Cote d'Ivoire, Seychelles, Curaçao, Serbia, Togo, and Ukraine. The general trend in international aviation is to do away with complicated and restriction-laden bilateral agreements and move toward Open Skies.

Characteristics of Open Skies

US Open Skies agreements generally contain eight key provisions.

The first, and probably the most important provision, is the removal of restrictions on international routes rights (DOS, 2016). This means that carriers from either country are free to fly between any two cities they wish, with whatever size aircraft they wish and as frequently as desired through the week. This freedom lowers barriers to entry for airlines, but it does not entirely eliminate them, as carriers may still require landing slots at foreign airports in order to initiate a new flight. Nonetheless, open competition will allow airlines to bid for these rights, which will ultimately be assigned to the highest-valued economic bidder.

The second major provision is that airline pricing should be determined by market forces (DOS, 2016). While true Open Skies would exclude governmental involvement in airline pricing, the US model does include a "double-disapproval" stipulation, whereby a fare can be rejected if both countries agree (DOS, 2016). In practice, carriers are allowed to set whatever fares they want. However, double-disapproval could possibly prevent some low-cost carriers (LCCs) from entering certain international markets and offering extremely discounted fares, if rejecting such fares happened to be politically attractive to the two governments involved.

The third major provision contained in US Open Skies agreements is a clause ensuring fair and equal opportunity to compete (DOS, 2016). This clause covers a wide variety of issues, including non-discriminatory airport slot allocations and user fees. Furthermore, it addresses concerns pertaining to the availability of ground handling and the establishment of sales offices. In essence, countries should allow airlines of both countries equal opportunity to compete fairly.

The fourth major provision enables airlines to enter cooperative marketing agreements (DOS, 2016). As we will point out later in the chapter, alliances play a critical role to the success of airlines. Prior to Open Skies agreements, restrictions could be placed on the air carriers' ability to enter alliance agreements with airlines of both countries. For instance, while both British Airways and American Airlines are founding members of the Oneworld Alliance, they were not permitted to code share on each other's flights under the previous Bermuda II Agreement. In the realm of Open Skies, airlines are permitted to enter whatever code share agreements they wish. Casting one's mind back, recall the Open Skies agreement between the United States and the Netherlands; Northwest Airlines and KLM were able to form a strong alliance that included revenue sharing between the carriers. In order for this cohesive agreement to occur, Open Skies had to be in place. Moreover, the extensive code share arrangement was given antitrust immunity from the US Department of Justice. While US Open Skies agreements allow full code sharing, they do not address issues pertaining to foreign ownership of airlines.

Other provisions encompassed within Open Skies agreements are mechanisms for dispute settlement, consultation pertaining to unfair practices, liberal legal charter agreements (the choice to operate under either country's charter arrangement), and agreements pertaining to the safe and secure operation of flights between the two countries (DOS, 2016). In Open Skies treaties, the United States also seeks the provision that there be seventh freedom rights for all-cargo flights (DOS, 2016). This permits carriers to transport cargo between the partner country and a third country, via flights that are not linked to its homeland. Under this stipulation, companies like FedEx and UPS can operate cargo hubs in foreign countries. Currently, only about half of the Open Skies agreements signed by the United States contain this optional provision (DOS, 2021). Likewise, fifth freedom rights are rarely provided. The most notable exception is the new United States–Canada Open Skies agreement, whereby Canadian carriers receive unilateral fifth freedom rights from the United States in exchange for seventh freedom all-cargo rights for US carriers.

Benefits of Open Skies

The benefits stemming from Open Skies agreements are similar to the benefits obtained from liberalization and deregulation; airlines are able to fly more routes, a development which ultimately increases competition and lowers average airfares. Open Skies also opens up new city pairs (domestic to foreign) that were previously unavailable. In general, passengers benefit significantly, as they receive more frequent service and lower prices from stiffer competition. However, it is noteworthy that Open Skies can also cause greater fluctuations in airline profits. Indeed, carriers benefit from these agreements, but the benefits vary depending on the airline's position in the market. For example, the airline that already has extensive rights to the foreign country is currently receiving some windfall profits from the protection it is receiving in the market. However, with Open Skies, that airline would no longer receive the protection and would face more competition. Conversely, carriers that are currently excluded from a market (or have limited service) gain more from Open Skies agreements compared to carriers with extensive existing route rights. This is the major reason why airlines such as Continental and Delta lobbied hard for an Open Skies agreement between the United States and the United Kingdom, while American Airlines, with its extensive London access rights, remained relatively quiet.

As mentioned above, the United States signed one of the first Open Skies agreements with Canada. In a study conducted by the Department of Transportation (DOT), three years after the signing, it was found that trans-border traffic averaged an 11.1% yearly growth rate compared to 1.4% per year for the three years prior to the agreement (DOT, 1998). Moreover, the number of nonstop markets with over 50,000 annual passengers increased from 54 in 1994 to 77 in 1997 (DOT, 1998). As a consequence of this agreement, it is estimated that 38 new city pairs were opened up between Canada and the United States (DOT, 1998). While this tremendous growth rate will naturally plateau, the figures clearly show the large latent demand, from both business and tourism, which was being suppressed before the Open Skies treaty. Moreover, the original agreement was amended in 2005, to provide both countries with increased freedoms. Even still, former Air Canada President Robert Milton stands among those who want to see a European-like market in North America, in which a Canadian carrier has US cabotage rights, and vice versa (Field, 2005). Unfortunately, the likelihood of such rights being granted is slim.

Open Skies in Europe

> The outspoken boss of Ireland's Ryanair, Michael O'Leary, says that losing access to the single aviation market will raise airfares and slash profits as airlines back out of the UK market. Ryanair's O'Leary warns that it is "highly unlikely" that the UK will be allowed to remain in the so-called Open Skies agreement.

Europe has had a successful experience of Open Skies, materializing through the establishment of a unified EU aviation market since 1997 (Kinnock, 1996). The agreement took over a decade to negotiate, but under a single market, EU carriers have unlimited traffic rights on any intra-EU route, without restrictions on investment by EU nationals in EU carriers. For instance, British Airways could fly from Paris to Frankfurt or from Amsterdam to Rome. This granting of seventh freedom rights also included the granting of eighth freedom rights, or cabotage, which further enabled British carriers to offer Frankfurt-Munich flights or Barcelona-Madrid flights. In fact, British Airways even created a German subsidiary to fly domestic routes within Germany. The notion of national ownership has become irrelevant for intra-European flights, and this is the primary reason why LCCs such as easyJet and Ryanair have been able to expand so rapidly. As a matter of fact, the number of destinations served by UK airports has doubled since 2000. However, with the UK vote to leave the EU (Brexit), the future of Open Skies agreements negotiated by the EU on behalf of its members is uncertain.[6] The United Kingdom decided not to join the likes of Norway, Iceland, and other members in the European Common Aviation Area (ECAA), which would have allowed continued access to the European single market and the permission to fly under the US-EU Open Skies agreement (Walker, 2016). Instead, a new trade agreement with the EU came into force at the end of 2020, which preserved most of the previous rights. Third and fourth freedoms remain, but UK airlines have no cabotage rights within the EU. Ownership rules were fudged so that UK airlines can be EU-owned if that was the case before the end of 2020, but not for new UK airlines after that threshold. A new agreement was also agreed with the United States at the end of 2020, with similar ownership agreements. The effects of the Brexit vote are yet to be fully experienced, but IATA estimates that the number of UK air passengers may drop 3%–5% by 2020.

Despite future uncertainty, intra-European travel remains liberalized, although global travel from Europe is still largely dominated by each country's respective flag carriers (de Palacio, 2001). For instance, German Airlines cannot fly from London to the United States just as British Airlines cannot fly from Paris to Japan. This is a result of the current bilateral treaties between individual European countries and other nations around the world; these agreements limit international flights to airlines with full national ownership (de Palacio, 2001). The existence of these separate treaties can be problematic, considering Europe's trend toward becoming a single market. While the United States currently has separate Open Skies agreements with most European nations, these clauses that enforce nationality-based restrictions were deemed illegal in a 2002 European Court of Justice (ECJ) ruling. This has placed pressure on the EU to create multilateral aviation agreements with foreign countries (Baker, 2005). The largest such agreement involved the EU and the United States.

The second stage of the Open Skies agreement between the EU and the United States was adopted on June 24, 2010 as part of the mandate set forth in the first stage to reach a balanced agreement in 2010.[7] The ultimate objective of the agreement is a single air transport market between the EU and the United States, without restriction and with full access to the domestic markets of both parties. Mutual consensus has been reached to remove the remaining barriers, which include a legislative change in the United States regarding foreign ownership. Currently, foreign ownership in US airlines is limited to 25% of voting rights, and the EU has stated its intentions of reciprocally allowing majority ownership of EU airlines by US nationals. Canada also has a 25% restriction but granted exemptions to Ultra Low-Cost Carriers (ULCCs) and pushing the limit to 49%. Australia permits an airline to own 100% of its domestic airlines, and Qantas limits to 49%.

Open Skies in Asia and the Pacific

Southeast Asia is already the home to some of the busiest routes, such as Singapore-Jakarta, Singapore-Kuala Lumpur, and Bangkok-Hong Kong. While numerous aviation industries have adopted liberalized markets, the Asia-Pacific region has not yet collectively implemented Open Skies. This delay is primarily due to perceived national interests. ASEAN Single Aviation Market, also known as ASEAN Open Sky Agreement, is the region's major aviation policy. The agreement is geared toward the development of a unified and single aviation market among ASEAN members in Southeast Asia projected to commence on January 1, 2015, even though all agreements have not been signed. These are the same national interests that initially kept the United States and Europe from liberalizing their air space. One major deterrent in the Asia-Pacific region is the fact that the aviation industry here is still in the developmental stage compared to Europe and North America. As these markets have illustrated, the benefits of Open Skies far outweigh the benefits of protectionism. However, it might take some period of time before it is fully realized in Asia. Nonetheless, two of the most prominent carriers in the region, namely Emirates and Singapore Airlines, have taken steps in this direction. Both play a significant role in promoting their relatively small countries, and through the adoption of Open Skies agreements, they have remarkably succeeded in the creation of global aviation hubs.

Australia is another country that has implemented Open Skies, by creating a single aviation market with New Zealand and eliminating foreign ownership restrictions. This liberalization was what enabled Richard Branson to start up Virgin Australia, formerly Virgin Blue. On the other hand, Australia did deny Singapore Airlines' request to fly from Sydney to Los Angeles. This action was no doubt an effort to protect Qantas Airways from competition on this route.

India, a long-time highly regulated aviation market, has slowly become more liberalized as the economy has grown. The country's initial focus was on liberalizing its domestic market. Only recently did the Indian government permit local carriers to fly internationally, and many of these bilateral agreements began with severe capacity restrictions. However, India revealed a new Civil Aviation Policy in 2016 that will aid in the liberalization of the international market (Ch-Aviation, 2016a). The country will now be seeking Open Skies polices and has already signed such an agreement with Greece. This bilateral treaty allows Indian carriers access to any destination in Greece, and it gives Greece access to six cities in India: Delhi, Mumbai, Hyderabad, Bengaluru, Kolkata, and Chennai (Mishra, 2016). Liberalization in India has spurred tremendous growth in air travel, and the nation has created several successful LCCs. Furthermore, the new Civil Aviation Policy changed the 5/20 rule that has been in effect since 2004. The 5/20 rule required Indian carriers that wanted to start flying internationally to have been in operation for at least five years and to have a fleet of at least 20 aircraft. While originally intended to safeguard the domestic market, this regulation inadvertently hindered the growth of many carriers in India. Under the modified rule, the age requirement is eliminated, and carriers that wish to operate internationally must allot the highest number of either 20 aircraft or 20% of total capacity to domestic flights (Ch-Aviation, 2016a).

In northern Asia, both Japan and Korea are still highly regulated, with most international routes containing capacity restrictions. Liberalization of the Japanese market is even more difficult due to airport restrictions at congested facilities such as Tokyo Narita. Notably it was since 2010 that Japan has an Open Skies agreement in place with the United States, one of few in the Asia-Pacific region.

China is arguably the most attractive Asia-Pacific country for foreign carriers. For political reasons, however, China has also historically been one of the most restrictive countries in the region. One particular aviation sanction was the prohibition of direct flights between China and Taiwan. While this policy posed challenges for both Chinese and Taiwanese carriers, the regulations actually benefited Macau, which was used as a transit point between China and Taiwan. Over time, China has begun to loosen its borders for foreign business, but the liberalization of the aviation sector has progressed at a much slower pace as compared to the rest of Asia. The nation's first Open Skies agreements were still quite restrictive. For example, the treaty with Singapore forbade Singapore LCCs from flying into Shanghai and Beijing (Francis, 2005). In this respect, the agreement was not truly Open Skies.

Previously, the Chinese domestic aviation industry was exclusively government-owned and was operated by multiple small carriers. However, consolidation has resulted in three main carriers: Air China, China Southern Airlines, and China Eastern Airlines, which are based at Beijing, Guangzhou, and Shanghai respectively (Francis, 2004). This consolidation set the stage for progressive, albeit slow reform, and has enabled the Chinese airlines to obtain a stronger international presence. Additionally, China has allowed private ownership of airlines, and the current cap of 49% could possibly be raised in the future (Francis, 2004).

China also began experimenting with other liberalized air policies, such as the creation of an entirely Open Skies policy for the Hainan region (Francis, 2004). Under this policy, foreign carriers are permitted unlimited access to the Hainan region, along with full fifth freedom rights and limited cabotage rights to other Chinese cities, with the exception of Beijing, Guangzhou, and Shanghai (Francis, 2004). This policy was an effort to open up aviation markets outside China's three dominant cities, but it could be argued that it still retained some protectionist elements, as these three cities also happen to be the hubs of China's three largest airlines (Francis, 2004).

The first nonstop flight between the United States and China took place in 1996 (Ke and Windle, 2014). While there are currently no Open Skies agreements between the two countries, China has been steadily granting access to several routes to major cities. In 2016, Hainan Airlines launched the eighth North America-China route, from Changsha to Los Angeles, and service is expanding to and from Seattle, San Francisco, and even Las Vegas (TAAF, 2016). Furthermore, China signed an official Open Skies treaty with Australia in 2016, effectively eliminating all capacity restrictions for carriers of both countries (TAAAF, 2016). This groundbreaking initiative is expected to benefits airports, airlines, and local economies.

Probably the most ambitious economic liberalization project to occur in the Asia-Pacific region is the multilateral Open Skies agreement between the ASEAN (Association of Southeast Asian Nations) countries. The ten members of the ASEAN are Brunei, Singapore, Thailand, Cambodia, Indonesia, Laos, Malaysia, Myanmar, the Philippines, and Vietnam. As part of the broader ASEAN Air Transport Liberalization Plan, ASEAN member countries aim to have a single aviation market, known as the ASEAN-SAM. In 2016, Indonesia and Laos became the last two member states to sign the agreement (Ch-Aviation, 2016b). These pivotal reforms represent a giant step forward for air transport liberalization in the region, since many of the ASEAN countries have historically had very protectionist viewpoints toward air travel. The anticipated outcomes of such liberalization are expected to benefit not only individual countries, but also the economic region as a whole in both the short term and long term (Forsyth King and Rodolfo, 2006). However, certain member countries still maintain restricted access due to worries of congestion and increased competition. For example, the Philippines opened up all cities except for Manila Ninoy Aquino International. Likewise, Laos still prohibits Thai carriers from accessing Vientiane and Luang Prabang. Although, the ASEAN Open Skies agreement shows promise, the Asia-Pacific region still remains a heavily regulated industry in comparison to Europe and North America.

Global Airline Strategic Alliances

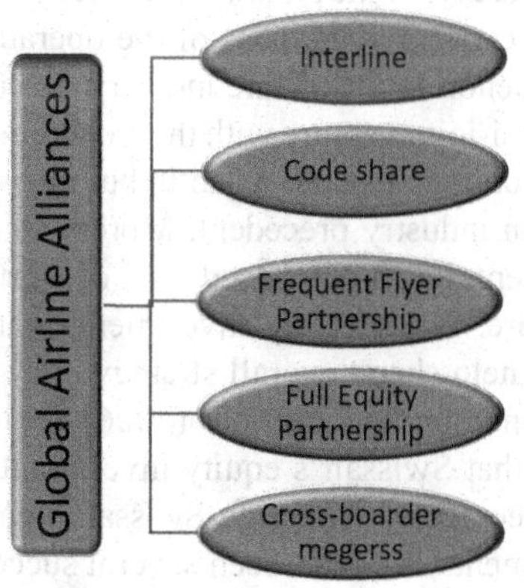

In an effort to overcome restrictive barriers to entry in international air transport markets, airlines have formed alliances with foreign carriers. An alliance signifies an agreement among two or more airlines to cooperate, coordinate, and share resources on a substantial level for mutually beneficial operations. The purpose of these alliances has generally been to introduce service in those countries and regions where there have been legal or financial restrictions. Different degrees of cooperation include: interline (using one ticket for a trip involving multiple airlines), code share, frequent flyer partnership, full equity partnership, and cross-border mergers.

While the initial global alliances started as simple interline and code share agreements between airlines, they have evolved into global alliances with multiple airlines that span the globe. The introduction of global alliances has also magnified the prominence of global and regional hubs. A codeshare agreement is a marketing arrangement in the airline industry, in which two or more airlines publish and market the same flight under their own airline designator and flight number as part of their published timetable or schedule. Most of the major airlines today have code sharing partnerships with other airlines, and code sharing is an important aspect of the major airline alliances.

History of Global Airline Alliances

In 1986, the first international airline alliance was signed between Air Florida and British Island, where Air Florida provided a passenger feed for British Island's London–Amsterdam route. This fundamental alliance between two carriers, commonly called a code share, enables an airline to place passengers onto the flight of another carrier. Code share agreements can be signed to cover a few particular routes or flights, or they can cover all of the airline's flights. While the initial concept was quite simple, code sharing has evolved to the point that carriers may even block out seats for code share partners. For instance, in 1993, Air Canada and Korean Air entered into a code share agreement whereby each airline purchased 48 seats per departure on the other airline's flight. In this example, the inventory assigned to the other airline is fixed. It may be variable in other cases, depending on demand. After this initial code share agreement was signed, other carriers followed suit: Japan Airlines and Thai Airways in 1985, American and Qantas on Qantas's transpacific flights in 1986, and Air France and Sabena with a blocked space agreement on the Paris-Brussels route in 1992.

In 1992, Dutch carrier KLM and US-based Northwest formed a major transatlantic airline alliance, establishing an extensive code share agreement. In 1993, the alliance received antitrust immunity (ATI) from the US Department of Transportation, thereby enabling the two airlines to closely coordinate their flights across the Atlantic. This led to a joint venture where revenues were divided between the two carriers, regardless of the operating airline. The notion of joint ventures are not a new phenomenon to the airline industry, as both Braniff and Singapore Airlines had already operated a quasi-joint venture with the Concorde aircraft. Remarkably, because it covered so many flights not only across the Atlantic but also in Europe and North America, the KLM/Northwest deal set an industry precedent. Moreover, there were equity investments for both airlines. In the agreement, KLM purchased 25% of Northwest's voting rights and 49% of Northwest's total equity share. While equity investments bring carriers closer together and enable the investing airline to help shape overall strategy, they also limit the flexibility of an alliance. For instance, Gudmundsson and Lechner (2006) contend that one of the downfalls of the Qualiflyer alliance was that Swissair's equity investments made it difficult for the alliance partners to enter new agreements.[8] Although Swissair's equity investment highlights the pitfalls involved in such agreements, we have seen several successes, such as British Airways'

25% investment in Qantas in 1993, Air Canada's 27.5% investment in Continental in 1993, and Singapore Airlines' current 49% investment in Virgin Atlantic.

The next development in the airline alliances model was the creation of global alliances. While Delta, Swissair, and Singapore had experimented with this in 1980s, the first truly global alliance was formed in 1997 between United, Lufthansa, SAS, Air Canada, and Thai Airways. This was called the Star Alliance,[9] and it was shortly followed by similar global partnerships: the Qualiflyer in 1998 that originally included Swissair, Sabena, Turkish Airlines, Air Liberte, and TAP Air Portugal; the Oneworld Alliance in September 1998 between American, British Airways, Qantas, and Cathay Pacific; and the SkyTeam alliance in September 1999, originally between just Delta Air Lines, Air France, and Aeromexico (Baker, 2001). Additional airlines have since joined, and these alliances reach all corners of the globe. Many airlines have joined not only for the obvious benefits, but also because they do not want to be left out of the game. However, several large carriers continue to remain unaligned with any alliances, including Emirates (UAE), Southwest Airlines (US), Ryanair (UK), easyJet (UK), JetBlue Airways (US), and Virgin Atlantic Airways (UK). Some unaffiliated carriers feel that despite having code share agreements, such alliances would not provide them with any additional benefits. Another commonly cited reason is the concern for other carriers' service standards. In the United States, Alaska Airlines has chosen not to join a global alliance but does operate multiple broad code share agreements with carriers from both Oneworld and SkyTeam. On the other hand, Aer Lingus decided to back out of the Oneworld Alliance when it redefined itself as an LCC.

Figures 12.2–12.4 display the global scope and membership numbers for the "Big Three" alliances.

Together, the three largest airline alliances account for 53.4% of total market share for 2022. Table 12.1 displays the ranking and breakdown.

All three alliances have expanded to provide geographical coverage to all areas of the world. A significant stride was made by Star Alliance to solidify its coverage in Africa in

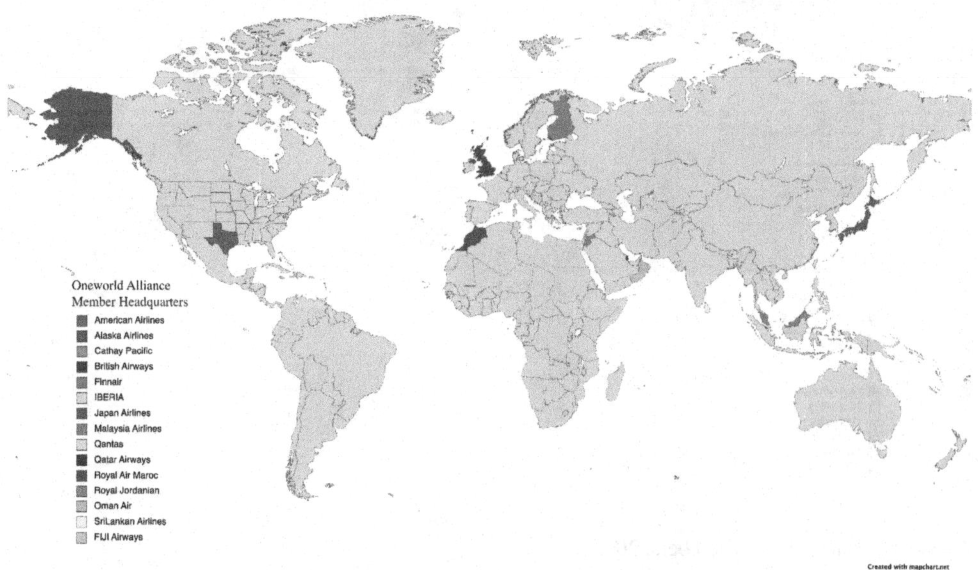

Figure 12.2 Oneworld Alliance Members, 2023.

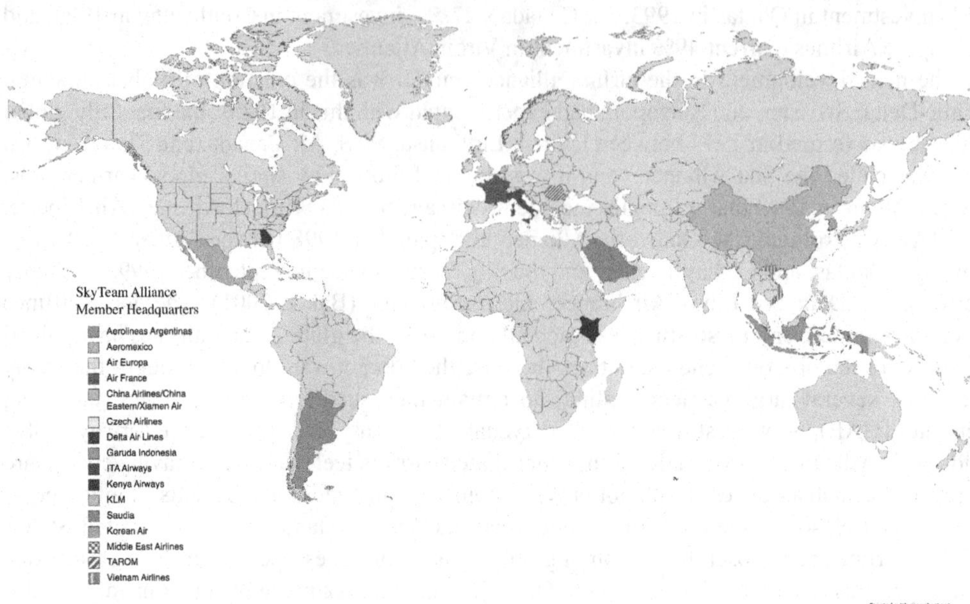

Figure 12.3 SkyTeam Alliance Members, 2023.

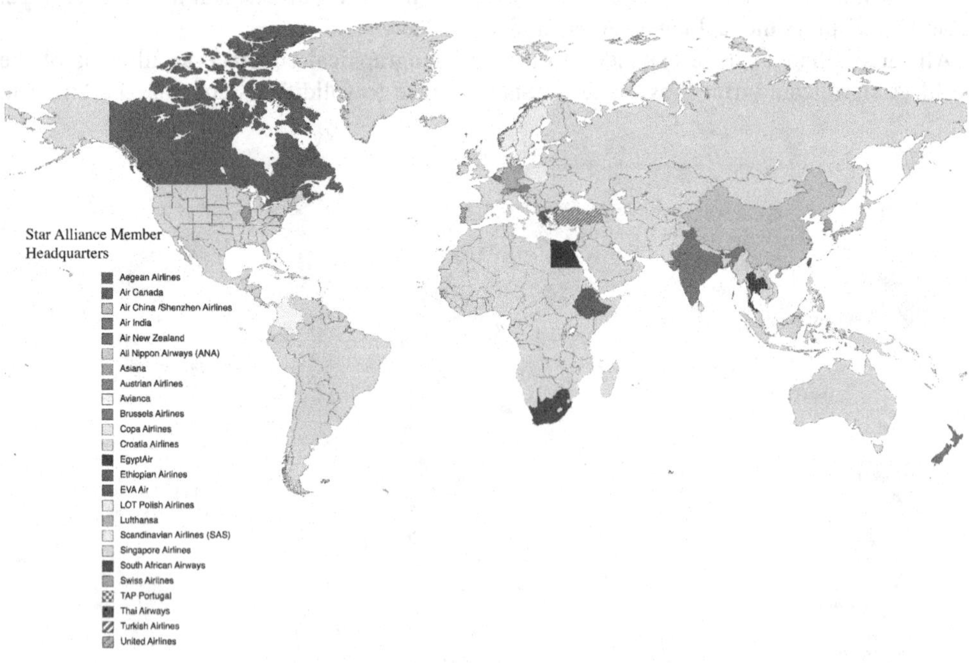

Figure 12.4 Star Alliance Members, 2023.

Table 12.1 Global Airline Alliance Statistics

	Star Alliance (2019)	*SkyTeam (2022)*	*Oneworld*
Member Airlines	26	18	15
Revenue ($billions)	179.05	152.9	108
RPKs (billions)	1,739	1,362	1,189
Passengers (millions)	762	676	535
Countries served	195	170	180
Destinations Served	1,330	1,036	1,100
Employees	4,32,603	4,81,691	4,00,000
Fleet	5,033	5,152	3,553

Source: Alliance Facts and Figures 2019 and 2022.

2012 when Ethiopian Airlines joined its ranks. Concurrently, SkyTeam welcomed Saudia as its first Middle-Eastern member. SkyTeam has also been heavily focused on Asia, with the addition of China Southern and China Eastern. Figures 12.5–12.7 provide comparison statistics, including the number of countries served, number of destinations served, and fleet size.

One major alliance trend has been to focus on the growing region of Eastern Europe. For instance, Czech Airways was the first Eastern European carrier to join a formal global alliance, but several others have followed in recent years. Another current trend is the creation/acceptance of smaller regional airlines. However, both Star and SkyTeam have created regional/associate members for niche airlines that serve a particular need, but these carriers must have a sponsoring member for entry into the alliance.

Global Alliances and Competitiveness

It is pertinent to acknowledge that the strategy of every airline is to weaken competition on certain routes and to gain market share. In this context, global alliance helps achieve that particular goal. As legacy carriers on both sides of the Atlantic have been faced with substantial and growing competition from LCCs on short and medium-haul routes, they have been rapidly expanding their global networks. This strategic maneuver makes their overall costs more competitive with the growing LCCs. The advent of global airline alliances gave rise to concerns that increased monopoly power of major carriers, leading to higher prices and lower service level (Migdadi, 2022).

Figure 12.8 displays the impact of global alliances on the top ten airports in the world in terms of flights. The market share for each airline is calculated based on the flight share published by Flight Global on each airport profile. In terms of concentration, Oneworld has the greatest market share, averaging 29% of flights originating from the world's ten busiest airports. SkyTeam is second, averaging 23% market share, while Star is a close third with 21% share of these markets. Dallas-Fort Worth is the most concentrated airport, where the Oneworld Alliance, largely driven by American Airlines, commands an 85% market share of the airport.

Almost all the airports are highly concentrated when grouped by global alliances—much more so than when grouping the airlines individually. Of the top ten airports, Los Angeles is the least concentrated, with all three alliances and non-member carriers having a fairly even market distribution. Even market distribution results in greater competition and lower airfares, while greater concentrations generally lead to reduced service and higher fares—a negative effect for consumers, but a positive effect for the airlines.

If two airlines with hubs in large cities at either end of a city-pair combine their networks, their cooperation as part of the alliance may grant them market power to raise prices, alter capacity and/or reduce the quality of service on that route. When an airline alliance is granted antitrust

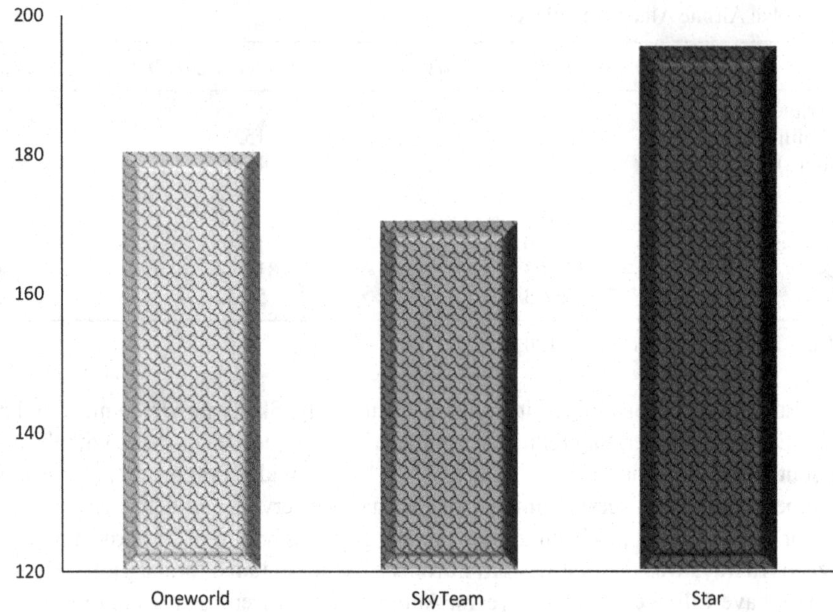

Figure 12.5 Global Airline Alliances: Countries Served as of 2022.

Source: Alliance Facts and Figures 2021

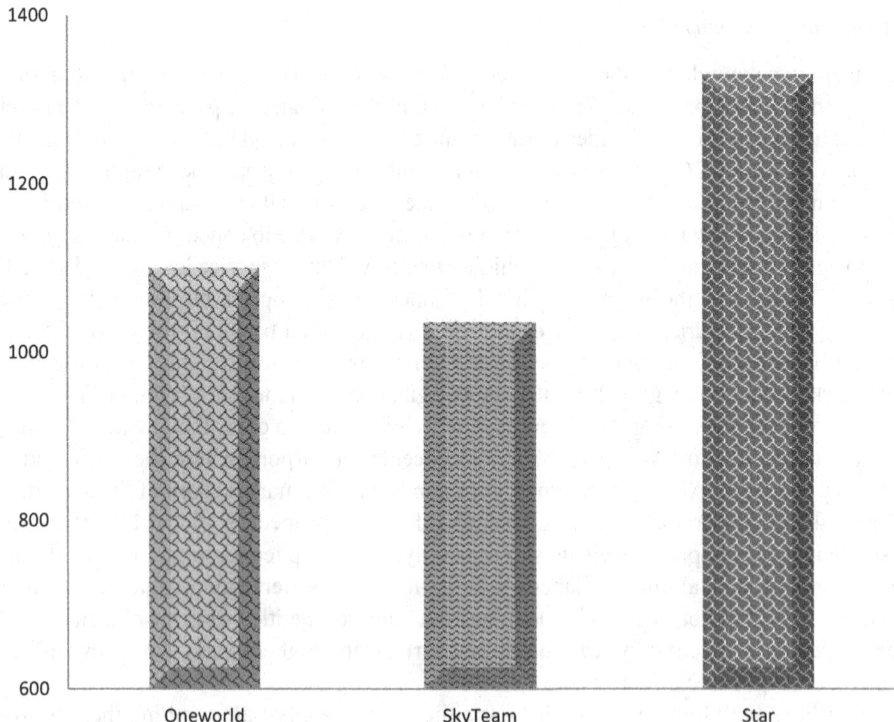

Figure 12.6 Global Airline Alliances: Destinations Served as of 2021.

Source: Alliance Facts and Figures 2019–2021

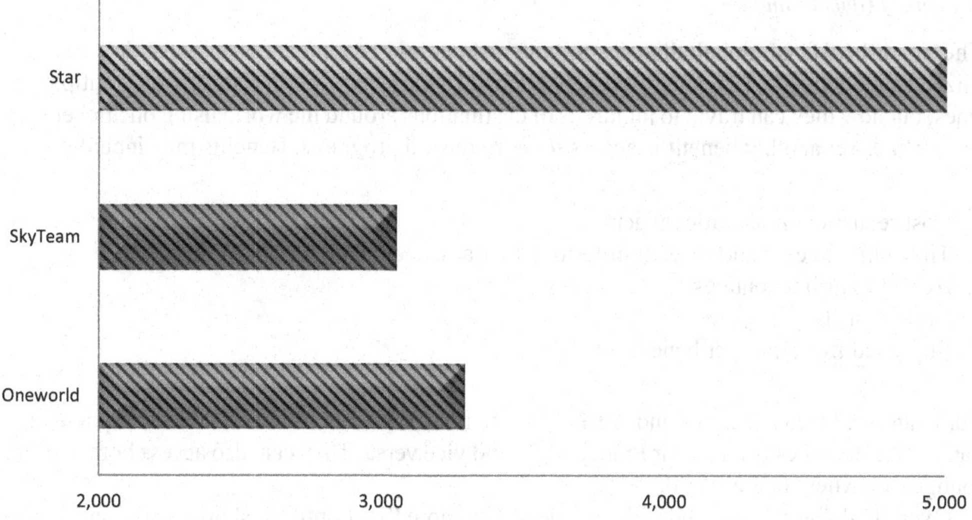

Figure 12.7 Global Airline Alliances: Aircraft Fleet as of 2022.
Source: Alliance Facts and Figures 2021

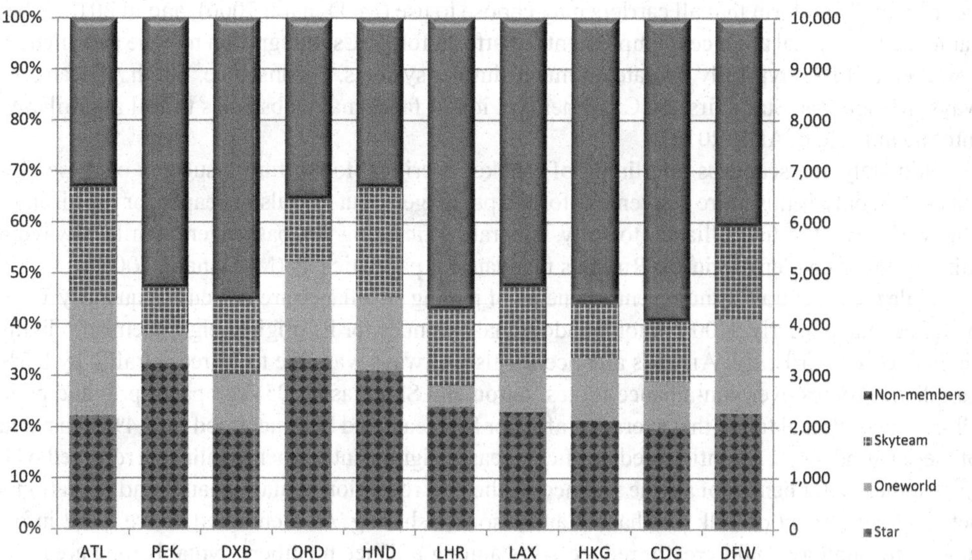

Figure 12.8 Concentration of 10 Global Airports by Alliance in Terms of Concentration.
Source: Compiled by the author from ifly.com and Airport Webpage

immunity (ATI), the number of independent competitors decreases significantly. In an effort to prevent unfair advantage, the US DOT and the European Competition Commission (ECC) carry out competitive assessments before granting ATI privileges to these alliances. Under EU competition rules, the Commission conducts an analysis of possible negative competitive effects, whereas the DOT weighs the potential efficiencies or benefits before it grants an ATI.

Benefits of Global Alliances

The major benefit of global alliances to both airlines and passengers is an expanded and optimized route network. Previously, passengers had to purchase multiple tickets on multiple airlines, but now they can travel to hundreds of destinations around the world using one ticket from one airline. Yet another benefit is access to more reward programs. Benefits may include:

- Cost reduction in operational activities
- The ability to earn and redeem miles on other alliance members
- Access to airline lounges
- Easier ticketing
- Improved frequent flyer benefits

For example, Delta Air Lines and Air France are both SkyTeam members. As such, passengers can earn Delta miles from an Air France flight and vice versa. They can also access both carriers' lounges anywhere in the world.

Overall, global alliances provide travelers with more flight options, shorter trips, and a more streamlined experience. Likewise, airlines achieve benefits from economies of scope, which is the reason that the alliances are seeking a strong presence in every major market in the world. To be successful, however, the connections between member carriers must be seamless and easy. Information technology and ticketing structure integration is critical. Star Alliance created a common IT platform that all carriers may choose to use (McDonald, 2006), and in 2015, it became the first global alliance to implement a platform for LCCs. Integration may be a challenge, however, as LCCs typically operate on much simpler systems. For instance, South African Airways' Mango was Star's first LCC partner, yet it still faces many obstacles to full assimilation into the alliance (CAPA, 2016).

Ultimately, the seamless interlining of e-ticket is critical to the future success of these alliances. Not only is this more convenient for the passengers, but it is also cheaper for the airlines. Oneworld was the first alliance to fully integrate e-ticketing for passengers, while SkyTeam initially faced challenges due to Russia's mandate for paper tickets (McDonald, 2006).

While the exact traffic and revenue benefits of joining an alliance are difficult to quantify, Oneworld estimated nearly $400 million in additional revenues for its original eight members. In the short-lived USAir/British Airways alliance, British Airways was able to increase traffic by 8.3% on alliance routes over non-alliance routes. Iatrou and Skourias (2005) compared pre- and post-alliance periods and found that average traffic for SkyTeam and Star increased by 9.4% as a result of these partnerships. As anticipated, traffic increased significantly when an alliance received ATI.

Another major benefit of airline alliances is the cost reduction in maintenance and operational activities as a result of bulk purchasing and resource sharing. As mentioned above, joint information technology could greatly reduce costs among alliance members. Notably, one area that the Star Alliance has pioneered is joint purchasing; this is in an effort to receive greater volume discounts. Star Fuel Co. launched in December 2003 (Mecham, 2004), which successfully reduced fuel costs for alliance members at Los Angeles, San Francisco, and London Heathrow by $50 million the following year (Mecham, 2004). Star Alliance members, namely, Air Canada, Austrian, Lufthansa, and SAS, all explored a joint regional aircraft purchase in the same year, but the initiative was unsuccessful, as Air Canada and Austrian made independent decisions. While the airlines managed to develop common specifications for the aircraft, the failure of the joint purchasing agreement highlights the difficulties that may be encountered when separate alliance members have unique and different requirements and objectives. Although the Star

Alliance intends to pursue joint aircraft purchasing again in the near future, a better strategy may be to focus only on fuel and aircraft parts.

The other major area where alliances are looking at reducing costs is at the airports. While airlines commonly use personnel from alliance members to help reduce costs, alliances are seeking to extend this further by hosting operations all under one roof. Under this scenario, not only would the carriers be able to share airport resources, but they would also provide passengers with easier connections. This concept occurred at London Heathrow with the opening of Terminal 5 in 2008. Dedicated alliance terminals not only help reduce costs, but they enable alliances to have shared business lounges, self-service check-ins, and possibly ground services. Star Alliance initiated its "one roof" initiative in the early 2000s, and now has dozens of integrated single terminals at airports around the world. Additionally, in an effort to improve customer service, the Star Alliance began assigning teams to meet incoming passengers at the gate, saving approximately $3.3 million per year in re-routing and baggage claim costs.

Having a strong global presence also enables the alliances to obtain global corporate travel contracts. For example, SkyTeam offers business reward programs, meeting assistance, and tailored agreements for companies in China (SkyTeam, 2017a). This additional source of revenue can be substantial for alliances, and the appeal of their offerings in comparison to rival alliances depends greatly on the alliances' global market coverage.

Disadvantages of Global Alliances

Some critics argue that global alliances have allowed some airlines to elude international antitrust regulations and effectively eliminate competition on certain routes. In 2020, Star Alliance was the leading airline alliance, accounting for 18.7% of the market share, followed by SkyTeam with 16.3%, Oneworld with a 12.7%, and the Non-aligned with 52.3% market share. Star Alliance gained the ability to optimize its existing infrastructure use and costs to meet the plummeting air travel demands around worldwide in response to COVID-19.

The second disadvantage is cost, namely the resources required to integrate IT systems. Depending on the carrier, this can take between six months and two years to complete. Moreover, further costs may trickle down from the additional overhead required to run such a large organization. To illustrate, each alliance staffs a global team of full-time employees.

Another potential concern among alliance members is the reduced, or shared exposure as more airlines join the network. This entails the possibility that carriers can be in competition with their own alliance partners. For example, Delta battled former Continental on transatlantic routes, even though both airlines were technically supposed to collaborate as SkyTeam members. Gudmundsson and Lechner (2006) argue that airlines will drop out and switch alliances in order to achieve the greatest benefits. As evidence, Continental announced its exit from SkyTeam in 2008. Subsequently, on October 27, 2009, the carrier subsequently joined the Star Alliance as part of a code sharing agreement with United, an existing Star member.[10] Likewise, Aer Lingus and Mexicana both dropped out of Oneworld and Star Alliance respectively. Airline alliances were criticized on a number of points including:

- Alliance members may collude to prevent other airlines from the market in violation of fair competition standards.
- Alliances could lead to the bankruptcy of some airlines that have to compete with less capital resources.
- Higher ticket prices due to a lower level of competition in the market.
- Less competition in the market.

Future for Global Alliances

As of 2022, Oneworld, SkyTeam, and Star Alliance have emerged as the dominating airline alliances, comprising 26 members, a fleet of 5,000 aircraft, and 130 destinations. This trend is expected to continue, as each alliance seeks new carriers to close coverage gaps between existing members. There are no current plans for the creation of a fourth global alliance. It is more likely that new and non-aligned carriers will join one of the Big Three; however, simplified alliances and cooperation between LCCs may continue to occur within the domestic networks.

Global alliances are expected to continue to be driven by economies of scale, scope, and density in addition to liberalization and shifts in market power. However, as the potential number of alliance members begins to decrease, more strategic decisions will be made by the Big Three global alliances to include members who can fill in any network gaps. There is also a new focus on creating antitrust immune joint ventures between fewer airlines (such as the "Blue Skies" transatlantic ATI JV between Delta, Air France/KLM and Virgin Atlantic), which appear to enable joint services that achieve most of the benefits of a quasi-merger. Currently, the biggest risk to alliances is the rise of the Persian Gulf carriers (Emirates, Etihad, and Qatar Airways). These airlines are now serious competitive threats to every major airline.[11] Emirates Airlines, boasting a revenue of $25.10 billion (2019–2020), has famously steered clear of involvement in any of the major alliances. But in July of 2022, Emirates and Air Canada announced a codeshare agreement.

In the past few decades, low-cost airlines have enjoyed significant gain in market share. Over the last decade, LCCs have rapidly expanded their share of the global air travel market. As of 2020, low-cost carriers accounted for 35% of the world's total seat capacity. In 2020, LCCs accounted for 35% of the world's total seat capacity. Despite the fact that there are several very high-quality, low-cost airlines operating in both domestic and international markets, no independent low-cost airline has become a member of any of the three global alliances.

Summary

Liberalization has led to substantial economic and traffic growth. Bilateral and multilateral Open Skies agreements have provided a framework that encouraged competition, enhanced connectivity, and expanded international air traffic. For example, the European Open Skies Agreement have allowed any airline registered in the EU or America to fly to and from any location within the European Union, as well as operate flights to and from America. Throughout this chapter, we have provided a detailed discussion of aviation agreements and the concept of Open Skies. The most comprehensive example of liberalization is the EU single aviation market (ECAA, signed on May 5, 2006 in Salzburg) that resulted in an almost fully deregulated EU single aviation market. We introduced the readers to the nine freedoms of the sky and to the key agreements that continue to shape the industry. Finally, we explored the history and strategy behind the three major global airline alliances, with the associated benefits and costs of belonging to a global alliance today. Many airlines have joined the global airline alliances because they offer several advantages in operations, marketing, financial, and operational areas. More recently, smaller ATI JVs have been a successful recent development on major international markets. However, none of the low-cost airlines are members of the three main alliances. Airports, aircraft manufacturers, and non-member airlines may experience both positive and negative impacts from the existence of global airline alliances.

Discussion Questions

1 List and briefly explain the eight provisions of Open Skies agreements.
2 Global airline alliances were created with the intention of growing the networks of airlines and providing greater access to more parts of the world. Recently, three major global alliances started to accept smaller, regional airlines. How do such members benefit an alliance?
3 Identify and describe some of the costs associated with joining a global alliance.
4 Define Cabotage Law and explain the impact of cabotage agreements on international travel.
5 How did the Open Skies agreement between the European Union and the United States reduce the barriers to entry?
6 How were LCCs in Europe affected by the EU Open Skies agreement?
7 What are the main provisions of Open Skies agreements and why have some countries avoided such agreements?
8 Which freedom is not likely to be extended to foreign airlines and why?
9 Name the three major world alliances. What are some of the benefits and costs associated with these alliances?
10 Why is aviation particularly well suited to Open Skies agreements, and what are the potential gains for individual airlines?
11 Why do legacy airlines have an advantage over LCCs in the international market?
12 What is a joint venture between airlines?
13 Explain why airlines originally formed alliances with foreign carriers.
14 What are code share agreements between airlines?
15 What are some of the pros and cons of equity investments between airlines?
16 What are the major trends in global alliances?
17 Which airport has the greatest concentration of a single global alliance network?
18 How does this affect traffic (domestic vs international) at the airport?
19 What is the difference between the way the EU and the DOT evaluate the grant of antitrust immunity?
20 Briefly summarize the future for global alliances as outlined in the chapter?

Notes

1 Carnegie Endowment for International Peace, Division of International Law, International Conferences of American States, vol. 1 (1934).
2 The SDR is an artificial currency unit based upon several national currencies. SDR is used by the International Monetary Fund (IMF) for internal accounting purposes and by some countries as a peg for their own currency and is used as an international reserve asset.
3 *Flight International, Bermuda 2 initialed*, July 2, 1977.
4 DOT order 93-1-11.
5 The U.S. - EU Air Transport Agreement signed April 30, 2007. Available at http://www.state.gov/e/eeb/rls/othr/ata/e/eu/114768.htm.
6 Brexit could lead to doors closing on Open Skies, Air Transport World, June 27, 2016.
7 Business Wire, A Berkshire Hathaway Company, March 22, 2011.
8 The Qualiflyer alliance was a European alliance led by Swissair and Sabena.
9 Star Alliance was founded in 1997 and is currently the largest airline alliance in the world.
10 Star Alliance, Alliance Customer Benefits Remain in Place until 31 May, 2012. Press Release 2012.
11 *Forbes*. In Debate Vs. Persian Gulf Carriers U.S.'s Big Three Airlines Can't Win - Even If They Win. March 18, 2015.

References

Baker, C. (2005). Back to the Table. *Airlines Business*, September. Retrieved on September 28, 2006 from Air Transport Intelligence.

CAPA Center for Aviation. (2016). *Star Alliance the First Global Alliance with an LCC Platform: SAA's Mango Becomes the First Partner*. Retrieved on November 10, 2016 from: http://centreforaviation.com/analysis/star-alliance-the-first-global-alliance-with-an-lcc-platform-saas-mango-becomes-the-first-partner-258088

Chicago Convention. (2006). *Convention on International Civil Aviation.* Signed at Chicago, on December 7, 1944.

Competition Commission. (1999). British Airways Plc and CityFlyer Express Limited: A Report on the Proposed Merger, Appendix 4.2 *Bermuda 2.*

de Palacio, L. (2001). Open Skies: How to Get the Airlines Airborne Again. *Wall Street Journal (Europe)*, September 11.

Ch-Aviation. (2016a). *India Unveils Its New Civil Aviation Policy.* Retrieved on November 9, 2016 from: http://www.ch-aviation.com/portal/news/47087-india-unveils-its-new-civil-aviation-policy

Ch-Aviation. (2016b). *Indonesia, Laos Ratify ASEAN Open Skies Agreement.* Retrieved on November 9, 2016 from: http://www.ch-aviation.com/portal/news/46254-indonesia-laos-ratify-asean-open-skies-agreement

Department of Transportation (DOT). (1978). *Air Services Agreement between the Government of the United States of America and the Government of the United Kingdom of Great Britain and Northern Ireland.* Washington, DC: DOT.

Department of Transportation (DOT). (1998). *The Impact of the New US–Canada Aviation Agreement at Its Third Anniversary.* Retrieved on August 15, 2012 from http://ostpxweb.dot.gov/aviation/intav/canada2.pdf.

Federal Aviation Administration (FAA). (2017). *Overflight Fees.* Retrieved on February 27, 2017 from http://www.faa.gov/air_traffic/international_aviation/overflight_fees/

Field, D. (2005). True Open Skies? *Airline Business*, March. Retrieved on September 28, 2006 from Air Transport Intelligence.

Forsyth, P., King, J., and Rodolfo, C. (2006). Open Skies in ASEAN. *Journal of Air Transport Management*, 12, 143–152.

Francis, L. (2004). Liberal Values. *Flight International*, October.

Francis, L. (2005). Singapore–China "Open Skies" Has Restriction on LCCs. *Air Transport Intelligence News*, December 2.

Gudmundsson, S.V. and Lechner, C. (2006). Multilateral Airline Alliances: Balancing Strategic Constraints and Opportunities. *Journal of Air Transport Management*, 12(3), 153–158.

Iatrou, K. and Skourias, N. (2005). An Attempt to Measure the Traffic Impact of Airline Alliances. *Journal of Air Transportation*, 10(3), 73–99.

International Civil Aviation Organization (ICAO). (2004) *Manual on the Regulation of International Air Transport* (Doc 9626, Part 4).

Ke, J. and Windle, R. (2014). The Ongoing Impact of the US-China Air Services Agreements (ASAs) on Air Passenger Markets. *Transportation Journal*, 53(3), 274–304. doi:10.5325/transportationj.53.3.0274.

Kinnock, N. (1996). The Liberalization of the European Aviation Industry. *European Business Journal*, 8(4), 8–13.

McDonald, M. (2006). When to Tie the Knot. *Air Transport World*, August. Retrieved on October 12, 2006 from lProQuest.

Mecham, M. (2004). Fueling Star. *Aviation Week & Space Technology*, 161(17), 29.

Migdadi, Y.K.A.A. (2022). The Impact of Airline Alliance Strategy on the Perceived Service Quality: A Global Survey. *Journal of Quality Assurance in Hospitality & Tourism*, 23(2), 415–446.

Mishra, M. (2016). India Signs Open Skies Agreement with Greece. *The Economic Times*. September 7.

Montreal Convention. (2006). *Convention for the Unification of Certain Rule for International Carriage by Air.* Montreal May 28, 1999.

SkyTeam (2017a). *SkyTeam Announces Global Meetings Enhancements.* Press Release, July 17, 2016.

The Australian Aviation Associations' Forum (TAAAF) (2016). A New Partnership for the Aviation Industry. Aviation Policy, 2016. Retrieved from http://abaa.com.au/downloads/TAAAF-Aviation-Policy-Summary-2016.pdf March 1, 2017.

US Centennial of Flight Commission (USCOF). (2006). *International Civil Aviation*. Retrieved on October 3, 2006 from http://www.centennialofflight.gov/essay/Government_Role/Intl_Civil/POL19.htm.

US Department of State (DOS). (2021). *Open Skies Partners*. https://www.state.gov/open-skies-partners

Walker, K. (2016). Brexit Could Lead to Doors Closing on Open Skies, Editor's Blog. *Air Transport World*.

Warsaw Convention (WC). (2006). *Convention for the Unification of Certain Rules Relating to International Carriage by Air*, Signed at Warsaw on October 12, 1929.

13 Aviation Infrastructure

Operations and Ownership

Traditionally, airports, airlines, and air traffic control systems were financed, built, and operated by government entities, either at the local or state level or the national level. Beyond North America and Europe, many nations maintain public ownership of their airlines. Air transport firms, including airports and airlines, were originally publicly owned because they were considered critical infrastructure that served the public interest—important pieces of infrastructure that are vital to the economy and national security. However, a number of national airlines have moved to the private sector such as British Airways, Air France, Qantas, Iberia, Lufthansa, Turkish Airlines, and Air Canada. The British and Spanish governments privatized British Airways and Iberia in 1987 and 2001, respectively.

The rise of global aviation is, in many ways, the story of how the industry has slowly moved away from pervasive government ownership and regulation to private sector management. The concept of direct regulation of fares and routes is, for the most part, no longer stifling competition. However, numerous political rules remain. While many countries have privatized, at least to some extent, airports and parts of air traffic control services, that has not been the case a number of countries, including the United States or New Zealand. Presently, air traffic controllers in the US work for the Federal Aviation Administration (FAA), a government agency. Australia, France, Germany, and the United Kingdom are among the dozens of countries that have spun off air-traffic control services into some type of private or government-owned corporation.[1] More than 36 years have passed since the first airport privatization occurred with British Airport Authority (BAA) in the United Kingdom in 1987. There are some indications that the United States will follow, but local federal agencies continue to control many aspects of aviation, including air traffic and the direct ownership of airports. Naturally, government regulators are, for better or worse, the de facto partners of virtually every business, yet very few face as much direct government control of day-to-day operations as air transport infrastructure firms. This level of oversight presents many unique challenges to the aviation industry.

This chapter applies the tools of economic analysis to the operational infrastructure of the industry, namely, Air Traffic Control (ATC) and airports. It begins with a brief history of air traffic control, followed by an economic analysis of the existing system, and finally, the prospects for reform. The concluding segment is devoted to an economic analysis of airport ownership and the likely outcomes when public or private ownership is considered. The chapter is outlined as follows:

- Air Traffic Control System
- Institutional Problems in US Air Traffic Control
- Air Traffic Control in a Government Corporation
- Political Obstacles to Reform

DOI: 10.4324/9781003388135-13

- Solutions to Air Traffic Control Problems
  - Regulation
  - Air Traffic Control Charges
- Airport Ownership and Management
  - Trends in Airport Ownership
  - Reasons for Privatization
  - Opposition to Privatization
  - Types of Privatizations
  - Privatization in the US Airport Industry
- Unmanned Aerial Systems
  - Classification of the Unmanned Aerial Systems
  - Drone Technology Commercial Uses and Applications
- Summary
- Discussion Questions
- Appendix

Air Traffic Control Systems

The privatization of America's air traffic control network has long been a contentious issue. The initial management of air traffic began in the 1920s and was mainly concerned with navigation. This rudimentary system involved the use of flags, lights, and bonfires to locate and identify airports and runways as a means to communicate with pilots. In the early 1930s, this system was replaced by a more formal set up that consisted of a series of light towers. The system was called the Transcontinental Lighted Airway, and this system once encompassed a vast expanse of over 1,500 beacons and 18,000 miles of airways. Thus, early technology forced aircraft to rely on point-to-point navigation over predetermined routes rather than the more direct routing that the aircraft were capable of. As radio technology advanced, it gradually replaced these earlier systems. At the same time, traffic between major metropolitan areas began to increase, and it became apparent that a more centralized system was needed to facilitate separation and navigation.

Accordingly, in the mid-1930s, an airline consortium established the first three centers to pool information on specific flights. These centers were taken over by the Bureau of Air Commerce within the Department of Commerce when it assumed responsibility for air traffic in the United States. Separation was primarily accomplished mainly through flight scheduling over the already established prescribed routes. Once more, the existing technology was forcing the aircraft to fly predetermined routes along ground-based paths. At the end of the 1930s, Congress passed the Civil Aeronautics Act, which transferred civil aviation responsibilities from the Department of Commerce to a newly created agency called the Civil Aeronautics Authority. In 1940, President Roosevelt separated the Authority into two agencies, the Civil Aeronautics Administration (CAA) and the Civil Aeronautics Board (CAB). The newly created CAA was tasked with certification, safety, airway development, and ATC (Kent, 1980). Meanwhile, the CAB was spun off from the CAA and was charged with the economic regulation of the transport industry.[2] The Federal Aviation Agency was subsequently created by the Federal Aviation Act of 1958, inheriting the responsibilities of the old CAA as well as the new responsibility of establishing safety rules. By 1967, the agency's name changed to Federal Aviation Administration

(FAA) and it was finally placed under the Department of Transportation (DOT). In the United States, the ATC System Command Center (ATCSCC) is responsible for all air traffic control, while Air Route Traffic Control Centers (ARTCC) manage traffic within all sectors of its center.

Throughout the 1970s, the FAA installed new radars, computers, and radio communications to upgrade and enhance the ATC system. However, a significant issue with these developments was the fact that they were created under the same foundational principles as the older systems. The Terminal Radar Approach Control (TRACON) directs approaching and departing aircraft within the airspace, while the Flight Service Stations (FSS) supply critical information, such as terrain, route, weather, and flight plan. This entailed that aircraft were still expected to travel between ground-based navigation points, the effect of which was a linear line of traffic along each route. Subsequently, controllers would then use various techniques to maintain predetermined separation standards. As one would expect, the flow of traffic was regulated based on the slowest aircraft and/or the largest separation distances. This of course is analogous to a ground-based highway system, and it was often called the highway in the sky. The problem here was the fact that this system ignores the capability of an aircraft to travel in three dimensions and directly through an airspace. Nonetheless, this system worked reasonably and efficiently with the existing volume of traffic and level of technology. It's worth noting that the system's effectiveness was strongly linked to weather. The system operated well under good weather conditions; pilots could see and be seen so that separation standards could be reduced. Given that good weather conditions are generally the norm, the problems with the system and the procedures were generally not apparent.

However, as traffic increased and technology advanced, it became increasingly evident that the system was outdated and there was an urgent need to modernize.[3] Unfortunately, bureaucratic tendencies and political considerations took over, which meant that meaningful reform and modernization were increasingly difficult if not impossible.[4] Although there were expensive efforts that were undertaken to improve the system, none of these yielded significant results. But, by the end of the 1990s and with the advent of the twenty-first century, the volume of traffic was overwhelming the system. While the tragic events of 9/11 slowed growth temporarily, traffic returned to and exceeded previous levels by 2006.

One of the principal advantages of air travel is the speed with which an individual can arrive at their destination. Therefore, factors that contribute to delays in the system certainly reduce the demand for air traffic. We discussed supply and demand models in the previous chapters, but Figure 13.1 displays the short-term economic effects of traffic delays. It is evident that there is an equilibrium price (PE) and a quantity supplied (QE) of air travel. Recall from the earlier chapters that any price above equilibrium will result in a supply surplus; that is, too many empty seats. In this situation, competition between airlines will lower the price to fill the seats and return to the equilibrium position. Any price below the equilibrium will result in a shortage and consumers will bid up the price to obtain the seating.

Consider a scenario that the ATC system imposes repeated and prolonged delays in the form of ground or airborne holds, which can be the result of separation standards or the controller's inability to handle the volume. This situation can be perceived as an externally imposed cost or tax to both the consumers and the producers of air travel. For consumers, it is an unanticipated delay that can be monetized as lost time, or in the case of the business travelers, as forgone opportunities. To the producer, the cost can be measured in terms of higher crew wages, more fuel burn, and the loss of utilization for other flights.

Flight delays present economic and environmental problems that cause aggravations for both airlines and airline passengers. The costs in Figure 13.1 are shown as the straight-line AB that joins the demand and supply curves. These costs can be considered as a parallel shift in the

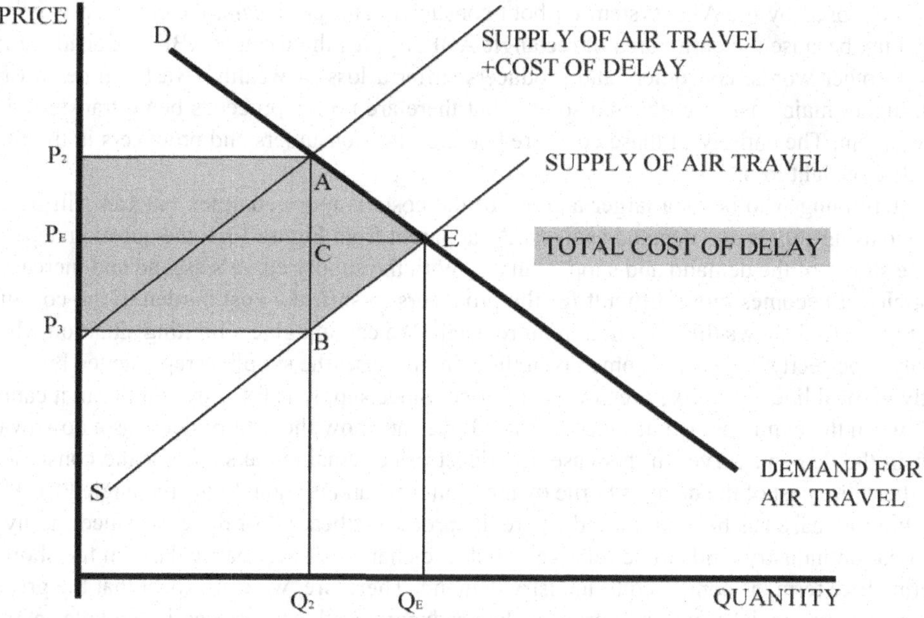

Figure 13.1 Short-Term Economic Effects of Air-Traffic Delay.

supply curve so that the new supply curve intersects the demand curve at point A. However, since these are extra costs, the new equilibrium quantity and price will be defined by the intersection of the new supply curve with the old demand curve at P_2 and Q_2. On the other hand, the effective price received by the producers is determined from the old supply curve, net of the cost introduced by the externally imposed delay at P3. It can also be seen that the consumers are also compelled with the equilibrium price P_2, which is clearly higher than the original equilibrium price. Therefore, the cost of the delay is shared between the consumers and the producers.

Traffic delays seem inevitable, especially during the busy holiday travel season. Between the mechanical issues, missing crew, computer glitch, weather, and air traffic control delays. The airline costs consist of increased operating expenses such as for crew, fuel, maintenance, and others, and come from two sources: schedule buffers and unforeseen delays. On the other hand, passenger costs result from time lost due to schedule buffers, delayed flights, flight cancellations, and missed connections.

The consumer pays a new higher ticket price, while the producer receives less from the new ticket price. The total amount of the cost is equal to the rectangle ABP3P_2 plus the triangle ABE. From the consumer standpoint, the costs are equal to the rectangle P2ACPE plus the triangle ACE. For producers, the costs are equal to rectangle PECBP3 plus the triangle CEB.

The cost of delay is analogous to the impact of a conventional tax on air travel, although congestion costs are much worse. Suppose that a tax, equal to congestion cost, is imposed. In conventional demand and supply tax analysis, the entire rectangle ABP3P2 is the amount that the taxing authority receives from the tax, while the triangle ABE is the dead weight loss that results from the imposition of the tax. This dead weight loss can best be thought of as the transactions between buyers and sellers that failed to materialize because of the imposition of the tax. In essence, it refers to the consumers who would have purchased tickets in the absence of the tax just as the producers would have sold them the tickets absent the tax. In the case of a delay that is imposed by the ATC system on both consumers and producers, the situation is graver than a tax because the entire area of rectangle ABP2P$_3$ plus the triangle ABE is a dead weight loss. In other words, consumers and producers suffer a loss of wealth—wasted time, wasted fuel, higher maintenance costs, and so on—but there are no tax proceeds being transferred to government. The entirety of these costs are borne by the consumers and producers in the form of a dead weight loss.

Determining who bears a larger amount of the costs is more complex but can still be addressed using supply and demand analysis. As apparent from Figure 13.1, the question depends on the slopes of the demand and supply curves. With the supply curve's ascend and increasing elasticity, it becomes more difficult for the producers to shift the cost burden to the consumers. Figure 13.2 shows this situation in more detail. We can imagine a limiting situation where supply is perfectly inelastic at some given time. In this case, the supply is represented by a perfectly vertical line and is fixed regardless of price. Since supply is fixed by definition, it cannot shift when the extra cost is introduced. Instead, we can show the cost of delay as a downward shift in the demand curve. In this case, the ticket price remains the same for the consumers, and the entire cost of the delay is borne by the producers and is equal to the rectangle PEEAP2. The limiting case has been presented where the producers bear all of the costs since supply in the aviation industry tends to be relatively inelastic characteristics, particularly in the short to intermediate term, as compared to industry demand. Therefore, we can expect that the greater part of the cost of delay will be borne by the producers. And, as it is seen in the latter part of the chapter, this appears to be true when we observe the preferences of the market participants.

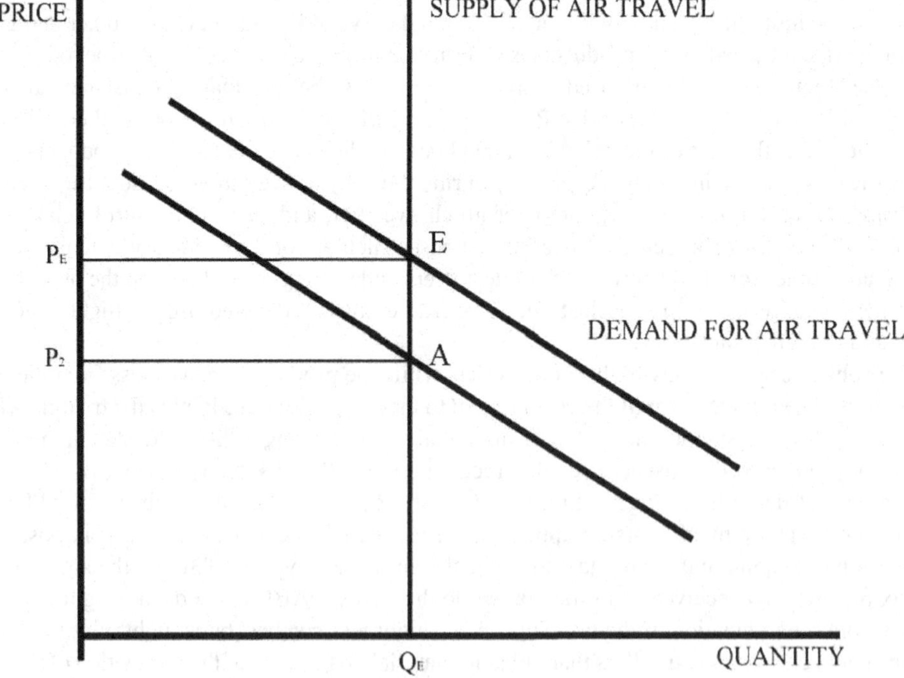

Figure 13.2 The Cost of Delay with Inelastic Supply.

However, this narrative does not conclude the story. Unfortunately, there are other longer-term supply and demand effects that must be considered. On the supply side, if the cost of delay is persistent and longer lasting as appears to be for the foreseeable future, then the value of the specialized resources presently in use in the aviation industry will be diminished accordingly. These resources include, among other inputs, the production of aircraft, the supply of spare parts, the manufacture of avionics, airport-related concessions, air travel-related accommodations, automobile rental concessions, pilots, flight attendants, mechanics, and a host of other related factors. As these specialized resources gradually deteriorate, they will not be replaced at the same rate, and this will further reduce output in the industry. This progression is illustrated in Figure 13.3 where the initial supply decrease occurs and then a further decrease takes place as these specialized resources wear out or exit the industry. As shown in the figure, the long-term effect further lowers quantity and raises price.

On the demand side, a shift is expected in preferences with demand veering away from air travel to alternate modes of travel where feasible. Although air travel is clearly the fastest mode of travel when considering relative speed, it is the total trip time that is of primary interest to the traveler. Due to extended delays during peak time at the security line and persistent air traffic system delays, the inherent speed advantage of air travel is severely compromised. If this continues, more and more consumers will opt for surface travel which will most likely be by private automobile. Since automobile traffic is inherently riskier than air travel, there will be a concurrent rise in accidents and fatalities.

This process is illustrated in Figure 13.4, featuring both an initial demand decreases and a long-term demand decrease. Initially, demand decreases immediately with delay since the quality and speed of air travel are reduced. However, this initial reaction is multiplied over time, reducing demand further as air travelers have more time to adjust their behavior, work out other travel arrangements, cut down on the number of trips, and so on.[5] The demand decreases

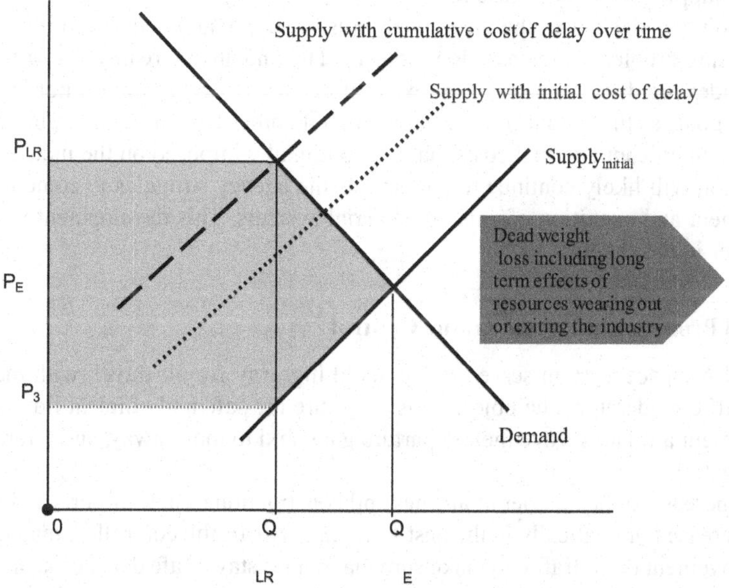

Figure 13.3 Costs of Delay over Time.

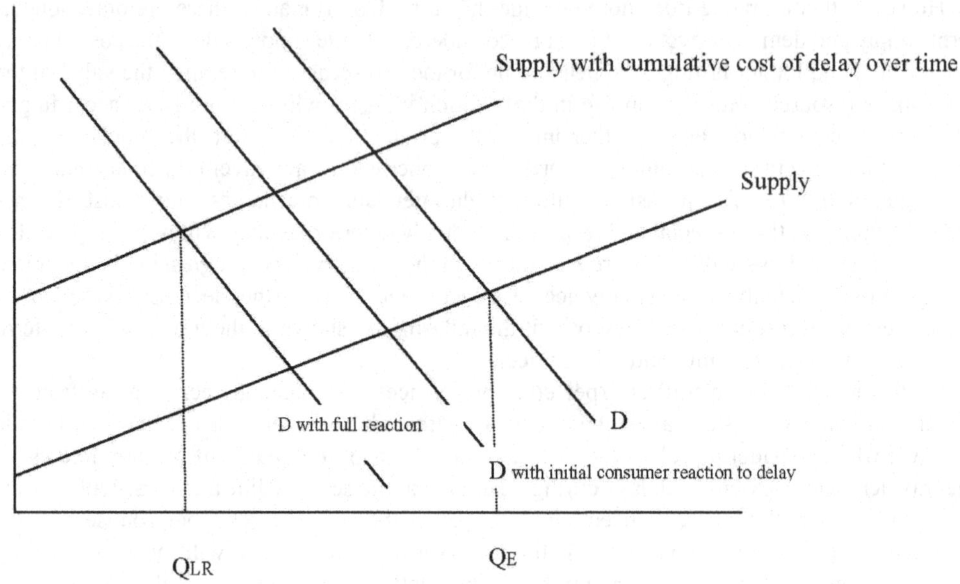

Figure 13.4 Market Reaction to Changes in Supply.

reinforce the decline in total air travel caused by the supply decreases. Consequently, the industry is substantially smaller and less efficient than it would be without these delays. However, the impact on price becomes theoretically ambiguous since falling demand tends to reduce price while falling supply tends to increase it.

The preceding analysis uses the theoretical tools of supply and demand to illuminate a very real and pressing problem in the aviation industry. The undeniable reality is that the consumer product is under the direct control of an external agency (FAA) that does not have the same incentives or goals as the producer, especially when it comes to profitability. This disparity has culminated in significant external costs that are continually imposed on the industry. On top of that, congestion will likely continue to increase as the agency struggles to come to terms with the development and operation of unmanned aerial systems. This development will be further discussed later in the chapter.

Institutional Problems in US Air Traffic Control

The National Airspace System serves as the aerial highway for air travel, with the FAA serving as the traffic moderator. The objective is to ensure the safe and efficient flow of air travel, from the moment airplanes leave their departure gate, taxi to the runway, and returning back to a deplaning gate.

With the increase in the number of airlines and construction of new airports and runways, air traffic has increased dramatically in the past few years. Air-traffic controllers manage and coordinate the movement of air traffic to make sure that planes stay a safe distance apart. Apart from ensuring safety, efficient air traffic must direct planes to minimize delays. The FAA is facing increased criticism for its role in governing ATC. A number of studies have concluded that ATC management in the United States is inherently flawed and in need for major reform. Authors of such studies include:

- The Aviation Safety Commission in 1988
- The National Commission to Ensure a Strong Competitive Airline Industry in 1993
- The National Performance Review in 1993
- The Secretary of Transportation's Executive Oversight Group in 1994
- The National Civil Aviation Review Commission (Mineta Commission) in 1997

The issue often highlighted is that funding flows from an unpredictable revenue stream subject to the federal budget process. At times, there also seems to be an inability to attract and retain needed managers and engineers who are skilled at implementing complex technology projects, stemming in part from limitations in the civil service system.

The lack of mission focus and clear accountability is at the root of much of the criticism because authority is shared by Congress and the FAA in a confusing bureaucracy. A prime example of this complexity is future implementation of NextGen, which will be complicated by the fact that numerous outdated FAA operations around the United States will need to be closed. However, Congressional representatives are reluctant to vote in favor of shutting down any operation that "provides jobs in their district."

A possible solution to this type of problem, according to some economists, could involve transitioning to a private, non-profit corporation, as Canada did in 1996 with Nav Canada Corporation. While the common belief is that this is not politically feasible, there is broad support for establishing a government corporation to address the concerns that have stymied previous attempts at major ATC reform.

The Next Generation Air Transportation System (NextGen) stands as an initiative for modernization set to render air travel safer, more flexible, and efficient. The present air traffic control system in the United States relies on ground-based radar and voice communication between air-traffic controllers and pilots. By using Automatic Dependent Surveillance-Broadcast (ADS-B), a GPS-based technology, aircraft are able to fly more safely and efficiently in previously challenging areas. NextGen has enhanced surface traffic operations at 39 of the 40 busiest airports in the United States by providing electronic communications to clear aircraft for departure. This technology has the potential to accelerate clearances and minimize error.[6] The NextGen system involves sharing data between airlines, airports, and air traffic control facilities to make more informed decisions about the management of flights and the use of airspace. The FAA began work on NextGen improvements in 2007 and anticipates completing the final implementation segment by 2030.

Political Obstacles to Reform

The primary contention against ATC commercialization centers on user fees. General aviation has been particularly fearful of user fee impact. However, it is very feasible, and arguably, politically necessary to exempt piston aircraft flying under visual flight rules (VFR) from user fees. For those that sometimes fly instrument flight rules (IFR), reasonable accommodations can be made. In Canada, for example, operators pay a modest annual fee based on aircraft weight. Moreover, the envisioned board of directors for a US government corporate ATC system would include representatives of general aviation that would have to approve any changes in user fees.

Business jets would be subject to some user fees, but experience shows that these can be reasonable. Notably, both Canada and Europe have experienced strong growth in business aviation after ATC commercialization (Poole, 2007).

One might expect public employees to be potentially strong opponents of commercialization. However, The National Air-Traffic Controllers Association, the main FAA union, supported the Clinton Administration's proposal to divest ATC to a government corporation, structured along the lines discussed here. Moreover, commercialization could readily include no-layoff guarantees for all current controllers and technicians.

Ultimately, government reform often proceeds at a glacial pace. Regardless of how inefficient existing institutions may be, there are always interest groups who perceive a vested interest in maintaining the status quo. Nonetheless, concerning ATC, it is plausible that the United States has reached a stage where the problems are so severe that the political logjam blocking major reform may soon be broken.

Air Traffic Control in a Government Corporation

Air-traffic controllers coordinate the movement of aircraft, including within the vicinity of airports and between altitude sectors and control centers, ensuring the maintenance of safe distances. The FAA is responsible for two basic functions: air safety regulation and air traffic control. A key feature of a government corporation is non-political funding, as user fees replace taxes and Congressional budgeting. The existence of an independent revenue stream allows access to private capital markets to fund modernization. In turn, the elimination of tax funding creates an exemption from government procurement rules that have previously tended to impede the acquisition of new technology. Likewise, independent funding allows exemption from Civil Service regulations that might otherwise impede the attraction, management, and maintenance of the appropriately skilled workforce.

In 1987, New Zealand converted its ATC operation from a government division to a self-supporting government corporation.[7] As of 2007, over 40 countries implemented similar commercialization reforms, including Australia, France, Germany, Switzerland, the UK, the Benelux countries, and Scandinavia. Only a few of these are privatized in the sense of being outside of government; most are government corporations. All of these commercialized and self-supporting Air Navigation Service Providers (ANSPs) belong to the Civil Air Navigation Services Organization (CANSO), which has become a key participant in international aviation policy debates. All ANSPS are subject to safety regulations and some form of economic regulation because of their monopoly on ATC services.

In 2005, the Government Accountability Office (GAO) conducted a large-scale evaluation of the performance of commercialized ANSPs.[8] The GAO collected extensive data from five major ANSPs—Australia, Canada, Germany, New Zealand, and UK. Their findings indicated that after commercialization of ATC, safety had either been unaffected or even improved since implementation. They also found that all five of the systems studied had taken significant steps to invest in new technology and equipment and had taken meaningful steps to reduce operating costs. Similarly, a 2005 FAA study (FAA, 2005) found that commercialized systems were more cost-effective in airspace with equivalent traffic density. In short, commercialized ATC has become the norm for most of the industrialized world and apparently has a solid record of improved efficiency with no decline in safety.

Solutions to Air Traffic Control Problems in the United States

The surge in the global air passenger traffic underscores the imperative to effectively manage air traffic. To tackle this challenge, the FAA has taken an ambitious, multi-year, multi-billion-dollar effort, known as the Next Generation Air Transportation System, to modernize its aging infrastructure. The FAA's annual budget for 2023 is $23.6 billion, with $1 billion earmarked for NextGen. The FAA expects flight operations to increase by over 35% in the next decade, and it also foresees a corresponding escalation in the aforementioned delay costs. Therefore, an increase in air passenger traffic across the globe is driving the growth of the commercial aircraft NextGen avionics market.

The possibility for a meaningful reform to take place is problematical, since it is challenging to envision an organization with a set of incentives and goals that are fundamentally different from the aviation industry will be able or willing to implement any of these changes. The following quote is taken from the Airlines for America "Smart Skies" initiative:

> Without dramatic change in the way our airspace is managed, congestion and resulting delays will be overwhelming for passengers, shippers, consumers, and businesses. Failure to meet future airspace demand could cost the US economy $40 billion annually by 2020.

While ATC in the United States remains under government control, federal agencies have begun to address the current problems with several recent developments.

Regulation

In response to numerous instances of passengers experiencing lengthy tarmac delays, the Department of Transportation (DOT) issued a final ruling entitled "Enhancing Airline Passenger Protections," also referred to as the three-hour tarmac rule, effective from April 29, 2010. This new regulation requires that when an aircraft is delayed at a large and medium hub airport, passengers must be given the opportunity to deplane no later than three hours after the cabin door has been closed. Exceptions to this rule are when an aircraft is returning to the gate, when the tarmac poses a safety or security risk, or when deplaning would severely disrupt airport operations. Particularly applicable to regional operations is the requirement that food and potable water must be made available no later than two hours after push-back or touch-down. This includes operable lavatory facilities while the aircraft remains on the tarmac. Furthermore, an airline that violates these rules can face a fine of up to $27,500 per passenger. Foreign flag carriers were initially exempt from the ruling, but in 2011, amendments required all foreign carriers with at least one aircraft with 30 or more seats to adopt and adhere to tarmac delay contingency plans. For international flights, the rule dictates that they are not allowed to remain on the tarmac at a US airport for more than four hours without allowing passengers to deplane subject to safety, security, and ATC exceptions.[9] In addition to these restrictions, the ruling also prohibits airlines from scheduling chronically delayed flights.

It is noteworthy to observe that in the eight months directly after the three-hour rule went into effect, cancellation rates at US airports rose 24%. Proponents of the ruling counteract this rise in cancellations with the fact that the data does not take into account variables like weather (one of the common causes for cancellations).

Air Traffic Control Charges

Another prospective strategy to control delays and congestion involves airports changing the charges levied on airlines from a uniform pricing structure (or one based on weights) to a congestion and peak-load pricing method. This pricing methodology was originally developed for roads where peak road usage is excessive because individual users do not take into account the delays imposed on other users. Economists have long argued for a similar pricing system at airports, according to each user and the marginal cost imposed on the other users of the system. This pricing system takes into account the differences in willingness to pay as well as the incremental costs of meeting demand during peak times when delays and congestion occur. European airports typically adhere to a weight-based system of charges with variations for day and night periods, alongside a slot coordination system. However, none of the major European airports makes use of a true congestion pricing method. The differences in charges between day and night are in accordance with strict noise abatement policies and not based on peak/off-peak periods.

Advocates of congestion pricing for airports point out that mid-sized airlines will redistribute their flights to off-peak hours. This strategic shift would enable hub airlines to operate more efficiently because of the reduced number of flights during peak hours and the airport benefits from increased revenues. Despite these economic benefits, peak-load pricing has encountered heavy criticism and has yet to be implemented in a North American airport. Presently, landing fees at North American airports are currently a function of landing weights and are unrelated to time of day or airport conditions. Instead of moving toward congestion pricing, some of the more congested airports are opting for slot controls where capacity is fixed to reduce congestion and delays.

Internal Efforts and Reform

At the present time, and for the foreseeable future, the FAA has been engaged in an ongoing program with the generic name of "NextGen." The need for NextGen became obvious during the summer of 2000, when air travel was hampered by significant delay and air-traffic congestion. The objective of this initiative is to enhance integrated communications and navigational devices to improve the flow of information and air traffic control. NextGen involves complex integrated, and interlinked programs, portfolios, systems, policies, and procedures. It has modernized air traffic infrastructure through fundamental changes in communications, navigation, and surveillance. Much like previous programs, the stated objectives of this program promise a huge improvement in some of the more outdated procedures and protocols that now exist.[10] As far as satellite navigation and communication are concerned, there is existing technology that can markedly improve the present system of point-to-point navigation and reliance on instrument landing systems. However, the actual implementation of these new technologies is a different matter altogether. Past experience has shown that it is challenging, if not impossible, to implement radical new technology and procedures under the present structure of the FAA. Again, bureaucracy tends to slow and hinder the development and use of these new technologies, which circles back to the question of reform. Can the FAA be streamlined enough to meet the challenges of the twenty-first century?

Recently, the industry itself has mounted a strong lobbying campaign in favor of reform. This effort has been led by the Airlines for America (formerly the Air Transport Association of America) and involves a political campaign aimed at influencing Congress to change the ATC system. Basically, the intent of the effort is to replace the existing ground-based radar and voice communication system with a more advanced technology. The new system will be based on a much more accurate surveillance technology, namely, the Automatic Dependent Surveillance Broadcast or ADS-B. This upgrade will also provide a more open standards-based architecture to replace the existing National Airspace System software. It will incorporate feature like airborne collision avoidance and shared intent information within the cockpit. Furthermore, the present communication method is to be replaced by a data link system allowing direct exchange of messages between controllers and pilots. Lastly, the new navigation systems that allow for direct routing will replace the current airway system.

Airport Ownership and Management

Privatization refers to the transfer of ownership or shifting of governmental responsibilities, and functions, in whole or in part, to a private party.

The concluding section of this chapter analyzes and discusses the appropriate ownership of airports and the use of pricing mechanisms to allocate and improve the scarce resources. According to Airports Council International (ACI), as of January 2022, ACI serves 717 members, operating 1,950 airports in 185 countries. In 2020, almost 55% of all employment in the aviation sector was at airports and airports worldwide managed 3.6 billion arriving and departing passengers, transported 108.5 million metric tons of cargo and 61.8 million aircraft movements. Furthermore, according to the FAA, there are 514 commercial airports in the United States. Among these, 422 feature more than 10,000 annual enplanements and are categorized as commercial service airports. Furthermore, the landscape includes 33 large hubs, with 379.14 million enplanements, 35 medium hubs, with 100.7 million enplanements, 68 small hubs, with 50 million enplanements in 2021. At present, almost all of the airports in the United States are under some type of government control. As mentioned earlier, a common product of this control is typically a pricing system (landing fees) that is fixed over the entire day. Consider Figure 13.5. If the airport authority sets a price below equilibrium for a particularly advantageous period of the day, it is easy to perceive that the quantity demanded would exceed the available supply by the amount of QE – QD. In this scenario, an alternative method must be found. This typically takes the form of delay for some or all of the aircraft and/or, in some cases, a rationing of the available landing times (slots) for the airport in question. Both of these solutions have inherent efficiency problems when considered from an economic point of view. Moreover, in case of slot controls, the airlines that are awarded the slots benefit from an economic rent.[11] Therefore, the issue becomes the appropriate ownership of airports. Many economists would maintain that private ownership of the airports would provide a better set of incentives for the long-term viability of the industry. The subsequent few sections discuss this question in more detail.

Trends in Airport Privatization

Across the globe, an increasing number of countries are rethinking the appropriate role for government in operation and ownership structure of aviation infrastructure. In Japan, Fukuoka Airport was privatized in 2019, with New Chitose in Hokkaido.[12] In another transaction, Vinci Airports of France was granted the right to acquire and operate Kansai Airport and Osaka International Airport for a 44-year duration, starting April 2016.[13] In 2012, the Brazilian government raised a total of $14.3 billion through the sale of a controlling interest in São Paulo Guarulhos International (GRU), Campinas Viracopos (CPQ), and Brasília International airports (BSB), three of the country's largest air travel facilities.[14] Many countries have privatized airports, with the understanding that the private sector can run airports more efficiently, akin to how it operates with airlines and aircraft manufacturers.[15]

In 1987, the British government led the way when it completely privatized seven major airports, selling BAA to the public for $2.5 billion. Subsequently, in 2006, the company was

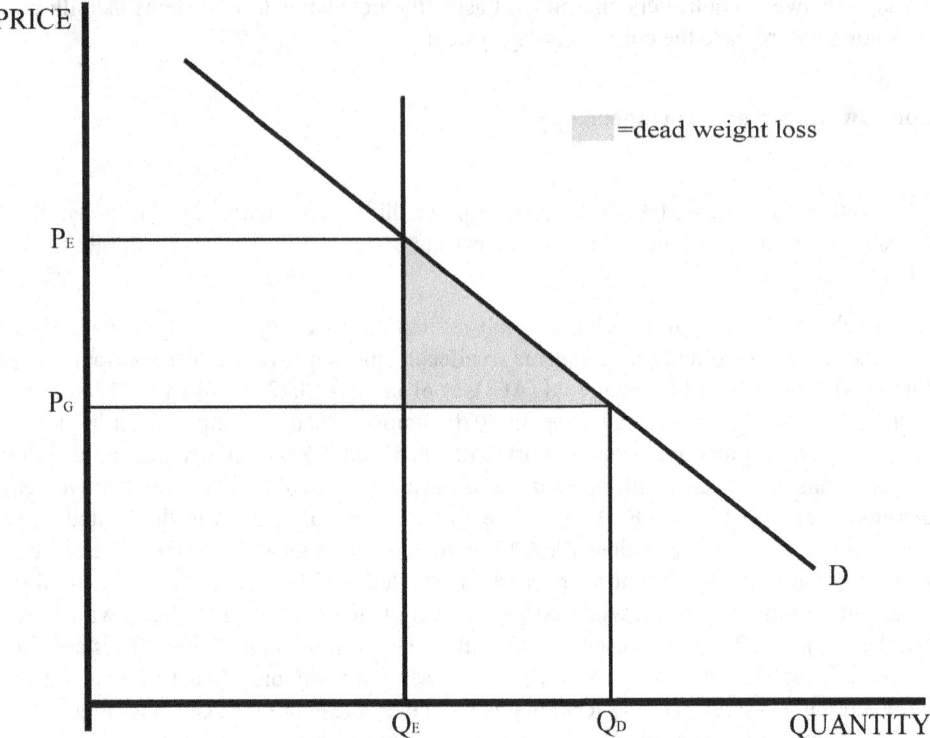

Figure 13.5 Demand for Airport Services.

purchased by the Spanish firm Ferrovial with a market value of $18 billion. At a certain juncture, BAA owned and operated five airports in the United Kingdom, including Heathrow, Stansted, Southampton, Glasgow, and Aberdeen in Scotland. It also operated Indianapolis International Airport from 1995 to 2007 and had retail-management agreements at Baltimore-Washington, Boston Logan, and Pittsburgh International, which eventually spun off into a new company, AirMall Inc. BAA was forced by the Competition Commission of Britain to sell Gatwick and Edinburgh in late 2011 on anti-competitive concerns. Subsequent sales followed, but the company is currently the largest airport operator, albeit under the name Heathrow Airport Holdings, which in turn is owned by a larger consortium. The remarkable achievements of BAA has led many countries to follow suit.

Over 100 airports worldwide have undergone at least partially privatized, including those in Belfast, Brussels, Budapest, Copenhagen, Düsseldorf, Frankfurt, Hamburg, Rome, South Africa, Argentina, Chile, Colombia, Mexico, Auckland, Brisbane, Melbourne, Sydney, and many other cities and countries. Consequently, dozens of companies are in the business of airport management. In fact, financial company, Macquarie, created a privatized airports mutual fund for global investors (Poole, 2007). About 75% of all passenger traffic in Europe and 66% of all passenger traffic in Latin America and the Caribbean passed through privately run airports in 2019.[16] Table 13.1 illustrates the 15 largest global airport groups based on the number of airports and annual passengers handled.

Numerous factors such as government regulation, availability of credit, and economic growth impact privatization initiatives. Following the 2008/9 financial crisis, many privatizations were suspended or aborted due to global credit issues. For example, Spain's attempt to divest its

Table 13.1 Largest Global Airport Groups

Company	*Base Country*	*Status*
Heathrow Airport Holdings	United Kingdom	Private
Aena SME, S.A.	Spain	Part-privatized: (51% Government, 49%)
Aeroports de Paris	France	Part-privatized: (51% French Sate)
Fraport AG	Germany	Part-privatized
Kansai International	Japan	Privatized[a]
TAV Airports	Turkey	Private
Beijing Capital International	China	Part-privatized[b]
Airports of Thailand	Thailand	Part-privatized
Manchester Airports Group	United Kingdom	Part-privatized
Aeroporti di Roma	Italy	Private
Flughafen Zürich	Switzerland	Private
Southern Cross Airport Holdings	Australia	Private
Gatwick Airport	United Kingdom	Private
Malaysia Airport Holdings	Malaysia	Part-privatized
SEA Group	Italy	Part-privatized
Schiphol	Amsterdam	Different governmental entities[c]
Narita International Airport	Japan	Privatized IN 2004

Source: Annual Privatization Report, and Reason Foundation.

[a] 80% owned by Orix and Vinci, with the remaining 20% owned by Kansai-based enterprises.
[b] The company's shares were listed on the Hong Kong Stock Exchange on February 1, 2000.
[c] State of the Netherlands (69.77%), Government of Amsterdam (20.03%), Groupe ADP (8.0%), and Government of Rotterdam (2.2%).

El Prat airport in Barcelona and Barajas airport in Madrid was put on hold when German airport operator Fraport, Spain's Fomento de Construcciones ContraFtas SA, and Singapore's Changi Airports International all pulled out of the bidding citing the difficult market situation (Dominguez and Perez, 2012).

In the United States, Luis Muñoz Marín International Airport in San Juan, Puerto Rico, stands as the sole airport with a private operator under the provisions of the Airport Investment Partnership Program (AIPP). As of December 2022, Hendry County Airglades Airport, a general aviation airport in Clewiston, FL, is another participant in the AIPP[17].

Reasons for Privatization

While there is no conclusive empirical evidence to definitively support the proponents of selling or long-term leasing of airports to the private sector, several perceived principal advantages are:

- Greater efficiency of operations, particularly in developing the non-aviation side of the airport
- Capital infusion from non-traditional sources
- Lower labor costs resulting from either lower wages or less input
- Conversion of a public airport to a tax-paying corporate entity
- Risk transfer

In addition to their general efficiency, private companies can readily raise funds for needed airport projects without entanglement in the political problems and delays that often plague government airports looking for grants to expand or renovate. Moreover, these companies can engage in equity financing, while government is only able to issue debt. Of course, potential problems with privatization (Vasigh and Gorjidooz, 2006) do exist. Concerns have been raised that, even with continued government regulation, a private company may not be motivated to properly maintain infrastructure. However, two decades of experience seem to indicate that such issues are relatively rare. Most economists would probably argue that profit motives provide strong incentives for proper maintenance of airport infrastructure. Given that consumers tend to be hyper-sensitive to safety concerns in air travel, even a hint of corner-cutting in this regard is likely to depress demand and sink profits. Additionally, private airports are more likely to be held accountable by liability laws since it is generally easier to sue a private party for damages than the government.[18] In essence, a private airport appears to maintain the regulatory incentive for safety as a government airport since there is no change in safety regulations with privatization. However, the incentive of stricter legal liability and of a profit motive prevails. Indeed, these added safety incentives for private companies may explain why one seems more likely to encounter dangerous infrastructure failures of government-owned levies, bridges, and roads than on private roads, parking lots, or other structures.

Opposition to Privatization

Airline and passenger dissatisfaction with privatization typically arises when the service level deteriorates and airport users face skyrocketing prices. Following a complaint by British Midland International of discriminatory pricing, the UK Civil Aviation Authority launched a formal investigation into passenger and landing charges at London Heathrow during April 2011 (Buyck, 2011). Another concern occasionally voiced is that private airports might go bankrupt. While this is a valid possibility, bankruptcy is more a financial disaster for stockholders than an operational problem for air travelers. Just as airlines have continued to operate normally in bankruptcy, viable airports would likely do the same. Furthermore, if management is markedly at fault, then a bankruptcy judge might just as well eject such management. Thus, bankruptcy provides a new channel, one not available in the case of mismanaged government airports, for eliminating poor management.

The main objection to airport privatization is that airports have monopoly power and, if private, will raise landing fees to inefficiently high levels. Ultimately, airports can only charge airlines higher fees if airlines are able to pass on those higher costs to customers. It is probably safe to assume that the leisure traveler will not bear such costs. In other words, leisure travelers will likely either travel by other modes of transportation or fly via more distant airports if prices go up substantially at their home airports. Business travelers might be more inclined to pay higher prices but even in their case, the monopolist airport must consider competition from other transportation modes, secondary airports, modern telecommunications, corporate jets, and the developing "air taxi" competition from the very light jets that can operate from smaller airports. The situation is similar to that discussed under "contestability" theory in Chapter 9. In other words, the potential for competition may be sufficient to preclude extreme monopoly pricing behavior on the part of privatized airports. Smaller airports and those airports acting as significant hubs for connecting passenger flows may face sufficient competition for airport charging to be efficient. However, numerous large city airports are dominated by passengers traveling to and from the city, and they often encounter very little competition, resulting in substantial market power over the level at which they set charges. In such circumstances, most economists strongly advocate independent, incentive-based, economic regulation to mimic a competitive market.

Although the theoretical grounds for supporting airport privatizations seem solid to most economists, actual experience may be the most persuasive evidence. The very fact that so many different governments are abandoning control of their airports is a strong statement in favor of privatizing. After some initial skepticism, there now seems to be strong support for the argument that divestiture can enhance the efficiency of airport operations (Truitt and Michael, 1996). Vasigh and Hamzaee emphasize the benefits of privatization of airports in Western Europe, Latin America, and Asia, providing inspiration for officials in search of new economic opportunities to transform publicly run airports into private businesses (Vasigh, Yoo and Owens, 2004).

Types of Privatizations

The techniques used to privatize airports vary in terms of the scope of responsibility and the degree of ownership transferred to the private sector. Each type of privatization has its own advantages and disadvantages, and the decision to privatize depends on the specific context and goals of the government. Several types of privatization exist, which are discussed here.

Build-Operate-Transfer (BOT) and Build-Own-Operate (BOO)

These approaches are mainly used when the requirement to expand airport capacity arises. They have the characteristics of a long-term franchise for infrastructure facilities under which projects are built, operated, and eventually transferred to the government in contractual agreements with private sectors parties. The private sector shifts risk, effectively reducing the burden from the private sector. In addition, the upfront and operating costs can be reduced, generating long-term profitability. In the build-operate-transfer (BOT) method, a private investor or pool of investors will build and operate the airport and then transfer it back to the government. This approach aims to generate enough revenue to build large infrastructures. Under the Build-Own-Operate (BOO) method, the private entity remains the owner of the project for the lifetime of the project.

Airport Concessions

A traditional privatization tool involves the contracting of selected services (restaurants, parking, security services, cargo, baggage handling, and/or fueling services) to the private sector, while the government retains overall operating responsibility for the airport. More comprehensively, under the contract management approach, the government transfers all responsibility for all airport operations and implementation of strategy to the private sector, while retaining the ownership and investment responsibilities. For example, AIRMALL is the developer and managing company of retail at Pittsburgh International, Cleveland Hopkins, and Boston Logan.[19] As airlines have consolidated and focused on controlling aeronautical costs, many airports depend significantly on non-aeronautical sources of revenue. Today, airports' largest income is generated from restaurants and parking.[20]

Management Contract

Under a management contract, the operator is responsible for the day-to-day operation, security, and routine maintenance of the airport facilities under the direction of the airport commissioner. Presently, several US airports currently operate under management contracts, including Westchester County Airport in New York, Orlando-Sanford in Florida, and Bob Hope Burbank Airport in California, which are jointly owned by the cities of Burbank, Glendale, and Pasadena. TBI Airport Management Inc. has been managing Burbank Airport for over a decade, receiving a fixed management fee plus expenses for the services it provides the facility. However, the airport authority is responsible for capital improvements. Burbank Airport, which ranks fifty-ninth in size among US airports (as measured by annual passenger enplanements), is commonly considered a viable model of public–private partnerships in airport operations. However, in October 2011, airport employees voted to affiliate themselves with the International Union of Operating Engineers due to pay below industry averages.

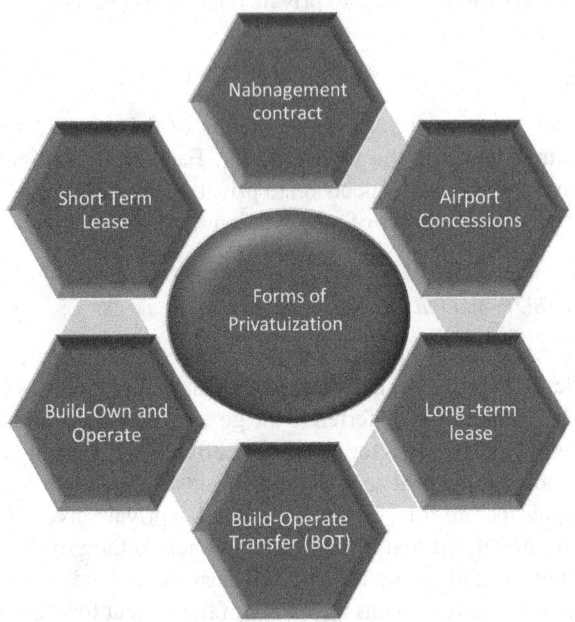

Similarly, in October of 1995, the BAA assumed the management of Indianapolis International Airport promising to raise non-airline revenues by $32 million within the ten-year contract period. The contract was renegotiated in 1998 and extended until 2008. Between 1995 and 1999, costs per passenger were reduced from $6.70 to $3.70, and in spite of a moderate passenger annual growth rate of 3.5%, non-airline revenue per passenger more than doubled by 2003 (Vasigh and Haririan, 2003). The private management of the airport ended on December 31, 2007, and control was smoothly transitioned back to Indianapolis International Airport management.

Long-Term Lease

This approach allows the government to legally (and politically) retain ownership but to transfer investment, operational, and managerial responsibilities to a private tenant. The duration of lease must be long enough to motivate the private tenant to more or less behave as an owner. This method can be employed to facilitate financing of airport construction or an associated project by the private sector, which must then relinquish control at the end of the lease term. Recent instances of this form of public–private partnership exist. Examples include the 99-year lease of Sydney Airport, and Brazil's recent awarding of three concession contracts (20, 25, and 30 years) for its busiest airports. One well-known example of such a lease arrangement is Teterboro Airport in New Jersey. The lease to operate Teterboro was established in 1970, when Pan American World Airways (now known as Johnson Controls World Services) secured a 30-year lease with Teterboro's owner, the Port Authority of New York and New Jersey. The lease expired in 2000, and the Port Authority resumed operation as scheduled. The Luis Muñoz Marín

International Airport in San Juan, Puerto Rico entered into a 40-year long-term lease concession with Aerostar Airport Holdings in 2013 in a deal valued at $2.6 billion over the life of the lease.[21] In 2022, American Corporate Airport Partners (ACAP) signed a long-term lease with Jefferson County to develop 30 acres for business aviation use at Rocky Mountain Metropolitan Airport (BJC) in Broomfield.

The third widely used method of privatization is the sale of either a part of the airport or the entire airport itself. Governments put up the airport for auction, to which the highest bidder will receive a portion or the entire airport ownership. In this scenario, the earnings from the sale usually go to reducing outstanding government debts or for other investment projects. Governments usually sell when they believe the airport is more efficiently operated by the private sector, or when the government is experiencing economic loss from operating the airport.

The Initial Public Offering is based on the first time offering of shares to public investors. The most widely known IPO transaction took place in 1987, when Prime Minister Thatcher proposed to sell off the British Airports Authority. Australia, on the other hand, raised more than $2.6 billion through the sale of Melbourne, Brisbane, and Perth airports. Some governments prefer to retain a minority or majority vote in the airport, leading to a sale of partial interests. A pioneering example of approach was witnessed in 1992 with the Vienna airport, Austria, and again in 1994 for the Copenhagen airport, Denmark.

An IPO can be part of a full sale, as in the case of BAA in 1987, or a partial sale, as in the cases of Bangkok in 2002 (30%) and Hong Kong (49%). It should be noted that even when an airport is sold, the government still retains substantial regulatory control in many areas, including safety and landing fees (Figure 13.6).

Privatization in the US Airport Industry[22]

In many countries around the world, except the United States, governments own and operate aviation infrastructure, including gates. These gates are assigned dynamically to airlines as needed (common-use gates). Airlines pay landing fees and space rentals, at pre-set rates, based on how much of the facilities they use. This model has continued under privatization, implying limited change for the airlines.

In contrast, the customary approach in the United States differs. Here, the typical approach involves anchor-tenant airlines signing long-term lease agreements with charges based on residual cost. In other words, the cost of operating the airport would first be covered by revenue sources other than the airlines, such as parking, concessions, and so on. Any remaining costs that are not covered by these revenues would then be assessed on the airlines via landing fees and space rentals.

In effect, these signatory airlines became joint owners of the airport. During prosperous periods, airports would take in more of the non-aviation revenues and the airlines would enjoy

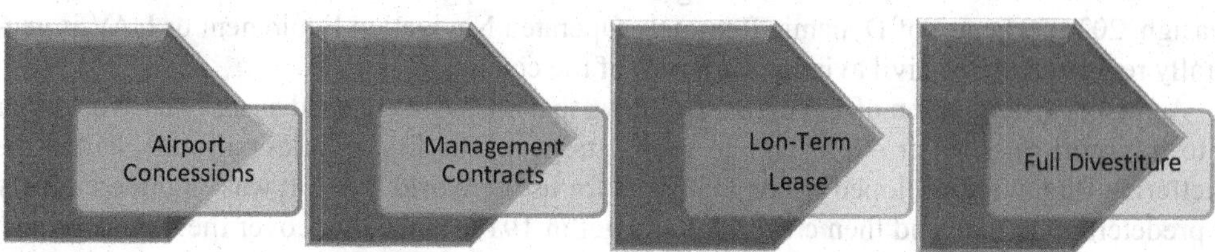

Figure 13.6 Levels of Airport Privatiozation.

lower fees. Conversely, during bad years with fewer passengers and therefore lower airport revenues, the airlines would have to pay higher fees. Thus, unfavorable years for the airlines become even worse.

One might expect the airlines to refuse an arrangement that makes their profits even more cyclical. However, two considerations make such an agreement worthwhile. First, the federal funding system for airport expansion is often so cumbersome that joint airport ownership/funding by airlines is the only viable way for the timely expansion of the airport. Second, airlines gain the ability to veto airport spending that they see as wasteful and might lead to more fees and charges. Consequently, US legacy carriers tend to have a vested interest in maintaining the status quo, opposing airport privatization because it might indirectly open their markets to more competition.

With the surge of airport privatization in the 1990s, there was a call for legislation to eliminate federal regulations hostile toward private airports. A key problem was that regulations were interpreted to imply that any local government that sold an airport would then have to repay all previous federal airport grants and, of course, that airport would be ineligible for any future grants. In order to tackle these concerns, the 1996 Airport Privatization Pilot Program was passed and supervised by the FAA. Under this program, cities whose airports were accepted for the pilot program would not have to repay previous grants.

However, political pressure, largely from the airlines, resulted in a provision that rendered the program essentially useless. In order to make use of lease or sale proceeds, a city must secure the approval of 65% of the airlines serving the airport. Otherwise, all profits must be reinvested in the airport, making the whole exercise, from the viewpoint of the airport owners, devoid of significant benefit.

The only airport actually privatized under the 1996 law was Stewart Airport in Newburgh, New York. However, this only lasted six years of the 99-year lease before being bought out by the Port Authority of New York and New Jersey, ironically, to initiate a $500 million expansion project that the firm wasn't willing to undertake. Furthermore, the project failed to secure the necessary airline endorsement, which in this case meant that the city could not have gained from the profit. As such, the sale or lease of US airports is likely to remain politically unfeasible for the foreseeable future, unless airline opposition weakens. Contractual privatization, either in part or its entirety, remains the only viable alternative.

Unmanned Aerial Systems

Dynamic Remotely Operated Navigation Equipment (Drones) are obviously disruptive technology that will change the way we think about deliveries, surveillance, exploration, disaster relief, inspections, and countless other domains. Concluding this chapter is presenting the work being done to develop and implement unmanned aerial vehicles (UAVs). Dangerous jobs, particularly infrastructure inspections, are being performed by commercial drones using high-resolution imaging with artificial intelligence packages, which can spot problems from afar (Jenkins and Vasigh, 2021). The use of Dynamic Remotely Operated Navigation Equipment or UAV is generally regulated by the civil aviation authority of the country.

A cursory examination of UAV history shows that drones were used as early as World War I to transport missiles or explosives to enemy targets. The first pilotless aircraft, called the Kettering Bug, was developed by the US Army for use in World War I. It was engineered to fly a predetermined path and then crash into a target in 1917. Since then, over the course of past century, drones have evolved from strictly military uses to hobby, civil, and commercial operations. The development of Global Positioning System (GPS) technology made it possible to program drones to fly autonomously, paving the way for their use in various applications beyond military use. The demand for drones is rapidly increasing in today's economy. The global defense industry is investing heavily in drone research and development. UAVs are considered a disruptive technology as they are changing the way various industries and services are approached. Disruptive technology refers to an innovation that disrupts an existing market, or technology by either creating a new market or changing the way existing markets operate. Cell phones serve as an exemplary disruptive technology in multiple ways since their introduction, and they have replaced landline communication. Since their inception, cell phones have been a disruptive technology, transforming the way people access information and communicate.

Classification of the Unmanned Aerial Systems

Drones come in a variety of sizes, from small handheld models that can fit in our palm to large industrial drones that can carry heavy payloads. The classification of UAS lacks a singular standard. The size of a drone is typically measured by its diagonal size, which is the distance between two diagonal motor centers. According to the US Department of Defense, UAVs are classified into five categories, as illustrated in Table 13.2.

Drones are capable of performing many tasks more efficiently than traditional methods, leading to cost savings for operational entities. According to a report by Grand View Research, the global commercial drone market size was estimated at $29.86 billion in 2022 and is anticipated to expand at a compound annual growth rate (CAGR) of 38.6% from 2023 to 2030. This section will explain the future demand, opportunities, and challenges associated with drones.

Numerous companies globally engage in manufacturing commercial drones, ranging from small startups to large multinational corporations. The French manufacturer Parrot produces consumer drones and professional drones for use in industries such as agriculture and construction. On the other hand, the Chinese company DJI is considered the largest drone manufacturer in the world. DJI produces a wide range of drones, from consumer-level to professional-grade drones used in the film industry and for search and rescue missions.

General Atomics is a US company that produces a range of military drones, including the MQ-1 Predator, MQ-9 Reaper, and Avenger drones. These drones are used for surveillance, reconnaissance, and strike missions. The Predator boasts a range of up to 1,000 nautical miles and can carry a payload of up to 450 pounds. As for the Reaper, it has a range of up to 1,850 nautical miles and can carry a payload of up to 3,750 pounds. This drone serves dual roles in both surveillance and strike missions.

Table 13.2 UAVs Classification According to the US Department of Defense

Category	*Size*	*Maximum Gross Takeoff Weight (lbs)*	*Normal Operating Altitude (ft)*	*Airspeed (knots)*
Group 1	Small	0–20	<1,200 above ground level	<100
Group 2	Medium	21–55	<3,500	<250
Group 3	Large	<1,320	<18,000 mean sea level	<250
Group 4	Larger	>1,320	<18,000 mean sea level	Any airspeed
Group 5	Largest	>1,320	>18,000	Any airspeed

Another notable player, Northrop Grumman, produces the RQ-4 Global Hawk, a high-altitude, long-endurance drone used for reconnaissance and surveillance missions. The Global Hawk has a range of up to 14,000 nautical miles and can carry a payload of up to 3,000 pounds.

The Federal Aviation Administration (FAA) is a national authority that has the power to regulate all aspects of civil aviation. All drones that weigh between 0.55 and 55 pounds must be registered with the FAA, including drones used for hobby or recreational purposes. In the recent development, the FAA has introduced new regulations that require drones to be equipped with remote identification (RID) technology, which allows for the identification of drones in flight. This technology is intended to enhance safety and security by allowing law enforcement and other authorities to identify drones that may be operating illegally or posing a threat to public safety.[23] All drone pilots required to register their UAS must adhere to the guidelines outlined in the final rule on remote ID beginning September 16, 2023.[24] In 2012, the federal government entrusted the FAA with determining how to integrate UAS into the National Airspace System (NAS). The US National Airspace System is composed of air traffic control facilities, navigational aids, airways, airports, rules, and regulations that support civil aviation and in many cases, military aviation.

Commercial Uses and Applications of Drone Technology

The main inhibitor of US commercial and civil development of UAS is the lack of a regulatory structure. Due to the prevailing airspace restrictions, non-defense use of UAS has been extremely limited. However, the combination of greater flexibility, lower capital, and lower operating costs could allow UAS to be a transformative technology in many diverse fields. In fact, UAS are already being used in a variety of applications, and many more areas will benefit by their use, including

- Aerial imaging/mapping
- Agricultural monitoring
- Disaster management
- Environmental monitoring
- Freight transport
- Infrastructure inspection
- Law enforcement
- Oil and gas exploration
- Telecommunication
- Television news coverage, sporting events, moviemaking
- Thermal infrared power line surveys
- Weather monitoring
- Wildfire mapping

Globally, drones have been used to monitor crop health, identify pest infestations, and assess crop yield. These applications furnish farmers with better decisions to increase their yield. UAVs equipped with high-quality cameras can capture dramatic aerial pictures and videos for various industries such as construction, film-making, and real estate. Additionally, drones can be used to inspect infrastructure such as bridges, pipelines, and power lines, without more flexibility and less cost. China has become a leader in drone technology and applications, using drones for agriculture, surveillance, disaster response, and transportation. In Brazil, drones are used for forest monitoring, crop management, and wildlife conservation. In Costa Rica, drones are used to capture stunning aerial footage of the beaches, mountains, and other natural beauties.

In the contemporary landscape, the UAS has longer operational duration and require less maintenance than earlier models. In addition, they can be operated remotely using more fuel-efficient technologies. These aircraft can be deployed in a number of different terrains and may be less dependent on prepared runways. Proponents argue that the use of UAS in the future will be a more responsible approach to certain airspace and airport operations from an environmental, ecological, and human risk perspective. Upon integration of airspace, numerous other markets will also use UAS. As of January 2022, several countries are working on new regulations, ranging from beyond line of sight (BLOS)[25] operations to unmanned traffic management (UTM) activities, which include the United States, the EU, India, South Korea, Japan, and Australia. Aviation authorities typically regulate drone BLOS operations to ensure safety and compliance with local laws.

In order to maintain a safe distance from airplanes, helicopters, and other aircraft systems and help prevent collisions, FAA restricted drones from flying in controlled airspace, but they must also stay away from crowded areas, be grounded during night-time, and fly only within a 400-foot altitude ceiling. However, BLOS operation imposes significant complications and endangers, including the risk of collisions with other aircraft or obstacles, loss of communication with the drone, and difficulty in detecting and avoiding dangers. To minimize aviation accidents, drone operators need to follow safety guidelines and best practices, including registering their drones, obtaining appropriate permits and certifications, and following airspace restrictions and regulations.

Summary

This chapter introduces the reader to some more practical applications of supply and demand that were introduced in the previous chapters, particularly within the context of air transport infrastructure. It explores the substantial control that government exerts over air traffic and the aviation industry as a whole. Privatization and liberalization can both play important roles in shaping the aviation industry, and policymakers need to carefully consider the costs and benefits of each approach when making decisions about privatization of State-Owned Enterprises (SOE). Employing supply and demand models, this chapter analyzes the costs of delay imposed by regulatory solutions as an external tax that has been levied on the industry through the failure of the regulatory agency to modernize and use effective technologies. The effects of these costs are not only large in the short run, but they are likely to grow even larger over the foreseeable future. Moreover, this chapter also uses supply and demand analysis to introduce the reader to the concept of airport privatization and the use of the market price system to allocate scarce resources at the airport. In Europe, many airports are owned and operated by private companies. Conversely, all US commercial airports are owned and operated by public entities, including local, regional, or state authorities with the power to issue bonds to finance some of their capital needs. Furthermore, more than 50 governments have commercialized their air traffic control (ATC) systems. Various approaches to privatization, both internationally and domestically, are discussed and critiqued in the last half of the chapter.

Discussion Questions

1 In what sense can it be said that the government controls the means of production for the airline industry?
2 In what ways are the effects of the regulatory delay tax more burdensome than the effects of an ordinary tax?
3 Why can it generally be assumed that the supply curve for the airline industry is relatively inelastic?

4 What are some of the benefits of airport and ATC privatization?
5 What are some of the ways in which the effects of an airport monopoly might be countered in the marketplace?
6 Suppose an airport has an inverse demand curve for landing aircraft where the demand: $P = 500 - 2 \times Q$. Assume that the airport is a monopoly and has negligible costs associated with landing aircraft.

 a Calculate the price that could be charged with this demand for the airport to maximize revenue.
 b Now suppose that the airport sets a price of $300. Calculate the dead weight loss that would result from this policy.

7 What are some of the problems associated with air traffic control commercialization?
8 If the supply of air travel is relatively inelastic, then who will bear the greater cost of congestion delay, the passengers, or the airlines?
9 What will be the long-term effects of continued congestion delay on the airline industry?
10 Explain how congestion pricing would alter traffic flow at an airport.
11 How has the historical development of air traffic control contributed to the point-to-point navigation that now exists?
12 Why might the air traffic control union oppose fully automated air traffic control?
13 Why might airlines that already had intercontinental route and slot positions oppose a more open navigation regime provided by satellite control?
14 What tends to happen over time to the regulating agency in a regulated industry?
15 List some reasons why the airlines might desire commercial air traffic control.
16 Would congestion pricing completely do away with delay at busy airports?
17 Discuss the various forms of privatization that are available for airport operation. Has one been more successful than the others?
18 Why is it so difficult to expand airports in the modern age?

Appendix

Airport	*Airport Code*
Auckland, New Zealand	AKL
Beijing, China, Capital	PEK
Belfast City Airport, Ireland	BHD
Berlin, Germany, Schoenefeld	SXF
Berne, Switzerland, Belp	BRN
Birmingham, AL, USA	BHM
Bologna, Italy, Guglielmo Marconi	BLQ
Boston, MA, USA, Logan International Airport	BOS
Brasilia, Distrito Federal, Brazil	BSB
Bristol, UK	BRS
Brussels, Belgium, National	BRU
Budapest, Hungary	BUD
Charlotte, NC, USA, Charlotte/Douglas Intl Airport	CLT
Chicago, IL, USA, O'Hare International Airport	ORD
Cincinnati, OH, USA, Greater Cincinnati Intl Airport	CVG
Copenhagen, Denmark	CPH
Dallas/Ft Worth, TX, USA	DFW
Denver, CO, USA	DEN
East Midlands, UK	EMA
Frankfurt, Germany	FRA
Hamburg, Germany	HAM
Haneda, Japan, Tokyo International Airport	HND
Helsinki, Finland	HEL

(*Continued*)

Airport	*Airport Code*
Houston, TX, USA	IAH
Leeds/Bradford, UK	LBA
Lisbon, Portugal, Lisboa	LIS
London, UK, Gatwick	LGW
London, UK, Luton	LTN
Madrid, Spain, Barajas	MAD
Narita International Airport, Japan	NRT
Newcastle, UK	NCL
Paris. France, Charles De Gaulle Airport	CDG
Rio De Janeiro, Brazil	GIG
Rio De Janeiro, Brazil, Santos Dumont	SDU
Rome, Italy, Ciampino	CIA
Rome, Italy, Leonardo Da Vinci/Fiumicino	FCO
Singapore Airport, Singapore	SIN
Sydney, Australia	SYD
Toronto, Ontario, Canada	YYZ
Vancouver, British Columbia	YVR
Verona, Italy	VRN
Warsaw, Poland, Okecie	WAW
Zurich, Switzerland, Zurich	ZRH

Notes

1 *The Wall Street Journal*, April 27, 2016.
2 The effect of this regulation is covered in greater detail in later chapters.
3 Principal among these developments were precise methods of navigation and the ability to accurately locate the position of any aircraft in the sky.
4 Among these considerations were the location of facilities and the question of union job loss.
5 In essence, this is merely a way of expressing the standard principle that demand (and supply) in the long run is more elastic than in the short run. For simplicity, we have omitted the long-run curves and focused on the additional shifts in the short-run curves.
6 Air Traffic Control Modernization. GAO 17-450, August 31, 2017.
7 Annual Privatization Report. Reason Foundation. March 2014.
8 Ibid.
9 Department of Transportation, Rules and Regulations: Federal Register Vol. 76, No. 79, April 25, 2011.
10 The Federal Aviation Administration, Next Generation Air Transportation System (NextGen), 2020.
11 An economic rent, also known as Ricardian theory of rent, is the payment over and above that needed to keep a factor of production in its current use.
12 *Asian Review*, December 30, 2015.
13 Ibid.
14 Dow Jones Newswires, February 3, 2012.
15 See Chapter 2 for a discussion of why efficiency tends to be enhanced by reducing the government's role.
16 *The Atlantic*. Privatizing airports is a no-brainer. January 18, 2022
17 Congress established the Airport Investment Partnership Program (formerly Airport Privatization Pilot Program) in 1997 to explore privatization as a means of generating access to various sources of private capital for airport improvement and development.
18 Of course, overly harsh liability laws can be an impediment to economic efficiency and consumer well-being, and many would argue that tort reform would render liability laws less harsh. However, tort reform is not a necessary pre-condition to airport privatization—many companies are clearly interested in buying airports under the existing tort system, whatever its faults.
19 AIRMALL Selected to Manage Concessions at New York's John F. Kennedy International Airport Terminal 5, Press Release, August 31, 2016. www.airmallusa.com.

20 How Airports Handle Non-Aeronautical Revenue. Aviation Pros. August 26, 2016.
21 Project Profile: Luis Muñoz Marín International Airport Privatization, Federal Highway Administration, July-August 2014.
22 This section draws heavily from Poole (2007) and Vasigh, Yoo, and Owens (2004).
23 Federal Aviation Administration, UAS Remote Identification.
24 Ibid.
25 BVLOS refers to the operation of a drone when it is not in direct visual range of the operator.

References

Buyck, C. (2011, July 7). London Heathrow Charges Investigated by CAA after BMI Complaint. *Air Transport World.*

Dominguez, P. and Perez, S. (2012, January 12). Spain Grounds Airport Privatization Plan. *The Wall Street Journal.*

Federal Aviation Administration. (2005). *International Terminal Air Traffic Control Benchmark Pilot Study.* Federal Aviation Administration.

Jenkins, D. and Vasigh, B. (2021). Drone Economics: Succeeding with the World's Newest Form of Transportation.

Kent, R. (1980). *Safe, Separated, and Soaring: A History of Federal Civil Aviation Policy, 1961–1972.* Washington DC: DOT/FAA.

Poole, R. (2007). *Will Midway Lease Re-Start U.S. Airport Privatization?* Reason Foundation, Public Works Financing.

Truitt, L. and Michael, J. (1996). Airport Privatization: Full Divestiture and Its Alternatives. *Policy Studies Journal*, 24(2), 100–124.

Vasigh, B. and Gorjidooz, J. (2006). Productivity Analysis of Public and Private Airports: A Causal Investigation. *Journal of Air Transportation*, 11(3), 142–162.

Vasigh, B. and Haririan, M. (2003). An Empirical Investigation of Financial and Operational Efficiency of Private Versus Public Airports. *Journal of Air Transpiration*, 8(1), 91–110.

Vasigh, B., Yoo, K., and Owens, J. (2004). A Price Forecasting Model for Predicting Value of Commercial Airports: A Case of Three Korean Airports. *International Journal of Transport Management*, 1(4), 225–236.

14 Climate Change and the Contribution of Transport

Climate change is now widely accepted by scientists as posing a serious threat to our wellbeing, through increasing global temperatures, sea level rise, and more volatile and extreme weather events. These climate impacts, in themselves, have operational consequences for aviation. For example, they affect the location of low-level airports and management of flight operations in the face of more volatile weather. However, it is the indirect impacts of climate change that might have the most significant effects on the economics of air transport. Government policymakers are reacting in different ways, but with a similar intention to incentivize a switch away from fossil fuels to low or no carbon aviation fuels. That typically has resulted in a higher cost to fly. Passengers and shippers might also be changing their behavior in response to a growing ethical concern about man-made climate change. So far, this has been limited, with the 'flygkamm' or 'flying shame' movement in Scandinavia and a number of companies limiting business air travel being the most significant. If science is correct, then climate change could become the most influential public policy impact on air transport in the future.

The challenge for air transport lies in its inherently high energy intensity. It requires a lot of fuel to keep several hundred passengers and their luggage airborne within an aluminum or composite tube at 35,000 feet. Additionally, some low-carbon alternative fuels are impractical for air transport due to issues like freezing at typical aircraft altitudes or insufficient density or excessive weight for practical purposes. However, because the cost of fuel is such a high proportion of total operating costs, typically 25%–30%, the air transport industry and its suppliers put a lot of effort into fuel efficiency, which has improved more than seven-fold since the introduction of the jet engine in the 1950s. Not many industries can match that fuel efficiency improvement. The challenge is that the demand to fly from both passengers and shippers has surged far more than fuel efficiency has improved. Although airlines use much less fuel to fly a passenger or a cargo load today than they did 10 or 20 years ago, the total volume of greenhouse gas emissions from fuel combustion has increased substantially due to the substantial increase in the frequency of flights. Aviation is still a small proportion of man-made emissions, at around 2% of CO_2 emissions. However, it is growing fast, and the emissions are difficult or costly to mitigate. Moreover, scientific evidence suggests there exists only a limited capacity for additional greenhouse gases to be released in the atmosphere if we are to prevent catastrophic climate change. As a result, pressures are mounting for more significant industry action or more stringent government policy measures. If these significant changes are to be implemented, while preserving the benefits of connecting cities with air transport, then it is critical to have a good understanding of the economics of climate change in this important economic sector.

DOI: 10.4324/9781003388135-14

This chapter will examine the following topics:

- Greenhouse Gas Emissions from Air Transport
- Impacts on the Climate
- Economics of Emissions Abatement
- Government Policy Response
    - o Emissions Trading and Baseline and Credit Schemes
    - o Carbon Taxes
    - o Low or No Carbon Fuels

Greenhouse Gas Emissions from Air Transport

Air transport is, not surprisingly, highly energy-intensive. It takes a lot of fuel to keep several hundred passengers and their luggage flying in an aluminum or composite tube at 35,000 feet. In 2019, each airline passenger, on average, used almost 20 gallons of fuel on their average flight distance of 1,188 miles (ATAG 2021), which is around half way from New York to San Francisco. Interestingly, flying can be more fuel-efficient that driving. Modern aircraft such as the Boeing 787 or the Airbus A350 have a fuel efficiency of 2.3–3 L per 100 km per passenger, which is better than most cars. However, it is crucial to note that each flight covers a greater distance than the typical car journey, and the automotive fleet is currently undergoing electrification. Commercial airlines use almost exclusively Jet-A1, which is a refined kerosene-type fossil fuel derived from oil. A small portion (around 0.1%) of flights use Sustainable Aviation Fuels, currently derived from waste oils. The combustion of all these fuels generates a number of greenhouse gas emissions from the engine tailpipe, the most significant of which is Carbon Dioxide (CO_2). According to Air Transport Action Group (ATAG) (2021), the commercial airline industry worldwide generated just over 900 million tons of CO_2 in 2019.

Figure 14.1, taken from Lee et al. (2021), illustrates the challenges facing air transport. While fuel efficiency (measured here by kilos of CO_2 per RPK) has improved dramatically and continuously, due to the exponential growth in demand to fly, the total amount of CO_2 emitted from air transport has grown significantly. Europe and the Americas constitute the biggest emitters, but the fastest expansion, and the issue for resolving this problem in the future, lies in China and other large emerging Asian markets.

Carbon dioxide is such a damaging greenhouse gas due to its long-lasting existence in the atmosphere, sometimes persisting for centuries. As a result of this, any CO_2 emission mixes thoroughly in the atmosphere and so it bears no significance whether the emission takes place on the ground or at 35,000 feet; they have the same climate impact. This characteristic renders a global economic policy instrument, such as a carbon tax or an emissions trading scheme, highly suitable for delivering the type of financial incentive across sectors and countries to mitigate CO_2 that economists would recommend. More elaboration on this will follow.

However, flying at 35,000 feet does have an impact on the climate that differs from ground transport. The most significant among these (non-CO_2) climate impacts comes from aircraft condensation trails (contrails), when flying through ice-saturated, low-temperature air, and from the soot and sulfur found in aircraft emissions prompting the formation of clouds, as shown in Figure 14.2 (Lee et al. 2021). The reaction of aircraft NOx emissions with sunlight at altitude also increases ozone, a greenhouse gas, but it destroys methane, another greenhouse gas. The net effect seems to be a small addition to air transport's climate impact, but much less than either contrails or CO_2. A feature of these non-CO_2 climate impacts is that they are typically

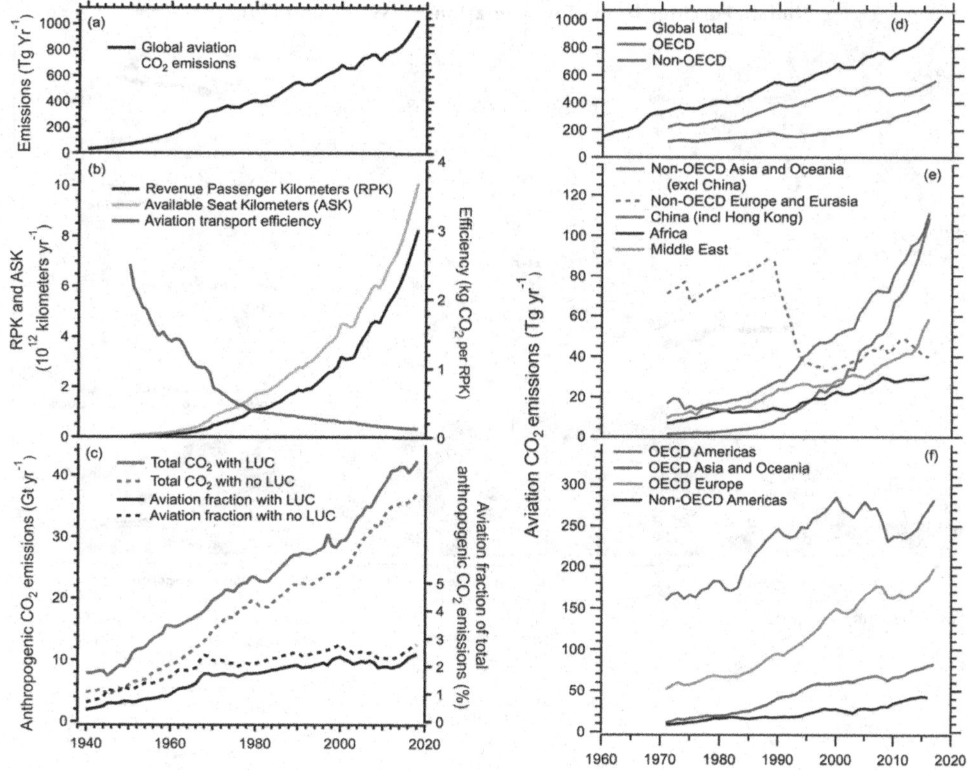

Figure 14.1 Historic CO_2 Emissions from Air Transport.

Source: Lee et al. (2021)

short-lived. As a result, and unlike CO_2 global impacts, the impacts from contrails and NOx are seen concentrated along heavily used routes. This feature implies that the economics of air transport might be influenced by more local policy measures, such as requirements to fly at altitudes where the air is not ice saturated. Such measures could impact the competitiveness of some routes compared to others, in a manner that a global carbon price on CO_2 emissions would not. At present, most policy attention revolves around CO_2 emissions, with less emphasis on other climate impacts.

Impact on the Climate

Climate scientists have measured the impact of CO_2 on global temperature change with a fairly high degree of precision, which is why Figure 14.3 illustrates quite narrow 5%–95% confidence bands around the mean impact estimate. Figure 14.3 also demonstrates that aircraft contrails have potentially a significantly larger effect than CO_2, although the broader 5%–95% confidence bands underscore the lower level of certainty in this case. Nevertheless, this highlights that mitigating greenhouse gases beyond CO_2 will be necessary for air transport in the future.

The most commonly used metric of climate impact on surface temperatures is called radiative forcing. This metric pertains to the change caused by a particular greenhouse gas on the net balance of inward energy from the sun and outward reflected radiation from the earth, measured

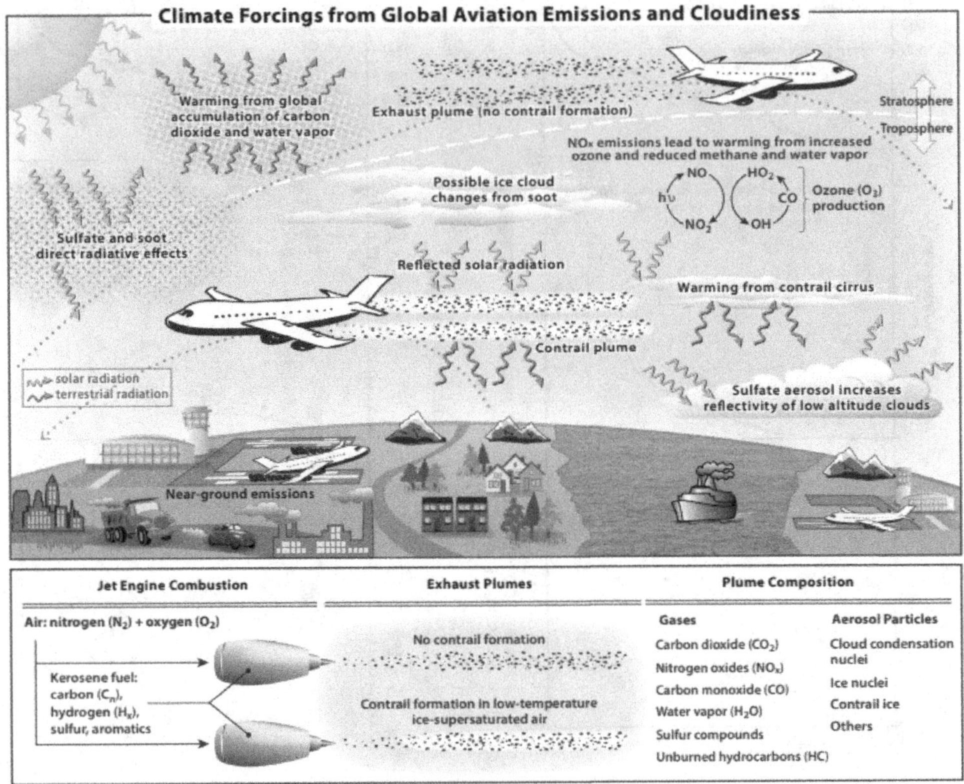

Figure 14.2 Emissions and Climate Effects from Air Transport.

Source: Lee et al. (2021)

in Watts per square meter. Both CO_2 and contrails act as a blanket trapping some of the outward radiation of solar energy from the earth, thereby contributing to the warming of surface temperatures. According to Figure 14.3, the current estimates of the climate impact of commercial air transport around the world from all its greenhouse gas emissions over 1940–2018 are a mean radiative forcing of 100 milliwatts per square meter, relative to pre-industrial levels.

A potentially more intuitive approach of understanding the importance of air transport's impact on the climate involves acknowledging a principle from climate science: global surface temperature change is correlated to the stock, the atmospheric concentration, not the flow of greenhouse gases (IPCC 2018). This observation is an important issue for CO_2. IPCC (2001) estimated an atmospheric residence time for CO_2 of 5–200 years. Further studies (Archer et al., 2009) have found that 20%–35% of the CO_2 remains in the atmosphere after equilibration with the ocean over a span of 2–20 centuries.

However, the focus of the debate on aviation climate policy has been on the sector's greenhouse gas emissions, specifically, the annual flow of CO_2 (and other gases) into the atmosphere. ICAO (2019), in it's 40th Assembly resolution on environmental protection, asserts, "Acknowledging that international aviation emissions, currently accounting for less than 2 per cent of total global CO_2 emissions, are projected to increase as a result of the continued growth of air transport." The principal policy measure to control aviation climate impacts in international airspace is ICAO's (ICAO 2016) Carbon Offsetting and Reduction Scheme for International

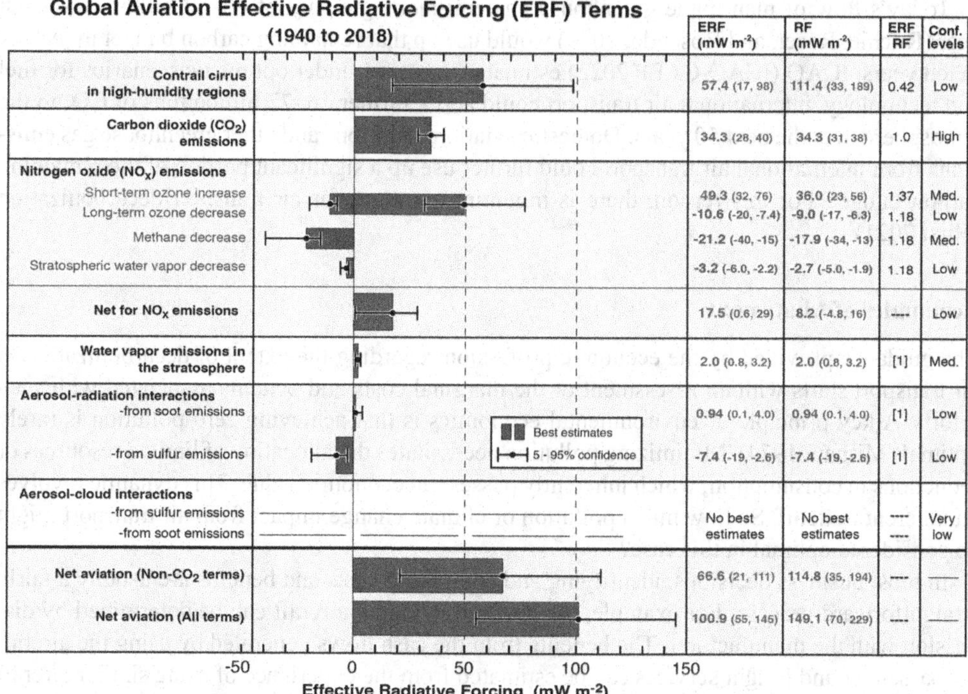

Global Aviation Effective Radiative Forcing (ERF) Terms
(1940 to 2018)
ERF (mW m⁻²)
RF (mW m⁻²)
ERF/RF
Conf. levels
Contrail cirrus in high-humidity regions 57.4 (17, 98) 111.4 (33, 189) 0.42 Low
Carbon dioxide (CO2) emissions 34.3 (28, 40) 34.3 (31, 38) 1.0 High
Nitrogen oxide (NOx) emissions
Short-term ozone increase 49.3 (32, 76) 36.0 (23, 56) 1.37 Med.
Long-term ozone decrease -10.6 (-20, -7.4) -9.0 (-17, -6.3) 1.18 Low
Methane decrease -21.2 (-40, -15) -17.9 (-34, -13) 1.18 Med.
Stratospheric water vapor decrease -3.2 (-6.0, -2.2) -2.7 (-5.0, -1.9) 1.18 Low
Net for NOx emissions 17.5 (0.6, 29) 8.2 (-4.8, 16) ---- Low
Water vapor emissions in the stratosphere 2.0 (0.8, 3.2) 2.0 (0.8, 3.2) [1] Med.
Aerosol-radiation interactions
-from soot emissions 0.94 (0.1, 4.0) 0.94 (0.1, 4.0) [1] Low
-from sulfur emissions -7.4 (-19, -2.6) -7.4 (-19, -2.6) [1] Low
Aerosol-cloud interactions
-from sulfur emissions
-from soot emissions
No best estimates
No best estimates

Very low
Net aviation (Non-CO2 terms) 66.6 (21, 111) 114.8 (35, 194) ----
Net aviation (All terms) 100.9 (55, 145) 149.1 (70, 229) ----
Best estimates
5 - 95% confidence
-50
0
50
100
150
Effective Radiative Forcing (mW m⁻²)

Figure 14.3 A Measure of the Impact on the Climate of Air Transport Greenhouse Gas Emissions.

Source: Lee et al. (2021)

Aviation (CORSIA), designed to cap the flow of emissions at the rate at which CO_2 was being emitted in 2019. Therefore, if successful, then international air transport will still continue to emit into the atmosphere each year some 600 million tons of CO_2, as estimated by ICAO CAEP (2021). A stable flow, even if capped, implies a still increasing stock and therefore an increasing contribution to global temperature rise resulting from air transport.

ICAO has now adopted what it calls a "long-term aspirational goal" of achieving net zero CO_2 emissions by 2050 (ICAO 2022). This step begins to address the issue of air transport's increasing impact on the climate. A (net) zero flow of emissions would stabilize the stock, but it would only stabilize air transport's impact on the climate rather than eliminate the associated damage. The question facing this, as well as other sectors and countries attempting to meet "net zero" goals, is whether this would be sufficient to achieve the legally-binding target of the Paris Agreement (UNFCCC 2015). These targets aim to limit temperature rise above pre-industrial levels to 2°C, or the 1.5°C target that States have committed to striving for.

A key issue is that climate science modeling (IPCC 2018) suggests that adding little more to the stock of greenhouse gases in the atmosphere would be necessary to have a good chance of avoiding a surface temperature increase of more than 1.5°C. The integrated assessment models of climate scientists estimate that if another 500 billion tons of greenhouse gases were added to the atmosphere, there would only be a 50% chance of limiting the global surface temperature rise to 1.5°C. To achieve an 83% chance, it would require limiting the addition to the stock of greenhouse gases in the atmosphere to no more than 300 million tons.

Today's flow of man-made greenhouse gas emissions globally of 45–50 billion tons each year (Ritchie, Roser, and Rosando, 2020) would use up that remaining carbon budget in just six to ten years. ICAO (ICAO CAEP 2022) estimates that even under optimistic scenarios for fuel and technology, international air transport could add a further 16–72 billion tons of CO_2 to the atmosphere over the next 50 years. Domestic aviation emissions and other greenhouse gas emissions from international air transport could further use up a significant portion of the remaining carbon budget. For this reason, there is mounting pressure for air transport decarbonization (Hirst 2021).

Economics of Abatement

The guidance provided by the economic profession regarding the extent of decarbonization in air transport starts with an assessment of the marginal costs and benefits associated with such efforts. A key principle of environmental economics is that achieving zero pollution is rarely optimal (Misham 1974). Minimizing pollution necessitates the allocation of limited resources or reductions in consumption, which inherently possess an economic value. This dynamic involves an inherent tradeoff. So how much pollution or climate change impact from air transport might be considered optimal in this case?

In most business decisions, identifying and comparing costs and benefits are usually a fairly straightforward process. For example, the cost of buying an aircraft can be determined by discussion with the manufacturer. The benefits from the cash flows generated by using the aircraft for passenger and freight services can be estimated from the experience of using similar aircraft in similar markets in the past, even if the future is less certain. A decision can be made on whether to buy the aircraft or not. The challenge posed by the climate change issue is that the benefit of preventing temperature change is not traded and thus lacks monetary value revealed by a market. This serves as an example of what economists call an externality or external cost (external to markets). In some jurisdictions, governments have attempted to fill that gap in markets by imposing a carbon tax or an emissions cap and trade scheme. In the absence of such mechanisms, air transport companies lack a market incentive or benefit to abate greenhouse gas emissions, beyond the incentive provided by the cost of jet fuel. Nor is there an easily available monetary value for the benefit of abatement for governments to use to compare with marginal abatement costs in order to assess the optimal level of greenhouse gas abatement across the industry.

An answer to this problem is provided by environmental economists, who employ various techniques to value externalities, in this case the economic value of the damage caused by climate change and, in particular, the value society places on a marginal reduction in such damage to our climate. Perhaps unsurprisingly, a wide range of such estimates exist, which are subject to change over time and influenced by different assumptions, particularly, the social discount rate. Nordhaus (2017), using the DICE-integrated assessment model, estimates the social cost of carbon (SCC) to be 37.3 \$/Ton CO_2 in 2020, projecting to increase to \$51.6 by 2030 and \$102.5 by 2050. As he reports, higher estimates can be derived by imposing a hard limit on (predicted) temperature rise, generating a 2030 SCC of \$351, which is close to that derived using a lower social discount rate in the Stern Review (Stern 2007).

If the Nordhaus estimate of \$51.6 is taken as the marginal benefit of reducing 1 ton of CO_2 in 2030, the point of optimal CO_2 abatement can be derived from the point where that crosses the air transport industry's marginal CO_2 abatement cost curve.

McKinsey (2009) illustrates the results of an exercise with IATA and others in the air transport industry. This initiative aimed to estimate a marginal abatement cost (MAC) curve for global commercial air transport, as depicted in Figure 14.4. This was constructed by estimating

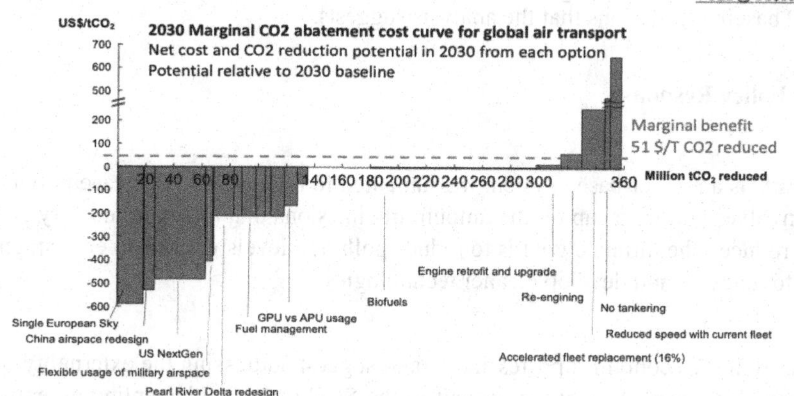

Figure 14.4 Comparing the SCC or Marginal Benefit with an Estimated Marginal Abatement Cost Curve for Global Commercial Air Transport.

the potential reduction in CO_2 emissions that could be achieved through each of the measures shown, such as the airspace improvements in the US NextGen project or engine retrofits. The abatement possible is shown on the horizontal x-axis of Figure 14.4. The value of the net fuel and any block hour savings minus the amortized capital cost of the measure is shown on the vertical y-axis, in US$ per ton of CO_2 abated. Each of the measures is ordered in the marginal abatement cost curve, ranging from the cheapest to the most expensive options.

The Nordhaus estimate of the SCC or the marginal benefit of reducing a ton of CO_2 of $51 crosses the MAC curve at a CO_2 abatement level of 300–320 million tons, which is approximately 25% of baseline emissions in 2030. Importantly, even if a very low social discount is employed and the estimated SCC is much higher, at $350, the optimal level of CO_2 abatement is not much higher at 340 million tons or 28% of 2030 baseline emissions. The MAC curve rises very steeply beyond this point, as known abatement options become very costly. Even at a SCC of $600 the optimal level of CO_2 abatement in air transport globally would be no more than 360 million tons or 29% of 2030 baseline emissions.

Nordhaus (2017) reports the wide range of estimates for the SCC. The MAC curve is also uncertain. Keseicki (2011) discusses the issues arising from adopting different approaches to estimating a MAC curve, ranging from the partial or general equilibrium model-based to the expert-based, bottom-up, engineering-cost approaches. The MAC curve in Figure 14.1 is based on an expert-based, bottom-up, engineering-cost approach, rather than being derived from a model. As such, each of the individual technology levers in Figure 14.1 represents the technical maximum potential abatement. Although the full capital and operating costs of implementing each CO_2 reducing measure was taken into account, there will be market imperfections imposing costs not included. The significant abatement opportunities from airspace improvements shown in Figure 14.1, with negative abatement costs, fail to consider the costs of the political barriers that hinder implementation. Nor are any behavioral impacts taken into account in this approach. Note that the impact on demand of imposing an SCC on air transport is not included in this MAC curve. Hourcade, Jaccard, Bataille, and Ghersi (2006) report that bottom-up modeling of MAC curves is likely to underestimate costs and overestimate optimal abatement due to omitting micro and macro feedbacks, while the opposite is true for top-down model base approaches, which tend to overestimate abatement costs. Consequently, although the MAC curve in Figure 14.1 is subject to considerable uncertainty, it probably underestimates abatement costs. Therefore, optimal CO_2 abatement may be even less than the 25%–29% reduction from the 2030 baseline emissions that the analysis suggests.

Government Policy Response

Cap and trade is a market-based system instrumented to regulate and decrease pollution levels. It involves putting a cap on the amount of emissions that a certain industry is allowed to produce. The ultimate goal is to reduce pollution levels while also encouraging industries to innovate and develop cleaner technologies.

The advice from the economics profession would suggest addressing the externality by imposing a carbon price through a tax equivalent to the SCC or by implementing an emissions cap and trade scheme across the economy. This approach would anticipate other sectors, where abatement costs are lower, would undertake more abatement efforts compared to air transport, where abatement is costlier (Helm 2005). Indeed, this is the approach that has been implemented in jurisdictions such as the European Union (expanded to include all EEA-EFTA states) with the EU Emissions Trading Scheme (EU ETS) (European Commission, 2023a), which includes all CO_2 emissions from air transport within its borders. The EU ETS emerged due to the failure of attempts to introduce a carbon tax in Europe during the 1990s and skepticism about the effectiveness of voluntary schemes. However, reviewing the evidence of the scheme's first two phases from 2005 to 2012 Laing, Sato, Grubb, and Comberti (2013) found an emissions reduction of only 2%–4%, in part due to excessive issuance of emission allowances. The Kyoto Protocol's attempt to establish a global market-based mechanism to control greenhouse gas emissions ended in failure (Napoli 2012). Many attempts to introduce carbon taxes have also ended in failure, such as the proposal in France in 2009 (Bremner 2009). So, apart from the EU ETS (with doubts about its effectiveness), there are few market-based policy instruments that impose a consistent carbon price across sectors in which air transport would participate as envisaged by standard economic advice.

A further issue is whether our standard tool of economic analysis, the cost benefit analysis of a marginal change is appropriate for an issue like climate change, where both the benefits and costs are non-marginal. Dietz and Hepburn (2010) demonstrate, using the DICE integrated assessment model, that the standard marginal cost benefit analysis can produce misleading results when the measure or impact is sufficiently large.

As a result, there are proposals for the decarbonization (beyond just facing decisions with the social cost of carbon) of hard-to-abate sectors, including air transport. These proposals came from entities such as the Energy Transitions Commission (2018). Some mainstream economists are now advocating for more radical measures, beyond the standard economics advice outlined earlier: "Short of a technological transformation, and quickly, if climate change is to be mitigated, shipping and air travel will have to diminish" (Helm 2020).

Little is being done by the government to bring about such a radical transformation in air transport's climate impact. At present, policies are doing little more than to slow the increase in air transport's damage to the climate (Larson, Elofsson, Sterner, and Akerman, 2019).

A significant challenge faced by governments aiming to reduce air transport greenhouse gas emissions is that 65% of CO_2 emissions take place in international airspace (Fleming and de

Lépinay, 2019), falling outside the direct control of individual governments. Governance in international airspace relies largely on UN bodies and their agencies, but that requires States to agree. The political climate today is not helpful for getting the agreement between governments necessary to decarbonize air transport in international airspace. Multilateralism has declined and protectionism risen for trade and many other cross-border issues (Fize, Martin, and Delpeuch, 2021). The same has been true for climate policy with the failure of the Kyoto Protocol (Napoli 2012) and, arguably, the failure of the ongoing COP process (Helm 2021).

The UNFCCC has delegated the management of greenhouse gas emissions from international air transport to ICAO (UNFCCC 1997). However, many are critical about the effectiveness of ICAO on this kind of issue in air transport. Lyle (2018) asserts, "ICAO's past and ongoing success has lain predominantly with air navigation, safety, and security matters. The Organization has never managed to reach a multilateral aviation agreement on economic issues, despite several attempts."

In 2019, the ICAO States did reach a multilateral agreement on capping the growth of CO_2 emissions from international air transport (ICAO 2019) with its Carbon Offsetting and Reduction Scheme for International Aviation (CORSIA). However, several important States (including China, India, Russia, and Brazil) formally expressed reservations about the resolution, suggesting that their future participation is not assured. Moreover, CORSIA represents an Assembly resolution, not a treaty, so there are no enforcement powers, except by individual states on their own airlines. The scheme undergoes a review every three years, potentially leading to increased stringency but also the possibility of weakened provisions. Notably, the baseline has already been weakened by raising it to pre-COVID-19 2019 levels. Consequently, no offsetting will occur until emissions fully recover. Until then, the effective carbon price from CORSIA will remain zero (Schneider 2022). The more fundamental problem with CORSIA has already been discussed at the start of this paper that, even if emissions growth is successfully capped, there will still be baseline CO_2 emissions of approximately 600 million tons (ICAO CAEP 2021) cumulating in the atmosphere each year, contributing to air transport's damage to the climate.

International policy has, so far, failed to even stabilize air transport's increasing damage to the climate.

There has been much more cohesion between States within the European Union, but even here regional policy for the decarbonization of air transport has largely failed. According to EASA (2022), the full-flight CO_2 emissions of aircraft departing from EU27+EFTA airport reached a new all-time high of 147 million tons in 2019. In 2020, the 57% fall witnessed was due to the COVID-19 pandemic, not policy. Laing, Sato, Grubb, and Comberti (2013) assert that attempts in the 1990s to introduce a carbon tax were rejected in favor of a carbon tax and that, unfortunately, appears to have proved too vulnerable to the lobbying of vested interests (Helm 2009). Only 22% of full-flight CO_2 emissions from departing flights in 2019 were covered by allowances in the EU ETS (EASA 2022), and the EU ETS allowance or carbon price for most of the life of the cap and trade scheme had been too low and too volatile, far below estimates of the social cost of carbon and little incentive for innovation and low carbon investment.

This situation changed from 2019 with the introduction of the Market Stability Reserve to "address the current surplus of allowances" (European Commission, 2023b) by directly adjusting the supply of allowances in order to manipulate the price. As a result, EU Allowance prices rose from around 20 €/ton CO_2 in early 2019 to €100 by early 2023. The current price is close to, or above, the central range of estimates of the social cost of carbon (Nordhaus 2017) and should now incentivize innovation and low carbon innovation. However, although air transport within European airspace should now face a carbon price close to the SCC, we have ended up with what is in effect an extremely complex and costly European carbon tax.

Emissions Trading and Baseline and Offset Schemes

Traditional forms of government regulation would impose absolute limits on an air transport company's greenhouse gas emissions or mandate the use of the "best available technology" in a command-and-control approach. Economic analysis demonstrates that this approach is often unnecessarily bureaucratic and inefficient. Tradeable allowances schemes with an overall cap on emissions such as the European Union Emissions Trading Scheme are an example of market-based instrument, in contrast to the command-and-control regulatory approach.

In an emissions trading scheme, a limit or cap is established on the emissions released within a particular jurisdiction, such as the EU, during a specific time period. Allowances are then issued up to the allowed cap. Various methods exist for the initial distribution of allowances among firms. A common way is to base the distribution on historic emissions, which is known as grandfathering. This approach does nothing to reduce emissions until the cap is reduced below historic emissions. Any firm generating fewer emissions that the allowances given to them receives a credit, which is tradeable. Some firms will find that reducing emissions by a certain amount is more economical than the price of allowances. If the firm's marginal cost of abatement is below the allowance price, then there is an incentive to abate and sell allowances. If marginal abatement costs are higher than the permit price and if emissions are higher than the firm's allowance allocation, then the firm will buy allowances.

The tradability of allowances stands as the key feature of this form of market-based instrument, as it is designed to keep the overall cost of complying with the cap lower than that of command-and-control regulations. Through trading, the cost of controlling greenhouse gas emissions should be concentrated among those firms who can efficiently reduce their emissions inexpensively. Allowance holdings should be concentrated in those firms who find it costly to abate. In the EU ETS, for example, airlines are typically buyers of allowances since they possess few cheap options to reduce emissions and sectors such as power, having switched to low-carbon fuels, have sold allowances. However, the overall environmental damage from these emissions remains capped because nothing has happened to alter the total number of allowances, and this is what determines the overall quantity of emissions and environmental impact.

To demonstrate how emissions trading schemes work, consider a hypothetical example involving two companies from different sectors, one an airline and the other a power company. In this example, each is emitting 10 tons of CO_2 each year. The bars depicted in Figure 14.5 and the first row of Figure 14.6 illustrate the (marginal) cost faced by each firm when attempting to reduce or abate 1 ton of CO_2.

Assume the regulator decides to implement a command-and-control regulation for each firm to abate 1 ton of CO_2. The cost to power company A is £20 and for the airline, where emissions are difficult to abate, it is £50. So the overall cost for the two firms to meet the environmental objective of limiting CO_2 emissions to 18 tons is £70.

Alternatively, within an emissions trading scheme, the regulator would issue 18 allowances, each representing permission to emit 1 ton of CO_2. If a grandfathering allocation method is employed, each firm would get nine allowances. The regulator allows trading of allowances and so they have a monetary value due to their potential for sale. Assume the allowance price is £25, as shown in Figure 14.5. Power company A can reduce its emissions from 10 to 9 tons, aligning with allowances at a cost of £20 (its marginal abatement cost). But it pays firm A to abate by more. If power company A abates by 2 tons, they can trade one allowance with airline B. Airline B will wish to pay firm A £25 for an allowance in order to avoid having to cut emissions by one ton at a cost of £50.

The outcome will be that the regulator achieves the objective of cutting overall emissions by 2–18 tons. However, within the trading framework, power company A cuts 2 tons, while there are no cuts in the hard-to-abate airline firm B. Figure 14.6 illustrates that each firm gains from

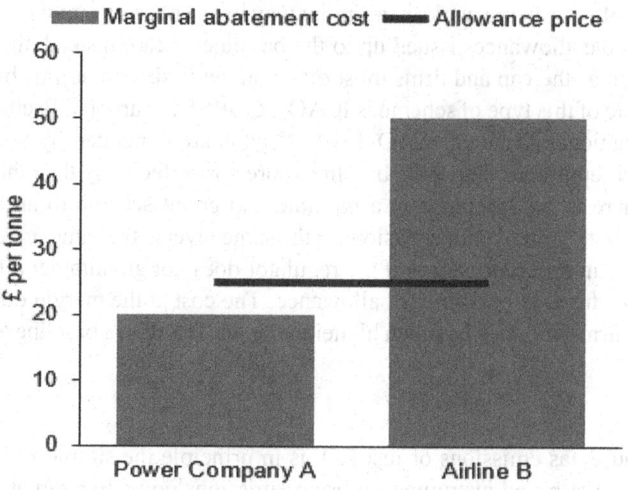

Figure 14.5 An Example of Marginal Abatement Costs and Allowance Price in an ETS.

	Power company A	Airline B
Cost of abating emissions by 1 ton, with no trading	£20	£50
Actual abatement with trading	2 tons	0 tons
Actual abatement cost with trading	£40	£0
Less sale of allowance	£25	
Plus purchase of allowance		£25
Net cost with trade	£15	£25
Gains from trade	£20-£15=£5	£50-£25=£25

Figure 14.6 An Example of the Gains from Trade in an ETS.

this trading arrangement. The net cost for the power company A under an emissions trading schemes (ETS) is £15, the cost of abating 2 tons less the revenue from selling one allowance. Under a command-and-control regulation to cut 1 ton without trading, the cost would have been £20, resulting in a net gain of £5 for Power Company A. Airline B faces a net cost of £25 for buying an allowance to avoid abating 1 ton of CO_2. Under a command-and-control regulation, it would have been £50, resulting in a net gain of £25 through trade for airline A.

This demonstrates that where the cost of abatement varies across companies and sectors, a market-based instrument, like an emissions trading scheme, can achieve the same reduction in emissions as a command-and-control regulation, but at a much lower cost.

A baseline and offset scheme works in a similar way to an emissions trading scheme. However, there are no tradeable allowances issued up to the baseline or cap. Instead, the baseline level of emissions is treated as the cap and firms must offset any emissions over this baseline by buying credits. An example of this type of scheme is ICAO's CORSIA (Carbon Offsetting and Reduction Scheme for International Aviation, ICAO 2019). Credits are generated by those in the scheme who can abate their emissions below the baseline more cost-effectively than the price of a credit. At the margin, there is no difference in a baseline and credit scheme to an emissions trading scheme. They can both limit overall emissions to the same level at the same price for an allowance or credit. A significant difference arises if the regulator does not grandfather allowances for free, but instead requires firms to pay for each allowance. The cost at the margin does not change but the overall cost to firms will then be much higher under an ETS than a baseline and credit scheme.

Carbon Tax

A tax on greenhouse gas emissions or just CO_2 is in principle the simplest way for a regulator to implement a market-based instrument to bring emissions down to a target level. In practice, it has proven to be, politically and practically, challenging for carbon taxes to be introduced.

This political difficulty has been despite the likelihood that a tax would be much cheaper than a command-and-control regulation. Figure 14.7 illustrates the difference for Airline A and Power Company B of a tax at £5 a ton of CO_2 and a regulation requiring both to abate emissions to point C2. If instead the regulator used a tax, at £5 as depicted in Figure 14.7, then Airline A with steeply rising abatement costs, would abate its emissions up to the point where the tax crosses its marginal abatement cost (MAC) curve at X, implying abatement of C1. Power Company B, with lower and more slowly rising abatement costs would find it pays to abatement more at point Y on its MAC curve, implying abatement of C3.

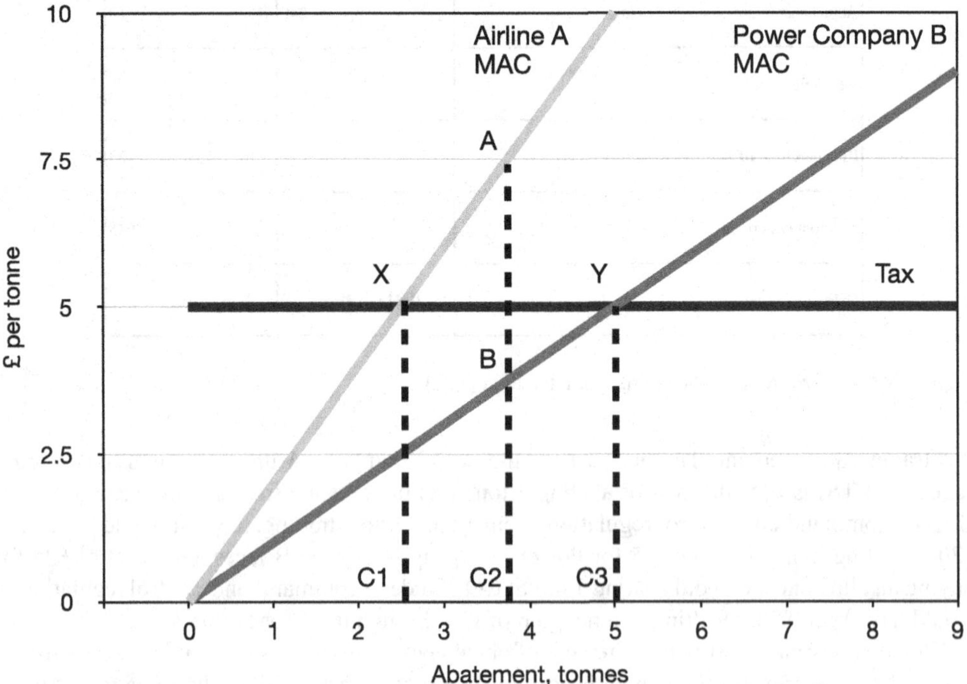

Figure 14.7 The Costs of a Carbon Tax Compared to a Command and Control Regulation.

This outcome closely resembles to an emissions trading scheme or baseline and credit scheme. Abatement takes place where it is most cost-effective. Airlines are a hard-to-abate sector with only very costly options for abatement. So under all these market-based instruments, they will end up achieving very little abatement but financially supporting other sectors to do more. Since there is a cost to undertaking abatement, this is the most efficient way of achieving the emissions target. As depicted in Figure 14.6, both firms stand to gain from trading. It also holds true that both firms under a tax-based approach will gain compared to complying with a command-and-control equal "burden sharing" regulation.

Under the command-and-control regulation to limit emissions:

Abatement cost (ACcac) = 0AC2 + 0BC2

Under the tax:

ACtax = 0XC1 + 0YC3

So, to compare the cost of both policy instruments, from Figure 14.7 it can be seen that:

ACcac - ACtax = C1XAC2- C2BYC3

It can be seen that C1XAC2 is larger than C2BYC3.

Therefore, the command-and-control regulation costs more than the tax. A tax would be more cost-effective for industry and the wider economy.

Low- or No-Carbon Aviation Fuels

CO_2 emissions and other pollution generate external costs as they are not traded in markets; however, they have an impact on others. The purpose of market-based instruments like a tax or an ETS is to introduce a price or a cost to the externality of emitting greenhouse gases like CO_2. This approach creates a financial incentive for firms to be as CO_2 efficient as possible, in the same way how fuel prices incentivize airlines to minimize their consumption of jet fuel. Airlines possess a number of options to reduce or abate CO_2: buy allowances or pay the tax, reduce emissions through more efficient operations, airspace efficiency improvements or better technology. Each of these abatement options will be incentivized to varying degrees by the carbon price created through a tax of an ETS.

The analysis of ETS and tax is made on the basis that airlines have limited cost-effective options to independently abate emissions through operations, infrastructure, or technology. In other words, the airline's CO_2 marginal abatement cost curve rises steeply, with much of it lying above the carbon price generated by any tax or allowance price within an ETS. The price of jet fuel in an industry as energy-intensive as airlines is such a strong incentive that most of the affordable options to reduce emissions have already been implemented through efficient operations and the purchase of fuel-efficient aircraft. Therefore, economists have always advocated for industries like air transport to be subject to a market-based instrument, to financially support other sectors to do most of the greenhouse gas abatement the world needs to stop damaging climate change. It is important to note that in order for market-based instruments to work effectively, by incentivizing the easy-to-abate sectors to do much of the abatement of CO_2, other sectors need to be included. A tax or ETS on air transport alone will do little to reduce emissions.

A relatively new concern arises from climate scientists' models, indicating that the world is on the brink of experiencing detrimental climate change. These models emphasize that only a limited number of emissions can be added to the stock of greenhouse gases in the atmosphere. Market-based instruments that work by establishing a carbon price to incentivize abatement and innovation is clearly uncertain and takes time to work. Climate scientists underscore the urgency of the situation, prompting policy makers to propose that air transport should focus on its own decarbonize, rather than relying on paying others through a tax or ETS.

Current technical analysis suggests that the only way to decarbonize air transport is through a low or no carbon fuel. Engines and airframes keep getting more efficient. Airspace could be made more efficient. However, air transport is such a competitive industry that any such efficiencies get passed through to passengers and shippers in lower air fares. The stimulus to demand more than offsets the fuel savings from efficiencies. Taking carbon out of aviation fuels seems the only answer at present.

It is challenging to replace Jet Kerosene because it is just the type of energy dense fuel needed, with the properties required to fly several hundred people and their baggage in an aluminum or composite tube at 35,000 feet. Many biofuels freeze at altitude and batteries for electric propulsion are heavy. But a number of Sustainable Aviation Fuels (SAF) have now been certified, at least as a 50% blend with Jet Kerosene, and widely used in flights around the world. These are what are known as 'drop-in' fuels that can use existing fuel infrastructure and engines, and can fuel long-haul flights.

The majority of biofuels in use by air transport in 2023 were created from waste oils through the Hydroprocessed Esters and Fatty Acids (HEFA) process. But a number of other processes for generating renewable jet fuel have been approved: Fisher-Tropsch hydrocracking (FT), Methanol to jet (MtJ), Ethanol or Alcohol to jet (AtJ). These all have renewable feedstocks such as waste oil, tires and plastic, or biomass. Early generations of biofuel used crops that competed with the land required for food crops, which was not sustainable. Concerns have been raised that waste oil and biomass will not be available in sufficient quantities over the long future periods required. Today SAF production is around 200,000 tons. To meet net zero targets by 2050, it would need to expand by 1,600× to around 360 million tons. That would require a 500 million liter output SAF facility coming online every 11 days until 2050, which is quite a challenge.

A significant problem today is that SAF is not commercially viable. Production costs are typically two times or more than the cost of Jet Kerosene. No commercial airline will use such an expensive fuel, except in minor quantities for Corporate Social Responsibility purposes. This issue is being addressed in the United States with substantial producer subsidies. In the EU, another approach is being adopted and that is a fuel mandate requiring 30% of aviation fuel in 2030 to be SAF and 63% by 2050. Unless economies of scale reduce costs, or the EU introduces US-style subsidies, this will significantly increase the cost of aviation fuel and air transport.

Biomass- or waste-based SAF is likely to be the focus for decarbonizing air transport over the next decade. But aside from competing with food crops and doubts about water and biomass supply, biomass-based SAF does not completely eliminate greenhouse gases. In fact, the emissions from aircraft tailpipes using SAF are almost identical to using Jet-A1. Both fuels consist of the hydrocarbons that generate CO_2 and NOx emissions. The reduction in CO_2 with SAF comes through the absorption of CO_2 in growing the biomass used to make the fuel. These fuels can reduce net or "life-cycle" CO_2 emissions by up to 80%, but there remains 20% or more than needs to be dealt with.

SAF is produced from renewable resources such as feedstocks, including waste oils and fats, agricultural residues, and non-food crops.

SAF has the potential to reduce greenhouse gas emissions from aviation by up to 80% compared to traditional aviation fuels.

A newer generation of SAF uses renewable electricity to produce green hydrogen, which is combined with carbon from direct air capture or electrolysis, to produce a synthetic aviation fuel. This process is called power to liquid (PtL) creating a SAF sometimes known as eJet. This process can reduce life-cycle CO_2 emissions by 90% or more. Electric power using lighter batteries is also now looking feasible for narrow-body short-haul aircraft. However, more than 60% of CO_2 emissions are produced on long-haul international flights, for which electrification looks unsuitable. PtL SAF and liquid hydrogen look to be the future for long-hail air transport. PtL SAF can use existing fueling infrastructure and aircraft engines. Liquid hydrogen will need a new generation of aircraft. Both, however, require very large increases in the infrastructure for renewable energy and producing and storing green hydrogen. Some estimates suggest investment of up to $2 trillion will be required. It seems highly likely that this will significantly add to the cost of air transport in the future.

Conclusions

Anyone interested in the economics of air transport will need to take climate change into account in the future. Today this public policy issue is only impacting air transport at the margins, but if achieving net zero CO_2 emissions targets by 2050 is sincere, then air transport faces imminent impacts. Two to three decades is a relatively short time span in aerospace and air transport investment and development. Air transport is one of the hard-to-abate sectors in the economy and its emissions are relatively small. With no "climate emergency" the sensible and expected option would be for air transport to be subject to a carbon price via more widespread and consistent emission trading schemes or carbon taxes. However, given climate scientists warnings that little more can be added to the atmospheric concentrations without damaging climate change, there is growing pressure for air transport to decarbonize. That means low or no carbon fuels. Over the next decade, that looks likely to mean biomass or waste-derived SAF, if production can be scaled up. The US approach is to offer a carrot in subsidies, the EU a stick in the form of mandates. In the longer term, then short-haul electrification with PtL and liquid hydrogen fuels may be the future. It seems likely this will mean higher prices for air transport users.

Discussion Questions

1. What greenhouse gases are produced by aircraft engines?
2. Is it the stock or the flow of CO_2 emissions that is more important for climate impacts?
3. How do aircraft condensation trails impact the climate?
4. What are the consequences of a limited "carbon budget" on air transport?
5. Describe the shape and consequences of aviation's CO_2 marginal abatement cost curve.
6. Is a command-and-control regulation or a market-based instrument better for controlling air transport CO_2 emissions?
7. Why is an Emissions Trading Scheme cheaper for air transport than a command-and-control regulation?
8. In which way are a carbon tax and an ETS equivalent policy instruments?
9. What has been the experience of governments introducing market-based instruments?
10. Why is there policy pressure for air transport to decarbonize further than under a market-based instrument?
11. Why might biofuels not be Sustainable Aviation Fuels?
12. If SAF costs twice as much as Jet Kerosene to produce, what will be the consequence of the EU's mandates?
13. Compare and contrast the US and the EU approaches to stimulating SAF production.
14. What will air transport look like in a world that achieves net zero CO_2 emissions?

References

Archer, D., et al. (2009). Atmospheric Lifetime of Fossil Fuel Carbon Dioxide. *Annual Review of Earth Planetary Science*, 37, 117–134. http://climatemodels.uchicago.edu/geocarb/archer.2009.ann_rev_tail.pdf (accessed 23 February 2023).

ATAG (2021). *Tracking Aviation Efficiency*. https://aviationbenefits.org/media/167475/fact-sheet_3_tracking-aviation-efficiency-v2.pdf (accessed 14 March 2023).

Bremner, C. (2009). Blow to President Sarkozy as carbon tax is thrown out. *The Times*, 31 December 2009. https://www.thetimes.co.uk/article/blow-to-president-sarkozy-as-carbon-tax-is-thrown-out-zll2jvr92jw (accessed 26 February 2023).

Dietz, S. and Hepburn, C. (2010). On non-marginal cost-benefit analysis. Centre for Climate Change Economics and Policy Working Paper No. 20 Grantham Research Institute on Climate Change and the Environment Working Paper No. 18. https://www.lse.ac.uk/granthaminstitute/wp-content/uploads/2014/02/Workingpaper18.pdf (accessed 26 February 2023).

EASA. (2022). *European Aviation Environmental Report: Emissions*. https://www.easa.europa.eu/eco/eaer/topics/overview-aviation-sector/emissions (accessed 5 March 2023).

Energy Transition Commission. (2018). Mission Possible: Reaching Net-Zero Carbon Emissions from Harder-To-Abate Sectors by Mid-Century. Green Industry Platform.

European Commission. (2023a). *EU Emissions Trading Scheme*. https://climate.ec.europa.eu/eu-action/eu-emissions-trading-system-eu-ets_en#about-the-eu-ets (accessed 26 February 2023).

European Commission (2023b). *Market Stability Reserve*. https://climate.ec.europa.eu/eu-action/eu-emissions-trading-system-eu-ets/market-stability-reserve_en (accessed 5 March 2023).

Fize, E., Martin, P., and Delpeuch, S. (2021). *Trade Imbalances and the Rise of Protectionism, CEPR*. https://cepr.org/voxeu/columns/trade-imbalances-and-rise-protectionism (accessed 1 March 2023).

Fleming, G. and de Lepinay, I. (2019). *ICAO Environmental Report 2019, Environmental Trends in Aviation to 2050, ICAO*. https://www.icao.int/environmental-protection/Documents/EnvironmentalReports/2019/ENVReport2019_pg17-23.pdf (accessed 1 March 2023).

Helm, D. (2005). *Climate-Change Policy*. Oxford University Press.

Helm, D. (2009). *EU Climate-Change Policy - A Critique, The Economics and Politics of Climate Change*. Oxford University Press.

Helm, D. (2020). *Net Zero: How We Stop Causing Climate Change*. London: William Collins.

Helm, D. (2021). *COP26 – So Was That It?* http://www.dieterhelm.co.uk/energy/climate-change/cop26-so-was-that-it/ (accessed 1 March 2023).

Hirst, D. (2021). *Aviation, Decarbonization and Climate Change*. House of Commons Library. https://commonslibrary.parliament.uk/research-briefings/cbp-8826/ (accessed 24 February 2023).

Hourcade, J.-C., Jaccard, M., Bataille, C., and Ghersi, F. (2006). Hybrid Modeling: New Answers to Old Challenges - Introduction to the Special Issue of The Energy Journal. *Energy Journal*, 27, 1–11.

ICAO. (2022). *States Adopt Net-Zero 2050 Global Aspirational Goal for International Flight Operations*. https://www.icao.int/Newsroom/Pages/States-adopts-netzero-2050-aspirational-goal-for-international-flight-operations.aspx (accessed 23 February 2023).

ICAO. (2016). *Resolution A41-22: Consolidated Statement of Continuing ICAO Policies and Practices Related to Environmental Protection - Carbon Offsetting and Reduction Scheme for International Aviation (CORSIA)*. https://www.icao.int/environmental-protection/CORSIA/Documents/Resolution_A41-22_CORSIA.pdf. (accessed 22 February 2023).

ICAO. (2019). *Assembly Resolution A40-18: Consolidated Statement of Continuing ICAO Policies and Practices Related to Environmental Protection - Climate Change*. https://www.icao.int/environmental-protection/Documents/Assembly/Resolution_A40-18_Climate_Change.pdf (accessed 22 February 2023).

ICAO. (2019). *Summary Listing of Reservations to Resolutions A40-18 and A40-19*. https://www.icao.int/Meetings/a40/Documents/Resolutions/a40_res_sum_en.pdf (accessed 1 March 2023).

ICAO CAEP (Committee on Aviation Environment Protection) (2021). *CAEP Inputs to the 225th Session of the ICAO Council on the 2022 Corsia Periodic Review*. https://www.icao.int/environmental-protection/CORSIA/Documents/CAEP_CORSIA Periodic Review (C225)_Executive Summary.pdf. (accessed 22 February 2023).

ICAO CAEP. (2022). *Report on the Feasibility of a Long-Term Aspirational Goal*. https://www.icao.int/environmental-protection/LTAG/Documents/REPORT ON THE FEASIBILITY OF A LONG-TERM ASPIRATIONAL GOAL_en.pdf (accessed 23 February 2023).

IPCC. (2001). *Third Assessment Report, Working Group 1: The Scientific Basis*. https://archive.ipcc.ch/ipccreports/tar/wg1/016.htm (accessed 22 February 2023).

IPCC. (2018). *Global Warming of 1.5°C*. An IPCC Special Report on the impacts of global warming of 1.5°C above pre-industrial levels and related global greenhouse gas emission pathways, in the context of strengthening the global response to the threat of climate change, sustainable development, and efforts to eradicate poverty. https://www.ipcc.ch/site/assets/uploads/sites/2/2019/06/SR15_Full_Report_High_Res.pdf (accessed 23 February 2023).

Keseicki, F. (2011). Marginal abatement cost curves for policy making – expert-based vs. model-derived curves. UCL Energy Institute. https://www.homepages.ucl.ac.uk/~ucft347/Kesicki_MACC.pdf (accessed 25 February 2023.

Laing, T., Sato, M., Grubb, M., and Comberti, C. (2013). *Assessing the Effectiveness of the EU Emissions Trading System*. Centre for Climate Change Economics and Policy Working Paper No. 126. Grantham Research Institute on Climate Change and the Environment Working Paper No. 106. https://www.lse.ac.uk/granthaminstitute/wp-content/uploads/2014/02/WP106-effectiveness-eu-emissions-trading-system.pdf (accessed 26 February 2023).

Larson, J., Elofsson, A., Sterner, T., and Akerman, J. (2019). International and National Climate Policies for Aviation: A Review. *Climate Policy*, 19(6). https://www.tandfonline.com/doi/full/10.1080/14693062.2018.1562871 (accessed 5 March 2023).

Lee, D.S., Fahey, D.W., Skowron, A., Allen, M.R., Burkhardt, U., Chen, Q., Doherty, S.J., Freeman, S., Forster, P.M., Fuglestvedt, J., Gettelman, A., De León, R.R., Lim, L.L., Lund, M.T., Millar, R.J., Owen, B., Penner, J.E., Pitari, G., Prather, M.J., Sausen, R., and Wilcox, L.J. (2021). The Contribution of Global Aviation to Anthropogenic Climate Forcing for 2000 to 2018. *Atmospheric Environment*, 244, 117834. https://doi.org/10.1016/j.atmosenv.2020.117834.

Lyle, C. (2018). Beyond ICAO's CORSIA: Towards a More Climatically Effective Strategy for Mitigation of Civil Aviation Emissions. *Climate Law*, 8(1–2), 104–127. https://www.researchgate.net/publication/345656962_Beyond_the_icao's_corsia_Towards_a_More_Climatically_Effective_Strategy_for_Mitigation_of_Civil-Aviation_Emissions (accessed 1 March 2023).

McKinsey & Company. (2009). *Pathways to a Low Carbon Economy: Version 2 of the Global Greenhouse Gas Abatement Cost Curve*. https://www.mckinsey.com/~/media/mckinsey/dotcom/client_service/sustainability/cost curve pdfs/pathways_lowcarbon_economy_version2.ashx (accessed 25 February 2023).

Misham, E.J. (1974). What Is the Optimal Level of Pollution? *Journal of Political Economy*, 82(6), 1287–1299. https://www.jstor.org/stable/1830678 (accessed 24 February 2023).

Napoli, C. (2012). Understanding Kyoto's Failure. *SAIS Review of International Affairs*, 32(2), 183–196.

Nordhaus, W. (2017). Revisiting the Social Cost of Carbon. *PNAS*, 114(7). https://www.pnas.org/doi/epdf/10.1073/pnas.1609244114 (accessed 24 February 2023).

Ritchie, H., Roser, M., and Rosando, P. (2020). *CO_2 and Greenhouse Gas Emissions*. Published online at OurWorldInData.org. https://ourworldindata.org/greenhouse-gas-emissions (accessed 23 February 2023).

Schneider, L. (2022). Fit for Purpose? Key Issues for the First Review of CORSIA, Oeko-Institut e.V. https://www.oeko.de/fileadmin/oekodoc/Key-issues-for-first-review-of-CORSIA.pdf (accessed 1 March 2023).

Stern, N. (2007). *The Economics of Climate Change: The Stern Review*. CUP.
UNFCCC. (1997). *Emissions from Fuels Used for International Aviation and Maritime Transport*. https://unfccc.int/topics/mitigation/workstreams/emissions-from-international-transport-bunker-fuels.
UNFCCC. (2015). *The Paris Agreement*. https://unfccc.int/process-and-meetings/the-paris-agreement (accessed 23 February 2023).

Abbreviations

AFC	Average Fixed Cost
AOC	Air Operator's Certificate
ASL	Average Stage Length
ASM	Available Seat Miles
ATA	Air Transport Association
ATC	Air Traffic Control
ATI	Air Transport Intelligence
AVC	Average Variable Cost
BAA	British Airport Authority
BOP	Balance of Payments
BRIC	Brazil, Russia, India, & China
BTS	Bureau of Transportation Statistics
CAA	Civil Aviation Authority
CAB	Civil Aeronautics Board
CASM	Cost per Available Seat Mile
CPI	Consumer Price Index
DOC	Direct Operating Cost
EMSR	Expected Marginal Seat Revenue
EU	European Union
FAA	Federal Aviation Administration
FAR	Federal Aviation Regulation
FC	Fixed Cost
FFP	Frequent Flyer Programs
GATT	General Agreement on Tariffs and Trades
GDP	Gross Domestic Product
GECAS	GE Commercial Aviation Services
GSE	Government Sponsored Entity
HHI	Herfindahl-Hirschman Index
IASB	International Accounting Standards Board
IATA	International Air Transport Association
ICAO	International Civil Aviation Organization
ILFC	International Lease Finance Corporation
IOC	Indirect Operating Cost
IRR	Internal Rate of Return
JAA	The Joint Aviation Authorities
LCC	Low-Cost Carrier

MAD	Mean Absolute Deviation
MC	Marginal Cost
MP	Marginal Profit
MR	Marginal Revenue
MSE	Mean Squared Error
MTOW	Maximum Takeoff Weight
NOC	Non-Operating Cost
O&D	Origin and Destination
OAG	Official Airline Guide
RASM	Revenue per Available Seat Mile
ROA	Return On Assets
ROE	Return On Equity
ROI	Return On Investment
RPK	Revenue Passenger Kilometer
RPM	Revenue Passenger Mile
RRPM	Revenue per Revenue Passenger Mile
RTM	Revenue Ton Miles
TC	Total Cost
TCAS	Traffic Collision Avoidance System
TFC	Total Fixed Cost
TOC	Total Operating Cost
VC	Variable Cost
VLA	Very Large Aircraft
WTO	World Trade Organization

Glossary of Terms

A

AEA: Association of European Airlines.

Aircraft Utilization: Aircraft utilization is calculated by dividing aircraft block hours by the number of aircraft days assigned to service on air carrier routes and presented in block hours per day.

Air Carrier: Any airline that undertakes directly, by lease, or other arrangement to engage in air transportation.

Aircraft Crews Maintenance Insurance (ACMI): A lease between two parties where the first party is a lessor with an AOC responsible for the aircraft crews, maintenance, and insurance and the second party is the lessee, usually with an AOC, who is responsible for schedules, flight charges, cargo handling, crew support, flight operations, ramp handling, and aircraft servicing and fueling.

Aircraft daily utilization: Aircraft hours flown (block-to-block) divided by aircraft days available.

Alliance: Several airlines participating in a commercial relationship or joint venture.

Available Seat Kilometer (ASK): A measure of a passenger airline's carrying capacity that is calculated as follows

ASK = *number of seats* × *number of kilometers flown*

Available Seat Mile (ASM): A measure of a passenger airline's carrying capacity that is calculated as follows

ASM = *number of seats* × *number of miles flown*

Available Ton Mile (ATM): A measure of a cargo airline's carrying capacity that is calculated as follows

ATM = weight in non-metric tons × number of miles flown.

Average Stage Length (ASL): The ASL is the average distance flown per aircraft departure.

$$\text{ASL} = \frac{\text{Plane miles}}{\text{Departures}}$$

B

Bankruptcy: The inability of an airline to pay its creditor is called bankruptcy.

Block Hour: Block hours are the airline industry basic measure of aircraft utilization. Block hour is the time from the minute the aircraft door closes at departure of a revenue flight until the moment the aircraft door opens at the arrival gate.

Break-Even: It is the volume of goods or services that have to be sold in order for the business to make neither a loss nor a profit.

Break-Even Load Factor: The load factor that covers the necessary operating costs for scheduled traffic revenue.

$$\text{Break-Even}_{LF} = \frac{\text{CASM}}{\text{R/RPM}} = \frac{\text{CASM}}{\text{Yield}}$$

Bumped: Airline lexicon for a passenger being offloaded from a flight. Most commonly due to a flight being oversold, although "bumped" can also mean being "upgraded" or "downgraded" where a seat in your booked class is not available.

C

Cabotage: Cabotage is the transport of passengers between two points in the same country by an aircraft registered in another country.

Carbon budget: Climate scientists estimate CO_2 concentration in the atmosphere cannot rise much further without damaging climate change, so they have calculated a carbon budget, the cumulated emissions that can be emitted without breaching this concentration.

Certified Air Carrier: An air carrier that is certified by the DOT to conduct scheduled or nonscheduled services interstate. The certificate issued to the air carrier by the DOT is the Certificate of Public Convenience and Necessity.

Code-sharing: An arrangement where an airline might place its own code to another carrier's flight. The airline that is actually operating the flight is called the operating carrier, and the airline that is marketing the flight is called the marketing carrier. Both carriers may sell tickets for the flight.

Commercial Service Airport: Airport receiving scheduled passenger service and having 2,500 or more enplaned passengers per year.

Commuter Air Carrier: A passenger air carrier operating aircraft with 30 seats or less and performs at least 5 scheduled roundtrips per week. It operates for hire or compensation under FAR Part 135.

Concentration ratio: Measure the proportion of an industry's output accounted for by several largest firms.

Consumer surplus: Consumer surplus is the difference between the maximum that a consumer is willing and able to pay for a good or service and the total amount that he actually pays.

Cost per available seat mile (CASM): It is represented in cents and is calculated as follows:

$$\text{CASM} = \frac{\text{Operating costs}}{\text{ASM}}$$

CRS: Computer Reservation System.

D

Deregulation: The term refers to the Airline Deregulation Act of 1978, which ended US government regulation of airline routes and charges.

Derived demand: It is the demand that is generated as the result of the demand for other goods or services.

Duopoly: Any market that is dominated by two firms. Commercial aircraft industry may be considered as a duopoly.

Duopsony: Two major buyers of a good or service in a market.

E

Economies of density: Cost reductions that result when a company utilizes a bigger plant size in the production a single product.

Economies of scale: The decrease in unit cost of a product, or the increase in efficiency of production as the number of goods being produced increases.

Economies of scope: Cost reductions that result when a company provides a variety of products rather than specializing in the production a single product.

Enplanement: The boarding of scheduled and nonscheduled service aircraft by domestic, territorial, and international revenue passengers for intrastate, interstate, and foreign commerce and that includes in transit passengers.

EASA: The European Aviation Safety Agency is an agency of the European Union (EU) which has been given regulatory and executive tasks in the field of civilian aviation safety.

Extended-Range Twin-Engine Operations (ETOPS): This rule allows twin-engine aircraft (such as the Airbus A300, A310, A320, A330, and A350, the Boeing 737, 757, 767, 777, and 787, the Embraer E-Jets, ATR) to fly longer distance routes that were previously off-limits to twin-engine aircraft.

F

Federal Aviation Administration (FAA): A US government agency responsible for air safety and operation of the air traffic control system.

Federal Air Regulation (FAR): Title 14 of the US government's Code of Federal Regulations. The FAR covers all the rules regarding aviation in the United States.

Financial Leverage: A measure of the amount of debt used in the capital structure of the airlines.

An airline with high leverage is more vulnerable to downturns in the business cycle because the airline must continue to service its debt regardless of how bad business is.

Flight stage: The operation of an aircraft from takeoff to its next landing.

Form 41 Data: Information collected from airline filings with the Bureau of Transportation Statistics. Airline financial data is filed with the BTS quarterly; traffic and employment numbers are filed monthly.

Fourth Freedom: The right to fly from another country/territory to one's own, e.g. British Airways carrying passengers from London to Sydney as a British airline.

Fifth Freedom: The right to fly between two foreign countries or territories while the flight originates or ends on one's own country/territory, e.g. American Airlines flying Sydney to Tokyo before flying to Los Angeles.

Freight: Any commodity other than mail and passenger baggage transported by air.

Freight-Ton Mile: A ton mile is defined as 1 ton of freight shipped 1 mile.

Frequent Flyer Programs: A service in which airline customers accrue points corresponding to the distance flown on an airline. These points can be used for free air travel, increased benefits such as airport lounge access, or priority bookings, and other products or services.

First Freedom: The right to fly over a foreign country/territory without landing there, e.g. Mexico City-Montreal flying over the United States.

G

Gross Domestic Product (GDP): GDP is a measure of the total market value of all final goods and services produced in our country during any quarter or year.

H

Hub and Spoke: Many airlines designate an airport as a hub through which they transit passengers from spoke (origin) to spoke (destination).

Herfindahl–Hirschman Index (HHI): A standard measure of industry concentration, expressed as the sum of the squares of the market shares of the firms in the same industry.

Homogeneous Good: The outputs of different firms are identical and indistinguishable.

I

International Civil Aviation Organization (ICAO): ICAO is a UN specialized agency that serves as the global forum for civil aviation and works to achieve safe, secure, and sustainable development of civil aviation through co-operation among member states.

Inflation Rate: The percentage change in the price level from one period to the next.

ILS: Instrument Landing System.

In Transit Passengers: Revenue passengers on board international flights that transit an airport for non-traffic purposes domestically.

International Air Transport Association (IATA): IATA is an international organization that regulates many of the world's scheduled airlines.

Involuntary Bumping: Involuntary denied boarding occurs when an airline removes a ticketed passenger from a flight without their consent.

J

The Joint Aviation Authorities (JAA): JAA was an associated body of the European Civil Aviation Conference (ECAC) representing the civil aviation regulatory authorities of a number of European States implementing safety regulatory standards and procedures.

L

Lease: A lease is a contract granting use or occupation of property during a specified period in exchange for specified lease payments.

Lessee: A person who leases a property from its owner (lessor).

Lessor: The owner of an asset who grants another party to lease the asset.

Leverage: The use of debt to supplement investment.

Load Factor: Load factor is the ratio of revenue passenger miles over available seat-miles, representing the proportion of aircraft seating capacity that is actually sold and utilized.

$$\text{Load factor} = \frac{\text{ASM}}{\text{RPM}}$$

M

Major Airlines: Airlines earning revenues of $1 billion or more annually in scheduled service.

Marginal Abatement Costs (MAC) Curve: The schedule of individual measures that could be taken to reduce an additional tonne of CO_2, ordered by their unit cost, including amortized capital costs.

Marginal Cost: The marginal cost is the cost of producing an additional output.

Market Failure: Market failure happens when free markets fail to deliver an efficient allocation of resources.

Maximum Certificated Takeoff Weight (MCTOW): The maximum weight at which the pilot of the aircraft is allowed to attempt to take off due to the aircraft's structural limitation.

Maximum Zero Fuel: MACRS allows for greater depreciation during the initial stages of the capital asset's life, enabling the tax deductible depreciation expense to be claimed sooner.

Monopsony: Monopsony is a market structure similar to a monopoly except that one buyer and many sellers of a particular product.

N

Narrow-Body Aircraft: An aircraft with a single aisle.

Net Profit Margin: Net profit after interest and taxes as a percent of operating revenues.

No Frills Airlines: Also known as "Low Cost" airlines.

Nonscheduled Service: Revenue flights not operated as regular scheduled service, such as charter flights, and all non-revenue flights incident to such flight.

O

Operating Expenses: Expenses incurred in the performance of air transportation, based on overall operating revenues and expenses.

Operating Lease: A short-term lease, for example, an aircraft which has an economic life of 30 years may be leased to an airline for four years on an operating lease.

Operating Leverage: A measure of the extent to which fixed assets are utilized in the business firm.

Operating Profit Margin: Operating profit (operating revenues minus operating expenses) as a percent of operating revenues.

Operating Revenues: Revenues from air transportation and related incidental services.

Overbooking: Selling more seats than the available capacity.

P

Passenger Load Factor: Load factor is the ratio of revenue passenger miles over available seat-miles, representing the proportion of aircraft seating capacity that is actually sold and utilized.

$$LF = \frac{RPM}{ASM} \times 100$$

Passenger Revenue per Available Seat Mile (PRASM): The average revenue received by the airline per unit of capacity available for sale.

$$PRASM = \frac{Revenue}{ASM}$$

Pax: Abbreviation passenger.
Payload: The part of an aircraft's load that generates revenue (freight and passengers).
Penetration Pricing: A pricing policy used to enter a new market, usually by setting a very low price.
Price Discrimination: Price discrimination happens when an airline charges different prices to different passengers for an identical service, for reasons other than costs.
Price Ceiling: A legally established maximum price.
Price Floor: A legally established minimum price.
Primary Market: The market for raising of new capital for the first time.
Profitability Ratios: They are a group of ratios that are used to assess the return on assets, sales, and invested capital.

R

Return on Investment (ROI): The percentage amount that is earned on a company's total capital, calculated by dividing the total capital into earnings before interest, taxes, or dividends.
Revenue Passenger Enplanement: The total number of revenue passengers boarding aircraft including origination, stopover, or connecting passengers.
Revenue Passenger Load Factor: (Scc Passenger Load Factor) Revenue passenger load factor is the ratio of revenue passenger miles over available seat-miles, representing the proportion of aircraft seating capacity that is actually sold and utilized.
Revenue Passenger Mile (RPM): RPM is computed by the summation of the products of the revenue aircraft miles flown by the number of revenue passengers carried on that route. RPM is a principal measure of an airline's turnover.
Revenue per available seat mile (RASM): The revenue in cents received for each seat mile offered. This is computed by dividing operating income by Available Seat-Miles and is not limited to ticket sales revenue.
Revenue Ton Mile (RTM): One non-metric ton of revenue traffic transported 1 mile.

S

Secondary Market: The markets for securities that have already been issued and traded among investors with no proceeds go to the company.
SEC: US Securities and Exchange Committee.

SLOT: The scheduled time of arrival or departure allocated to an aircraft movement on a specific date at an airport.

Small Certificated Air Carrier: An air carrier holding a certificate issued under section 401 of the Federal Aviation Act of 1958, as amended, that operates aircraft designed to have a maximum seating capacity of 60 seats or fewer or a maximum payload of 18,000 pounds or less.

Sunk Costs: Sunk costs cannot be recovered if a business decides to leave an industry.

T

Tariff: Import tax.

Trade Deficit: Imports of goods and services exceed exports of goods and services.

Trade Surplus: Exports of goods and services exceed imports of goods and services.

Treasury Bill: A short-term bond issued by the US government.

U

US Flag Carrier: One of a class of air carriers holding a Certificate of Public Convenience and Necessity issued by the US Department of Transportation (DOT) and approved by the President, authorizing scheduled operations over specified routes between the United States and one or more foreign countries.

V

Variable Costs: A variable cost is a cost that changes in proportion to a change in a company's activity or business.

Variance: A measure of how much an economic variable varies across the mean.

Voluntary Denied Boarding: When the flight is overbooked and the airline is looking for volunteers to give up their seats and change their travel plans.

W

Wet Lease: Refers to the leasing of an aircraft and includes the provision of crew and supporting services such as fuel, airport fees, and insurance.

Wide-Body Aircraft: A commercial aircraft with two aisles.

Y

Yield: Average revenue per revenue passenger mile or revenue ton mile, expressed in cents per mile.

Answers to Selected Questions and Problems

Chapter 1

1 As mentioned in the chapter, the principal factors affecting world traffic are the level of economic prosperity in a region, the increases in the real cost of air travel (for example, fuel costs), an increase in population rates, and economic liberalization.

7 Historically, mergers in the airline industry have not been overly successful. The mergers have had difficulty in dealing with labor groups and the merging of corporate cultures has been an underestimated barrier to successful mergers.

9 During the period of regulation, airline ticket prices were set to cover the average costs of the regulated airline. Setting prices to cover the average cost of an airline will result in no particular attempt to minimize costs on the part of the regulated airline, which will naturally result in a higher fare prices to the consumer.

11 The direct effects of the economic impacts of air transportation are the direct payments that are made to the participants in the industry. An example of this would be salaries paid to the employees of an airport or airlines that use the airport. The indirect economic impacts are those that are not directly attributable to the industry itself but come about because of the presence of the industry. An example of this would be to salaries of people employed in a hotel that is adjacent to the airport.

13 Low-cost carriers generally have an inherent cost advantage over legacy carriers due to the fact that they are free to negotiate wages and prior agreements without the encumbrance of contracts that were negotiated during the regulated era, or even more recent contracts shaped by attitudes and labor culture that are still influenced by traditions established in the regulated era.

14 International routes have traditionally been less competitive than domestic routes because of the fact that political considerations are always involved in international air travel and airlines must get political approval before instituting new international routes.

15 The principal advantage that airline travel has over all other modes of transportation is the speed of travel, particularly over distances in excess of 300–400 miles.

Chapter 2

1 Opportunity cost, as it is used in economics, is defined as the alternative cost of using a resource; that is, the benefits that would accrue if the resources were being used in its next best allocation.

3 Economics may be defined as the science of decision-making and resource allocation under scarcity.

4 Microeconomics deals with the behavior of individual households and businesses; that is, individual decision-making units that are responding to either the supply or demand for scarce resources. On the other hand, macroeconomics studies the decision-making process for the entire economy; movements in gross domestic product, interest rates, inflation rates, exchange rates, balancing trays, and their interrelationships are all considered macroeconomic.

6 The two main categories of market failures are externalities and the lack of any competitive outcome in the market; in other words, some type of monopoly pricing.

7 What is unique about the regulatory environment of the airline industry is the fact that the delivery of the product, that is, an airline seat to a specific destination, has been completely controlled by the federal government. Therefore, airlines have generally not been free to adjust their schedules and reactions to market conditions, but must respond to the control of the Federal Aviation Administration with respect to the delivery of their product. Pockets of such oppressive regulation continue, and even in more deregulated markets, the FAA's ATC and influence on airport policies continue to hinder airlines' decisions.

11 Prices constitute the central allocating mechanism in economics and are the decision-making parameters by which individuals and businesses organize their actions. Prices in market economies reflect both the scarcity of resources and the valuation that consumers place on the products that are produced by those resources.

13 If a freeway has one lane reserved for only those drivers who are considered to be on urgent business, as defined by themselves, the economic principle of self-interest (not greed) would result in that lane being as crowded as all the other lanes, since the majority of drivers would naturally consider that their own business is urgent.

16 Some amount of unemployment is essential to the functioning of a market economy, since individuals must be free to change occupations and to search for those jobs that they are best suited for. This specialization increases the overall output of the economy.

25

	Total Population	*In Labor Force*	*Employed*		*In Labor Force*	*Employed*	*Employed Rate*	*Unemployment Rate*
High School	35,450,000	23,042,500	21,199,100	High School	23,042,500	21,199,100	0.92	0.08
Bachelors Degree	45,233,000	29,401,450	27,343,349	Bachelor's Degree	29,401,450	27,343,349	0.93	0.07
Post Graduate	41,150,000	26,747,500	25,945,075	Post Graduate	26,747,500	25,945,075	0.97	0.03

Chapter 3

1 Price elasticity of demand is defined as the percentage change in the quantity demanded divided by the percentage change in the price. A product with elastic demand might be fresh tomatoes, since there are a variety of good substitutes for tomatoes. A product with inelastic demand might be gasoline, since it is difficult to change driving patterns right away.

3 Give an example for the airline industry and show it graphically. The law of demand states that, all else equal, consumers will buy less of a given time when the price of a product increases and buy more as the price decreases. The law of supply states that the higher the price, the more producers are willing and able to produce. All else constant, the quantity

supplied increases as the price increases and decreases as price decreases. An increase in demand is a shift in the entire demand curve. An increase in the quantity demanded is a movement along a given demand curve.

4 We would expect that the elasticity of demand in short-haul markets would be more elastic than long-haul markets because the automobile and rail transportation can compete with airlines in a short-haul market, whereas it is more difficult for other modes of transportation to compete with airline travel in the long-haul market, especially with regard to time of travel.

8 If fuel prices go up, then we should expect to see a shift in the supply curve to the left, a decrease in response to the increase in cost. The leftward shift in the supply curve will cause an increase in price and a decrease in the quantity demanded. That is, the movement of the supply curve will be along a given demand curve. If fuel prices go down, we should expect to see a shift in the supply curve to the right or in a downward direction. This will cause a decrease in price and an increase in the quantity demanded. That is, the movement of the supply curve will be along a given demand curve.

11

a

$$E_d = \frac{800-735}{435-515} \times \frac{435+515}{800+515}$$

$$E_d = \frac{65}{-80} \times \frac{950}{1,315}$$

$$E_d = -0.59$$

b Inelastic

c The number of ticket sold doesn't change as much as the price does

d Percentage change in the number of ticket sold = −0.59 × 10% = 5.90% increase

12

First, we need to find the equilibrium quantity and price:

$600 - Q_d = 300 + 2Q_s$

$3Q = 300$

$Q = 100$ units, and $P = \$300$

$$CS = \int_0^{100} \left[600 - Q\right]dx - \left(300 \times 100\right)$$

$$CS = \left|600\ Q - 0.5Q^{2}\right._{o}^{100} - 30,000$$

$$CS = 60,000 - 5,000 - 30,000 = 25,000$$

13

a $P = 200 - 2Q$

b $P = 200 - 2 \times 5$

$P = \$190$

c $TC\ (Q = 5) = 104 - 14 \times 5 + 5^2$

$TC\ (Q = 5) = \$59$

18 The short-term results of this policy would undoubtedly be a shortage of available airline seats on those flights affected by the policy. That is, the quantity demanded would exceed the quantity supplied at a price that is below the market-determined equilibrium price.

21

a $55 - 3Q_D = 5 + 2Q_S$

$Q = 5{,}000$ gallons

$P = 55 - 3(5) = \$40$

b

$28 = 55 - 3Q_D$

$Q_D = 9$

$28 = 5 + 7Q_S$

$Q_S = 3.28$

The shortage is therefore $9 - 3.28 = 5.72$ units

c

With this price floor, we know that $Q = Q_D + 15$

$$Q_S = \frac{1}{7} + \frac{P}{7}$$

$$Q_D = \frac{55}{73} - \frac{P}{3}$$

$$\frac{1}{7} + \frac{P}{7} = \frac{55}{3} - \frac{P}{3} + 5$$

$P = 48.70$

22

a and b

$P = 20 - 0.20 \times Q_d$

$P = 7.50 + 0.20 \times Q_S$

c

$$7.50 + 0.20 \times Q_s = P = 20 - 0.20 \times Q_d$$

$$12.5 = 0.4Q$$

$$Q = 31.25 \text{ units}$$

$$P = 20 - 0.20 \times (31.25)$$

$$P = \$13.75$$

Chapter 4

3 Economies of scale refer to the advantages gained when in the long run the average costs decrease with an increase in the quantity produced. Economies of scope occur when the company or airline can reduce its unit costs by leveraging efficiencies through the sharing of resources for multiple projects or production lines.

6 A sunk cost is an investment that cannot be recovered due to its very nature. An example of a sunk cost for an airline might be a hangar or storage facility which can no longer accommodate new aircraft that the airline might purchase. Such costs have already been incurred and should not affect managerial decision-making in the present time.

7 Historical costs are those incurred for the original purchase of an asset. Replacement costs are the costs required to duplicate productive capabilities using current technology. Some costs for the investments made in productive facilities cannot be recovered.

12

$$\text{VC}(Q) = -9Q^2 + 0.002Q^3$$

Set derivative equal to zero

$$\text{AVC}(Q)' = -18Q + 0.006Q^2$$

$$Q = 3{,}000 \text{ units}$$

13

a $$Q_{B-E} = \frac{\text{FC}}{P - \text{VC}}$$

$$Q_{B-E} = \frac{24{,}000}{190 - 150}$$

$$Q_{B-E} = 600 \text{ units}$$

b

$$\text{TC} = 24{,}000 + 150 \times Q \quad \text{In millions}$$

$$\text{TR} = 190 \times \text{Q} \quad \text{In millions}$$

14 The cost of producing anti-icing 40 is the cost of producing 40 minus the cost of producing 39 units:

a $TC\ (Q = 39) = 4{,}000 + 35 \times 39 - 0.01 \times 39^2$

$TC\ (Q = 40) = 4{,}000 + 35 \times 40 - 0.01 \times 40^2$

The cost of producing 40 units is $34.21

b $MC = TC'\ (Q) = 35 - 0.02 \times Q$

$MC = 35 - 0.02 \times 40$

$MC = 34.20$

Chapter 5

1 The four basic market structures are perfect competition, monopolistic competition, oligopoly, and monopoly. An example for a monopsony market structure is the Lockheed Martin F-22 Raptor which was developed for the United States Air Force (USAF) only.

2 Normal profit can be thought of as the going rate of return for an average firm in the economy. Rates of return that are significantly above this are called economic profits.

3

a Set MC = MR

$MC = 2$

$MR = 80 - 2Q$

$80 - 2Q = 2,\ Q = 39$

$P = 80 - 39 = \$41$

b $TR = P \times Q = \$41 \times 39$

$TR = \$1{,}599$

$TC = 1{,}500 + 39 \times 2$

$TC = \$1{,}578$

Profit = $21

5

a Many buyers and many sellers (none of which is large to impact the price)
b Homogeneous (identical) products
c Full dissemination of information
d Easy entry and exit

11 It is not true that a monopoly can charge any price that it wishes. The maximum price that a monopoly can charge is limited by the extent of the market; that is, the maximum price that a demander is willing to pay. The profit maximizing price for the monopolist is the point

on the demand curve where marginal revenue equals marginal cost for the monopolist. This may or may not result in normal profits, economic profits, or losses depending upon the average cost curve.

12

a $MC = MR$

$MC = 10Q$, $MR = 50$

$10Q = 50$, so $Q = 5$ units

b Profit = Total revenue – Total cost

Profit = (5) × ($50) – [40 + 5 × (5)²]

Profit = $250 – ($40 + $125) = $85

16 When some firms do not cover the average total costs in the long run, they will be forced to leave the industry. When this happens, the market supply curve will shift to the left and the equilibrium price will rise. Eventually, the price will just cover the average total cost curve which contains the normal rate of profit for the remaining firms in the industry.

17 It is not true that a monopoly firm will always make a profit. The reason for this is the fact that it depends upon the location of the average total cost curve with respect to the industry demand curve. If the average total cost curve is above the industry demand curve, then even the monopolist will not make a profit because he or she cannot charge a price that covers all costs, because demand is simply too weak.

Chapter 6

2 In an oligopolistic market, the actions of one firm substantially affect the market. In this case, there is a complex interdependence among firms; that is, each firm's action depends upon what they believe the competitors will do. Therefore, pricing, in this market, tends to be unpredictable in the short run. However, in the long run, pricing will have to be such as to cover all costs for some of the firms will exit the industry.

4 In a monopolistically competitive market prices will be set with marginal cost equals marginal revenue. However, the demand curve that faces a monopolistically competitive firm will be closer to that of a perfectly competitive firm, so that the difference between marginal revenue and price will be small. In the long run, prices will be set by the forces of competition so as to cover all costs, to include the normal rate of profit.

5 The government appears to support certain monopolies, since the public seems to be convinced that certain products cannot be brought into the marketplace in the presence of competition. It is also true that some industries have successfully lobbied for government protection through extremely high barriers to entry; for example, the drug. However, it is worth noting that medical drugs exist in an unusual and complex, regulated market.

10 In the airline industry the upper portion of the kinked demand curve is assumed to be more elastic because it is assumed that price increases on the part of the airline will not be followed by competing airlines. Therefore, passengers will shift from the airline that raises its price to those that have the less expensive fare, thereby making the demand curve elastic at

this point. The lower portion of the demand curve is assumed to be inelastic, since in this area it is assumed that a decrease in price by any airline will be followed by competing airlines, thereby making this portion of the demand curve inelastic; that is, the decrease in price will not result in an increase in total revenue.

13

a Set MR = MR

$Q = 50 - P$

$P = 50 - Q$

$\text{MR} = 50 - 2Q$

$\text{MC} = -25 + 3Q$

$50 - 2Q = -25 + 3Q$

$Q = 15$

$P = \$35$

c Profit = TR − TC

$\pi = P \times Q = 35 \times 15 - [375 - 25 \times 15 + 1.5 \times 15^2]$

$\pi = 525 - [375 - 375 - 337.5]$

$\pi = \$187.50$

16 The fact that rental cars must be returned with a full tank of gas means that gas stations which are close to the rental car location will have a higher demand for their gas than gas stations which are further away. This enables the gas stations that are nearer to the rental car location to charge a higher price.

17 This would be a classic oligopoly situation where the actions of one competitor directly affect the market of the second competitor. In this case, the second airline would be forced to match the sale price of the first airline or the second airline would lose some of its market share.

18 If one of the airlines opted out of the market, the other airline will most likely not adopt a monopoly pricing practice because of the fact that an airline market is a classic example of a contestable market where it would be quite easy for another airline to enter the market, if prices were exceptionally high.

19 In addition to the better service that is advertised by the airline, the information obtained from the questionnaire would most likely allow the airline to distinguish between price-sensitive, time-sensitive, and service-sensitive travelers and they would be able to allocate seats accordingly.

20

a Profit maximization output

$P = 1{,}000 - 10 \times (q_{\text{DirectJet}} + q_{\text{MyJet}})$

$P = 1{,}000 - 10q_{\text{DirectJet}} - 10q_{\text{MyJet}}$

$\text{MR}_{\text{DirectJet}} = 1{,}000 - 20q_{\text{DirectJet}} - 10q_{\text{MyJet}}$

$\text{MR}_{\text{MyJet}} = 1{,}000 - 10q_{\text{DirectJet}} - 20q_{\text{MyJet}}$

To find the level of profit for airlines we just need to set MC = MR

$MR_{DirectJet} = 1{,}000 - 20q_{DirectJet} - 10q_{MyJet} = 50$

$MR_{MyJet} = 1{,}000 - 10q_{DirectJet} - 20q_{MyJet} = 50$

$20q_{DirectJet} + 10q_{MyJet} = 950$

$10q_{DirectJet} + 20q_2 = 950$

Solving the function simultaneously:

$20q_{DirectJet} + 10q_{MyJet} = 950$

$-20q_{DirectJet} - 40q_{MyJet} = -1{,}900$

$-30q_2 = 950 \geq q_{MyJet} = 31.67$

And

$20q_{DirectJet} + 10q_{MyJet} = 950$

$-20q_{DirectJet} - 40q_{MyJet} = -1{,}900$

$-30q_2 = 950 \geq q_{MyJet} = 31.67$

$P = 1{,}000 - 10\ (q_{DirectJet} + q_2)$

$P = 1{,}000 - 10 \times (31.67 + 31.67)$

$P = \$366.60$

b Profit level

Profit = TR − TC

Profit = (\$366.60 × 31.67) − (\$50 × 31.67)

Profit = \$10,027

c $MR_{DirectJet} = 1{,}000 - 20q_{DirectJet} - 10q_{MyJet} = 100$

$MR_{MyJet} = 1{,}000 - 10q_{DirectJet} - 20q_{MyJet} = 50$

$20q_{DirectJet} + 10q_{MyJet} = 900$

$10q_{DirectJet} + 20q_{MyJet} = 950$

Solving the above two equation leads to:

$q_{DirectJet} = 22.50$ seats

$q_{MyJet} = 45$ seats

Chapter 7

1 Qualitative forecasting is the process of making predictions based on past and present quantitative observations and data. Qualitative forecasts do not use statistical databases or provide measures of forecast accuracy, since they are based on opinions, surveys, and

beliefs. Quantitative methods use statistical data to analyze and forecast future behavior of specific variables. An advantage of qualitative forecasting is its flexibility, and a limitation is a lack of tests of accuracy. An advantage of quantitative forecasting is that there are tests of reliability to determine forecast accuracy and a limitation is that the economy may change and distort the forecast.

2 A dummy variable is a binary number that takes on only two values (0 or 1). It requires no additional economic information. Regression analysis with dummy variables may be used to identify the actual nature of the relationship between the dependent variable and the independent variables. Therefore, dummy variables may be used to introduce qualitative variables into regression analysis.

3 Multicollinearity occurs when two or more independent variables are highly correlated with each other. In the limit, when the two independent variables are perfectly related, the estimates of the coefficients cannot be computed. The problem arises since regression cannot separate the effects of the perfectly correlated independent variables.

5 Seasonal variations occur because of the natural tendency of consumers to vary their purchase of airline tickets based upon the time of year. Cyclical variations on the other hand occur because of the business cycle and whether it is in an upswing or a downswing.

6 The four different components of time series analysis are trend analysis, which accounts for the movements of a time series over a long period of time, seasonal variations, which account for regular patterns of variability within certain time periods, cyclical variations, which account for variations because of the business cycle, and random factors, which account for short-term unanticipated and/or nonrecurring factors that affect the values of the series.

7 R^2 is always between 0% and 100%. R^2 of 0.89 means 89% variation in the dependent variable has been explained by variation of independent variables.

10 In a simple regression model, it is not possible that all the actual Y values would lie above or below the true regression line, since the regression line is selected to minimize the sum of the squared error terms which lie above and below the true regression line.

15

a MR = MC

$\text{MR} = 4{,}485.8 - 0.3206Q$

$\text{MC} = \$150$

$Q = 13{,}440$ passengers

$P = \$2908.\ 67$

b $\text{TR} = 38{,}658\text{P} - 8.67P^2$

$$\frac{\text{dTR}}{\text{dP}} = 38{,}658 - 17.34P$$

$P = \$2{,}229.41$

19 The t statistic is used to test the significance of individual variables within a multiple regression, whereas the F test statistic is used to test the significance of more than one independent variable within a regression.

21 Answers:

a

b Excel output

$$PAX = 56{,}301 + 3.83 \times BUS$$

$$PAX_{2019} = 56{,}301 + 3.83 \times BUS$$

$$PAX_{2019} = 56{,}301 + 3.83 \times 16{,}500$$

$$PAX_{2019} = 119{,}556$$

Regression Statistics

Multiple *R*	0.967344222				
R^2	0.935754844				
Adjusted-R^2	0.927724199				
Standard error	3532.110848				
Observations	10				
ANOVA					
	df	*SS*	*MS*	*F*	*Significance F*
Regression	1	1,453,718,544	1,453,718,544	117	4.78296E-06
Residual	8	99,806,456	12,475,807		
Total	9	1,553,525,000			
	Coefficients	*Standard Error*	*t Stat*	*P-Value*	*Lower 95%*
Intercept	56,301	3,085.59	18.25	0.00	49,185.79
BUS	3.83	0.36	10.79	0.00	3.01

Chapter 8

1 Peak-load pricing is the policy of charging higher prices at times when demand for a service/product is at the peak. Cell phone companies and electrical companies have been using peak-load pricing for years.

2 Markup pricing is the practice of adding up all of the costs that a firm might have and then adding a set percentage to these costs as the price of the product. The problem with this approach to pricing is the fact that it totally ignores the demand for the product and could result in a price that is too high for the market or in some cases a price that might be significantly below that might be charged in a market with high demand.

3

a $$MU_{Cost} = \frac{P - C}{C}$$

$$MU_{Cost} = \frac{6 - 4}{4}$$

$$MU_{Cost} = 50\%$$

b $MU_{Cost}^{Optimum} = \left(\frac{E}{1+E}\right)$

$$MU_{Cost}^{Optimum} = \left(\frac{-2}{1-2}\right) = 200\%$$

4 Reservation price is a term referring to the maximum price that a buyer is willing to pay for a good or service. Consumer surplus is the difference between the highest amount the consumer is willing to pay and the amount they actually pay.

6 Airlines and other service industries use price discrimination that is based on elasticity of demand, by charging a higher price to those with a low elasticity of demand and a lower price to those with a high elasticity of demand. If a passenger books the tickets late, chances are the passenger is desperate to fly and therefore doesn't mind paying a little more. The airfare will also depend on the months during which you will travel. Most families have limited options and would usually take off during school holidays. Knowing this, airlines differentiate between peak and off-peak demand periods and charge different rates of airfares.

7

$$P_{BUS} = \frac{150}{1+\frac{1}{-1.5}} = 450$$

$$P_{ECN} = \frac{150}{1+\frac{1}{-3.0}} = 225$$

9 Average cost pricing (ACP) is a tool used by the government to regulate a monopoly market. Generally, ACP may increase production and reduce price.

10 The basic idea behind the expected marginal seat revenue (EMSR) is the use of historical data on fares and past booking to calculate the expected revenue generated from selling the marginal seat. Or the $EMSR_i$ is the expected revenue for class i when the number of seats available to that class is increased by one.

$$EMSR_i = f_i \times Pr_i$$

11 Assume that two days before the flight departure the airline recognizes that there are still some seats left in the aircraft and passengers are willing to pay \$600, but the probability of this happening is only 40%. Hence, the EMSR for holding the seat is:

$$EMSR_i = f_i \times Pr_i$$

$$EMSR_i = \$600 \times 0.40$$

$$EMSR_i = \$240$$

13 $CS = \int_0^Q (100 - Q^2)dQ - P_e \times Q_e$

$$Q^2 = 100 - 75$$

$$Q = 5 \text{ units}$$

$$CS = \left| 100Q - \frac{1}{3}Q^3 \right|_0^5 - (\$75 \times 5)$$

$$CS = \left[100 \times 5 - \frac{1}{3} \times 5^3 \right] - (\$75 \times 5)$$

$$CS = (500 - 41.67) - (375)$$

$$CS = \$83.33$$

16 Price discrimination would allow a company to manage its demand more effectively. Without price discrimination, airlines may not be able to optimize their load factor. On the negative side, passengers pay higher prices than in the absence of price discrimination.

20

$$EMSR_{\$500} = f_{500} \times Pr_{500}$$

$$EMSR_{\$500} = \$500 \times = 0.50 = \$250$$

$$EMSR_{\$300} = f_{300} \times Pr_{300}$$

$$EMSR_{\$300} = \$300 \times 0.90 = \$270$$

$$EMSR_{\$220} = f_{220} \times Pr_{220}$$

$$EMSR_{\$220} = \$220 \times 100\% = \$220$$

22 Spoilage = certain number of seats that is not sold because too few seats are allocated to low-priced fare classes.
Spillage = certain number (or percentage) of passengers that could not buy a seat due to flight being fully booked at the time of request

23 Average = Number of passengers booked × Probability

Average = 50 × 0.88 = 44 passengers

24

$$Pr(Q \le X) = \frac{C_U}{C_U + C_O}$$

$$Pr(Q \ge X) = \frac{\$800}{\$800 + \$475}$$

$$Pr(Q \le X) = 37.25\%$$

From the above information the $Z = 0.32$
Thus, the maximum number of booking should be:
Booking = 300 + (0.32 × 40)
Booking = 312.80 seats

Chapter 9

2 Some of the strategic policies that Southwest Airlines and Ryanair have followed to allow them to be so successful are first and foremost low-cost and low-fare operations coupled with point-to-point flight operations that avoid hub airports. In addition:

- Fast aircraft turnaround to maximize aircraft utilization
- Fleet uniformity (one type of aircraft to minimize maintenance and training expenses)
- Optimum use of seating space
- Minimum cabin service

3 The biggest difference between low-cost airlines and legacy airlines is the cost structure, especially labor costs, and diseconomies of scale.

4

a From a passenger's point of view the advantage of low-cost airline is the fare structure.
b The disadvantage of a low-cost airline would be the lack of an extensive route structure.

5 Having a single type of aircraft makes it much easier to recover from irregular operations since all of the spare parts and maintenance are common to the fleet and the same thing is true of the flight operations crew; that is, flight attendants and pilots.

7 The challenges and problems faced by low-cost carriers to expand into international markets would revolve around the ability of the low-cost carriers to convince foreign governments that they should be given permission to operate in the country in the face of determined opposition and lobbying from the legacy airlines, which in many cases are owned and operated by the governments that will have to give permission.

10 The attempts to create low-cost carriers on the part of the legacy airlines have failed primarily because the low-cost carriers that were created by the legacy airlines have essentially the same management style, relatively the same cost structure of the legacy airline, and hence did not achieve any appreciable comparative advantages.

11 In general, the bankruptcy proceedings of many of the legacy airlines have allowed the legacy airlines to terminate many of the high labor contracts that were created and sustained during the regulatory period. This has allowed the legacy airlines to compete on a more cost-effective basis with the low-cost carriers.

12 Some reasons why a low-cost airline would choose to locate at a secondary airport that is close to a major hub would be the fact that the low-cost carrier is still providing the customer with access to the major metropolitan area, but at the same time, the low-cost carrier does not have to deal with the congestion and delay that is usually present at a major hub.

Chapter 10

1 Some of the major incentives for airlines to continuously improve safety are the facts that any major accident may cause a substantial decline in passenger traffic for the airline, adverse publicity on an ongoing basis, and a large decline in the capital markets for the airline.

2 The three major causes of aviation accidents are:

- Human error,
- Aircraft malfunction, and
- Weather-related accidents.

3 The improvements in air safety can be categorized as new technologies, advanced computer simulation and modeling, better flight training, and better research into crew resource management.

4 Similar to traffic regulations, aviation regulations are designed to deter airlines from violating safety procedures. The Federal Aviation Administration has the authority to order any airline to cease operations and this would effectively cut off revenue while imposing sizable costs and penalties. Therefore, safety regulation has increased overall safety, but it is unclear that this would not have occurred for market-related concerns anyway.

5 Passengers can decide how important safety is too. Therefore, an airline that is perceived to be less safe, as a result of an accident or investigation, is likely to see a decrease in demand compared to other airlines. Similar to passengers' reaction, labor supply may also react adversely to an aviation accident. Employees do not want to work in an environment perceived to be unsafe. Therefore, airlines may experience two labor issues as a result of an accident: increased turnover and/or increased wage demands.

6 The often heard statement that "airline safety must be preserved at any cost" is obviously incorrect from either an economic or practical standpoint. There is virtually no activity that can be performed without some possibility of an accident or injury. Therefore, any regulations that contribute only marginally to the safety of air travel should be subjected to the same cost–benefit analysis that is typically applied to other forms of transportation or possible activities that might be undertaken in the modern world.

Chapter 11

1 Open Skies agreements established liberal ground rules for international aviation markets and minimize government involvement.

4 Cabotage allows a foreign airline to fly between different domestic markets in a country. Cabotage agreements, where applicable, increase competition within the domestic market by allowing for airlines to compete for air travelers.

5 Open Skies agreements enable airlines to fly more routes, which ultimately results in increased competition, resulting in lower average airfares. Open Skies also enable new city pairs (domestic to foreign) that were previously not possible. Consumers benefit from Open Skies as they receive more frequent service and lower prices.

6 Open Skies agreements have generally affected LCCs in a positive way by allowing them to fly more destinations to complete effectively with legacy airlines.

8 The freedom that is not likely to be extended for airlines is the Cabotage freedom, since that increases domestic competition and is likely to be strongly resisted by domestic airlines using the legal power of the government.

Chapter 12

2 If country A takes 100 hours to produce 20 aircraft or 10 jet engines, then the domestic terms of trade for country A will be 2 aircraft for 1 jet engine. If country B takes 100 hours to produce 15 aircraft or 5 jet engines, then the domestic terms of trade will be 3 aircraft for 1 jet engine. Country A has an absolute advantage in the production of both products. However, country B has a comparative advantage in the production of aircraft. So, trade can take place between the two countries. The limits of the terms of trade would lie between one jet engine for two to three aircraft or one aircraft for between 1/2 and 1/3 jet engine.

4 Nations trade because they have different natural resource endowments, different capabilities within the population, different capital infrastructures, and different valuations on economic products. All of these things lead to specialization in one product or another, and this leads to trade, which increases the wealth of the countries themselves. The advantages of free trade are that it reduces the price of items sold in the market, increases the supply of products that in turn helps the global economy, increases the number and variety of products, and results in a higher standard of living for the trading partners. Arguments against free trade are a loss of jobs in a particular industry, national security concerns, environmental concerns, and a desire to avoid too much specialization.

5 Three barriers to trade are tariffs, quotas, and subsidies. Tariffs are taxes that are levied on imported goods. Quotas limit the quantity of commodities that can be imported. Subsidies decrease the costs of imported goods.

7 Imports that exceed exports reduce foreign currency reserves, causing a decrease in the foreign currency supply (supply shifts to the left), driving up the value of foreign currency relative to the local currency (depreciation), and decreasing the exchange rate.

9

a $P = 1{,}000 - 5Q = \$700$

$5Q = 300$

$Q = 60$ units

At this price

$700 = 500 + 5Q$; 40 units of the product will be produced domestically and 20 units will be imported.

b With a tariff of \$25 per unit of the product, the price will now be \$725, and the quantity demanded will be:

$1{,}000 - 5Q = \$725$

$Q = 55$ units, at a price of \$725

At the price of \$725

$500 + 5Q = 725$

$Q_{Produced} = 45$ units of the product will be produced domestically

$Q_{Demanded} = 55$ units will be demanded

$Q_{Imported} = 10$ units

13 The negative slope of the production possibilities curve indicates that it is not possible to get more of one product without giving up some of the other. The convexity indicates that less and less units of a commodity are sacrificed to gain an additional unit of another commodity (increasing opportunity cost).

Chapter 13

1 It can be said that the government controls the means of production for the airline industry because the flow of traffic from location to location, which is the product that the airline industry is providing, is totally under the control of the Federal Aviation Agency and that flow can be suspended or altered at any time at the discretion of the FAA.

2 The regulatory delay tax is more burdensome than an ordinary tax due to the fact that the costs of the tax are totally borne by the consumers and the producers of the product, in this case air travel, and there is no offset amount that a taxing authority would receive from the tax.

3 It can be assumed that the supply curve in the airline industry is relatively inelastic due to the fact that airline schedules must be published well ahead of time and it is difficult to change them, either to increase or decrease the number of seats available in a short period of time.

6 From the demand function, we can get

$P = 500 - 2 \times Q$

$\text{MR} = 500 - 4 \times Q$

Set

$\text{MR} = \text{MC}$

$500 - 4 \times Q = 0$

$Q = \$500/4 = 125$

$P = 500 - 2 \times (125) = \$250$

a $P = \$300$, there for $Q = 100$ units

$$\text{Deadweight} = \frac{125-100}{2} = 12.5$$

7 The concept of privatizing air traffic control operations is not new. Opponents of spinning off air traffic system voiced worries that the passengers may be put at risk if the FAA is removed from ATC operations.

8 If the supply curve of the airline industry is relatively inelastic, then the majority of the cost of congestion delay will be borne by the airlines and traveling public.

Index